The Silver Market Phenomenon

Florian Kohlbacher • Cornelius Herstatt
Editors

The Silver Market Phenomenon

Business Opportunities in an Era of Demographic Change

 Springer

Editors

Dr. Florian Kohlbacher
German Institute for Japanese Studies (DIJ)
Jochi Kioizaka Bldg. 2F
7-1 Kioicho
Chiyoda-ku, Tokyo 102-0094
Japan
E-mail: kohlbacher@dijtokyo.org

Prof. Dr. Cornelius Herstatt
TU Hamburg-Harburg
Institut für Technologie- und
Innovationsmanagement
Schwarzenbergstrasse 95
21073 Hamburg
Germany
E-mail: c.herstatt@tu-harburg.de

ISBN: 978-3-540-75330-8   e-ISBN: 978-3-540-75331-5
DOI: 10.1007/978-3-540-75331-5

Library of Congress Control Number: 2008930071

Cover design: WMX Design GmbH, Heidelberg

Printed on acid-free paper

9 8 7 6 5 4 3 2 1

springer.com

Looking at the Bright Side of Things

Ageing is central to human experience. The spectacular extension of the average Japanese life expectancy by one third over the past half century has pushed ageing into the foreground of public attention: as a social concern, as a policy issue and as an economic variable. Population ageing is a phenomenon experienced in most countries throughout the industrialized world. "The highest age to the greatest number" seems to be the maxim of our age. Japan is leading the way. In no other country have politicians, scholars and business people paid more attention to changes in the population structure, past and present, because further gains in life expectancy are to be expected. According to the most recent projections, Japan's median age will rise to an astounding 57 years by mid-century, that is, half of the population will then be 57 or older, while the total population continues to decline.

In the 1930s, when Japan's median age was less half that, economist Kaname Akamatsu proposed "the flying geese model of development" in order to explain the catching-up process of industrialization in East Asia. Japan was the leader, pointing the way for other economies. Today, the process is no longer industrialization but the transition into a hyper-aged society, defined as one where the population aged 65 years and older exceeds 20%. Japan is already there, others will follow suit. It is for this reason, and because the time needed for the elderly population to double from 7% to 14% was shorter by a large measure in Japan than in other industrialized countries, that Japan is of special interest in this regard. It has had less time to accommodate to the new population structure, but in many respects has done more to come to terms with it than others.

The "silver market" bears testimony to this development. The term itself originated in Japan. It has nothing to do with precious metals investments, as unsuspecting readers might be mislead to believe. Rather, it bears witness to a certain cultural inclination towards euphemism. Compare, for instance, "silver market" with "Gray Panthers", the American organization established in the early 1970s to defend the rights of senior citizens. Albeit ironically, this name combines two terms with decidedly negative connotations, "gray" indicating mediocrity, lack of colour and feebleness, while "panther" (in analogy to the Black Panthers) signals aggressiveness. By contrast, "silver" bears only positive connotations.

On 15 September, Respect for the Elderly Day, 1973, the Japanese National Railway first introduced "silver seats", for silver-haired senior citizens and the infirm. In the meantime, all public transport systems throughout Japan have renamed them "priority seats", while "silver" has become a common epithet for all sorts of institutions, activities and products designed for and catering to senior citizens. There are "silver workers", "silver homes", "silver fees" (rebates) and "silver employment agencies" (*shirubā jinzai sentā*); there is "business directed at the baby boom generation senior silver stratum" (*dankaisedai shinia shirubā sō muke bijinesu*) and, of course, the "silver market".

Surely, silver is more promising than gray. The silver market, as it has evolved over the past two decades, is widely perceived in Japan as an opportunity rather than a threat to business. Whether ageing is seen as a dark cloud overshadowing our future or an auspicious new horizon lies in the eye of the beholder. The Japanese business community, on the whole, has chosen to take a bright view of things. As demonstrated in several chapters of this book, Japanese companies of various sectors are today at the vanguard of developing and marketing products for senior citizens. The German Institute for Japanese Studies (DIJ) has taken an active interest in the development of this market for years and continues to study it as one important consequence of Japan's changing population situation. It is our considered opinion that demographic change – ageing and population decline – is the greatest challenge Japan faces today, which is why all of our research resources are at present focused on this phenomenon.

It goes without saying that in a capitalist economy much depends on market forces when it comes to meeting this challenge. In our studies on the consequences of Japan's population development, the silver market, therefore, occupies a special place. The government, too, cannot sidestep the issue, but its means for engineering a hyper-aged society capable of maintaining its present high level of affluence are limited. Much depends on the business sector in this adjustment process.

It is a matter of great satisfaction that DIJ was able to co-sponsor the joint research project that has resulted in this book. Its chapters help us gain a deeper insight into the implications of ageing for business, putting Japan in international perspective. It is a project to be continued.

Tokyo, Japan   *Florian Coulmas*
Director, German Institute for Japanese Studies

From the World Demographic Association

Long life expectancy is both a privilege and an achievement that is due largely to successful economic development and improvement in public health. However, it is also a challenge that will impact on all aspects of twenty-first century society. For example, the consequences of improved life expectancy on demographics is illustrated by the fact that the number of people aged 60 and over is expected to rise from the approximately 600 million people reported in 2000 to 1.2 billion in 2025 and 2 billion in 2050. Likewise, whereas today about two-thirds of all older people live in the developing world, by 2025 it will be three-quarters. At the same time, the fastest-growing population group in the developed world is the over-80s, and because women outlive men in virtually all societies, women constitute the majority at a ratio of 2:1.

Thus, population growth and population ageing pose great challenges to industrialised and developing countries alike. As with every challenge, it is not just about facing the problem but about seizing the chance to identify and shape the opportunities that lie within. We have the right and the responsibility to define today what effect and impact population ageing will have on our society, on our social and political framework, on our economy and on our position within the global framework. It is our task and opportunity to shape our future and to think for generations ahead. The World Demographic Association strives to identify these unique opportunities by looking at the broad spectrum of issues so that sustainable solutions can be developed. For that purpose, the World Demographic Association has created an international, interdisciplinary, intergenerational and permanent platform for demographic and generational issues – a forum designed to facilitate the analysis, discussion and exchange of ideas.

We believe that addressing this challenge requires serious effort and cooperation, not just from the public sector but from all stakeholders. Yet, the action plans and programmes initiated to date, the most prominent being the 1982 First World Assembly on Ageing (Vienna, Austria), and the 2002 Second World Assembly on Ageing (Madrid, Spain), point to few correlations between facing this challenge and global political agendas. Rather, we are still far from an actual global coordination of the multiple initiatives and projects suggested locally, let alone adequate institutionalisation to deal with the challenge.

Moreover, whereas the international debate is important in raising awareness, it is also vital to realise that all people are highly affected by this change on both an individual and a collective level. As the challenges are multiple, so must the responses be manifold, because every human being will deal with the situation in his or her own individual way. Thus, it is important to acknowledge that ageing is not disconnected from social integration, gender progression, and financial and economic stability or poverty.

As a result, modern societies, with their complex social security systems and social infrastructure, will be confronted with effects that are not easily estimated let alone absorbed. However, the individual too will have to face the consequences of an unexpectedly extended lifespan and will have to adapt their life course in terms of career, family and financial planning. These challenges will be of particular concern to the so-called Baby Boomers, those individuals born between 1946 and 1964, who will make up a large portion of those over 60 by 2030.

These boomers do and always have innovated and redefined trends and values, challenging the standards and practices of pre-modern society through their political, social or economic views. Indeed, they founded social modernism through their legendary "anti-war" and "free love" movements in the 1960s, reinvented professional careers by aiming for the professional integration of women, and redefined social concepts like family life and active ageing.

Today, the boomers continue to "do it their way" and forge new ground as they go. Thus, because of the high population percentage their group represents, they are challenging today's notion of retirement and, even more, today's perception of "being old". Never before have retirees been so well-educated, so healthy and so active. Most importantly, this generation grew up comfortable with a consumption-based lifestyle of which they still, because of their high purchasing power, are a main pillar. Thus, whereas earlier generations would refrain in old age from spending their hard-earned money, today's retirees are active: travelling, serving in Senior Expert Service (SES), renovating their houses or even buying high-end cars. Consequently, it comes as no surprise that the average age of a Porsche buyer is said to be 58.

As a result, being above 60 no longer means looking, behaving and acting like a grandfather or grandmother. Rather, instead of simply adapting their services and products to this newly discovered consumer group, multiple commercial services and industries are creating and redefining "age" as sexy, inventing euphemisms for "old" and making it easy for the older consumer to identify with the "young old". Much of this change in mindset manifests among the "Woopies" (well-off old people) or "Best Agers". Above all, this phenomenon reflects a change in the perception of what it means to be old today.

Nevertheless, today's and tomorrow's retirees are more than just the 1968 generation. They are selective consumers with several decades of consumer experience: not only do they know what they want, what quality they strive for and what price they are willing to pay, most importantly, they can afford to be selective. These trends are particularly reflected in housing and banking for the elderly, but are apparent in many areas.

Despite these changes, and no matter how great the opportunities for new markets, it is imperative that the international community, including all stakeholders, respond to the extraordinary variability in opportunities and challenges. Specifically, we must recognise the limits as well as the benefits of ageing societies by offering our older citizens the opportunity to contribute in a meaningful way.

Thus, we must start thinking of what can be, and learn to cooperate to achieve what should be: a meaningful and peaceful community of all generations. Or, as Nitin Desai, Special Advisor to the Secretary-General, United Nations, stated in the foreword to the World Ageing Situation 2000: "*We are all constituents of an ageing society, rural and city dwellers, public and private sector identities, families and individuals, old and young alike. It is crucial that societies adjust to this human paradigm as record numbers of people live into very old age, if we are to move towards a society for all ages. [Let us]... continue the dialogue and build on partnerships that can bring us closer to a society that weaves all ages into the larger human community in which we thrive.*"

St. Gallen, Switzerland   *Prisca Boxler, Academic Director*
                                                 Alfonso Sousa-Poza, Executive Director
                                                 World Demographic Association

Preface and Introduction

The Silver Market Phenomenon

In the developed countries, the dominant factor in the next society will be something to which most people are only beginning to pay attention: the rapid growth in the older population and the rapid shrinking of the younger generation.

Peter F. Drucker

The current shift in demographics – aging and shrinking populations – in many countries around the world presents a major challenge to companies and societies alike. As a matter of fact, this is true both for a number of industrialized nations as well as for certain emerging economies. However, even though this crucial issue has recently started to attract the attention of scholars, business leaders, and politicians, research on the implications of the demographic change on businesses is still in its infancy.

Most accounts of the so-called demographic "problem" deal, as the term already suggests, with the challenges and threats of the demographic development. These discussions feature, for example, the shrinking workforce, welfare effects, social conflicts, etc. At the same time, chances and opportunities are often neglected. The emergence of new markets, the potential for innovations, the integration of older people into jobs and work places, the joy of active aging, and their varied roles within society are just a few examples of how what at first sight appears to be a crisis could be turned into an opportunity. All in all, countries and industries are reacting very differently – from still neglecting to proactively looking for and developing solutions.

One particularly essential implication of the demographic shift is the emergence and constant growth of the "graying market" or "silver market," the market segment more or less broadly defined as those people aged 50 or 55 and older. Increasing in number and share of the total population while at the same time being relatively well-off, this market segment can be seen as very attractive and promising, although still very underdeveloped in terms of product and service offerings. Note that this is both true for the B2C as well as the B2B sector, as the workforce of organizations is also aging. This means that machines and tools etc. also need to be adapted to fit the needs of an aging workforce.

Given the importance and the vast implications of demographic change for the business world, it is surprising to see how little academic research in the field of business and management studies has been conducted so far. Academia is only slowly taking up this challenge. In particular, empirically grounded work is missing. We need to know how companies and whole industries are coping with demographic change. We need to know what the needs of aging/aged people are compared to other age groups, and we need to look for practical solutions to their needs. There is also a lack of concepts, processes, and practical solutions in various fields and functions of management: How to segment and approach the silver market? How to adapt product development, design, and delivery of value to the silver market? How to grasp the latent needs and wants of the potential silver customers?

Japan is the country most severely affected by the demographic shift and it is the most advanced in terms of product development and innovation, with very affluent, free-spending but also demanding customers. Japanese companies were among the first to react to the challenge of the demographic change and are constantly coming up with product and service innovations. Nevertheless, they have only touched the tip of the iceberg of the huge potential of this market. Overall, Japan can be seen as the lead silver market, which offers the opportunity to study the silver market phenomenon and learn from the successes and failures of pioneering Japanese firms. Therefore, we have made an effort to include a variety of contributions about Japan from both Japanese and non-Japanese authors. But, other countries and their political decision-makers, as well as industries, are paying more and more attention to the silver market phenomenon and are developing concrete solutions. In this volume, we can only present a first fraction of these, including examples from the USA, Finland, Germany, and India. Furthermore, we can only present examples from some, but not all, industries working on solutions towards catering for the needs of elderly people. We did not aim for "completeness" but rather for variety and to illustrate the differences between distinct industries and countries.

This book offers a thorough and up-to-date analysis of the challenges and opportunities in leveraging innovation, product development, and marketing for elder consumers and employees. Key lessons are drawn from the "lead market" Japan as well as other selected countries. This book wants to reach a rather broad target audience. We are positive that it will offer helpful guidance for decision makers, managers responsible for innovation, technology and R&D, marketing managers, the strategic management (including CEOs, governmental and political decision-makers), but also interested scholars, teachers, and students.

We strongly believe in the relevance of the topic and hope that this work helps to stimulate the development of innovation on different levels (product, services, and social). We further want to bridge between disciplines, such as the social sciences, engineering, health care/medical etc. and to foster networking among these, favoring the creation of valuable silver market solutions.

This is an edited volume and without the positive response and active (writing) support of all the contributing authors it would never have been thinkable, nor possible. We therefore want to express our gratitude and thanks here to all authors. Further, we would like to thank our publisher Springer and specifically Dr. Martina Bihn and her colleagues for accepting and realizing this ambitious project. We would also like to thank Dr. Michael Prieler for his invaluable help in mastering the format template and properly formatting all chapters in the book.

This book will arrive on the market right on time for the international symposium "The Silver Market Phenomenon: Business Opportunities and Responsibilities in the Ageing Society" (2–4 October, 2008 in Tokyo, Japan), co-organized by the German Institute for Japanese Studies, Tokyo, the United Nations University, Tokyo, the Tokyo Institute of Technology and the Institute of Technology and Innovation Management (TIM) of the Technical University Hamburg–Harburg. This global forum focuses on innovation, product and service development, technology management, and marketing and business models for the 50+ market. Additionally, policy makers, academics, and practitioners will debate business responsibilities, challenges, and solutions for coping with changing demographics around the world. We see this event as a cornerstone and hope it will also initialize and stimulate other researchers from all over the world to start initiatives in order to better understand the silver market phenomenon, its chances, challenges, and opportunities for societies and industries.

Structure of the Book: Overview

This book is structured into four parts: In the first section (Part I, The Demographic Shift: Challenges, Chances, Perspectives) we take a closer look at the demographic shifts from a global (macro-) economical perspective. Authors in this section present and discuss the specific challenges and chances of aging, and give perspectives for future developments. They further look at impacts for decision makers on and discuss avenues for responding to these.

The second part of the book (Part II, Innovation, Design and Product Development for the Silver Market) has more of a micro-perspective nature. Within this part, authors present their concepts and processes for successfully approaching the silver markets, leading to innovative solutions in the form of new products and services that better fulfill the specific needs and desires of this target market. The authors clearly demonstrate that an important element of these approaches is to carefully segment the silver markets, to ensure adequate and early integration of representatives of this market (customers and users) into product and service development and to design solutions that truly correspond to their needs and desires. The concepts of universal design and transgenerational design are of particular interest in this context.

Part III (Marketing for the Silver Market) of this book addresses marketing-related issues in combination with serving the silver market. Authors in this section look at pricing, distribution, and promoting and positioning issues corresponding to silver markets. They discuss the applicability of classical marketing-mix related activities in combination with silver markets and present innovative approaches in applying these within this specific context.

The final section of the book (Part IV, Industry Challenges and Solutions) presents a series of concrete examples or solutions (innovative products and services for the silver market) in very different industries, including the automotive, health care, medical devices, media, education (life-long learning), housing sectors etc. Besides B2C strategies, the impact for B2B is also discussed.

The book ends with an afterword that shifts the focus once again onto the lead market, Japan. Going beyond the silver market phenomenon it explores a number of cultural and business particularities in Japan and relates them to the topic of demographic change, thus serving as a skillful wrap-up and outlook of the book.

Structure of the Book: Detailed Overview

Part I: The Demographic Shift: Challenges, Chances, Perspectives

The first part of our book consists of six contributions. In the paper on "Demographic Change and Economic Growth," *Thomas Fent, Bernhard Mahlberg* and *Alexia Prskawetz* discuss the relationship between changes in a country's age structure and its economic growth and productivity. Based on recent literature and results of their own empirical findings, the authors indicate a (surprisingly) positive impact of the age group 50–64 on economic growth. Moreover, they can demonstrate that a high proportion of people in the age group 15–29 facilitate technology absorption. They further estimate age–productivity profiles at the firm level, based on the use of matched employer–employee data. Considering all firms in the data set, they show a negative productivity effect of the share of older workers (50+). Considering only large firms, where no impact of the age structure is the case, a negative impact of the share of younger workers is shown.

The second paper, by *Gabriele Vogt* (Talking Politics: Demographic Variables and Policy Measures in Japan), looks at the three core variables of demographic change: a population's fertility behavior, structures of migration, and people's life expectancy. These translate into policy fields as family, replacement, and old-age policies. Her study shows how Japan, one of the most rapidly aging and shrinking nations, addresses this demographic change through various policy measures. She argues that Japan is putting much effort into old-age policy, thereby addressing the present needs of a growing elderly population. In her perspective, Japan, however, only hesitantly takes on the issues of family and replacement policy. Historical and ideological taboos here prove to be too persistent to allow for radical policy changes. However, such changes are necessary in order to comprehensively deal with the future challenges of demographic change.

Naohiro Yashiro (The Silver Markets in Japan Through Regulatory Reform) takes a closer look at Japan's health care service industry, which he claims to be one of the most promising sectors because of a constantly growing customer base. From his perspective this sector is still underdeveloped, regulations impeding new entries hindering its development. If these obstacles can be removed, Yashiro argues, the potential demand for health care services will be stimulated, and the productivity level improved. Major issues here are a revision of the rules that today are banning the mixing of public and private health insurances. He further looks at the growing demand for nursing care services. Yashiro argues that regulatory reforms are the key to developing the silver industries in Japan.

Norbert Malanowski (Matching Demand and Supply: Future Technologies for Active Ageing in Europe) delivers a European perspective. He starts his discussion based on his statement that extending the average human life expectancy shall go hand in hand with non-suffering. This demand is mirrored by "active aging," put forward by the World Health Organization. Active aging in this context refers to a continuous participation in social, economic, cultural, spiritual and civic affairs, not just the ability to be physically active or part of the labor force. Active aging views elderly people as active participants in an age-integrated society. A way to advance policy concepts to match supply and demand can be derived from focusing on promising fields of application for future technologies that generate age-based innovations. Malanowski further argues that future technologies for active aging provide a new and promising policy concept to tackle the challenges of aging societies, to transform them into opportunities and to use as many as possible of the opportunities presented by aging societies by matching demand and supply.

The paper "How Baby-Boomers in the United States Anticipate Their Aging Future: Implications for the Silver Market" by *Merril Silverstein* and *Alexis Abramson* examines three types of aging anxiety among baby-boomers in the United States and discusses their implications for the silver market of older consumers. The authors use data from an US sample of 473 baby-boomers to examine the structure and predictors of aging anxiety. They find that three dimensions adequately describe the apprehensions that this generation has about growing old: anxiety over the loss of autonomy emerged as the most powerful factor, followed by uneasiness over the physical manifestations of aging, and optimism/pessimism with regard to expecting continuity and contentment in old age. A variety of factors are associated with these dimensions, including gender, marital status, income, knowledge about aging, and exposure to older adults. The authors discuss how an appreciation of the sources of aging anxiety among baby-boomers can help marketers and advertisers better understand the pre-elderly consumer market, and suggest ways of addressing baby-boomers' fears with positive images of growing old.

Chikako Usui with her paper "Japan's Demographic Changes: Social Implications, and Business Opportunities," argues that the so-called "aging problem" should not be viewed as an economic encumbrance, but better viewed in the context of the robustness of the economy. In her view, an expansion of the carrying capacity of the active labor force, as well as active aging among older adults, will decrease the burden on a society. Her work draws out social and cultural implications of demographic changes in the context of Japan's transformation from a Fordist to post-Fordist economy. This distinction shifts attention to the social organization of technology-based service industries. The growing number of older persons and senior households means immense business opportunities for developing new solutions, products, and services. Older adults are potent consumers, willing and economically able to secure independent living and a high quality of life. This chapter discusses a number of emerging silver industries, including housing and real estate, food, pets, robotics, senior care appliances, and the funeral market.

Part II: Innovation, Design and Product Development for the Silver Market

The second part of our book includes five chapters. The first paper in this section by *Pia Helminen* (Disabled Persons as Lead Users for Silver Market Customers), looks at the key aspect of integrating customers/users into the process of developing innovative products and services. She argues how important it is to deeply understand needs of (silver-)customers when developing new products. User-centered design provides tools for learning about user needs in question, but studying only the target market customers may result in constricted need data because of the functional fixedness of these customers. The lead user approach, in contrast, aims to learn from the lead users of a certain target group in order to find better solutions for the needs in the target market. In this chapter, Helminen shows through a study on mobile phones how disabled persons can be seen as lead users when developing products for silver market customers. She also presents methods to explore the needs and solutions that disabled users possess.

The second paper in this section (Integration of the Elderly in the Design Process), by *Karin Schmidt-Ruhland* and *Mathias Knigge*, is somewhat related to the work of Helminen. They argue that with demographic change looming in the background there is an ever-greater need for products and aids for the growing target group of elderly people. Both authors state that classical methods in product development and design have often failed to develop attractive and helpful solutions that meet the wishes and needs of this age group. They then introduce new approaches and concepts, which have been developed in the "sentha Research Project." "sentha" stands for Everyday Technology for Senior Households. In this interdisciplinary research project designers from the Berlin University of the Arts work closely in cooperation with the Technical Universities of Berlin and Cottbus as well as the Berlin Institute for Social Research. The goal was to develop products and services for an increasingly aging society so that seniors can maintain their independence in daily life as long as possible. This includes the development and positioning of senior-friendly products and services. In their projects, the focus was on specific wishes and needs of elderly people, without limiting themselves in form and function solely to this one target group. The article elucidates specific design approaches, methods for integrating elderly people, and shows a selection of real-world designs.

Oliver Gassmann and *Gerrit Reepmeyer* introduce a different perspective with their work (Universal Design – Innovations for All Ages), since they strongly argue for a product design that bridges between the needs of different age groups. In their view, demographics require companies to abandon the concept of solely targeting young customers. They need to create new products that are attractive to *both* younger *and* older customers. For both authors the key to success is Universal Design. Products that follow the principles of Universal Design don't separate but integrate customer groups, and they substantially increase a company's target markets. This chapter not only highlights the economic potential of Universal Design, it also shows how Universal Design can be implemented within any corporation. A successful implementation requires: (i) to define a suitable Universal Design strategy, (ii) to establish adequate processes within the firm, (iii) to design the products correctly, and (iv) to market the products appropriately to customers. The chapter concludes by illustrating attractive areas for universally designed innovations.

James Pirkl writes his chapter on the design of living, or what he calls transgenerational housing (Transgenerational Design: A Heart Transplant for Housing). Responding to his past research and the realities of the aging process, the author describes why and how he designed and built the first fully accessible house aiming directly at baby-boomers and beyond. His project offers a vehicle for broadening consumer awareness of, and increasing the demand for, "transgenerational" housing and household products. This uniquely innovative design neutralizes many restrictive effects of aging, accidents, illness or chronic conditions. It also demonstrates that attractive transgenerational houses can be designed to promote, provide and extend independent living, remove barriers, offer wider options, supply greater choices, and enhance the quality of life for all – the young, the old, the able, the disabled – without penalty to any group.

The last paper in this section of the book takes the perspective of services and innovations in service (Service Innovation: Towards Designing New Business Models for Aging Societies, by *Patrick Reinmoeller*). This author claims that the aging of industrialized countries requires firms to fundamentally rethink their business models. Firms active in Japan have to reconsider how to deal with unprecedented demographic change that alters the resources available to satisfy the shifting demand. Throughout the supply chain, aging of human talent and retirement requires firms to anticipate and prevent the negative effects of losing knowledge and skills. Adjusting the supply chain, developing new products, and/or augmenting products with services to target the silver market may offer short-term benefits but is not enough to sustain success. Firms need to develop and implement new business models, leveraging service innovation to meet the needs in aging societies. Examples of service innovations and the case study of Seven Eleven Japan and Yamato Transport's Takkyubin's shared business model innovation illustrate how companies can seize the opportunities to create and capture more value in aging societies.

Part III: Marketing for the Silver Market

This section includes nine chapters. *Gunnar Arnold* and *Stephanie Krancioch* (Current Strategies in the Retail Industry for Best-Agers), take a closer look at retailing in combination with the silver market. In their view of the demographic transformation, the retail trade faces a clear challenge to reconsider existing retailing concepts, and to better include older target groups in marketing planning. In the present paper, the authors look first at the factor location, one of the central success factors in the retail trade. Next, they examine the preferences of German best-agers for certain types of businesses, such as shops close to home in comparison with out-of-town malls. They then proceed to discuss the effects of changed customer needs on the design of the assortments and of packaging because of their decreasing physical capabilities. Finally the authors present examples from the daily practice of the trade, and conclude with a brief overview of foreseeable trends in the retail trade.

Stefan Lippert (Silver Pricing: Satisfying Needs is Not Enough – Balancing Value Delivery and Value Extraction is Key) presents the next work. Also in his view, the silver market provides a highly lucrative opportunity for businesses willing and able to meet the needs of Japan's senior generation. International and domestic players have been pursuing the new opportunities in the last few years. Thoroughly understanding the needs of the silver generation is a key to capitalizing on it. However, he argues, this is just one side of the value coin, since a need is not the same as demand, and demand is not the same as profitable business. To turn into a profit, companies have to balance value delivery and value extraction. Value delivery is relatively easy: it requires market research, appropriate products and services, and an effective distribution system. Value extraction is difficult: companies need to set and implement the "right" prices across products, regions, and channels. A business strategy based solely on demographic and socioeconomic data, customer needs, and buying power is simplistic, misleading, and in some cases even dangerous. Capitalizing on the silver market requires a systematic approach to developing and profitably selling products and services tailored to the older generation. It takes a solid understanding of customer requirements, value-to-customer, ability and willingness to pay, price elasticity, and revenue and profit functions. The best way to achieve this, so he argues, is by means of a professional pricing process covering and connecting pricing strategy, price setting, and price implementation.

Takako Yamashita and *Takashi Nakamura* (Macro-Structural Bases of Consumption in an Aging and Low Birth-Rate Society: An Application of Bayesian Cohort Models) also start their argument based on the observation that, at first glance, the silver market provides a highly lucrative opportunity for businesses willing and able to meet the needs of Japan's senior generation. The purpose of their study is to clarify the driving factors in the changing structure of consumption at the macro-level caused by an aging society in Japan. To describe the macroscopic, dynamic, and structural bases of consumption, the authors used cohort analysis, which is a method of separating age, period, and cohort effects from time-series household accounts data, classified by age and period. Many items of expenditure are susceptible to the age effect. The effect of changes in the number of household members due to changing life stages and the effect of changing expenses due to aging of consumers can also be seen. Other expenditure items are susceptible to plural effects. For example, fish and shellfish, vegetables and seaweed, and fruit are all susceptible to both age and cohort factors. Eating out, private transportation, communication, and books and other reading material are susceptible to all three factors at different levels of effectiveness. Observing the profile pattern on the cohort analysis result graph, the authors consider how market aging and the alternation of generations, which are viewed from a population theory perspective, affect the consumption structure.

The paper "Changing Consumer Values and Behavior in Japan" by *Nozomi Enomoto*, looks (again) closer at issues concerning retailing for the silver market. Retailers in Japan now face various changes in the business environment, including that of demographic change, economic globalization, development of information technology, and changes in consumers' values and behavior. The consumers' values and behavior in Japan reflect a characteristic transition in the retail sector, in which department stores have been a major force. Keio Department Store Shinjuku has been gearing its business toward seniors since the mid-1990s. The purpose of Enomoto's study is to examine how an organization like a department store adapts to a changing business environment, by exploring Keio Department Store Shinjuku as a case of a senior-focused retailer, extracting factors that are important in tailoring business practices.

The next paper in this section, "Grey Power: Older Workers as Older Customers" by *Sue Tempest*, *Christopher Barnatt* and *Christine Coupland*, explores the increasing importance of "gray power" in the labor market and the marketplace. In their perspective, to fully understand gray market potential, companies need to develop an understanding of individual older customers and their broader social contexts in terms of both their varying immediate household compositions, and their intergenerational relationships. The authors first challenge stereotypes and then introduce a model of older-person segmentation. The frame of analysis is then extended beyond the individual older customer in order to assess the range of "future households" in which the old will increasingly play a key role when purchasing decisions are being made. They then provide a wealth/health segmentation for firms seeking to develop older customer strategies, and supplement this with a categorization of future households and the issues raised by intergenerational dynamics. This is then used to challenge false assumptions about older household compositions in the twenty-first century. In turn, this provides a segmentation of the old as workers and as customers in a variety of social contexts, which we hope offers some useful tools for companies seeking to capitalize on grey power now and into the future.

Simone Pettigrew with her work on "Older Consumers' Customer Service Preferences," discusses her observation that older consumers have distinct customer service preferences that can constitute a source of competitive advantage for forward-thinking marketers who seek to attract this large and relatively affluent segment. Her chapter focuses on the supermarket, financial planning, and healthcare industries to demonstrate the importance of providing personalized attention to allow for the older person's deteriorating physical and cognitive abilities and shrinking social networks. In particular, emphasis is placed on the need to allow older customers to form meaningful relationships with service staff. This strategy has implications for the recruitment, training, and retention of staff members who are able to demonstrate genuine concern for the welfare of the older consumer.

Michael Prieler (Silver Advertising: Elderly People in Japanese TV Ads) looks closer at the role of aged people in advertising in Japanese TV ads. He observed that about 10% of Japanese commercials show elderly people. They advertise a relatively small range of product categories, such as pharmaceuticals/health products, financial/insurance plans, and food. Elderly people are the main target group, especially for the first two product categories, and often are the only age group that appears in the ads. In contrast, for products targeted at more age groups or for which elderly people are not the explicit targets, elderly people either do not appear at all, appear in a family setting, or in a more general way as a representative of one generation, e.g., in commercials showing that all generations use the product. This leads to the situation in which only about 20% of commercials with elderly people advertise products that are explicitly for elderly people. The representation and function of elderly people in commercials is not only connected with the age groups they are appearing with, but there also are differences within the representation of elderly people. This is especially the case of male versus female representations, in which the latter are clearly underrepresented. On the whole, most of the findings of this study confirmed previous research results from other parts of the world.

Chuck Nyren (Advertising Agencies: The Most Calcified Part of the Process), also looks into the issues of advertising in connection with the silver market. From their perspective, today's advertising industry needs a minor revolution. Talented men and women in their 40s, 50s, and 60s must to be brought into the fold if you want to target the silver market. This includes copywriters, graphic artists, producers, video directors, and creative directors. If companies plan on implementing a marketing strategy that includes baby-boomers as a primary, secondary, or tertiary market, and turn it over to only people in their 20s and 30s, they will forfeit the natural sensibilities required to generate vital campaigns. Companies can analyze marketing fodder all day and night, read countless books about marketing to baby-boomers, attend advertising and marketing conventions around the world, and soak up everything all the experts have to say. But, the bottom line is this: if the right people aren't in the right jobs, what happens is what happens in all arenas of business – failure and mediocrity. And the reverse is true. If a company had a product or service for the late-teens and twenty-somethings, and had walked into an advertising agency with a creative team made up of only people in their 50s and 60s, the company should and would be very, very worried.

The last chapter in this section (The Importance of Web 2.0 to the 50-Plus) by *Dick Stroud* looks into the importance of Web 2.0 for older people. This paper addresses this issue and provides suggestions on how organizations can use Web 2.0 to improve their online interactions with the older market. The chapter analyses the differences between the historical way that web sites have been created and used and the opportunities and dangers of using Web 2.0 technologies. Social networking and web video are the two best-known applications of Web 2.0 and are discussed in detail. The author shows that whilst both these applications are associated with young people they are intrinsically "age neutral" and are equally appropriate to older Web users. The chapter describes how social networking and web video are likely to develop and the resulting implications upon the channel strategy of organizations targeting the older web user.

Part IV: Industry Challenges and Solutions

Altogether we present 13 papers here: The first, "The Business of Aging: Ten Successful Strategies for a Diverse Market" by *Hiroyuki Murata*, starts with the observation that in Japan, an increasing number of enterprises have been focusing on developing new products and services for older adults or for the baby-boomer generation, but actually most of them failed to do so. One reason for this is because often their visions or approaches were too narrowly defined. Many enterprises consider the older adult market or the boomer market as single homogeneous icebergs. However, it seems not to be enough to say that the boomers represent a large part of the market just by sheer numbers. Another reason is that the nature of today's markets is very different from those of the past. This paper gives readers a perspective of how to view at the baby-boomer market or senior market and gives insights in how to successfully serve markets in this realm.

The next paper looks closer at the case of Germany (The Discovery and Development of the Silver Market in Germany). The authors *Peter Enste, Gerhard, Naegele,* and *Verena Leve* report a paradigm shift in Germany, which is emerging regarding the silver economy and resulting in an increasing focus on the economic potential and the economic power of the elderly. Given the much increased buying power of the elderly, the increased heterogeneity of consumption wishes and needs corresponding to the differentiation of old age, as well as the empirical evidence for an age-specific change in consumption requirements, it stands to reason to look for inherent impulses for economic growth and employment by dint of new "age-sensitive" product ranges and services and to promote their development and expansion. Today, in fact, the silver economy comprises products and services in very diverse and by no means only "social" market segments and, in addition to the health economy, affects such diverse sectors as mobility and IT. The contribution provides an insight into the development of the silver economy in Germany and its future prospects.

The perspective of India is presented by *Suresh Paul Antony, P.C. Purwar, Neelam Kinra,* and *Janakiraman Moorthy* (India: Emerging Opportunities in a Market in Transition). India is in the middle of its demographic transition. The 60+ age group will treble by 2050 while the 0–14 group will remain stagnant. India's population structure and distribution would then closely resemble that of nations like Russia and UK, as seen now. Their high aging index indicates that the 60+ age group is larger than the 0–14 group. Such changes in the size, structure and distribution of the population will have implications for public policy as well as business. The Government has launched a slew of initiatives to meet this challenge. On the business front, many products and services have been launched that specifically target the elderly. However, there are many other products and services used by all age groups. These may have to be repositioned if the motivations of the different age groups are not similar. Both from the angle of public policy and business, decision makers in India could closely examine the experience of nations with a high aging index and respond to the challenges of demographic transition.

The chapter "Silver Markets and Business Customers: Opportunities for Industrial Markets?" by *Peter Mertens*, *Steve Russel* and *Ines Steinke*, looks at the impact of demographic change on industrial markets and B2B. The ratio of people over 65 years of age will rise in all triad countries. At the same time, the number of younger people, and thus recruits in all education levels, will drastically decline in Japan and Germany. In the USA, a shortage of highly skilled and educated workers is expected. The employment rate of aged people will therefore rise. Companies can react on many different levels. On the one hand, they can make it a business opportunity by developing and selling products and services that support older people. On the other hand, companies will have to cope with fewer younger workers. The authors discuss several ways to do this: (1) to prevent loss of skills from retirement, (2) to accommodate older workers, and (3) to survive with fewer workers. These could lead to B2B products and services that can help companies to solve the issues involved. The authors look at these possibilities in turn and find that they each lead to ideas that have one or more of the following properties: (a) they are actually B2C products, (b) they are management or organizational solutions or services, or (c) their benefits are not specific to older workers but benefit all employees. Thus, the authors are led to the conclusion: the technical products best suited for the B2Industry silver market will not be "silver-specific" products, but products "designed for all" with an emphasis on usability and problem solving.

Part IV includes further a number of papers discussing different industries, and solutions within these, for the silver market automotive industry. The first paper (Business Chance in Personal Transportation: Traffic Safety and Strategy for Older Adults) by *Kazutaka Mitobe* starts with a view on business opportunities in the safety of personal transportation for older adults. In order to achieve traffic safety for older adults, it is important to support the declining sense and cognitive function. The author discusses the process of how to reduce traffic accidents involving pedestrians in an aged society. A first business opportunity lies in the establishment of inspection technology. A second business chance would be the establishment of training technology. A third business chance would lie in the establishment of the market of assistive devices that can compensate for older adult's sense and cognitive functions. From the human factor study using a VR technology, the detailed situations of pedestrian traffic accidents will become clear. Effective assistive technology might be developed based on the risk factor of traffic accidents.

A related work is next presented by *Joachim Meyer* (In-Vehicle Telematic Systems and the Older Driver). He starts his argument on the fact that cars in general are rapidly changing. In addition to its traditional driving-related functions, the car has become a platform for various services and devices. Some of these are involved in the driving task and can improve its ease, comfort, and safety. Others are unrelated to driving and allow the driver to engage in various activities while driving. The aging of the driving population and the tendency of older people in many parts of the world to continue driving for as long as possible pose major challenges regarding the design of such devices and their deployment in cars. Some advantages, as well as some limitations, these devices may have for older drivers are pointed out. Design of future in-vehicle telematic systems will have to consider these issues in order to provide maximum benefits for the older driver.

Emi Osono (Taking Advantage of Adversarial Demographic Changes to Innovate Your Own Business) focuses on adversarial change. What if a new customer segment emerges but has a very different set of needs? What if the growing customer segment brings subtle shortcomings in firms' offerings to the surface? Such is often the case with the silver market segment. These changes bring with them great opportunities for the company to innovate itself. The question is how? Various scholars noted that the distance of the organizational units and the leaders who are in charge of both the new and old businesses is critical. Also, others noted that when a company starts a new business, it has to carefully manage three processes, namely, borrowing, forgetting, and learning. Focusing on organizational distance and the three processes, the author has conducted comparative case studies of Toyota's adaptation to demographic changes in the US, which has led to an insight about how organizational distance has contributed to innovation.

"The Golden Opportunity of Silver Marketing: The Case of Housing and Financial Services" by *Kenneth Grossberg*, examines two areas that promise major commercial opportunities because of such a vast socio-demographic change linked to a huge pool of liquid assets. Those areas are, firstly, catering to the financial needs of the country's senior citizens and, secondly, responding to their particular preferences and requirements for housing. In Japan's generally sluggish market for housing and financial services, the silver market provides one of the richest segments available, but successfully offering such services to this population requires skill, sensitivity, and an understanding of the evolving consumer mindset in Japan. The following work concentrates on the medical sector in Japan (Institutional Reforms of Medicine and Medical Information Systems in Japan). The author *Noboyuki Kishida* discusses how Japan needs to undertake medical system reforms in order to suppress the ballooning national medical expenses of the aging society. Medical computerization is one of the focal issues. The government stated a plan to mandate the online billing of medical service fees to all medical institutions. The prevalence of EMR (electronic medical record), which has been delayed due to unsophisticated IT (information technology) and the limited IT literacy of elderly medical staff in general, should be promoted in this opportunity. Without the prevalence of EMR, several social innovations, the regional coordinated medical service and the future NHR (national health record) service etc., will not become reality. The author strongly advocates inducing newcomers to innovate business models by means of deregulations, so as to promote more investments in the medical information market from the business sector, and accelerate the build-up of regional medical information networks based on networked EMR systems.

In the next paper, the author *Mark Miller* takes the perspective of the media industry (The End of Mass Media: Aging and the US Newspaper Industry). Miller observes that the baby-boom generation, the largest in US history, grew up with mass media and is by far the largest constituency for newspapers, television, and magazines. But, as audiences age and fragment, the economic foundations of these traditional media are challenged. The pain is especially sharp in the newspaper industry, giving rise to worries about the future of American journalism.

Junichi Tomita (Material Innovation in the Japanese Silver Market) takes again another industry perspective. His work argues what the material innovation process in the Japanese silver market should be like. Material suppliers are continualy attempting to contribute to an aging society through material innovation. Although they are not always successful in their intentions to meet the needs of users, they at times discover the actual needs of the users, which are slightly different from the perceived needs. Subsequently, these suppliers work on improving the new materials so as to meet the actual needs of users by developing a close contact with them. The case of superabsorbent polymer (SAP), studied in this chapter, is a typical example of this. We term this material innovation process an emergent process. The SAP "Aqualic CA" launched on the market by Nippon Shokubai Co., Ltd., in 1983 is a raw material that facilitated the popularity of disposable diapers in the Japanese market. It also currently holds a large share in the American and European markets. However, it was not originally designed for use in disposable diapers, and the process it underwent from development to marketing was not linear. His case study describes how after failure in its technological development and supply agreements, success was finally achieved. Further, it indicates the effectiveness of developing evaluation technologies in the process through an end-user oriented approach. As a result, his study should prove to be a valuable aid in helping material suppliers understand effective innovation management.

Another industry perspective is presented by *Helinä Melkas* (Potholes in the Road to Efficient Gerontechnology Use in Elderly Care Work). The use of information and communication technologies (ICT), including safety alarm technologies, is increasing. Its influence on service personnel in elderly care has implications on the possibilities for rooting technological innovations into care work. Human impact assessment methodologies have been employed to assess competence related to technology use, needs for orientation into technology use, and well-being of care personnel. Safety alarms are considered useful both for actual care work and for the administrative part of the care organization. Care personnel appeared not to be fully informed on the technical characteristics and resulting organizational changes. At individual and work community levels, regular human impact assessment of new technologies may stimulate their adoption by the professional carers. The chapter is based on empirical research in a large research and development project in Finland. The research focused on safety telephones and high-tech well-being wristbands.

Finally, in their paper "Senior Educational Programs for Compensating Future Student Decline in German Universities," the German authors *Doreen Schwarz, Janine Lentzy,* and *Christiane Hipp* discuss the opportunities of the silver market for (German) universities. Germany's population is expected to fall from about 82.4 million people to between 69 and 74 million people in 2050. Simultaneously, the average age of the population is increasing. In particular, the next few years in East Germany will be characterized by a strong decline in the number of young people and a significant increase in the number of elderly. However, demographic change does not automatically imply negative consequences but also creates room for opportunities. In this chapter, the authors explore opportunities to enlarge the purpose of the educational silver market by an economic component due to two developments: firstly, current and upcoming generations of seniors increasingly spend their spare time studying intellectual and cultural subjects and, secondly, traditional universities suffer from a low number of students. We make considerations regarding incentives to include more people aged 65 and over in educational issues, and thus to create a win–win situation for third-agers and institutions of higher education.

In the very last chapter of the book, we – as editors – try to give a brief wrap-up and outlook by looking at the lessons learned and the challenges and opportunities ahead.

Tokyo, Japan   *Florian Kohlbacher*
Hamburg, Germany   *Cornelius Herstatt*
May 2008

Contents

Part III Marketing for the Silver Market

Part IV Industry Challenges and Solutions

Contributors

Alexis Abramson
Vice President of Research, Retirement Living TV, Atlanta, GA, USA

Suresh Paul Antony
Doctoral Candidate, Marketing Area, Indian Institute for Management, Lucknow, India

Gunnar Arnold
Project Manager, Market Research, Center for Innovation and Education, Wartenberg(wibz GmbH), Berlin, Germany

Christopher Barnatt
Associate Professor in Computing & Organizations, Nottingham University Business School, United Kingdom

Prisca Boxler
Programme Director, World Demographic Association, St. Gallen, Switzerland

Florian Coulmas
Director, German Institute for Japanese Studies, Tokyo, Japan

Christine Coupland
Associate Professor in Organizational Behaviour, Nottingham University Business School, United Kingdom

Nozomi Enomoto
Junior Associate Professor, School of Management, Tokyo University of Science, Saitama, Japan

Peter Enste
Research Assistant, Institute for Gerontology, Technical University of Dortmund and Institute of Work and Technology, Gelsenkirchen, Germany

Thomas Fent
Research Scientist, Vienna Institute of Demography, Austrian Academy of Sciences, Vienna, Austria

Oliver Gassmann
Full Professor and Managing Director, Institute of Technology Management,
University of St. Gallen, Switzerland

Kenneth Alan Grossberg
Professor and Director, Waseda Business School, Waseda Marketing Forum,
Waseda University, Tokyo, Japan

Pia Helminen
Researcher, BIT Research Centre, Helsinki University of Technology, Finland

Cornelius Herstatt
Full Professor and Director, Institute for Technology and Innovation Management,
Technical University of Hamburg-Harburg, Germany

Christiane Hipp
Full Professor and vice-dean, Chair of Organization, Human Resource Management
and General Management, Department of Economics and Business Sciences,
Brandenburg University of Technology Cottbus, Germany

Neelam Kinra
Professor, Marketing Area, Indian Institute of Management, Lucknow, India

Nobuyuki Kishida
Management Consultant, Ph.D. Candidate, Graduate School of Commerce,
Waseda University, Tokyo, Japan

Mathias Knigge
General Manager, Grauwert – Office for Demografically Proven Products and
Services, Hamburg, Germany

Florian Kohlbacher
Research Fellow, Business and Economics Section, German Institute for Japanese
Studies, Tokyo, Japan

Stephanie Krancioch
Client Relationship Consultant, Account Management, German Institute for Value
Management and Value Analysis (DIWA), Frankfurt a. M., Germany

Janine Lentzy
Research Assistant, Chair of Organization, HRM, General Management,
Brandenburg University of Technology, Cottbus, Germany

Verena Leve
Research Assistant, Institute for Gerontology, Technical University of Dortmund,
Germany

Stefan Lippert
Managing Partner, Simon-Kucher & Partners Strategy & Marketing Consultants
Japan K.K., Tokyo, Japan

Bernhard Mahlberg
Researcher, Institute for Industrial Research, Lecturer, Institute for European
Affairs, Vienna University of Economics and Business Administration, Austria

Norbert Malanowski
Senior Researcher and Project Coordinator, Future Technologies Division, VDI
Technology Center, Düsseldorf, Germany

Helinä Melkas
Senior Research Fellow, Adjunct Professor, Lahti Unit, Lappeenranta University of
Technology, Lahti, Finland

Peter Mertens
General Manager, Corporate Technology, Siemens KK, Tokyo, Japan

Joachim Meyer
Associate Professor, Department of Industrial Engineering and Management Ben
Gurion University of the Negev Beer Sheva, Israel

Mark Miller
President, 50+Digital LLC, Author, Retire Smart syndicated newspaper column,
Publisher/Editor, RetirementRevised.com

Kazutaka Mitobe
Associate Professor, Faculty of Engineering and Resource Science, Akita
University, Akita, Japan

Janakiraman Moorthy
Professor, Marketing Area, Pearl School of Business, Gurgaon, India

Hiroyuki Murata
President, Murata Associates, Inc., Tokyo, Japan, Professor, Faculty of Global
Strategy, Tohoku University, Japan

Gerhard Naegele
Full Professor and Director, Institute for Gerontology, Technical University of
Dortmund, Germany

Takashi Nakamura
Professor and Director, Department of Data Science, The Institute of Statistical
Mathematics, Tokyo, Japan

Chuck Nyren
Author, Advertising to Baby Boomers – copyright 2005, 2007 Paramount Market
Publishing, A Classroom Resource for The Advertising Educational Foundation

Emi Osono
Associate Professor, Graduate School of International Corporate Strategy,
Hitotsubashi University, Tokyo, Japan

Simone Pettigrew
Senior Lecturer in Marketing, UWA Business School, University of Western
Australia, Australia

James J. Pirkl
Professor Emeritus and Former Senior Research Fellow, All-University
Gerontology Center, Syracuse University, Syracuse, NY, U.S.A.

Michael Prieler
Visiting Researcher, German Institute for Japanese Studies, Tokyo, Japan

Alexia Prskawetz
Professor, Institute for Mathematical Methods in Economics (Research Unit
Economics), Vienna University of Technology, Austria, Deputy Director, Vienna
Institute of Demography, Austrian Academy of Sciences, Vienna, Austria

P.C. Purwar
Professor, Marketing Area, Indian Institute of Management, Lucknow, India

Gerrit Reepmeyer
Research Fellow, Institute of Technology Management, St. Gallen, Switzerland

Patrick Reinmoeller
Associate Professor, Strategic Management and Business Environment, Rotterdam
School of Management, Erasmus University, The Netherlands

Steve Russell
Senior Consultant, Knowledge Management, Siemens Corporate Research,
Princeton, New Jersey, USA

Karin Schmidt-Ruhland
Professor, Design of Playing and Learning, Burg Giebichenstein, University of Art
and Design Halle, Germany

Doreen Schwarz
Research Associate, Chair of Organization, Human Resource Management (HRM),
General Management, Brandenburg University of Technology, Cottbus, Germany

Merril Silverstein
Professor of Gerontology and Sociology, Davis School of Gerontology and
Department of Sociology, University of Southern California, Los Angeles,
California, USA

Alfonso Sousa-Poza
Executive Director, World Demographic Association, St. Gallen, Switzerland, Full
Professor, Economics University of Hohenheim, Germany

Ines Steinke
Consultant, Corporate Technology, User Interface Design CT IC 7, Siemens AG,
Munich, Germany

Dick Stroud
Managing Director, 20plus30 consulting, Salisbury, UK

Sue Tempest
Associate Professor in Strategic Management, Nottingham University Business
School, United Kingdom

Junichi Tomita
Lecturer, Faculty of Business Administration, Toyo University, Tokyo, Japan

Hugo Tschirky
Professor Emeritus, ETH Zurich, Switzerland

Chikako Usui
Chair and Associate Professor, Department of Sociology, University of Missouri-St. Louis, St. Louis, U.S.A

Gabriele Vogt
Deputy Director, German Institute for Japanese Studies, Tokyo, Japan

Takako Yamashita
Associate Professor, Faculty of Commerce, University of Marketing and Distribution Sciences, Kobe, Japan

Naohiro Yashiro
Professor of Economics, International Christian University, Tokyo, Japan

Part I
The Demographic Shift: Challenges, Chances, Perspectives

Chapter 1
Demographic Change and Economic Growth

T. Fent, B. Mahlberg, and A. Prskawetz

Abstract In this chapter we discuss the relationship between changes in a country's age structure and its economic growth and productivity. We summarize the recent literature on the impact of a country's age structure on economic growth and relate the results to our own empirical findings. Our results indicate a positive impact of the age group 50–64 on economic growth. Moreover, a high proportion of people in the age group 15–29 facilitate technology absorption. The use of matched employer–employee data sets allows us to estimate age-productivity profiles at the firm level. Considering all firms in the data set reveals a negative productivity effect of the share of older workers (50+). Considering only large firms reveals no impact of the age structure in the mining and manufacturing industries and a negative impact of the share of younger workers for the non-manufacturing sector.

Introduction

During recent years there has been an increasing awareness of a direct influence of population age structure on macro-economy. The theoretical foundations of the reduced form models applied in econometric studies are: (1) the life cycle model of savings and investment, and (2) age-specific variations in labor productivity. Because people's economic behavior and needs vary at different stages of life, changes in a country's age structure can have significant effects on its economic performance. While young people require investment in health and education, prime-age adults supply labor and savings, and the aged require health care and retirement income.

Several studies explain that a falling youth dependency ratio (the population below working age divided by the population of working age) contributed to the economic growth miracle in East Asia. More general, recent evidence suggests that falling youth dependency ratios in developing countries can create an opportunity for economic growth, provided that policies (openness to trade, labor-market

3

flexibility, etc.) to take advantage of the "demographic dividend" are in place. Regarding Bloom and Canning [6] "... the combined effect of this large working-age population and health, family, labor, financial, and human capital policies can effect virtuous cycles of wealth creation." On the other hand, if a large share of the population is constituted by the elderly (as projected for Europe and most industrialized countries during the next decades, and for all other world regions except Africa until the middle of the twenty-first century), the effects may be similar to those of a very young population. In this case, a large share of the population depends on the output produced by a shrinking productive working-age population and might constitute a "demographic burden."

It needs to be said that age structure is only one of several relevant factors that determine economic growth and this is equally relevant for the EU where the role of R&D and human capital formation are particularly relevant. R&D expenditures need to go hand in hand with other measures, such as human capital development, to increase the absorptive capacity of a country (i.e., the ability to absorb and take advantage of technologies initially developed abroad) and to facilitate international technological spillover. Demographic changes will intervene with these other forces of growth and in particular the foreseen aging of the European population requires intensified and longer utilization of existing human capital.

In this chapter, we first review empirical evidence at the macro level that relates demographic structure to economic growth (section "Empirical Studies on Population Structure and Economic Growth"), and will introduce the concept of the first and second demographic dividend (section "Demographic Transition and the First and Second Demographic Dividend"). In the second part of the paper (sections "Demographic Structure and Economic Productivity at the Micro and Firm Level" and "Firm Productivity, Workforce Age and Educational Structure in Austrian Mining and Manufacturing in 2001") we briefly review studies on age-productivity profiles estimated at the firm level using linked employer–employee data sets. Our exposition is based on two recent reports [15, 16] for the European Commission.

Demographic Transition and the First and Second Demographic Dividend

Since World War II developing countries have passed through a demographic transition at varying rates and times [12]. During the standard demographic transition scenario, infant mortality declines and fertility falls with a lag only after the mortality decline has begun. As a consequence, a demographic transition leads first to a demographic "burden" because population growth is faster than the growth of the working-age population. Later, as fertility declines, the demographic transition leads to a demographic "dividend" because the growth of the working-age population is faster than the growth of the total population [8]. In addition, as argued in [14], the working-age population also increases due to lower mortality. However, as soon as the further decline of mortality happens only at higher ages and fertility stays at low levels the demographic dividend turns into a demographic burden as the retired population increases.

As in developing countries, the demographic dividend could also be observed in industrialized countries that experienced a baby boom, followed by a baby bust and continued low fertility since World War II. As a consequence, the demographic change first led to a demographic dividend when the baby boom generation entered the labor market because population growth was slower than the growth of the working-age population. In the coming decades, the fertility decline that set in will lead to a demographic burden because the growth of the working-age population will fall short of the growth of the total population.

The demographic dividend leads to opportunities for growth of output per capita for two reasons. First, there is an accounting effect because a rising ratio of the working-age population to the total population increases the ratio of "producers" to "consumers." Obviously this contributes positively to the growth of output per capita. Second, there might also exist "behavioral effects" on the growth of output per capita. As Bloom and Williamson [5] stress, a rising growth rate of the working-age population leads, on the one hand, to capital dilution, that is, a reduction of the ratio of capital to the working-age population. On the other hand, a rising ratio of the working-age population to the total population implies a falling dependency ratio. Bloom et al. [7], using aggregate data of developing and developed countries, show that a falling dependency ratio increases aggregate savings (see, among others [11]). As argued in [14] further mortality decline at retirement age reduces the first demographic dividend.

In a cross-section of countries, but applying age profiles of production and consumption observed in the USA in 2000, Mason identifies the population aged 24–57 to contribute positively to the first demographic dividend. To estimate the magnitude of the first dividend, Mason computes time series of the support ratio, which gives the ratio of effective workers per effective consumers. The growth of this ratio during a 5-year period is interpreted as dividend. While the support ratio exceeded 1.1 in the USA in 1950 it was below 0.9 in Mexico. Therefore, the USA had a clear advantage, which is expected to remain until 2015. In both countries this ratio declined during the 1950s and 1960s as a result of relatively high fertility. Fertility decline caused an increase of the growth rate of the support ratio beginning in the USA in 1970 and in Mexico in 1975. In the USA this increase lasted until 2000 and in Mexico it is expected to persist until 2025. Comparing the total increase of 12.7% over a 30-year period in the USA with an increase of 46.4% during a 50-year period in Mexico reveals that Mexico gained much more from the first demographic dividend – albeit starting from a lower support ratio.

Comparing world regions, Mason finds that the dividend period started in the industrial countries in 1970, followed by Latin America, the Pacific Islands (around 1975), the Middle East and North Africa, East and Southeast Asia, the transitional economies (around 1980), South Asia (around 1980), and sub-Saharan Africa (just before 2000). The duration of the dividend period ranges from 30 years in the industrial countries to 60 years in South Asia. Comparing individual countries with respect to duration and magnitude of the dividend reveals a positive correlation between duration and magnitude for countries with a dividend period lasting less than 40 years. Despite the comprehensive comparison of dividends (i.e., increases of support ratios) among countries and regions Mason shows that it is not only the increase but also the absolute level of the support ratio that matters. Although the first demographic dividend may last for several decades, it is temporary in its nature since the increase of the working-age population due to demographic transition cannot be sustained.

When the first demographic dividend turns negative due to an increase in the retired population, the second demographic dividend comes into play. Its magnitude depends on the foresight of consumers and policymakers. Therefore, it is highly policy-dependent. Aging populations face a substantially reduced labor income. Since individuals are aware of increases in life expectancy they adopt their savings behavior and accumulate wealth to compensate for the lack of labor income during their retirement, in particular but not only in countries that do not provide a pay-as-you-go pension system. Investing these savings in the domestic economy results in capital deepening and accelerated growth in output per worker. Foreign investments, on the other hand, increase the current account and national income. Both types of investment result in more rapid growth of income per capita.

Calculating the magnitude of the second demographic dividend is more difficult than for the first dividend, partially because it is forward looking. Capital accumulation typically takes place during the late working age when peak earnings coincide with completed childrearing responsibilities. Thus, Mason takes the ratio of the wealth of the age group 50 and older to total labor income as an input to estimate the second dividend. Comparing world regions reveals that the wealth to output ratios varied between 0.4 for the Pacific Islands to 2.2 for the industrial countries. The wealth ratios exhibited a pronounced increase from 1950 to 2000 for all regions except sub-Saharan Africa. While between 1950 and 1975 the most rapid annual growth occurred in the industrial countries (1.1%), from 1975 to 2000 East and Southeast Asia (2.8%), the Pacific Islands (2.6%), Latin America (2.1%), the Middle East and North Africa and East and Southeast Asia (both 1.7%), and the transitional countries (1.4%) clearly surpassed the industrial countries, exhibiting a growth rate of 1.3% on average.

Comparing the first and second demographic dividend with the actual growth in gross domestic product per effective consumer for the period 1970–2000 reveals that only in three regions of the world, (the industrial countries, East and Southeast Asia, and South Asia) did the economies succeed in achieving a rate of economic growth exceeding the sum of the first and second demographic dividend. The other world regions failed to exploit the growth potential provided by demography and savings behavior. In contrast to the first demographic dividend, the second demographic dividend can be sustained and it is usually about twice as high in magnitude.

Empirical Studies on Population Structure and Economic Growth

According to the neoclassical growth model [18], population growth reduces economic growth due to capital dilution. However, various studies using cross-country data found an insignificant effect of population growth on economic growth for the 1960s and 1970s. Barro [1, 2] introduced a set of demographic variables into "convergence" models of economic growth. In general, fertility, population growth, and mortality turned out to be negatively related to per capita output growth, and population size and density to be positively related. In the late 1990s several studies confirmed that population growth has no effect on economic growth in growth equations with the growth rate of the total population as the only demographic variable. However, they show that demography matters for economic growth if changes in the age structure of the population are considered.

As argued in [11] "What has changed with the evolution of modeling in the 1990s is a clearer interpretation of the channels and sizes of demographic changes on the economy." Regarding Feyrer [10], demographic variables offer a great opportunity for empirical growth estimates since they are (a) strongly predetermined and (b) they possess important time series variation. The time series variation allows exploitation of the panel nature of the data.

In their study on the demographic structure and interdecade changes in output per capita growth rates, Kelley and Schmidt [11] find positive economic impacts in the 1980s and 1990s and growth-enhancing demographic trends throughout. However, the accounting effects were exhausted after the 1970s. These average worldwide impacts, however, concealed a considerable variability across decades and regions.

While the impact of core economic variables differ across region and time, core demographic variables have a positive impact in four out of the five regions considered. A closer look at core economic variables indicates that human capital (as measured by life expectancy and education) had a strong growth-inducing effect over all periods and regions, while financial and political components had more ambiguous impacts. Among the demographic core variables, declines in youth dependency ratios had a strong positive impact, while elderly dependency ratios did not yet have an impact. Obviously, the variation in elderly dependency ratios is still rather limited for past decades. While life expectancy has been attributed to the economic core variables, possibly some of the impacts from life expectancy would also account for demographic changes.

Similar to Kelley and Schmidt [11], Bloom and Williamson [5] calculate the contribution of demographic change to past economic growth by world regions. In addition, they also present the contribution of demographic change to future economic growth. As their results indicate, population dynamics can explain 1.64 and 0.52 percentage points in GDP per capita growth rates for Asia and Europe, for the period from 1965 to 1990. Expressed as a ratio of the observed GDP per capita growth rates yields: 1.64/3.33 = 0.49 and 0.52/2.83 = 0.18. Hence, population dynamics can explain almost half of the economic growth miracle in Asia and contributed about 20% to the growth observed in Europe over the same time (1965–1990). In the future, population dynamics will contribute less to economic growth and in the case of Europe even hold back economic growth prospects. As the authors underline, after having enjoyed the demographic gift phase, East Asia will get a negative demographic contribution to growth rates by entering the last stage of the demographic transition.

Based on Bloom and Williamson [5] the paper by Bloom and Canning [6] further dwells upon reverse causality, i.e., in what way demography and economy affect each other and how this relationship may change over time. The authors discuss three different mechanisms by which demography may influence economic growth: (a) labor-market effect, (b) an effect on savings and capital accumulation, and (c) an effect on educational enrolment and human capital.

Labor market effects can be determined by looking at dependency ratios, which reveal significant age structure effects. Several studies indicate that accounting effects are accompanied by strong behavioral elements, although it is not fully clear through what channels these behavioral effects operate. Effects on saving and capital accumulation are based on the assumption of imperfect international capital markets, thus implying that national savings roughly equal national investment. However, life cycle theory cannot explain the strong rise in East Asian saving rates over the past decades, but rising life expectancy with the need for a retirement income seems to be a promising explanation. Effects on educational enrolment and human capital work through life expectancy, which is a robust predictor of school enrolment rates, according to a cross-country study by Behrman et al. [4]. While this is due to increased rates of return for education, high youth dependency ratios may impede high school enrolment rates.

As the authors argue, reductions in the death rate can therefore increase the labor force per capita, generate higher savings, and increase returns to education. Later on, a higher proportion of old age dependents may increase productivity through higher capital intensity; however, this is less probable in a pay-as-you-go pension system. Besides age structure, population density may affect economic growth. The empirical evidence on this is not clear though. Population density may impede economic growth through resource constraints or enhance it through economies of scale.

While the previously discussed papers have focused on samples of all world regions, the contribution by Beaudry and Collard [3] concentrates on industrialized countries. The authors investigate the impact of growth in the working-age population on economic performance across the richest industrialized countries. They ran cross-country regressions covering the periods 1960–1974 and 1975–1997 in those countries where income per adult in 1985 exceeded US$10,000. The exclusive consideration of only rich industrialized countries allows for the assumption that all countries in the sample are affected by the same technological forces.

The results obtained for the 1960–1974 period differ significantly from those obtained for the 1975–1997 period. While the coefficients capturing the influence of the working-age population were small and insignificant in the first period, Beaudry and Collard observed a significant correlation for the second period. Between 1975 and 1997, countries with higher growth of the adult population exhibited lower growth in output per worker but higher growth in employment per adult. Thus, in the second period, countries exhibiting slow growth in the adult population showed an increase in output per adult at the same rate as those countries with higher population growth rates, but at a lower rate of exploitation of the potential labor force. It is then postulated that the difference observed between the periods of 1960–1974 and 1975–1997 can be explained by a major technological change. To motivate this explanation, Beaudry and Collard developed an analytical model that was based on the standard growth model [18].

While former papers on demographics and economic growth tended to concentrate on the dependency ratio, the paper by Feyrer [10] takes the internal demographic composition of the workforce into account. Therefore the author focuses more on the age structure of the workforce rather than on the age structure of the entire population. Based on a panel of 5-year intervals from 1960 to 1990 the author studied the role of demographic structure on economic growth for two country samples: one consists of 87 non-oil countries and the second consists of 19 OECD countries.

Applying these estimates to explain cross-country productivity differences Feyrer [10] concludes that a lower proportion of 40-year old workers in the poorer nations compared to the richer nations is associated with lower productivity. One-quarter to one-third of the observed logarithmic productivity gap between poorer and richer nations is associated with differences in workforce demographic structure. The author then suggests that the acceleration in the increase of the gap after 1980 may be associated with divergence in the demographic structure.

In [16] we studied the role of demographic structure for the EU-15 countries over the time period 1950–2005. Our results indicate that the middle-aged group 50–64 contributes positively to economic growth while the young and old-age population negatively effects economic growth. These age effects may support our hypothesis that for convergence, highly educated youngsters drive the absorption process while mature adults drive the productivity process.

For the same set of EU-15 countries we tested whether demographic variables (like proportions in different age groups and their change over time) are robust determinants of long-run economic growth in the EU-15 by taking into account the variation in parameter estimates depending on the set of variables being controlled for. We implemented a robustness exercise in order to evaluate the robustness of demographic variables as growth determinants in Europe for the period under study. Through the robustness analysis we identified the key demographic variables that were related to economic growth during the period 1960–1990. Our results of the robustness analysis are completely compatible with the first study. However, as previously shown by Lindh and Malmberg [13] and several other authors, the hump-shaped pattern of the age structure effect shifts to the right as life expectancy increases.

In the same report, we also investigated the nature of the demographic effects by empirically analyzing the influence of age structure on technology adoption (and, subsequently, on GDP per capita growth) in the EU for a panel setting from 1950 to 2005. The demographic variables used are the proportion of the workforce aged 15–29 (*L1529*), 30–49 (*L3049*), and 50–64 (*L5064*) in the initial year of each period, the ratio of *L5064* to *L1529*, and the standard deviation of the three work-force age groups. While our results do not indicate any significant effects for the variables measuring the standard deviation of age groups, we find that economies with a relatively low proportion of the workforce in the youngest age group present insignificant absorption rates, as opposed to economies with high proportions, which tend to catch up with the technological frontier. For the other age groups (that are of course closely correlated with the youngest age group) we find that countries with low shares in the 30–49 and the 50–64 age groups have positive and significant absorption parameters. We find similar results for the ratio of *L5064* to *L1529*. These results support our hypothesis that for convergence it is highly educated youngsters who drive the absorption process, while mature adults drive the mature productiv-ity process. Inclusion of demographic variables as extra regressors did not change the results concerning the location of the thresholds and the sign and significance of the technology absorption parameter estimates. However, the demographic vari-ables did not appear significant as linear regressors. This may indicate that the effect of age structure on growth in this case takes place through its interaction with the relative level of development of a given country, and thus might be understood as an effect whose channel to growth is technology absorption.

Summing up the empirical evidence on population structure and economic growth, it is evident that over the time period 1965–1990 almost half of the eco-nomic growth miracle in Asia and about 20% of the observed economic growth in Europe can be linked to changes in the demographic structure. Estimates on the world sample over the 1960s to 1990s indicate that declines in the youth dependency ratio and increases in life expectancy (as a measure of human capital and health) have a robust positive impact on economic growth. Overall, empirical evidence indicates that the demographic dividend (a decreasing youth dependency ratio) is more likely to boost economic growth under conditions of open economies, a flex-ible labor force, and modern institutions, though the results are not robust to the specifications and samples chosen. A more differentiated analysis by age structure indicates a hump-shaped effect of the age structure on economic growth whereby increasing life expectancy shifts the hump to the right. For industrialized countries it is particularly the advanced work force age group (50–64) that positively con-tributes to economic growth. While mature adults therefore drive the productivity process, empirical evidence has shown that it is the younger age groups who drive the absorption process in a sample of EU-15 countries over the second half of the twentieth century.

Demographic Structure and Economic Productivity at the Micro and Firm Level

While the relation between changes in the adult population and aggregate produc-tivity at the macro level has been rather clear-cut, recent evidence of the relation between age and individual productivity is less clear-cut. Understanding the age productivity profile at the individual and firm level (i.e., micro level) is central to understanding retirement incentives at the individual and firm level. Strategies of encouraging older workers to remain longer in the workforce need to be evaluated in tandem with the productivity profile of older workers. It is well known that workers of different ages may have different levels of productivity (as well as capacities of learning), although the exact shape is still highly disputed and strongly dependent on the occupation, technological progress, and possible cohort effects that work through schooling levels.

Studies that estimate the influence of age on individual productivity are based on different indices, including supervisors' evaluations, piece-rate studies, analyses of employer–employee datasets, age-earnings profiles, and entrepreneurial activity. Most piece-rate studies, which measure the quantity and quality of the workers' output, and analyses of employer–employee datasets, where companies' productivity is measured, suggest that productivity follows an inverted U-shaped profile where significant decreases are found after the age of 50. A problem with most estimates of age-specific productivity is that older individuals who remain in the workforce are positively selected and have a higher productivity than those leaving the workforce, which might bias the estimates. Although supervisors' evaluations on average show little or no relationship between the assessment score and the age of the employee, subjective opinions may be biased, where for example the management's opinions of older employees may be inflated for loyalty reasons. Since the relation between individual performance and wages is often distorted, age-earnings profiles cannot replicate the age–productivity profiles. Most commonly, the latter profiles peak earlier than the former ones.

An important cause of age-related productivity decline is likely to be age-specific reduction in cognitive abilities. Some abilities, such as perceptual speed, show relatively large decrements even from a young age, while others, like verbal abilities, exhibit only small changes throughout the working life. Experience in a firm or plant boosts productivity up to a point beyond which, however, additional tenure has little effect. Older individuals learn at a slower pace and have reductions in their memory and reasoning abilities. In particular, senior workers are likely to have difficulties in adjusting to new ways of working.

Earlier studies tend to neglect the causes of age-related job performance differences and the impact of changing labor market demands when measuring age differences in productivity. Skirbekk [17] estimates the productivity potential by weighing age-specific ability levels against the labor market demand for these abilities. Evidence from both employment shifts between industries and changes caused by relative wage levels of unskilled and skilled employees suggests that there has been an increase in the demand for cognitive abilities over a long period of time. Physical strength and bodily coordination have lost much of their importance, while analytic, numerical, and interpersonal abilities are increasingly in demand. Basing the estimates on the causes of productivity differences allows an assessment of the impact of structural changes in the labor market. The age–productivity profile is found to vary over time, in accordance with changing labor market needs. Assuming a reasonably strong effect of experience, we estimate that productivity peaks for the 35–44 year old age group. If the demand for experience falls, the productivity peak shifts towards younger ages. Conversely, if the minimum ability requirement dropped over time, age differences in productivity would decrease. Estimations of the productivity profile reflect that job performance on average tends to decrease in the second half of the working life, given almost any calibration of the model. The only exception to this would be if an individual's productivity gains from experience continued for several decades and if this effect more than outweighed the functional decreases with respect to other job-related factors. Given available empirical evidence on how additional work experience affects productivity, this may seem unlikely. Hence, these findings support the theory of delayed payment contracts, where the relatively high wages of older workers create loyalty to the firm and represent a compensation for high productivity earlier in the career.

Continuous increases in life expectancy have raised the concern that the number of years spent in the labor market in order to maintain old-age social security needs to increase both from an individual as well as social point of view. Understanding how health develops over the life cycle is crucial to understanding individuals' work potential at older ages. The health effects of age represent a particularly important issue if frail health makes it difficult to work or if employment represents a health hazard for older individuals. As one grows older, blood circulation deteriorates, maximum oxygen uptake decreases, muscle strength and endurance are lowered, bone mass decreases (particularly among women), hearing and eyesight decline with age, and individuals are more likely to fall sick. Older individuals' work capacity can therefore be lower in many occupations, although adjusted working environments, technical aids, and ergonomic equipment can improve the situation. Moreover, physical exercise, less smoking and alcohol, and a healthier lifestyle with better nutrition would improve the working capacity of older individuals, and presumably this also holds true for younger individuals. As we argue in our recent report [15], productivity is a system attribute and can only be understood within its social context. However, the hump-shaped pattern of age–productivity differentials seems to be ubiquitous across various studies. To investigate the relationship between age and productivity, considering firm-level-specific factors, in the next section we will look at a new matched employer–employee data set for Austria.

Firm Productivity, Workforce Age and Educational Structure in Austrian Mining and Manufacturing in 2001

We use a cross-section of employer–employee matched data from Statistik Austria for the year 2001.[1] The data set emerged from matching individual data from structural business statistics[2] with the population census of Austria. It

---

[1] For a more detailed description of the data and variables see [15].

[2] Our data are collected from the Structural Business Survey (year 2001) of Statistik Austria. The Structural Business Statistics are produced by extrapolating the results of the survey to the main part of the Austrian economy. For details of sample selection and the focus of the survey as well as the extrapolation mechanism see [19].

Table 1.1 Effects of employee's age structure on firm productivity in Austria

Table	All firms	Small firms	Large firms
Share of young employees (below 30)	Negative effect on productivity	Negative effect on productivity	Negative effect on productivity
Share of older employees (over 49)	Negative effect on productivity	Negative effect on productivity	No effect on productivity

covers Nomenclature générale des activités économiques dans les Communautés européennes (NACE) sections C (mining and quarrying) to K (real estate, renting and business activities) and contains selected economic indicators of 34,375 enterprises as well as selected socio-demographic indicators of 1,563,873 employees. The economic indicators include, e.g., information about branch affiliation, number of white-collar and blue-collar employees at the end of 2001, and the value added in 2001 from structural business statistics. Socio-demographic indicators taken from the population census provide information on age, education, and occupation of individuals employed in establishments on 15 May 2001. Like Crépon et al. [9], we divide our sample into firm-level data from mining and manufacturing sectors (NACE sections C and D) and non-manufacturing sectors (NACE sections E through K).

Summing up the micro-evidence for Austrian industries (see also Table 1.1), we find a negative productivity effect of the share of older workers (50 years and older) for the whole sample and for small firms (irrespective of the economic sector we consider), which is similar to the findings of most employer–employee studies. If we restrict our sample to large firms, the age–productivity profile changes. For firms in the mining and manufacturing industries, the age structure of the workforce cannot be related to productivity whereas for firms in the non-manufacturing sectors only the share of younger workers can be related to productivity, namely negatively. Our results are similar to the findings of Crépon et al. [9] for large firms; they also found a concave age–productivity profile. Though the sample size decreases when we move to large firms, we are more confident in our results for this sub-sample since in larger firms we may expect that all age and educational shares are represented. For educational shares we found mixed results. In the mining and manufacturing sector it is the share of upper-secondary education that increases productivity. For firms in the non-manufacturing industries we find a positive educational gradient: the higher the education, the greater the increase in productivity.

Results for a more detailed workforce composition that includes the interaction of age and educational shares do not yield new insights. We may therefore conclude that the age and educational share coefficients are rather stable across educational and respectively large age categories. Our results for the other control variables (size and age of firm, occupational structure, gender composition of the workforce) are similar to findings in the literature so far. For instance, Crépon et al. [9] also found that an increase in the female share of employees decreases productivity, though to a smaller extent (about 11% in manufacturing and 7% in non-manufacturing) than in our results.

These results need to be interpreted with caution since we cannot control for endogeneity of the regressors within our cross-sectional data set. A clear result of our study is the differing age–productivity profile in small versus large firms. We find that the share of older workers is negatively related to productivity only for small firms. As we argued, this result may indicate that larger firms are more able to optimize their age structure, or that alternatively within larger firms the age structure of the employees is less important. A third alternative hypothesis, more related to the mode of production, could be that the substitutability of workers at different ages is different in small versus large firms. In our econometric setup of the model we assumed perfect substitutability of workers at different ages. Future research needs to verify this assumption.

In [16] we demonstrated throughout a series of simulations that in a pure labor economy the substitutability of workers at different ages has a stronger impact on aggregate productivity than variations in the age–productivity profile. Our study cannot offer definite policy advice regarding the productivity of older workers. Our study does indicate, however, that part of the negative effect of the share of older workers on productivity we find may be firm-specific rather than individual-specific, given that the effect disappears for large firms.

Summary and Conclusion

While previous estimates indicated that population dynamics had and will have an impact on economic growth and labor productivity, the channels though which these effects work remain largely unspecified. Empirical evidence indicates that demographic factors matter just as much, or sometimes even more, for economic growth as the factors commonly stressed in the growth literature, such as technological change, innovation, and political/institutional explanations.

At the very least this indicates that any economic growth study that does not control for heterogeneity with respect to age is very likely to suffer from omitted variable bias. The general finding is a significant hump-shaped pattern for the impact of the age structure of the workforce on economic growth. One channel through which demography may impact economic growth is labor productivity. As we have shown in the second part of our review, labor productivity by age again exhibits a hump-shaped pattern at the individual as well as at the firm level. The peak of this hump, however, seems to be sensitive to the time period on which the estimates are based. By including more recent time periods, it seems that the peak of the hump-shaped age pattern moves to the right.

The potential role of demographic variables doubtlessly lies in the fact that they are better measured and more well-defined and suffer from less endogeneity problems (except possibly the younger age groups) than the core economic variables. Nevertheless it needs to be kept in mind that macro-level econometric studies are not adequate to identify the mechanisms and causalities that operate between the link of economic and demographic factors (although our results on technology adoption offer such an explanation, where we have shown that the absorptive capacity is related to the age structure). Further research is definitely needed to disentangle the mechanisms through which demographic change operates at the macro level. The next steps in the research agenda are clearly in-depth micro studies on economic–demographic interactions.

Aging is often negatively associated with economic growth; however, as we have shown this depends on the context. So far, most countries are still in the midst of a window of opportunity. The youth dependency ratio has decreased essentially and the old age dependency ratio has not yet increased to its forecasted maximum value. This opportunity needs to be reaped from the economy. Labor markets, social security systems, etc. need to be adapted to be ready for the compositional change of the demographic structure to be expected. Of course, what has changed is the age structure of the labor force. Still, this does not automatically imply that an old labor force is negative for the economy. In macro-level studies it has been shown that the hump-shaped pattern of the age structure shifts to the right when life expectancy (i.e., economic development) increases. That is, in industrialized countries older workers seem to add positively to economic growth. Also, at the individual/firm level the deterioration of productivity with age cannot be shown to be taken for sure. Whether productivity decreases with age depends on many factors, like the firm, the occupation, etc. that the employee works in. Hence productivity is a system attribute! Keep in mind that these are all ceteris paribus assumptions if we project findings on the past to possible future impacts of aging. In fact, it will be more complicated and most likely also more optimistic as the shift of the hump-shaped pattern of age structure to the right already indicates. If life expectancy (and in particular healthy life expectancy) increases, the behavior of people will change. Savings, investments, etc. may increase, people may start to work longer, etc. These effects may all counteract the negative productivity effect of aging.

The empirical results presented in this chapter rely on data sets from the EU-15, but also provide insights for other economies. Our estimates reveal that the highly educated young workers drive the process of technology adoption and the experienced old workers contribute positively to economic growth. While most developing countries are just entering the period of a growing share of the working-age population (first demographic dividend), the industrialized countries are approaching the end of this period and are moving into an era where accelerated capital accumulation may sustain high levels of economic growth. Therefore, in the developing countries investments in human capital will be crucial for the economic performance, and in industrialized countries the utilization of existing human capital (experienced workers), individual savings, and the effective investment of these savings either in the domestic economy or abroad will be the key determinants in fostering productivity and economic growth.

We conclude that population aging should be considered a challenge and opportunity for society and the economy and not just a negative impact on economic growth and productivity.

References

1. R.J. Barro, Q. J. Econ. **106**(2), 407 (1991)
2. R.J. Barro, *Determinants of Economic Growth: A Cross-Country Empirical Study* (MIT Press, Cambridge, MA, 1997)
3. P. Beaudry, F. Collard, Scand. J. Econ. **105**(3), 441 (2003)
4. J.R. Behrman, S. Duryea, M. Székely, *Human Capital in Latin America at the End of the 20th Century* (University of Pennsylvania, Mimeo, 1999)
5. D.E. Bloom, J.G. Williamson, World Bank Econ. Rev. **12**(3), 419 (1998)
6. D.E. Bloom, D. Canning, in *Population Matters: Demographic Change, Economic Growth, and Poverty in the Developing World*, ed. by N. Birdsall, A. Kelley, S. Sinding (Oxford University Press, Oxford, 2001), p. 165
7. D.E. Bloom, D. Canning, B. Graham, Scand. J. Econ. **105**, 319 (2003)
8. D.E. Bloom, D. Canning, J. Sevilla, *The Demographic Dividend: A New Perspective on the Economic Consequences of Population Change* (Rand, Santa Monica, CA, 2003)
9. B. Crépon, N. Deniau, S. Perez-Duarte, *Wages, Productivity and Worker Characteristics. A French Perspective* (INSEE, Mimeo, 2002)
10. J. Feyrer, Rev. Econ. Stat. **89**(1), 100 (2007)
11. A.C. Kelley, R.M. Schmidt, J. Popul. Econ. **18**(2), 275 (2005)
12. R.D. Lee, J. Econ. Perspect. **17**(4), 167 (2003)
13. T. Lindh, B. Malmberg, Demographically based global income forecasts up to the year 2050. Working Paper 7, Institute for Futures Studies, Stockholm, 2004
14. A. Mason, in *Proceedings of the United Nations Expert Group Meeting on Social and Economic Implications of Changing Population Age Structure*, Mexico, 31 Aug–2 Sep 2005
15. A. Prskawetz, T. Lindh, The Impact of Ageing on Innovation and Productivity Growth in Europe. Research Report No. 28, Vienna Institute of Demography, Austrian Academy of Sciences, 2006
16. A. Prskawetz, T. Lindh, The Relationship Between Demographic Change and Economic Growth in the EU. Research Report No. 32, Vienna Institute of Demography, Austrian Academy of Sciences, 2007
17. V. Skirbekk, *Age and Individual Productivity: A Literature Survey* (Vienna Yearbook of Population Research, Vienna, 2004), p. 133
18. R.M. Solow, Q. J. Econ. **70**(1), 65 (1956)
19. Statistik Austria, *Leistungs- und Struturerhebung 2002 (Structural Business Statistics Manufacturing and Services 2002)* (Statistik Austria, Vienna, 2003)

Chapter 2
Talking Politics: Demographic Variables and Policy Measures in Japan

G. Vogt

Abstract The three core variables of demographic change: a population's fertility behaviour, structures of migration and people's life expectancy, translate into policy fields as family, replacement and old-age policies. The study at hand shows how Japan (one of the most rapidly ageing and shrinking nations) is addressing this demographic change through various policy measures. It will be argued that Japan is putting much effort into old-age policy, thereby addressing the present needs of a growing elderly population. Japan, however, only hesitantly takes upon issues of family and replacement policy. Historical and ideological taboos prove to be too persistent to allow for radical policy changes. These, however, are necessary in order to comprehensively deal with the future challenges of demographic change.

Introduction

The core variables of demographic change are changes in a population's fertility behaviour, the dynamism of migration, and changes in people's life expectancy. All three variables have a comprehensive political dimension inherent to them. Issues of a population's fertility behaviour translate into politics as "family policy", issues of emigration and immigration as "replacement policy", and issues of people's life expectancy as "old-age policy".

The paper at hand addresses these three political dimensions of demographic change: family, replacement, and old-age policies. The study is concerned with exemplified policies and the political process alike. It is based on a notion of governance, as opposed to government, thereby arguing that any comprehensive approach to policies and politics needs to deal with the multiple layers of the political system. That is, not only should traditional political actors such as political parties and governmental agencies be studied, the power of new political actors such as civil society organizations and lobbying groups within the business world should also be taken into account. The political process (agenda setting, policy formation, policy implementation) is both a top-down and bottom-up process.

Japan, a country that is facing an enormously rapid demographic change, and which might become a role model with regard to the puzzle of how to address demographic change in politics, will be in the focus of my study. Wherever appropriate I will put the case study of Japan in comparative perspective to policies evolving around demographic change in other nations.

Family Policy

In January 2007, in a talk to supporters of the Liberal Democratic Party (LDP) in Matsue (Shimane Prefecture, Hakuo Yanagisawa), Japan's Minister of Health, Labour and Welfare labelled women "birth-giving machines". He is quoted as follows: "The number of women aged 15–50 is fixed. As we have a fixed number of birth-giving machines and devices, all we can ask of them is that each do their best." [1]. Only a month later, the Bishop of the diocese of Augsburg/Germany, Walter Mixa, harshly criticized the German Minister for Families, Seniors, Women and Youth, Ursula von der Leyen, herself the mother of seven children, for introducing a new policy guideline that aims to introduce additional child-care for 500,000 children under the age of three within the next 6 years. Creating more child-care facilities for young children, the Bishop argued, means expecting women to go back to work soon after having had a baby, denying them the opportunity to be full-time mothers, and thus treating them as birth-giving machines [25].

Rarely do politicians, religious leaders or other public figures express their personal opinions so openly when it comes to the issue of people's fertility behaviour. Fertility behaviour is probably the most private decision of individuals, and to most citizens it is unacceptable to see the state interfering in this matter. When it comes to fertility behaviour, in other words, to designing a nation's future demographic structure, the power of political guidelines is limited.

Japan currently faces the hardship of learning this lesson. It is confronted with the puzzle of how limited the state's range of action is when it comes to boosting its population's total fertility rate (TFR). Ever since the "1.57 shock" of 1990, when the nation's TFR fell to a record post-war low of 1.57, the Ministry of Health, Labour and Welfare (MHLW) has implemented a broad variety of measures aiming at curbing the falling birth rate. The underlying reason for these measures is straightforward and pragmatic; political scientist Schoppa [23] put it this way: "Today's babies are [...] seen as tomorrow's tax payers, and there aren't enough of them to pay for the health and pension benefits retiring baby boomers are counting on."

A falling birth rate immediately translates into a threat to the fundamental characteristics of modern welfare states, in particular to the inter-generational dependence, numerically measured as dependency ratio. For a nation of lowest-low fertility[1]

---

[1] Italian demographer Francesco Billari coined the term lowest-low fertility, indicating a TFR below 1.30.

such as Japan, with 1.29 TFR in 2004 [9], the total dependency ratio is predicted to change at a hitherto unknown high speed. The total dependency ratio is the sum of the child-dependency ratio (ratio of population aged 0–14 to population aged 15–64) and the old-age dependency ratio (ratio of population aged 65 and over to population aged 15–64). While the child-dependency ratio is decreasing (from 59.3% in 1950 to 20.8% in 2004), the old-age dependency ratio is increasing rapidly (from 8.3% in 1950 to 29.2% in 2004). In sum, this development over the course of the past half-century translates into a decreasing total dependency ratio (from 67.5% in 1950 to 50.1% in 2004). Noteworthy, however, is the fundamental change in the dependency structure, measured as the elderly–children ratio. While the elderly–children ratio in 1950 was at 14.0%, it rose to 140.3% by 2004. This indicates that nowadays there are ten times more elderly per child than there were 50 years ago [9]. The impact this development will have on Japan's social security system will be unprecedented.

Measures that have been taken in the context of balancing Japan's dependency ratio through family policy target in particular three groups of society: (working) mothers, "new fathers", and "parents of the next generation". The core measures of Japan's family policy, which – ironically enough – is not called "family policy" (*kazoku seisaku*) in Japanese, but is framed as "measures to counter the declining birth rate" (*shōshika taisaku*), are three successive action plans: the Angel Plan (1995–1999), the New Angel Plan (2000–2004), and the Children and Childrearing Support Plan (2005–2009).[2]

The main concern of the initial Angel Plan (1995–1999) lay with Japan's working mothers. It set numerical targets to increase the number of child-care facilities, including those with extended hours (from 2230 to 7000), emergency child-care facilities (from 450 to 3000) and after school clubs (from 4520 to 9000). The Angel Plan in its core aimed at enabling more women to participate in the workforce while relying on a dense support network for raising their children. The Angel Plan's second target group were stay-at-home mothers, with a specific focus on lightening their burden of isolation (an increasing phenomenon in Japan's urban areas) and thus making parenting a less stressful experience. The number of community childrearing support centres and drop-in child-care services was increased.

The New Angel Plan (2000–2004) increased efforts of supporting stay-at-home mothers and, for the first time, emphasized the need for alterations within Japan's economic world. It called for family-friendly workplaces, in particular for a reduction of working hours, encouragement for employees to take allotted vacation days, and facilitated child-care leave. In 2001, then Prime Minister Junichirō Koizumi furthermore initiated the "Zero Waiting for Day Care Program". Within 4 years under this program, 150,000 additional child-care spaces were established. The downside of the increase in the number of child-care spaces was the decrease in quality in many of the new places. Hitherto strict regulations with regard to personnel and facility standards had to be relaxed in order to license greater numbers of child-care spaces.

---

[2] If not indicated differently, the numbers introduced in the following paragraphs on family policy are drawn from Coleman [6].

The Children and Childrearing Support Plan (2005–2009) needs to be understood as the first step towards a paradigm change in Japan's family policy. There are two "innovative" target groups at the centre of this plan: Japan's "new fathers" and the "parents of the next generation". Among the plan's objectives is to shorten over-time hours at work and to encourage men to spend more time on childrearing and house working (from 48 min per day to 2 h). These goals reflect a substantial reor-ganization of the habits and traditions of Japan's working environment. Based on the 1999 Basic Law for a Gender-Equal Society (*Danjo Koyō Kikai Kintō-hō*) they aim to create a more equal partnership between men and women by ensuring the compatibility of professional and family life.[3]

While the policies that aim at creating "new fathers" reflect Japan's intention to catch up with Western countries when it comes to family policy, its scheme to create "parents of the next generation" is a cutting-edge policy approach. It has two objectives: first, it aims at demonstrating to young adults the enriching aspects of parenting through some hands-on experience. Young parents and their newborn babies, for example, are invited to visit school classes and to share their personal experiences of a life with children. Secondly, "parents of the next generation" are understood to be self-sufficient and responsible members of society.

The Tokyo Metropolitan Government (TMG) took over a leading role in imple-menting this new policy of building "parents of the next generation" by introducing a Volunteering Day into its public high schools' curriculum in the 2004/2005 school year. In 2006, Japan's Ministry of Education, Science, Sports, Culture and Tech-nology (MEXT) introduced a mandatory course entitled *hōshi* (service) in 893 pilot schools at all levels. The program aims to teach young adults through volunteer ser-vices at, for example, elderly care facilities, what it means to take responsibility for one's own life and the lives of dependants.[4]

Japan's family policy (its main actor being the MHLW) involves a broad range of policy issues such as work/life-balance,[5] employment structures, and educational reforms. Policy measures in this field target a variety of groups in Japan's society, such as (working) mothers, (modern) fathers, and young adults. The target groups are numerous and measures are comprehensive. Yet Japan's TFR is not increasing significantly. The reason behind this policy failure is threefold:

First, family policies to the representatives of the private sector are nothing more than non-binding guidelines. When it comes, for example, to parenting leave for fathers, the political and legal framework has been set. Yet, many companies put pressure framed as an issue of work ethic on their employees not to take the leave.

---

[3] Schad-Seifert [22] offers a thorough study on policy measures, initiated by the Gender Equality Bureau, to counter the falling birth rate following the 1999 Basic Law.

[4] See Ogawa [15] for more details on this program of "induced volunteerism" in Japanese schools.

[5] Work/life-balance was one of the central issues of debate during a two-day EU-Japan conference on the various challenges of demographic change. Kuniko Inoguchi, LDP politician and former Minister for Gender Equality and Social Affairs, pointed out that the hardship of balancing profes-sional and family life is the main reason behind Japan's low fertility rate [10]. Scholarly work on the topic of work/life-balance has been conducted, for example, by Gambles et al. [8] and – with a special focus on Japan – by Roberts [20].

Second, current family policies fail to target one growing group of Japan's society, the young women who "race for the exits" [24], those who opt for a life outside the traditional boundaries of Japan's social and economic system.

Thirdly, Japan's family policy cannot openly show any pro-natal characteristics. Following Japan's (pre-) war history of *umeyo-fuyaseyo* (give birth and multiply) policy, pro-natal policies in Japan (as well as, for example, in Germany) nowadays are considered a political and societal taboo.

Replacement Policy

The concept of replacement policy is straight-forward: When a national workforce is not large enough to fill job openings and/or to ensure economic growth, it can be compensated for by foreign workers. The practical side of replacement policy, however, is not all that simple. Often, politics need to balance the economic demand for foreign workers against societal fears of what German sociologist Georg Simmel has called "the stranger", that is, persons of social distance in general, and foreigners in particular.

Currently, just over 2 million foreigners reside in Japan. This comprises 1.63% of the population of Japan [14]. In international comparison, especially in comparison with other OECD nations, this number is extremely low. In Germany, for example, in 2005, 8.2% of the population held a foreign passport [3]. Demographic change, if counter-measured solely through replacement policy, would make migration flows to Japan need to rise tremendously. In 2000, the United Nations Population Division (UNPD) published a report entitled "Replacement Migration: Is It a Solution to Declining and Ageing Populations?" In it they introduce projections for eight industrial nations and two world regions.

For Japan, the report projects astronomic numbers: Were Japan, for example, to keep its old-age dependency ratio at its 1995-level solely through immigration of foreign workers, it would need a replacement migration of roughly 10 million persons per year. By 2050 Japan would have seen a migration flow of 553 million persons and the population of Japan would have risen to a total of 818 million persons, with 87% of them being post-1995-immigrants and their descendants [27].

An increase in migration flows to Japan can be observed from 1990 on. The 1990 revision of the Immigration Control and Refugee Recognition Act triggered the rise in the number of foreign residents in Japan to double (from 1 to 2 million persons) within one and a half decades. It has been the Chinese and the Brazilian populations of Japan that saw a particularly sharp increase in numbers.[6] This is due to the fact that two of the main revisions of the Immigration Control and Refugee Recognition Act opened new avenues for migration. That is, they created and redefined certain visa categories, which are mainly made use of by Chinese and Brazilians. Yet, the

---

[6] With more than half a million persons, the largest group among foreign residents in Japan still is Korean nationals. The overwhelming majority of these Koreans and their ancestors came to Japan, often as forced laborers, before the end of World War II. They nowadays reside in Japan as special permanent residents without any restrictions on their work permit.

official political guideline in Japan still reads: Japan is not a country of immigration, and Japan does not accept labour migration except for temporary migration (usually a maximum stay of 5 years) of the highly skilled.

Some 300,000 Brazilians are currently residing in Japan. They make up the majority of labour migrants to Japan coming from Central and South America. Some 89.6% of those labour migrants come to Japan as so-called *Nikkeijin*, that is, persons of Japanese descent. Descendents of Japanese emigrants can obtain a long-term resident status up until the third generation. This visa category is exceptional in that it does not imply any restrictions on work permission. More than three quarters of *Nikkeijin* residing in Japan work in jobs that do not require special qualifications, usually in the service and manufacturing industries. They usually reside in the prefectures of Aichi, Shizuoka and Gunma and work in Japan's automobile and electronic industries.

Nikkeijin employees are attractive to Japanese companies for a number of reasons. First, *Nikkeijin* usually are hired via intermediary companies located in Brazil. It is up to these intermediaries to cover the social security costs of the *Nikkeijin* employees. Secondly, *Nikkeijin* are remunerated on an hourly (not monthly) basis, which means that companies do not pay them extra allowances such as the biannual bonuses, a standard in Japan. Thirdly, *Nikkeijin* are almost exclusively hired on a basis of temporary work contracts. This means that for companies they are flexible human resources, a leeway for comparatively quick hiring and firing according to market developments. LDP-politician and then Vice Minister of Justice, Tarō Kōno [12] stated in a 2006 interview with the author that the terms of residence for *Nikkeijin* were created with the purpose of opening a side-door for labour migration of the not-highly skilled.

Another side door is the internship program, which caused the numbers of Chinese migrants to Japan to rise significantly. The program runs under the framework of overseas development aid. It created a special visa category of intern, with the officially stated purpose of enabling young workers from developing countries to come to Japan, gain some work experience in Japanese companies, and after a maximum of 3 years (1 year training on the job, followed by 2 years internship) to return to their various home countries. Ideally, this way a spill-over of knowledge and skills would take place.

The reality, however, particularly regarding working conditions, in many cases does not follow this altruistic line of argument. Ippei Torii, chairman of the *Zentōitsu Workers' Union*, Japan's largest labour union for foreign workers, reports hourly wages of just 300 Japanese Yen (roughly US$3) being paid. Breaks during work time, even a short toilet break, are deducted from working hours. Since there is no work contract between an intern and a company s/he works for, the intern does not have any access to legal remedies. Japan's internship program has come under severe international criticism as violating human rights. By now, influential political actors such as MHLW and *Nippon Keidanren*, the Japan Business Federation, are calling for a reassessment of the program.[7]

---

[7] Currently (spring 2008) the government of Japan is debating a bill that would allow interns to be covered by labour standard laws and minimum wage laws [11].

The internship program, as well as the *Nikkeijin* migration, feeds Japan's low-wage sector with an urgently needed workforce. Both open avenues for the migration of unskilled workers to Japan; Japan's politicians not only tolerate these systems, they initiated them. They did so because of a conundrum: on the one hand Japan needs labour migrants, in particular in the service sector and the manufacturing industries. On the other hand, there is a lack of political guidelines offering opportunities to these migrants; such guidelines would not be backed by a majority in society. In fact, the rising number of foreign workers in Japan is perceived to be a problem by more and more Japanese (53.1% in 2004) [18].

Yet, against the background of its demographic crisis, Japan is currently touching on the taboo issue of labour migration. For the first time ever, in the 2006 bilateral Economic Partnership Agreement (EPA) between Japan and the Philippines, Japan agreed to accept the labour migration of unskilled workers. The Japan–Philippines EPA will enable up to 1000 care givers to come to Japan and, after passing a Japanese language test as well as the national care givers examination, work in their professions. In 2007, yet another agreement on a bilateral EPA was reached. This most recent EPA, between Japan and Indonesia, will also allow for care giver migration to Japan. EPAs are a remarkable step for Japan's replacement policy, as they reflect a paradigm change: EPAs pose a pragmatic political answer to an economic need, defying concerns in society. The care giving sector is one of the sectors that is already suffering from labour shortages. The ratio of job openings to job applicants currently is around two and is expected to rise even higher with a growing older population.[8]

Economists and politicians alike argue that the number of foreign workers in Japan will need to rise in order to keep the nation's dependency ratio in balance. One of the most outspoken advocates of increasing the number of foreign workers in Japan is Hidenori Sakanaka, a former Ministry of Justice bureaucrat (1970–2005) and former chairman of Japan's Immigration Bureau. Sakanaka currently heads an independent think-tank, the Japan Immigration Policy Institute. His latest policy proposal is to accept 10 million labour migrants within the next 50 years [21].

Japan's need for labour migration is uncontested; yet translating any responses to this need into actual policies appears to be difficult, since: (a) there are numerous political actors involved in replacement policy, each of them advocating their own policy proposals; and (b) those policies not only target potential migrants, but also call for a change of mind-set within the receiving society. Moreover, replacement policy has been (and to some degree still is) a political taboo issue. Two aspects need to be highlighted in this context:

First, contemporary Japan is very much caught up in a discourse on the growing gap between rich and poor, between the urban centres and the nation's periphery. Inequality in, among others, education and income are at the centre of this discourse. Japan's society is facing the disappearance of the structure of its middle-strata society. Against this background, the influx of foreign elements is perceived

---

[8] The Japan–Philippines EPA as well as the Japan–Indonesia EPA are awaiting ratification. On the process of political bargaining around the Japan–Philippines EPA refer to Vogt [28].

as a threat to public order, national security and even economic security.[9] Reforms on migration policy in Japan first of all need to overcome this societal fear of de-homogenization.

Secondly, if migration flows to Japan were to be expanded, policies of integration would need to be implemented. This thought is taking root in Japan slowly and on a small scale. It was only in October 2006 that the term integration was first mentioned in an official political document. It appeared in the Ministry of the Interior's report on the concept of *tabunka kyōsei*, which is often translated into English as "multicultural coexistence". Political scientist and head of the ministry's in-house committee that created the report, Keizo Yamawaki, however, argues that the more fitting translation for this term was "multicultural community building". This term implies that not only foreigners but also the Japanese society is required to make an effort in order to ensure that a new and positive structure of society can emerge. It is only when the Japanese society willingly accepts its transformation (multiculturalization) ahead, that migration to Japan can become a win–win situation for both the migrants and the receiving society.[10]

Old-Age Policy

Is Japan's political system a democracy? Some agree; others might call it a "silver democracy" or "gerontocracy" [7]. These alternative terms hint at the fact that Japan's political system is dominated by elderly voters and elderly politicians. Moreover, old-age policy is a prominent and well-funded policy field.

The 2005 elections to the Lower House of the National Diet showed that 25.3% of eligible voters were 65 years or older. They comprise a large interest group among all eligible voters. Furthermore, they are also the most politically active group: The average turn-out at the 2005 election was 67.5%. While only 43.3% of the 20–24 age cohort (number of eligible voters 7,725,000) cast their ballot, the turnout among the 65–69 cohort (number of eligible voters 7,344,000) was 83.7%. The 65–69 cohort showed the highest turn-out among all voters. These numbers clarify the political power of the elderly voters, which is matched in the political power of elderly politicians: While the average age for Japan's overall population in 2005 was 43.1 years of age, for representatives in the Lower House it was 56.8 years and 59.2 years for prefectural governors [7]. A question that needs to be asked is whether the numerical dominance of elderly voters and elderly politicians is reflected in the contents of old-age policy and its underlying decision making process.

With regard to how old-age policy making developed in post-war Japan, political scientist Campbell [5] has conducted in-depth studies on all three steps of the

---

[9] See Yamamoto [30] on the discourse of foreigner crime in Japan and Lie [13] on the discourse of Japaneseness.

[10] In a survey among migrant support organizations in Japan, conducted by Vogt and Lersch [29], "Change the way foreigners are treated in Japan" was named as one of the most prominent purposes of those organizations. This hints at the (perceived) need of a changing attitude towards foreigners in Japan's society.

political process (agenda setting, decision making and policy implementation).[11] Campbell concludes his research with several main findings. On the academic controversy about policy making in Japan he argues that both bureaucrats and politicians participated in policy making with significant impacts. The role of individual bureaucrats and politicians in shaping the structure of Japan's welfare state was significant. The major actors, the MHLW and the LDP, generally agreed "that Japan should have a welfare state up to Western standards and that social programs must be [...] effective and not too expensive." [5]. Central issues of "a welfare state up to Western standards" are public pension, medical care, and long-term care, all three of which have seen alternating periods of expansion and contraction over the past decades. While bureaucrats tended to initiate small expansions and radical contractions, politicians, on the other hand, often opted for major expansions and tentative contractions of the welfare state. More than once expansion plans were linked to elections [5].

Conflicts between political parties over issues of the welfare state, however, were rare. To some degree, this also holds true today, although with the Democratic Party of Japan's (DPJ) electoral victory in the 2007 Upper House elections, the balance of power shifted. Political scientists argue that this election victory is the first step for Japan to develop a dual party system, after decades of LDP dominance, broken only for a short period in 1993–1995. Indeed, the DPJ is bringing new issues onto Japan's political agenda of old-age policy, such as a draft law for prevention of violence against the elderly in nursing homes. The LDP's coalition partner, the Buddhist New Kōmei Party, in the field of old-age policies calls for a mitigation of the growing social inequality, while the LDP itself places emphases on reducing the social burden of social security contributions and taxes to citizens. As political scientist Talcott [26] argues: "This priority fits with the longstanding interest of the LDP in promoting economic growth first, then distributing the benefits of growth later."

The budget very often drives the general political process and the specific policy outcomes. Budgetary distributions also allow insights into the importance the political elites ascribe to certain policy fields. Old-age policy is by far the most prominent and well-funded policy field taking up demographic developments in Japan. While government expenditures for family policies account for 3.8% of the social security budget, old-age policies draw some 70% of this budget [6]. Replacement policies only recently started to receive some modest funding: for example, 1.9 billion Yen for the education of care givers to come to Japan under the bilateral EPAs with the Philippines and Indonesia [1].

Despite having generous funds at their disposal, state-driven measures in the field of old-age policies are no longer able to match the growing societal needs for these policies. The importance of new political actors, above all, civil society organizations (CSOs) is growing. The importance of CSOs as political actors in Japan's old-age policy is based on two main aspects: First of all, and this is tightly connected to the state's budgetary constraints, volunteers take over functions that the

---

[11] For more details on the political process of old-age policy making refer to Campbell [4].

state is no longer willing or able to fulfil. They lower the costs of services while often improving the performance. Secondly, volunteers in the field of old-age policy are often senior citizens themselves. Their engagement in CSO activities equals what Pekkanen and Tsujinaka [17] call "a bulwark that mitigates enfeeblement and loneliness".

This phenomenon can be most clearly observed when studying the so-called *chōnai-kai* or neighbourhood associations (NHAs). With nearly 300,000 groups across the nation, NHAs are Japan's most numerous CSO, and about half of the adult population of Japan are active in NHAs. An NHA's budget is small for that of a political actor; it usually ranges between half a million and 6 million Japanese Yen, depending on the size of their membership (membership fees usually range from 100 to 500 Japanese Yen)[12] and the amount of subsidies the group receives from local governments [17].

NHAs contribute to the stock of regional social capital in two ways. First, they provide a forum for frequent interaction of people living in a certain area. To many elderly people this has important health benefits, since social connectedness in general correlates with better health for the elderly. Furthermore, close relations with their peers provide an opportunity for early detection of health concerns. Secondly, as research by the *Nihon Sōgō Kenkyūjo*, a think tank, founded in 1970 under the supervision of the Prime Minister's Office and the Ministry of Economy, Trade and Industry (METI), shows, participation in NHAs raises the levels of generalized trust at the individual level [17].

NHAs, however, fail to be powerful political actors when it comes to formulating or articulating new policy proposals. This failure is grounded in two aspects. Firstly, in the close relationship to local governments, which creates a dependency structure through the government's significant financial contributions to an NHA's budget [16]. Secondly, NHAs show a low level of professionalism when it comes to political advocacy. This becomes clear, for example, in comparison with the American Association of Retired Persons (AARP), which uses almost 10% of its US$689 million budget (fiscal year 2003) for lobbying activities in legislation and research [17]. NHAs are caught in what Pekkanen [16] coined "Japan's dual civil society". That is, they are strong actors in hands-on activism on a local level, but have little impact in designing alternative policies.

This duality holds true for other CSOs in Japan, such as the growing number of non-profit organizations (NPOs), as political scientist Potter [19] showed in a data-rich study. In addition, Potter argued that NPOs with their small size, limited resources and reliance on volunteer staffs, which translates into their character of low professionalism, face competition from other civil society and quasi-public entities. Another factor that hinders NPOs and other CSOs from playing a major political role in Japan's old-age policies is their uneven regional distribution. Rural areas with a high proportion of elderly residents tend to have low rates of NPO formation. The relationship between new and traditional political actors in Japan is a contentious one. This may best be illustrated in the field of old-age policy:

---

[12] At the time of writing this chapter (Spring 2008), 100 Japanese Yen equals approximately US$1.

Traditional political actors rely on new political actors to fill the rising number of gaps in old-age services resulting from (a) an increasing demand for those services and (b) a budget that, despite its focus on old-age policy among the demographically relevant policies, cannot match the demands. This relationship bears in it a danger to the independent role of CSOs. Being incorporated as partners, usually by local governments, CSOs cannot act as political watchdogs. Japan's political system is thus missing out on initiatives from a vital "third sector".

Old-age policy, despite its budgetary importance, is an astonishingly uncontested policy field. There is no political party of senior citizens for senior citizens that would be of vital importance[13], in contrast, for example, to the party Die Grauen (the grey), founded in Germany in 1989. The clientele is missing since the ruling LDP comprehensively covers the issues of the welfare state that senior citizens, a growing electorate, are interested in. The relevance of old-age policy in contemporary Japan may cause concern with regard to the representation of the "common good" in Japan's politics.

Summary and Conclusion

The three demographic variables translate into policy measures in three fields, namely family, replacement, and old-age policies. While family and replacement policies through a variety of measures aim at actively shaping the development of population figures, old-age policy is concerned with how to manage the existing demographic structure of a nation. This paper shows that politics in Japan (one of the most rapidly ageing and shrinking nations) is mainly concerned with issues of the welfare state and thereby with the question of how to practically manage the current demographic change. This becomes clear particularly with regard to the budgetary distribution among the three policy fields. By strongly focusing on how to cope with aspects of old-age policy, while largely neglecting the fields of family and replacement policy, Japan's political leaders are missing out on an opportunity to actively shape the nation's *future* demographic structure. Active interference in family policy and replacement policy, however, are extremely difficult since those policy fields are loaded with historical and ideological taboos.

"Demographic policy" in Japan is about to start to take on certain taboo issues, exemplified in a pro-natal campaign of building "parents of the next generation" or the paradigm change of accepting sector-specific labour migration to Japan of the not highly skilled. In order to respond more directly and in a more focused way to the needs of a society under the impact of demographic change, however, Japan's political elites need to grant even more direct access to the political process to new political actors. The new political actors – civil society organizations and business federations alike – are being presented with an adventurous prospect: creating policies rather than limiting themselves to hands-on activism in localities

---

[13] Japan's *Rojintō* (elderly-party), a web-based political party founded in 2003, so far has not grown into a significant political actor. Its website can be accessed from http://www.6410.jp.

and companies is the invitation given to the new actors by an increasingly irresolute state. This invitation comes along with a responsibility to strive for the "common good" and numerous opportunities to shape the specific settings of the "new state".

There are two main lessons other nations can learn from how Japan deals with issues of demographic change: First, a huge challenge calls for comprehensive policy measures. Demographic policy needs to overcome boundaries between policy fields. This also applies to budgetary distributions. Secondly, a huge challenge also calls for a broad variety of actors to address it. Traditional political elites need to accept that new political actors from within society and the business world can contribute significantly to the handling of the challenge of demographic change. Politicians, citizens and the business sector alike will need to be willing to walk down roads of even more radical and comprehensive policy changes when addressing one of the most fundamental changes of modern states. This holds true for Japan as well as for other nations.

References

1. Asahi Shinbun, Health minister hit for calling women baby machines (29 Jan 2007), http://www.asahi.com/english/Herald-asahi/TKY200701290091.html. Accessed 5 Mar 2007
2. Asahi Shinbun, Kaigoshira nennai ni mo rainichi (Care givers to come to Japan before the end of this year), (11 Feb 2008), p. 1
3. BAMF, Bundesamt für Migration und Flüchtlinge, Ausländerbestandsdaten (2005), http://www.bamf.de/cln_011/nn_442496/SharedDocs/Anlagen/DE/DasBAMF/Downloads/Statistik/statistik-anlage-teil-2-auslaendezahlen-auflage14,templateId=raw,property=publicationFile.pdf/statistik-anlage-teil-2-auslaendezahlen-auflage14.pdf. Accessed 28 Feb 2008
4. J.C. Campbell, *How Policies Change. The Japanese Government and the Ageing Society* (Princeton University Press, Princeton, NJ, 1992)
5. J.C. Campbell, in *The Demographic Challenge. A Handbook About Japan*, ed. by F. Coulmas, H. Conrad, A. Schad-Seifert, G. Vogt (Brill, Leiden, 2008), p. 653
6. L. Coleman, in *The Demographic Challenge. A Handbook About Japan*, ed. by F. Coulmas, H. Conrad, A. Schad-Seifert, G. Vogt (Brill, Leiden, 2008), p. 750
7. F. Coulmas, *Population Decline and Ageing in Japan – The Social Consequences* (Routledge, London and New York, 2007)
8. R. Gambles, S. Lewis, R. Rapoport, *The Myth of Work-Life Balance. The Challenge of Our Time for Men, Women and Societies.* (Wiley, Chichester, West Sussex, 2006)
9. IPSS, National Institute for Population and Social Security Research, Population statistics of Japan 2006 (2006), http://www.ipss.go.jp/p-info/e/PSJ2006.pdf. Accessed 28 Feb 2008
10. The Japan Times, Women key to fixing demographic crunch (1 February 2008), http://search.japantimes.co.jp/print/nn20080201f3.html. Accessed 25 Mar 2008
11. The Japan Times, Foreign trainees to get labor law safeguards (26 March 2008), http://search.japantimes.co.jp/print/nn20080326a7.html. Accessed 26 Mar 2008
12. Kōno Tarō (2006). Interview with the author, Tokyo, February 20, 2006
13. J. Lie, in *Japan and Global Migration. Foreign Workers in the Advent of a Multicultural Society*, ed. by M. Douglass, G. Roberts (University of Hawai'i Press, Honolulu, 2003), p. 70
14. MOJ, Ministry of Justice, *Immigration Control 2006* (Bureau of Immigration, Tokyo, 2007)
15. A. Ogawa, in *The Demographic Challenge. A Handbook About Japan*, ed. by F. Coulmas, H. Conrad, A. Schad-Seifert, G. Vogt (Brill, Leiden, 2008), p. 721
16. R. Pekkanen, *Japan's Dual Civil Society. Members Without Advocates* (Stanford University Press, Stanford, 2006)

17. R. Pekkanen, Y. Tsujinaka, in *The Demographic Challenge. A Handbook About Japan*, ed. by F. Coulmas, H. Conrad, A. Schad-Seifert, G. Vogt (Brill, Leiden, 2008), p. 707
18. PMO, Prime Minister's Office, *Gaikokujin rōdōsha no ukeire ni kan suru yoronchōsa* (Opinion poll on the acceptance of foreign workers) (2004), http://www8.cao.go.jp/survey/h16/h16-foreignerworker/index.html. Accessed 26 Feb 2008
19. D.M. Potter, in *The Demographic Challenge. A Handbook About Japan*, ed. by F. Coulmas, H. Conrad, A. Schad-Seifert, G. Vogt (Brill, Leiden, 2008), p. 721
20. G. Roberts, in *Challenges for Japan: Democracy, Finance, International Relations, Gender*, ed. by G. Latz, I. Koide (The International House of Japan, Inc. for the Shibusawa Ei'ichi Memorial Foundation, Tokyo, 2003), p. 75
21. H. Sakanaka, Economisuto 22 (2008)
22. A. Schad-Seifert, Coping with low fertility? Japan's Government measures for a gender equal society (2006), DIJ Working Papers 2006/4. http://www.dijtokyo.org/doc/WP0604-%20Schad.pdf. Accessed 26 Feb 2008
23. L. Schoppa, in *The Demographic Challenge. A Handbook About Japan*, ed. by F. Coulmas, H. Conrad, A. Schad-Seifert, G. Vogt (Brill, Leiden, 2008), p. 639
24. L.J. Schoppa, *Race for the Exits. The Uraveling of Japan's System of Social Protection* (Cornell University Press, Ithaca, NY, 2006)
25. Süddeutsche Zeitung, Bischof Mixa kritisiert Familienpolitik: "Von der Leyen degradiert Frauen zu Gebärmaschinen." (Bishop Mixa criticises family policy: "Von der Leyen reduces women to birth-giving machines") (22 Feb 2007), http://www.sueddeutsche.de/deutschland/artikel/96/102993. Accessed 5 Mar 2007
26. P. Talcott, in *The Demographic Challenge. A Handbook About Japan*, ed. by F. Coulmas, H. Conrad, A. Schad-Seifert, G. Vogt (Brill, Leiden, 2008), p. 667
27. UNPD, United Nations Population Division, Replacement migration: is it a solution to declining and ageing populations? (2000), http://www.un.org/esa/population/publications/migration/migration.htm. Accessed 28 Feb 2008
28. G. Vogt, Jpn Aktuell J. Curr. Jpn Aff. 3 (2007)
29. G. Vogt, L. Philipp, Migrant support organizations in Japan – a survey (2007), DIJ Working Papers 2007/1. http://www.dijtokyo.org/doc/WP0701_%20Migrant_%20Support_%20Organisation_Survey.pdf. Accessed 26 Feb 2008
30. R. Yamamoto, in *Japanstudien 16, Jahrbuch des Deutschen Instituts für Japanstudien*, ed. by A. Germer, A. Moerke (Iudicium, Munich, 2004), p. 27

Chapter 3
The Silver Markets in Japan Through Regulatory Reform

N. Yashiro

Abstract As the aging of Japan's population is rapidly proceeding, the market for the elderly is growing too. The health care service industry is one of the most promising because the customers are increasing and it is still underdeveloped, with various regulations impeding new entries. If these obstacles are removed, the potential demand for health care services would be stimulated, and the productivity level could be improved. Major issues here are revision of the rules on banning the mixing of public and private health insurance, and financing for profit hospitals. Demand for nursing care services are also expanding, and nursery schools for children become more important as more Japanese women start to work full-time under tightening labor market conditions. Both are affected by the changes in Japan's family structure with the continuously declining share of three-generation households, and both are also under heavy government intervention. Thus, regulatory reform is a key to developing these silver industries in Japan.

Introduction

Though the aging of the population is a common feature in many developed countries, Japan's aging process is marked by its high speed by international standards. The ratio of the elderly had been stable at around 5% of the population until the 1960s, but rose to 20% in 2005 and is projected to rise to over 30% in 2025. It is attributable to a continuous decline in the total fertility ratio, which is now below 1.3, and to extension of longevity to the top level in the world. This aging process is associated with a declining population, which peaked in 2006, and the declining trend will continue through the twenty-first century. Declining population as well as increasing numbers of the elderly will exert a strong pressure on the social security budgets, in particularly on the public pension and health expenditures. Thus, the aging issue is often considered a dismal phenomenon to the economy and society. As the aging process proceeds, the trade-off between an increase in tax and social security contributions for the working generation and cutting the benefits to the beneficiaries becomes more prominent.

However, if we focus on the market demand side, the aging of the population means an increase in the demand for goods and services by the elderly customers. The elderly population (age 65 and above) is projected to increase by 7.7 million between 2008 and 2020, despite the decline in total population by 4.8 million. Besides, the current elderly households are not particularly poor; their average household income in 2003 was 290 million yen, which is about half of the average household, but the per capita income was 185 million yen or over 90% of the average. Also, 85% of the elderly households owned their own house compared with 61% of the average households, and the average financial assets of the elderly households[1] was 20 million yen compared with 9.5 million yen of the average. In particular, those who were born in the postwar baby-boom period, and worked through the era of high economic growth, will be more affluent when they are retired than the current elderly who were born before World War II. The new elderly group has accumulated household savings out of the growing earnings in the process of postwar economic development, catching up rapidly to the level of OECD economies. Also, they have enjoyed huge capital gains in their real and financial assets, even after the bursting of the bubble in the early 1990s.

Besides, a major characteristic of the elderly is the large disparity in household incomes and assets, so that consumption by the upper/middle income group should become more important. The Gini coefficient of the households headed by those aged 70–75 is 0.78, which is much higher than the 0.31 of those aged 30–35. Major sources for the disparity among the elderly are the following: First, under the seniority-based wage structure in Japan, the earning disparities grow with one's age or years of experience in a particular firm. The second factor is the difference between those who stay in the labor markets and have earnings and those who have left the labor markets, which is important in Japan where participation of the elderly in the labor force has remained high by international standards. The third factor is the difference in capital income; the average rate of return of financial assets is quite low in Japan, mainly because over a half of the household assets are directed to bank or postal savings deposits. If their financial assets are utilized more efficiently, there is a plenty room for increasing the income and consumption of the elderly.

Thus, the population aging in Japan can bring about abundant consumer-oriented markets, as there will be a growing number of elderly households that maintain sufficient purchasing power after retirement. There are many industries where the elderly are particularly important customers, but we will focus on the professional service sectors like the health care and nursing care services. This is because the developments in these professional services rely not only on the efforts of the providers, but also on the regulatory reforms for opening up the markets for both domestic and foreign companies and workers.

---

[1] Here, the definition of the elderly household is one with the head of household aged 60 and above.

Health Care Services

The health care service industry is the most promising industry in the silver markets because of the following factors: first, the demand for health care services is particularly strong among the elderly group (Fig. 3.1). The average expenditures on health care services of those aged 70 and above are about three times those of the age average. Though this is largely affected by the subsidies from the health insurance schemes, it is obvious that the potential demand for health care services should increase with increasing numbers of the elderly.

Second, just as other professional services, the income elasticity of health care services is generally higher than unity [1]. This means that people are willing to pay for the quality rather than quantity of the services. In this sense, the health care service industry should be profitable by producing the higher value-added services that people are willing to consume. Nevertheless, most prices of the health care services are fixed by the government with less consideration for the quality differences. This often leads to inefficient resource allocations, including the creation of black markets.

Third, the provision of health care services is highly regulated by two layers of regulations. One is the regulation on hospitals and clinics, and the qualification of doctors and other medical service staffs. Another is on the way that public health insurance is applied to the respective health care services. These regulations were originally set for the benefit of patients, but faction fact are often utilized for the protection of existing poor health care providers. Thus, they actually prevent the increase in supply of qualified health care services meeting with the potential

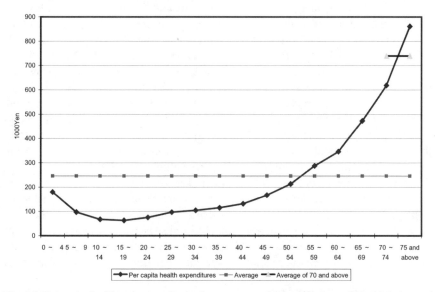

Fig. 3.1 Per capita health care expenditures by age group. Source: Ministry of Health Labor and Welfare, National Health Expenditure Survey (2001)

demand. If these regulations were removed, the health care service markets could grow substantially.

Supply-Side Policies

A major constraint for the development of health care service markets is "prohibition of profit seeking" in the majority of health care services. This seems to be natural as health care meets basic human needs, just like elementary education. However, the definition of "profit-seeking behavior" is not clearly defined by law, and the poor substitute of the definition of "non-profitability" is the prohibition of issuing dividends by hospitals and clinics. This is an odd definition, because it is a regulation on the means of financing the capital of medical institutions. In other words, the law actually defines that financing the hospital buildings or equipments through bank lending is "non-profit," while that through issuing stocks in the capital markets is "for profit." However, according to the textbook of economics, interests and dividends are both defined as the "costs of financing capital" for a firm, even though interest payments are classified as "costs" while dividends are "distribution of profits" in the company's balance of payments. This regulation on financing in the capital markets de facto works for the protection of small hospitals and clinics by excluding new entrants of large hospitals of both domestic and foreign origin[2] [2].

If this inefficient regulation is removed, the huge capital markets for M&A of private hospitals and clinics would be developed. Currently, most of the large-scale hospitals in Japan are publicly owned, and there are not many first-class private hospitals, while there are many small clinics with only one doctor. This is partly because the capital costs are not explicitly covered by public health insurance. Thus, without being financed by public funds like publicly owned ones, many private hospitals have to finance their capital through bank lending. The total amount of lending is limited by the collateral value and thus the scale of the hospitals is limited. However, if capital costs for hospitals can be financed by issuing stocks, the financing of large scale private hospitals or chain of many medium-size hospitals could be increased. Moreover, financing the capital through issuing of stocks would stimulate the mergers and acquisitions of hospitals and clinics, so that well-managed hospitals meeting the demand by patients could take over the less well-managed ones. As a result, the existing hospitals and clinics would be more efficiently allocated, resulting in a dynamic efficiency mechanism in hospital markets.

"No-profitability" in the health care service markets could be guaranteed by setting a form of "supply obligation," which means that they have to supply their services even in the local areas with less profitability, just as in the cases of electricity or gas companies. Setting the rule for obligation of mandatory health care service supply to a certain extent has to replace the current regulation on prohibiting company

---

[2] Most of the small hospitals and clinics in Japan are like small companies based on private funds. Though issuing of dividends is prohibited, withdrawal of the capital gains by a member of the original fund raisers is possible.

hospitals. The regulatory reform on the supply side of the health care services is a combination of liberalization of the regulations in the means of financing capitals and setting an effective means to provide health care service more efficiently.

Demand-Side Policies

In OECD countries, the share of health care expenditures to GDP varies, though that of public health expenditures is less varied than the total (Fig. 3.2). Japan's share currently is not large by international standards, but is projected to grow to a similar level as the current US level in 2020. In that sense, not only the total scale of health care expenditure, but the ratio of the public health care expenditures financed by mandatory social security contributions or taxes has to be reviewed.

A major constraint in the demand side is a ban on mixing public health care with private expenses. This is the rule that two medical treatments, of which one is covered by the public insurance and another is not, cannot be combined in the same treatment. Otherwise, the reimbursement by the public insurance cannot be made to the treatment originally covered by the insurance. For example, if a patient wants to use a new medicine or materials that are not admitted by the public health insurance, he has to pay not only the costs of these additional ones but the total cost of the treatment, i.e., public insurance cannot be used in this treatment. This is in contrast with normal insurance contracts where costs originally covered by the insurance are paid regardless of the extra services voluntarily paid by the insured.

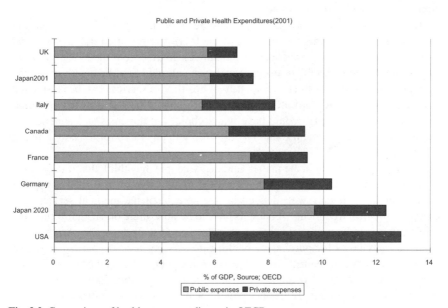

Fig. 3.2 Comparison of health care expenditures in OECD

This uncommon rule in Japan's health insurance can be rationalized by the following considerations: one, an egalitarian nature of health care services cannot be maintained if only the rich purchase the better health care services at additional costs; two, the public insurance might be abused by combining with treatments for health services other than basic health care; three, doctors may well induce their patients to buy unnecessary drugs or treatments by using their advantageous knowledge over the patients.

This rule on banning the mixing of public and private health insurances has brought about several problems. The first is concerning the egalitarian rule between different types of peoples; the rule does care for the equality between those who can afford to pay extra costs other than covered by public health insurance and those who cannot, but simply ignores the one between those who can afford to pay the total costs of the qualified health care services and those who can pay for the extra costs other than covered by public insurance. In this sense, a too-strict egalitarian rule can be unfair to the majority of people.

Another issue concerns whether the current banning rule contributes to reducing the public health insurance costs, which is not clear. The logic entirely depends on the assumption that patients give up using health insurance if the combination with uncovered treatments is not allowed. However, there is a possibility that the costs covered by the public insurance could be even larger, because the patients have to use less desirable treatments rather than being combined with the best practices not covered by the public insurance. The conclusion depends on the results of empirical tests. Finally, concerning the risk of selling unnecessary treatments, the banning rule can be relaxed only for those qualified hospitals and clinics. With assessments by the insurance companies on the mixed treatments, the qualification could be removed if unnecessary treatments are found.

If the banning rule is waved, there would be ample possibility for the expansion of health care service markets because of the following factors: First, the qualified hospitals could have extra revenues to maintain the high level of medical treatments, which is not easy under the uniform reimbursement rule of public health insurance. Second, competition for the better quality of health care services can be stimulated, as compared with the current competition for quantity, i.e., that of having more patients. Thirdly, patients would have wider choices in the costs and benefits of a variety of medical treatments, and may be willing to pay more for the better quality of services.

The final point is a delicate matter, and many people may think that it may not be a merit but a demerit that patients have a wider choice, the extent of which depends on their income. It may well depend on the content of the medical services: for example, medical treatments of patients have to be done more on an egalitarian rule, while others can be more selective as an extension of their daily life. After all, the voluntary payments for purchasing health care services are less burdensome than the mandatory social security contributions or tax payments. As the costs of health care services grow with technical development and population aging, the share of the mandatory payments by the tax payers or patients will eventually have to be limited.

Thus, a key to realizing the scheme smoothly is deciding how to set the boundary of the health care services that have to be fully covered by public insurance. So far, the authorities have allowed hospitals to ask for extra charges on, for example, making a reservation for outpatients, amenities, and certain highly specialized medical treatments. But, they are a list of exceptions to the regulations. It is necessary to set an exemption from the ban, either by type of diseases, or by the quality of hospital or clinic, as above, to establish a route for the developing health care service industry.

Nursing Care and Nursery Services

The need for nursing care services should also grow in the aging society with the increasing number of the frail elderly. The possibility of being a frail elderly in some form is 3.8% between ages 65 and 74, but rises to 24% at age 65 and above (Table 3.1). The nursing care services used to be provided in principle within a family, and public nursing services were supplied as a part of the welfare services for those who did not have family support. However, on one hand the number of family having frail elderly has risen over time with aging, and on the other the family's capability in taking care of them has declined. This is because there is a trend decline in the co-residence ratios between the elderly and their children's family, as well as an increasing ratio of working women in the labor markets. As a result, those frail elderly are being hospitalized under a rule of free access to medical services, which is one of the major causes for an expansion in health care costs.

Under such circumstances, a new social insurance covering the costs for nursing services for the frail elderly was established in the year 2000. This has several important characteristics for the growth of a silver market. The first is to allow private firms to provide nursing care services, which is important in stimulating the supply in the market to meet the growing demand. The second is to share the costs of purchasing nursing care services through the public insurance, so that users of nursing care services are granted 90% of the costs. This is compared with the previous welfare system where only a limited group of beneficiaries are granted free nursing care services. However, the shifts of the costs from health insurance to nurs-

Table 3.1 Probability of being a frail elderly by age group

	Age 65–74	Age 75+
Need assistance	0.5	3.2
Level 1	1.1	7.1
Level 2	0.8	4.4
Level 3	0.5	3.2
Level 4	0.4	3.2
Level 5	0.5	3
Total	3.8	24.1

Source: MHLW 2001.

ing insurance were limited, so that it is not sufficient to suppress the demand for health care for the elderly.

Nevertheless, the nursing care insurance has the following important implications for the growth of the silver markets: One, entry to the markets has been opened to new entrants of any form, which is not in the case for the health care services with the banning of the entry of corporate firms to hospital businesses. Two, public supports though public insurance benefits are directed to consumers rather than providers as in the case of welfare services, so that consumers have a wider selection of services. Three, the options for consumers in combining extra nursing services with those covered by the public insurance is larger than is the case for health services. This is true even though the differentiated services with additional costs are not allowed, and the private firms have difficulty in providing the better services with higher prices as in the case of most of the service industries [3].

Nursery services for children are also expected to grow in the silver markets. The increasing labor shortage due to aging of the population as well as the higher ratio of women's college enrollment should stimulate the labor force participation of married women. In that case, a major bottleneck is the child-raising in a family, which needs to be substituted by the market services. In fact, about 70% of married women leave their company on the occasion of the first born baby, despite various policy measures supporting their child rearing. The major obstacle for not staying at work for married women is a lack of child-care facilities, particularly for the children aged 0–2 years. Nevertheless, nursery services have long been supplied by the public sector as a welfare program for children who are not well taken care of by the family.

Like other public services, the high cost of the provision of nursery services managed by public employees with seniority-based wages is a major factor for the lack of efficient supply and a long queue on the waiting list. As this is a similar situation to the nursing care services before the public insurance for frail elderly was introduced, the policy implication is the same. If the new social insurance for nursery services were implemented, the supply of nursery services should increase substantially and the quality may well be improved with the extra expense by consumer.

Summary and Conclusion

In Japan, with a substantial increase in the elderly population in the coming decades, the silver market is expected to grow significantly. But, most of the promising areas in the silver markets such as health, nursing, and nursery services are under heavy regulation by the government. These services were originally provided by the public sector or de facto monopolized by non-profit organizations as a part of the welfare policy. However, in order to expand the supply to meet the huge potential demand with aging of the population, regulatory reform to vitalize the economy has to be implemented.

There are two types of regulations that are most important impediments to the development of the silver markets. The first type of the regulation is the "non-profit principle," which is based on the view that corporate firms are seeking profits, and thus they have to be kept away from the markets. This in reality works for the protection of existing so-called no-profit providers at the cost of consumers, as competition between firms and other providers in the markets is the most important factors for improving user-friendly services. Another type of regulation is based on the "uniform principle," which is based on the view that services supported by the public or public insurance have to be equally provided regardless of the individual income levels. This sets a limit to the extension of the markets by excluding the choice of consumers for the better services with higher prices.

In summing up, the conditions for successful development of the silver markets in Japan are basically the same as the task of structural reform of the economy. Competition of providers needs to be stimulated in the markets, so that the suppliers with better services can expand their business through mergers and acquisition of the others. The socialist view that remains, particularly in the aging-related service sector in Japan, is a major obstacle that has to be overcome.

References

1. N. Yashiro, R. Suzuki, W. Suzuki, in *Health Care Issues in the United States and Japan*, ed. by D.A. Wise, N. Yashiro (The University of Chicago Press, Chicago, 2006), p. 17
2. N. Yashiro, in *Economic Analysis of Social Regulatory Reform*, ed. by N. Yashiro (Nihonkeiza-ishinbunsha, Tokyo, 2000)
3. Y. Zhous, W. Suzuki, in *Economic Analysis of Social Regulatory Reform*, ed. by N. Yashiro (Nihonkeizaishinbunsha, Tokyo, 2000)

Chapter 4
Matching Demand and Supply: Future Technologies for Active Ageing in Europe

N. Malanowski

Abstract There are several paradigms concerning the general aim of extending the average human life expectancy without extending suffering. The most challenging one is "active ageing", put forward by the World Health Organization. Active ageing in this context refers to a continuous participation in social, economic, cultural, spiritual and civic affairs, not just the ability to be physically active or part of the labour force. Active ageing views elderly people as active participants in an age-integrated society. An interesting way to advance policy concepts to match supply and demand can be derived from focusing on promising fields of application for future technologies that generate age-based innovations. This contribution to the book argues that future technologies for active ageing provide a new and promising policy concept to tackle the challenges of ageing societies, to transform them into opportunities and to use as many as possible of the opportunities presented by ageing societies by matching demand and supply.

Introduction

The world is experiencing an important demographic transformation: the unprecedented ageing of the population of almost all developed and developing countries. Some observers are already describing it as a demographic revolution in all cultures and societies. In addition, the ageing society is a phenomenon that has been apparent in developed countries like Japan, Italy and Germany for a number of years. The increasing presence of older people in society makes people of all ages more aware that they are living in a multi-generational society, and not in the "forever young" society shown in so many magazines, advertisements and popular movies. Ageing populations are having more and more influence on global patterns in labour and capital markets, and on services and traditional social support systems like health care and pensions in the European countries [1]. Against this background, society and policy makers cannot ignore the ageing phenomenon, regardless of whether they view it positively or negatively.

In almost all Member States of the European Union (EU) the current fertility rates are low. This means fewer births, which eventually translates into smaller cohorts of young persons. If birth rates continue to decrease as predicted, the proportion of young and old citizens will undergo a historic crossover. Further, the particularly sizeable generation known as the baby-boomers (born between 1945 and 1965) has started to retire. In addition, there is an enormous increase in life expectancy due to factors like better nutrition, medical treatment and health services. According to figures from the Economic Policy Committee/European Commission [5] the outcome of these demographic developments will be a remarkable shift in the age structure of the population. A moderate projection for the EU for the period between 2004 and 2050 suggests that the population of those aged 65+ will increase by 58 million or 77%, and that at the same time the working-age population will drop by 48 million or 16%. This might mean that in the EU the ratio of people of working age to the elderly is two to one, instead of four to one at present. But, although all EU Member States will experience an ageing population there will be some differences in timing, nature and scale.

Quite often the demographic challenges are discussed in the media as a serious problem for social support systems and in a fairly negative way (focusing on the likely "cost explosion"). This is one way to look at this topic, but another way is to discuss the opportunities provided by ageing societies, such as for instance innovative markets for new applications and products/services for elderly people [8, 10]. Both ways can be combined and discussed in a way that focuses on how we might prepare ourselves for the consequences of demographic change, and shape our ageing societies, instead of thinking that the ageing of our societies will come over us like a hurricane, damaging the heart of our civilization. Hence, the policy challenge is to decide how to tackle the issues and to use the opportunities presented by ageing societies in the best possible way.

The intention of this contribution is to provide a stimulus for further discussion of the scientific and policy options in this thematic field. Applications based on information and communication technologies (ICT) were chosen as a focus for this work, since ICT can be used in a number of very promising ways to promote active ageing: for instance in medical treatment, education and housing. The key question is how to tackle the challenge of matching demand and supply by using the suggested policy framework of future technologies for active ageing (FT4AA), which is from the author's point of view complementary to other concepts for active ageing such as better nutrition, sports and health promotion services. This contribution discusses FT4AA mainly in the European context, and on the macro-level of policy and politics. Recent developments and discourses on the micro- and meso-level have been described and analysed elsewhere and will not be discussed in detail here.[1]

---

[1] For a solid work on the micro-level developments in ageing societies see for instance [2].

Policy Aspects of Active Ageing

According to the World Health Organization (WHO; [14]), active ageing (a term increasingly used in current policy discourses on the international level) is "the process of optimising opportunities for health, participation and security in order to enhance the quality of life as people age". A similar term (ageing well) was used in a recent communication by the European Commission [8] on *Ageing Well in the Information Society*. Active ageing/ageing well applies to both individuals and groups. It allows people to realize their potential for physical, social and mental well-being throughout their lives, and to participate in society according to their needs, desires and capacities, while providing them with adequate protection, security and care when they require assistance.

"Active" refers to a continuous participation in social, economic, cultural, spiritual and civic affairs, not just the ability to be physically active or part of the labour force. Another important element in this policy framework is quality of life. This is an individual's perception of their position in life in the context of the culture and value system in which they live, and in relation to their goals, expectations, standards and concerns. It is a broad-ranging concept of the complex relationship between a person's physical health, psychological state, level of independence, social relationships and personal beliefs. As people age, their quality of life is largely determined by their ability to maintain autonomy and independence. Autonomy means in this context the perceived ability to control, cope with and make personal decisions about one's life on a day-to-day basis, according to one's own rules and preferences. Independence is understood as the ability to perform functions related to daily life: that is, the capacity to live independently in the community with little or no help from others.

The WHO points to six categories that are important determinants for active ageing and quality of life (see Table 4.1). Culture and gender are cross-cutting determinants. On the one hand, culture shapes the way in which people age because it influences all the other determinants of active ageing. On the other hand, gender is a "lens" that helps us to consider how policy options affect the well-being of both men and women. The behavioural determinants are often of very high importance for active ageing. Maintaining a healthy lifestyle is up to the individual. Engaging in appropriate physical activity, healthy eating, not smoking and using alcohol and medication wisely, for instance, can prevent diseases and support active ageing considerably. Determinants related to personal factors are the individual's genetic endowment, and psychological factors, including intelligence and the cognitive capacity to adapt to change, which may affect susceptibility to disease. Determinants related to the physical environment are for instance safe housing and the likelihood of suffering from falls. Most injuries to older people could be avoided if they enjoyed appropriate physical environments. Social support, opportunities for education and lifelong learning, protection from violence and others are important determinants related to the social environment. Finally, economic determinants like income, social protection and work are of high importance. By "work" in this context the WHO does not mean just the formal labour market, but also the work that

Table 4.1 Determinants of active ageing, based on WHO data [14]

Culture and gender (cross-cutting)	Determinants related to the physical environment
Health and social services	Physical environments (e.g. transportation)
Health promotion and disease prevention	Safe housing
Curative services	Falls
Long-term care	Clean water
Mental health services	Clean air and safe food
Behavioural determinants	*Determinants related to the social environment*
Tobacco use	Social support
Physical activity	Violence and abuse
Healthy eating	Education and literacy
Oral health	
Alcohol use	*Economic determinants*
Medications	Income
Iatrogenesis	Social protection
Adherence	Work
	Determinants related to personal factors
	Biology and genetics
	Psychological factors

older people do in the informal sector, and their unpaid work at home and/or for their family.

Most of the determinants presented in Table 4.1 have an implicit technology component: for instance this is self-evidently an aspect of safe housing, education, curative services and transportation.

The EU is tackling the economic, employment and social implications of ageing as part of an overall strategy of mutually reinforcing policies, launched at the Lisbon European Council in March 2000. It confirmed this approach at subsequent European Council meetings in Nice, Stockholm, Goeteborg and Laeken, since the ageing of the population is being observed in most EU Member States. The Social Policy Agenda, annexed to the Nice European Council conclusions, lists EU policy priorities in employment and social affairs, outlining how Member States can deal with the wider social and work–life-related implications of ageing through mutually reinforcing employment, social protection and economic policies. Active ageing policies and practices in this sense are being encouraged, for instance by approaches like lifelong learning, working longer and retiring more gradually, being active after retirement, and engaging in health-sustaining activities.

Since the Lisbon European Council in 2000 there have been a number of EU initiatives linked to the field of ageing societies and active ageing. For instance, at the beginning of 2005 the European Commission published a Green Paper, *Confronting Demographic Change: A New Solidarity Between the Generations* [6], with the aim of launching a debate among all relevant stakeholders and in the wider society on ageing populations, and particularly on educational/learning aspects. The launching of this paper was intended to contribute to finding answers to the key question of how to cope best with the impacts of an ageing population.

A new step towards a broader active ageing strategy was taken recently when, for the first time, it was suggested explicitly that ICT-based applications could provide support for active ageing. The EU initiative "i2010: A European information society for growth and employment", announced in June 2005, aims to promote an inclusive European information society and make Europe more attractive to investment and innovation in knowledge-based goods and services. Linked with i2010 are three "Flagship initiatives on key social challenges." One of these is the initiative "Needs of the ageing society". In addition, actions have been suggested to overcome the geographic and social digital divide, culminating in a European initiative on e-inclusion.

The Ministerial Declaration of the Ministerial Conference "ICT for an inclusive society" in June 2006 underlined the use of ICT options for active ageing. This declaration explicitly stressed the need to address "ICT solutions for active ageing" [7]. In line with the 2008 European initiative on e-inclusion, it also stressed that "the contribution of civil society, industry and all other stakeholders is essential ..." (p. 6). The declaration suggested that particular attention should be given to four areas of needs of older people:

Exploiting the full potential of the internal market of ICT services and products for the older people, amongst others by addressing demand fragmentation by promoting interoperability through standards and common specifications where appropriate. Barriers to innovative ICT solutions for social security and health reimbursement schemes need to be addressed, particularly at the national level.

Improving the employability, working conditions and work–life balance of older workers to improve productivity by supporting innovative ICT solutions which can be easily used everywhere including at home, and encouraging the provision of training from the public, private sectors and from civil society, making special efforts on ICT skills for older people.

Enhancing active participation in the society and economy and self-expression, through innovative ICT-enabled access to goods and services, and relevant content, to facilitate interactions with public and private entities, entertainment, and social contacts.

Realising increased quality of life, autonomy and safety, while respecting privacy and ethical requirements. This can be done through independent living initiatives, the promotion of assistive technologies, and ICT-enabled services for integrated social and healthcare, including personal emergency and location-based services.

A recently published European Commission Communication, *Ageing Well in the Information Society* (2007), makes even stronger reference to learning and quality of life for older people:

The information society should enable older people – where they wish to do so – to fully participate in the society and the economy and to be active and empowered citizens and consumers, thereby contributing to a positive perception of ageing in Europe [8].

The Action Plan that accompanies the communication foresees the need to raise R&D investment in ICT to over €1 billion, addressing three further areas of user needs: active ageing at work, daily life at home, and continuing to participate actively in society.

The key points of this chapter are the following:

- The World Health Organization's policy concept of active ageing was the first to refer to the continuous participation of older people, linking this to the use of technology, but not focusing solely on paid work.
- In the EU, different policy streams from different backgrounds have culminated in the concept of ageing well. This concept explicitly focuses its ideas about active ageing/ageing well on future technologies.
- The concept of ageing well in the information society stresses the need for matching demand and supply to make the best use of R&D investment.

The Silver Market

Selected Research Findings

Currently, there is quite a lot of discussion in public about the high economic potential of appropriate products for older people and the enormous "silver" market. Usually, it is reported that companies need to develop the adequate "technological" capabilities (or in other words, applications, products and services) to enable them to make use of the opportunities resulting, for instance, from the existing purchasing power of the older population. However, it is not as simple as it might seem at first glance to find ways to harness the opportunities presented by ageing societies. In other words, it has not proved easy to convert the technology-related needs of older people into a strong demand for products specifically designed for this age group.

There have been only a few studies on the key question of why there has not yet been a major breakthrough in exploiting the silver market with new ICT applications and products/services (e.g. [8, 9, 11]). Cutler [3] reports that new technologies tend to be developed by young people and aimed at a "young" market. Besides this, he states that major companies in the USA started to develop a growing interest a few years ago. Some companies like Microsoft, Hewlett Packard and Intel have launched initiatives to meet the specific technology-related needs of older people when developing new or improving existing ICT-products. But at the moment there are no scientific findings available on how influential these initiatives are within American companies.

Gassmann and Keupp [10] did a survey on age-based products in Switzerland. According to this study, a vast majority of Swiss companies think that it is important to align with demographic change. However, just one-third have ideas about how to supply age-based products. A few companies are already supplying age-based products (such as Phonak, which offers products for hearing-impaired (older) people, and Schindler, which creates intelligent systems to give (older) people better mobility). These companies state that these products have a successful market performance. The authors assume that small enterprises in particular are not yet active in this sector because of a lack of resources for getting more information on the silver market.

In addition, the authors underline the point that there is a lack of studies and sur-veys on the market potential of age-based products and their market segments. It seems that we are confronted with a chicken-and-egg-problem. On the one hand, there are older consumers (and the market) waiting for age-based products (supply) and on the other, there are companies waiting for signals by the market (demand). It is suggested that public start-up finance could help to solve this problem. Gassmann and Keupp recommend that most product innovations for older people be regarded as merit goods (in the same category as, for example, education, sports and vacci-nations). Usually, consumers do not recognize the value of such goods right from the beginning. However, since the state has more information on the value of merit goods for society it has the possibility to use this information to support age-based goods in the start-up phase.

Advancing Implementation

An interesting way to advance the implementation of concepts to match supply and demand, and the operability of such concepts, can be derived from a suggestion by Gassmann and Reepmeyer [9]. They recommend differentiating between a num-ber of promising application fields for age-based innovations, for instance, medical technology, housing technology and transportation technology. In almost all of the fields mentioned, ICT-based applications can be found. From the author's point of view at least two important application fields have to be added: work/employment and learning. These are also important fields for age-based innovations since these innovations could enable older people to stay healthier, and probably continue for longer in the employment sector or carry out voluntary work. Two additional points have to be kept in mind. The perception of changes in applications and prod-ucts/services is very important. The step from established and well-known products to new products should not be too abrupt. Besides this, the new applications and products must be affordable. The best age-based application or product is of no use if no one can afford it. All these aspects have to be considered when thinking about appropriate forms of stakeholder involvement and the implementation of ways to match demand and supply.

The key points of this chapter are the following:

- Currently, there is a lot of discussion about the high potential of the silver market. However, there is still a lack of high-quality studies of this phenomenon.
- At the moment, it seems, we are confronted with a chicken-and-egg problem. The older consumers are waiting for convincing age-based products whereas the companies are waiting for signals from the older consumers.
- In addition, too-abrupt changes in product offerings for older consumers might not be appropriate. The older consumer wants to be convinced about the value of a new product. A product that is perceived merely as "trendy" might be not convincing for these groups of consumers.

The Involvement of Stakeholders

Selected Research Findings

Currently, it is more or less the theoretical mainstream approach in most scientific, political and industry communities, as well as in most interest groups of older people, to stress the point that the involvement of older people in the development of future applications and products/services would be of high value for society in general. It is seen as an appropriate participatory approach, tackling the challenges and using the opportunities presented by ageing societies. The involvement of older people and their interest groups in finding ways to match supply with demand is a major pillar in policy concepts like the WHO's Active Ageing Framework and the European Commission's latest concepts (2006, 2007) on e-inclusion and ageing well.

The stakeholder group "older people" is part of Walker's [13] work on the political participation of older people. He concludes that "the growth of political participation among older people has been openly encouraged in several countries by policy-makers" (p. 346). He suggests that senior citizens should not be regarded as a homogenous group represented by interest groups with a homogenous membership base. "In fact, older people are just as deeply divided ... as younger people" (p. 350). From the author's point of view, "grey power" is more hype than substance. Older people's interest groups usually have few if any staff, and often struggle with a lack of resources. Besides this, there are also a large number of older people actively involved in caring for their partners and others in need. Therefore, they might not have the physical energy and mental space to be active in participatory processes. The asymmetry between the lack of resources available to older people and their interest groups, and the resources available in most companies and their interest groups, might be seen as a factor that makes it more difficult for the elderly to participate.

Advancing Implementation

The German Centre for Research on Ageing [4] stated 10 years ago that sustainable communication platforms are necessary to promote interdisciplinary and multi-professional work in which older people are able to participate. Such discourse tools would offer all involved stakeholders the opportunity to understand each other in a better way. Usually "understanding" each other on a general level is not a problem for the actors. It is quite easy to find a basic consensus on specific higher-level needs like health, safety, independence, mobility and participation. But it will become more and more important to get more differentiated knowledge on the specific technology-related needs of different groups of older people, which will make it possible to provide a supply of applications and products/services that matches their "real" needs.

There are also some possible pitfalls. Since the stated technology-related needs of older people can be interpreted in different ways, it is necessary to learn an "easy common" language to communicate and understand each other. In order to achieve this there also has to be a process of continuous exchange of information. Industry and science would have the role of informing older people in a competent way about possible new technological solutions that could be applied to provide products and services that are relevant for them. On the other hand, the availability of such information would help older people to get a clearer idea about their specific technology-related needs, especially when it comes to the stage of predicting their future needs and developing common visions. Thus there would be a process of continuous rapprochement and exchange.

The key points of this chapter are the following:

- The assumption of the so-called grey power of older people and their interest organizations is at least questionable, since many older people and their interest groups suffer from a lack of resources.
- A continuous exchange of information between older people and companies in a common language is needed to match demand and supply in a better way.
- It is especially important for companies, but also for policy-makers, to get a clearer idea about the specific needs of older people.

Future Technologies for Active Ageing

From the discussions of the previous chapters it is possible to develop and suggest additional input for the active ageing/ageing well policy concept of the European Commission. This additional input focuses on FT4AA using the example of ICT-based applications (for more details see [12]). These ideas are compatible with and complementary to other concepts for active ageing such as improved nutrition, sports and health promotion, which are being used on the political macro-, meso- and micro-levels.

The aim of active ageing in this case is not to reverse ageing. The policy of using future technologies to promote active ageing is directed at preventing significant physical and cognitive impairments, enhancing the perceived quality of life of elderly people, using the experience and knowledge of the elderly for society as long as possible and stabilizing the cost to the public purse. Where there are possible ethical challenges (for example, concerning the independence of older people) it is suggested that these should be discussed case by case. The approach of active ageing also takes into account some very important characteristics of "the elderly" or in other words "the complexity of ageism". Instead of only using the traditional categories for age groups (categories 55–64, 65–74 and 75+), the concept suggests that in addition we should use more differentiated categories such as:

- Time to formal retirement, for individuals who are (a) in good health, and (b) in poor health

- Autonomous age as a pensioner (period of independent living)
- Age with increasing handicaps (start of period of dependent living)
- Dependent pensioners' age

Furthermore, intergenerational justice is a necessary additional element. It empha-sizes burden-sharing and solidarity between generations in ageing societies where distributional conflicts among generations certainly exist as a result of serious chal-lenges for public finances. FT4AA has a strong focus on the specific technology-related needs of older people. To match these technology-related needs (demand) with the technological supply (applications and products/services) specific tools are needed (e.g. Design for All). FT4AA distinguishes between compensatory, preven-tive and competence-supporting applications. It is also necessary to have adequate communication tools to build bridges between the relevant stakeholders. Sustain-able communication platforms for the stakeholders (e.g. elderly people, industry, science, governmental organizations and others like trade unions) are another pillar of the FT4AA approach.

As mentioned, the suggested FT4AA approach aims to prevent significant phys-ical and cognitive impairments, enhance the perceived quality of life of elderly people, use the experience and knowledge of the elderly for society as long as possi-ble, and stabilize the cost to the public purse. Besides this, it takes into account that political support for age-based products/services is needed because most of them are merit goods. In order to lower the development and mismatch risk of future age-based products and services, and applications that could be using them, it is important for industry to get more knowledge about the specific technology-related needs of older people. The development and mismatch risk ranges between low and high. The level of technology-related needs of older people ranges between con-crete and vague. But, both factors are related and represented on the same axis. If the technology-related needs are diffuse, the development and mismatch risk is high, and vice versa: if the technology-related needs are concrete the develop-ment and market risk is low. At present this means that we find the majority of products and services in the group of compensatory applications, and that most eco-nomic and societal resources are used to make up for the significant physical and cognitive impairments of elderly people. But, with the implementation of FT4AA (see Fig. 4.1) it is intended to reduce the need for compensatory applications, while there will be a clear increase in preventive applications as well as those that support competences.

Preventive applications aim at preventing or retarding significant physical and cognitive impairments right from the beginning. The aim of preventive applications is prevent people from needing compensatory applications at such an early stage. Competence-supporting applications go a step further. Whereas compensatory and preventive applications focus basically on impairments, competence-supporting applications proactively support the special capabilities of older people. The devel-opment and mismatch risk for industry will decrease, since older people's specific technology-related needs will be more concrete because of the use of specific tools to match demand and supply described above.

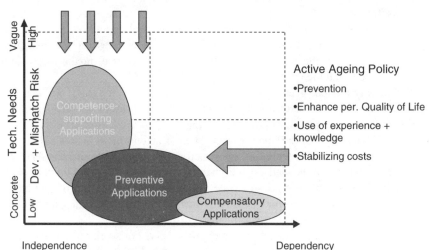

Fig. 4.1 Different applications and development and mismatch risk compared with (tomorrow's) technology-related needs of older people

The key points of this chapter are the following:

- It is necessary to distinguish between different groups of older people when approaching the issue of special technology-related needs.
- At the beginning, support from policy-makers is needed for the development of age-based products and services, since most of them are merit goods.
- A differentiation between compensatory, preventive and competence-supporting applications is highly recommended since it shows where older people's needs are more concrete on the one hand, and less concrete on the other hand.

Summary and Conclusion

As has been argued throughout this contribution, future technologies for active ageing is a new promising approach for tackling the challenges of ageing societies, to transform them into opportunities and to use as many as possible of the opportunities presented by ageing societies. It is a broad approach focusing on the macro-level of politics and also inspiring discussion, policy initiatives and coordinated actions on the meso- and micro-levels, thus supporting multi-layered politics in the EU and its Member States. Nevertheless, some further work is needed before starting its broad implementation.

The topics of the agenda for further work can be clustered in the following way:

- Multi-layered politics: In order to strengthen and coordinate the ways in which active ageing policy can be linked with technology, comparative research would be useful on multi-layered policies in core policy fields such as health, education, housing, transportation and employment, as well as on how they overlap and interact. This would also help to produce more knowledge on how the active ageing policy on the macro-level influences the discourse on the meso- and micro-levels, and vice versa.
- Technology-related needs of older people: In order to meet the specific technology-related needs of older people, it is necessary to develop more differentiated categorizations of older people.
- Economic potential of the silver market: There is an enormous lack of solid studies on the economic potential of age-based applications and products/services. More knowledge is needed on the characteristics and segments of the silver market. This might help to solve the chicken-and-egg-problem of age-based applications and products being basically seen as merit goods, which are difficult to sell at the beginning.
- Sub-concepts (tools) to match demand and supply: For work on new concepts and to modify existing concepts (e.g. Design for All, Ambient Assisted Living) to match demand and supply, it is important to focus on application fields (such as health, education and housing). It is also suggested that in further work it would be useful to distinguish between different types of applications (e.g. compensatory, preventive and competence-supporting).
- Communications tools: It is very necessary to use appropriate communication tools in participatory processes with older people, to simplify finding a common language while working on concepts to match demand and supply in ageing societies.
- Supporting practical use: The suggested approach of future technologies for active ageing, which in this contribution has been discussed in the context of ICT-based applications, has to be "practised". This means working on visions, tools and concrete steps to match demand and supply. Its applications could be supported either in policy areas (clustered application fields) or in application fields using a differentiation of applications (e.g. compensatory, preventive and competence supporting).

The ageing of the population is not occurring only in developed countries, but it is a general demographic trend all over the world, though at a slower rate in some cases. In this respect, the EU and its Member States could be a model for other parts of the world in using the concept of future technologies for active ageing, which is complementary to other concepts like good nutrition and health promotion. In order to match demand and supply in the silver market in a sustainable way, the support of policy-makers is needed. This is especially necessary at the beginning, since the logic of these actors allows them to have a broader view on the issue and not a narrow view just focused on a set of products from one company.

Acknowledgements The views expressed in this article are the sole responsibility of the author and do not necessarily reflect the views of the European Commission. The author would like to thank Rukiye Özcivelek and Marcelino Cabrera for comments on a draft of this article.

References

1. A. Boersch-Supan, in *Information and Communication Technologies for Active Ageing: Opportunities and Challenges*, ed. by M. Cabrera, N. Malanowski (IOS-Press, Amsterdam, 2008)
2. C.B. Cox, *Community Care for an Aging Society* (Springer, New York, 2005)
3. S.J. Cutler, in *Handbook of Aging and the Social Sciences*, ed. by R. Binstock, L.K. George (Elsevier Academic Press, Amsterdam), pp. 257–276
4. Deutsches Zentrum für Alternsforschung (DZFA), *Bedürfnistrukturen älterer Menschen* (Forschungsbericht Nr. 1 aus dem DZFA, Heidelberg, 1997)
5. Economic Policy Committee/European Commission, *The Impact of Ageing on Public Expenditure* (EPC/European Commission, Brussels, 2005)
6. European Commission, Confronting Demographic Change: A New Solidarity Between the Generations. Green Paper, European Commission, Brussels, 2005
7. European Commission, ICT for an Inclusive Society. Ministerial Declaration of the Ministerial Conference in Riga, Brussels, 2006
8. European Commission, *Ageing Well in the Information Society* (An i2010 Initiative. Com 332 of the European Commission, Brussels, 2007)
9. O. Gassmann, G. Reepmeyer, *Wachstumsmarkt Alter* (Hanser Verlag, Munich and Vienna, 2006)
10. O. Gassmann, M. Keupp, in *Information and Communication Technologies for Active Ageing: Opportunities and Challenges*, ed. by M. Cabrera, N. Malanowski (IOS-Press, Amsterdam, 2008)
11. Y. Hedrick-Wong, *The Glittering Silver Market: The Rise of the Elderly Consumers in Asia* (Wiley, New York, 2006)
12. N. Malanowski, in *Information and Communication Technologies for Active Ageing: Opportunities and Challenges*, ed. by M. Cabrera, N. Malanowski (IOS-Press, Amsterdam, 2008)
13. A. Walker, in *Handbook of Aging and the Social Sciences*, ed. by R. Binstock, L.K. George (Elsevier Academic Press, Amsterdam), pp. 339–359
14. World Health Organization, *Active Ageing: A Policy Framework* (WHO, Geneva, 2002)

Chapter 5
How Baby-Boomers in the United States Anticipate Their Aging Future: Implications for the Silver Market

M. Silverstein and A. Abramson

Abstract This chapter examines three types of aging anxiety among baby-boomers in the United States and discusses their implications for the silver market of older consumers. We use data from a national sample of 473 baby-boomers to examine the structure and predictors of aging anxiety. We find that three dimensions adequately describe the apprehensions that this generation has about growing old: anxiety over the loss of autonomy emerged as the most powerful factor, followed by uneasiness over the physical manifestations of aging, and optimism/pessimism with regard to expecting continuity and contentment in old age. A variety of factors are associated with these dimensions, including gender, marital status, income, knowledge about aging, and exposure to older adults. We discuss how an appreciation of the sources of aging anxiety among baby-boomers can help marketers and advertisers better understand the pre-elderly consumer market, and suggest ways of addressing baby-boomers' fears with positive images of growing old.

Introduction

January 1, 2008 was an auspicious date in American gerontological history as it marked the year when the first members of the baby-boom generation began receiving early retirement benefits from the Social Security Administration. In 2011, the first baby-boomers (that cohort of Americans born between 1946 and 1964) will reach age 65 and begin a long anticipated cascade of 76 million individuals who will enter their retirement years over the next several decades. How informed are baby-boomers about the realities of aging? Given their temporal proximity to old age, are they fearful of the experience? If so, are their fears based on fact? Does Franklin D. Roosevelt's rallying proclamation regarding World War II that "we have nothing to fear, but fear itself" apply as well to fears about aging? In this chapter we examine the meaning of aging anxiety and identify its sources in middle-aged Americans who stand on the threshold of old age. The graying of the US population, indeed of the world's population, is the product of three forces that have converged in a unique way. First, increased life-expectancy has meant that most individuals can now expect to live into old age, and many into advanced old age. The average American can expect to live to 78 years, 30 years more than they could expect to live in 1900 [18]. Second, historical reductions in fertility over the twentieth century have shifted the age composition of most developed societies from having a preponderance of children to having a preponderance of adults. Third, the post-World War II baby-boom created a bulge in the population structure that will bring to fruition an aged society with the percentage of older adults rising from 12.4% in 2000 to more than 20.6% in 2050 [9].

These demographic changes have sharpened personal expectations about what it means to grow old, with active and engaged life-styles held up as the model of successful aging. Expectations of old age have been redefined, empowering individuals with adequate means to spend their retirement years in fulfilling and interesting ways. Yet knowledge about aging and the older population is relatively low in the general population. On at least one standard, the *Facts on Aging Quiz* [21], a 25-question test of knowledge about aging and the older population, the American public received an average score of 50%, a putative failing grade that has not changed over the last 10 years [1]. In part, lack of knowledge about aging is fostered by continued age-segregation in most of America's major institutions and social arenas [8], as well as ageist depictions in the media that reinforce negative stereotypes of older adults. Western culture continues to place great value on youth and the characteristics associated with being young, while ascribing primarily negative characteristics, such as being unhealthy, grouchy and physically unattractive, to older adults [4]. However, some argue that these images are beginning to fade, as the elderly population becomes healthier and more active than in previous times [6].

Positive images of aging have emerged in advertisements and have tended to emphasize the use of products that resist or even reverse the physical and mental changes that accompany aging. These ads are a double-edged sword, on the one hand, proffering an image of old age that seems to defy aging itself, and, on the other hand, raising expectations about successful aging to unrealistic, and, in many cases, unattainable heights [7]. Anti-aging products have been criticized as capitalizing on false hopes and capitulating to the cultural imperative that age-related changes are to be avoided at all costs, or at least hidden. Even so, scientific findings about products or behavioral changes that delay or reverse declines associated with aging have instilled a degree of optimism about the aging experience. Converting these findings into behavior has proven to be difficult, as much of the research is contradictory or inconclusive, creating confusion about the strategy that will best promote successful aging. The proliferation of pseudo-scientific findings has increased misconceptions about aging, particularly when improbable claims about the effectiveness of anti-aging products are represented as empirical truth [2]. The resulting uncertainty can be a basis for aging anxiety.

Aging anxiety can be functional if worries about the changes wrought by aging, even if exaggerated, reflect legitimate concerns that motivate preventive activities (e.g., improving health behaviors) and forward-thinking consumer behaviors (e.g., purchasing long-term care insurance). Unrealistically positive perception of what risks lie ahead may be problematic if it inhibits precautionary actions. As the next few years represent a long-awaited watershed period with respect to population aging, we believe that it is a propitious time to examine the anxieties and concerns of baby-boomers, a large cohort at the cusp of old age.

Anxieties about aging may stem from lack of factual knowledge about the aging process [5]. In a national study, Lynch [16] found that having accurate knowledge about aging and older adults correlated inversely with aging anxiety, implying that having accurate knowledge about the future reduces anxiety about it. While younger adults tend to have the least knowledge and the most anxiety about aging [19], this tendency is not immutable. Following their participation in courses on aging, young adults developed more accepting attitudes toward older people and experienced reduced discomfort about their own aging [3, 13]. Another study showed that medical students increased their sensitivity to older patients after receiving training in gerontological topics [22].

Exposure to older adults has also been found to alleviate aging anxiety [12]. Lasher and Faulkender [15] found that having more frequent contact with older adults relieved anxieties about changes in physical appearance, the loss of loved ones, and declines in health and financial well-being due to aging. Exposure to elders in the family also shapes attitudes towards the aging process; contact with grandparents contributed to positive attitudes about aging and lessened fear of growing old [17].

By and large, aging anxiety declines with increasing chronological age; generally, older adults hold the most positive views of later life and young adults the most negative, with the middle-aged in between [20]. However, the argument has been made that aging anxiety is not a relevant concept for younger and older adults [16]. Young adults are temporally too far from old age to make a reasoned assessment about their state of anxiety, and the elderly are contemporaneously experiencing the condition about which anxiety is assessed. Midlife thus represents an age at which anxiety is most relevant because it is imminently anticipated. While there is considerable debate about the contribution of aging anxiety to the so-called midlife crisis [14], some evidence points to a heightened salience of aging concerns among middle-aged adults [16, 23]. Countering the gender stereotype that aging is more threatening to women than to men, research has found that among the middle-aged, men tend to more negatively anticipate aging than women [15], providing support for another gender stereotype – that of the male midlife crisis.

Aging anxiety in middle-age might result from a generalized fear of old age as a time of decline and marginalization, but may also stem from one's particular personal circumstances. Baby-boomers with fewer economic resources and worse health may rightfully be concerned about the quality of their impending retirement years [11, 16]. In addition, those who have launched children and achieved an "empty nest" stage of life, or who have lost a spouse to death, may view old age as a potentially alienating period of life [10].

Research questions. In this investigation we examine the structure and determinants of aging anxiety in American baby-boomers in order to better understand the nature and sources of such anxiety in a generation on the threshold of old age. Specifically, we ask the following questions:

1. What set of concerns do baby-boomers have about their future aging? Do their worries cohere around a consistent set of themes?
2. Do the current health, social, and economic circumstances of baby-boomers affect whether they anticipate aging with fear or acceptance?
3. Does familiarity with the realities of aging and exposure to the older population affect how aging is anticipated?
4. What implications do these questions have for older consumers, and what lessons do they provide to businesses catering to the silver market?

We hypothesize that baby-boomers with fewer personal resources – defined in terms of physical, economic, social, and psychological well-being – will be more pessimistic about their future aging than those with greater personal resources. We also anticipate that baby-boomers with relatively little exposure to older adults and who are relatively misinformed about the realities of aging will have greater anxiety and less hopefulness about their aging futures. We propose that knowledge of aging is a multifaceted construct in terms of its utility as a predictor of aging anxiety. We expect that negatively cast misunderstandings about older adults will add to anxiety over aging, while an appreciation of the positive potentials of later life will reduce aging anxiety. Further, we speculate that greater understanding of the *true* declines associated with aging will induce "healthy" anxiety. Finally, exposure to older adults is expected to allay fears about aging by providing a realistic image of what it means to be old that, in most cases, will be more positive than existing preconceptions.

Images of Aging Study

Sample

The data used for this investigation were derived from the *Images of Aging Study*, a joint project of the University of Southern California (USC) and AARP. A random sample of 1202 adults 18 years of age and older living in the continental United States was surveyed by telephone (see [1] for details). The main purpose of the study was to explore images, perceptions, and attitudes that Americans have toward aging and the older population (methodological details are provided in point 1 of Appendix 1).

We restricted our analyses to 473 respondents who were born between 1946 and 1964 (the most liberal definition of the baby-boom), which at the time of the survey represented those ranging in age from 40 to 58 years. Characteristics of the sample are described in Table 5.1, both for the total sample and for younger (40–49) and older (50–58) cohorts of the baby-boom. In examining age-group differences in characteristics, we note that respondents 40–49 years of age were significantly more likely to have at least one parent alive and more likely to have children living at home compared to those aged 50–58. In addition, the younger group tended to have higher incomes and was more likely to be employed full-time than the older group.

Measures

We measured aging anxiety with the Kafer Anxiety Scale (KAS), a 13-item sub-scale of the Aging Opinion Survey [12]. Examples of items found in KAS included "I worry others will have to make decisions for me when I'm older," "the older I become, the more I worry about my health," and "I have become more content with the years" (see Table 5.2). Items were scored on a 4-point scale with responses ranging from 1 = *strongly disagree* to 4 = *strongly agree*.

To evaluate knowledge of aging and the older population we relied on Palmore's Facts-on-Aging Quiz (FAQ) [21]. FAQ consists of a series of 25 statements about aging that respondents assessed as either true or false. We used 22 statements from this test to represent three domains that relate to factual (accurate vs. inaccurate) and evaluative (positive vs. negative) aspects of the assessment. Accurate negative perceptions of the aged are labeled *negative realism*, (e.g., "All five senses tend to decline in old age"; "Older people tend to take longer to learn something new"), inaccurate negative perceptions of the aged are labeled *negative falsism* (e.g., "The majority of older people are senile"; "In general, older people tend to be pretty much alike"), and accurate positive perceptions of the aged are labeled *positive realism* (e.g., "The majority of older people say they are seldom bored"; "Older workers have fewer accidents than younger workers"). In this way we were able to explore warranted anxiety about aging grounded in objective truth, and unwarranted anxiety about aging based on false negative stereotypes of older adults.

To ascertain exposure to older adults in daily life we asked respondents how often they talked to, or got together with anyone age 65 or older (other than a spouse), measured as daily, weekly, monthly, or less. To measure exposure to an older generation in the family, we compared respondents with at least one parent alive to those with both parents deceased.

Measures of demographic characteristics and personal well-being included age, gender, race/ethnicity, marital status, education, yearly household income, home ownership, having a child living at home, being employed, health status, and life satisfaction (details provided in point 2 of Appendix 1).

What Are Baby-Boomers Anxious About?

We used twelve of the Kafer items to examine whether anxiety can be parsed into meaningful substantive categories. We found three discernable types of anxiety (the results of principal components analysis of these items are shown in Table 5.2). We label them: (1) "dependence worries," reflecting fear over losing autonomy and resource depletion; (2) "physical worries," reflecting fear of declining health, outward signs of aging, the aging process itself, and death, and (3) "aging optimism," reflecting an affinity for older people, growing contentment with aging, and expectation of continued friendships and sexual relations in later life. We note that while dependence and physical worries are moderately correlated at 0.4, the correlation of these two dimensions with aging optimism is only modest (0.11 and 0.16, respectively) suggesting that fears over the negative prospects of aging do not necessarily inhibit optimism about aging.

We review the absolute amount of anxiety with regard to the three types identified (see Table 5.3). Average anxiety about dependency in old age and physical aging varied only slightly from the midpoint of the scale (i.e., 2.5), implying that baby-boomers are generally moderate in their level of apprehension. Comparing the two "fear" factors reveals that fear of dependence supersedes fear of physical aging, signifying that practical concerns about lack of autonomy and resources are more intense than existential fears about the physical manifestations of aging. That aging optimism averages above the scale midpoint (approximately between "agree" and "strongly agree") suggests that baby-boomers feel a degree of hopefulness about their aging future. In comparing levels of anxiety between younger and older baby-boomers, we find that younger boomers worry more than older boomers about physical changes associated with aging, although this difference is only marginal.

Taken together, these results support the view that aging is viewed by baby-boomers with mixed feelings that include elements of both fear and optimism. This suggests that *ambivalence* may be a good operant term to describe how those at midlife anticipate their old age.

How Knowledgeable Are Baby-Boomers About Aging?

Examining the index that signifies the number of correct responses about positive aspects of aging, we note that the sample averaged slightly more than three correct responses out of six (see Table 5.3). This represents only a 51% accuracy score for *positive realism*. For the index of correct responses about negative aspects of aging, the sample averaged 3.7 correct responses out of five for a 74% accuracy rate, providing moderate evidence of *negative realism*. However, this statistic must be balanced against a mean of 3.8 incorrect responses (out of 11) concerning negative aspects of aging that have no basis in fact. Thus, the average baby-boomer can be said to have 34% negative stereotyping error about aging and the aged. These results not only confirm other studies that find a general lack of knowledge in the general population about the realities of aging, they further suggest an exaggerated view of the declines associated with aging and a pessimism concerning the adaptive potential and resilience of older adults. When knowledge about aging is compared across younger and older baby-boomers, we see that the number of negative misconceptions about aging is greater in the younger than in the older group, a finding consistent with the former's greater personal anxiety over growing old, the late-boomers apparently fearing and misunderstanding what for them is more distant on the horizon.

Which Baby-Boomers Are Particularly Anxious About Aging?

We next examine social and demographic characteristics that are uniquely associated with the three dimensions of aging anxiety. While a detailed discussion of our statistical approach is beyond the scope of this chapter, we note that the results discussed are statistically significant effects from multiple regression analyses in which all variables cited earlier are simultaneously controlled (see Table 5.4).

Dependence worries. We first address worries about dependence in old age. Baby-boom women have greater fears of dependence than do baby-boom men, reflecting legitimate differences in resources, health, and life expectancies between the two genders. Curiously, married respondents were more fearful of dependence than previously married respondents – those who were divorced/separated or widowed. This result may reflect fear of the anticipated consequences of widowhood among the married. Having higher income appears to allay fears of dependence (those who did not report their income, a group that tends to have higher socioeconomic status, were less fearful as well). Neither poor health status nor low life-satisfaction influenced anxiety about dependence; their associations with this type of anxiety (not reported) having been fully mediated by the lower-than-average incomes of the less healthy and less satisfied.

In terms of knowledge about aging, we found that having greater negative misconceptions about aging increased personal anxiety over dependence in later life. Because knowledge is positively correlated with income (higher income respondents tended to have greater knowledge), the influence of household income on dependence anxiety is weakened but still present when knowledge is considered simultaneously. Having daily contact with older adults marginally reduced worries about dependence in later life.

Physical worries. Turning to anxiety about the physical manifestations of aging, we find that never-married respondents had greater anxiety about physical aging than married respondents, and those who were employed full-time reported less anxiety than those working less than full-time or not at all. As expected, baby-boomers who were more satisfied with their lives and who were in better health had less anxiety about physical aging compared to those who were less satisfied and in worse health, respectively.

We found that respondents with more negative misconceptions about aging tended to have greater fear over physical changes due to aging compared to those with fewer such misconceptions. We also note that baby-boomers of 50–58 years of age had significantly less fear than those 40–49 years of age, but this was fully explained by the fact that the older age group made fewer negative stereotyping errors about the aged than the younger group. That is, the "natural" optimism of the older age-group ceased to be important when their more accurate knowledge about aging was controlled. Exposure to older adults did not assuage or strengthen this type of anxiety.

Aging optimism. Finally, we examine optimism about aging. Baby-boomers who never married were less optimistic about their aging futures than those who were currently married. In addition, those who were more satisfied with life tended to have greater optimism than those who were less satisfied.

We found that realistic views of aging affected the degree of optimism felt about one's own old age; positive realistic views increased optimism and negative realistic views decreased optimism. Because we controlled for the number of false negative beliefs about aging, it is possible to conclude that the effect of negative realism is free of stereotyping error in that it explains that aspect of low optimism that has a factual basis and therefore reflects legitimate concerns about growing old. This awareness may be important in guiding protective action and adaptive behaviors in advance of these declines.

We found that exposure to older people was particularly important with regard to this aspect of aging anxiety. Respondents who had more contact with older adults, particularly those with daily contact, were more optimistic about their aging futures than those with less contact. Ostensibly, points of contact with older individuals provided a more accurate perception of aging and increased comfort with it.

What Are the Implications for Older Consumers?

Our results suggest that middle-aged consumers will need to be gently introduced to products and services that help redress, avoid, or delay the deficits and challenges associated with aging. Products such as self-help books and DVDs to promote healthy aging through diet and exercise may appeal to baby-boomers who are forward thinking and predisposed to being proactive about their prospective aging. Literature and services that assist with retirement planning may also be of interest. Consumers with greater economic means who are concerned with outward appearances of aging may be attracted to aesthetic-enhancing procedures such as botox injections and cosmetic surgery.

Baby-boomers, the generation that defined its culture at each stage of life, will reshape retirement to fit their life-styles. Residential choices in retirement living that assume a preference for age-segregated housing may be outmoded. Senior retirement complexes that begin at age 50 are beginning to break down age barriers by catering to a more active, engaged, and younger retiree than in the past. Age-integrated housing that is organized around shared interests, hobbies, previous occupations, or cultural and religious backgrounds may prove attractive to both pre-retired and retired empty-nesters. Such communities will find particular interest among baby-boomers anticipating an active old age. Engaged and healthy seniors may be reluctant to "put down their Harley for the hammock." Baby-boomers in poorer health – who our research shows to be particularly anxious about physical changes of aging – have legitimate concerns that may be addressed by protective products such as long-term care insurance and assisted living facilities.

Virtual communities will abound with the anticipated growth of on-line communication among the elderly. This will surely change the image of retirement from one physically bounded within "gray ghettos" to one that is fluidly interactive with "silver surfers" communicating both within and across generational lines. Online programs that match older volunteers with volunteer positions offer opportunities for continued engagement after retirement. Ergonomic and high-technology products that promote independence and autonomy (e.g., Jitterbug large button cell phone; GPS navigational devices) will likely find an attentive audience among the tech-savvy baby-boomers.

While discourse in the popular press argues that women are less comfortable than men in their "aging skin," our results suggest that women are more fearful than men of cognitive, social, and monetary dependence. Facing the likelihood of widowhood, middle-aged women may worry about the loss of resources that typically follows the loss of a spouse. Therefore, mature women may be particularly receptive to financial services that help build, protect, and transfer assets in the event of widowhood.

How will baby-boomers, this vast and heterogeneous cohort, approach and experience old age as consumers? Our hunch is that much will depend on which segments of the baby-boom generation are considered. Some older adults of the near future will be motivated by their fears, others by their needs, and still others by their preferred life-style choices, or some combination of the three. This consumer market will likely have multiple motivations and create demand for goods and services accordingly.

What Are the Implications for Marketers and Advertisers?

Marketers and advertisers face the challenge of addressing aging consumer markets about sensitive issues, such as death, illness, chronic care, and stressful life transitions, which tend to provoke anxiety. We suggest several ways that marketing strategies can capitalize on the anxiety of consumers as a motivator of action, without alienating those consumers by triggering excess anxiety. Long-term care insurance faces this particular challenge, as most people would prefer not to dwell on their need for chronic care. Marketing approaches that focus on the capacity of such insurance to save children the burden of care may appeal to altruistic tendencies of older adults interested in preserving their legacy. Financial and estate planning services can tap into the elderly's desire to insure the economic well-being of their descendants and guarantee generational continuity.

Advertising has been effective at defusing the stigma of embarrassing conditions in order to propose a remedy (e.g., the use of Viagra to address the problem of erectile dysfunction). To do this, advertisers have positioned products to appeal to a desirable identity as much as much as to "fix" an external problem. For instance, an advertisement for a drug that helps with urinary problems could focus less on the embarrassment of having the problem and more on presenting positive consequences from using the product (such as engaging in sports activities with friends). Advertisements for moisturizers and cosmetics that reduce signs of aging have only recently begun to show women in their true "skin." These ads let middle-aged and older adults know that it is acceptable that their bodies have changed, and suggest almost second-handedly that the product will make them look younger. In other words, a flattering image offsets the less-than-flattering nature of the problem. In general, marketing will be more successful if it avoids identifying consumers as "old" or "sick," and offers a more nuanced message of continued youthfulness and functionality with use of the product.

Finally, niche markets in the older population will become more sizable as baby-boomers bring their unique demographic characteristics into later life. There are greater numbers of never-married, previously married, and childless persons in the baby-boom cohort than in preceding cohorts. Our research showed greater aging anxiety and lower levels of aging optimism among never-married baby-boomers, possibly reflecting concerns about entering old age without a spouse or children. These concerns may predispose unpartnered baby-boomers to have an interest in amenities and supportive environments that provide social alternatives to family such as singles-cruises and online "reunion" friendship/dating services.

Summary and Conclusion

In this chapter we have endeavored to illuminate the central concerns about aging expressed by the baby-boom cohort in the United States. From policy, planning and marketing perspectives, this segment of the population is notable both for its sheer size, formidable resources, and potential for reinvention. Trends toward healthy aging are cause for optimism about this cohort's potential for achieving a high quality of later life. At the same time, media convey images of older adults that magnify traits of illness, confusion, and marginalization, devaluing them in the public mind. Uncertainties about what to expect in old age – stemming from either lack of knowledge or fearful images – has created ambivalence about aging, and in some cases outright dread of growing old. While we do not suggest that it is the responsibility of the business community to rectify negative images based on misinformation and false stereotypes, we do conclude that is in the interest of those marketing to the baby-boomers to softly educate them about the aging experience and bring to them the goods and services that can improve their quality of life as they grow old.

What do the three dimensions of aging anxiety we identified imply for older consumers? Anxiety over financial and social dependence emerged as the most powerful factor. Products and services, such as long-term care insurance, congregate housing, and investment counseling, may find a welcome reception among the now near-elderly baby-boomers who are concerned about their continued autonomy. Having a poor factual understanding of the aging process was implicated in escalating fears of dependence in old age. Public education campaigns about the realities of growing old may partially assuage such fears. Low income also appeared to be a risk factor for this type of anxiety and may require public–private partnerships to resolve.

In general, fear over physical decline was characteristic of those with fewer health and social resources. Products and services that change the course or appearance of aging, such as cosmetics, anti-oxidant vitamins, and preventive health regimens of various types, may be particularly attractive to middle-aged individuals who have these fears.

We found that greater exposure to older adults enhanced aging optimism. Middle-aged individuals who interact with, and enjoy the company of, older adults may find leisure-oriented retirement communities and senior cruises appealing. Aging optimism was also influenced by greater realism about growing old. Positive perceptions about the potential of later life made for greater personal hopefulness about aging. In addition, the accurate perception that physical declines accompany aging – what we label "healthy awareness" of physiological changes in the aging body – caused reductions in optimism. These reality-based perceptions may be characteristic of a market segment that is predisposed toward products and amenities (such as driving aids and home modifications) that can accommodate expected physical and sensory declines in later life.

Negative misconceptions about the elderly increased fears of dependence and physical decline with aging. Although such fears are based on false notions about what it means to be old, we must acknowledge the possibility that a more dire view of aging may be accurate when reported by members of disadvantaged groups.

While the desire to remain autonomous as long as possible is not a particularly American trait, the dominant cultural ideology in the United States clearly values individualism and personal responsibility. Market and public policy solutions to problems of aging in the baby-boom generation will necessarily cater to underlying preferences to avoid dependence and maintain self-reliance. This notion is summarized by the powerful metaphor of "successful aging" that describes goals universally valued in life: avoiding disease and disability, engaging in social relations, and maintaining high cognitive and physical functioning [24].

It is somewhat worrying that the general public, even those close to old age, know so little about the realities of aging and that misconceptions of the older population are generally pejorative in nature. Perhaps it is only human nature to fear an unknown future (in this case a future that turns out to be not as bad as anticipated). However, being misinformed about the aged implies ignorance about our future older selves. Although a more gerontologically educated, age-integrated society is a lofty goal, even modest movement toward that objective may bring expectations of aging more in line with actual experience. Ultimately, this will provide a better basis for preparatory action and informed consumer behavior when anticipating both the promise and the inevitabilities of growing old.

Appendix 1: Methodology

1. The core sample consisted of 1202 adults 18 years of age and older selected by telephone random digit dialing of residential locations in the continental United States between March and April 2004. For households in which several adults resided, residents whose birthdays were closest to the interview date were chosen to participate. The overall response rate to the survey was 50%, a figure in line with most random national telephone surveys. We applied sample weights in our regression analyses to adjust for non-response and insure that the sample reflected a national profile on age, gender, educational attainment, race, and

Hispanic origin based on Current Population Survey data in 2002 from the US Census Bureau.

2. Demographic characteristics were measured by dichotomous indicators for age (50–58 vs. 40–49), gender (female vs. male), race/ethnicity (Hispanic, non-white race vs. white); marital status (divorced/separated/widowed, never married vs. married), education (having graduated college vs. not having graduated college); yearly household income ($35,000–$75,000, more than $75,000, income not reported vs. less than $35,000), home ownership (owns vs. rents); child at home (at least one child at home vs. no child at home); employment (full-time vs. not full-time). Measures of well-being include self-rated health (excellent/good vs. fair/poor) and satisfaction with life (somewhat/very satisfied vs. somewhat/very dissatisfied).

Appendix 2: Supporting Tables

Table 5.1 Characteristics of baby-boom respondents (40–58 years) in *AARP Images of Aging Study, 2004*

Characteristic	Total sample 40–58 ($N = 473$) %	Age group 40–49 ($N = 289$) %	Age group 50–58 ($N = 184$) %
Age			
40–49	55.2	–	–
50–58	44.8	–	–
Gender			
Male	41.0	41.4	40.6
Female	59.0	58.6	59.4
Race/ethnicity			
White non-Hispanic	76.5	74.0	79.7
Hispanic	10.6	10.7	10.4
Non-white/non-Hispanic	12.9	15.3	9.9
Marital status			
Married	67.2	67.1	67.4
Divorced/separated/widowed	21.8	20.3	23.6
Never married	11.0	12.6	9.0
Education			
Less than college graduate	63.5	64.4	62.7
College graduate or more	38.4	35.6	37.3
Household income			
Less than 35K	26.4	22.6	30.7[+]
35–74K	30.0	34.1	25.0
75K or more	33.5	33.7	33.5
Income not reported	10.1	9.6	10.8
Home ownership			
Rents	23.3	24.9	21.2
Owns	76.7	75.1	78.8

Table 5.1 (continued)

Characteristic	Total sample 40–58 ($N = 473$) %	Age group 40–49 ($N = 289$) %	Age group 50–58 ($N = 184$) %
Children at home			
No child at home	45.7	30.3	64.6***
At least one child at home	54.3	69.7	35.4
Employment			
Not employed full-time	37.4	34.1	41.5+
Employed full-time	62.6	65.9	58.5
Satisfaction with life			
Somewhat or very dissatisfied	12.5	13.4	11.3
Somewhat or very satisfied	87.5	86.6	88.7
Self-rated health			
Fair or poor	18.2	16.1	20.8
Excellent or good	81.8	83.9	79.2
Parents' survival			
Both parents deceased	24.7	14.6	37.3***
At least one parent alive	75.3	85.4	62.7
Contact with older people			
Monthly or less	21.7	18.8	25.5
Weekly	45.5	45.6	45.3
Daily	32.8	35.6	29.2

$^+ p < 0.10$, $*p < 0.05$, $**p < 0.01$, $***p < 0.001$ denote significance levels of chi-square test for age-group differences.

Table 5.2 Rotated factor loadings of principal components of Kafer Aging Anxiety Scale among baby-boom respondents (40–58 years) in *Images of Aging Study, 2004* ($N = 473$)

Kafer Aging Anxiety statements	Principal components		
	Dependence worries	Physical worries	Aging optimism
I worry about not being able to get around on my own when I'm older	0.751		
I worry others will have to make decisions for me when I'm older	0.795		
Financial dependence on my children in old age is one of my greatest fears	0.684		
The older I get, the more I worry about money matters	0.650		
The older I become, the more I worry about my health		0.536	
Thinking about dying doesn't bother me much (score reversed)		0.764	
The older I become, the more anxious I am about the future		0.540	
I always worried about the day I would look into the mirror and see gray hairs		0.535	
I enjoy talking to older people			0.596
I have become more content with the years			0.503
I know I'll enjoy sex no matter how old I am			0.546
I am sure that I will always have plenty of friends to talk to			0.639

Note: Factor loadings below 0.5 not shown. A 46.9% variance explained by three-factor solution.

Table 5.3 Mean scores on dimensions of Kafer Aging Anxiety Scale and Facts-on-Aging Quiz for baby-boom respondents in *AARP Images of Aging Study, 2004*

Dimensions	Total sample 40–58 ($N = 473$) Mean (SD)	Age group 40–49 ($N = 289$) Mean (SD)	Age group 50–58 ($N = 184$) Mean (SD)
Kafer Aging Anxiety dimensions			
Dependence worries	2.65 (0.87)	2.67 (0.89)	2.62 (0.85)
Physical worries	2.30 (0.77)	2.35 (0.78)	2.23 (0.75)
Optimism about aging	3.32 (0.53)	3.31 (0.53)	3.33 (0.53)
Facts on Aging dimensions			
Positive realism (0–6 items)	3.12 (1.22)	3.04 (1.17)	3.22 (1.27)
Negative realism (0–5 items)	3.72 (1.19)	3.75 (1.19)	3.68 (1.18)
Negative falsism (0–11 items)	3.76 (2.21)	4.00 (2.14)	3.47 (2.26)

Scores are the means of variables coded as 1 = strongly disagree, 2 = disagree, 3 = agree, 4 = strongly agree.

Table 5.4 Unstandardized OLS regression estimates predicting three dimensions of aging anxiety for baby-boom respondents in *AARP Images of Aging Study, 2004* ($N = 473$)

Independent variables	Dependence worries	Physical worries	Aging optimism
Demographic and well-being			
Age group 50–58	−0.02	−0.12	−0.06
Female	0.23*	0.07	0.00
Hispanic	0.02	−0.04	0.02
Non-white/non-Hispanic	−0.15	−0.04	−0.18
Divorced/separated/widowed	−0.28*	−0.03	0.09
Never married	0.19	0.48**	−0.43**
College graduate or more	0.07	−0.14	−0.10
Household income 35–74K	−0.27*	−0.03	0.01
Household income >75K	−0.38*	0.18	−0.09
Household income not reported	−0.22	0.08	0.12
Owns home	−0.10	−0.09	−0.13
Child at home	−0.01	−0.01	0.03
Employed full-time	0.12	−0.22*	−0.06
Very or somewhat satisfied with life	0.01	−0.12	0.52***
Excellent or good health	−0.19	−0.26*	0.15
Knowledge of aging			
Positive realism scale (FAQ)	−0.03	−0.04	0.07*
Negative realism scale (FAQ)	0.04	0.06	−0.08*
Negative falsism scale (FAQ)	0.14***	0.08***	−0.01
Exposure to older adults			
At least one parent alive	0.06	0.11	−0.05
Daily contact with older people	−0.21+	−0.07	0.51***
Weekly contact with older people	−0.18	−0.18	0.24*
Constant contact	−0.16	0.15	−0.47
R^2	0.19	0.15	0.13

Note: Data are weighted based on 2002 US Census for age, gender, and educational attainment, race, and Hispanic origin. Dependent variables are standardized factor scores from earlier principle components analysis $^+p < 0.10$, $*p < 0.05$, $**p < 0.01$, $***p < 0.001$.

References

1. AARP, Images of aging in America 2004 (2006), http://assets.aarp.org/rgcenter/general/images_aging.pdf. Retrieved 8 Mar 2008
2. R.H. Binstock, J.R. Fishman, T.E. Johnson, in *Handbook of Aging and the Social Sciences*, 6th edn., ed. by R.L. Binstock, L.K. George (Academic, San Diego, 2005), p. 436
3. E.M. Blunk, S.W. Williams, Educ. Gerontol. **23**, 233 (1997)
4. W.H. Crockett, M.L. Hummert, in *Annual Review of Gerontology and Geriatrics*, vol. 7, ed. by K.W. Schaie (Springer, New York, 1987), p. 217
5. K. Doka, Int. J. Aging Hum. Dev. **22**, 173 (1986)
6. K.F. Ferraro, Gerontologist **32**, 296 (1992)
7. C. Haber, Generations **25**, 9 (2001–2002)
8. G.O. Hagestad, P. Uhlenberg, J. Soc. Issues **61**, 343 (2005)
9. W. He, M. Sengupta, V.A. Velkoff, K.A. DeBarros, *U.S. Census Bureau, Current Population Reports, P23-209, 65+ in the United States: 2005* (U.S. Government Printing Office, Washington, DC, 2005)
10. B. Hiedemann, O. Suhomlinova, A.M. O'Rand, J. Marriage Fam. **60**, 219 (1998)
11. D. Holtz-Eakin, T.M. Smeeding, in *Demography of Aging*, ed. by L.G. Martin, S.H. Preston (National Academy Press, Washington, DC, 1994), p. 102
12. R.A. Kafer, W. Rakowski, M. Lachman, T. Hicket, Int. J. Aging Hum. Dev. **11**, 319 (1980)
13. R. Katz, Int. J. Aging Hum. Dev. **31**, 147 (1990)
14. A. Kruger, Psychol. Rep. **75**, 1299 (1994)
15. K. Lasher, P. Faulkender, Int. J. Aging Hum. Dev. **37**, 247 (1993)
16. S.M. Lynch, Res. Aging, **22**, 533 (2000)
17. K. McGuinn, P.M. Mosher-Ashley, Educ. Gerontol. **28**, 561 (2002)
18. National Center for Health Statistics. *The State of Aging and Health in America 2004* (U.S. Department of Health and Human Services, Centers for Disease Control and Prevention, Hyattsville, MD, 2004)
19. S.M. Neikrug, Educ. Gerontol. **24**, 287 (1998)
20. A.M. O'Hanlon, C.J. Camp, H.J. Osofsky, Educ. Gerontol. **19**, 753 (1993)
21. E.B. Palmore, Gerontologist **17**, 315 (1977)
22. E.B. Palmore, *Facts on Aging Quiz* (Springer, New York, 1988)
23. C.E. Ross, P. Drentea, J. Health Soc. Behav. **39**, 317 (1998)
24. J.W. Rowe, R.L. Kahn, *Successful Aging* (Pantheon, New York, 1998)

Chapter 6
Japan's Demographic Changes, Social Implications, and Business Opportunities

C. Usui

Abstract The "aging problem" should not be viewed as an economic encumbrance. It is better viewed in the context of the robustness of the economy. Expansion of the carrying capacity of the active labor force as well as active aging among older adults will decrease the burden on society. This chapter draws out social and cultural implications of demographic changes in the context of Japan's transformation from a Fordist to post-Fordist economy. The distinction shifts attention to the social organization of technology-based service industries. The growing number of older persons and senior households means immense business opportunities for developing new solutions, products, and services. Older adults are potent consumers, willing and economically able to secure independent living and a high quality of life. This chapter discusses a number of emerging silver industries, including housing and real estate, food, pets, robotics, senior care appliances, and the funeral market.

Introduction

The aging of the population in developed societies has taken on a kind of doomsday patina in many policy circles. It has brought foreboding and predictions of impending calamity. Yet the problem of population aging should not be viewed as operating in a static societal black box. The determination of the "aging problem" rests, in part, with the changing economic conditions in each country and the "carrying capacity" (productivity) of active workers. Relatively small increases in economic growth have the potential to substantially moderate the ill effects of demographic factors [6, 30]. Expansion of the carrying capacity of active as well as non-active groups will decrease the burden for the dependent older population. In the twenty-first century, developed countries are shifting from a "Fordist" to "post-Fordist" economy with new levels of productive capacity. Any discussion of aging society must take this change in productive capacity into account [40, 41].

The "aged dependency ratio" is a common measure for gauging the burden of the "dependent" population in an aging society. It is the number of actively working population divided by the number of "aged dependents" in the population. In 2000 in Japan, there were 3.9 active workers supporting each person 65 years of age and older. By 2010, there will be fewer than three workers, and by the year 2025 the figure is predicted to drop to two active workers for every aged dependent member. Although the aged dependency ratio has become conventional in describing economic burden in an aging society, it is based on questionable assumptions. For example, the productivity and consumption patterns of different age groups are based on past patterns and are assumed to be static. On average, people of working age (aged 15–64) are considered productive and consumption-oriented, while the older population (aged 65 and over) is considered unproductive with relatively low incomes and low levels of consumption. In addition, policy-makers often focus exclusively on the denominator in the aged dependency ratio (i.e., older population) and look for solutions that reduce the burden of the aged dependents. The aged population is viewed in isolation and presumed to provide little or no contribution to society, while the active population is assumed to have a static carrying capacity with little change in their production or consumption patterns.

In contrast, this chapter presents a different set of views. First, demographics are an intrinsic part of the social organization of society. Historically, demographic patterns have been altered by socio-economic, technological, and political changes in society. Second, expansion of the productive and consumption capacities of either group will decrease the level of dependency for the same proportion of elderly. Third, productivity and consumption of any age group are more variable and dynamic than presently supposed. The logic that the working population will have to support the dependent population is based on assumptions of social organization and life cycle that characterized the Fordist economy of the twentieth century. In the twenty-first century, industrialized countries are shifting to a new logic of the post-Fordist economy.

"Fordist" refers to an industrial organization system associated with the Ford Motor Company in the early twentieth century [13,20]. A Fordist economy is based on mass production and mass consumption, with products having relatively long life cycles. Worker skills, once acquired, also have relatively long life cycles. The auto, steel, and rubber industries are examples of the leading sectors in this type of industrial economy. In contrast, a post-Fordist economy is more oriented to the application of information technology. The economy is geared to the flexible production of selective goods and the consumption of a variety of goods. Goods and services have relatively short production life cycles, requiring continuous innovation. The computer software, telecommunications, and information-based service industries represent examples of the leading sectors of this type of economy.

The OECD [23] notes that a key to promoting the service sector is the diffusion of technology, and future increases in productivity can offset labor shortages in certain sectors. In other words, Japan's future hinges on whether new, post-Fordist growth industries will emerge and raise economic productivity and whether labor-market fluidity will accommodate these new industries. Some authors maintain that the key to sustaining a healthy economy is a continuous 2–3% economic growth rate [6,30]. It is not the ratio of the working to dependent population but rather the economy's capacity that largely determines whether an aging population becomes a problem [9,30,41].

Japan's economy has considerable room for future productivity gains compared to other advanced nations, and it can produce more even though the labor force may shrink. Japan is ranked third among 24 countries in the labor productivity of the manufacturing sector, reaching $78,680 [23]. However, when the comparison was made for overall labor productivity among 30 OECD nations, Japan ranked nineteenth with $59,651. Luxemburg ranked first ($90,683) and the USA second ($83,129).

Seniors as Consumers

Recent changes in living arrangements and life-styles among older adults have a significant impact on emerging business and industries. Today's older population is better off economically than other generations, creating a potent consumer market. Japan now has a larger number of older persons (aged 65 and older) than young persons (0–15 years of age), and the number of senior households without any non-senior household members surpassed 6 million in 2000. Unlike their parents' generation that depended on their children's income and support in old age in co-residential arrangements, the current generation of older adults is healthy and places more emphasis on self-reliance and quality of life. These older adults provide a boost to productive and consumption capacity. Multifaceted social changes involving the household structures, living arrangements, intergenerational relations, and attitudes towards the source of support in old age have given rise to robust silver industries. The growing markets for senior adults are called silver markets or mature markets. They involve the production of specialized goods and services in medical and health services and equipment, home care, real estate, construction, financial services, education and learning, food, cosmetics, travel, and entertainment. The current generation of older persons commands a larger disposable income and national financial assets than their previous generations did. They are willing consumers of goods and services that promote independent living. Their concerns about living and dying have fueled the development of innovative products and services. Innovations in telecommunications technology and equipment, telecare and telematics (both addressing new forms of health care deliveries), consumer electronics, robotics, and other high-tech engineering address new demands arising out of the social and cultural changes surrounding their living environments. There is a potential for active aging, which changes the current assumptions about the aged dependency ratio.

Senior households have large assets and are a key to the future expansion of the silver market. According to a national livelihood survey in 2002, the average per capita income of senior households (defined as those without anyone between the ages of 19 and 64) was 91% of the national average [32]. A government white paper in 2003 found that almost 80% of Japanese seniors considered themselves "free of financial difficulties." In addition, the average financial assets held by senior households rose to ¥24.7 million ($226,440 when US$1 = ¥110) compared to the national average of ¥16.5 million ($150,000) among all households in 2002 [32]. These senior households possess nearly 50% of the entire national savings ($11.3 trillion) and spend $95 billion per year on products and services that make their lives more comfortable [4]. The Nomura Research Institute estimates that senior households aged 75 and above will have the largest increase in annual spending from 2005 to 2010 [36].

The retirement of baby boomers will bring additional expansion of consumer markets in silver industries. Japanese baby boomers were born between 1947 and 1949; these roughly 6.8 million people account for 5.3% of the total population and hold even greater assets than the current generation of older persons. According to JETRO [21], the total value of financial assets held by baby boomers was approximately $1.13 trillion in 2004. A Dentsu report (2006) indicates that direct spending by baby boomers prior to and after retirement will amount to ¥7.78 trillion ($70.7 billion), and the impact of this increased consumption will lead in the medium term to total economic outlays of ¥15.3 trillion ($139.3 billion) [7].

Of the ¥7.78 trillion in expected direct spending by baby boomers, the biggest outlays derive from house remodeling, real estate, and related sectors, yielding ¥4,092 billion ($37.2 billion) or 52.6% of the estimated consumption. The next largest category of estimated spending is hobby pursuits and education (¥1,196 billion or $10.9 billion). The third category is travel, with ¥1,116 billion ($10.1 billion). Purchase of durable goods, such as automobiles, is estimated at ¥404 billion ($3.7 billion) and purchase of financial products (e.g., stocks, bonds) at ¥675.5 billion ($6.1 billion) [7].

Emerging Silver Industries

Japan's demographic changes have important social consequences, affecting business in the emerging silver industries. We examine these issues in housing and real estate, food and food safety, pets, robotics, senior care appliances, and the funeral market.

Housing and Real Estate

According to JETRO [21], spending on housing and home renovation in 2005 was highest among the 65–69 age group, and this group spent twice as much as the 55–59 age group. Upgrading homes with seismic retrofitting, insulation, heating and ventilation, energy efficiency, security, and safety (barrier-free homes, wheelchair accessibility) are the most popular types of renovation. Japan is the world leader in developing energy-efficient homes and accounts for nearly 50% of the total solar cell production in the world. The use of solar panels in homes has become popular, and power companies purchase excess electricity generated from ordinary consumers [11].

Luxury home remodeling and vacation homes have attracted affluent seniors and are expected to increase with the retirement of baby boomers who have higher standards for comfort than the previous generation. Installation of home elevators, for example, is no longer out of reach for ordinary families, and sales by Mitsubishi Electric Elevator Products have risen steadily [4]. The Nomura Research Institute estimates the housing renovation market will rise to ¥8 trillion ($72.7 billion) by 2010 [21].

Today's older adults tend toward "active aging" not just because they enjoy good health, but because they are the first generation willing and economically able to support themselves in old age. Post-material values such as quality of life and independent living have become important goals. A "quiet revolution" is taking place in their attitudes toward spending time and money [1]. Today's seniors are more willing to focus on their lives and spend money for their own independent life-styles rather than saving for their children.

The Japanese government facilitated the development of new living arrangements among seniors when it introduced the Long-Term Care Insurance (LTCI) (*kaigo hoken*) in 2000. In 2003 the government deregulated the industry to increase private-sector participation in nursing care sectors [16]. The government subsidizes much of the remodeling costs for seniors' homes, including the remodeling of disabled-access toilets and the installation of banisters, non-slip guides, and ramps, and the availability of LTCI has led to greater choices for older persons in private-sector facilities. In addition, there are affluent older persons willing to pay more for high-quality services and facilities that provide long-term care.

Food and Food Safety

Food accounts for 23% of expenditures by Japanese households [3]. The Japanese food market is estimated at over $700 billion, and the market for high-quality, safe food is booming [22]. The Japanese people are concerned with health and are more likely to seek dietary health through foods than through supplements. The aging population is driving a range of new trends in food markets. Due to the rapid growth in single person and senior couple households, mini-size packaging is popular. "Bulk" items and "super-size" products are no longer the standard [38]. Instead of low-priced products, older adults seek high-quality, high-priced, specialty products [3]. Market demands for ready-to-eat meals, take-out foods (including box lunches or *obento*), and food delivery services have sharply increased [22]. Shopping for food on TV, the Internet, and by mail-order has also expanded, aided by door-to-door home-delivery services (*takuhaibin* or *takkyubin*).

"Nutraceutical" and organic foods are gaining larger market shares [3]. Nutraceutical foods (also called functional foods), claimed to have health benefits, make up a huge market in Japan: $27.1 billion in 2005 (compared to $22 billion in the USA). Examples of nutraceuticals are red wine as an antioxidant and an anticholestorolemic, broccoli as a cancer preventative, and soy and clover to improve arterial health in women. Some nutraceuticals are well known, including gamma-linolenic acid, beta carotene, and anthocyanins. According to Nitta [21], the health boom that began in 2001 is expected to continue with the retirement of baby boomers. More recently, people's interest in mineral water and the health benefits of water generated sales in the water market of $1.6 billion in 2006, a 32% increase from 2005 [22, 34]. Food safety and traceability, freshness, and visual appeal are important features in this market. The Nomura Research Institute reports that older adults are much more likely to use cooperatives (group purchasing of foods shipped directly from organic farm producers) out of concerns for food safety [36].

Food markets are integrating information technologies to improve food safety, including the use of devices that identify the origin and quality of products, such as the "protected designation of origin" (PDO) or "protected geographical indicator" (PGI), both developed by the European Union in 1992. Specialty food stores based on the 7-Eleven business model, not Wal-Mart, are gaining appeal [22] as seniors find it more convenient to shop close to home rather than traveling farther away to discount stores offering a huge selection. Small and medium-sized retailers hold a large market share and are expected to dominate in the future.

Pets

Japanese people's attitudes toward pets have changed from "animals" to "family members" due to decline in family size, increase in the number of empty nest households, and population aging. Following a recent but explosive pet boom, Japan now has more dogs and cats than children, over 12 million dogs in 2004 or about equal to the human population of Tokyo [14]. This market is assessed as a "trillion yen" ($9 billion) market and is expected to grow even larger. The popularity of pets has triggered vigorous demands in related industries, including pet food, books and magazines, pet insurance (for health/medical care), pet training, grooming, pharmaceuticals (including medicines for aging pets and vitamin supplements), and clothing. Rising concerns over the quality of life for pets also mean more demands for pet health care, veterinary clinics, vaccines and medication, and other health products.

The pet business has the potential to improve the quality of life among older adults [43]. Living with pets is known to improve the well-being of older adults because of benefits such as countering feelings of loneliness and provision of social interaction. Owning pets helps regulate the daily routines of elders, and pets induce more physical activities, help maintain emotional balance, and provide objects of affection, leisure opportunities, and extended circles of friendships (e.g., pet-loving circles). According to one study, Japanese pet owners spend 35% more on pets each year than their US counterparts [10]. One pet-insurance company, Amicom, grew to a $13 million business with 2200 participating care providers and 70,000 subscribers in 2004 [10]. Leisure activities for pets and the pet-grooming business have expanded, including amusement parks and hot springs for dogs, spacious tracks for exercising dogs, and dog runs.

Robotics

Of particular note is the Japanese ability to adapt to changing circumstances and embrace new products and services, including machines and new technologies [18, 27]. Japan had an early romance with robots. Tetsuwan Atom (Iron Arm Atom or Astro Boy) began as a successful comic strip in the 1950s, followed by Tetsujin No. 28 in a 1963 television series, and Doraemon, a robotic cat. Doraemon was one of the most famous manga characters in the 1980s and became a cultural icon in Japan.

Japanese tendencies to anthropomorphize machines are critical to our understanding of their attitudes toward, and embrace of, new technology, including robots. Machines have become companions in everyday life whether they are office machines, factory robots, or automobile navigators. Tamagotchi (virtual/digital pets with morals and ethics), created in 1996, illustrate the scale of business and people's attitudes toward a mechanical pal. More than 13 million Tamagotchi were sold in less than a year. Between 1996 and 2007, some 37 versions of Tamagotchi were made and sold [19, 37]. Robots will play a major role in assisting the daily lives of older adults as well as the rapidly aging labor force [8, 24]. Japan is "a kingdom of robots" [29]. Factories use over 410,000 robots, and Japan, a major exporter of robots, accounts for 60% of the world's supply, with an additional $4.4 billion worth of other robots. A robotic entertainment dog, AIBO, introduced by Sony in 1999 turned out to be Sony's biggest success in years [33]. AIBO is an autonomous robot integrated with a computer, vision system, and articulators. It is equipped with 100 voice commands and can learn and mature from interaction with its owner and the external environment. Owners enjoy teaching their robotic pets new behaviors. Priced at $2500 each in 1999, all 3000 units in Japan sold out in just 20 min, and 2000 units sold in 4 days in the USA. Exceeding expectations, Sony provided 10,000 more AIBO units for sales in Japan, Europe, and the USA in late 1999 [33]. Other robots include NEC's R-100, a toddler-sized robot on wheels that can turn on the TV, send and receive email, and do a little entertainment. Mitsubishi, OMRON, and Matsushita have robot pets that send reminder messages for taking medications. These robots are linked to family members, hospitals, and community centers for monitoring via the Internet. They can fill a critical void at home in a society where an increasing number of seniors live alone. Another successful example is Paro, a furry robotic baby seal, manufactured for alleviating stress and tensions for people with dementia in nursing homes. It is priced at ¥350,000 ($3180) and is sold as medical equipment. Paro is equipped with sensors and responds to petting by fluttering its eyes and moving its flippers. It won the service prize at the government-sponsored Robot Awards 2006 [26].

Service robots will likely become part of everyday life in the near future and will make homes safer and assist in care giving. At present, service robots perform a wide variety of tasks such as cleaning, making coffee and serving tea, making the bed, and even feeding. A sophisticated type of service robot is the personal assistant robot. According to Research Horizon Magazine [28], the global market for personal robots is growing at 400% per year. Mitsubishi's Wakamaru, a companion and nursing robot, for example, is 3 ft tall, rolls on wheels and is equipped with an integrated mobile phone, Web camera (to allow family members and doctors to keep an eye on the owner), and a dictionary. It can recognize some 10,000 words and is priced at $10,000 [2]. Although Wakamaru turned out to be a failure and was discontinued in 2007, Japanese companies are developing robots that can communicate better and incorporate sophisticated functions. A confluence of smart materials, low cost, high-speed computing power, complex wireless communication systems, improvements in batteries, and continuing research on human–robot interactions (especially perception and reliability) is making this industry explosive.

Senior Care Appliances

In 2004 the Sanyo Electric Company developed a new elder care product, the human washing machine. One hundred companies bought Sanyo's new washing machines for people. According to a *New York Times* article [5], residents of nursing homes welcome the new technological help because the machines warm the whole body and protect their privacy. For staff members, it means less lifting of residents and physical burdens. The user sits in a chair that is rolled backward into place. The sides of the machine then close like a clamshell, forming an instant tub with the person's head sticking out the top. Shampooing and hair drying is done by hand. The human washing machine was developed by Mitsuru Haruyama, a businessman crippled by muscular dystrophy [5].

Other examples that integrate modern technology include mobile-phone based health care management and a "robot suit." Tokyo Mobile Healthcare Inc. provides mobile phone-based health management and patient care services, including assistance in the management of diabetes and chronic conditions [31]. A "robot suit" was developed as a motorized, battery-operated pair of pants designed to help the aged and infirm move around on their own. The project was led by engineering professors at Tsukuba University, and the product will be available in the second half of 2008 [12]. Similarly, Tokyo University of Agriculture and Technology has developed a product to help Japan's aging farmers. It is a power-assisted robot suit that provides physical strength. The robot suit gives support to the shoulders, knees, arms, and legs so that the wearer can withstand strenuous work without getting tired. The project engineers expect to commercialize the product in 2012 [25]. These devices and others in development will push Japanese sales of domestic robots to \$14 billion in 2010 and \$40 billion in 2025 from nearly \$4 billion currently, according to the Japan Robot Association.

Although human washing machines cost almost \$50,000 a unit – enough to pay a year's wages for two immigrant nurses – they save money in the long run and make care-giving tasks less labor intensive. These practical applications of new technologies in care giving offer promising solutions for the future. Fueling the demand are the decision by the government to push for home care and rehabilitation to promote more independent living among the elderly, rapid changes in family structure, and older adults' desire for independent living with a high quality of life.

Funerals

Funerary practices in Japan have been a topic of academic inquiry because of the long tradition of ancestor worship [35]. The industry is being transformed from religious ritual to a thriving death industry [42]. In 2004 there were over one million deaths, and more than 6000 death-related business establishments/operators offered diverse funeral services. In an industry estimated at \$1.7 billion, the cost of funerals in Japan ranks among the highest in the world [15]. It used to be socially improper to discuss the cost of funeral arrangements in advance. More recently, however, the industry began offering transparent pricing, and pricing has become competitive. Hotels and railway companies have entered the market. These new businesses involve franchises and offer packaged funeral services. Cremation is the rule.

Funeral industries are not regulated [15]: there is no government approval system or regulation over entry. The first foreign firm to enter the Japanese funeral market was All Nations Society (an American funeral business) in 2004. Its success is attributed to open pricing and affordability. Traditionally, funerals are held in people's homes. However, due to changes in family structure and community networks, the use of packaged funeral services at franchised ceremonial halls is gaining popularity.

Japan's custom of ancestor veneration entails the continuity of family line and connections to family members. Family graves are the place where the dead are housed and remembered; graves are maintained and visited regularly. However, with falling fertility rates, increasing frequency of divorce, and increase in single-person households, people are concerned about their descendants' ability to care for the dead. In 1997, a movie entitled *Ohaka ga nai!* (I have no grave for myself) depicted modern grave-related problems (*haka mondai*) [39].

A variety of new businesses have emerged in response to *haka mondai*. Time of death has become a predictable event with the advancement of medical technology, enabling people to make funeral arrangements in advance. One prominent example is a permanent ritual care (*eitai kuyo*) in cemeteries. These graves are permanently cared for, usually for 33 years after death. Such care primarily targets people without successors or those who feel they could not expect ritual care from their children. According to Kawano [17], the costs of permanent ritual care ranged between ¥100,000 and ¥500,000 ($900–$45,000) per person in 2000, and over 230 cemeteries provided such services.

Summary and Conclusion

In this chapter I have questioned demographic predictions of a societal catastrophe based on the aging of Japanese society. This popular view is based on a static view of the capacities of the population, economy, and institutions. Instead, this chapter has focused on the social aspects of demographic changes involving the family structures, living arrangements, and the older generation's attitudes towards independent living and consumption. It has drawn out some business implications for the productivity-enhancing social and organizational changes in the context of the transformation from a Fordist to post-Fordist economy. The distinction between the Fordist and post-Fordist economies shifts our focus to the future expansion in the carrying capacity of technology-based service industries and consumption capacity of older population. I have argued that the current and future generations of older population tend towards active aging and are in a position to consume more than is currently assumed. Quality of life becomes an important goal in the post-Fordist economy, creating new demand for more selective goods and services. An increase in the older population creates demand for new industries in the sliver industries and increases consumption. Population aging requires adjustments in markets, corporate practices, and government policies, but it should in no way be interpreted as the bankrupting of Japan's economy.

To illustrate elements of the transition from a Fordist to post-Fordist economy, this chapter has reviewed a number of emerging silver industries, including housing and real estate, food and food safety, pets, robotics, senior care appliances, and funerals. The robotics and senior care appliances markets are based on the intensive use of new information technologies and demonstrate future improvements in quality of life among senior adults.

Significant attitudinal and behavioral changes among older adults have often been overlooked. The older Japanese population is healthy and is a vital resource to society as volunteers, care givers, childcare providers, and consumers. Goods and services that promote active and healthy aging as well as those that meet the needs of changing family structures are some of the key factors that will ensure the success of business in the Japanese market.

There are three lessons to be learned from this chapter. First, today's older population constitutes a distinctive and capable force affecting the Japanese economy and society. Second, the current generation of older persons has fueled demands for diverse goods and services as they tend toward an independent life-style and quality of life. Third, the demands for innovative goods and services are mediated by social and cultural sensitivities to the issues of living and dying.

As the first country to test innovative solutions in the silver market, Japanese experiences have several lessons for other countries. First, the social and cultural dimensions of aging should not be overlooked. Technological innovations and adaptations are modulated by social and cultural contexts of aging in any society. They condition the relationship between demographic changes and societal consequences. Japanese willingness to adapt to modern technological solutions described in this chapter is a good example. Second, Japan's experience shows the significance of generational and age-cohort changes that are a key to understanding new consumption trends. It is a common error to view each successive cohort of older persons as an unchanging, static group resistant to new ideas, products, or services. Third, the rising consumption capacity among the older population, and their desire to lead a healthy and active aging mean expanding new business opportunities. Japan provides an excellent testing ground for how new business can succeed.

References

1. T. Aritake, Japan's elder power: most Western CEOs have yet to discover the nation's imminent spending power, Chief Executives January 1 (2005), http://findarticles.com/p/articles/mi_m4070/is_205/ai_n13787906
2. Artificial Intelligence and Robotics (2007), http://smart-machines.blogspot.com/2007/06/mitsubishi-robot-receptionist-available.html. Accessed 19 June 2007
3. Asia Pacific Trade Council, Report of the Japan Market Advisory Group April 2007, British Columbia (2007), http://www.asiapacifictradecouncil.ca/pdf/japan_report.pdf
4. K. Belson, These oldies look golden to Japan Inc. Business Week Online (17 July 2000), http://www.businessweek.com/2000/00_29/b3690152.htm
5. J. Brooke, Japan seeks robotic help caring for the aged. New York Times (5 Mar 2004), http://www.nytimes.com/2004/03/05/international/asia/05JAPA.html?ex=1393822800&en=eb854fe2a4e6c9bd&ei=5007&partner=USERLAND
6. J.C. Campbell, Population aging: hardly Japan's biggest problem. *The Demographic Dilemma: Japan's Aging Society*, Asia Program Special Report, No. 107 (Woodrow Wilson International Center for Scholars, Washington, DC, 2003), p. 10
7. Dentsu Inc., Dentsu survey estimates the economic impact on consumption resulting from the retirement of baby boomers, News release by Dentsu Inc. Communications Division, No. 21-2006 (30 Mar 2006), http://www.dentsu.com/news/2006/20060210330html
8. N. Dethlefs, B. Martin, Sci. Public Policy **33**(1), 47 (2006), http://www.uow.edu.au/arts/sts/bmartin/pubs/06spp.html
9. International Institute for Applied Analysis, in *Populations Aging, Pensions, and Health,* Options. vol Summer (International Institute for Applied Analysis, 2003), p. 2, 6
10. Japan Entrepreneur Report, Report No. 20 (June 2004), http://www.japanentrepreneur.com/200406.html
11. Japan moving toward more efficient solar power. Japan Today (16 Dec 2004), http://www.japantoday.com/jp/feature/797
12. Japan unveils "robot suit" that enhances human power. Space Daily (7 June 2005), http://www.spacedaily.com/news/robot-05zq.html
13. D. Jaffee, *Organizational Theory* (New York: McGraw Hill, 2001)
14. JETRO, Invest Jpn **8**(Spring), 8 (2005), http://www.jetro.go.jp/en/invest/newsroom/newsletter/pdf/ij_08.pdf
15. JETRO, Trends in the Japanese funeral industry. Japan Economic Monthly (February 2006), http://www.jetro.go.jp/en/market/report/pdf/2006_13_p.pdf
16. JETRO, Attractive sectors: medical care – policy initiatives. http://www.jetro.go.jp/en/market/attract/medical/policy.html

17. S. Kawano, in *Demographic Change and the Family in Japan's Aging Society*, ed. by J.W. Traphagan, J. Knight (SUNY Press, Albany), p. 147
18. T. Larimer, Man's best friend. Times Asia (1 May 2000), http://www.time.com/time/asia/magazine/2000/0501/japan.bestfriends.html
19. List of Tamagotchi Releases, http://en.wikipedia.org/wiki/List_of_Tamagotchi_releases
20. J. Myles, in *Beyond the Marketplace: Rethinking Economy and Society*, ed. by R. Frieland, A.F. Robertson (Aldine de Gruyter, New York, 1990), p. 271
21. H. Nitta, Capitalizing on retirement of Japan's first baby-boomers. JETRO Japan Economic Report, April–May (2006), http://www.jetro.go.jp/en/market/report/pdf/2006_18_u.pdf
22. J. Noguchi, Food business line. Japan Market Development Reports (USDA Foreign Agricultural Service GAIN Report), VII (3) (March 1–31) (Global Agriculture Information Network, Tokyo, 25 April 2007), http://www.calwinexport.com/content/Market_Info/FAS%202007/Japan%20Development%20Report%202007.htm
23. OECD, Economic Survey of Japan 2006 (20 July 2006), http://www.ceri-sciences-po.org/archive/sept06/artoecd.pdf
24. A. Oreback, A Component Framework for Autonomous Mobile Robots. Ph.D. Dissertation, KTH Numerical Analysis and Computer Science, Stockholm, Sweden, 2004. http://www.nada.kth.se/~oreback/publik/oreback-thesis.pdf
25. Physical strength-enhancing wearable 'power-assist robot suit' for farmers developed (11 Jan 2008), http://www.gizmowatch.com/entry/physical-strength-enhancing-wearable-power-assist-robot-suit-for-farmers-developed/
26. Robotic baby seal wins top award (22 Dec 2006), http://news.bbc.co.uk/2/hi/technology/6202765.stm
27. D. Rosen, C. Usui, UCLA Pac. Basin Law J. **13**(1), 32 (1994)
28. J. Sanders, From science to fiction to reality: personal robots emerge to improve quality of life at work, home and school. Research Horizons Magazine, Georgia Institute of Technology (8 June 2007), http://gtresearchnews.gatech.edu/newsrelease/personal_robotics.htm
29. F.L. Schodt, *Inside the Robot Kingdom: Japan, Mechatronics, and the Coming Robotopia* (Kodansha International, Tokyo, 1988)
30. J.H. Schulz, *Economics of Aging* (Auburn House, New York, 1995)
31. D. Scuka, Mobile Internet for the silver market (2003), http://unjobs.org/authors/daniel-scuka
32. Silver Years, Jpn Echo, **33**(2) (2006), http://www.japanecho.co.jp/sum/2006/330214.html
33. SONY, Press releases (25 Jan 2000), http://www.sony.net/SonyInfo/News/Press_Archive/200001/00-002E/
34. Success and failure in functional water (Nov 2006), http://www.piribo.com/publications/dietary/1181/success_failure_functional_water.html
35. H. Suzuki, *The Price of Death: The Funeral Industry in Contemporary Japan* (Stanford University Press, Stanford, CA, 2000)
36. H. Takei, K. Kudo, T. Miyata, Y. Ito, Adaptive strategies for Japan's retail industry facing a turning point. Nomura Research Institute Papers 110 (1 Oct 2006), http://www.nri.co.jp/english/opinion/papers/2006/pdf/np2006110.pdf
37. Tamagotchi, http://en.wikipedia.org/wiki/Tamagotchi
38. Targeting the over 60s key to the Japanese market (7 Aug 2006), http://www.scoop.co.nz/stories/BU0608/S00140.htm
39. J.W. Traphagan, J. Knight (eds.), *Demographic Change and the Family in Japan's Aging Society* (SUNY Press, Albany, 2003)
40. C. Usui, Int. House Jpn Bull. **21**(1), 42 (2001). Also published in Japanese as Kokusai Bunka Kaiho **12**(1), 54
41. C. Usui, in *The Demographic Dilemma: Japan's Aging Society,* Asia Program Special Report 107 (Woodrow Wilson International Center for Scholars, Washington, DC, 2003), p. 16
42. A.L. Webb, Japan's dying industry. Newsweek International (23 Dec 2002), http://www.newsweek.com/id/66864. (Updated version 29 Oct 2007, http://www.newsweek.com/id/66864/output/print)
43. L. Wood, B. Giles-Corti, M. Bulsara, Soc. Sci. Med. **61**, 1159 (2005), http://www.ncbi.nlm.nih.gov/sites/entrez?db=pubmed&uid=15970228&cmd=showdetailview&indexed=google

Part II
Innovation, Design and Product Development for the Silver Market

Chapter 7
Disabled Persons as Lead Users for Silver Market Customers

P. Helminen

Abstract It is important to understand user needs when developing new products. User-centered design provides tools for learning about the user needs in question, but studying only the target market customers may result in constricted need data because of the functional fixedness of these customers. Lead user approach, on the contrary, aims to learn from the lead users of a certain target group in order to find better solutions for the needs in the target market. In this chapter, I show through a study on mobile phones, how disabled persons can be seen as lead users when developing products for silver market customers. I also present methods for exploring the needs and solutions that disabled users possess.

Introduction

The customers of the so-called silver market are people who are often beginning to suffer from deterioration in their eyesight, hearing, or mobility. Product development has traditionally concentrated on developing products for the general, able-bodied public. It should not be forgotten that up to 25% of the population in industrialized countries are older people or people with a disability, most of them in the silver market. The target market of most of the products, such as mobile phones, being virtually all consumers, means that the aging population should not be shrugged aside, as it continues to fill an ever-increasing part of the target market.

I first introduce the concepts of user-centered design, user innovation, and lead users. Then I show through a study on mobile phone user interfaces that disabled persons can be seen as lead users, when developing products for the silver market. The study also shows how methods like photo-diary and contextual inquiry can be used in order to better understand the needs of silver market customers.

User-Centered Design and Lead Users

It is common understanding among designers and product developers that user needs
have to be taken into account when developing a product. The roots of user-centered
design are in the military industry. In World War II it was found that the performance
of technology can be improved if attention is paid to the ergonomic requirements
of those who use the technology. The goal of user-centered design is to transfer
user needs into product specifications, and thus ensure the satisfaction of the future
customers. What is common in all user-centered design methods is that they provide
the designer with information that he or she can use when designing the product.
The role of the user is to be purely an information source for the designer who then
hopefully is able to innovate.

User innovation means innovation carried out specifically by users. Users are
individual consumers or companies that expect to benefit from using a product or
a service, whereas manufactures expect to benefit from selling a product or a service. Traditionally, users have been seen as passive consumers who just consume
the products that manufacturers develop. In reality, users have always made modifications to products when needed. In fact, when users need something badly and
there is no solution in the market, they will generate a solution by themselves – they
will innovate.

Often, user innovation is confused with user-centered design. The user-centered
design approach offers a variety of methods for user needs assessment: interviewing
(group, open, structural, etc.), contextual inquiry [1], probing [5], observing, etc. All
of these methods help the designer learn about the needs of the targeted user. Thus,
the company first learns about user's needs and then develops a responsive product
to fill that need. Even if the user has developed some type of solution to his/her need,
companies very often overlook user's solution but only register the need. The main
difference between user innovation and user-centered design is who carries out the
actual innovation. *In user-centered design the innovator is the designer who works
in a company. In user innovation it is the user himself.*

Users innovate because they have to, and they benefit directly from the innovation
they develop. Users do not care how the need is filled as long as it is. Companies
on the other hand need to struggle with many things other than the optimal solution: product portfolios, strategy, manufacturing capability, etc. Users can come up
with the most creative solution, because they are searching for the best possible
functional solution to their own problem.

To better grasp the concept of user innovation, von Hippel [19] developed the
term *lead user*. These are the users that companies need to find in order to benefit
from user innovation. In order to understand what lead users are, we need to understand what diffusion is. Rogers's [11,12] ideas on diffusion are well known. He talks
about diffusion of new ideas through a society, and the fact that a considerable time
lag exists from the introduction of a new idea to its widespread adoption. The main
elements in the diffusion of new ideas are: (i) an innovation that is (ii) communicated
through certain channels, (iii) over time (iv) among the members of a social system.
In spite of the fact that the communication of most innovations involves a time lag,

there is certain inevitability in their diffusion. Most attempts to prevent innovation diffusion over an extended period of time have failed. For instance, the Chinese were unsuccessful in their attempt to maintain sole knowledge of gunpowder. And today, the secret of the nuclear bomb is no longer a secret [11–13].

According to the diffusion model, an innovation is completely diffused when it has been adopted by 100% of the members of the social group to which it has been introduced. Rogers divides the adopters into five categories [11]: innovators (the first 2.5% to adopt), early adopters (13.5%), early majority (34%), late majority (34%), and laggards (the final 16% to adopt) [11].

The theory of lead users relies on the idea that there is always somebody who has the need first, and that the rest of the marketplace will have the need later. As all new things diffuse through a society over time, there are always users whose present needs foreshadow general demand [13]. Von Hippel defines lead users of a novel or enhanced product, process, or service as those displaying two characteristics with respect to it:

1. Lead users face needs that will be general in a marketplace – but face them months or years before the bulk of that marketplace encounters them.
2. Lead users are positioned to benefit significantly by obtaining a solution to those needs [19].

According to the first lead user characteristic, the "ahead on an important market trend" variable, there are users who experience new needs and are prepared to generate innovations that substantially differ from existing market offers. The second characteristic, the "expected benefits variable" reflects the possibility of the users initiating the development of a new solution if the solution would bring them significant benefit [18, 19]. In other words, lead users are well ahead of market trends and have needs that go far beyond those of the average user [17].

It is important to distinguish lead users from the categories defined by Rogers. *Lead users acts solely on their needs*, when Rogers's innovators and early adopters are driven by their interest in the new technology. In other words, as stated by von Hippel [18]: "Note that lead users are not the same as early adopters of an innovation. They are typically ahead of the entire adoption curve in that they experience needs before any responsive commercial products exist – and therefore often develop their own solutions." See Fig. 7.1.

Classical research on problem-solving shows that it may be inhibited by the functional fixedness of solution objects [4]. This means that if we examine users that are already familiar with the product, we might find them not able to generate new ideas for its use. They are functionally fixed and then not able to think out of the box. If a person is asked to perform a task that requires the use of a wire, he is less likely to unbend a paper clip if he is given the clip attached to papers than if he sees the clip loose. Or, for example, a screwdriver is designed for handling screws but as it is long and sharp, it could also be used as a crowbar or a chisel.

In user-centered design, we take a look at the targeted customers. The problem with the targeted customers is that however well we study them, they are going to be functionally fixed and therefore not able to reveal information that enables us to

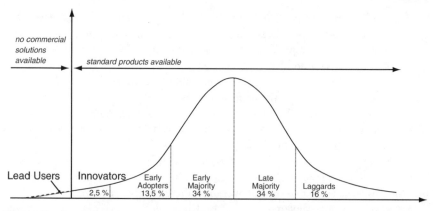

Fig. 7.1 Lead users' position on a market trend compared to Rogers's diffusion curve

create breakthroughs. *Lack of functional fixedness makes lead users very appealing to product development*, i.e., lead users do not base their views on existing products but on their needs. As Lilien et al. state: "In contrast, lead users would seem to be better situated in this regard – they 'live in the future' relative to representative target-market users, experiencing today what representative users will experience months or years later" [9].

Who are lead users then? A leead user is often somebody who is trying to improve their way of working, rather than consciously trying to invent. Like the developer of World Wide Web Tim Berners-Lee says: "It was something I needed in my work." Berners-Lee wanted simply to solve a problem that was hindering his efforts as a consulting software engineer at CERN, the European particle-physics laboratory in Geneva. Mainly to become more efficient, he developed a system that provided easy-to-follow links between documents stored on a number of different computer systems and created by different groups [2].

Very often lead users will have already invented solutions to meet their needs. This is particularly true among highly technical user communities, such as those in the medical or scientific fields [8, 10]. Also, innovations in sporting equipment are often developed by lead users. Shah [14] shows that innovations in skateboarding, snowboarding, and windsurfing have typically been developed by a few early expert participants in those sports. The idea for the heart rate monitor was originated by a Finnish professor, Seppo Säynäjäkangas, in the early 1970s. He enjoyed cross-country skiing, and he started wondering what methods could be used to monitor the development of his condition. The Finnish Ski Association soon became interested in the idea and started developing a prototype with Säynäjäkangas. Later this invention was utilized by all competitive athletes, and nowadays the heart rate monitor has diffused to serve a big part of the population who enjoy recreational sports. Also, the energy bar is a user innovation. It was invented by an Olympic marathoner, who cooked up the first PowerBar in his kitchen.

Lead users can also be found among those who function in harsh conditions, such as aerospace or the military, for example.

When 3M, a diversified technology company, was trying to develop cheaper and more effective infection control in the area of surgical drapes,[1] they gathered information outside the target market, in order to find lead users. They traveled to hospitals in Malaysia, Indonesia, South Korea, and India, and learned how people in less than ideal environments attempt to keep infections from spreading in the operating room. They interviewed veterinarians who had great success keeping infection rates low despite cost constraints and the fact that their patients were covered with hair and didn't bathe. They interviewed Hollywood makeup artists who had learned effective ways to apply nonirritating, easy-to-remove materials to skin, which is important to the design of infection control materials. With the help of these lead users, 3M was able to create three new product-line concepts [17].

In the following study I show that disabled persons can be lead users for able-bodied users, and especially for the silver market customers.

Disabled Persons as Lead Users in Mobile Phone Design

The purpose of this study was to (i) investigate if disabled persons could be seen as lead users in mobile phone user interface design, and (ii) to evaluate the suitability of the selected research methods on the examined user groups.

Traditionally mainstream consumer product design has not explicitly considered the needs of older or disabled people. Instead, their needs have been considered in the design of niche products, e.g., disability aids, providing separate and also stigmatizing solutions for these user groups. Yet in many ordinary circumstances we all suffer from a "situational disability": When there is no light, we cannot use our eyesight, for example. When there is a lot of noise, we are not able to hear. When driving a car, we should not use our hands for anything other than driving nor look away from the road. Moments of situational disability are even more common among the silver market users.

I argue that if a mobile phone user interface is designed based on the user needs of the target market (i.e., the majority of consumers, who are people that hear and see well), we end up leaving out everyday situations, where the use of eyesight and hearing is limited or completely prevented. Yet, it is a significant advantage for a mobile phone to work well in all possible situations. I suggest that if a mobile phone user interface was designed based on the needs of disabled persons, the special disability situations would be covered as well.

In this study I investigated whether the needs of a disabled user in an "ordinary" situation correspond to the needs of an "ordinary" user in a special situation. In other words, are specifications derived from an actual disability equal to those derived from a situational disability? Three members of three different groups of

---

[1] Surgical drapes are thin adhesive-backed plastic films that are adhered to a patient's skin at the site of surgical incision, prior to surgery. Surgeons cut directly through these films during an operation.

mobile phone users were studied and compared: deaf, blind, and "ordinary users" who see and hear well. The methods that were used in the study are photo-diary and contextual inquiry combined with an open-ended discussion. Contextual inquiry was used for learning about users needs. Photo-diary and open-ended discussion provided information both on user needs but also on the leading edge behavior of the disabled persons. The methodology of the study is presented in detail in the appendix.

I will present the results of the study on how disabled persons can be lead users for silver market customers, firstly by showing the comparison between the user needs of the disabled users and the ordinary users (situationally disabled users), and secondly, by showing examples of the leading-edge behavior of the disabled users, and how they indeed face needs that the ordinary public, and especially the silver market customers, may encounter. I will also show some design guidelines for visually and hearing-impaired users. These guidelines apply not only to completely blind and deaf users but also to users with milder impairments that are common among silver market customers.

User Needs of Disabled Users vs. Ordinary Users

Photo-diaries documented the course of the participant's day, and the objects and devices that had been used during the day. The photographs taken by the blind participants turned out well. Only aiming at the target was slightly inaccurate, but it did not impede recognition of the photographed object (see Fig. 7.2). The contextual inquiry and open-ended discussion were able to widen the understanding of the actual user needs of each participant.

All ordinary users articulated situations when use of mobile phones is difficult because of not being able to hear well: urban noise, rock festival, library (when the phone should be silent and no speaking is allowed). Speaking on the phone when walking in the city center was found difficult and uncomfortable since it is not possible to clearly hear the voice on the other end. In noisy environments you cannot talk on the phone and you cannot hear the phone ring.

Fig. 7.2 Photographs taken by a blind person

Table 7.1 Ability to perform given tasks (situationally blind vs. blind)

Task	Situationally blind (complete darkness)			Blind		
	Ordinary 1	Ordinary 2	Ordinary 3	Blind 1 *no TALKS*	Blind 2 *TALKS*	Blind 3 *TALKS*
Can he find the silent phone, when not holding it, and make a call?	No	No	No	No	No	No
Can he find the ringing phone, when not holding it, and answer the call?	Yes	Yes	Yes	Yes	Yes	Yes
Keypad locked, can he unlock it and make a call?	Yes[a]	Yes[b]	No[c]	Yes[b]	Yes[d]	Yes[d]
Keypad unlocked, can he make a call?	Yes[e]	Yes[e]	Yes[e]	Yes[f]	Yes	Yes
Keypad unlocked, can he send a text message?	Yes[e]	Yes[e]	Yes[e]	Yes[f]	Yes	Yes

[a] Pressing one determinate key lights the screen and makes the instructions to unlock the screen visible. *User knows the determinate key by heart.*
[b] Pressing two determinate keys is needed to unlock the keypad. The screen is not lit until unlocked, i.e., the instructions to unlock the screen not visible. *User knows the determinate keys by heart.*
[c] Pressing two determinate keys is needed to unlock the keypad. The screen is not lit until unlocked, i.e., the instructions to unlock the screen not visible. *User does not know the determinate keys by heart.*
[d] *TALKS* speaks out the instructions to unlock the screen.
[e] The screen is lit.
[f] *User knows the menu structure and keys by heart.*

Two blind participants have TALKS[2] speech output software on their mobile phones. It speaks out the words and letters that are shown on the screen. The third participant is not a TALKS user, but uses the mobile phone just by touch. She has a limited access to mobile phone functions since she has to memorize the menu structure.

Both blind and situationally blind users performed equally in given tasks (see Table 7.1). None of the users were able to find a silent phone if it was placed in an unknown location, but if the phone was ringing, they found it easily guided by the sound.

Some phones require pressing two determinate keys to unlock the keypad. The screen of the phones will not be lit until the keypad is unlocked, i.e., the instructions to unlock the keypad that are shown on the screen cannot be seen. In order to unlock the keypad without instructions, one must remember the correct key combination by heart. One situationally blind and two blind users did not remember the

---

[2] SpeechPAK TALKS converts the display text of a cellular handset into highly intelligible speech, making the device completely accessible for blind and visually impaired people. SpeechPAK TALKS runs on Symbian-powered mobile phones to speech-enable contact names, callerID, text messages, help files, and other screen content.

combination. These two blind users were, however, able to listen to the instructions on the screen through TALKS and were then able to successfully unlock the keypad, where as the situationally blind user was not. In other words, the blind users had found a solution to their need by installing TALKS on the mobile phone.

One ordinary user drives a lot and uses a hands-free holder for the mobile phone in the car. He finds it very difficult to drive and simultaneously hit the right buttons when phone is placed in the holder. This problem is very similar to the one of unlocking the keypad in the dark.

Also, deaf and situationally deaf users performed equally in given tasks (see Table 7.2).

All users talked about the importance of a good keypad. None of the ordinary users were satisfied with their current keypad. One ordinary user hoped for a keypad with good tactility that would enable the use of it without watching. She also wanted to wear a protective cover on the mobile phone but found using the keypad difficult through the cover. She uses the protective cover on the phone not only in order to protect the phone but also in order to get a better grip when digging out the phone from a bag without looking. Two blind users had found a solution to their tactility need: They had modified the keypad by adding a small "lump" on the 5-key or all keys in order to make the keypad more tactile.

What is found is that the needs that ordinary (situationally disabled) users face in special situations are similar to those of disabled users in ordinary situations.

Table 7.2 Ability to perform given tasks (situationally deaf vs. deaf)

Task	Situationally deaf (noisy environment)			Deaf		
	Ordinary 1	Ordinary 2	Ordinary 3	Deaf 1	Deaf 2	Deaf 3
Can he find the ringing phone, if not holding it?	No	Yes[a]	No	No	No	No
Incoming call, can he find the phone, if the phone placed in a pocket or a handbag? (phone vibrating)	No	Yes	Yes	Yes	Yes	Yes
Incoming text message, can he find the phone, if the phone in pocket or handbag? (phone vibrating)	No	Yes	Yes	Yes	Yes	Yes
Can he make a call...	Yes	Yes	Yes	Yes	Yes	Yes
...and communicate the message?	Yes[b]	No[c]	No[c]	No	No	No
Can he send a text message?	Yes	Yes	Yes	Yes	Yes	Yes

[a] User notices the blinking light on the screen.

[b] User notices when the call is answered, and then speaks out the message on the phone.

[c] User does not notice when the call is answered. User speaks out the message on the unanswered phone.

Leading-Edge Behavior of Disabled Users

It was found that disabled persons experience needs that ordinary users may also experience, and that in many cases they have already obtained solutions to those needs. There are examples of solutions the disabled users have found that have later become general among ordinary users. There were also several examples of solutions currently used by disabled users that may become common in the future.

Deaf users rely heavily on text messages, and in Europe they have, in fact, adopted text messaging much earlier than the ordinary public. This, however, requires writing in a language other than native, which for the deaf is sign language. One deaf user sends her husband photos of products from stores, in order to avoid time-consuming text messaging. For ordinary users this would in many cases be more efficient than trying to describe something using words.

One blind participant still actively uses Memona Plus (see Fig. 7.3) for making notes. Memona Plus is a pocket-sized electronic, portable Braille note-taker that weighs 180 g and can be connected to a PC or to a mobile phone. The storing capacity is 30 A4 pages. The written texts can be checked sign by sign through the inbuilt digitized speech output. The notes can be stored as different files and they can easily be transferred to a PC. Short voice messages can be recorded through the inbuilt microphone. Memona Plus also tells the time and date. The predecessor of Memona Plus was Memona (introduced in 1992), which had a smaller storing capacity and no voice message recording. The first personal digital assistants (PDAs) had practically the same functions. One of the first was Palm Pilot that came to market in 1996, 4 years later than Memona.

One blind user actively uses Navicore Personal[3] navigation software through TALKS, as he is not able to see the map on the phone screen. Although Navicore was

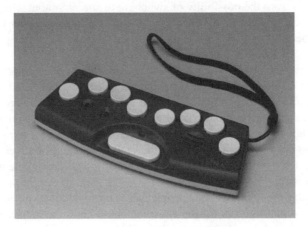

Fig. 7.3 Memona Plus

---

[3] Navicore Personal is a software application that is installed on the mobile phone by memory card, and used together with an external Bluetooth GPS-receiver (http://www.navicore.fi/).

designed to be used when driving, he uses it for personal navigation when walking. Separate navigation systems especially designed for car-use tend to have a speech output option for exactly the same reason, i.e., not being able to look at the map when driving.

To compensate for the missing possibility to make calls, all deaf users have been using MSN messenger[4] service on the internet for years. Nowadays, MSN messenger and the like have also been adopted by the general public. The next step, from using the messenger service with a webcam, is making two-way video calls, which two deaf users already do on their clamshell phone that has two cameras: one on the outer side and one on the same as the screen (inner side).

The majority of current mobile phone users have not yet started using two-way video calls or even sending one-way video messages. There are several reasons why video calls and messages may become popular among all users.[5] In the modern world we live in, families and friends often live geographically far away from each other. By making two-way video calls instead of phone calls, grandparents could stay in tighter contact with their grandchildren, for example. A parent would be able to show the other parent the first steps of their child as he or she is taking them. Instead of sending a holiday text message stating it is sunny and the beach is beautiful, one could send a video message actually showing it. Also, working life has become more dispersed over the years and people spend more and more time on business trips. Video conferencing is used but it requires special equipment, which makes organizing such a conference complicated. A two-way video call could be established right then and there, whenever needed.

The deaf users also indicated that there should be a small light source integrated in the phone. Otherwise it is not possible to make two-way video calls or send one-way video messages in the dark. That naturally would apply for all users.

Two blind users had installed TALKS on their mobile phones, but all users would clearly benefit from the possibility of switching to speech output when in the dark or driving a car, for example. Most silver market customers need special reading glasses for being able to see clearly at a short distance, so when the glasses are not available, a speech output function would help.

One visually impaired participant described a problem considering routing when outdoors. He is able to notice signboards but not able to see what is written on them. He suggested image recognition as a solution to this problem: User would take a photo of the signboard and have TALKS read out the text. This would be a handy tool for anybody visiting a foreign country. Before departing for a trip, one would just download a suitable dictionary on the mobile phone. For silver market customers with deteriorating eye sight, image recognition on the mobile phone would be really practical.

An everyday problem that blind people face is trying to locate objects. One blind user suggested that in order to stop worrying about keys, the mobile phone could be used to lock and unlock the home door. That would clearly help everybody, as

---

[4] Internet messaging service by Microsoft (http://messenger.msn.com/).

[5] This study was carried out in 2005. Now (September 2007) video messages and video calls have become popular in Japan and are also becoming so in Europe.

we all seem to be carrying more and more objects every day, and especially silver market customers that suffer from memory disorders.

These multiple examples show that the disabled users do indeed exhibit leading-edge behavior in adapting and developing new communication aids.

Critical Attributes for Visually Impaired Users

Examining altogether six blind or visually impaired users gave information on attributes that are critical for these users to be able to successfully use a mobile phone. These guidelines apply well not only to blind users, but also to users with the milder visual impairment common for silver market customers.

Good keypad is essential. Since blind users are not able to perceive the keys visually, they need to rely on the tactile feeling of the keypad. There are a few attributes that define a good keypad:

- Keys need to be separate from each other. When the keys are clearly separate from each other, it is easy to know when your finger is on a key.
- Good tactile response when pressing a key. The sensation of "click" signals the user that a key has in fact been pressed. A feather-touch switch, for example, is not a good choice.
- Keys in straight rows, no strange arrangements, such as U-shape. If keys are not arranged in straight rows and columns, it is not easy to know which key is which. In a U-shaped arrangement, for example, when you go to the left from the 5-key, you can accidentally end up on the 7-key instead of the 4-key.
- Tactile cue on the 5-key. To facilitate the positioning of fingers on the keypad, there should be a tactile cue on the 5-key. The cue needs to be on the key, not beside or below the key like in some phone models.
- Surface of the key not slippery. For better touch, the keys should not be slippery. A rubber-like surface, for example, was preferred by the research participants.

Not many changing functions on one key was a common wish. If one key has changing functions depending on what is shown on the screen, the use of the keypad becomes complicated for users who cannot see the information shown on the screen. Softkeys[6] like the NAVI-key[7], for example, was mentioned as problematic.

For visually impaired users that are not using speech output software like TALKS, a *logical menu structure* is essential. When you are not able to see the screen, you must be able to create a mental model of the menu structure.

---

[6] A multifunction key usually positioned beneath the mobile phone display with the corresponding textual or graphical function label shown on the display [6].

[7] Navi™-key: Nokia's one-softkey interaction style; first applied in the Nokia 3110 phone model [6].

Critical Attributes for Hearing-Impaired Users

Since a mobile phone interface relies heavily on visual information, there are not as clear critical attributes for hearing-impaired users as there are for visually impaired users. As long as the interaction with the mobile phone is based on text, symbols, or images, a hearing-impaired user is able to use the phone. For two-way communication, deaf users can apply two-way video calls.

For hearing-aid users an inductive loop set[8] is essential. Even with severe hearing impairment, the use of an inductive loop set enables calling on a mobile phone. Without the loop set, the user would have to rely on the use of text-messages only.

Summary and Conclusion

The customers of any product are not alike, but they differ in their capability to perform tasks on and interface with the product. The importance of taking user needs into account when developing new products is nowadays common knowledge. To be able to satisfy the needs of a market where – mainly due to the aging population – user needs have become increasingly heterogeneous, concepts like "universal design" (USA and Japan), "design for all" (Europe), and "inclusive design" (UK) have been developed. In addition, more labeling concepts such as "design for disability," have come up. All of these concepts fall under the umbrella of user-centered design, where the user needs are indeed considered but where the designer of the solution is an engineer. The lead user approach, in contrast, sees lead users as a source of possible solutions.

This study shows that the user needs of situationally disabled users, i.e., ordinary users in special situations, overlap with the needs of disabled users in ordinary situations. Also, several examples of leading-edge behavior in disabled users were found. When we look at the data gathered through this study in reference to von Hippel's definition of lead users, we find that the second lead user characteristic clearly applies to disabled users: Disabled users surely benefit significantly by obtaining a solution to their needs. As for the first characteristic, there are examples showing that disabled users have found solutions like text messages that have later become common among all users. There seems to be a similar trend in two-way video calling. This suggests that *disabled users can be seen as lead users* when developing products – in this case mobile phone user interfaces – for the ordinary public who undergo moments of situational disability.

The aging customers of the silver market often suffer from deterioration of eyesight and/or hearing. They, in fact, are even more often situationally disabled than the younger and more able-bodied customers, which means that many products, such as mobile phones, are more difficult for them to use.

---

[8] All hearing aids support the induction loop technology. When the hearing aid is on the T-mode, it captures the signal supplied from the loop.

As explained earlier, user-centered design concentrates on gathering user needs from the targeted customers, but the targeted customers may be functionally fixed and not able to give us information that could help develop breakthrough products. The targeted customers are seldom able to articulate the latent needs behind their fixedness. For an aging customer, this can be even more so, because deteriorating eyesight, for example, might be a delicate matter for them. Therefore it is possible that they are less willing to expose their actual, everyday needs, when approached by a designer.

In this study, only visually and hearing-impaired users were examined as possible lead users. The aging population suffers not only from visual and hearing impairments but also from deterioration of mobility. I assume that if the user needs of persons with a physical disability were examined, we would get a similar result.

The study also showed that the selected methods were applicable for studying deaf and blind users. Photo-diary was found to be an effective and easy method for self-documentation, also when studying blind users. No other equipment is needed for documentation, as long as the photos are later gone through in a separate discussion. No major difficulties occurred in carrying out the contextual inquiry and open-ended discussion.

When working with visually and hearing-impaired users, the designer should remember the role of language in interaction. Common language means fluent and more personal communication. Sign language is the native language of the congenitally deaf. For a blind person it is easier to contact the designer by e-mail or by phone, since he or she can do it in their native language. The deaf participants can feel uncomfortable and perhaps even shy about sending a written message. It should not be presupposed that a deaf person can fluently write in the predominant language. Having to book a sign language interpreter makes scheduling more complicated and the meetings a little less personal.

This study concentrated on the mobile phone user interfaces, but this approach can easily be transferred to any other products. I recommend that when developing products for the customers of the silver market, disabled persons should be seen as lead users and therefore as a valuable source of not only user need data, but also as a source of possible solutions.

Appendix: Overview of the Study

Three members of three different groups of mobile phone users were studied and compared: deaf, blind, and "ordinary users" who see and hear well. Deaf and blind groups were selected to represent disabled persons, because of the clear definition of these groups, and the fact that it was rather easy to access these groups. Blind and deaf persons were contacted through several associations and societies, such as Finnish Federation of the Visually Impaired and Finnish Association of the Deaf, and through personal contacts. The three deaf persons were deaf since birth. Two of the blind participants were congenitally blind, and one had lost his eyesight in adulthood.

The methods used were *photo-diary* based on a theme, and *contextual inquiry* combined with an *open-ended discussion* (further details are given below). Contextual inquiry was used for learning about users needs. Photo-diary and open-ended discussion provided information both on user needs but also on the leading-edge behavior of the disabled persons.

Photo-diary and self-photography have been used in various disciplines. Gaver et al. [5] included a disposable camera in the cultural probes package when studying the elderly, and Brown et al. [3] used photo-diary followed by semistructured interviews to capture information on working life.

Contextual inquiry is a field data-gathering technique developed by Beyer and Holtzblatt [1]. The most basic requirement of contextual inquiry is the principle of context. Staying in context enables the interviewer to gather ongoing experience rather than summary experience, and concrete data rather than abstract data. Gathering data on an ongoing experience means that the interviewer is present when work is being done. If a person is asked a question, the answers tend to be summarized, for it is very difficult to go into detail and describe exactly what happened. The job of the interviewer is to recognize the actual work structure, which arises out of details of mundane work actions. In order to discover concrete data instead of abstract data it is very important to talk in concrete terms. When the customer says "generally I do this" or "usually..." the interviewer must pull the customer back to a real experience. To gather concrete data you need to ask questions like "what did you do last time" instead of "what do you do usually."

Contextual inquiry helps us to understand the real environment people live in and work in, and it reveals their needs within that environment. It uncovers what people really do and how they define what is actually valuable to them [7].

There were two meetings with every participant. The first meeting was a short 30-min meeting where participants were given the photo-diary assignment. Approximately 2 weeks later in the second meeting the contextual inquiry and the open-ended discussion were carried out. At the same time, the photo-diary results were talked through and used as inspiration in the discussion. An outside interpreter took part in the meetings with the deaf participants.

The study was piloted with one ordinary user. The pilot revealed that in the photo-diary assignment, the use of flash on the disposable camera was a bit complicated. This problem was addressed by giving the participants step-by-step instructions on the use of the disposable camera. The tasks to be performed by ordinary users in special situations were shaped during the pilot study.

In addition to the nine participants presented above, two open-ended interviews were carried out. The first interview included two persons who have progressively lost a major part of their eyesight in adulthood. The second interview included one person who had a similar visual disability but who also suffered from a severe hearing impairment. Two of these persons were found through personal contacts. One was a volunteer found through a society of the visually impaired. The purpose of these interviews was to gain a wider perspective on disability in general, since these persons had literally seen both worlds. Besides, all three had tried out a variety of mobile communication devices. All participants are listed in Table 7.3.

Table 7.3 List of participants and their mobile phones

User	Sex	Age	Mobile phones
Blind 1	Female	34	Nokia 8310 (personal), Nokia 1100 (personal)
Blind 2	Female	58	Nokia 3660 (personal)
Blind 3[a]	Male	36	Nokia 6600 (personal)
Deaf 1	Male	25	Nokia 6100 (personal), SonyEricsson Z1010 (personal), Nokia 6600 (work)
Deaf 2	Male	33	Nokia 9110 (personal), SonyEricsson Z1010 (personal), Nokia 6310i (personal), Nokia 9110 (work)
Deaf 3	Female	28	Nokia 6820 (personal)
Ordinary (pilot)	Female	27	Nokia 3510 (personal)
Ordinary 1	Male	29	Siemens ST60 (personal)
Ordinary 2	Female	30	Nokia 6600 (personal)
Ordinary 3	Male	60	Nokia 9210i (personal, work), Nokia 6230 (personal, work)
Severe visual impairment	Male	43	Nokia 6600 (personal, work)
Severe visual impairment	Male	37	Nokia 6600 (personal, work)
Severe visual and hearing impairment	Male	57	Nokia 9300 (personal)+Nokia LPS-4 inductive loop set

[a] Not congenitally blind. Not able to read braille.

Photo-Diary

The photo-diary assignment consisted of a disposable camera and a stamped return envelope. Instructions on how to use the camera were given verbally in the first meeting, and also on paper or by e-mail depending on the person's choice. The theme of the photo-diary was to take a picture of "everything you use for communication, or use for receiving or transmitting information." Some general examples were given:

- If you read a newspaper, take a picture of the newspaper
- If you listen to the radio, take a picture of the radio
- If you check the temperature, take a picture of the thermometer
- If you use a mobile phone, take a picture of the mobile phone

The time frame within which the photo-diary was supposed to be carried out was one day, starting from waking up in the morning until going to sleep in the evening. The participants could choose the day themselves (see pictures in Fig. 7.4).

The blind participants were advised in practice on how to use the disposable camera. Since the pilot study had showed that there might be problems with the flash when using a disposable camera, step-by-step instructions were given to all participants on paper or by e-mail.

No additional equipment was required, just the disposable camera.

Fig. 7.4 Photo-diary pictures

It was possible to take 28 pictures with the camera, but participants were advised not to worry, if at the end of the day they had taken only ten photos. The important thing was to document all possible things and equipment that were used according to the given theme. After finishing the photo-diary, the camera was to be sent back to me (within 2 weeks) in the stamped return envelope, in order for me to develop the pictures.

Contextual Inquiry and Open-Ended Discussion

In the second meeting the pictures taken in the photo-diary assignment were discussed one-by-one. The participant explained the meaning of each picture in the order they were taken. Each object in the pictures was discussed in detail: how many times it was used during the day, why, and for which purposes.

The use of mobile phone was discussed following the principles of contextual inquiry: What have you done with your mobile phone today? Show me how you do it. What devices have you used this week? For which purposes? Why? Show me.

The disabled users were observed when using their own mobile phones in their ordinary environment, such as home or work environment.

The ordinary users were observed when using their mobile phones in special situations that included complete darkness, and a noisy environment. These special situations were created in the participant's home. Complete darkness was achieved in a walk-in closet or in a bathroom. A noisy environment was created by using an industrial hearing protector headset that included total noise-canceling and an FM radio. This way, all sounds from surrounding environment were blocked out and replaced with music. To assure total canceling of surrounding sounds, disposable foam ear plugs were used under the headset.

The special situations were chosen to be such that really simulate a possible everyday disability situation. Therefore, the "situational blindness" was not simulated by concealing user's eyes. It is highly unlikely that a person ends up in a situation where their eyes are concealed, but it is possible that eyesight is limited by lack of light.

In these special situations the ordinary users were asked to perform basic tasks, such as calling, receiving a call, sending a text message, and receiving one. The starting point of the tasks varied: the mobile phone was to be found in the pocket, in the bag, or in the surroundings in proximity of the user. The use of mobile devices was studied also in the ordinary environment in the same manner as was done with the disabled users.

After going through the pictures of the photo-diary, and the contextual inquiry, the participants widely expressed their views on their current mobile devices, their expectations, and desires. They told about problems they have faced, and shared their visions on what kind of devices they would like to use and how.

References

1. H. Beyer, K. Holtzblatt, *Contextual Design: Defining Customer-Centered Systems* (Morgan Kaufmann, San Francisco, 1998)
2. H. Brody, Technol. Rev. **99**(5), 32 (1996)
3. B.A.T. Brown, A.J. Sellen, K.P. O'Hara, in *Proceedings of the SIGCHI Conference on Human Factors in Computing Systems* (ACM, New York, 2000), p. 438
4. K. Duncker, Psychol. Monogr. **58**(5), 270 (1945)
5. B. Gaver, T. Dunne, E. Pacenti, Interactions **6**(1), 21 (1999)
6. H. Kiljander, *Evolution and Usability of Mobile Phone Interaction Styles*, Helsinki University of Technology, Publications in Telecommunications Software and Multimedia, Espoo, Finland (2004)
7. M. Kuniavsky, *Observing the User Experience: A Practitioner's Guide to User Research* (Morgan Kaufmann, San Francisco, CA, 2003)
8. C. Lettl, Technol. Health Care **13**(3), 169 (2005)
9. G.L. Lilien, P.D. Morrison, K. Searls, M. Sonnack, E. von Hippel, Manage. Sci. **48**(8), 1042 (2002)
10. C. Lüthje, in *Proceedings of the 32nd EMAC Conference*, Glasgow, UK, 2003
11. E.M. Rogers, *Diffusion of Innovations*, 4th edn. (Free Press, New York, 1995)
12. E.M. Rogers, *Diffusion of Innovations* (Free Press, New York, 1962)
13. E.M. Rogers, F. Shoemaker, *Communication of Innovations: A Cross-Cultural Approach* (Free Press, New York, 1971)
14. S. Shah, *Sources and Patterns of Innovation in a Consumer Products Field: Innovations in Sporting Equipment*, Working Paper, No. 4105 edn, Sloan School of Management, Massachusetts Institute of Technology, Cambridge, MA, (2000)

15. E. von Hippel, Manage. Sci. **32**(7), 791 (1986)
16. E. von Hippel, *The Sources of Innovation* (Oxford University Press, New York, 1988)
17. E. von Hippel, S. Thomke, M. Sonnack, Harvard Bus Rev **77**(5), 47 (1999)
18. E. von Hippel, *Horizontal Innovation Networks – By and For Users*, Working Paper, No. 4366–02 edn, Sloan School of Management, Massachusetts Institute of Technology, Cambridge, MA, (2002)
19. E. von Hippel, *Democratizing Innovation* (MIT, Cambridge, MA, 2005)

Chapter 8
Integration of the Elderly in the Design Process

K. Schmidt-Ruhland and M. Knigge

Abstract With demographic change looming in the background there has been an ever greater need for products and aids for the growing target group of elderly people. Previous methods and ideas in the areas of product development and design have not proven to be satisfactory enough to develop attractive and helpful solutions that meet the wishes and needs of this age group.

New approaches and product concepts have been developed in the *sentha* research project. *sentha* stands for Everyday Technology for Senior Households. Working in this interdisciplinary research project are designers from the Berlin University of the Arts in cooperation with the Technical Universities of Berlin and Cottbus, as well as the Berlin Institute for Social Research.

The goal was to develop products and services for an increasingly aging society so that seniors can maintain their independence in daily life as long as possible.

At the Institute for Product and Process Design (Prof. Achim Heine) of the Berlin University of the Arts, designers Karin Schmidt-Ruhland and Mathias Knigge have been working on the development and positioning of senior-friendly products and services. In their projects they have focused on specific wishes and needs of elderly people without limiting themselves in form and function solely to this one target group. The article elucidates the specific design approach as regards this user group, the methods for integrating elderly people, and shows a selection of designs that have been realized in the *sentha* project (Table 8.1).

Introduction: The Research Project *sentha* and Demographic Change

Demographic change poses an enormous challenge for product manufacturers and service providers because conventional offers do not always meet the demands of elderly people, who complain about lack of user-friendliness and being overtaxed. For many needs and requirements at this age there are no offers at all.

Table 8.1 Overview of the articles presented in the *sentha* project

Title	Contents	Result
Image – age in images and the image of age	Analysis of the age image as depicted in advertising (print media)	• Images do not correspond to the self-image of elderly people • They don't feel they are being taken seriously • They think depictions are exaggerated (positive/negative) • Elderly prefer realistic images; like to see themselves pictured as part of different generations • They highly regard positive values such as knowledge, experience, affluence
Small helpers – product range and sales channels in the market for seniors	Analysis of products developed especially for seniors with regard to design, functionality, and evaluation of the attendant sales channels	• The design of many products is slipshod or old-fashioned and does not appeal to elderly people • The solution of a deficiency is almost always in the foreground, lack of positive reasons to buy the product • Sales structures or forms of presentation do not correspond to the wishes or the needs of elderly people
Digital productions – stories of aging and of things	Photo project in which stereotypical ideas of age are countered by the self-image of elderly people	• Research of biographies, life circumstances and objects used • Photographic production on the basis of discovered "histories"
Who rests gets rusty – on the search for and finding of short-term parking spots	Design of products for public spaces for resting, relaxing, or putting aside one's cares	"The bench" – The construction site fence as chance to sit down
My wonderful bathroom – new bathtubs for old users	New design solutions for bathrooms that provide support and take user habits into consideration	"Sea saw" – bathtub and shower in one
Handicapping – Speculating and manipulating with senses	Design of "tools" in order to make aging capable of being experienced and comprehended	• Different "tools" that simulate and represent individual aspects, e.g., hearing, seeing, feeling, smelling, moving • Taking the representation of change and positive changes into consideration, not just the deficiencies
Designing crosswise – I'll do it… for elderly people	Interdisciplinary cooperative exercise between engineers and designers. Joint re-designing of daily objects	• Definition of age demands (product quality, how convenient, safe, self-explanatory, etc) • Design of numerous variations (Products such as electrical outlets, scissors, bags, etc.)

Table 8.1 (continued)

Title	Contents	Result
Living longer – changes in living areas	Design of new solutions for living areas that allow adaptive methods of use	"Time to read" – comfortable book support with integrated reading lamp "Upside-down" – aids for daily action sequences in the kitchen "Upset" – chairs and sofas as aids in getting up
My first Sony – investigation on the subject of "easy operation"	Study on elderly-friendly operating panels and sequences	"My first Sony" – an answering machine with intuitive operation and tactile interface
Alternatives – products for a new elderly generation	Design competition with the goal of enthusing up-and-coming designers for the subject and to offer a platform for good designs	"A-Button" – a button that you can close with one hand "Footwear" – shoe with spring mechanism that you can put on and take off without bending over "Listening to newspapers" – barcodes are scanned under newspaper articles and the corresponding article is read aloud via the internet

Until now, one resorted to solutions for this target group from the field of aid provision for handicapped persons. However, the methods and ideas in product development and design are not sufficient for providing helpful and attractive solutions. One essential reason for this is the lack of empathy, especially on the part of young developers dealing with elderly to very old consumers [11].

Therein lies a great chance for manufacturers, commerce, and service providers in the development of such user-oriented solutions. Equipped with innovative quality features, thesolutions for such a financially strong target group range from being interesting to being necessary in order to become old with the greatest amount of self-determination possible in their own homes [2].

This is where the research project *sentha* has its starting point for developing new approaches and product concepts. *sentha* is the abbreviation for Everyday Technology for Senior Households.

With the background of a steadily growing share of elderly people in the total population, together with a great increase in life expectancy, the project has researched products and services that in the future can enable people to lead their lives as independently as possible in old age.

This field, which in the meantime has become important, hardly received any attention in the past and the usual senior-friendly solutions were rejected by elderly users because these solutions obviously originated from handicapped and rehabilitation technology. Consequently, innovative products should be developed that are of interest for all ages in the sense of a "design for all" concept, but that especially offer elderly people more safety and comfort in their everyday home life [10].

The group of researchers selected an integrative and interdisciplinary approach for this plan, financed by the Germany Research Society (Deutsche Forschungsgemeinschaft – DFG) for over six years:

- Integrative through the strong orientation and integration of elderly people in the development processes, within which user- and product-related questions were combined. A senior citizen advisory council was available, which was continuously integrated in the work.
- Interdisciplinary through the integration of the most diverse competencies, which made a synthesis of disciplinary perspectives possible.

Members of the joint research group included designers from the field of industrial design, scientists from the Technical Universities of Berlin and Cottbus, and the Berlin Institute for Social Research. As a result, experts were available for the joint work from the fields of social sciences and manpower studies, design, construction engineering, as well as biomedical and communications technology.

Particular importance was placed on the partial project for design. Here methods were developed and practiced with which the wishes and needs of elderly people could be recognized and taken into account in the development process. Furthermore, prototypical designs were worked out in the project work that showed what future solutions for elderly users could look like without limiting the form and function solely to this one target group.

The main point of departure was a specific design approach.

How the Discipline of Design Views Itself Within the *sentha* Project

For us, product formation and design do not simply mean the design of the form/shape. "With design" does not mean that we are only dealing with the product "in itself," but that the design is always embedded in cultural and social interrelations. This integrates both the dealings with things as well as an understanding of the target group – in this case the senior citizens. We have thus abandoned the traditional fixation of designers on objects. We understand design as an integral concept in which complex social, economic, and cultural contexts for the design process are also reflected. This is the understanding of design we have pursued as part of *sentha*.

Of course, this does not exclude "making things beautiful," something we placed a great deal of value on as part of *sentha*. In addition, concentrating exclusively on shape and formation is an understanding of design that we at the Berlin University of the Arts view as being too limited. For us, design is a comprehensive phenomenon and a multilayered process in dealing with things and technical systems. Everyday culture, consumer habits, life styles and thus also the pluralization of life styles and corresponding product worlds are all embedded in the goal of design [15].

In this respect, we have had an interdisciplinary orientation per se: always with a view toward neighboring fields, disciplines, and the formulation of questions about our actual task, namely the final design of the objects.

This implies a holistic, interdisciplinary approach. Instead of designing the results of the other disciplines at the end, it was always important for us in the research project to start as a whole and to be correspondingly integrated in all work steps.

Concretely, this means that we have expanded the narrow questions, in contrast to other disciplines thatcooperated in the *sentha* research project, which always had very concrete questions and concrete work steps. For example, we were not only concerned with the optimized, senior-friendly design of a video recorder, but also always included the importance of video and television in general, the viewing habits of senior citizens, etc. in our work.

Senior-Friendly Product Design: Going Beyond Stigmatizing Aids

From the very beginning we concerned ourselves with the question of how can one find and develop a new product language that is less stigmatizing and transcends the marginalizing form language of senior-friendly products. Therefore, what does a product and its adequate marketing strategy (catchword: image) have to look like so that it fulfills the needs of senior citizens but is not recognized and decoded at first sight as "a product for old people." The felt age of the majority of people over 60 lies 10–15 years under their calendar age [16], while at the same time bodily limitations are felt as a sign of age but are especially perceived in other people [17].

If the things that elderly people need in the sense of aids can be made hip and trendy, then the design of the things has to be changed to such a degree that they look normal, and that is then design in the narrower sense. Thus, design also means "making something beautiful" in a specific, non-stigmatizing manner.

In this connection, it was an important concept for us to keep the subject open. This meant that we not only had aids for seniors in mind, but also did not focus exclusively on elderly people. We thus developed sponsorship models in which we observed and asked elderly people. In this way, ideas for new products emerged. It was, however, constitutive of our approach toward senior-friendly design always to keep in mind that the results were just as usable and appropriate for other people, i.e., that the elderly people were only an indicator for the deficits in their everyday home lives, but product design was intended to stretch beyond this specific target group and its handicaps.

The partial project for design did not conceptualize the subject of the problem from the very beginning as being something completed, i.e., only for a certain age group. On the other hand, this is connected with our general understanding of design: for a designer, every product is an aid because people generally cannot do many, many things. Consequently, they make use of different aids in order to be able to do something. They cannot open a tin can with their mouth or their fingers, which is why we have can openers. They cannot fly, which is why we have airplanes. It is not possible to carry much, consequently there are cranes. From the time of birth there are aids. In this respect, every person is a "disabled person" and design has developed to a certain extent prostheses for everyone. This perspective is assuredly not new since Sigmund Freud in the 1920s characterized the bodily inadequate human being as a "prosthesis god" [9]. This perspective, however, was particularly important as part of *sentha*. Even if the project naturally focused on elderly persons and their situational needs, we were always concerned with overcoming the problem-centered view toward seniors in the sense of "handicapped people." We succeeded in our concept because we expanded our view to all of society, because that which can provide relief to elderly people, can also be helpful and useful for younger people [4]. In the area of "senior-friendly products" there are very many things that not only elderly people want to have, but that in principle are of interest for many. There are many things that can be done without any problem but you ask yourself again and again: why am I actually doing this?

Why am I dragging this so tediously? Isn't there any better solution? Even a 40-year-old's back hurts when he has to carry something laboriously. That is why we decided on opening up the subject. We have always said: "these are simply aids." We never spoke of specific aids for seniors. This approach helped us to view the problematic matter of age as a quite normal problematic matter. Therefore, we were able to work against the cultural marginalization of seniors. At the same time, we were able in our ideas and through the age-transcending design to overcome the stigmatization through product design. This understanding also found expression of course in the form and design of senior-friendly helpers in everyday home life – senior-friendly does not mean senior-specific, but means an aid for seniors and others.

Design as an Empirical–Experimental Process

The well-known procedure in other disciplines consists of establishing hypotheses beforehand to be verified or negated. This is connected very closely with the actual formulation of questions or way of looking at a problem. However, it can become more difficult to open up toward phenomena or knowledge that have not been drawn up within the research approach. Such an approach is relatively closed toward new, surprising, previously unthought-of influential factors and questions. Therein lies the strength of our approach: Quite consciously we take the naïve point of view exploratorily and experimentally: "I will now pretend that I don't know anything and as if I had no premonition or hypothesis and then look and see what kinds of answers I get to my questions."

There are different methical approaches in the design process, which we have worked out and quite consciously employed in project work at the Berlin University of the Arts. These techniques and methods were conceived and tested especially in the expert group of Prof. Hans (Nick) Roericht [14]. For example, in exercises such as "Jumping into the matter," products are created without any previous research directly on the basis of our own experiences and influences. In the "Unconventional thinker exercise" completely diverse objects are combined: fusion as design methodology. In the *sentha* projects with the title "... Lifting and aging" the characteristics of things were changed, i.e., young becomes old and vice versa. Here, primarily formal and aesthetic aspects and social placement are investigated, questioned, and altered. The result is products and visualizations that are stimuli for further creative approaches in product development. "Design has a great deal of room for improvised use of its methods and can take over or reject methods or also cut its specific occurrences to its own use.... Since design is not obliged to produce accurate depictions of reality it can experiment in a way which would not be tolerated in other sciences" [13].

That design works empirically–experimentally means in concrete terms that we basically combine scientific survey and analysis methods with rather artistic– experimental methods. This means that the participatory observation and qualitative social research, the hermeneutic interpretation – whereby understanding certain processes or phenomena play just as an important role in our approach as experiments and association – observation, interviews, scientific analysis, and experiments are interlocked [15].

We are dealing here with a multistage, cyclical research process in dialogue form rather than a stringent linear one. The point of departure was taking stock: what products are there at present for elderly people? How functional and senior-friendly are these offers really? What image is used in advertising to stage-manage and communicate these products?

With this knowledge we then turned to elderly people.

Participatory Observation

The situation in the everyday home life is such that the sequence of most household actions is performed routinely and proceeds unconsciously. Who really thinks about why he makes coffee in such a way or why he makes certain hand movements when taking a shower? Formulated in another way: especially in everyday home life, many things take place unconsciously and unreflectively. Consequently, they can only be partially opened to analysis in linguistic terms. You can only reflect upon things and give information when you take note of them yourself.

The rest remains uninvestigated "tacit knowledge," know-how that one has, but cannot reflect upon because it has already become such an obvious matter that one no longer thinks about it, indeed, it no longer even strikes one as special know-how.

With this background for our research, participatory observation for *sentha* acquired quite fundamental importance. Participatory observation has the advantage of being sensitive even for unreflective, habitual, everyday actions. It is thus no accident that participatory observation is regarded as the "royal road" in field research because it is also in a position to train one's sights on things that cannot be explored by linguistic–interrogative methods such as interviews and group discussions. Whoever can take part in routine everyday processes as a sensitive observer sees more as a rule than the observed person can communicate in an ensuing talk. Participatory observation is thus, unlike an interview, a very usable and sensitive instrument for researching everyday life. Motions and hand movements, which go on in a perfectly routine manner, can especially be a point of departure for one's work. Here is such a trick from the everyday life of an elderly person: for example, a screwed-in light bulb as a darning mushroom that is illuminated from within because elderly people can no longer see well in dim light. You often experience people who are very forgetful and stick post-its on their door when they go out. These are small things, which are not even noticed by the source person and which people do not even talk about. These are unreflective routine actions that are carried out completely unconsciously. You can only perceive them when you deliberately look at them. Only then can you ask specific questions.

This was deliberately practiced with students. "Digital stage-managing" was the title of a project in which we, by observing the users on location, got an idea of how elderly persons deal with things that surround them. What things are important and what is the relationship to them? The resulting relationship was to be produced and recorded in a picture, an intensified observation. In the illustrated example, the love of an old married couple for books and reading was the theme. Intensive research and close cooperation with the seniors preceded the photos (Figs. 8.1 and 8.2).

The project "Who rests gets rusty" about the search for and finding of short-term resting spots dealt with exact observation and not just of elderly people, but in particular of what surrounds us. It dealt with places where people hang around,

Fig. 8.1 Breakfast at the Gorisch's

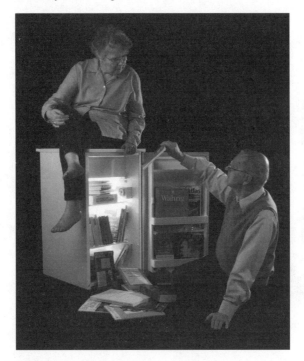

Fig. 8.2 ... and at night they like to have a second helping

take a break, and put aside their cares. Using a camera, we looked for, observed, and recorded places. The result of good observation is the draft "The bench" (Fig. 8.3) by Andreas Bergmann. The beginning of the draft is: "many visitors and curious onlookers at Berlin construction sites and construction site fences." The motto was that the barrier fence became a kind of bench for lingering and resting. In doing so, not only the needs and wishes of elderly people were taken up. The work was given an award in a competition by the Deutsche Bank [7].

The Dialogue: Participative Principle of Our Research

From the beginning of the project, the dialogue principle was a fundamental matter of concern in our research. As in modern ethnology (in which the research objects are increasingly integrated into the research process), by commenting on one's own interviews or on the concrete research results, we thus wanted to actively involve the seniors in the research process. This means that the research objects, i.e. the seniors, became subjects who consequently became the experts of our research. In several dialogue phases the seniors in a so-called senior council followed, discussed, checked, and commented on our work steps in the *sentha* project. From the very

Fig. 8.3 The bench

beginning, we integrated our user group not only through questioning and participatory observation, but especially through sponsorship models and joint trial and error. The members of the senior council were also involved right from the beginning of the project (Figs. 8.4 and 8.5). They were, so to speak, motivated to play along and thus had the possibility of discovering their own needs in the design and production processes. Every student picked up the theme directly on location in the form of sponsorship models and looked for solutions together with the users. By means of this direct contact to later users it was possible to come up with user typologies in order to vary use and production characteristics, e.g., according to age, sex, educational level, culture, etc.

This integration and consideration of the user leads to consideration of the needs of the greatest possible group of addressees through the designer in the sense of "inclusive design" [6]. This happens by integrating the needs of groups that had so far been excluded from consideration, e.g., because of their age, their handicap, or on the basis of changing technologies or work structures. Thus, the exclusion of special user groups in events and actions is prevented.

Roger Coleman describes this by using an example of a train journey in which many questions are asked, for example, in the beginning by obtaining information about a selected destination, about advice, orientation, transportation, and comfort up to the final destination. The trip by train can thus be seen as a chain of individual products and services, the availability of which is only as strong as the weakest link in this chain. In order to reach one's destination, all areas have to be available to

Fig. 8.4 Participation I: discussion in the packing project

Fig. 8.5 Participation II: discussion at a table with seniors

everyone. Therefore, we have to illuminate the process and design the weakest links in such a way that they are manageable for everyone.

If you look at the action from one particular point and then build a chain of the most diverse possibilities, then a great deal of design leeway is evident: both the focusing on detailed solutions as well as the conceptual opening of the point of departure. Design can therefore begin at any point [5].

Empathy: The Foundation for the Designs in the Sense of the Later User

How can I put myself in the position of the later user, or how do the individual small steps of an action become clear to me? In order to answer these questions, we in the *sentha* project have attempted in the most diverse places to "feel into" the user group of elderly people. We looked for and invented exercise, methods, and aids that give you a feeling of how one feels in certain situations or how detailed certain actions in the course of everyday life actually are. These methods help in the analysis of products and in describing the requirements specifications.

The actual sequence of actions, e.g., a series of single photos of washing in the morning, was recorded in the project "My wonderful bathroom – new bathtubs for old users." Every activity was written down in a log book and subsequently analyzed (Fig. 8.6).

In the project "Handicapping, speculating and manipulating with senses" we, together with the students, experimentally pushed an empathetic approach into the forefront. What would happen if a sense was dropped or was added?

What does it mean when someone can no longer sit or stand up or if one's hand shakes? In this respect we are dealing with experimental designs in order to experience these feelings on our own bodies. The task was then to "conceive of a tool with which one's own and other senses can be weakened, strengthened, shifted, channeled, expanded, limited, exchanged, and instrumentalized."

The photos show a few examples of experimental designs such as the "thebrush feet" for an unsteady gait, "gaping straight ahead" for tunnel vision, or the "ax in the nape of the neck" for the stooped-over gait. This series of experiments has been further developed for the permanent exhibition "Man" in the Hygiene Museum in Dresden and are exhibits that visitors can try out [19] (Fig. 8.7).

Interdisciplinarity: Stimuli Through the Disciplines Involved in the Research Project

Both in the projects with students and in the dialogue with seniors we dealt with a reciprocal feedback process: a briefing for the students was formulated from the subject area. The young male and female designers then developed concrete ideas

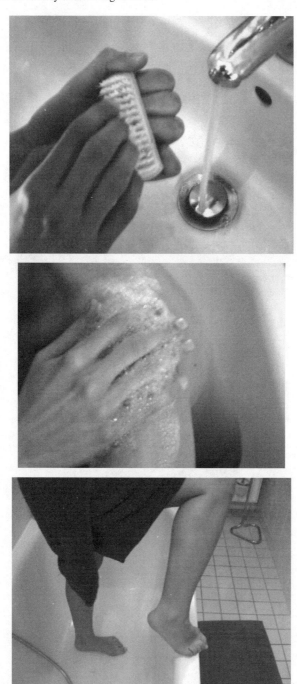

Fig. 8.6 Washing photo sequence

Fig. 8.7 Handicapping photo sequence. (Examples: Berit, Michael, Harald)

and innovative solutions, which in turn were incorporated into the *sentha* research project and discussed with the seniors. This ping-pong effect is very important especially because new impulses can be generated through the feedback of others, from the outside, which in the end constitutes innovation and creativity. Without this opening we would have argued, thought about, and developed within our own closed horizons and surely less interesting ideas would have originated [12].

This expresses a very fundamental catchword: interdisciplinarity. One could indeed say that the project interrelationships of *sentha*, consisting of labor and social scientists, construction and communication engineers, and biomedical doctors and including the senior and industrial council, have already genuinely taken into account the way designers see themselves. As part of the design process, a designer in the end always makes eclectic use of the level of knowledge of other disciplines – from the psychology of perception, to the cultural sciences and the engineering sciences. Consequently, the interdisciplinary approach belongs to the way designers see themselves and it practically goes without saying that we have ourselves profited from the interdisciplinary nature of the research project.

A concrete example of this interdisciplinary cooperation is the joint project "Designing crosswise." Within the period of a week, from Monday to Friday, we gave ourselves the concrete task of "Senior-friendly technology in everyday home life."

We had four archetypical products – an iron, knives and forks, a bottle of mineral water, and an electrical outlet – that we wanted to optimize for senior-friendliness with respect to previously defined product qualities: more demanding, safer, simpler, and more entertaining. We then set up teams of two consisting of a labor scientist and a designer who were supposed to reflect upon the archetypes and translate them into a specific product quality. Each day the teams moved on to the next product in order to improve its product quality. This means that the product quality of every archetype was further developed by every team. On the last day, all products were presented. Needless to say the project included discussions, differences of opinion, and a transfer of knowledge between the labor scientists and the designers. What does "safer" actually mean? Why does it have to be "more demanding" for elderly people at all? What do we mean when we speak of "simpler"?

We also understand interdisciplinarity in a further sense: all perspectives and results do not always have to be integrated into a harmonious, interdisciplinary whole. Much would surely be lost if one had to limit oneself to a very small common denominator. This means that we comprehend interdisciplinarity not in the sense that texts and ideas that point in different directions are argued over in a different way and disparate thoughts are formulated in order to be swirled together in a kind of cerebral blender. It is more the idea (exactly because of this polyphony) of acquiring new stimuli from other voices: to simultaneously see two or more ways of looking at things, to be able to think about things and then come up again with new ideas. In the end something arises out of this mixture of different texts and thoughts, a point of knowledge or innovation, which could not have developed in any single discipline.

In this respect you can establish a cross-connection to the association so important for male and female designers, namely, everything that can stimulate the mind, release ideas associatively, and give new impulses can serve the design process. Knowledge and information from neighboring or even distant disciplines can have a stimulating effect and provide new impulses.

This supports our fundamental point of view, namely, that research and design always take place in a dialogue, associative and as partners.

Product Development

This section introduces some exemplary designs from projects that originated at the Institute for Product and Process Design at the Berlin University of the Arts as part of our research project. The aim of the design work was to develop products and services that support peoples' independent living in everyday home life and that do not use any kind of stigmatizing senior-specific product language.

As long as an object is used, so goes the hypothesis, there will be people who make functional inadequacy the driving force of their attempts to improve it [1].

That is how we proceeded in our design projects with expanding the questions and considering the products in their context [3]. Similarly, we focused on user habits and actions, especially of the age group we set our sights on. In addition, there are analogies and the consideration of other sequences of action.

In addition to observation, participation, and the empathetic approach to understanding processes and phenomena, experimentation and association play for us just as important a role, whereby all levels interlock in an integral project: observation, interviews, scientific analysis, association, and experiments.

An example of such a design comes from the project "Living longer – transformation in living areas," a case in which the kitchen cutting board meets a work bench. A kitchen cutting board that facilitates work in the kitchen was developed here in an analogy to other work steps and locations.

First of all, the different "tools" are hidden in the work surface and are used in the work steps when needed, i.e., they reduce complexity. The principle of the guillotine shears from a paper or metal workshop was integrated in the design, or the rings on the top of old kitchen stoves are given new functions. For example, a mixing bowl can be lowered and stirring with one hand becomes possible. There are many such situations, be it when making a telephone call, carrying a child in your arm, or when there is not sufficient strength in the other arm.

By means of such tools, support for the motor movements of the hands is provided and the exertion of force for these actions is minimized.

The design "Upside down" by Nicolas Möbius and Karen Olze has received several awards in the "My way" competition and in the "Life dreams" competition by IF Hannover (Industrie Forum Design Hannover). In the meantime, the work has been integrated into the collection of the kitchen appliance producer Alno (Fig. 8.8).

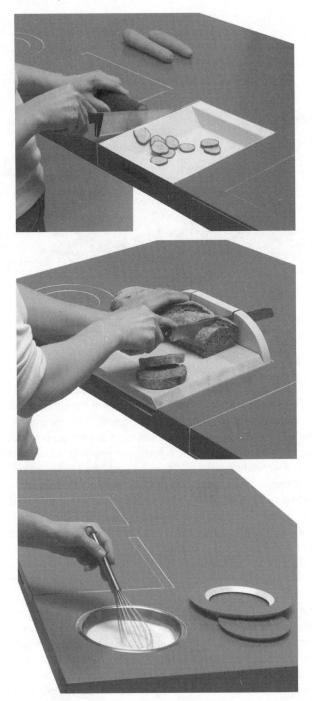

Fig. 8.8 Kitchen photo sequence

Fig. 8.9 Cushion

The title of the project "Living longer" stood for the demographic change in our society. The greater life expectancy and the desire for independence in old age require new products as well as new ways to use them. Here concepts and products for living areas have been developed that meet the demands of elderly persons. Design solutions were sought in which form and function are attractive to a wide circle of users. The reading cushion "Time to read" by Lucie Grünzig and Sandra Hirsch is an example. It is a symbiosis of static and textile elements, which makes extended reading more pleasant. The book support with pull-out reading lamp can be integrated into the cushion with a one-hand movement (Fig. 8.9). The weight of the book is reduced and the reader can then sit in a relaxed position. Reading in bed becomes more comfortable for young and old.

Diploma theses have also been written on this research subject in addition to the projects, for example, "My first Sony – investigations on the subject of easy operation" by Christoph Eberle [8].

The fundamental thought was the fact that with every new device, people often reach the point where their initial curiosity and pleasure with their new possession turns into helplessness. Thick instruction manuals, incomprehensible symbols on the operating panel, and numerous switches and pushbuttons with multifunctions frustrate the first-time user. As a rule, they are finally satisfied when they can manage to handle some of the functions. Sometimes the device disappears back into the cardboard box. The users often think the fault lies with them. Again and again you hear the remark; "I am probably too stupid to do it."

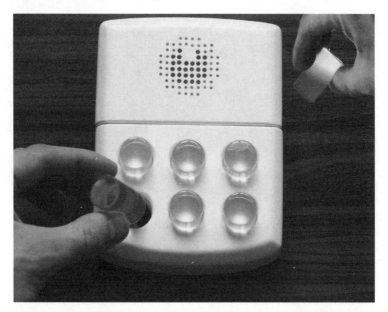

Fig. 8.10 Answering machine

One result of this diploma thesis was to re-design an answering machine (Fig. 8.10) with new, unconventional and easier operating elements [8].

One important aspect of the research project was to motivate and promote up-and-coming designers, which was also the trigger for launching a professional competition for young male and female designers. The "Alternative products for a new elderly generation" competition was offered twice within the project.

The question posed was: what can technical products and devices look like that meet the needs of elderly people and are at the same time also attractive for many age groups. Students and recent graduates majoring in design and architecture were asked to develop new products and concepts. Even minimal products were submitted and received awards, for example, the "A-Button" by Antonia Roth, which can be threaded through button holes more easily because of its formal design, or concepts such as "Newspapers for listening" by Harald Kollwitz (Figs. 8.11 and 8.12).

The concept provides for more social integration of elderly people in daily life, but also offers other target groups interesting uses. That is why newspaper articles are provided with individual barcodes. With the aid of a device you can call up an article and the publishing firm can load it as an audio file onto the device. The user can then listen to the selected spoken text using headphones. This is not only advantageous for people who can no longer see well, but also when one's attention is distracted, such as when driving [18].

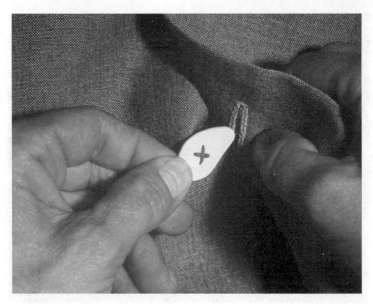

Fig. 8.11 The A-button

Soforthilfe / Entwurf für umfangreiches Paket / Schutz vor Schaden

WASHINGTON, 20. September. Die amerikanische Regierung will Folgen des Terroranschlags besonders betroffene Fluggesellschaft Dollar Soforthilfe in bar gewähren, um einen Teil des Schadens auszugleichen, der durch das Flugverbot in der vergangenen Woche entstanden ist. Weitere 3 Milliarden Dollar sollen den Unternehmen bei der Umsetzung der Sicherheits-

kanischen Fluggesellschaften zuvor während einer Anhörung des Verkehrsausschusses des Repräsentantenhauses gefordert hatten. Darüber solle erst in einem zweiten Schritt verhandelt werden, hieß es aus dem Weißen Haus.

Die Unternehmensvertreter wiesen die Abgeordneten auf die Dringlichkeit finanzieller Unterstützung aus Washington hin. Werde sie nicht gewährt, dann drohe eini-

Fig. 8.12 Listening to newspapers

Summary and Conclusion

In conclusion, we can state that the *sentha* project approach has proven to be worthwhile. With the aid of a multistaged, cyclical (not linear) process and the intensive integration of elderly users solutions could be found that stood up to the demands of universal design as well as our own demands on design.

In addition to participatory observation, the fundamental elements in this process are the participatory elements such as user tests of the hypotheses, which produced important feedback from the seniors' trial actions. With this help we were able to optimize, complement, and further develop our own ideas.

The research project clearly confirmed that elderly people did not like products that were developed solely for the "elderly" or for "seniors." They preferred "solutions for everyone" and exactly that is possible by taking into consideration the wishes and needs of the older user group in the process described in the beginning. At the same time product attractiveness has to be achieved, which is also of interest to other target groups. Therefore, emphasis should be placed on the combination of good design and additional product advantages.

A very important task in the research project was putting the subject in the curricula of the Design Department at the University of the Arts in Berlin. The inclusion of this subject in courses can sensitize the younger generation to the needs of the elderly. The theme "Design for the elderly," as illustrated in the examples above, can be integrated in an attractive and lasting manner by means of interesting project work and by involving the "elderly person" user group in the process. In this way new areas were and are being established and designers trained who are specialized in products for elderly people and, as experts, will help in the future to reduce present deficits in product development.

We see a very large need for participatory approaches in the future, such as user tests in order to check products for their "demographic steadfastness" and to work out suggestions for optimization. Only in this way can producers and service providers make positive use of the challenges posed by demographic change. In doing so, the innovative potential of such approaches should not be underestimated since new concepts in the future, which will be of great interest to a wide target group, can arise with the user-centered occupation with existing solutions.

References

1. G. Basalla, in *Messer, Gabel, Reissverschluss. Die Evolution der Gebrauchsgegenstände*, ed. by H. Petroski (Birkhäuser, Basel, 1994)
2. K. Bastuck, N. Keil, Wachstumschance Senioren – Potenziale seniorengerechter Produkte, Rölfs MC Partner, Frankfurt am Main 2004
3. L. Burckhardt, *Die Kinder fressen ihre Revolution* (Köln, DuMont, 1985)
4. R. Coleman, *Design Für Die Zukunft* (Köln, DuMont, 1997)
5. R. Coleman, (o.J.), *Living Longer – The New Context for Design*, (Design Council, London, 2001)
6. R. Coleman, S. Keates, P.J Clarkson, C. Lebbon, *Inclusive Design, Design for the Whole Population* (Springer, Berlin, 2002)

7. Deutsche Bank (Hrsg.) Internationaler Design-Wettbewerb Die Deutsche Bank für die deutsche Bank, Katalog Frankfurt am Main: Selbstverlag 1999
8. Ch. Eberle, *My first Sony, Diplomarbeit, Institut für Produkt- und Prozessgestaltung* (Universität der Künste, Berlin, 2003)
9. S. Freud, *Das Unbehagen in der Kultur, Wien: Internationaler Psychoanalytischer* (Verlag, Erstdruck, 1930)
10. W. Friesdorf, A. Heine (Hrsg.), *sentha – seniorengerechte Technik im häuslichen Alltag – Ein Forschungsbericht mit integriertem Roman* (Springer, Heidelberg, 2007)
11. M. Knigge, J. Hofmann, Auf dem Prüfstand der Senioren – Alternde Kunden fordern Unternehmen auf allen Ebenen, DB Research, Frankfurt am Main 2003
12. A. Peine, H.-L. Dienel, in *Living Old Age,* ed. by A. Guerci, S. Consigliere. Defining a Common Framework of Objectives – A New Methodological Focus for Developing Senior Household Technology, (L'Occidente e la modernizzazione, Genua, Erga Edizioni, 2002)
13. R. Rickenberg, R. in *Wörterbuch Design*, ed. by M. Erlhoff, T. Marshall. Entwurfsmethoden (Birkhäuser, Basel, 2008), p. 128
14. H. Roericht, die Lehre an der hdk/udk berlin 1972–2002: http://www.roericht.de/_ID_IV/index.html (01/2008)
15. K. Schmidt-Ruhland, M. Knigge, *Third International Conference on Gerontechnology,* München 10–13, Oktober 1999
16. J. Smith, P.B. Baltes, in *Altern aus psychologischer Perspektive: Trends und Profile im hohen Alter,* ed. by K.U. Mayer, P.B. Baltes. (Die Berliner Altersstudie Berlin, Akademie-Verlag). pp. 221–250
17. W.C. Thomas, Gerontologist **21**(4), 402 (1981)
18. Universität der Künste Berlin (ed.) *Alternativen – Produkte für eine neue alte Generation* (Ausstellungskatalog, Berlin, 2001)
19. K. Weining, *Deutsches Hygiene-Museum Dresden* (München, Prestel, 2005)

Chapter 9
Universal Design – Innovations for All Ages

O. Gassmann and G. Reepmeyer

Abstract Demographics require companies to abandon the concept of solely target-ing young customers. They need to create new products that are attractive to both younger and older customers. The key to success is Universal Design. Products that follow the principles of Universal Design don't separate but integrate customer groups, and they substantially increase a company's target markets. This chapter not only highlights the economic potential of Universal Design, it also shows how Universal Design can be implemented within any corporation. A successful imple-mentation needs: (a) to define a suitable Universal Design strategy, (b) to establish adequate processes within the firm, (c) to design the products right, and (d) to mar-ket the products appropriately to customers. The chapter concludes by illustrating attractive areas for universally designed innovations.

Introduction: Opening New Markets by Integrating Young and Old Customers

The demographic time bomb is ticking: The society in most Western economies is getting older every day. However, while the "Generation 50+" turns out to be one of the most attractive target groups for many companies, the term "aging" itself is controversially discussed. It is still fairly prevalent that everybody will become old, but no one wants to be old. But this antiquated perception of age has become outdated itself. The "new" elderly generation is much more vital, has a higher pur-chasing power and increasingly loves to experiment with new products compared to "older" elderly generations. This is not very surprising if it is considered that today's 50+ generation grew up under totally different circumstances than the traditionally known "older generation." Today's 50- to 65-year-olds grew up in a cultural environ-ment with Rock 'n' Roll, Elvis Presley, and The Beatles. They identify themselves with people such as Tina Turner, Robert Redford, Sean Connery, or Mick Jagger. It is simple but true: someone who was 26 years old in 1968 is 65 years old today.

Despite this development, many companies still haven't launched appropriate initiatives that intentionally include this fairly new and fast-growing market segment of people over 50 years of age into product planning and development activities. Research by the Arizona State University has shown that only 12 out of 125 Fortune 500 companies mention on their websites that they proactively consider the specific needs of the elderly in their product strategy. Upon request, only two of these companies were able to provide more detailed information about these initiatives.

Our explorative study in 2003 with 105 companies in 11 different industries showed similar results. Eighty-five percent of companies considered it important to align product offerings with demographic developments. However, only 29% of respondents have proactively thought about opportunities to launch the respective initiatives. Only around 20% of companies have conducted or even read market research reports discussing the potential of demographic change. This negligence has fatal consequences because companies miss out on real opportunities. The survey asked companies who already offered age-friendly products about the products' performance. Seventy percent of the respondents confirmed that they are very satisfied with this type of product diversification and that these products are successful on the market. Fifty-nine percent of all companies expect that age-friendly products will lead to at least average if not above-average growth. Only 2% believed that age-friendly products will lead to growth rates below average (see Fig. 9.1). This study is of explorative character and needs further research with larger samples in different regions.

In addition to the lack of awareness among companies, the amount of research on the economic potential of demographic change is fairly limited as well. The only available studies relate to customer segmentation approaches and defining the needs and special demands of older consumers [2, 10, 18]. Hupp [8] observed the decision making of older people, whereas Trocchia and Janda [24] analyzed Internet usage of senior users. Szmigin and Carrigan [23] looked at the societal construction of aging and the resulting self-perception of the elderly. Wolfe [26] has taken this approach a step further and analyzed the thought structures of the elderly. Silvers [22] did research about marketing-relevant events for people of older age, and Bristol [1] analyzed the impact of the "endorser age" on the value of brands. All authors collectively came to the conclusion that a focus on only younger customer generations is wrong [4,8,12,14,16]. Some other researchers analyzed advertising and sales concepts targeting the elderly as well as the role of older customers in advertising and commercials [3,14,19]. In addition, there are some studies available that analyze the consumer behavior of older customers. Lazer [13] was one of the first researchers who observed the purchasing power and consumer acceptance of seniors. Hock and Bader [7] have built upon this approach and analyzed the purchasing and consumer behavior of the 55+ generation.

Most companies are still overwhelmed with the opportunities and corresponding challenges of the demographic development. Some companies have tried to address older customers by offering products that are particularly declared and promoted as products for the elderly. However, developing products especially for seniors hasn't shown to be effective in addressing these customers. As most of the people over 50

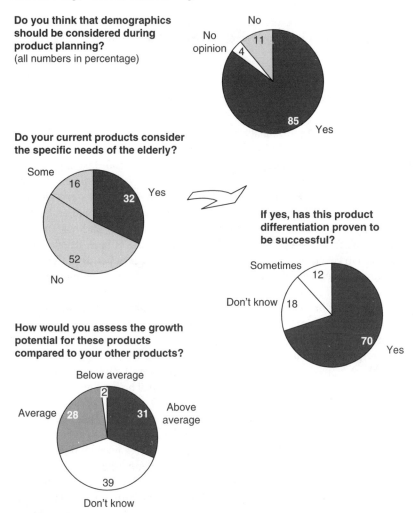

Fig. 9.1 Many companies consider demographic developments to be important for their product offerings, but only a few companies have launched corresponding initiatives: The potential of age-friendly products seems to be significant

are still physically fit and vital, they prefer to buy their products in the same locations where younger generations prefer to shop. They do not want to be separated from younger and healthier generations by shopping for products that have a connotation "for seniors."

This leaves companies with no other choice than developing products and services independent of the customers' age. These products and services need to combine the product requirements (logic, complexity, dimensions, functions, handling) with the special capabilities of the elderly (sensory and cognitive capabilities, mental agility, physical condition, technical experience). Successful innovations follow the motto: "Creating products for younger generations excludes the elderly. Creating products for all ages, however, includes all generations – young and old."

The Potential of Universal Design

In this context, innovation management has recently started to become engaged with the new paradigm of "Universal Design." Universally designed products are attractive to all customers, independent of their age. Universal Design integrates. It doesn't differentiate between disabled, normal, old, and young. Universal products take into account the needs and requirements of all possible users and customers. Therefore, Universal Design conceptually represents a standard, not an exception. Universal Design intentionally avoids highlighting the users' and customers' different capabilities. A 30-year-old won't buy a car that has been developed for a 60-year-old. However, the 60-year-old won't buy this car either. By offering products that are independent of their users' age, companies can eventually maximize their possible target customers.

The Center for Universal Design at North Carolina State University in the United States is one of the pioneers in promoting Universal Design as a product standard. The Center has come up with principles for universally designed products. These principles have found broad acceptance in product development around the world. Table 9.1 provides a brief overview of the seven Universal Design Principles. The application of all principles ensures a universal product design that is truly independent of the customers' age.

The origins of Universal Design date back to the early 1950s. Because of the high number of veterans of World War II, the public has slowly developed an interest in the needs of disabled people and people who cannot live a normal, regular life due to physical impairments. Many people were either directly affected by disability or knew someone in their immediate social environment who was disabled due to the consequences of the war. It was during these times that efforts were made to develop products that were motivated to take disabled people's needs into account. However, those products were usually designed and declared as "products for the disabled." Besides a lack of aesthetics in design, the prices were comparatively high as well.

It took another couple of years (it was only after the end of the Vietnam War in the mid-1970s) till the first laws came into effect that constituted favoring situations and environments for people with disabilities. The USA introduced in the 1990 the "American Disability Act," and the UK passed in 1995 the "Disability Discrimination Act." Only in 1998 did the first real tangible benefits for people who were physically challenged become eminent with the introduction of "Section 508" of the "Workforce Investment Act." This section describes that public contracts may only be issued to companies that design their products in a way that they can be also used by disabled customers. The advantage of this act was that it left a lot of freedom to the companies to decide what actions they prefer to take in order to achieve this goal – and if they intend to achieve it at all.

Table 9.1 The seven Universal Design principles (source: The Center for Universal Design)

Principle	Explanation
1. Equitable use	The design is useful and marketable to people with diverse abilities
	Guidelines
	(a) Provide the same means of use for all users: identical whenever possible; equivalent when not
	(b) Avoid segregating or stigmatizing any users
	(c) Provisions for privacy, security, and safety should be equally available to all users
	(d) Make the design appealing to all users
2. Flexibility in use	The design accommodates a wide range of individual preferences and abilities
	Guidelines
	(a) Provide choice in methods of use
	(b) Accommodate right- or left-handed access and use
	(c) Facilitate the user's accuracy and precision
	(d) Provide adaptability to the user's pace
3. Simple and intuitive use	Use of the design is easy to understand, regardless of the user's experience, knowledge, language skills, or current concentration level
	Guidelines
	(a) Eliminate unnecessary complexity
	(b) Be consistent with user expectations and intuition
	(c) Accommodate a wide range of literacy and language skills
	(d) Arrange information consistent with its importance
	(e) Provide effective prompting and feedback during and after task completion
4. Perceptible information	The design communicates necessary information effectively to the user, regardless of ambient conditions or the user's sensory abilities
	Guidelines
	(a) Use different modes (pictorial, verbal, tactile) for redundant presentation of essential information
	(b) Provide adequate contrast between essential information and its surroundings
	(c) Maximize "legibility" of essential information
	(d) Differentiate elements in ways that can be described (i.e., make it easy to give instructions or directions)
	(e) Provide compatibility with a variety of techniques or devices used by people with sensory limitations

(continued)

Table 9.1 (continued)

Principle	Explanation
5. Tolerance for error	The design minimizes hazards and the adverse consequences of accidental or unintended actions
	Guidelines
	(a) Arrange elements to minimize hazards and errors: most used elements, most accessible; hazardous elements eliminated, isolated, or shielded
	(b) Provide warnings of hazards and errors
	(c) Provide fail-safe features
	(d) Discourage unconscious action in tasks that require vigilance
6. Low physical effort	The design can be used efficiently and comfortably and with a minimum of fatigue
	Guidelines
	(a) Allow user to maintain a neutral body position
	(b) Use reasonable operating forces
	(c) Minimize repetitive actions
	(d) Minimize sustained physical effort
7. Size/space for approach/use	Appropriate size and space is provided for approach, reach, manipulation, and use regardless of user's body size, posture, or mobility
	Guidelines
	(a) Provide a clear line of sight to important elements for any seated or standing user
	(b) Make reach to all components comfortable for any seated or standing user
	(c) Accommodate variations in hand and grip size
	(d) Provide adequate space for the use of assistive devices or personal assistance

Many countries in Europe have adopted the thought of caring about people with disabilities as well. For example, the European Union declared the year 2003 as the "Year of People with Disabilities." In this context, the EU launched a big initiative to fund research projects focusing on issues related to Universal Design.

Despite the clear governmental mandate, industry, however, still has little experience when it comes to Universal Design. The tasks and costs are frequently considered to be still unknown, and many companies have not yet responded to this trend. Only a few examples exist that show the real tangible benefits of Universal Design, but this number is growing. Sometimes, other notations are used for the concept of age-independent design, such as transgenerational design. However, the idea behind all those initiatives remains the same – to create products and applications that can be used by all customers, independent of their age or physical and mental conditions.

It doesn't always take a lot of effort and energy to come up with a universally designed pathway to impact. The company Whirlpool, for example, might serve as a good case in this context. Whirlpool (one of the world's leaders in appliances, especially washing machines) received a few years ago an unusual amount of letters and complaints from their customer indicating that the company's products are hard to understand and use. As a response, Whirlpool conducted a few smaller modifications, such as placing an easily understandable manual with large letters right underneath the cover of the machine. While the older customers didn't send any complaints to Whirlpool any more, the younger customers have not complained either. In addition, the younger customers were indifferent towards the new design. Thus, Whirlpool was able to make only small adjustments to its current product, but was able to increase the group of satisfied customers quite substantially which is right at the heart of the meaning of the concept of Universal Design.

Implementing Universal Design Within the Corporation

Define a Suitable Strategy

Anchoring the concept of Universal Design in the product strategy is the first step towards a successful implementation of Universal Design. Top management has to make clear how strategic initiatives should be conceptualized and implemented. The following questions need to be addressed:

- Should Universal Design be implemented within the entire company, certain business units, or only some selected product lines or groups?
- What resources and competencies are necessary, and how can the company's own core competencies best be leveraged?
- What are the potential applications and what is their market potential?

A successfully implemented Universal Design strategy defines how the company intends to position itself towards its stakeholders, what message the company wants to promulgate, and what products and services it should offer. Every company can rely upon three generic strategies to define its degree of implementation of Universal Design (see Fig. 9.2):

1. *Marketing existing products customized for seniors*: This strategy simply relies upon redirecting the company's marketing concept. The yet-neglected target group of the elderly will intentionally be integrated into the marketing of existing products and services. However, the existing products and services are usually not adapted accordingly. The company only changes its way of communicating and addressing the possibly new customers in order to attract older customers.
2. *Adapting existing offerings according to the customers' age*: This strategy systematically analyzes all existing products and services and determines if they fulfill the Universal Design requirements. If some products or services do not meet these criteria, the company can try to come up with possible adaptations in order to make the products and services more attractive for the elderly.

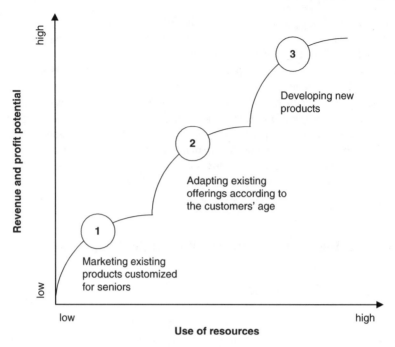

Fig. 9.2 Universal Design can be implemented in the corporate strategy in multiple ways and can have different scopes [5]

3. *Developing new products*: This strategy includes the development of entirely new products and services that strictly follow all Universal Design principles, from ideation to market introduction. The elderly are proactively included during product development phases in order to ensure adherence to Universal Design standards.

The first strategy entails fairly low market risks. Small changes in product marketing may lead to comparatively quick market success. The strategy's implications on sales and profit may be limited though.

The second strategy requires more resources. The higher effort, however, will most likely lead to greater leaps in revenues and profits because this strategy indeed offers more attractive products and services for the older generation, in addition to an age-friendly marketing. The increased attractiveness of the products and services is usually based upon an improved design of the interfaces between the product and the user (i.e., the technology and the older customer). Good examples are telephones with enlarged number keys as well as high-resolution and high-contrast digital displays.

The third strategy is characterized by the highest development and market risks. It also requires the largest amount of resources. Due to comparatively longer lead times in development, this strategy will usually increase sales and profits with a slight delay. By contrast, these products and services are most appropriately suited to include satisfying the needs of the elderly as they proactively include their opinions and perspectives.

All three strategies are not exclusive. They can be applied in parallel, and they are applicable in a broad range of industries ranging from high-tech to consumer goods. The textile and fashion company Betty Barclay, for example, has broadened its product offering – purposely including the elderly – and has achieved great success since then. While most textile and fashion companies in Germany have posted declining revenues and profits, Betty Barclay, however, was able to present an increase of sales in 2003 of 1.6%. The average Betty Barclay customer is 39 years of age or older.

Another example of a company that has radically shifted its strategy a couple of years ago, and now primarily, but not exclusively, offers products that target the market of the elderly is the Swiss company Synthes-Stratec. Initially, the company produced high-quality Swiss watches. The company's engineers were experimenting with new materials, with the objective of discovering non-magnetic alloys that are resistant to shocks and corrosion. Today, these alloys are still used in well-known brands such as Rolex or IWC. The company's management recognized that these new alloys were not only applicable in watches but in a couple of other market segments that were characterized by high growth rates. Because of that, the company engaged in cooperation with the Association for Osteosynthesis. This cooperation represented the company's entrance into prosthetics, a market segment that primarily, but not exclusively, includes older customers. In the following years, Synthes-Stratec has substantially changed gears, and now focuses on prosthetics. Today, the company is world leader in osteosynthesis and generates revenues of more than CHF 1.5 billion.

In most instances, small changes in the company's product strategy are sufficient to make products and services attractive and applicable to users of all ages. While all age groups will benefit from these adjustments, it is most often the group of the elderly that benefits the most. Whereas younger users are usually able to adapt to new circumstances and new situations, older users usually don't have these capabilities. That is the reason why they appreciate universally designed products the most.

Establish Adequate Processes

In order to identify and define processes that allow implementing Universal Design strategies, a closer look at the older customers' specific capabilities and abilities has proven to be a very effective first step. Physical and mental capabilities usually worsen with old age. Many age-related medical conditions lead to the fact that sensory capabilities and velocity-related activities decline. Vision usually starts to deteriorate at an age of around 40. The eye's abilities relating to contrast and colors are usually impaired by then. Starting at around 60 years of age, more severe constraints frequently occur. Hearing impairment usually starts at an age of around 60, the same age where the muscular strength usually starts declining as well. For example, a 60-year-old has on average 15–35% less muscular strength than a

20-year-old. In addition, problems of the joints usually occur. Taking all these factors into account, many researchers in gerontology came to the general belief that people beyond their mid-60s face considerable multi-morbidity issues [10, 11, 17]. However, studies have shown that substantial losses of physical fitness only correlate for people with an average age of over 85.

Besides physical capabilities, the mental capabilities of older customers also face significant challenges. For example, older people tend to overly rely on their previous experiences. Due to their life experience, older people usually have accumulated highly specific knowledge systems. The part of their intelligence that is based on experience is usually fairly high. This has led to the situation that older people tend to assign new information to familiar schemes and thinking [6, 20]. Therefore, the ability to understand novel technologies and functional principles usually declines with increasing age. However, this should not be confused with generally lower intelligence. Only the "fluid" intelligence, i.e., the intelligence that is used to process new and complex information (also referred to as comprehensive power), is lower for people with older age [27]. The "crystallized" intelligence, by contrast, which contains factual knowledge and relies on capabilities acquired during the course of a person's lifetime, rarely declines with old age. Moreover, the crystallized intelligence can even partly compensate for the declining fluid intelligence in older people.

Considering the situation of many older people, the main problem of product development becomes eminent: In many cases, fairly young engineers, designers, and marketing experts are creating products that are expected to be purchased by the elderly. Simply because of the difference in age, they have never been exposed to the special physical and mental challenges that most of their customers are facing. They usually know the perspectives and opinions of younger customer generations quite well, but they mostly lack the knowledge and empathy to grasp and understand the special capabilities and needs of older customer generations. A successful implementation of Universal Design therefore always requires merging of both the innovative products' features with the special capabilities and abilities of the older consumers (see Fig. 9.3).

In order to make it happen that both the product's requirements and features as well as the customers physical and mental capabilities match, three generally accepted strategies can be applied to address this challenge:

1. *Checklists for product features*: Multiple groups of researchers (including the Center for Universal Design in the USA) have already developed guidelines that describe the characteristics of age-friendly products and services. Companies can use these guidelines to identify potentials for improvement of their current product and service offerings. However, they should keep in mind that concrete design implications can usually not be generalized. Every product or service design needs to be handled as an individual case.

2. *Deficit simulation*: Besides theoretically elaborating the needs and capabilities of older customers, physically experiencing these challenges is an even more powerful tool for really understanding the special issues related to serving the elderly. The company Meyer-Hentschel Management Consulting has developed an "Age

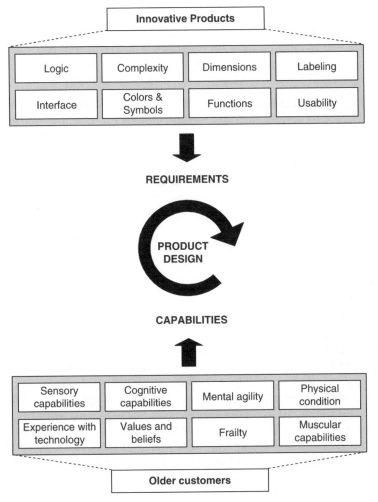

Fig. 9.3 Successful product development under the Universal Design paradigm matches the requirements of the innovative products with the abilities of older customers

Explorer" that uses glasses, headsets, weights, and other tools to simulate the physical and cognitive capabilities of older people. If a younger designer or engineer uses the "Age Explorer," his or her own capabilities are literally reduced, and the "Age Explorer" allows them to have the same experience using products and services that the older customers would have. That way, the deficits of old age can be made recognizable and experience-able.

3. *Participative design*: Participative design describes a method that directly includes elderly customers in product development activities, ideally from idea generation to final market testing. This allows giving a voice to older customers and lets them articulate their needs and expectations. In addition, the

designers also get a much closer understanding of the older people's opinions and perspectives. Companies could proactively employ older people in their R&D departments in order to allow for participative design. A well-balanced mix of young and old designers and engineers seems to be a promising approach to a successful implementation of Universal Design product strategies.

The needs and requirements of customers can only be appropriately considered during the product development process if the customers that actually use the product are included in the products' development process. In addition, the capabilities of the users need to comply with the requirements of the product. Only under this constellation, will innovations be adopted and actually used. Products fulfill the requirements of Universal Design if all of these aspects are taken into account and, simultaneously, the younger customer groups are not excluded or scared away by the products' design. If these conditions are met, the product has the best prerequisites for becoming a market success.

Design the Products Right

The product's design and interface to the user is becoming particularly important. If a customer uses a product for the first time, this usage should be a success. Particularly, studies among the elderly have shown that the first-time use is highly predictive of a product's success [9]. While the technology adoption and implementation theory of Rogers [21] came to the conclusion that early adopters are usually neither older nor younger than late adopters, the fact that age has no relevance on technology adoption has been critically discussed by many researchers. Rogers [21] himself has noted in this context that there is inconsistent evidence about the relationship of age and innovativeness. Martinez et al. [15] have come to the conclusion that the likelihood of customers being among the early adopters of certain household appliances declines with increasing age.

However, Wahl and Mollenkopf [25] have shown that there is converging evidence that older adults are neither "enemies" of technology nor uncritical users of technological innovations. The authors suggest two dimensions of attitudes among the elderly:

- Cognitive–rational aspects of technology (e.g., "technological progress is necessary and therefore one has to accept some inevitable disadvantages")
- Emotional–affective aspects of technology (e.g., "technology is more a threat than a benefit to people")

The combination of these attitudes resulted in four types of older people's relation to technology, namely:

1. Positive advocates
2. Rationally adapting
3. Skeptical and ambivalent
4. Critical and reserved

A survey among 1417 older people has shown that all four types are distributed roughly equally among the sample (see Fig. 9.4). It is interesting to note that the study revealed that there were no significant gender differences within the four types of older people.

Market the Products Appropriately

After developing and designing a new product that follows Universal Design principles, companies need to introduce the product to the market appropriately. The field of "senior marketing" has found fairly broad resonance in research so far. Most experts usually differentiate between two marketing concepts:

- Integration marketing: Target younger and older customers comprehensively; however, explicitly take older customer's needs into account
- Modern senior marketing: Target only the elderly specifically with a specially designed marketing program

In the context of Universal Design, both approaches are acceptable. Although the actual product development has been done universally, marketing the products doesn't necessarily have to follow the same comprehensive approach. A targeted marketing approach might work better in some industries or environments to sell universally designed products. This segmented approach might even allow increasing the overall number of targeted customers.

However, differentiating the elderly into "young" and "old" elderly should be avoided. Successful marketing for seniors uses a high level of individualization. For example, a 50-year-old has other needs and a totally different purchasing behavior to a 75-year-old. In particular, the new group of elderly stemming from the Babyboomer generation is expected to be very demanding when it comes to individualized and customized products and services.

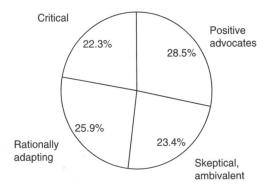

Fig. 9.4 Different types of technology acceptance [25]

In addition, every Universal Design strategy should take into consideration that older customers expect both an intensive and competent consultation while they make their purchase decision, as well as fast customer service after they have made the purchasing decision and in case there are additional questions of shortcomings of the product. Experienced sales support and consultation is therefore critical to success. Older customers will only become loyal long-term customers if they find both.

Thus, while necessary, it is not sufficient to simply sell age-friendly or age-adjusted products. The products' application by the customer needs to be accompanied by the company as well, and therefore should be included in the company's marketing approach. In particular, a well structured and aligned after-sales approach may allow success to be achieved quickly. A simple phone call to check if the older customer is happy with the product, if it meets his or her expectations, and/or if it may cause any problems during usage could significantly increase customer satisfaction.

After-sales service also allows for substantial improvements in customer loyalty as older customers seem to value this type of service. Even if this type of consultation is time-consuming, it is a key success factor in selling a product to an older customer, and it is oftentimes regarded as a requirement for a successful sale. The right design of an innovative product for an older customer always depends on the company's understanding of the user's behavior in the context of his/her capabilities and opportunities. If the use of a product asks for a higher sophistication than the user has to offer, it is the product that is responsible for its non-usage, not the user.

Summary and Conclusion: Identifying Attractive Areas for Innovation

Market success of innovations is neither defined simply by technology determinism nor by the pure existence of customer needs. Only the interconnection of both technologies and market needs substantially increases the economic success of an invention. When discussing the potential of Universal Design, companies frequently ask which products or bundles of products represent the highest potential for innovation. In order to derive and identify attractive areas for innovation, the intersection between novel technologies, markets, customers, and applications needs to be analyzed in greater detail. The largest potentials for innovation are right at the intersection between technologies and markets where both merge in a well-balanced proportion. Figure 9.5 represents this intersection of specific customer needs of the 50+ generation and a couple of selected gerontechnologies (i.e. technologies that can be applied specifically to improve the day-to-day life of the elderly). The objective of gerontechnologies is to provide older people with the opportunity to live and experience an "active aging".

In general, innovative solutions targeting the elderly can be found everywhere, because every industry is principally affected by the demographic development – some industries more, some less. Industries that offer products that are preferably

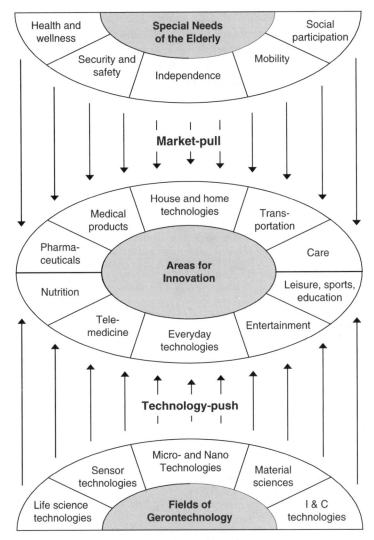

Fig. 9.5 Attractive areas with a high potential for innovation emerge where markets meet technologies

consumed by older customers offer, of course, the highest potential for innovation. However, industries that have a broad customer profile and target all age groups can also benefit substantially from applying Universal Design principles. It can be assumed that the areas for innovation in Fig. 9.5 are characterized by a comparatively high innovation potential due to their strong technology affinity. Besides the innovation areas in Fig. 9.5, there are additional sectors that might benefit from the demographic development. However, they usually depend less on innovative technologies. Examples of these "soft" innovation areas include financial services, religion and esotericism, gero-transcendence, culture, and traditions.

In summary, the importance of demographic change requires addressing one high-level issue: the awareness and sensitivity around the potential, chances, and opportunities that arise from demographic change need to be taken into account not only by politicians and society, but also by leaders in the corporate world. Products and services that include older generations but don't exclude younger generations have a high value for society, and therefore for companies. Only if the mindset of all stakeholders fully grasp the meritoric character of age-friendly products, is it possible to find the necessary reforms in society and business that address one of the most pressing challenges of the future – demographics.

References

1. T. Bristol, J. Curr. Issues Res. Advert. **18**(2), S59 (1996)
2. B.O. Brünner, *Die Zielgruppe Senioren – eine Analyse* (Peter Lang, Frankfurt, 1997)
3. M. Carrigan, I. Szmigin, Bus. Ethics. Eur. Rev. **9**(1), S42 (2000)
4. M.K. Dychtwald, J. Consum. Mark. **14**(4/5), S271 (1997)
5. O. Gassmann, G. Reepmeyer, *Wachstumsmarkt Alter. Innovationen für die Zielgruppe 50+* (Hanser, München, 2006)
6. T. Hess, in *Aging and Semantic Influences on Memory*, ed. by T.M. Hess (Amsterdam, North-Holland), p. S93
7. E.-M. Hock, B. Bader, in *Thexis – Fachbericht für Marketing*, vol. 2001/3, ed. by C. Belz, T. Tomczak, T. Rudolph (2001)
8. O. Hupp, *Seniorenmarketing: Informations- und Entscheidungsverhalten älterer Konsumenten* (Kovaè, Hamburg, 1999)
9. T.W. King, *Assistive Technology: Essential Human Factors* (Allyn & Bacon, Boston, MA, 1999)
10. B. Kölzer, *Senioren als Zielgruppe: Kundenorientierung im Handel* (Deutscher Universitäts-Verlag, Wiesbaden, 1995)
11. C. Krieb, A. Reidel, *Senioren-Marketing: so erreichen Sie die Zielgruppe der Zukunft* (Ueberreuter, Wien, 1999)
12. C. Krieb, A. Reidl, *Seniorenmarketing – So erreichen Sie die Zielgruppe der Zukunft* (Landsberg am Lech, Moderne Industrie, 2001)
13. W. Lazer, J. Consum. Mark. **3**(3), S23 (1986)
14. H.G. Lewis, *Seniorenmarketing – Die besten Werbe- und Verkaufskonzepte* (Landsberg am Lech, Moderne Industrie, 1997)
15. E.Martinez, Y. Polo, C. Flavián, J. Consum. Mark. **15**(4), S323 (1998)
16. Meyer-Hentschel, *Handbuch Senioren-Marketing: Erfolgsstrategien aus der Praxis* (Meyer-Hentschel Management Consulting, Dt. Fachverlag, Frankfurt a.M., 2000)
17. H. Meyer-Hentschel, G. Meyer-Hentschel, *Das goldene Marktsegment: Produkt und Ladengestaltung für den Seniorenmarkt* (Dt. Fachverlag, Frankfurt a.M., 1991)
18. G.P. Moschis, E. Lee, A. Mathur, J. Consum. Mark. **14**(4/5), S282 (1997)
19. J. Nielson, K. Curry, J. Consum. Mark. **14**(4/5), S310 (1997)
20. G.E. Rice, M.A. Okun, J. Gerontol. Psychol. Sci. **49**, S119 (1994)
21. E.M. Rogers, *Diffusion of Innovations. 5. Auflage* (The Free Press, New York, 2003)
22. C. Silvers, J. Consum. Mark. **14**(4/5), S303 (1997)
23. I. Szmigin, M. Carrigan, Psychol. Mark. **18**(10), S1091 (2001)
24. P.J. Trocchia, S. Janda, J. Consum. Mark. **17**(6/7), S605 (2000)
25. H.-W. Wahl, H. Mollenkopf, in *Impact of Everyday Technology in the Home Environment on Older Adults' Quality of Life*, ed. by N. Charness, K.W. Schaie (Springer, New York, 2003)
26. D.B. Wolfe, J. Consum. Mark. **14**(4/5), S294 (1997)
27. M. Yom, T. Wilhelm, D. Beger, Planung und Analyse **28**(6), S.22 (2001)

Chapter 10
Transgenerational Design: A Heart Transplant for Housing

J.J. Pirkl

Abstract Time and circumstances reshape one's expectations and priorities. Responding to his past research and the realities of the aging process, the author describes why and how he designed and built the first fully accessible house aimed directly at Baby Boomers and beyond. The project offers a vehicle for broadening consumer awareness of, and increasing the demand for, "transgenerational" housing and household products. This uniquely innovative design neutralizes many restrictive effects of aging, accidents, illness or chronic conditions. It also demonstrates that attractive transgenerational houses can be designed to promote, provide, and extend independent living, remove barriers, offer wider options, supply greater choices, and enhance the quality of life for all – the young, the old, the able, the disabled – without penalty to any group.

Introduction

Forty-five years ago, I led one of three design teams that developed the General Motors *Futurama* exhibit at the 1964 New York World's Fair. Our assignment was to envision the "world of tomorrow" that would demonstrate how knowledge could be used to span the new challenges of time, distance, and environment.

Futurama transported 70,000 visitors a day on an imaginative three-dimensional panoramic adventure to experience technology's future possibilities on a global and cosmic scale. They witnessed the moon's exploration, polar ice cap mining, undersea oil drilling, atomic-powered submarine transportation, laser beam tree harvesting, remote control desert farming, and highways connecting remote residential communities. The climax was a ride through a "city of tomorrow" punctuated with sleek high-rise buildings, covered "moving sidewalks," "containerized" freight terminals, and "automated parking facilities," all laced by expansive ribbons of "automatic highway lanes" [6].

The experience convinced us that future "dream cars," "kitchens of tomorrow," and robotic household products would pamper our every whim and extend our pursuit of happiness into an ageless future. The thought of growing old and retiring never entered our minds.

But, time and circumstances reshape and reorder one's expectations and priorities. As a young designer, I never confronted the fragility of ability or longevity – or the probability of acquiring a physical or sensory impairment – until my mother's stroke underscored the frustrating lack of supporting environments and products. A decade ago, after several bouts of medical repairs, my wife and I began to experience similar environmental frustrations and recognized our own growing need for a new kind of supportive housing.

Looking back, I can't point to any particular time where I began to morph into an aging senior. But here I am, along with hundreds of millions like me, who have also experienced. or will experience, the physical and sensory effects of discriminating environmental challenges.

I'm now living in that "world of tomorrow." I've enjoyed owning a "dream car" or two, and discovered retirement in my 60s. And I'm still exploring new challenges, this time, age-related design projects having a "transgenerational" focus.

An Emerging Design Challenge

A quiet revolution is taking place – the world's population is aging. Never before has our planet contained so many older people, or such a large percentage of them. Throughout the world today, there are more people age 65 and older than the populations of France, Germany, Japan, and Russia combined [13]. Thirty-six million Americans are aged 65 and older, a number larger than the combined populations of New York, London, and Moscow. Twenty-five years ago, Japan was the youngest society in the world. Today, it is the oldest [9]. In one generation, the life expectancy of Japanese people has already increased by more than 30% with the number of older people expanding from 15 to 25% by 2025 [3].

Still, the numbers continue to grow. Fifty million American Baby Boomers, the driving force behind yesterday's youth culture, are aging toward retirement. Many will experience periods of illness, accidents, and normal declines in their physical and sensory abilities while, at the same time, trying to balance the needs of their children with those of their aging parents.

In the decade ahead, according to the National Association of Home Builders (NAHB), Boomers will be the fastest growing segment of the home-buying public. Clearly, this is an emerging market for "transgenerational" housing and household products that respond to their changing needs. And, while this realization has attracted the attention of forward-thinking manufacturers and homebuilders, many others fail to accept the challenge of developing and offering alternative choices within today's housing, retirement community, and elder care markets.

In his book, *Age Power*, Dychtwald [4] observes, "aging is not something that begins on one's 65th birthday. Rather, all of the choices we make regarding how we care for ourselves, how we manage our lives and even how we think about our futures, shape who we ultimately become in our later years. It [is] obvious that many of the painful, punishing challenges of old age could be prevented if informed choices were made earlier in life."

Builders and manufacturers, aware of the exploding aging Baby Boomer population and the effect that their informed choices will have on sales, increasingly speak in terms of "universal and "transgenerational" design. But, Bauer [2] suggests that "mainstream companies are sometimes fearful of the term "universal design" because they interpret these words to mean that a product must satisfy persons of every level of ability." Feeheley [5] concurs, asserting that "the term Universal Design has not lived up to or inspired people to its promise…having become associated with a design movement that targets only the aged and the handicapped."

As a result, transgenerational design is emerging as the favored terminology for housing and household products that offer informed aging Baby Boomers a new generation of attractive, accommodating choices.

Why Transgenerational Design

A Matter of Terminology

We don't see much in the popular press about transgenerational design, nor hear it being discussed at cocktail parties. Yet an increasing number of astute global manufacturers and research organizations are embracing the transgenerational design concept, recognizing its competitive advantage for attracting the attention – and collective buying power – of the exploding aging market. Researchers like Leahy [7] have "found it beneficial to speak of transgenerational design (TD) rather than universal design (UD) when making presentations to company executives" because "TD piques the interest of corporations trying to tap into the aging Baby Boomer market."

It is unfortunate, however, that those who benefit the most from the application are those who know the least about it. Yet, when confronted with an example, most people immediately recognize the benefits. When introduced to a new transgenerational product or environment, the accommodating design helps transcend the frustration of a painful impairment or disability. Such designs promote graceful aging, soften the impact of the aging process, extend independent living, and enhance the quality of life for all – the young, the old, the able, the disabled. In short, the designs *sympathize* rather than *stigmatize*.

Let me further clarify the issue.

Transgenerational design is *not* about producing more cynical elderly housing, homes for the aged, or adult retirement communities that provide only bland code-compliant environments outfitted with such adaptive add-ons as grab bars, ramps, and raised toilet seats that reek with medical, aging, and institutional connotations.

It *is* about designing *all* residential environments and household products to be attractive and accommodating to the widest possible spectrum of those who would use them – the young, the old, the able, the disabled. And it does so by integrating human-sensitive architecture, living spaces, appliances, fixtures, products, and communications designed for safety, comfort, convenience, beauty, accessibility, cleanability, adjust-ability, ease of use, and bodily fit. These are all transgenerational features that neutralize the effects of age and disability.

We call it transgenerational design because it bridges the generations by making products and environments compatible with those physical and sensory impairments associated with human aging, and which limit major activities of daily living [10].

I coined the term in 1986 conducting a research project at Syracuse University with gerontologist Anna L. Babic under a grant from the US Department of Health and Human Services. Our published guidelines and strategies for designing transgenerational products were the first to accommodate one's changing limitations in vision, hearing, touch, dexterity, and mobility that lead to impairments and disabilities [11].

It is a mistake, however, to inseparably link age with disabilities and impairments. While most physical and sensory limitations do occur in older people, we tend to forget that one does not have to be old to acquire them. Indeed, they can, and do, occur during our younger years. And because they do, transgenerational design extends its supporting benefits to those temporary disabilities that most of us acquire throughout out lives: falls, sprains, burns, broken bones, and even pregnancy, which limit our activities and curtail our independence. Consider, in the USA today:

- Some 49 million people, of all ages, have some form of disability; 35 million are under age 65 [12].
- Over 46 million Americans, of all ages, suffer from arthritis. It is the leading cause of disability among Americans aged 15 and older, limiting activities for over 7 million individuals [1].
- Problems related to stiffness or paralysis affect 5 million households, including about 60% of all elderly households.
- Falls are the second leading cause of unintentional deaths, accounting for 50% of all injury deaths [8].

In the light of such statistics, shouldn't a kitchen, bath, laundry, patio, or even a garage or a thermostat, be as readily and easily used by a child with a sprained ankle, a Baby Boomer with heart disease, an octogenarian with a broken hip, or a pregnant twenty-something housewife with an arthritic spine? We think they should.

A fair question would be: what kind of housing will extend independence and improve the quality of life for all who use them – young or old, able or disabled? My answer is, transgenerational housing, which:

- Bridges the transitions across life's stages
- Responds to the widest range of individual differences and abilities

- Offers a variety of ways to accomplish one's activities of daily living
- Provides an opportunity to maintain one's dignity and sense of self-worth
- Enables personal and social interaction, and inter-generational relationships

This is why transgenerational design is so important. A transgenerational house accomplishes each by removing barriers, promoting and extending independent living, providing wider options, offering greater choices, and enhancing the quality of life for all, and at no group's expense.

The Transgenerational Paradigm

As an industrial designer, I look at a house as a product, albeit a very large product. But, whether a product is large or small, people of all ages and abilities desire, buy, and use a product based on a blend of three perceived consumer value categories: humanics, aesthetics, and technics. I call them the "HAT" values of transgenerational design (see Fig. 10.1).

- Humanics refers to the humane aspects of a product's value: Is the product safe and easy to use or operate? Is it comfortable? Does it fit one's body? Does it accommodate different age groups or physical and sensory abilities? Without humanics, a product lacks the values of safety, comfort, convenience, accommodation, ease of use, and ergonomic fit, regardless of its aesthetics and technics values.
- Aesthetics denotes the visual/sensory aspects of a product's value: Is the product attractive? Does its form, color, texture, and sound reflect one's taste? Does it symbolize one's group, clique, or coterie? Does its appearance reflect the products function? Without aesthetics, a product may be unattractive, ugly,

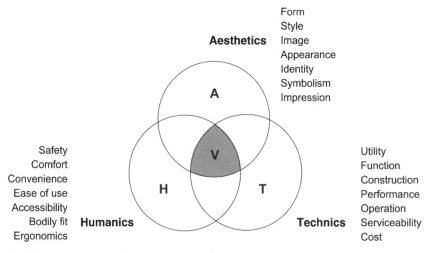

Fig. 10.1 Primary product design value categories

intimidating, discriminating, or demeaning, regardless of its humanics and technics values.

- Technics deals with the technological aspects of the product's value: Does it perform its intended function? How is the product constructed? How effective is its operation? Is it affordable? Can it be repaired or serviced? Without technics, a product cannot work, function, operate, perform, or be repaired, regardless of its eesthetics and humanics values.

The design of our 2700 ft^2 transgenerational house – its concept, plan, furnishings, appliances, materials, lighting, and attention to details – is a seamless blend of each HAT value category articulated in the design program. The following case study may offer additional insight.

The Transgenerational House: A Case Study

Project Goals

We began our experimental transgenerational house project by establishing a guiding set of three achievable goals:

1. Demonstrate that accommodating "accessible" housing can be attractive, appealing, and desirable to the widest spectrum of people
2. Stimulate consumer interest by informing the general public about the advantages that transgenerational design can bring to housing, interior environments, and household products
3. Communicate the competitive advantages of transgenerational design to the home building, remodeling, and household product industries

The Design Program

Before beginning the design phase of the project, we prepared a 12-page design program setting down our needs, desires, and requirements – our "wish list." It included such objectives as:

- Provide safety, comfort, convenience, beauty, accessibility, and easy use for the widest diversity of potential users
- Create an attractive, upbeat, contemporary design that appeals to young as well as older residents
- Create an aesthetic blend of structure, open floor plan, and large glass openings with "universal" access
- Produce a passive solar structure with low-maintenance, utilizing energy-efficient and environmentally sensitive materials

- Design the kitchen, dining, and living room as one flowing flexible space that accentuates the site's dramatic mountain views
- Develop a wheelchair-friendly plan that reduces the need to bend, squat, lift, or stand for long periods of time

The program also included an extensive room-by-room inventory of our "value" needs. In addition to the usual grab bars, lever door handles, extra wide doors, and level thresholds, our list also included such specific items as:

- Keyless entry locks
- Movable partitions and sliding panels
- Radiant heating sympathetic to legs and feet
- Multilevel counters and work surfaces
- Curb-less, dual-use showers with adjustable seating
- Sustainable materials like cork and bamboo flooring
- Adjustable-height bathroom vanities
- Extended bathtub deck for easy transfer
- Easy-to-reach, side-mounted bathtub controls
- Flexible-use, indoor and outdoor spaces
- Sliding pocket doors to eliminate wheelchair interference
- Multiple 5-ft diameter wheelchair turnabouts
- Internet, entertainment, and communication systems
- Remote security, medical, and environmental control systems
- Higher electrical outlets and lower light switches
- Remote controls for operating high window blinds
- Level no-step thresholds

The Site

We selected a site in a new residential community called Sundance Mesa, located about halfway between Albuquerque and Santa Fe, New Mexico. The site had an elevated plateau with magnificent views of the Sandia Mountains to the southeast and a sweeping horizon of mesas and plains to the west, across and beyond the Rio Grande. To the north, a natural rolling expanse of foothills offered freedom to stroll, hike, or walk a dog. A small arroyo cut diagonally across the lot, supporting a variety of southwestern vegetation – chemise, purple sage, juniper, and four-wing salt-bush.

We also selected the site because it challenged accepted principles of accessibility – it was not a flat lot. "Why," we thought, "should one be limited to flat lots when building a house accessible to all?" Building on the site's elevated plateau, however, was not without design problems. We located the driveway along the edge of the site, bridging an arroyo and raising the grade gradually to the parking apron and garage. Thus, the car became the elevating conveyance from street level to house level, providing equal access to all without using ramps. Our plan integrated the house with the site's natural contours and existing landscape. It also preserved most of the site's natural environment – another of our early design priorities.

The Plan

The plan of the house evolved from numerous schematic layouts in which we explored our desire to:

- Capture the site's dramatic views of the Sandia Mountains and the Rio Grande valley
- Provide a private, walled courtyard "oasis" accessible directly from all major living areas
- Produce a dramatic visual and functional interplay of both indoor and outdoor spaces
- Utilize natural, "green" sustainable materials
- Achieve single-level wheelchair accessibility throughout

We accomplished our objectives by positioning and integrating four function-defining activity zones:

- **Zone A** contains the "public" areas: the main entry, kitchen and laundry, and the living/dining areas that access an outdoor dining patio and the private courtyard.
- **Zone B** includes a library/media/activity room, which overlooks the courtyard and links the "public" and "private" areas. An adjacent guest bedroom has a connecting guest bath, which is also accessed from the connecting tiled hallway. Guests access the courtyard from a door opposite the guest bathroom.
- **Zone C** contains the "private" areas. The master bedroom suite, with direct access to the courtyard and exercise pool, contains a fully accessible master bath. The office/studio opens onto its own private courtyard. The nearby utility/storage room offers an expedient transition from house to garage.
- **Zone D** encloses the private courtyard "oasis" conveniently accessed from each of the other zones. Upon entering the courtyard, wide sidewalks direct one past raised flower and herb beds to the solar-heated, self-cleaning exercise pool.

All indoor and outdoor spaces are equipped with lever door handles, level thresholds, non-slip floors and walkways, and multiple 5-ft diameter, 360° turning circles to accommodate wheelchair users (see Fig. 10.2).

Green Design

In addition to applying the tenets of universal and transgenerational design, we also applied such green and environmentally sustainable principles as:

- Design for energy efficiency
- Utilize renewable energy

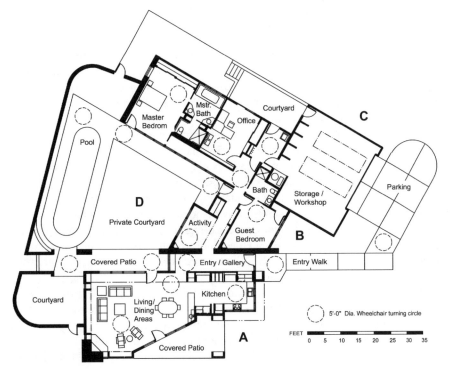

Fig. 10.2 Plan of the transgenerational house

- Optimize use of materials
- Install water-efficient, low-maintenance landscaping
- Design for durability and low maintenance
- Plan for future reuse and adaptability
- Avoid materials that give off gas pollutants
- Utilize renewable materials like cork and bamboo flooring

Such green principles save health, energy, and resources. They help simplify the activities of daily living and contribute to the mutually inclusive objectives of both universal and transgenerational design.

Tour the Transgenerational House

Our experimental transgenerational house project provides an informative case study meant to spark discussion, initiate innovation, offer alternate solutions, increase public awareness, and generate market demand. The tour begins at the entry and proceeds through the four activity zones, focusing on the most innovative solutions.

Zone A

Entry: One approaches the house – set on a raised acre with southwestern vegetation – by climbing a steadily rising, curved driveway to the parking apron. Approaching the door, a wide level walkway, flanked by natural vegetation, leads directly to the weather-protected entry. A full-length sidelight permits residents to view visitors before opening the door.

A raised recessed platform adjacent to the entry provides a convenient, protected spot to set down packages or groceries. A 5-ft diameter wheelchair turn-around area provides ample maneuverability while unlocking and opening the front door, which is fitted with an optional keyless lock (see Fig. 10.3).

Once inside, a handy pass-thru counter provides a convenient place to set down grocery bags and packages intended for the adjacent kitchen. Below it, a convenient seating *banco* with storage drawers offers a place to remove hiking boots, gloves, etc. A 5-ft wide, slip-resistant tiled floor stretches from the entry to a ceiling-high window at the end of the hallway, extending one's view into the courtyard and framing a view of the mesa beyond.

Kitchen: The window-wrapped kitchen features a resilient cork floor and multilevel work surfaces designed to ease body pain from bending or standing. The line of windows follows the counter tops around the corner, offering a panoramic view of the mountains. Horizontal mini-blinds moderate the natural light while, outside, an exterior overhang keeps out direct sunlight. Indirect cove and task lighting supplement the kitchen's central skylight.

Fig. 10.3 Entry view from the parking apron

All base cabinets are raised 8 in. instead of the usual 4 in., making cleaning easier and minimizing the need to bend or squat. Cabinets and drawers open with D-pulls or hand cutouts and are designed with slide-out storage shelves, pantry units, and towel racks. The multiheight countertops offer fingertip-grasping edges designed for steadying or, if in a wheelchair, pulling closer to the counter. The sink cabinet's doors and floor are easily removed, permitting clear knee space for easy wheelchair access. A trash-recycling drawer pulls out and separates trash into four easily accessed bins with self-closing lids.

A rolling trolley locks onto the countertop's finger lip-edge detail, offering the option of temporarily reconfiguring the countertop layout. It is also useful as a serving cart, or for transporting items within the kitchen, or throughout the house or patio. It docks conveniently within a cabinet cavity when not in use. A stack of display cabinets, appearing to be fixed, pull out individually revealing a hidden storage area behind the shelf's vertical display panel.

The under-counter dishwasher is also raised 8 in. This permits easier loading and unloading. Its countertop, used as the pass-through from the entry to the kitchen, doubles as a work surface. The easy-to-reach built-in microwave and convection ovens are installed at convenient heights. The shallow side-by-side refrigerator, with in-the-door water and ice dispensers, offers cooling and freezer access to users of different sizes and reach abilities.

Laundry: The raised, front-loading washer and dryer are conveniently located at the edge of the kitchen within a matching set of cabinets. Their proximity allows cooking and laundry chores to be carried out simultaneously. (The utility room in Zone C, which contains a utility sink, is also plumbed to accept the washer and dryer as an alternate location.) The appliances' solid-surface cabinet top provides a convenient place for sorting and folding clothes.

An adjacent drawer-mounted ironing board folds out at sitting height to accommodate both chair and wheelchair users. Laundry and ironing supplies can be stored in one of the nearby hidden display/storage areas. The kitchen's rolling trolley is also useful for transporting clothes and supplies to and from other rooms.

Living/Dining Area: High ceilings and bamboo flooring set a "natural" theme for the area's light-filled flowing spaces. Translucent floor-to-ceiling roll-up window blinds fill the bright open space with soft natural light. Privacy, light control, and height adjustment are controlled remotely.

In the far corner, a raised remote-controlled gas-fired fireplace, flanked by thin vertical windows, offers a wide, chair-height hearth for sitting or wheelchair transfer. Recessed walls, fitted with easy-access cabinets and bookcases, provide overhead glare-free lighting for hanging artwork.

The area's generous maneuvering space also offers raised electrical outlets (18 in.) and lower light switches (42 in.), which reduce bending and reaching. Two 3-ft wide glass-paneled doors open onto two wheelchair-accessible outdoor areas: a dining patio with a gas barbeque hook-up and the central courtyard located in Zone D. "Easy-to-use" thermostats offer oversize, high-contrast, three-dimensional numerals with tactile feedback for those with sensory or tactile impairments.

Zone B

Library/Media/Activity Room: A wide, slip-resistant tile walkway extends from the entry hall, through the area, and connects with Zone C. To the left, resilient cork flooring extends to a row of desk-high windows that look out onto the central courtyard "oasis." To the right, recessed cabinets and shelves provide easy access to storage cabinets, shelves, and books. Recessed lighting complements the natural light controlled by the windows' adjustable blinds. A vertical pane of non-glare translucent glass diffuses the corner's built-in fluorescent light.

Guest Bedroom: The room's angled wall offers alternative furniture arrangements. The floor covering is commercial-grade, no-pad, low-pile carpeting, which provides easy-rolling wheelchair travel. Remote controlled, translucent floor-to-ceiling window blinds provide privacy and light control. The corner's built-in fluorescent light, diffused with a vertical pane of non-glare translucent glass, echo's the one in the library.

The room's 3-ft wide door has an 18-in. frosted glass sidelight, which permits natural light from the adjacent courtyard to enter. It also offers additional space for a person in a wheelchair to grasp the handle and pull the door open. A well-lit closet provides adjustable height shelves and clothes rack. An identical door with sidelight, directly across the walkway from the guest bedroom, offers access to the central patio and exercise pool.

Guest Bathroom: The guest bath serves both the public spaces and the guest bedroom. Twin 3-ft wide sliding pocket doors provide easy wheelchair access and maneuverability from either the guest bedroom or the connecting walkway. A skylight delivers diffused natural light for glare-free illumination.

The slip-resistant tile floor provides clear 5-ft diameter wheelchair turnabouts for easy access and transfer to the raised, off the floor, wall-hung water closet. The wall-mounted fingertip flusher can be removed, providing access to an in-wall water tank and flush mechanism. Blue accented stainless steel sidewall grab bars offer added safety and transfer assistance. Motion sensors control lights and fans.

The one-piece fiberglass roll-in shower is equipped with grab bars, an adjustable-height showerhead and hand spray, and an adjustable fold-down seat. An overhead built-in light provides glare-free lighting.

An off-the-floor vanity with a recessed front and a single-lever faucet adjusts in height to accommodate a chair, a wheelchair, or people of any height. Its one-piece solid surface top with integral basin has grasping fingertip edges. A row of incandescent bulbs above the medicine cabinet provides even illumination for makeup or shaving.

Zone C

Master Bedroom: One approaches the master bedroom through a wide tiled passageway flanked on one side by a floor-to ceiling, south-facing window–wall that borders the central courtyard. A roof overhang and translucent window shades shield the summer sun, keeping the floor and opposite wall in cool shadow. During the winter months the low-angled sunlight heats the floor and the adobe trombe wall, providing sustainable solar heat.

One enters the bedroom through a 3-ft wide sliding pocket door onto an expanse of bamboo flooring. A no-threshold glass-paneled door at the end of the window-wall opens into the central courtyard, permitting wheelchair access to the exercise pool.

At the opposite end of the room, four side-by-side sliding mirrored doors enclose a deep wall-wide closet system with fully adjustable clothes racks, shelves, and drawer units. Overhead recessed lighting provides glare-free illumination. A nearby set of narrow recessed shelves extends from floor to ceiling, offering a convenient place for books, photos, and mementos.

Master Bathroom: The bamboo floor of the master bedroom flows into the master bath, through a 3-ft sliding pocket door, which visually joins the two areas. The tub and vanity units encircle an open 5-ft diameter turnabout, affording easy wheelchair maneuverability.

The whirlpool tub is centered within a wide 17-in. high wall-to-wall surface for sitting or wheelchair transfer. A narrow shelf above the surrounding grab bars provides a short reach for bath items, plus added safety and stability for all ages and abilities. Side-mounted controls and a retracting hand-held showerhead offer easy water temperature and spray adjustment prior to and after entry.

Off-the-floor twin corner vanities adjust to accommodate users of any height; the mirrored medicine cabinets feature diffused sidelights. A 3-ft wide sliding pocket door, located between the two vanities, leads past pull-out drawer and storage units into a "wet room" containing the shower and water closet.

The no-slip, roll-in shower offers an adjustable-height fold-up seat and an adjustable hand-held showerhead. Stainless steel grab bars provide additional safety and security. The shower's glass door can be removed if additional maneuverability is required, utilizing the room's "wet room" function. The raised, wall-hung off-the-floor water closet makes floor cleaning easy, while stainless steel grab bars and a wall-hung telephone provide additional safety and convenience. Like the guest bath, motion sensors control lights and fans, and a skylight provides diffused natural daylight.

Zone D

The house wraps around a walled central courtyard and exercise pool, underscoring the advantage of indoor and outdoor living in the semi-arid climate of New Mexico. Accessed by level thresholds, the area is wheelchair accessible throughout. The raised flowerbeds and herb gardens offer the benefits of no-bend gardening. Wide level walkways, with 5-ft diameter turnabouts at each end, lead to and surround the self-cleaning lap pool. Sitting, dining, and entertaining areas are positioned beneath the roof overhangs in the courtyard and the patio adjacent to the dining area. The 5-ft high wall provides privacy, while offering dramatic views of the mesas and the western horizon beyond the Rio Grande.

Summary and Conclusion

It is time to explore better ways to design for the needs of a transgenerational population. Achieving results, however, requires us to re-conceptualize our association of age with disability. In reality:

- Young people grow old
- Disabled people grow old
- Young people can be disabled
- Old people can be disabled

Such understanding can help to change the prevailing mindset from one of *compliance* to one of *assistance*. Conventional practice suggests that "accessible" housing is best achieved through laws, statutes, standards, codes, or regulations.

History, however, clearly reveals the limitations of this approach. It takes more than just complying with mandated principles and dimensioned templates to achieve genuine transgenerational environments and products. Code compliance, while important, only addresses the *functional*, *utilitarian*, and *liability* aspects of accommodation. It does not address the environmental "HAT" values that help define our humanity, individuality, dignity, and self-worth.

As innovative examples of transgenerational designs begin to emerge, attract attention, stimulate sales, and create demand, the competition for a share of this swelling market will cause discerning designers, builders, and manufacturers to respond with an ever-increasing flow of attractive and desirable transgenerational designs.

I have learned that the best kind of design requires not simply the ability to envision a direction, not simply the courage to take an unpopular one, but also the belief that perseverance is essential for transforming rigid attitudes. There is no limit to what can be accomplished when everyone genuinely has a stake in the outcome and in achieving the possibilities.

Working – and aging – together, we can help provide a "heart transplant" for housing and live in the "world of tomorrow" that we collectively envision.

References

1. Arthritis Foundation. Arthritis facts (2007), http://www.arthritis.org/facts.php. Accessed 6 Sep 2007
2. S.M. Bauer, Invisible no longer: Newsletters June 2005. The Family Center on Technology and Disability (June 2005), http://www.fctd.info/resources/newsletters/displayNewsletter.php? newsletterID=10022. Accessed 20 Dec 2007

3. K. Bole, Graying Japan poses golden opportunity. San Francisco Business Times, 16 Dec 1996
4. K. Dychtwald, *Age Power: How the 21st Century Will be Ruled by the New Old* (Tarcher/Putnam, New York, 1996)
5. T. Feeheley, PROTEUS web site. Transgenerational design (2007), http://www.proteusdesign. com/transgenerational_design.aspx. Accessed 20 Dec 2007
6. General Motors, Futurama, New York World's Fair, 1964–65. Visitor handout booklet (General Motors Corporation, Detroit, 1964)
7. J.A. Leahy, Transgenerational design and product differentiators in product development (2004), http://t2rerc.buffalo.edu/pubs/conference/fulltext_2004_leahy_2.htm. Accessed 20 Dec 2007
8. National Safety Council, What are the odds of dying? (2006), http://www.nsc.org/mem/ educ/slips.htm. Accessed 6 Sep 2007
9. P.G. Peterson, *Gray Dawn: How the Coming Age Wave Will Transform America and the World* (Random House, New York, 1999)
10. J.J. Pirkl, *Transgenerational Design: Products for an Aging Population* (Wiley, New York, 1994)
11. J.J. Pirkl, A.L. Babic, *Guidelines and Strategies for Designing Transgenerational Products* (Copley, Acton, MA, 1988)
12. US Bureau of the Census, *Statistical Abstract of the United States: 1195*, 115th edn. (US Bureau of the Census, Washington, DC, 1995)
13. US Bureau of the Census, Table no. 1334. Population by Country: 1980 to 2000. *Statistical Abstract of the United States: 1997*, 117th edn. (US Bureau of the Census, Washington, DC, 1997)

Chapter 11
Service Innovation: Towards Designing New Business Models for Aging Societies

P. Reinmoeller

Abstract The aging of industrialized countries, led by Japan, requires firms to fundamentally rethink their business models. Firms active in Japan have to reconsider how to deal with unprecedented demographic change, which alters the resources available, to satisfy the shifting demand. Throughout the supply chain, aging of human talent and retirement requires firms to anticipate and prevent the negative effects of losing knowledge and skills. Adjusting the supply chain, developing new products, and/or augmenting products with services to target the silver market may offer short-term benefits but are not enough to sustain success. Firms need to develop and implement new business models leveraging service innovation to meet the needs in aging societies. Examples of service innovations and the case study of Seven-Eleven Japan and Yamato Transports' shared business model innovation illustrate how companies can seize the opportunities to create and capture more value in aging societies.

Introduction

Large-scale environmental changes and rivalry increase the volatility and uncertainty for companies [1]. Climate change, political instability, or shifts in the demographics such as the mass retirement of baby boomers in Japan and other aging societies (including the industrialized countries) all question organizational strategies and shake the foundations of corporations. By 2020, one retiree's pension in Japan, Germany, the UK, and France will rely on only two workers; a drop from three and a half in 2000. The successful one-child policy of Chinese administrations, intended to limit the growth of China's population, is expected to have unintended consequences including the rapid aging of China. These changes will affect societies, economies, and companies. Often highly disruptive, these changes lead to dwindling demand for companies' offerings, loss of knowledge through retirement and competitive hiring, and lack of quality supply. However, these changes also offer opportunities to develop new products and services, to conquer new markets, and to add more value to existing offerings. Opportunities are for the well-prepared; companies need to anticipate such large-scale shifts and embrace emerging opportunities in advance.

Japan lives in the future of the West. Japan is now the largest and richest emerging silver market. In other words, Japan may well be the lead silver market that allows for learning. The research, development, and design efforts of Japanese firms and foreign firms in Japan today may generate and even foreshadow superior products, service, and public design for decades to come. Unfortunately, many existing offerings are not able to satisfy the needs of aging societies; many products were designed for young segments and services are often accessories to tangible products. Better services not only need to make hardware usable, better services need to create new business opportunities by delivering value in a changing market. Today's organizations are designed to procure, produce, and promote products for the society of baby boomers. The future of aging societies demands different products and services and the organizations able to create these. Adapting to the requirements of the aging society can be done most effectively with business model innovation. While other chapters describe the shifts the leading economies are experiencing, clearly define the silver market, and expertly show how they influence company performance, this chapter focuses on the creation of new business models that are aligned to the emerging reality of silver markets.

Aging Societies and Business Issues

The size, financial volume, and sophistication of demand in the silver market offer opportunities for businesses capable of adjusting to the silver society. The notion that advancing age in society poses a threat only to industrialized countries is illusionary. How China's rapid development and the one-child policy contribute to this society's graying has been mentioned before. Industrial success has so far reduced birth rates in most industrialized nations and it seems not implausible that India will also succumb to this effect with enduring economic growth. While the scale of this global phenomenon, especially in areas such as healthcare and social support, focuses much attention, it should not be forgotten that the retiring generation of baby boomers is the richest generation of retirees ever in the USA, Europe, and especially in Japan. McKinsey reports the disposable income of baby-boomers in the USA to be 40% higher compared to the previous generation. The opportunity measured in terms of size of the market and the financial resourcefulness is unrivaled. At the same time, however, these relatively wealthy consumers are financially not ready to retire and are concerned about their future. In other words, the large demand for new offerings in financial services or social care waits to be served. Current supply often does not satisfy the sophisticated demand of these retirees who have seen their expectations rise over a lifetime and have become used to rising standards of living. This generation, having adapted to post-war, cold-war, and post-cold war times, is flexible and demanding. This offers large opportunities for firms able to create offerings that meet the needs in this silver market. Growing income disparity in Japan is linked to generational differences. While older generations still benefit from more generous employment contracts, members of younger generations often work part-time without lucrative salaries and benefits. Companies able to develop new business models are poised to seize the opportunities if they address the silver markets' new demand for financial wealth and security, a safe and adventurous life, healthy but not boring personal experiences, social activities, or opportunities to generate income after retirement.

Why Service Innovation in Japan Matters

The business potential of the silver market suggests that companies pay attention to the seismic shift. The potential for disruption of existing businesses and the challenges related to the sophisticated demand in the silver market require firms to innovate. Product innovation alone is not enough. Exploring some of the opportunities that businesses capable of adjusting to the silver society have, this chapter focuses on service innovation and why it matters. The broader economic development, the characteristics of demand in the silver market, and the scarcity of science show that our knowledge on developing new business models focused on services needs to grow.

Service Economies

Of late, the economy of each developed country becomes progressively more dominated by services [2]. The GDP in advanced nations has grown over the last decades mainly driven by growth in services, which are now the most important sector in all OECD economies. Since 1987 the share of services in advanced economies frequently exceeds 60% or even 70% of total GDP [3]. In times of resource scarcity and the importance of China as location of choice for many a manufacturer, it is often overlooked that not only India's service industries are growing rapidly. China's service sector had already reached 40% in 2005 and it continues to grow. Service innovation and growth in the service sector have driven the last decades' economic advances. However, a recent study by the OECD [4] suggests that in order to enhance overall economic growth in the future, improving the performance of the services sector is crucial. Growth is driven by factors such as globalization and innovation. Services innovation is an important driver for significant growth. In 2001, investment in R&D aiming at service innovation was as high as 40% of all business R&D in countries like Norway, Australia, and Denmark; service industries in Japan and Germany have shares of less than 10% of business R&D. Service innovation is needed to rekindle growth in advanced countries and prolong growth in countries that still rely on manufacturing.

Aging Markets Worldwide

Japan's aging society leads the development in other industrialized countries. We consider the characteristics of the silver market in the context of the world's demographic development. The global drama of senescence begins with the growth of world population; the population of 6.5 billion people today is expected to reach 9.1 billion in 2050. India is facing a baby boom. India's population will be the largest in 2050 with 1.628 billion compared with today's 1.104 billion. The average African mother will continue to give birth to more than five children. At the same time, the picture in the industrialized countries could not be more different. Fertility rates are declining in industrialized countries. Italy, Germany, Japan, and Korea watch their populations shrink. Improvements in living conditions together with better health care result in unprecedented longevity for large segments in these societies. This exacerbates the problem of seniority. The large population of senior people has to rely on fewer people to provide the basis for increasing living standards.

Looking at the net effect on global demographics, the ratio of elderly people aged 65+ stands today at 7.4%. At an elderly ratio of 7% societies are said to be aging, at 14% they are called aged societies. The world will be aged in 2040. By 2050 the forecasts see even more elderly; a group as strong as 16.1%. By then, 320 million elderly people will live in the developed countries and 1.14 billion in the developing countries.

Paying attention to the Japanese silver market is especially important because Japan's society is aging quickly, ahead of other countries. The general Japanese population peaked in 2006 [5]. In rural areas such as Shimane prefecture on the East Sea, from where young adults have long left for jobs in the cities, the population today has 26.7% aged 65 and above. Japan's population now has 19% seniors aged 65 and above. More than a million Japanese citizens are older than 90, twice as many as in 1996. Japan has 23,000 centenarians today. By 2050, about 40% of Japan's population will be over 65 years old. These elderly people want to maintain or even improve the high quality of their life. Japanese firms need to learn – quickly – how to serve its elderly and how to keep the younger generations needed to rekindle growth of the Japanese economy and society.

Service Innovation

Innovation

Reviewing the academic literature, one finds much theoretical and empirical research that describes, explains, and offers guidelines for the development of efficient supply chains and new products. Being an important area of innovation, developing new products is by far not the only area in which innovation is needed. Research on service innovation is still rare. Services are intangible and their production and consumption is often simultaneous. These commonly accepted characteristics of services make managing for new services more challenging than managing for new products. This has resulted in many offerings where services are tied to products and are often bundled with hardware. Packaged in this way, services appear more manageable but these ad-on services, such as maintenance or repair activities, often remain limited by the link to a physical product. Important as these activities may be, in focusing on them companies forgo the potential of more fundamental service innovation.

In recent research on innovation, three important themes have emerged that go beyond the development of products:

1. Academics have devoted much attention to specific functions, mainly management of technology and of research and development. Aiming to understand productivity increases of basic and applied research, many articles develop and test ideas on how management of technology and R&D is linked to performance, often measured by patents registered.
2. Management of knowledge, especially tacit knowledge to foster product innovation, has been a particularly rich area since the mid-1990s [6]. Creating knowledge individually or in small teams and disseminating it across units and organizations explains the successes of leading firms in industries such as the automotive, electronics, or optical and mechanical equipment industries.
3. Outside innovation (as a new approach to tap into external resources) has received much attention under the labels of inclusive or open or innovation [7–9]. Linked to entrepreneurship and new business development is the creation and integration of new venture leverage start-ups as the test-beds for new services and new kinds of organization, in order to develop ideas quickly by interacting with markets.

In what follows I shall focus on the way companies renew their capabilities and organize for ambidexterity [10–12], i.e., develop new business models by integrating specialized activities and creating new services.

Services

In silver markets the importance of services is exacerbated because service innovation has the potential to create value and meet the requirements of sophisticated and wealthy customers who experience disadvantage and constraints coming with age. Services, according to [13] are "deeds, processes and performances"[1] to satisfy customers [14, 15], either as supporting good and/or as the process for making this good. Service is defined as a process of more or less intangible activities that often take place in interactions between the customer and service employees or

---

[1] Lists of services include wholesale and retail trade, transportation and warehousing, information, finance, insurance, professional, scientific, and technical, management of companies, administrative and support, education, healthcare and social assistance, arts, entertainment and recreation, accommodation and food services, or public administration (e.g., US Bureau of Census).

artifacts, aimed at adding value for customers. The non-physical character of services hinders product and price comparisons [16]. Consumers cannot easily analyze the cost–value ratio given that the products are invisible and service quality is assessed based on their experience of the service (customer satisfaction). Customers use key components to judge a company's service [17], such as physical facilities, equipment, personnel and communication materials as well as intangibles such as reliability, responsiveness, assurance, and empathy.

Without including the level of integration with products, Välikangas and Lehtinen [18] categorize three types of services, which they term generic, specialized, and customized services. Generic services are categorized as basic services in which the focus lies on low price. Specialized services require resources or skills to create a superior or unique performance vis-à-vis competitors. Strategic service is customized services. New business models can include service innovations of the three types with different emphasis on key components. Often service innovations are hybrids of the three at different levels of integration with products.

Changing Business Models with Service Innovations

The term "business model" is defined in different ways [19]. In particular, the proliferation of information and communications technologies in the last 20 years has led to a broad discussion of the choice of the right business models [20–23]. Magretta [24] argues that a good business model stays important to every successful organization, whether it is an established player or a new venture. The foremost objective of a business model is to abstract the business [25] and to organize a firm and allows serving its customers in an effective way [26] Amit and Zott [27] define a business model as the structure, the design of transaction content, and governance as ways to create value while exploiting business opportunities.

We extend and clarify in two ways. First, better business models are systems that exploit opportunities and create value by using the intertwined and complementary nature of tangible and intangible elements. Raising the importance of services beyond the level of repair and maintenance to a vital element of the total offering, services can help differentiate more forcefully and to renew firms. Consider how Dell established itself as a leading computer retailer by developing customer service delivered by telephone marketing, complementing its system of low-cost assembly [28,29]. Second, better business models are dynamically expanding by interacting with customers and business partners. The dynamic expansion is opportunity-driven and resource-driven. Opportunities and resources reveal themselves in interaction. The business model allows integrating new opportunities and resources and helps to exploit them with existing resources. Amazon.com illustrates this point well. The online sites' ability to generate recommendations is one of the most important marketing and sales instruments, and it was developed by Amazon to enhance its basic proposition in the business of selling books. Multiple ways of offering suggestions to customers of the bookstore today drive not only book sales but also allowed Amazon to more quickly raise the profile of its ventures into other categories.

Being a vital part of a company's business model and service, innovation is an effective way to create new business models that withstand disruption by seismic shifts. Consider how Apple Computer has changed by designing its new business model by service innovation. Apple Computer's business model was based on selling computer hardware and earning a premium on computer software. Since the introduction of the iPod, Apple has entered the market space of portable music. The service innovation that brought about the new business model is linked to making the vast archives of the music industry searchable online with Apple's easy-to-use interface and expanding this into the online retail business iTunes. Apple now benefits from low margins on content because the music sales drive hardware sales. The dynamic expansion of its business since the introduction of the iPod into movies and with the recent launch of the iPhone shows how service innovation together with the complementary elements of its business model allow for exploration and exploitation of new opportunities.

Designing and Implementing Service Innovation

Designing and implementing service innovation has helped outstanding Japanese companies to develop new business models to meet the demand of silver markets. The cases presented below are based on empirical research conducted in Japan since 2005. Interviews, field observation, and archival research yielded a rich database from which the following illustrations of service innovation were selected. The cases show how service innovation enabled successful business model design and how two Japanese companies lead in satisfying the needs of the silver market.

Seven-Eleven Japan (SEJ) is the franchise system of convenience stores known also in other countries. Yamato Transport's Takkyubin (YTT) is a small-lot haulage service, which is less known abroad but illustrates clearly how important service innovations can be in creating value for senior segments in the market. As will be explained later, SEJ and YTT enhance the utility of each other's offering in a subsidiary of SEJ called Seven-Meal Service.

Seven-Eleven Japan

SEJ is the largest convenience store franchise operator in Japan. Concentrating with more than 11,000 stores in the larger metropolitan areas of Japan, SEJ has seen sales and profits grow for decades. SEJ's vision to adapt to changing customer needs led Seven-Eleven from introducing the concept of a convenience store in Japan to becoming one of the most admired firms in Japan. Initially licensing the Seven-Eleven brand and system, SEJ has over time succeeded in outshining the original owner of the concept. SEJ's continuous service innovation has turned the operator of convenience stores into an infrastructure platform supportive of Japanese lifestyle. Four points explain how SEJ continuously innovates: from product to service orientation, network of stores, assortment, and item-by-item stock management:

1. Seven-Eleven's brand name and practice emphasizes long opening hours, i.e., a store that opens early, stays open until late and sells convenience items. SEJ has emphasized the idea that adaptive capability is what underpins its success. Consequently, service innovations such as extending into financial services or online business have become successful service elements of a strengthened business model.
2. SEJ's extensive network of stores is accessible to large parts of the population. In metropolitan areas people live within walking distance of the next convenience store. In the popular press, this omnipresence has led to comparing SEJ's stores to private storage rooms for customers, i.e., powder room, kitchen, and refrigerator. Taken for granted to such an extent, the stores fulfill the needs of many who are not willing to stock home product or drive to a hypermarket.
3. Seven-Eleven has over the years developed a system that allows it to offer a standard group of basic offerings that are an important part of the assortment. These include, for instance, cosmetics, newspapers and magazines, snacks and beverages, and fresh bread and rice dishes. Besides these taken-for-granted products that can be found in all shops, SEJ developed a system to develop differentiated assortments so to adapt to the local demand even at a single store. Location and demographics are important in shaping the demand. Shops close to schools, for example, carry different items to shops close to office buildings. Stores in areas where many families reside have different offerings to stores in areas where more elderly people live. Other dimensions also matter; monitoring weather changes, SEJ's headquarters offer locally specific weather forecasts to help in adapting the assortment in time. New product development also benefits a lot from SEJ's awareness of local differences, which is a source of new ideas.
4. Item by item stock-keeping, together with sophisticated logistics, enables SEJ to avoid running out of stock. Local employees place orders based on the hypothesis (location-specific demand forecasts for items). These hypotheses are immediately tested by objective data available from the company's point-of-sales systems. Avoiding overstocking and opportunity loss are key elements in gaining trust, increasing reliability, and in enticing customers into trying some new offering.

Seven-Eleven's emphasis on offerings and service innovations have turned a retailer into a taken-for-granted institution providing services such as selling theatre tickets, postal services, and financial services. Accessible, innovative, and reliable, the stores are a supportive platform, especially for elderly customers because the small-scale mom-and-pop and neighborhood retailers are quickly disappearing. In the silver market, convenience stores fulfill important functions as they help seniors to manage their own lives and postpone the need of some for senior homes and caretakers.

Yamato Transport's Takkyubin

YTT service innovation has changed what haulage means in Japan. The YTT delivery comprises haulage of parcels, packages, suitcases for travelers, and also golf bags, clubs, or skis. Originally, haulage had been a packages service for mainly corporate customers. After years of striving to become a company that would transport any quantity to anywhere in Japan, Masao Ogura, who was the president of Yamato between 1971 and 1987, reconsidered the strategy [30]. The insight that Yamato and its customers might be better off if the firm offered only a focused service triggered a series of changes that created YTT and helped the company to regain profitability and reputation.

In January 1976, YTT inaugurated the home-to-home service with a distribution network that was modeled on the hub and spoke system of airlines. Satisfying demand from households required that Yamato's office network would expand. Tokyo and its surrounding prefectures were covered with a next-day delivery service. If a truck was to go to a household ¥500 were surcharged. Initially, YTT chose liquor shops as Yamato's agents for drop off and pick up because of their presence in every town. Today, SEJ has become a powerful partner.

The business model behind YTT's service innovation helped to charge standardized prices and to generate cash immediately (cash payment). Two years later the fundamental change towards the new business model became apparent when YTT withdrew from large-lot haulage and unattractive haulage contracts to concentrate on small-lot haulage. Five years after the start YTT broke even.

Four important points need to be made, i.e., delivery network, service standardization, next-day delivery, increasing quality:

1. YTT's delivery network covers Japan, which allows easy drop-off and pick-up at all locations. This service greatly increases the value YTT provides to customers.
2. Large simplification of package sizes, delivery rhythms, and prices made sending and receiving by YTT much easier for customers. YTT's house-to-house haulage system increases the ease with which citizens, especially seniors, can send and receive parcels.
3. Since 1981, YTT has increased the area in which it guarantees next-day delivery and introduced on-time delivery to satisfy the customers' need to have parcels delivered when they are at home and not when they are absent. YTT's service innovation was so successful that the number of 150 million parcels delivered in 1984 exceeded that of the Japanese postal system.
4. Increasing quality was an important part of the new business model design. YTT developed an excellent reputation for customer service and quality of delivery, despite the time pressure on delivery staff. YTT also increased its appeal further by the introduction of haulage of chilled cargoes introduced in 1988.

YTT's emphasis on service innovations has turned haulage from a service for corporations into a service for families and individuals to help their haulage needs. Today YTT has become a taken-for-granted institution providing services indispensable in large metropolitan areas where traveling with luggage is difficult or where quick delivery is needed. In the silver market, YTT fulfills important functions in helping seniors to manage their haulage needs.

Seven Meal Service

SEJ sells and YTT delivers goods. These complementary services of SEJ and YTT are now being taken beyond this evident link of firms in retail and logistics. The development from the first relationship to Seven Meal Service (7Meal), a new subsidiary of SEJ, is evidence of a dynamically expanding business model that has been jointly constructed by two companies.

Selling a wide variety of meals and submeals through catalogues, its website, and the Seven-Eleven chain of convenience stores, 7Meals offers also home delivery of the preordered meals. SEJ's skills and experience with fresh food sold in its stores was instrumental in developing 7Meal practices. This first-hand experience helped to gain a first understanding of what kind of meals may be needed at which price levels. Allying with YTT helped to solve the issue of affordable yet high quality transport. Interacting with customers and business partners, SEJ and YTT together exploit new opportunities and develop new capabilities to increase the value added by their service innovation, i.e., a for-profit, large-scale meal delivery service that includes the silver market as a key target segment. In what follows I illustrate how 7Meal exploits opportunities in the silver market and creates value by leveraging the complementary skills and capabilities of SEJ and YTT.

The alliance between SEJ and YTT had so far been centered on the SEJ stores serving as pick-up and drop-off points and complementing YTT's haulage system. Patrons leave their parcel so that YTT staff will pick it up and bring it to its destination, or the recipient may pick it up at any local store. This contributes to Seven-Eleven's taken-for-grantedness in everyday life in Japan, or to put it differently it has be come an institution. SEJ serves an assortment of prepackaged, often perishable, goods. Since 1988 YTT has offered Cool Takkyubin, the service of chilled cargo haulage, which enabled customers to send any products found at the convenience store and more to locations all over Japan. Having thus extended its capabilities, YTT's skills and know-how opened new opportunities for SEJ with the delivery of freshly prepared or on-demand merchandise. SEJ could now start thinking of selling and delivering fresh snacks anytime or proper meals and submeals (courses) for breakfast, lunch, and dinner.

In August 2000, SEJ established Seven Meal Service, a subsidiary focusing on home delivery of food and meals, which started services in September 2000 in the Tokyo metropolitan area. Since starting the service, 7Meal has been expanding the area covered by its service over 7 years. In summer 2007 Hokkaido was finally included in the coverage area, effectively completing full coverage of Japan. 7Meal had to address three main obstacles that made rapid extension of coverage difficult: variety, freshness, price. Learning from interaction with customers and slowly rolling out its business, 7Meal overcame the obstacles by building volume, cooperation, and affordable quality.

Successful meal services need to offer enough *variety* to guarantee being able to satisfy heavy users. Variety has two dimensions that increase costs considerably: increasing the choice on each given day increases the cost of new product development and production while at the same time it also reduces the sales of each specific dish (diminishing the benefit from scale economies, given stable demand). Variation over time means that 7Meals cannot enjoy cost benefits of repetition and increases the cost of new product development. In 2000, when 7Meal started operations, SEJ operated only about 8000 stores in Japan. In 2007 it operates 11,750 in Japan and 32,254 worldwide. The increase of almost 50% of stores in Japan helped SEJ to improve the economics of its supply chain.

Freshness of meals requires efficient production and delivery fit to the nature of the meals. Increasing economies of *scale* and learning increase SEJ's ability to reduce the production-related costs. Chilled transport, especially in the warm and hot seasons or Southern areas, is a critical capability only offered by YTT. This ability complements SEJ's business model design for 7Meal. Delivery of perishable meals to the home is costly. Allying itself with YTT, 7Meal is able to benefit from YTT's extensive service network and SEJ's shared history of a successful cooperation. The transport costs for each 7Meal delivery of ¥200 are charged in addition to the cost of the products, which range from approximately ¥500 to ¥2000. 7Meal offers its customers the choice between front-door deliveries by YTT or pick-up at a designated SEJ convenience store.

Meals services need to be affordable and may not compromise on quality. Building up the scale of operations over 7 years, the price–quality ratio has been upgraded continuously. 7Meal chose an alliance with YTT for reasons of quality and price. The longstanding cooperation between SEJ and YTT reassured SEJ that YTT would conduct deliveries professionally at highest quality levels. YTT offers to deliver a single meal for about ¥200 to the doorstep of a customer, which is much lower than the comparable delivery price for a parcel. Today 7Meals has 170,000 users, more than 50% of the patrons being seniors aged over 60. The other half chooses the service because of lack of time or preference. About half of the users pick up their meals at a close-by location. The number is somewhat smaller for the senior customers; however, many also choose the pick-up option because they enjoy the flexibility and also the social interaction with staff. Walking to the store, looking around and chatting with SEJ staff offers them an opportunity to complement their meals with other products and to overcome isolation by having a chat with the sales clerk.

Summary and Conclusion

Having shown how the aging of societies exacerbates the need for service innovation and renewal of business models, this chapter has explained how service innovation can help to change business models for the special case of Japan, the country that precedes all industrialized societies on the journey to senescence. Japan's companies are among the first to feel the changes in the demand for services and supply in the workforce related to the demographic changes that are occurring. Developing the notion of business models in the literature, I extend the concept by emphasizing service innovation as a means to better explore and exploit the opportunities of the silver market. Introducing the dynamics of new business model development as driven by service innovation, this chapter shows how interaction with customers (SEJ and YTT) and with business partners (Seven Meal Service) expands the range of what is possible and – over time – the skills and capabilities needed to seize opportunities.

Japan is a showcase for how societies change and its demographic changes antecede those in other markets. Such a lead market offers the attentive observer key lessons to be learned. Researchers need to emphasize more the service economy in seeking to build theory that better explains how innovation happens and how it matters. Dynamic capabilities and ambidextrous systems are here suggested to be the result of continued infusion of tacit knowledge. It is not well understood precisely how this upgrading of dynamic capabilities and innovation through informal, intangible, and implicit knowledge happens. The questions of "where do dynamic capabilities come from?" and "how do they emerge from tacit knowledge" have set the agenda for more empirical research.

Four lessons seem to be especially useful for decision-makers in business and governmental organizations, i.e., infrastructure and tacit knowledge, ambidextrous systems, innovation as strategy, and private solutions for public issues:

1. The importance of infrastructure to exploit opportunities in aging societies is shown. Lower mobility of seniors leads to more efforts to provide services and goods at home or at convenient locations nearby. However, retail outlets or car parks alone do not satisfy the new demand. Accumulating tacit knowledge over time through interaction with customers and partners in the supply chain is indispensable for innovation and renewal. At SEJ the shop clerks and at YTT the drivers of delivery trucks become invested in their regional network and highly attuned to the needs and behavior of "their" customers. While companies need to think how they can tap the tacit knowledge of stakeholders, regional government or country leadership needs to pay attention to what is happening in the leading silver market to learn from success and to avoid failure.
2. The widespread networks of SEJ's convenience stores and the YTT haulage system are two models for companies in industrialized countries because they show how one business model manages the paradox of pursuing localization and customization without the need to sacrifice scale. Exploring the new and emergent needs of customers helps the companies to offer more value. Safeguarding that volumes remain sufficiently large so that the benefits of economies of scale accrue to both firms, they successfully integrate scale and variety.
3. SEJ and YTT illustrate how the quest for innovation is the core of their strategy. The continuous expansion of their range of ideas and businesses show the strong growth orientation. The complementary services and the hardware platform allow tacit knowledge and insights to lead the business model to renewal.
4. Government intervention to solve societal problems can sometimes be flawed; often it is less efficient than market-based solutions. Market-based solutions often

seek profits more than the public good. This chapter shows how profit-oriented firms can renew and expand their business models and at the same time provide the organizational basis for one aspect of taking care of the elderly.

These four lessons learned seem useful for individual companies but also for regions or countries that also face the arrival of the silver market. Infusing tacit knowledge into organizational systems can enable firms to overcome paradox, i.e., to become ambidextrous, and succeed in contributing to the solution of societal issues by introducing new services and business model innovation.

References

1. R.A. D'Aveni, *Hypercompetition: Managing the Dynamics of Strategic Manoeuvring* (Free Press, New York, 1994)
2. D. Iacobucci, R.T. Rust, S. Shugan, V.A. Zeithaml, American Marketing Association, 10 (1999)
3. OECD, The Service Economy, Science Technology Industry Business Policy Forum Series (2001)
4. A. Woefl, The service economy in OECD countries, OECD Science, Technology and Industry Working Papers, 2005/3 (2005)
5. Ministry of Internal Affairs and Communications, *Statistical Handbook of Japan* (Statistics Bureau, Tokyo, 2007)
6. I. Nonaka, H. Takeuchi, *The Knowledge-Creating Company: How Japanese Companies Create the Dynamics of Innovation* (Oxford University Press, New York, 1995)
7. H. Chesborough, *Open Innovation: The New Imperative for Creating and Profiting from Technology* (Harvard Business School Press, Cambridge, MA, 2003)
8. E. Hippel von, MIT Sloan Manage. J. **42**(4), 82 (2001)
9. P. Seybold, *Outside Innovation* (Collins, New York, 2006)
10. K.M. Eisenhardt, J.A. Martin, Strateg. Manage. J. **21**, 1105 (2000)
11. C. O'Reilly, M. Tushman, Ambidexterity as a dynamic capability: resolving the innovator's dilemma, Stanford Graduate School of Business, Research Paper Series, No. 1963 (2007)
12. D. Teece, G. Pisano, A. Shuen, Strateg. Manage. J. **18**, 509 (1997)
13. V.A. Zeithaml, M.J. Bitner, D.D. Gremler, *Services Marketing: Integrating Customer Focus Across the Firm* (McGraw-Hill Irwin, New York, 2006)
14. C. Grönroos, Eur. J. Mark. **18**, 36 (1984)
15. C. Grönroos, Manag. Serv. Qual. **11**, 150 (2001)
16. L. Berry, M.S. Yadav, Sloan Manage. Rev. **37**, 41 (1996)
17. L.L. Berry, V.A. Zeithaml, A. Parasuraman, Sloan Manage. Rev. **31**(4), 29 (1990)
18. L. Välikangas, U. Lehtinen, Int. J. Serv. Ind. Manage. **5**, 72 (1994)
19. M. Morris, M. Schindehutte, J. Richardson, J. Allen, J. Small Bus. Strategy **17**, 27 (2006)
20. R.E.S. Boulton, B.D. Libert, S.M. Samek, J. Bus. Strategy **21**, 29 (2000)
21. K. Chaharbaghi, C. Fendt, R. Willis, Manage. Decis. **41**, 372 (2003)
22. S. Forge, Futures **25**(9), 923 (1993)
23. S. Shafer, H.J. Smith, J. Linder, Bus. Horiz. **48**, 199 (2005)
24. J. Magretta, Harvard Business Review, 10 (2001)
25. J.A. Zackman, *Concepts of the framework for enterprise architecture* (Zackam International, Los Angeles, 1996)
26. D.W. Mitchell, C.B. Coles, *Leader to Leader* **29**, 12 (2003)
27. R. Amit, C. Zott, Strateg. Manage. J. **22**, 493 (2001)
28. D. Darlin, Dell's world isn't what it used to be. The New York Times Company, 1 (2006)
29. K.L. Kraemer, J. Dedrick, S. Yamashiro, Inf. Soc. **16**, 5 (2000)
30. M. Ogura, Watakushino rirekisho. *Nippon Keizan Shimbun* (2001)

Part III
Marketing for the Silver Market

Chapter 12
Current Strategies in the Retail Industry for Best-Agers

G. Arnold and S. Krancioch

Abstract In view of the current demographic transformation, the retail trade faces a clear challenge to reconsider its existing concepts, and to include older target groups in its marketing planning to an increased degree. In the present paper, we will look first at the factor of location, one of the central success factors in the retail trade. Next, we will examine the preferences of German best-agers for certain types of businesses, such as shops close to home rather than out-of-town malls. We then proceed to discuss the effects of changed customer needs on the design of the assortments and of packaging because of the customer's decreasing physical capabilities. We will present examples from the daily practice of the trade. In conclusion, we will provide a brief overview of foreseeable trends in the retail trade.

Introduction

In view of the current demographic transformation, the retail trade faces a clear challenge to reconsider its existing concepts, and to include older target groups in its marketing planning to an increased degree. In the present paper, we will look first at the factor of location, one of the central success factors in the retail trade. Next, we will examine the preferences of German best-agers for certain types of businesses, such as shops close to home rather than out-of-town malls. We then proceed to discuss the effects of changed customer needs on the design of the assortments and of packaging because of the customer's decreasing physical capabilities. We will present examples from the daily practice of the trade. In conclusion, we will provide a brief overview of foreseeable trends in the retail trade.

The Retail Trade in the Face of Demographic Change

An adjustment to the needs of the older customers is necessary in the retail trade, since this area has, in some respects, a great need to catch up with developments, and because the potential of the best-agers is being underestimated. This very heterogeneous target group includes people over 50 years of age with different socio-demographic characteristics, value orientations, leisure time activities, and consumer preferences. It must always be considered that, regardless of the particular leisure preferences, interests, or consumption habits of older people, they share the basic wish to supply themselves via retail shopping as long as they are physically able to do so. The spending power of the German best-agers is also attractive. Those aged 50–59 spent about €24,000 in the retail trade during 2005. The 60+ generation had €20,000 per annum to spend, giving them €1000 more purchasing power, on average, than the target groups through age 49.

The demographic impact on retail trade substantially affects such matters as decisions on the location of commercial establishments. The demands of older target groups regarding convenience and comfort in shopping absolutely coincide with those of younger target groups. Purchase outlets must be accessible, and designed in such a way that the consumers feel good there [17].

The specific wishes and needs of older customers for the retail trade include (see p. 58 in [16]):

* Entry at ground level or by elevator
* Safe place to put shopping carts
* No turnstiles
* Wide corridors and short distances in markets
* Shallower shopping carts that are easier to push
* Help when shopping, personal contact, and opportunities for social contact
* Clear identification of sections at eye-level
* Products always located at the same place
* Easily legible price labels
* Pricing on items, not on shelves
* Magnifying glasses at the shelves
* Less depth in freezers and refrigerators
* No need to bend down or reach up
* Small portions and light packaging
* Less technology (e.g., bottle-return machines)
* Places to rest
* Standing supports at cash registers; less hectic atmosphere there
* Possibility to leave items in shopping carts during checking
* Packaging help and delivery service; installation of equipment
* Easily legible sales slips
* Convenient transportation of purchased items to the car

Effects on Location and Types of Business

Scientific examinations by the Institute for Trade Research at the University of Cologne (IFH) and by BBDO Sales GmbH confirm that two thirds (67%) of those aged 50–89 in Germany usually shop near home. More than half (52%) often shop in pedestrian shopping districts in city centers. Conveniently located out-of-town mall sites with good connections to transportation are frequented by 41% of those surveyed; shopping centers achieved 39% (cf. Fig. 12.1).

Even if older consumers frequently shop within walking distance and in city centers (39%), in malls outside of town (30%), and in shopping centers (29%), a significant difference is still apparent between the frequency of shopping close to home versus that at more remote locations.

Of those surveyed, 29% shop close to home, but avoid inner-city pedestrian districts; 37% shop close to home, but not in out-of-town malls; and 38% shop close to home, but not in shopping centers.

With regard to single age groups in the 50–89 range, it turns out that close-to-home locations for shops enjoy high market acceptance values in all groups (cf. Fig. 12.2). Although the willingness to shop in out-of-town malls increases slightly among those aged 50–69, it drops again noticeably among 70-year-olds. The 70–89 age group prefers to do its shopping close to home. All in all, it can be stated that

Where do you frequently shop?			
	Proportion of persons surveyed	Close-to-home and ...	Close-to-home, but not...
Close to home	67%	-	-
Inner-city pedestrian district	52%	39%	28%
Convenient out-of-town malls	41%	30%	37%
Shopping center	39%	29%	38%
n = 1370/multiple answers/rounded)			

Fig. 12.1 Locations frequented [14]

Prefered locations				
Age	Close to home	Convenient out-of-town malls	Shopping centers	Pedestrian shopping districts
50-59 years (n = 561)	67%	42%	43%	57%
60-69 years (n = 450)	69%	46%	43%	58%
70-79 years (n = 234)	63%	38%	31%	39%
80-89 years (n = 53)	70%	26%	13%	38%
(Values rounded)				

Fig. 12.2 Location preference, by age group [14]

older consumers prefer to shop within walking distance of home, and patronize inner-city pedestrian shopping districts, shopping centers, and out-of-town malls ever less frequently with advancing age [14].

In order to meet the demand of easy accessibility, the location of a market must be chosen so that it has an optimum connection to public transportation and to the road network. Customers want to shop near their place of residence or their workplace, and find the products they need quickly.

Up to the mid-1990s, the retail trade still pursued the concept of targeted steering of customers, forcing them to first walk past products of irregular demand (such as textiles, magazines, and CDs) before crossing the drinks and preserved-foods section and finally reaching the fresh-foods section. Today, there has been a change in attitude in that respect. In order to stimulate the customers to spontaneous purchases in specialty-store centers for example, clothing stores are purposely placed in various locations. Here, customers actually consumed up to a third more than they had planned. Overall, however, drops in sales volume were registered, since consumers shifted to other shopping centers that offered greater convenience.

Thus, a self-service market would have to be designed so that it would be up to the customer to decide in which order s/he wished to visit various sections. For specialty-store centers, such a reorganization could mean, for example, grouping several retailers that supply irregularly required products. Thus, clothing stores oriented toward different price levels could be located directly adjacent to one another. The establishment of a discount store and a drugstore in the immediate vicinity of a self-service department store would enable customers to obtain all their regularly required products without moving long distances [17].

The location decisions of retailers are usually closely connected to the selected type of business. The preferences of consumers for certain types of business must therefore also be included in considerations. Figure 12.3 shows that over 50-year-olds most frequently shop at discount stores (82.1%) and at supermarkets

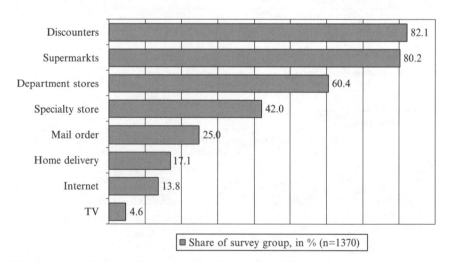

□ Share of survey group, in % (n=1370)

Fig. 12.3 Types of business frequented (50 to 89-year-olds) [14]

(80.2%). Of those surveyed by the IFH, 60.4% frequently shop at department stores, while 42% stated specialty stores. In that survey, 25% described themselves as frequent customers of mail-order houses, 17.1% stated that they often made use of home-delivery, and no less than 13.8% frequently shopped on the Internet (cf. Fig. 12.3). Overall, the best-agers prefer types of business that supply their daily needs and are typically located close to their residences. Other business types, which are more likely to provide for long-term requirements, are less frequently visited.

It should be noted with regard to particular age groups that those aged 50–69 like to shop in department stores and specialty stores, but that this frequency drops considerably among customers over 70. The trend of ever-fewer people frequenting various types of business is also shown in Fig. 12.4. This suggests strongly that best-agers also shop ever less frequently in supermarkets and discount stores with advancing age. Moreover, it is evident that home services are used mainly by the 70–79 age group. The 50–59 age group, however, like to shop on the Internet and by mail order (cf. Fig. 12.4).

These descriptions strongly suggest that locations near residential areas are likely to gain in significance again in the future [15]. Particularly, markets with small floor space stand a good chance of becoming close-to-home suppliers, and will be able to score points with personal contact, good counseling, and friendly service [21]. Already, a trend by discount stores to move away from the periphery and towards close-to-home and inner-city locations can be observed. Shopping centers too are being increasingly located in city centers [15].

The Consequences for Assortment Structuring and Packaging Design

In addition to location selection and store design, there is another problem involving the products in the market itself. Here, the packaging is often a problem for older customers as all senses (such as sight and touch) deteriorate with age, as

Preferred business types							
Age	Supermarkets	Discounters	Department stores	Specialty stores	Home delivery	Catalog / Mail order	Internet
50–59 years (n = 561)	80%	84%	62%	40%	18%	31%	23%
60–69 years (n = 450)	81%	84%	65%	47%	15%	20%	8%
70–79 years (n = 234)	85%	78%	59%	73%	20%	21%	5%
80–89 years (n = 53)	74%	72%	40%	28%	15%	19%	0%
(Values rounded)							

Fig. 12.4 Business form preferences, by age [14]

do motor skills and strength [10]. Viewed in this light, packaging is often not user-friendly [5]. A study by the European Association of Carton and Cartonboard Manufacturers (ProCarton) confirms that only 19% of the over-60s are very satisfied with the packaging of products. On the other hand, 83% of older customers stated that, for them, packaging is the decisive factor in purchasing [2]. Packaging can thus become an indicator for the success or failure of a product at the point of sale [16]. To attain a maximum level of comfort for the customer, the first thing should be to provide smaller packaging. A 10-kg package of detergent, while it may be an advantage for a family, is often a problem for older customers, since they may not be able to transport it home due to physical restrictions [5]. Another problem is too-complicated sealing mechanisms, which make it difficult to take the product out [16]. It is therefore not surprising that 36% of the more mature customers surveyed state that they would not repeat the purchase of a product if they could not open it comfortably [11].

The visual design is also very important. Thus, matted packaging is recommended to avoid a dazzling effect. An appropriately large type-face should be used for marking, due to deteriorating eyesight, and the color selection should avoid using blue and green, which older people can easily confuse [16]. Older consumers in particular include many diabetics, for whom the information on ingredients on the packaging must be easily recognizable. For this reason the following statements should be present:

• Exact price
• Expiration date
• Composition
• Method of application (dosage, preparation)
• Warnings for certain target groups (people suffering from allergies)
• Safety regulations and disposal instructions
• Information about manufacturer and origin

Unfortunately, this information is often entirely lacking, or only available in English, which can cause a problem for people whose native language is not English. Due to bad packing design, mistaken purchases often occur. This true not only for older customers, but also for younger ones, who are often pressed for time [5].

For this reason, the folding box manufacturer Edelmann has developed a number of packing solutions to meet these new requirements. From the point of view of the manufacturer, these involve particularly understandable instructions for opening and closing mechanisms, legible names and information, and contrasting backgrounds. Under the brand name CEasy, various innovative packaging types are now provided, including sliding packaging with recessed grips, column-shaped packaging with large flaps to be grasped, or folding boxes with opening aids (cf. Fig. 12.5) [2].

Moreover, the packing design is closely connected to the assortment selection, since here too certain characteristics can be determined for the older target groups. For example, not only the small packet sizes already mentioned are advantageous here, but organic products also have a high value [5]. This was also confirmed by a survey by TNS Infratest. A high affinity for organic products was ascertained,

Fig. 12.5 Packing solutions by the Edelmann company [3]

precisely among older people over 50 years of age [19]. This is due mainly to cultural, religious, and idealistic values. The consumer behavior of persons with this characteristic combination of values is regarded as extremely demanding. A high-quality diet is of great importance for them. The great confidence of this target groups in the organic-food quality label is also due to this factor [19].

Due to the low price sensitivity of the best-agers, there is great leeway in brand choice from a marketing point of view, particularly as regards trade brands. According to a current survey by KMPG, trade brands are enjoying ever-greater market acceptance, and are no longer to be found only in the lower price segment. On the contrary, given the largely similar assortment in the food retail trade for example, they can serve as a mark of distinction. The VivaVital and BioBio products of the discount store Plus, which have long since attained the price level of classic brand-name products, are successful examples here [9]. In addition, the convenience aspect of the products is very important for older people. A former professional woman who used to reach automatically for the frozen-food rack will continue to do so in old age. For that reason, the per capita consumption of frozen food more than doubled between 1983 and 2003 (cf. Fig. 12.6). This convenience boom thus also represents a great potential for the retail trade [18].

But, convenience alone is not enough for the older target group. A healthy diet is very important to them. The high value they place on maintaining their health is confirmed by surveys conducted by the Allensbach Institute, a polling agency. Older people in the 60–69 age group are the leaders here (cf. Fig. 12.7).

Convenience and staying healthy have long stopped being a contradiction [9]. In that sense, it is not surprising that best-agers prefer products that contain many additives of vitamins and vital substances, such as dairy products and local products. Thus, health and functional foods offer good growth opportunities for the retail

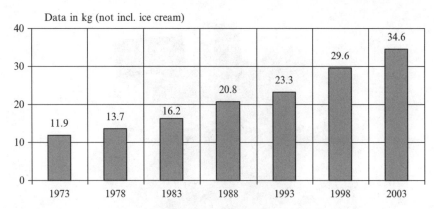

Fig. 12.6 Consumption of frozen food [18]

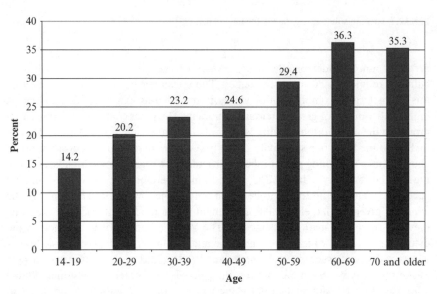

Fig. 12.7 People particularly concerned about their health [6]

trade. In 2005, the sales volume of such products as fluoridated table salt, wellness waters, and probiotic dairy products grew strongly, with an increase of 16.8%. These growth rates were reached both due to the successful introduction of new products and due to the discount stores. Particularly among the best-agers, the use frequency of products in the health and functional foods segment is growing. This circumstance reflects the value they place on a healthy, high-quality diet, with price playing a relatively subordinate role [4].

Implementation and Trends

Retailers are increasingly orienting themselves toward the needs of the older target groups, and are developing innovative concepts. In addition to the Swiss Coop and a Globus supermarket in Saarbrücken [15], the Austrian Adeg retail chain assumed a pioneering role in 2003 with the opening of *Aktiv Markt 50plus* stores. The parent company Edeka, too, followed that good example and, by 2006, had opened ten stores subtitled *Supermarket of the Generations* in Germany. The Metro Group is testing special concepts on the best-agers in the *future store* of the Galeria Kaufhof, and the mail-order house Otto is providing special assortments in its catalogues. Bus tours from all over Germany are bringing customers to Germany's first *senior's department store* in Großräschen in Lusatia. Additional stores on a franchise basis are planned [12]. Recently, the Tengelmann Group entered this new territory as well, with its Kaiser's *Generation Market* in Berlin. During selection of the location, it was ensured that approximately 57% of the population in the intake area were 50 years old or older. The share of single budgets is 56%, hence also above the national average. The market is to appeal to young and old target groups alike, but is to particularly take the needs of the older target groups into account. A good overview and good orientation are achieved by means of numerous signs identifying product groups, and colored product illustrations. The fresh-foods and dry-goods areas have been broken down both by design elements and by color-coding of the non-slip floor coverings. Good legibility is a priority in price and product information. There are numerous magnifying glasses on the shelves for fine print on the items, and also on the shopping carts, which are provided with integrated seats. Numerous bells are placed in the extra-wide walks, with which an employee can be called to certain places in the supermarket for questions and support (Fig. 12.8).

A pleasant shopping atmosphere was created by the remodeling of the facility and the lighting concepts of each of the sections. In addition to these individual services, the "Kaiser's Meeting Point" was established directly opposite the bakery. In this separate area, customers can enjoy coffee and cake, and socialize in a relaxed atmosphere. Moreover, a comfortable seating corner, a massage couch, an information monitor and Internet access are available. An additional special feature is the small and single packaging marked "for the small household," since older customers and singles have specifically asked for that [7]. The discounte store Plus, which is part of the Tengelmann Group, uses the brand "for the small purchase" to meet the increasing demand for smaller packets [13]. The gourmet division of Hertie in Frankfurt even spares its older customers the annoying repacking process at the register. With the aid of *Scanny*, a mobile scanner terminal, the customers enter the prices themselves, and are rewarded with a bonus book, which reminds many of trading-stamp booklets. On weekends moreover, a packing service and delivery to the car is provided [16]. Several studies indeed confirm that standing in line at the register is the greatest annoyance for customers [8]. The register area is normally marked by jams, customer stress, and impatience. The introduction of new technical solutions is an attempt being undertaken in many places to remove this sore spot in the conventional supermarket in a manner advantageous to all customers [20].

Shopping cart with seat   Magnifying glass on shopping cart

Massage couch in the "Kaiser's meeting point"   Product identification "for the small household"

Fig. 12.8 Kaiser's "Generation Market" in Berlin [7]

Summary and Conclusion

In order to be successful in the best-agers segment the retail trade has to provide well-accessible locations and a convenient store structuring. The assortment and packaging should address the specific target group needs. It so also offers good prospects for other industries, like the food and packaging industry. Distinctive features and additional income could be created through special services and offers with an additional benefit. If the retail trade fulfils all these needs it can also develop a higher attraction for younger target groups. This is because they are not at all put off by all these adaptations but, quite the opposite, they appreciate them too.

Nonetheless, only a few established service products in Germany have to date been able to demonstrate promise for the future. US retail chains provide not only an inviting ambiance, but also products targeted to older customers, in the marketing of fruits and vegetables. These include special product-friendly packaging, complete with health tips, for example. "Meal solutions" too are an area in which the German retail trade has some catching up to do. The integration of ready-to-eat products into the supermarket assortment holds added value potential and an opportunity to set oneself apart from the discount stores [1]. Marketing campaigns on such topics as cooking, health, regional, or seasonal products, and special offers for older target groups could contribute to such a counter-positioning of supermarkets and close-to-home stores [20]. In step with the needs of the older generation, the significance of service and counseling-oriented products for the retail trade will tend to increase [17].

References

1. S. Biester, *Lebensmittelzeitung* **21**, 32 (2007)
2. Die Best Agers im Fokus der Verpackungsentwicklung (Best-agers in the focus of packaging developments). *Neue Verpackung* **6**, 36, 2007
3. Edelmann Group, *CEasy, die Generation 50plus* (*CEasy, the 50plus generation*) (Edelmann Group, Heidenheim, 2007)
4. Health & Functional Food, *Lebensmittel Prax.* **24**, 40 (2006)
5. M. Hens, *Professionelle Ladengestaltung für 50plus Kunden* (*Professional store design for 50plus customers*) (BBE-Verlag, Cologne, 2006)
6. Institut für Demoskopie Allensbach, *Allensbacher Markt- und Werbeträgeranalyse* (*Allensbach Market and Advertising Media Analysis*) (Institut für Demoskopie Allensbach, Allensbach, 2003)
7. Kaiser's Tengelmann, Press release: *1. Kaiser's "Generationen-Markt" in Berlin!* (*1st Kaiser's Generation Market in Berlin!*) (Kaiser's Tengelmann, Viersen, 2006)
8. I. Kober, *Regal* **2**, 112 (2006)
9. T. Kreimer, M. Gerling, *Status quo und Perspektiven im deutschen Lebensmitteleinzelhandel 2006* (*Status quo and prospects in the German food retail trade 2006*) (KPMG, Berlin, 2006)
10. C. Krieb, A. Reidl, *Seniorenmarketing – so erreichen Sie die Zielgruppe der Zukunft* (*Seniors marketing – how to reach the target group of the future*) (Ueberreuter, Vienna/Frankfurt, 1999)
11. H. Krost, *Lebensmittelzeitung* **39**, 68 (2004)
12. M. Martell, *Handel entdeckt über 50-Jährige* (*The retail trade discovers the over-50-year-olds*) http://www.stuttgarter-zeitung.de/stz/page/detail.php/1273025, 2007. Accessed 11 June 2008
13. Plus startet Singelpackungen (Plus starts single packaging), *afz* **25**, 2 (2007)
14. M. Preißner, A. Knob, Handel im Fokus **2**, 101 (2006)
15. D. Rees, *Lebensmittelzeitung* **38**, 58 (2000)
16. A. Reidl, *Neue Verpackung* **5**, 54, 2006
17. B. Schoofs, *Immobilien und Finanzierung* **19**, 662 (2006)
18. SevenOne Media, *TrendReport – Die Anti-Aging Gesellschaft* (*Trend report: the anti-aging society*) (SevenOne Media, Unterföhring, 2005)
19. TNS Infratest, *Semiometrie – Die Zielgruppe für Biolebensmittel* (*Semiometrie, the target group for organic food*) (TNS Infratest, Bielefeld, 2007)
20. Verschlafen wir nicht den Zug der Zeit (Let's not oversleep and miss the train of our time!) *Regal* **2**, 3 (2006)
21. Wellness- und Energy Boom (Wellness and enery boom), *Rundschau für den Lebensmittelhandel* **3**, 36 (2007)
22. B. Will, *Lebensmittelzeitung* **20**, 38 (2007)

Chapter 13
Silver Pricing: Satisfying Needs is Not Enough
Balancing Value Delivery and Value Extraction is Key

S. Lippert

Abstract At first glance, the silver market provides a highly lucrative opportunity for businesses willing and able to meet the needs of Japan's senior generation. International and domestic players have been pursuing the new opportunities in the last few years. Thoroughly understanding the needs of the silver generation is a key to capitalizing on it. However, this is just one side of the value coin. A need is not the same as demand, and demand is not the same as profitable business. To turn a profit, you have to balance value delivery and value extraction. Value delivery is relatively easy: it requires market research, appropriate products and services, and an effective distribution system. Value extraction is difficult: you need to set and implement the right prices across products, regions, and channels. A business strategy based solely on demographic and socioeconomic data, customer needs and buying power is simplistic, misleading, and in some cases dangerous. Capitalizing on the silver market requires a systematic approach to developing and profitably selling products and services tailored to the older generation. It takes a solid understanding of customer requirements, value-to-customer, ability and willingness to pay, price elasticities, and revenue and profit functions. The best way to achieve this is by means of a professional pricing process covering and connecting pricing strategy, price setting, and price implementation.

Introduction: Japan's Silver Market

At First Glance, a Highly Attractive Opportunity

The rapidly aging population in Japan poses an unprecedented challenge to marketing. For many decades, marketers concentrated on consumers aged between 15 and 40. In some cases, such as in the premium automotive market, private banking, real estate, luxury goods, leisure, and healthcare, the age groups of 40–50 and 50–60 also played a role. The silver market is widely understood to start with the 60+ age

185

group, which is mostly uncharted territory from a marketing perspective. There are three reasons why Japan's silver market is so attractive:

1. *Size*: Today, 20% of the Japanese population is 65 or over. If the current demographic trends (low birthrate, rising longevity) continue, this figure will double to 40% by 2055. Over the same period, Japan's population is expected to drop by 30% to less than 90 million, after peaking near 128 million in 2005. These facts are having a huge impact on business. Both the supply side and the demand side are affected. On the supply side, the main challenge is a dramatic shortage of labor. The latest government forecast suggests there will be 1.3 workers per senior citizen in the 2050s, down from 3.3 in 2005. On the demand side, the overall domestic market will shrink significantly (30 million fewer people by 2055), *but the size of the silver segment will markedly increase – from currently 26 million to 36 million people by 2055*. Between 2012 and 2014 alone, the number of elderly people will increase by one million every year, since most baby boomers will turn 65 then. By 2015, senior citizens will account for 26% of the population. The "super-aged" society, in which one in four people is 65 years or older, will arrive in less than 10 years [1].

2. *Purchasing power*: In spite of the demographic challenge, Japan will most likely maintain its position as a global economic powerhouse. Current economic research suggests that even in 2050, Japan will be number five in a global GDP ranking, behind the USA, China, the EU and India.[1] The country's high level of wealth will be distributed among fewer people, and the elderly will have the lion's share of the assets. The key facts and figures are:

   • The total amount of retirement benefits the baby boomers are entitled to during the period 2007–2009 is estimated to amount to ¥50 trillion (US$450 billion).
   • The 6.8 million boomers account for 5.4% of the population, but they hold total financial assets worth ¥130 trillion (US$1170 billion), or 10% of the total financial assets held by individuals. If retirement benefits are included, the latter figure increases to 14%.
   • Elderly households have more financial assets than other generations. On average, households comprising people aged between 60 and 70 are worth ¥17 million (US$150,000). Households of people aged 70 and over are worth ¥15 million (US$135,000); households of people aged 50–69 are worth ¥11.5 million (US$100,000) [2].

3. *Value change*: Older generations of the past diligently saved their money to enable the next generation to receive a good education. They also saved money to balance out the expenses connected with caring for grandparents and older family members living at home. This behavior is now changing drastically. The baby boomers no longer expect their few children, who often live and work farther away, to care for them in their advanced years. On the other hand, they also feel less disposed to save for the younger generation. Leading financial institutes like

---

[1] Japan Center for Economic Research 2007 (ranking based on 2000 purchasing power parity, in US$).

JP Morgan, Goldman Sachs, and Nomura Securities believe that the demographic change in the coming years will be advantageous for Japan's economic growth. This conviction is strengthened by the fact that senior citizens spend substantially more than other age groups. Retirees draw on their savings (as they do in the USA), while workers over 60 years old accrue hardly any savings. This trend is spreading. In 2000, retirees spent about 15% more than they received in retirement. Their expenditures are now 29% higher than their income. These figures are also reflected in consumer spending: Japan's senior citizens consume more than the younger generation, with average per capita expenditure increasing clearly until the age of 70 [3].

At first glance, the silver market provides a highly lucrative opportunity for businesses willing and able to meet the needs of Japan's senior generation. International and domestic players have been pursuing the new opportunities in the last few years. Consider HSBC, which has decided to tap into the premium retail banking market. The bank targets the upper middle class, especially baby boomers receiving their retirement benefits and looking for good advice on how to invest the money properly. Citigroup has acquired Nikko Cordial, one of the top three brokerages, to expand its customer network and to sell its financial products. Allianz Group has entered the Japanese life insurance market. Other major insurance companies such as ING and Hartford have been successful in selling variable annuity (VA) products primarily to the older generation; the Japanese VA market skyrocketed from less than US$1 billion in assets in 2000 to over US$50 billion so far. Nomura Securities sells an investment fund that pays out dividends six times a year, when seniors get no payment from the public pension system, which pays only every other month. The fund raised ¥660 billion (US$6 billion) in the first year. International investors have acquired a large number of golf courses, restructured them and established new companies (e.g., Accordia Golf). Domestic companies focus on opportunities in the leisure, travel, fitness, wellness, education, entertainment, and real estate sectors, to name just a few. In particular, the healthcare market provides attractive opportunities. Healthcare costs have reached 8% of the Japanese GDP, compared with 4.4% in 1965. More than 40% of healthcare costs are related to patients aged 70 or above. Further massive growth in the healthcare market is expected, given the demographic shift and the low level of per capita health spending (about half of the US level) [4]. On the B2B side, companies providing solutions for the shrinking workforce (e.g., automation, robotics) are likely to profit from the demographic change.

It's Worth a Second Glance: Value Delivery and Value Extraction

Thoroughly understanding the needs of the silver generation is a key to capitalizing on it. We call this *value delivery*. However, this is just one side of the value coin. The other side is that *business is about making money, not just satisfying needs. A need is not the same as demand, and demand is not the same as profitable business. To turn a profit, you have to balance value delivery and value extraction.* Value delivery is relatively easy: it requires market research, appropriate products and services, and an effective distribution system. Value extraction is difficult: you need to set and implement the right prices across products, regions, and channels. A few real-life cases of silver market-related businesses in Japan illustrate this:

- You have read about the interest of retiring boomers in cultural travel and want to set up a conveniently located travel agency focusing on premium vacation tours. Assuming that you are able to address your target segment: What is the convenience and advice worth to your potential customers? Are they really willing to pay more for convenience and advice if the same trip is offered at a lower price over the web? Or, do they use your services and end up booking electronically? What kind of pricing levels, structures, and fencing mechanisms does it take to prevent this?
- You want to offer advice on financial planning to retirees and sell products accordingly. Market research has uncovered a huge need, and you have read the reports of investment banks that tend to indicate the same. Yet, you realize that it is by no means clear whether this need is actually backed by a sufficient willingness to pay. Can you compete with incumbents that offer low-level consultation for free? Apart from consultation, which features of your product (e.g., a lifecycle investment fund) really matter to your customers? How much are they willing to pay for them? Does your brand influence the buying decision? How would demand react if you change prices by 2.5, 5, or 10%?
- You make premium household goods. Your Japanese chief marketer recommends changing product specifications in order to better meet the needs of senior customers. In particular, handling and design should be modified. You like the idea, but you realize that this increases the costs of R&D, production, and handling. You ask your marketer about the possibility of charging a higher price that reflects the additional costs, but you hear that this would be difficult. You realize that the silver market wants specific products, but does not want to pay more for them. Is the assessment given by your marketer accurate? How much would sales decline if you actually charge a higher price? What would be the overall impact on revenue and profit?
- You are in the hospitality business. You know that your silver customers have specific preferences and are actually willing to pay a premium to get what they want (e.g., a room with an ocean view). However, you also have to develop an attractive offering for younger customers, while achieving various performance goals: occupancy, revenue, and profit. You deploy a dynamic pricing model, i.e., early but inflexible booking rates are highly discounted. Eventually you discover that your elderly customers, who can plan ahead over months (in comparison with the younger segment, which is busy and wants flexibility), book early according to their preferences and pay less than they are actually willing to do. You also realize that you have educated a core customer group to demand lower prices – behavior which is likely to extend to services offered at the hotel, restaurants, shops, etc. Of course, you didn't want this to happen. What went wrong? How should the price–product structure be designed to avoid profit-destroying booking behavior?

The silver market story sounds good, but it's not so easily cracked. Before venturing into the uncharted territory of the silver market, you should have a clear, profound understanding of both the ability and the willingness to pay.

The *ability to pay* may be affected in the long term by a reduction in savings and wealth due to a shrinking and aging population. A recent study suggests that the continuous increase in the standard of living in the post-war period will come to an end. Regardless of further GDP growth, savings will decline to almost zero over the next 20 years. The decline in the savings rate has a direct impact on wealth and economic growth. If new savings dry up, less wealth is created, and, consequently, dramatically less money is available to be spent. In concrete terms, financial wealth in Japan is projected to fall slightly from 2003 to 2024, after increasing by 5.5% a year from 1975 to 2003. Hence, if effective counter-measures (such as a broad shift towards higher-yielding asset classes or massively increased productivity) are not taken, the wealth of the average Japanese household in 2024 will be more or less the same as it was in the mid-1990s [5].[2]

However, this gloomy long-term perspective must not be mixed up with the optimistic short- and mid-term outlook. Here, the question is not whether enough money is available but how to extract it. Uncertainties stem particularly from the fact that the elderly face a long and unprecedented retirement period of about 18 years (men) and 23 years (women) after turning 65. Are they really big spenders, in spite of the weaknesses of the public pension system and the lack of family support? These questions boil down to the issue of *willingness to pay*.

Understanding Willingness to Pay: The Key to Smart Profit Growth in the Silver Market

Of the three factors of the profit equation – price, units sold, and costs – price is the most effective profit driver. In the silver market, the role of intelligent pricing cannot be exaggerated because a needs-based view still prevails. Understanding your silver

---

[2] The study argues that the decline in savings is driven by three main factors: Firstly, retired households will outnumber households in their prime saving years, so savings rates will naturally decline. The prime savers ratio – the number of households in their prime saving years (aged 30–50) divided by the number of elderly households (aged 65 and above) – has been below one since the mid-1980s. Secondly, the generational saving behavior has changed. The young generation saves less than the older generations have. This is particularly true for the generation born in the 1960s and 1970s, which has been moving into the prime saving years since 1990. These households have higher disposable incomes than earlier generations, but they also spend more. Thirdly, Japanese households traditionally build wealth through new savings rather than asset appreciation. Recent data indicates a slight shift towards asset classes with higher yields (e.g., mutual funds and life insurance products), but eye-catching media reports on Japanese housewives pursuing "carry trades" must not divert from the fact that low-yielding bank deposits still account for more than 50% of household assets. It is unlikely that the basic investment pattern, which is deeply rooted in a specific risk culture and the painful experience of stock market and real estate crashes in the 1990s, will change significantly over the next 10 or 20 years [5, 6].

customer's needs and developing products and services accordingly is necessary for successful sales, but it is not sufficient to make sure you turn a profit.

Serving the silver market can entail higher sales costs and stricter customer protection requirements. Consider the financial services sector. The new Japanese investor protection law, which took effect in fall 2007, requires banks to overhaul their practices of selling investment trusts (mutual funds) and other risk products to elderly customers. To avoid disciplinary action from the regulator, banks had already set up internal rules on how to deal with customers in their 70s or 80s. For example, SMBC requires that customers aged 70+ be accompanied by a family member when purchasing a variable annuity, while MUFG states it explains the risks involved in complex financial products at least twice to customers over 70. Banks also plan to increase their after-sales services by, for example, visiting elderly customers to explain the performance of investment products or inviting them to investment conferences [7]. All these activities cost money, and the question the bank (or insurance company) has to answer is whether the return on these activities is sufficiently high.

Further, silver pricing has to factor in the specific value structure and peculiarities of the target group. Consider variable annuities, an investment-linked, rather complex life insurance product, which is bought mostly by customers aged 60+ in Japan. Variable annuities are a booming product in the overall shrinking Japanese life insurance market. However, competition is fierce and the shelf space provided by the bank assurance channel is rather limited. To be successful in the challenging, but still highly promising market space, it takes an exact quantitative analysis of the product features from the perspective of the Japanese seniors: Which features do they really appreciate and how much they are willing to pay for them? The following chart exemplifies the differing value perception of the same age group in two countries (Fig. 13.1).

Investment security, for example, plays a high role for German customers, whereas Singaporeans prefer products that offer an option to withdraw money flexibly and high returns. Translated into willingness-to-pay, it becomes clear that these two markets require tailored, very different products to profitably meet the specific value structures. A one-size-fits-all-approach doesn't work. It is a no-brainer to say that these value structures are deeply rooted in mental and cultural history. It is less clear why international companies still tend to neglect the specific value structure of their Japanese customers. To sell profitably to the baby boomers, it takes pinpointed offerings that accurately reflect their needs and willingness to pay.

Whether or not age-based price discrimination is possible depends on the given business situation (sector, product group, intensity of regulation, etc.). In non- or less-regulated sectors such as travel, age-based discounting has become quite common in Japan; in particular, train tickets and vacation packages are sold with certain age-based discounts. In financial services, Kabu.com, a leading online brokerage, launched a commission discount program in 2006 for investors aged 50–60. According to the company, about 30% of its customers are aged 50 or over. However, the goal of silver pricing cannot be discounting. Rebates boost units sold rather than profits. In fixed cost-based businesses such as railway transportation and securities order processing, higher units sold translate quite directly into higher total profits,

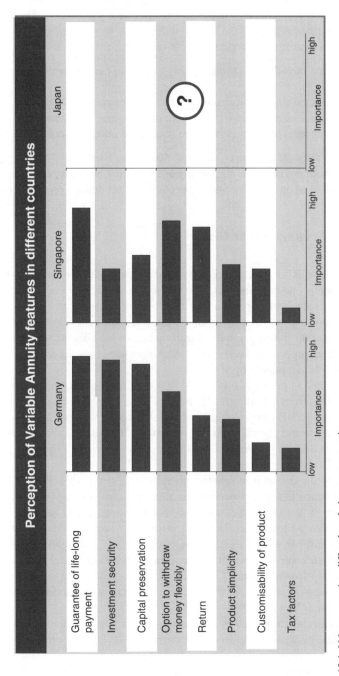

Fig. 13.1 Value perception differs largely between countries

but in businesses with high variable costs (e.g., manufacturing automobiles, mobile phones, or TV flat screens) discounts destroy margins and, in most cases, total profits. The goal of silver pricing is to make sure you get what you deserve. This requires an accurate understanding of the actual willingness to pay, the price–response function, the revenue function, and the profit function:

- How much are our silver customers going to pay for the product/service offered to them?
- How will demand shift if we change price levels or structures?
- What is the optimal price level/structure in order to maximize our revenues?
- What is the optimal price level/structure in order to maximize our profits?

To get the right answers to these critical questions, a well-structured pricing process is the key. If there are no clear, convincing answers, any business plan based upon silver needs is based on guessing and benevolence rather than on profit orientation.

Price is the Primary Profit Driver

Assume a bank sells its silver market-oriented account package for ¥10,000 and its sales volume is one million units. The variable costs per unit (sales, back office processing, etc.) are ¥8000, resulting in a contribution margin of ¥2000 per unit. The bank's fixed costs are ¥1 billion. In this situation, the bank earns a profit of ¥1 billion [= (¥10,000–8000) per unit ×1 million units – ¥1 billion fixed costs]. How does each of the four profit drivers – price, variable costs, volume, and fixed costs – change profit when improved by 10%?

A 10% increase in price (¥10,000 to ¥11,000) leads (ceteris paribus) to a profit increase of 100%, from ¥1 billion to ¥2 billion. The effect of the other profit drivers is clearly lower. A 10% improvement of variable costs, volume, and fixed costs (ceteris paribus) would yield a profit increase of 80, 20, and 10% respectively. This simple yet typical example undermines the key role of pricing. This is especially true in situations where unit margins are low (Fig. 13.2).

To facilitate the decision of whether to raise or lower prices, Fig. 13.3 shows the impact of price changes depending on different cost–income ratios. The percentages given in the tables indicate how much volume has to be gained (price reduction) or can be lost (price increase) in order to keep the cost–income ratio constant. The silver marketer should change a price only if the expected effect on volume is higher/lower than the given percentages. For example: at a cost–income ratio of 0.75, a price reduction of 10% increases profit only if a volume increase of 67% or more is expected. A 10% increase in price increases profit only if the volume decrease is less than 29%.

Increased margins stimulated by professional pricing immediately increase profit and do not require expensive upfront investments or severance payments. Relative to cost-cutting, price optimization offers three opportunities: it gains time, avoids additional upfront expenses, and has a stronger impact on profit. So, the crucial question is: how can these profit potentials be leveraged effectively?

A 10% improvement in...   ... leads to a profit increase of...

	Profit Driver		Profit (Yen)	
	Old	New	Old	New
Price (monthly account fee)	10,000	11,000	1.0 b	2.0 b	100%
Variable unit cost	8000	7200	1.0 b	1.8 b	80%
Sales volume	1 m	1.1 m	1.0 b	1.2 b	20%
Fixed cost	1.0 b	0.9 b	1.0 b	1.1 b	10%

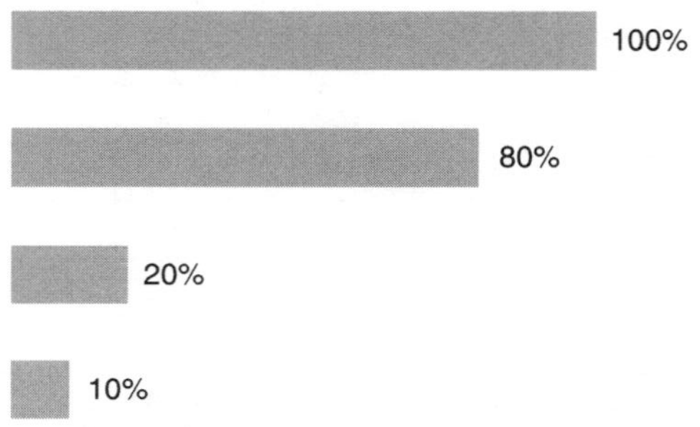

To be read as follows: **A 10% price improvement brings the price up to 11,000 Yen. Everything else unchanged, this increases profit by 100% to 2.0 billionYen.**

Fig. 13.2 Impact of profit drivers

Cost-Income-Ratio**

Price Increase in %	0.95	0.90	0.85	0.80	0.75	0.70	0.65	0.60	0.55	0.50	0.45	0.40	0.35
	Decrease of Volume in % to keep Contribution Margin constant												
2.0	29	17	12	9.1	7.4	6.3	5.4	4.8	4.3	3.8	3.5	3.2	3
3.0	38	23	17	13	11	9.1	7.9	7	6.3	5.7	5.2	4.8	4.4
4.0	44	29	21	17	14	12	10	9.1	8.2	7.4	6.8	6.3	5.8
5.0	50	33	25	20	17	14	13	11	10	9.1	8.3	7.7	7.1
7.5	60	43	33	27	23	20	18	16	14	13	12	11	10
10.0	67	50	40	33	29	25	22	20	18	17	15.0	14	13
15.0	75	60	50	43	38	33	30	27	25	23	21	20	19
30.0	86	75	67	60	55	50	46	43	40	38	35	33	32
40.0	89	80	73	67	62	57	53	50	47	44	42	40	38

** reads: At a price increase of 10% and a cost income-ratio of 0.75, volume can decrease by 29% to keep contribution margin constant.

Cost-Income-Ratio*

Price Reduction in %	0.95	0.90	0.85	0.80	0.75	0.70	0.65	0.60	0.55	0.50	0.45	0.40	0.35
	Increase of Volume in % to keep Contribution Margin constant												
2.0	67	25	15	11	8.7	7.1	6.1	5.3	4.7	4.2	3.8	3.4	3.2
3.0	150	43	25	18	14	11	9.4	8.1	7.1	6.4	5.8	5.3	4.8
4.0	400	67	36	25	19	15	13	11	9.8	8.7	7.8	7.1	6.6
5.0		100	50	33	25	20	17	14	13	11	10	9.1	8.3
7.5		300	100	60	43	33	27	23	20	18	16	14	13
10.0			200	100	67	50	40	33	29	25	22	20	18.2
15.0				300	150	100	75	60	50	43	38	33	30
30.0							600	300	200	150	120	100	86
40.0									800	400	267	200	160

* reads: At a price reduction of 10% and a cost-income-ratio of 0.75, an increase in volume of 67% is required to keep contribution margin constant.

Fig. 13.3 Decision table for price reductions and price increases

Pricing Process

"Simple" price increases are risky and mostly do not result in the projected effects. Just increasing existing prices or ordering sales staff to negotiate higher prices with silver customers will fail. Silver marketers must apply innovative price strategies that focus on the customers' needs (known as "value pricing") and implement such strategies using an effective pricing process. Otherwise, silver pricing is at risk of simply pushing units through discounts. A pricing process is a system of organizational rules, guidelines, and measures intended to determine, manage, and implement prices. When companies offer a large number of products, or prices are negotiated for each transaction, pricing processes are crucial. However, due to the high number of necessary price decisions, the effort involved in each decision has to be limited. Precisely defined processes are required to determine and implement prices and thereby garner optimal yields (Fig. 13.4).

A professional pricing process usually includes five basic steps: strategy, analysis, decision, implementation, and monitoring.

Pricing Strategy

The pricing strategy and vision should be developed well before the new product (or service) is launched. Typically the strategy is formulated in the early stages of product development, when there is already a clear concept and fixed specifications. The product managers in particular are responsible for creating the guidelines and framework for future pricing within the product strategy. The pricing strategy must involve a clear strategy for the market entry (skimming or penetration), premium potentials, lifecycle aspects, and regional differentiation where necessary or possible. Likewise, the pricing strategy must be developed for other new aspects such as parts, services, equipment, etc.

Price Analysis

To develop a pricing strategy and optimize prices, it is critical that all relevant data be collected and the right analyses be applied. These steps are basic elements of pricing processes and should be well-structured and considered as standard. The information regarding the strategic triangle – silver customers, products, and competitors – must be complete to ensure that pricing is performed correctly using all relevant data. Among the typical questions to be answered are: How successful are today's pricing processes? Which data and information is necessary for an optimal pricing decision? Which methods are used? How important is the price in the purchase decision process? How do the competitive situation and price–value relationships look from the silver customers' perspective?

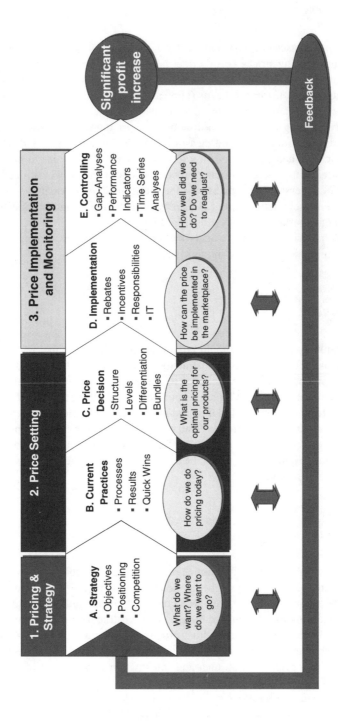

Fig. 13.4 Five phases of the pricing process

Price Decision

The price decision determines the optimal price and is subsequently confirmed by the decision makers. It is clear that all parties involved in the price decision must understand which price is being analyzed (list price, discounted price, transaction price, with/without VAT, etc.), for which product, in which configuration, and for which channel and/or region.

The value-based approach to pricing comes into play here. Cost-plus and competition-based pricing provide a certain range, but are not directly interrelated with the silver customer's buying decision. For example, the baby boomer couple looking for a brain-training video game do not care about the development and distribution costs of the software vendor. Neither are silver customers willing or able to compare the highly complex price–product architectures of competing medical insurance products. However, they know what they want and what they are willing to pay. Hence the best way to conduct silver pricing is to consider customer requirements, value-to-customer, and the customers' willingness to pay. To understand and quantify these factors, indirect, multivariate methods deliver the most accurate results. A particularly powerful approach is conjoint measurement. A conjoint measurement exercise basically simulates the real buying decision with real customers (through focus groups or telephone/web-based interviews). Because the customer has to indicate preferences for realistic price–product configurations, the pitfalls of direct, price-oriented methods are avoided. The buying decision is always a trade-off between the value the product delivers and the price. The most sophisticated versions of conjoint measurement are adaptive, i.e., the computer generates realistic product/price pair comparisons based on the previous answers. After 20 or 30 of these pair comparisons, the value structure of the individual customer is sufficiently understood. The relative utilities of the key attributes can be compared and the willingness-to-pay for different levels of each attribute and for the entire product can be calculated. By aggregating preference patterns, distinctive customer segments emerge. Such a segmentation based on value-to-customer and willingness-to-pay is extremely effective when it comes to designing new products and services for the silver market.

Further, up- and cross-selling potentials need to be taken into account. *Upselling*: what is the optimal price gap between a standard and a premium product in order to optimize total profits? *Cross-selling*: how would silver customers react to bundling offers? This field provides tremendous opportunities for smart silver marketers, especially in sectors in which convenience plays a larger role. For example, a car package that includes an easy-entry option as well as an insurance package pinpointed to the needs of the older generation (e.g., including travel repatriation insurance) might be an attractive offering. The same holds true in the insurance sector, where various policy types (e.g., health and life insurance) can be sold at a package price, profiting from extremely low additional sales costs.

Price Implementation

After determining optimal price levels and structures, implementation is key. It calls for a functioning organization, process/goal-oriented organization, effective IT systems, and clever incentive systems for both sales people and customers.

Pricing organization is, especially in Japan, an often overlooked success factor. A professional pricing organization has to set the framework for successful pricing processes. This involves clear responsibilities, availability of relevant information, and a structured feedback system to enable lessons to be learned from the past.

Clear responsibilities are the cornerstone of all pricing issues. In many cases responsibilities are not clearly defined. They vary for different pricing tasks and between divisions. Quite often, responsibility is borne by a group rather than a single individual.

There has to be a clear process owner for all relevant processes within price management. This process owner is responsible for the timely and correct execution of the process as well as for the involvement of relevant experts and the outcome of the process. As an important side effect, the responsible person can be easily identified by the company's employees who are not involved in the process in question.

The existence of a pricing department facilitates (but does not guarantee) the development of a formalized pricing process. A more important factor seems to be a direct link to senior management and good awareness at that level of the importance of pricing. If pricing is conducted decentrally, clear guidelines and monitoring are necessary.

Monitoring

Monitoring is an essential element in pricing to increase profitability. The implementation of the prices has to be checked continuously and adjusted if necessary. Daily statistics and transaction price studies support the checking and adjusting tasks by identifying negative price developments. This information also serves as input data for the initial pricing step. Key questions to be answered are: Which prices have been achieved in the market? How did prices, revenues and profits develop? Where and why have target prices not been reached?

Summary and Conclusion

The silver market offers tremendous potential, but it also harbors a lot of uncertainties and potential pitfalls. A business strategy based solely on demographic and socioeconomic data, customer needs and buying power is simplistic, misleading, and in some cases dangerous. This is even true for top-notch Western companies, whose Japanese ventures recently failed: Vodafone, Carrefour, Burger King, Pret a Manger, eBay and, in the 1980s, IKEA, to name just a few. Of course there are specific reasons in each of these cases – wrong hiring decisions on country manager level, lack of suitable sites in order to gain scale advantages and concessions from Japanese suppliers, insufficient will to invest in Japan-specific product design and infrastructure, roll-out of an American-centric service model, ineffective announcement policy etc. But all of them "suffered from rather serious lapses of judgment, employed flawed strategies and demonstrated a lack of understanding in regards to both the dynamics of the market to which they had come, and the highly particular demands of the Japanese consumer" [8]. Note that most of these businesses focused on the younger generation, which has been thoroughly studied by marketers for decades. The uncharted territory of the silver market bears a significantly higher risk of failing. Capitalizing on this market, with its specific value structure and peculiarities, requires a systematic approach to developing and profitably selling products and services tailored to the older generation. Specifically, it takes a clear, solid understanding of customer requirements, value-to-customer, willingness to pay, price elasticities, and revenue and profit functions to be successful in this attractive, but also difficult market. The best way to achieve this is by means of a well-structured, professional pricing process covering and connecting pricing strategy, price setting, and price implementation.

References

1. Cabinet Office, *White paper on aging society*, (Government of Japan, 2007)
2. Dai-Ichi Life Research Institute, *Following the first baby-boom generation's money: where the savings of the elderly go*, (Dai-Ichi Life Research Institute, 2005)
3. Financial Times, Deutschland, 4 June 2005
4. Japan Times, 4 Oct 2007
5. McKinsey Global Institute, *The coming demographic deficit: how aging populations will reduce global savings*, (McKinsey and Company, 2005)
6. B. P. Bosworth, R. C. Bryant, G. Burtless, *The impact of aging on financial markets and the economy: a survey*, (Brookings Institution, 2004)
7. The Nikkei Weekly, 1 Oct 2007, p. 12
8. G. Lane, *Failed businesses in Japan*, Japan Inc 7/2007, p. 6

Chapter 14
Macro-Structural Bases of Consumption in an Aging Low Birth-Rate Society

T. Yamashita and T. Nakamura

Abstract The purpose of this study is to clarify the driving factors in the changing structure of consumption at the macro-level caused by an aging society in Japan. To describe the macroscopic, dynamic, and structural bases of consumption, the authors used cohort analysis, which is a method of separating age, period, and cohort effects from time-series household accounts data, classified by age and period. Many items of expenditure are susceptible to the age factor. The effect of changes in the number of household members due to changing life stages and the effect of changing expenses due to aging of consumers can also be seen. Other expenditure items are susceptible to plural factors. For example, fish & shellfish, vegetables & seaweed, and fruit are all susceptible to both age and cohort factors. Eating out, private transportation, communication, and books & other reading material are susceptible to all three factors at different levels of effectiveness. Observing the profile pattern on the cohort analysis result graph, we can consider how market aging and the alternation of generations, which are viewed from a population theory perspective, affect the consumption structure.

Introduction

A number of researchers are actively involved in studying how the change in population structure with regard to age and generation due to the impact of a low birth-rate and aging population will transform the consumer market. Regarding the issue of generation in particular, quite a few reports refer to people in their 50s and older, including the *Dankai* (Japanese baby boomers) that are being referred to as the "New Fifties" or "Active Seniors," and predict that youthful consumer behavior, in contrast to that of conventional stereotypes will increase as new generations enter this age bracket [7, 12]. Japanese baby boomers currently at the cusp of retirement could dramatically transform household expenditure, and eventually transform Japanese macro-structure consumption through sheer weight of numbers.

This chapter questions the ambiguity of the cause of change in consumer behavior not clarified in terms like "New Fifties" and so on. No clarification is made as to whether that change is generated by features of consumer behavior belonging to a specific generation (*Dankai, Shin-Jin-Rui* etc.), brought about by a change in specific period of years behind the consumption, or caused by aging (or shift in life stage).

As an example, let us consider a hypothetical consumer behavior trait and compare it in relation to a generational hypothesis and another age-related hypothesis:

H1: *Dankai* (Japanese baby boomers) and newer generations prefer wearing jeans.

H2: Everybody 30 or younger prefers wearing jeans.

If generation-related hypothesis (H1) is true, it might be estimated that "Japanese baby boomers and younger generations prefer wearing jeans even after having reached the age of 30." Contrarily, if age related hypothesis (H2) is true, it implies "Anybody older than the age of 30 will not wear jeans regardless of generation." Furthermore and as follows, an additional hypothesis in relation to period should be taken into consideration:

H3: Casual fashion is a universal trend (the casual apparel industry, for example Uniqlo, is growing every year and an increasing number of people purchase casual clothing such as jeans regardless of age or sex).

If (H3) is true, then it can be predicted that "the majority of people prefer wearing jeans regardless of age or sex as they age." These are neither true or false propositions nor exclusive events; rather a problem of scale.

In some cases, dynamic continuous changes in the population structure due to a low birth-rate and aging population and/or unequal distribution of generations may lead to amplifying the impact people in a certain age bracket or generation can have on change prevailing throughout society in its entirety over the long run, and even further in macroscopically changing consumer trends. Clarification of changes in consumption is of substantial significance if it is pursued taking the age of the consumer, behavioral pattern specific to each generation, economic and social processes during their lifetime, and norms and technological renovations into consideration. Among others, demographic statistics are useful in making forecasts at high levels of certainty and are understood as a factor directly connected to demand for consumables and financial products. In addition, it is important to analyze just what the specific areas of household expenditure will be that will expand or shrink in the future when drawing up marketing strategies.

This chapter describes analysis that was implemented using Bayesian cohort models, based on data from the *Annual Report on Family Income and Expenditure Survey* (Statistics Bureau, Japan) [14, 15]. Cohort analysis can organically connect plural investigation results and divide them into the three factors of consumer age, consumer cohort, and survey year in analyzing their effects on consumer behavior from the perspective of expenditure.

Trends in Consumer Expenditure of Japanese Households

According to the percentage distribution by consumer item (of all households throughout the nation) in *the Annual Report on Family Income and Expenditure Survey*, the share of food expenses decreased from 60.4% in 1948 to 23.2% in 2003. Similarly, clothes & footwear expenses dropped from 9.2% in 1975 to 4.6% in 2003. In contrast to this, the share of transportation & communication expenses[1] and reading & recreation expenses against total consumer expenditure in 2003 increased in comparison with those of 1975: from 6.1 to 12.4% for transportation & communication and from 8.4 to 10.0% for reading & recreation. The weighting of consumer expenditure can definitely be seen to have shifted to preferential consumption from necessary consumption.

Actual consumer expenditure of all households continued to decrease from 1993 due to the impact of the slow economy, and particularly in 1998 actually dropped by 2.2% in comparison with the previous year, influenced by the drop in consumer confidence due to uneasiness in the financial system. With respect to the relationship between consumer confidence and consumer expenditure, Sano [13] indicated that psychological indicators exist, such as in the perspective that households exert predictive powers over trends due to preferential consumer expenditure. She also referred to a finding in a time-series analysis in that while there were parts that changed over the short term in response to the economic environment, there were also those that did not easily change due to individual attributes. The cohort analysis used in this chapter is capable of discriminating the period effects on changes in consumer expenditure, which reflect the influence of economic trends and others, from other effects (age effect and cohort effect).

Aging of householders is accompanied by a shift in the life stage of the household budget and changes in the content of consumer expenditure. Okamoto [10] proposed a cohort analysis based not on the ages of the householders but rather on the ages of the eldest children in those households, that is, consumer tendency cohort analysis based on the life stage of the household budget. He also indicated that the financial assets of the household are indirectly presented in the cohort effect,[2] and pointed out that cohort analysis concerning consumer tendencies could be adequately explained using models with ordinary consumption functions because the cohort effect could be alternatively obtained by taking into consideration the effect financial assets have. On the other hand, Okamoto applied the life stage cohort model to the ratio of fish & shellfish expenses to total food expenses based on the understanding that the cohort effect to be identified through usual cohort analysis would be presented in itemized consumer expenses such as fish & shellfish, even if the cohort effect

---

[1] Transportation & communication expenses are comprised of expenses for transportation, communication, automobile-related items, and others. The total amount for these items showed a real increase because cellular phone charges and automobile-related payments actually increased, although transportation expenses showed a real reduction.

[2] Okamoto [10] stated "...cohort effect is present as financial assets are an accumulation of saving and lending behavior in the past, ...it may be natural to infer that the average consumption tendency has a cohort effect which is indirectly presented through the effect of financial assets." (p. 23).

was not sufficiently meaningful in total food expenses. However, he did refer to the difficulty of making the most of the model as it was premised on the use of a public database, whereas he was showing the value of the life stage cohort model.

This chapter describes analysis implemented using the Bayesian cohort models introduced by Nakamura [4, 5, 8] with the conclusion that the magnitude of the influence of the three effects of consumer age, cohort, and period of years can be identified by way of analyzing the amount of consumer expenditure per item. This can be applied to forecasts for a given consumer market to some extent by observing the profile of fluctuations in addition to the range of fluctuations, which represent the magnitude of the influence of the three effects. Variables closely related to the amount of household consumer expenditure by age of householder might include persons per household and earners per household, to which Bayesian cohort analysis was also applied.

Data and Method

Consumer data by age group of householder (medium category) from 1980 to 2002 obtained from the *Annual Report on the Family Income and Expenditure Survey* [14] was used. For the analysis of household expenditure items, data on the amount of money deflated by the consumer price index corresponding to each item was used. The obtained cohort tables, ten age groups with 5-year age intervals ×23 survey year points were separated into the three effects of age, period of years, and cohort using Bayesian cohort analysis. (See Appendix 1 for the Bayesian cohort analysis and the three effects.)

Results

Persons per household and earners per household were first analyzed with Bayesian cohort models. The figure for persons per household (Fig. 14.1) has three frames and parameter values for period effect (<period>), age effect (<age>), and cohort effect (<cohort>) and are output in the three frames from top to bottom, respectively. The center frame indicates where the parameter value is equal to zero. The right side indicates an addition, i.e., an increase in number of persons per household. The left side indicates a subtraction, i.e., a decrease in the number of persons per household. <Grand mean> denotes the grand mean effect. According to them, the period effect of 23 years is rather small, whereas the age effect is quite large in the life stage phase estimated to be from someone's 30s to early 50s, where children are still being supported. The cohort effect has a left oblique profile, which means that the number of household members tends to decrease with newer generations.

The figure for earners per household (Fig. 14.2) shows that the period effect has a very smooth convex curve with its peak at the collapse of the bubble economy

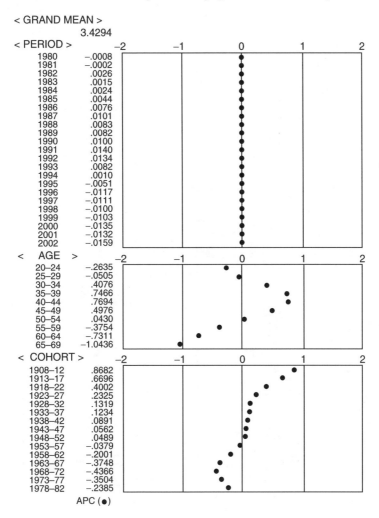

Fig. 14.1 Persons per household

around 1990, and very little width variation. This can be interpreted as being that the impact of job growth during the economic upturn phase, and women's social advancement that was encouraged in the *Law for Equal Employment Opportunities for Men and Women* and other measures does not clearly reflect in the earners per household category in the same terms the period effect does. On the other hand, age effect has a distinctive convex curve with its peak in the age range of householders from 55 to 59. The cohort effect has a right oblique profile where earners per household slightly increases with newer cohorts. When the fluctuation ranges (range = maximum value − minimum value) of the estimated values for the effects of age, period, and cohort (obtained as a result of analysis) are compared with each other,

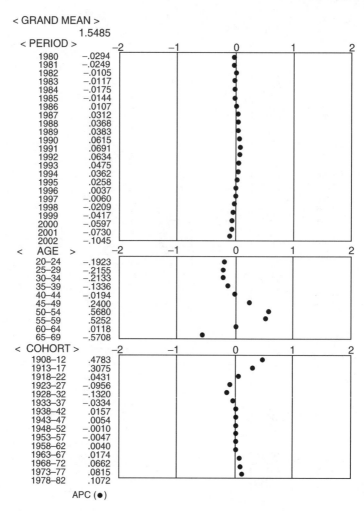

Fig. 14.2 Earners per household

the age effect is the largest, followed by the cohort effect, and then the period effect. More specifically, the most reasonable factor for an increase in the number of earners within the same household is the reemployment of a spouse after their children start school (as judged by the life stage estimated using the age of the householder). In further analysis, it would appear necessary to emphasize that the age of a householder does not merely mean their personal age but rather represents, as background, an image of the household using the premise of an average life stage model created with the householder age factor.

Table 14.1 summarizes the relative magnitudes of the three effects by adopting as an index the range of variation in respective effect parameter estimates as a result

Table 14.1 Results of cohort analysis on amounts of consumer expenditure by item (deflated)

Expenditure Items	GRAND MEAN	PERIOD Min(year)	PERIOD Max(year)	PERIOD Range	AGE Min(age)	AGE Max(age)	AGE Range	COHORT Min(cohort)	COHORT Max(cohort)	COHORT Range
Persons per household (persons)	3.4294	-0.0159 / 2002	0.0140 / 1991	0.0299	-1.0436 / 65-69	0.7694 / 40-44	1.8130	-0.4365 / 1968-72	0.8582 / 1908-12	1.2947
Earner per household (persons)	1.5485	-0.1045 / 2002	0.0691 / 1991	0.1736	-0.5708 / 65-69	0.5680 / 50-54	1.1388	-0.1320 / 1928-32	0.4783 / 1908-12	0.6103
Living expenditure (¥1,000)	5.7191	-0.0668 / 1981	0.0540 / 1992	0.1208	-0.2408 / 20-24	0.2195 / 50-54	0.4603	-0.0420 / 1913-17	0.0167 / 1943-47	0.0587
Food	4.3123	-0.0681 / 2001	0.0443 / 1980	0.1124	-0.2409 / 20-24	0.1779 / 40-44	0.4188	-0.1989 / 1978-82	0.0655 / 1908-12	0.2644
Cereals	2.0882	-0.2144 / 2002	0.2247 / 1980	0.4391	-0.3883 / 20-24	0.2695 / 45-49	0.6578	-0.0937 / 1973-77	0.0576 / 1938-42	0.1513
Fish & shellfish	2.1617	-0.0891 / 2002	0.0617 / 1992	0.1508	-0.1299 / 65-69	0.1227 / 45-49	0.2526	-0.9264 / 1978-82	0.4945 / 1908-12	1.4209
Meat	19.380	-0.1869 / 2002	0.0902 / 1982	0.2771	-0.3106 / 20-24	0.2949 / 45-49	0.6055	-0.0921 / 1973-77	0.0660 / 1943-47	0.1581
Dairy products & eggs	1.2785	-0.0612 / 1986	0.0439 / 1998	0.1051	-0.1084 / 20-24	0.1044 / 40-44	0.2128	-0.1448 / 1978-82	0.1057 / 1953-57	0.2505
Vegetables & seaweeds	2.1946	-0.1100 / 2001	0.1177 / 1980	0.2277	-0.2571 / 20-24	0.1287 / 50-54	0.3858	-0.4538 / 1978-82	0.1407 / 1938-42	0.5945
Fruites	1.1156	-0.1145 / 1996	0.1476 / 1983	0.2621	-0.0736 / 20-24	0.0647 / 40-44	0.1383	-0.9578 / 1978-82	0.3423 / 1928-32	1.3001
Oils, fats & seasonings	1.0560	-0.0455 / 1995	0.0322 / 1999	0.0777	-0.2863 / 20-24	0.1730 / 45-49	0.4593	-0.1240 / 1978-82	0.0695 / 1948-52	0.1935
Cakes & candies	1.6103	-0.0720 / 2000	0.0822 / 1993	0.1542	-0.2956 / 20-24	0.2666 / 40-44	0.5622	-0.0858 / 1978-82	0.0998 / 1953-57	0.1856
Cooked food	1.8696	-0.1911 / 1980	0.1559 / 2001	0.3470	-0.2279 / 25-29	0.2117 / 45-49	0.4396	-0.1939 / 1913-17	0.1100 / 1953-57	0.3039
Bevarages	1.1674	-0.1083 / 1986	0.1101 / 2002	0.2184	-0.1378 / 65-69	0.1130 / 45-49	0.2508	-0.0989 / 1908-12	0.0992 / 1958-62	0.1981
Alcoholic bevarage	1.2561	-0.0735 / 2002	0.0538 / 1980	0.1273	-0.3267 / 20-24	0.1686 / 55-59	0.4953	-0.2965 / 1978-82	0.1445 / 1943-47	0.4410
Eating out	12.8014	-1.3080 / 1980	0.7748 / 1991	2.0828	-4.9290 / 65-69	4.0311 / 40-44	8.9601	-1.0771 / 1923-27	0.5150 / 1948-52	1.5921

(continued)

Table 14.1 (continued)

Housing	3.0503	-0.1632 / 1980	0.1528 / 1996	0.3160	**-0.2348 / 50-54**	**0.4629 / 20-24**	**0.6977**	-0.0693 / 1948-52	0.1282 / 1978-82	0.1975
Fruel, light & warter charges	2.8455	-0.2683 / 1980	0.1527 / 2000	0.4210	**-0.3042 / 20-24**	**0.1594 / 45-49**	**0.4636**	-0.0349 / 1918-22	0.0272 / 1953-57	0.0621
Electricity	1.8741	**-0.4368 / 1980**	**0.2979 / 2002**	**0.7347**	-0.3929 / 20-24	0.1954 / 45-49	0.5883	-0.0117 / 1928-32	0.0109 / 1953-57	0.0226
Gas	1.7250	**-0.1518 / 1980**	**0.0763 / 1996**	**0.2281**	-0.1144 / 20-24	0.1105 / 45-49	0.2249	-0.0142 / 1928-32	0.0171 / 1978-82	0.0313
Other fuel & light	1.1688	-0.0994 / 1982	0.1741 / 1986	0.2735	-0.2423 / 20-24	0.1526 / 55-59	0.3949	**-0.3771 / 1973-77**	**0.1961 / 1928-32**	**0.5732**
Water & sewarage chrges	1.3725	-0.2097 / 1980	0.0944 / 1998	0.3041	**-0.3240 / 20-24**	**0.1580 / 45-49**	**0.4820**	-0.1624 / 1913-17	0.0975 / 1948-52	0.2599
Furniture & household utensils	10.3008	-1.1044 / 1981	0.7585 / 1991	1.8629	-2.6386 / 20-24	2.2592 / 55-59	4.8978	-0.8949 / 1913-17	0.4250 / 1953-57	1.3199
Household durables	1.1233	-0.2609 / 1980	0.2185 / 2001	0.4794	-0.2427 / 25-29	0.2659 / 55-59	**0.5086**	-0.0786 / 1913-17	0.0731 / 1933-37	0.1517
Interior furnishings & decotations	1.1128	-0.1327 / 1986	0.1813 / 1994	0.3140	-0.2841 / 20-24	0.2786 / 55-59	**0.5627**	-0.1039 / 1978-82	0.0954 / 1928-32	0.1993
Bedding	0.9542	-0.1555 / 2002	0.1411 / 1983	0.2966	-0.2840 / 25-29	**0.3023 / 50-54**	**0.5863**			N.S.
Domestic utensils	0.8738	-0.0625 / 1981	0.0644 / 1993	0.1269	-0.2264 / 65-69	0.0844 / 35-39	**0.3108**			N.S.
Domestic non-durable goods	0.5379	**-0.2136 / 1981**	**0.1925 / 2002**	**0.4061**	-0.2158 / 20-24	0.1001 / 45-49	0.3159	-0.2480 / 1908-12	0.1347 / 1958-62	0.3827
Domestic services	1.0267	-0.2016 / 2002	0.1627 / 1980	0.3643	-0.5087 / 20-24	**0.2958 / 65-69**	**0.8045**	-0.0799 / 1973-77	0.0847 / 1908-12	0.1646

Expenditure Items		GRAND MEAN	PERIOD			AGE			COHORT		
			Min(year)	Max(year)	Range	Min(age)	Max(age)	Range	Min(cohort)	Max(cohort)	Range
Living expenditure (¥1,000)	Clothes & footware	3.0045	-0.3165 / 2002	0.1715 / 1980	0.4880	-0.3288 / 20-24	0.3106 / 50-54	0.6394	-0.0366 / 1973-77	0.0520 / 1928-32	0.0886
	Japanese clothings	0.0579	-0.8044 / 2002	0.6105 / 1980	1.4149	-0.8978 / 30-34	1.0758 / 50-54	1.9736	-0.0949 / 1953-57	0.1131 / 1938-42	0.2080
	Clothings	2.0924	-0.2960 / 2002	0.1579 / 1980	0.4539	-0.4284 / 65-69	0.2888 / 45-49	0.7172	-0.0137 / 1948-52	0.0196 / 1928-32	0.0333
	Shirts & sweaters	1.2677	-0.1574 / 2001	0.1417 / 1990	0.2991	-0.2744 / 20-24	0.2227 / 45-49	0.4971	-0.1863 / 1978-82	0.1198 / 1933-37	0.3061
	Underware	0.6005	-0.3141 / 2002	0.1702 / 1980	0.4843	-0.2026 / 65-69	0.1522 / 45-49	0.3548	-0.2132 / 1978-82	0.0854 / 1948-52	0.2986
	Cloth & thread	-0.5512	-0.6588 / 2002	0.6854 / 1980	1.3442	-0.2830 / 20-24	0.3739 / 50-54	0.6569	-0.2036 / 1978-82	0.4897 / 1928-32	0.6933
	Other clothing	0.3096	-0.2424 / 2002	0.1522 / 1991	0.3946	-0.3039 / 65-69	0.1732 / 40-44	0.4771	-0.1224 / 1918-22	0.0767 / 1943-47	0.1991
	Footwear	0.6867	-0.1541 / 2001	0.0836 / 1990	0.2377	-0.4640 / 65-69	0.3546 / 40-44	0.8186	-0.0213 / 1963-67	0.0208 / 1931-35	0.0421
	Services related to clothings	0.4522	-0.4344 / 2002	0.1793 / 1992	0.6137	-0.4683 / 20-24	0.4107 / 55-59	0.8790	-0.1059 / 1978-82	0.0688 / 1958-62	0.1747
Medical care		2.3017	-0.1338 / 1986	0.1181 / 2002	0.2519	-0.0993 / 40-44	0.1639 / 65-69	0.2632	-0.1269 / 1908-12	0.0768 / 1958-62	0.2037
	Medicines	0.6158	-0.2289 / 1986	0.2943 / 2002	0.5232	-0.4086 / 20-24	0.3199 / 65-69	0.7285	-0.2596 / 1978-82	0.1130 / 1933-37	0.3726
	Medical supplies & appliances	0.5471	-0.3839 / 1980	0.3112 / 2000	0.6951	-0.0898 / 60-64	0.1292 / 45-49	0.2190	-0.1516 / 1943-47	0.2565 / 1963-67	0.4081
	Medical services	6.5011	-0.3609 / 1986	0.3353 / 1993	0.6962	-1.3860 / 50-54	1.2113 / 60-64	2.5973	-1.0397 / 1978-82	0.3823 / 1928-32	1.4220
Transportation & communication	Transportation & communication	3.4064	-0.3390 / 1980	0.2598 / 2002	0.5988	-0.4859 / 65-69	0.1527 / 20-24	0.6386	-0.0476 / 1918-22	0.0710 / 1958-62	0.1186
	Public transportation	7.0027	-0.6912 / 2002	0.6729 / 1992	1.3641	-2.1614 / 20-24	2.2656 / 45-49	4.4270	-0.1433 / 1928-32	0.2313 / 1963-67	0.3746
	Private transportation	17.0647	-3.5990 / 1980	2.1819 / 1996	5.7809	-3.2465 / 65-69	3.7733 / 50-54	7.0198	-8.6019 / 1918-22	8.3796 / 1973-77	16.9815
	Communication	1.8123	-0.4370 / 1980	0.5658 / 2002	1.0028	-0.3599 / 20-24	0.3753 / 50-54	0.7352	-0.2448 / 1933-37	0.8245 / 1978-82	1.0693

(continued)

Table 14.1 (continued)

		min	max	range	min	max	range	min	max	range
Education	2.2107	-0.1688 1990	0.1169 2002	0.2857	-1.2007 20-24	1.5144 45-49	**2.7151**	-0.1132 1928-32	0.2142 1908-12	0.3274
School fees	2.0306	-0.1298 2001	0.0956 1990	0.2254	-1.1024 65-69	1.3654 45-49	**2.4678**	-0.0455 1928-32	0.0383 1953-57	0.0838
School textbooks & reference books for study	-1.385	-0.3004 2002	0.1981 1990	0.4985	-1.3193 20-24	1.6082 40-44	**2.9275**	-0.0617 1938-42	0.0720 1908-12	0.1337
Tutorial fees	0.3198	-0.2346 1980	0.1647 1992	0.3993	-1.5765 20-24	1.9540 45-49	**3.5305**	-0.2107 1933-37	0.1513 1968-72	0.3620
Reading & recreation	28.9417	-4.1263 1980	2.3329 1999	6.4592	-10.4793 20-24	7.5514 40-44	18.0307	-2.3369 1913-17	1.8642 1958-62	4.2011
Recreational durable goods	0.6732	**-0.6411 1980**	**0.8994 2002**	**1.5405**	-0.4626 65-69	0.2064 40-44	0.6690	-0.1087 1913-17	0.1161 1953-57	0.2248
Recreational goods	6.0886	-1.2775 1980	0.7709 1993	2.0484	-1.8299 20-24	2.0480 40-44	3.8779	-0.5045 1928-32	0.6478 1958-62	1.1523
Books & other reading materials	1.6009	-0.0924 2001	0.1139 1980	0.2063	-0.1223 20-24	0.1082 35-39	0.2305	**-0.2698 1978-82**	**0.0960 1928-32**	**0.3658**
Recreational services	15.9551	-2.0073 1981	2.0664 1992	4.0737	-7.0680 20-24	4.4634 40-44	11.5314	-0.5811 1943-47	0.6623 1933-37	1.2434
Other living expenditure	4.3166	-0.0719 2002	0.0700 1992	0.1419	-0.3158 20-24	0.4147 50-54	0.7305	-0.1893 1978-82	0.0939 1943-47	0.2832
Miscellaneous	2.8838	-0.1111 1981	0.0813 1993	0.1924	-0.2694 25-29	0.3373 55-59	0.6067	-0.0270 1943-47	0.0442 1928-32	0.0712
Pocket money	3.1768	-0.1942 2002	0.1285 1989	0.3227	-0.8690 65-69	0.3717 50-54	1.2407	-0.2700 1973-77	0.1138 1943-47	0.3838
Social expenses	3.2893	-0.0644 2002	0.0852 1991	0.1496	-0.2954 20-24	0.3220 55-59	0.6174	-0.3498 1978-82	0.1272 1938-42	0.4770
Remittance	1.1571	-0.1487 1984	0.1214 1988	0.2701	-1.5325 25-29	2.1265 50-54	3.6590	-0.2077 1933-37	0.1320 1953-57	0.3397

"Range" column shows the maximum minus minimum values of respective effect. Bold typeface indicates the strongest effects among the three effects.

of separating household consumer expenditure. It also lists the categories in which the respective effects reveal their minimum and maximum values. Using the profile pattern on the cohort analysis result graph, the changing number of household members, product diffusion, and purchasing status characteristics can be seen.

Expenditure Items on Which the Age Effects Are Large

The profile of age effect indicates that the amount of consumer expenditure is influenced by an increase or decrease in household members and by a change in the number of people contributing to the household budget. In accordance with a shift in the life stage of the householder, there is a convex curve with its peak in the age range 40–50; the majority of their consumer expenditure items fall within this pattern.

Expenses for oil, fat & seasonings and others in food expenses; for electricity and gas in fuel; for light & water charges; and for bedding, domestic utensils, public transportation, and miscellaneous are reflected in the finding that the amount of consumer expenditure is determined by an increase or decrease in the number of householder members at a given life stage based on the age of the householder.

Although domestic services (e.g., wages for household helpers) is the factor most influenced by age, it does not have a convex profile but rather a right oblique profile. Therefore, it can be estimated that expenditure in this area will expand as the ratio of elderly increases.

Expenditure Items on Which the Age and Cohort Effects Are Large

While fish & shellfish, vegetables & seaweed, and fruit (Fig. 14.3) in food expenses have a convex profile for the age effect, they have a left oblique profile and a large fluctuation range for the cohort effect; the newer cohort markedly decrease their expenditure on these items. In other words, the expenditure amount of the new cohort has a relatively negative cohort effect. Furthermore, these expenses continue decreasing due to a switch into the old cohort because the number of household members also decreases.

Housing mainly refers to rent for dwellings & land. Its age effect has a left oblique profile, which means housing expenses for younger households without houses of their own are relatively large. In addition, younger cohorts show relatively large expenditure on this item. Okamoto [10] demonstrated that younger cohorts had the strong tendency for a decrease in financial assets by applying a life stage cohort model to household financial assets, and pointed out an increase in housing loans as the possible cause. According to the analysis of this paper, however, younger

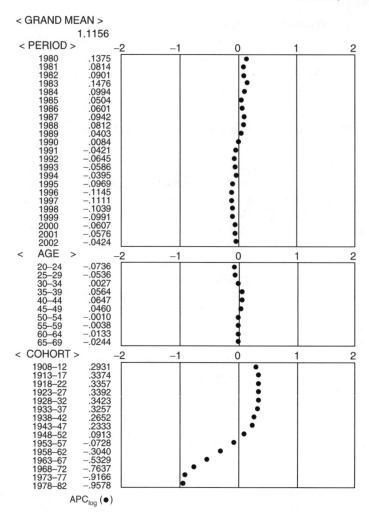

Fig. 14.3 Fruits

cohorts have large rent expenses, and the relationship with the increase in housing loans (increase in houses owned) was not sufficiently identifiable.

Regarding the age effect, social expenses have a right oblique profile, which means that the amount increases as people age. This is possibly because expenses for social norms such as marriage, funeral and ancestral worship ceremonies increase with age. Regarding the cohort effect, it has a left oblique profile, which means that younger cohorts tend to spend less on them. When both effects are compared with each other, the range of age effect is slightly larger. Entertainment expenses increase as the aging of the population advances, which can be interpreted as being repressed by the shift to younger cohorts.

Expenditure Items on Which the Age and Period Effects Are Large

Cereals and meat in food expenses, and shirts & sweaters and underwear in clothing & footwear have a convex profile of the age effect with its peak in the 40s, where the increase or decrease in number of household members is notable due to the householder's change in life stage. The period effect on them has a right oblique profile, which means that those expenses decrease as the years advance. The period effect on Japanese clothing *(kimono)* shows a left oblique profile where the expenses drastically decrease as years advance The age effect does not show a convex profile but rather an S-shape profile with its peak in the 50s and the bottom in the 30s. According to the *Sen'i-Touei data guide* (utilization guide for textile statistical data) [9], while the Coming of Age ceremony *(Sei-jin Shiki)* is the biggest event for stimulating demand in the *kimono* industry, the number of females aged 20 (age of the heads of households to which they belong is about 50), the target population of the event, decreased by 17% during the period 1995–2000. Analysis concludes that the decrease in population caused the falling demand for *kimonos*. It is estimated that the market for Japanese traditional clothing will continue to shrink due to the influence of the low birth rate.

The age effect on domestic non-durable goods, domestic durables, and recreational durable goods (including IT electronic appliances such as personal computers) shows a convex profile, which means that consumption is influenced by an increase/decrease in the number of household members. The period effect on them has a left oblique profile, which means that the consumption expenses expand as years advance. Recreational services include package tours and tuition fees. Both the age effect of a convex profile and the period effect of a convex profile with its peak in 1992 have a wide range of fluctuation.

Education and tutorial fees (Fig. 14.4) are large when the household head falls into the age bracket of those with children in school. Education expenses are of high expenditure elasticity.[3] The period effect decreases in line with economic recession. Medical care directly paid from household budgets is relatively small as the majority of it is covered by medical insurance. However, the self-pay ratio for patients has been raised through the medical insurance system being reformed and the portion not covered by public insurance is expanding. While the ratio of treatment received for infectious diseases to all diseases dropped sharply, the ratio of treatment received for adult diseases has been rising every year [14]. The aging of a population is typically accompanied by an increase in expenses for medicine and medical services (hospital charges and medical service fees) (Fig. 14.5). As the trend toward a nuclear family intensifies, the home is no longer used for nursing care and the ratio of hospitals as a "place to die" surpassed that of homes in 1980, recording over 70% in 1990. Since then, the ratio has continued to rise [15], and expenses for beds

---

[3] According to the *Annual Report on the Family Income and Expenditure Survey*, almost all items under education expenses, such as school fees and tutorial fees, are classified as "D (1.25 or over)", the highest category in terms of expenditure flexibility.

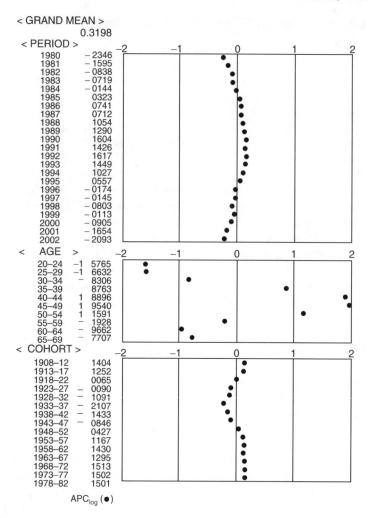

Fig. 14.4 Tutorial fees

incurring extra charges that are not covered by medical insurance and others will become increasingly necessary. The age effect has a concave profile, which means expenses increase in the age bracket of householders with aged persons, infants, and toddlers.

Expenditure Items on Which the Age, Period, and Cohort Effects Are Large

Regarding expenditure on eating out, a convex profile of age effect as well as gradual right oblique profiles of the period effect and cohort effect can be observed. The

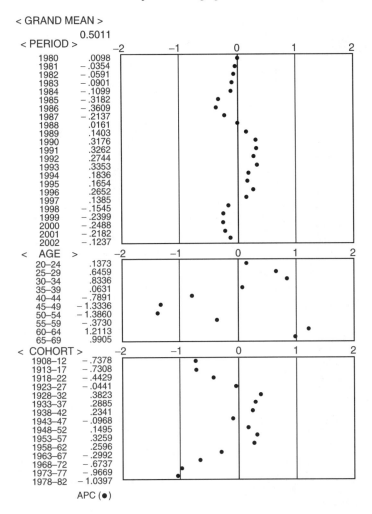

Fig. 14.5 Medical services

market will further expand as the children of the new cohort households, who have the ingrained habit of eating out, mature.

Regarding expenses for private transportation (Fig. 14.6), newer cohorts have larger expenses. The period effect has a right oblique profile, while the age effect has a convex profile with its peak in the 50s. More specifically, expenditure on private transportation continues to grow with age until some years have passed and people in the new cohorts enter their 50s. Based on the fact that the market share of Toyota out of the top three automobile manufacturers in the 1980s was distinctly high for the age range of middle-age and elderly people (40–59), and that Honda was highly supported by younger people in the age bracket 18–29, Ogawa [11] implemented simplified cohort analysis on those market shares. The results indicated that the age

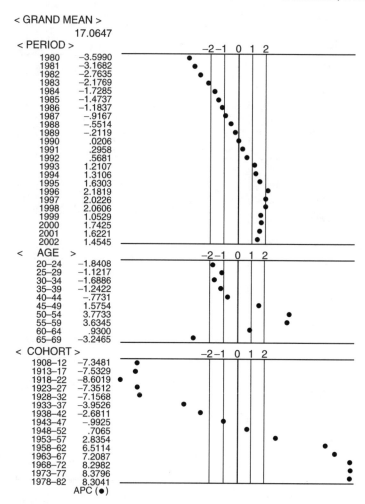

```
< GRAND MEAN >
            17.0647
< PERIOD >                      -2 -1  0  1  2
   1980    -3.5990
   1981    -3.1682
   1982    -2.7635
   1983    -2.1769
   1984    -1.7285
   1985    -1.4737
   1986    -1.1837
   1987     -.9167
   1988     -.5514
   1989     -.2119
   1990      .0206
   1991      .2958
   1992      .5681
   1993     1.2107
   1994     1.3106
   1995     1.6303
   1996     2.1819
   1997     2.0226
   1998     2.0606
   1999     1.0529
   2000     1.7425
   2001     1.6221
   2002     1.4545
<   AGE   >                     -2 -1  0  1  2
  20–24    -1.8408
  25–29    -1.1217
  30–34    -1.6886
  35–39    -1.2422
  40–44     -.7731
  45–49     1.5754
  50–54     3.7733
  55–59     3.6345
  60–64      .9300
  65–69    -3.2465
< COHORT >                      -2 -1  0  1  2
 1908–12   -7.3481
 1913–17   -7.5329
 1918–22   -8.6019
 1923–27   -7.3512
 1928–32   -7.1568
 1933–37   -3.9526
 1938–42   -2.6811
 1943–47    -.9925
 1948–52     .7065
 1953–57    2.8354
 1958–62    6.5114
 1963–67    7.2087
 1968–72    8.2982
 1973–77    8.3796
 1978–82    8.3041
            APC (●)
```

Fig. 14.6 Private transportation

effect dominated when selecting automobile manufacturers. He also demonstrated from that analysis that the market share of Toyota increased with age while that of Honda markedly decreased. This seems to reflect the tendency that people tend to buy higher class or more stylish cars from Toyota with age because the manufacturer has a wider range of luxury cars, and the increased number of middle-age and older drivers is expected to lead to a shift to high-priced luxury cars.

Communications (Fig. 14.7) includes postage, telephone bills, and charges for communication tools (cellular phones). Both the period and cohort effects have a right oblique profile while the age effect is convex with a wide range of fluctuation, which means that expenditure on communications will increasingly expand. In contrast, both the period and cohort effects on books & other reading material and cloth

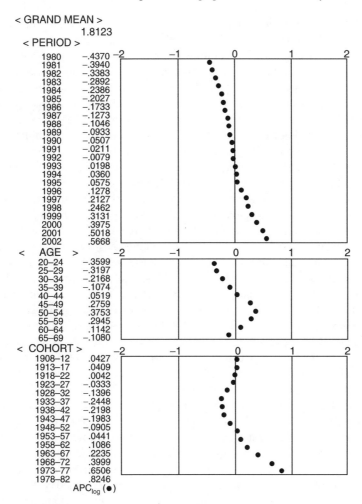

Fig. 14.7 Communication

& thread have a left oblique profile. The age effect has a convex profile, which is the true indication of a shrinking market.

Conclusion

By separating the household expenses into age, period, and cohort effects, the process difference of household consumption structure changes is clearly verified. Many expenditure items are susceptible to the age factor. The effect of changing the number of household members due to changing life stages and the effect of changing expenses due to aging of consumers can both be seen.

On the other hand, some expenditure items are susceptible to both cohort and age factors. It was confirmed that consumption behavior changed with the number of household members and with change in the cohorts of household members belonging to that of Japanese baby boomers or later cohorts, influenced by the volume of each cohort. It is necessary to qualitatively interpret how changes in the population structure of each cohort change the macro-level consumption structure. Based on the assumption that a direct relationship between the current consumer society and the aging society has developed during the period of modernization, a framework that can be organically integrated should be streamlined or reconstructed with the objective of clarifying consumer behavior changes in consideration of the parameters of consumer age, generation, and behavior patterns, the various systems as background to their lives, the socio-economic process involved, standards, technological advances, etc. Consumer behavior of individuals and households could be incorporated with actual living systems and the various factors that act upon each other. Yamashita and Nakamura [6] analyzed household account data in Japan and the USA using Bayesian cohort models. In the USA, most expenditure items are susceptible to the cohort effect; in contrast, many expenditure items are susceptible to the age effect in Japan. Figure 14.8 compares the results of the Bayesian cohort analyses of consumption expenses for fish and shellfish, as an example, in both Japan and the USA. The panels in the figure show that (i) the period effect for both countries follows a similar trend except in the late 1980s, (ii) in both, the age effects follow basically the same pattern and have peaks at the ages of 45–54, and (iii) cohort effects for the two countries have different movements. High age effects at age 30–55 of the household head suggest that children do not support themselves in those households. The cohort effects indicate that household heads born in 1948 or later (baby boomers and subsequent generations) tend to spend more money on fish and shellfish in the USA, which is the opposite extreme to the situation in Japan.

Not only economic factors but also non-economic factors should be classified and conceptualized in determining the mutual relationship between them. In the future, in order to more comprehensively explain the cause-and-effect chains of the three effects, a mutually complementary approach of quantitative and qualitative methods will be adopted. This will contribute to establishing an integrated theory, while respecting the existing theories of consumer behavior rather than ignoring them.

Appendix 1

Age, Period, and Cohort Effects

Age effect: This is due to changes in a person's opinions or attitudes as they age. For example, most people usually cease eating greasy foods as they get older. A

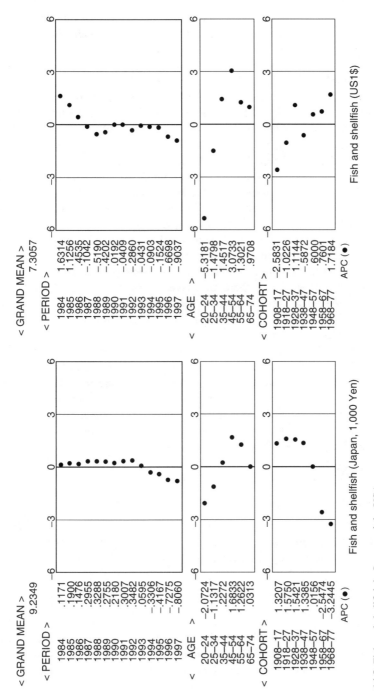

Fig. 14.8 Fish and shellfish in Japan and the USA

lot of research on consumer behavior changes due to aging, based on consumer functions, age, and family life cycle theory, has accumulated. As the data used in this chapter concerns households, changes related to the age of individual household members cannot be observed. However, with household expense data, the life cycles of average households and household life stages can be considered as the age of the household. More specifically, the age effect of the household head includes the effects of household structural changes caused by birth, growth, and the leaving of children due to self-sufficiency in average households, and economic changes such as changes in income. Assuming that no remarkable difference exists with the average household of each age group of the household heads, we represent the age of the household head as being that of the household.

Cohort effect: A cohort here denotes a group composed of individuals born within a specific period. People within the same cohort usually have similar mindsets and behavior patterns, and differ from those belonging to other cohorts. Cohort factors are considered to be independent of age and period factors. Individual cohorts may have been imprinted with fundamental differences in their way of thinking about consumption and saving in their youth. Having been exposed to a certain socioeconomic system from birth until their late twenties definitely determines a cohort's behavioral tendencies thereafter. Features of a cohort such as *Dankai-no-Sedai* (Japanese baby boomers) and *Shin-Jin-Rui* (New Species) are the most obvious during adolescence. Here, the cohort of the household head is regarded as that of the household.

Period effect: This is due to changes in the social environment and reflects that most people in a certain period move in the same direction, regardless of age and generation. Historical and environmental changes, which are related to the period effect, are considered common to all household members. They include economic, social, and sustainable changes such as trends of the time (for example, the so-called "bubble" economy), the increase in disposable income accompanying economic growth, and changes in being aware of what you eat.

Bayesian Cohort Model

Let y_{ij} be some quantity characterizing the ith age group in jth period. An age-period-cohort model can then be written as:

$$y_{ij} \text{ (or log } y_{ij}) = \beta^G + \beta_i^A + \beta_j^P + \sum_{k=1}^{K} c_{ij,k}\beta_k^C + \varepsilon_{ij}, \quad i = 1,\ldots,I; j = 1,\ldots,J,$$

where β^G, β_i^A, β_j^P, and β_k^C are the grand mean, age, period, and cohort effect parameters, respectively, and I, J, and K are the numbers of age, period, and cohort effect parameters, respectively. The parameters are subject to the following zero-sum constraints:

$$\sum_{i=1}^{I} \beta_i^A = \sum_{j=1}^{J} \beta_j^P = \sum_{i=1}^{I} \sum_{j=1}^{J} \sum_{k=1}^{K} c_{ij,k} \beta_k^C = 0.$$

The weights $c_{ij,k}$ are given as proportional to the degree to which the cohort intervals of the (i, j)th cell and the kth cohort parameter overlap ($c_{ij,k} \geq 0$ and $\sum_k c_{ij,k} = 1$). The terms ε_{ij} are assumed to distribute independently as normal with mean 0 and variance σ^2.

It is well known that the age-period-cohort model confronts an identification problem wherein the parameters of the model cannot be uniquely estimated [2,3]. To overcome the identification problem in cohort analysis, Nakamura [4,6,8] proposed a Bayesian cohort model incorporating a gradually-changing-parameter assumption or minimizing the following weighted sum of squares of first-order differences of adjacent effect parameters:

$$\frac{1}{\sigma_A^2} \sum_{i=1}^{I-1} (\beta_i^A - \beta_{i+1}^A)^2 + \frac{1}{\sigma_P^2} \sum_{j=1}^{J-1} (\beta_j^P - \beta_{j+1}^P)^2 + \frac{1}{\sigma_C^2} \sum_{k=1}^{K-1} (\beta_k^C - \beta_{k+1}^C)^2.$$

The model includes this assumption as a prior distribution with hyperparameters, σ_A^2, σ_P^2, and σ_C^2, which are determined by minimizing Akaike's Bayesian information criterion, ABIC [1]:

$$\text{ABIC} = -2\log \int f(\underline{y}|\underline{\beta}) \, \pi(\underline{\beta}|\underline{\sigma}) \, d\underline{\beta}_* + 2h,$$

where $f(\underline{y}|\underline{\beta})$ is the likelihood function, $\pi(\underline{\beta}|\underline{\sigma})$ the prior density, $\underline{\beta}_*$ the vector of effect parameters excluding β^G, $\underline{\sigma}$ the vector of hyperparameters, and h the number of hyperparameters. The estimate $\hat{\beta}$ of β is obtained by the mode of posterior density or maximizing $\log f(\underline{y}|\underline{\beta})\pi(\underline{\beta}|\hat{\underline{\sigma}})$.

We investigated and compared the magnitudes of age, period, and cohort effects using the range of their parameter variations (see Table 14.1).

Appendix 2

Descriptions of Japanese Cohorts

Silver (Year of Birth: 1935 or Earlier)

In general, the silver generation refers to those aged 60 or more. Those belonging to this generation experienced the Second World War and a period of high economic growth, but not uniformly. Therefore, it is difficult to express the silver market in a word. The 70s age group's sense of values, gained before the war, were completely reversed after it. The 60s age group are often called "people born in the Showa single-digit era." During the period of high economic growth, they were in the primes of their lives (30s). They worked hard as "self-sacrificing servants," transforming themselves into "economic animals," in order to catch up with Western living standards. The so-called Three Sacred Treasures (a television, washing machine, and electric refrigerator) or the 3Cs (a car, air conditioner, and color TV set) were respected as symbols of success in urban life.

Mature (Year of Birth: 1935–1946)

Together with the silver generation, this generation experienced the Japan–USA Security Treaty and student revolution periods, supported the high growth economy period, and were prominent throughout them. Their incomes leveled out and they eagerly sought affluence. Furthermore, their lifestyles changed to the modern Western style. Housework was simplified due to electric wiring in houses, the purchase of ready-made clothes, processed food, etc. A revolution in distribution also enabled people to buy daily necessities at superstores such as Daiei and Ito-Yokado, or GMS. With this generation, owning your own car also became popular due to the popularization of the motor industry that began in the latter half of the 1960s.

Dankai (Japanese Baby Boomers; Year of Birth: 1947–1949)

People in the baby boomer generation were born during 1947–1949 and went to school during a period of high economic growth and grew aware of foreign countries such as the USA through the Olympic Games, Project Apollo, and the World Trade Fairs. This generation wore flashy clothes and created markets together with Shiseido, Suntory, Honda, Sony, etc. In addition, they recognized that environmental pollution was behind economic growth, but that it was a trade-off for the affluence that resulted from economic growth. Their values differed from those of their parents, who were born before the war. They tried to destroy existing values and concepts through university protests that became increasingly disruptive in 1969. However, when they entered the workforce, tertiary service industries like securities and distribution were prominent choices. Many joined emerging industries, which are now being restructured due to the *Heisei* depression. As this generation is aging, we need to focus on this matter because of its sheer volume.

Heisei (New Family; Year of Birth: 1950–1960)

This generation was still in elementary school during the period of high economic growth of the 1960s. When they reached the age of discretion, the Three Sacred Treasures were already popular in their homes. They reached puberty in the 1970s when magazines such as *an an* and *non-no* were first issued. It is said that they have a greater appreciation of life than earlier generations.

Shin-Jin-Rui (New Species; Year of Birth: 1960–1970)

This generation was born in the 1960s amidst high economic growth, from which they enjoyed a heady consumer lifestyle. They have been in the limelight since youth, particularly women who experienced greater opportunities in education and work as a result of the *Law Concerning the Promotion of Equal Opportunity and Treatment Between Men and Women in Employment and Other Welfare Measures*. Furthermore, the enactment of the *Law Concerning the Welfare of Workers Who Take Care of Children* made it possible for them to continue working after giving birth. New products such as animation, TV games, Walkmans, VTRs, etc. were released on the market. As all those new products were fully available to them, this group became more selective in their tastes. In the bubble economy period of the 1980s, affluent single young people enjoyed overseas travel and purchasing brand-name products, which was further influenced by the emerging strength of the yen.

Dankai Jr. (Year of Birth: 1971–1983)

This generation refers to the second baby boomer generation born in the 1970s. Their parents belonged to the baby boomer generation and have the same postwar ideology that their parents had. They experienced a largely comfortable lifestyle as a result of improved social and living funds. Some 50–60% of elementary higher-class schoolchildren went to cram schools, which are private schools external to the national education system. The education industry represented by, for example, *Kumon-shiki* and *Shinken-zemi*, flourished. This generation has grown up surrounded by convenience stores, fast-food shops, family-style restaurants, Tokyo Disneyland, personal computers, etc., which have innovated their sense of values and life styles into that of an information-oriented society. This generation is becoming more individualistic; therefore, it is been said that the market has already been significantly subdivided.

Dankai Jr. graduated from university, but in time to coincide with the worst hiring slump in the mid-1990s. Most companies put a curb on hiring new workers as a result of weak business conditions following the burst of the economic bubble in 1990. That condition was often referred to as the "Ice Age" (a hard time to be a college-graduate job seeker) and peaked in 1997 when large banking agencies failed one after another. Therefore, this generation has quite a number of people who are not permanent employees. They are often categorized as "freeters" (job-hopping part-timers) or NEETs.

References

In English

1. H. Akaike in *Bayesian Statistics*, ed. by J.M. Bernardo, M.H. DeGroot, D.V. Lindley, A.F.M. Smoth (University Press, Valencia, 1980)
2. S.E. Fienberg, W.M. Mason, in *Sociological Methodology 1979*, ed. by K.F. Schuessler (Jossey-Bass, San Francisco, 1979)
3. W.M. Mason, H.H. Winsborough, W.K. Poole, Am. Soc. Rev. **38**, 242 (1973)
4. T. Nakamura, Ann. Inst. Statist. Math. **32**, 353 (1986)
5. T. Nakamura, in *Measurement and Multivariate Analysis*, ed. by S. Nishisato, Y. Baba, H. Bozdogan, K. Kanefuji (Springer, Berlin, 2002)
6. T. Yamashita, T. Nakamura, Comparison of the macro-structural foundation of consumption in aging and low-birth-rate societies of Japan and U.S. based on Bayesian age-period-cohort analyses. *Proceedings of Academy of Marketing Science*, 2003

In Japanese

7. Hakuhodo Institute of Life & Living, Kyodai Shijou "Elder" no Tanjou. President Sha, 2003
8. T. Nakamura, Proc. Inst. Statist. Math. **29**(2), 77 (1982)
9. K. Ogawa, Chan store Age **1996/4/5**, 65 & **1996/5/1**, 52 (1996)
10. M. Okamoto, Tokei **60**, 20 (2003)
11. Organization for Small & Medium Enterprises and Regional Innovation, JAPAN" (SMRJ), *Sen'i-Touei data guide* (utilization guide for textile statistical data) (2001), http://www.smrj.go.jp/jasmec/tira/jyohyo03/toukeidata.pdf, 43
12. K. Saitou, K. Matsuura, T. Fujino, C. Minami, Active senior no Syohi Koudou. Chuo Keizai Sha, 2003
13. M. Sano, Kokoro ga Shohi wo Kaeru. Taga Shuppan, 2004
14. Statistics and Information Department Minister's Secretariat Ministry of Health, Labour and Welfare JAPAN, *Heisei 14 Nen Kanja Chosa no Gaikyou.* (2002), http://www.mhlw.go.jp/toukei/saikin/hw/kanja/02/
15. Statistics and Information Department Minister's Secretariat Ministry of Health, Labour and Welfare JAPAN, *Heisei 15 Nen Jinkou Doutai Toukei.* (2003), http://wwwdbtk.mhlw.go.jp/toukei/data/010/2003/toukeihyou/0004652/t0098905/mc210_001.html

Chapter 15
Changing Consumer Values and Behavior in Japan: Adaptation of Keio Department Store Shinjuku

N. Enomoto

Abstract Japan has been the most aged society in the world since the early 1990s. Retailers in Japan now face various changes in the business environment, including demographic change, economic globalization, development of information technology, and changes in consumer's values and behavior. The consumer values and behavior in Japan reflect a characteristic transition in the retail sector, in which department stores have been a major force. The Keio Department Store in Shinjuku has been gearing its business toward seniors since the mid-1990s. The purpose of this chapter is to examine how an organization adapts to a changing business environment by exploring Keio Department Store Shinjuku as a case of a senior-focused retailer, extracting factors that are important in tailoring business practices.

Introduction

Learning from Western department stores, Japanese department stores, since their introduction in 1904, have developed in their socioeconomic and cultural characteristics and held a dominant position in the retail sector in Japan for many years. However, since Japan entered a period of slow economic growth after the first oil crises in 1973, department stores have experienced diminished sales. This revealed an inherent weakness of traditional department stores, and they seemed incapable of responding to changes in the competitive environment and to changing consumer values and behavior, particularly after the 1980s. Also, the short-sighted downsizing of merchandising efforts in the wake of plummeting sales after the 1991 collapse of Japan's bubble economy only served to make the department stores even more ill-equipped to attract customers during tough times.

Given such circumstances, Keio Department Store Shinjuku reached a turning point, combined with a fierce battle with a new Takashimaya department store in Shinjuku in 1996. Its strategic innovation in adapting to the changing business environment was to differentiate itself by making seniors its target demographic.

To analyze Keio's external environment, the changing business environment and consumer values and behavior will be explored in the following sections from the perspective of factors in the change and transition of the retail sector in Japan.

Mechanism and Factors in Changing Values and Lifestyle

Japan's current dynamic social environment, combined with economic globalization and the development of information technology, largely influences the diversification of people's lifestyles and values. With constant access to new information and knowledge, people become more tolerant toward different ways of thinking. The infiltration of the Internet and other information technology into everyday life has diversified not only people's lifestyles and values but also personal relations and communication styles. Between 1997 and 2006, the number of Internet users increased from 11.55 million to 87.54 million, and the user diffusion rate jumped from 9.2 to 68.5% ([11], p. 28). Nowadays, family members live far away from one another for educational or employment reasons. The number of Japanese students studying abroad, for example, increased from 18,066 to 76,464 between 1983 and 2000 [10]. Likewise, the number of foreign students in Japan increased from 10,428 to 121,812 between 1983 and 2005 [6]. Such exposure to a new social environment increases individuals' drive to seek out new information and pursue their own styles, whereas in the past, information was conventionally limited and mostly received in a passive manner.

Weakened demand for traditions or customs would be an indication of the diversification of values and lifestyles. Nowadays people enjoy their own time in their own way and value leisure time a great deal, but mostly this was not the case in the past. Valuing personal leisure time has influenced people's perspectives on conventional marriage, for example. Along with the increase in late marriages, the number of unmarried people in their 20s and early 30s has been increasing remarkably. The percentage of single people increased from 18 to 54% between 1970 and 2000, and more than half of all women in their late 20s were unmarried. In addition, the percentage of unmarried men in their late 30s increased from 12 to 43% in the same period. Because people still dominantly tend to have children after marriage in Japan, the decline in the marriage rate has led to a decline in the birth rate [14].

The enactment of laws and regulations can also be a factor that influences demographic change and value and lifestyle diversification. The Equal Employment Opportunity Law, enacted in 1985, for example, encourages women to be economically independent. When women pursue careers, and their work is incompatible with childcare, fewer women have children. In terms of the declining live birth rate, the gradual downward tendency continued into the late 1980s, and the rate hit its lowest postwar record of 1.29 live births per woman in 2003. The number of children born per year was about 2 million in the first half of the 1970s but decreased to around 1.1 million in 2006 [14].

Other environmental factors influencing changes in values and lifestyles are the spread of epidemics, such as avian flu and tainted food, and other natural or man-made disasters that result in greater concern for disease prevention and security. This heightened concern promotes consumer demand for safe, healthy food and other health-related goods. The factors related to changing values and lifestyles as above mentioned are only examples of the mechanisms to be explored in looking at how the diversification of values and lifestyles affects and is affected by ever-changing natural and social environments. Although it would be difficult to specify factors that influence things like consumer values and behavior and to analyze their degree of importance, the viewpoint that values and lifestyles and changing natural and social environments mutually influence one another is crucial, particularly for long-term assumptions about the business environment.

Figure 15.1 shows the mechanism of change and the key factors that interact with one another in society, lifestyle, and values.

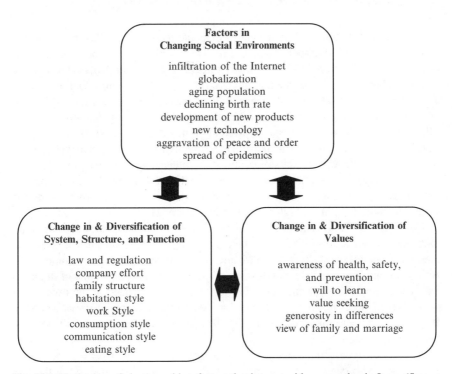

Fig. 15.1 Mechanism of change and key factors that interact with one another in Japan (*Source*: author's figure)

Transition of Department Stores and the Retail Sector in Japan

The consumer values and behavior in Japan generally reflect the characteristic transition in the retail sector. In the early post-war period, consumer demand was almost exclusively for daily necessities. However, the demand picture has changed as production and distribution of consumer goods increased and retail formats changed. The growth in consumer demand allowed growth of new retail formats ([9], p. 38). The department store was the first retail format and played an important role in the development of the retail sector in Japan. In the following sections, the transitions of department stores and the retail sector will be explored from the perspective of the changing external business environment.

Early Stage of Development of Department Stores

The prewar distribution system in Japan – characterized as a multilayered, complex system with a surplus number of small-scale retailers in relation to population – was often blamed for structural weakness, low effectiveness, and high distribution costs compared with those of Europe and the USA ([12], p. 4). The introduction and the development of the department store therefore had a great impact on distribution and retail businesses. Learning from Western department stores, the long-standing Mitsukoshi Gofuku-ten (Mitsukoshi Mercer Store) declared itself a "department store" in 1904, named itself Mitsukoshi Department Store, and targeted wealth in its early stages. After Mitsukoshi's reorganization, other major mercer stores, including Matuzakaya, Takashimaya, and Daimaru, followed ([7], pp. 27–28). Compared with other small retailers, the department stores were characterized by size and the wide selection of the latest high-grade goods ([22]. p. 2).

However, the Great Kanto Earthquake in 1923 brought an historic turning point to the department stores ([9], p. 18). The existing department stores in Tokyo geared their business toward seeking popularization and expansion of their customer base. As Jinbo cited from the histories of some major department stores, one of the main reasons for this change in direction was to fulfill a market need of the time. Most general retail stores had been destroyed by fire and the department stores that were able to restore operations quickly played a role in supplying daily necessities to the public ([7], pp. 28–29).

Also, a new type of department store, selling necessities such as food and household goods, with capital from the private railway companies, emerged in the late 1920s at the start of suburban rail service. As competition among department stores intensified, friction arose between the department stores and the small- and medium-sized retailers. As a result, the Department Store Law was passed in 1937, and control over the department stores was strengthened ([7], p. 30).

Dynamic Change in Retail Formats with Economic Growth

With the economic boom that followed the Korean War, Japan enjoyed unprecedented prosperity from the middle of the 1950s to the early 1970s. Its prewar
retailing system, consisting of a few powerful department stores and countless
small- and medium-sized retailers, revived. Although the Department Store Law,
enacted with the aim of ensuring business opportunities for small- and medium-
sized retailers, was reintroduced in 1956 ([9], p. 38), the department stores remained
remarkably competitive until the early 1970s. The number of railway-station department stores, for example, increased rapidly from the 1950s to mid-1960s, along with
growth of the suburban population ([7], p. 32).

With the rapid economic growth, a standardized mass popularized consumption
market appeared and developed large-scale retail businesses during the 1960s. These
new retail formats formed the base of the modern distribution establishments (e.g.,
large-scale household-appliance specialty stores), which did not have affiliated conventional distribution channels, and the chain stores. The outstanding development
of chain stores, particularly general superstores, shook the nationwide retail sector,
and the sales volume of the superstore segment surpassed that of the department
stores in1972 ([23], p. 59).

The first oil crisis in 1973 led Japan into a recession. At the same time, enactment of the Large-Scale Retail Store Law in 1973 hardened distribution and retail
systems, affecting rapid growth of the superstore segment. Instead, the popular consumption market disintegrated into many market segments, and the retail sector
became more diverse. The number of retailers whose business activities targeted
specific parts of the subdivided consumption market increased rapidly. Also, with
the growth in personal automobile ownership, the radius of shopping expanded,
and large roadside specialty stores dealing in toys and menswear, for example, and
suburban shopping centers appeared. Furthermore, convenience stores appeared in
the mid-1970s, and later developed with multifunctional services, including ATMs
and home delivery ([8], pp. 75–81). At the same time, general superstores and
department stores adopted a market segmentation strategy and sought differentiation and identity. Thus, new retail formats and the innovations in traditional business
appeared one after another during the 1970s.

Falling into Functional Insufficiency

Through the 1970s, 1980s, and 1990s, Japanese department stores had sluggish
sales, except for a short-lived recovery between 1986 and 1991, the days of the
bubble economy. The weaknesses of Japanese department stores during this time
were revealed in their functions and systems. Their multifunctional structure, adding
features such as cultural exhibitions, theaters, special displays, playgrounds, and
restaurants to attract customers, was one of the characteristics of Japanese department stores, but they caused malfunctioning. ([13], p. 61). Another important

characteristic of Japanese department stores that should be pointed out is an out-sourcing system of merchandising, using temporary sales staff. The system was introduced by an apparel wholesaler to gain competitiveness in 1953. The system was mutually beneficial for avoiding the risk for department stores of absorbing losses from unsold goods. Knowledgeable salespersons were sent to the department stores to reduce the risk of unsold goods. The system spread widely among depart-ment stores across the country, because of risk reduction, and department stores saw sales growth until the early 1970s ([7], pp. 39–40). However, this system resulted in weakness of department stores in the areas of their own managerial capabilities, lack of integrated management, and above all, limited room for creating differentiation and innovations.

The weakened integrated management capability of these retailers was evidenced by their practices after a protracted recession and after the collapse of the bubble economy in the early 1990s. To cut costs, conventional functions and merchandizing were reduced and externalized during this restructuring period. Departments such as women's apparel and medical supplies were expanded, while furniture, household appliances, and sporting goods were eliminated. For example, sales of women's clothing rose from 21.5 to 25.3% of the total sales volume of Japanese department stores between 1991 and 2001, whereas sales from furniture fell from 6.0 to 2.7% ([1], p. 9).

In addition, many large specialty retailers such as Bic Camera, Yodobashi Camera, Best Denki, and Otsuka Furniture opened concessions in department stores. Urban department stores such as Kyoto Kintetsu, Shinjuku Mitsukoshi, and Sukiyabashi Hankyu department stores converted part of their buildings for such tenant use ([13], p. 62). Such measures reduced the possibility of their own domain for department stores in management and innovation. In addition, they created similar merchandise selections and compromised a store's unique characteristics. Thus, while strong administrative management capability was required for Japanese department stores, the reforms narrowed their management range by externalizing merchandise dealings. In other words, Japanese department stores diverged from originality of functions and innovations. The inertia in this direction of depart-ment stores made them incapable of responding to changes in the competitive environment and to changing consumer values and behavior after the 1980s.

Changing Consumer Values and Behavior

Consumer demand was generally for the same daily necessities as in the early postwar period. However, this changed with increased production and distribution of consumer goods. When Japan experienced rapid economic growth for about 20 years starting in 1955, the demand for daily necessities was met, and people moved on to fulfilling special needs ([9], p. 33). However, consumer values and behavior were still characterized at that stage as conformist and with the same desires, largely because of the appearance of a standardized, large-scale, popularized consumption market accompanied by development of a mass-targeted retail sector.

When the postwar economic boom ended with the first oil crisis in 1973, many consumers became more selective and started seeking individual lifestyles. At the same time, the popular consumption market fragmented into many market segments. The remarkable tendencies seen in the early 1980s were a differentiated quality-of-life orientation, fashion orientation, and smart consumption. Combinations of these orientations made for extreme diversity ([12], pp. 13–14). Younger people respect diversity more than traditional ways. These trends reverse for both men and women in their 40s. Views of marriage are becoming liberalized, drifting away from the traditional mindset that "one should get married" ([16], p. 10). The number of households with no sons or daughters is increasing, and more people live alone. This is also true among seniors. However, more consumers take word-of-mouth as reliable opinion despite positions to the contrary from the Internet, and from communication with family and friends ([16] p. 13).

Different approaches and research studies have revealed some trends in consumer values and behavior. For example, consumers enjoy more relaxation services in their free time, and they pursue lifestyles and consumption patterns that attach great importance to their individuality. Accordingly, consciousness in terms of collecting and searching for information about lifestyles has increased. "The cheaper, the better," which dominated in the 1970s, was no longer the most important issue for consumers ([20], pp. 9–10).

Japanese consumers have traditionally been described as displaying "bipolarization": a high-grade orientation toward buying goods regardless of the price, and price-oriented to buy inexpensive goods without being particular. Shiozaki's research group suggests a new framework for analysis of current consumers' behavioral patterns. Setting high and low prices on the vertical axis, and stronger and weaker particularities about things toward the right and left on the horizontal axis, consumer behavioral patterns can be classified into four styles: high-grade seeker, convenience seeker regardless of price, reasonable-price seekers of particular things, and price seeker, "the cheaper, the better" ([20], pp. 15–18). The increased number of Internet users reveals that customers enjoy a social environment that makes it easy for them to search for information. Also, even divided into the four categories, the individuals change their inclination depending on items and occasions. Although the percentage and absolute number of people in each group are not shown, the obvious trend is toward diverse consumer values and behavior, with more careful consideration of purchases by searching and collecting reliable information.

Even among seniors, the characteristics of their consumption styles tend "to involve caring about the reputation or comments from other people about the product" or "to examine whether a price is reasonable for good quality." For example, in research in 2000, 2003, and 2006, the numbers of male and female consumers who considered the validity of price and quality increased. Likewise, the number of seniors who are particular about what they want is also increasing, especially among males ([19], pp. 24–25)

According to research from the Bank of Japan, the individual propensity to consume is firm, including among youths, and it has been remarkable among seniors in recent years. The factors in seniors' consumption trends can be the structural factors of demographic change such as the aging population, changes in consumer values and company efforts, and the introduction of the nursing-care insurance system. Generally, the propensity to consume decreases from youth to middle age then increases with age. Taking a long-term view of the propensity to consume, a cohort analysis to break down the propensity into the age effect, the generation effect, and the period effect was also applied. As a result, it has been confirmed that the change in the composition of the aging population steadily pushes up the overall propensity among the population to consume ([3], pp. 11–18).

In terms of changing lifestyles, seniors who have more financial security want to "enjoy life." Businesses view "active seniors" who can afford to buy as an important target group. A trend in a "tertiary industry activity index" shows that travel agencies, fitness clubs, and bars are experiencing high growth rates. Also, expanding distribution channels for consumption include convenience stores, drugstores, specialty stores, and shopping malls, as well as TV and online shopping. However, a study from Nomura Research Institute clearly shows that seniors are more inclined to go the way of one-stop shopping (purchasing as many items as possible at one store) than are those of other generations, and the radius of consumption for seniors is smaller [22]. This means that distant and large-sized stores are not appropriate for frequent patronage by seniors.

Thus, Japanese consumer values and behavior, in general, are becoming more diverse, more oriented toward quality of life in terms of health, safety, and relaxation than in the 1960s. They are also more selective and wary of value-oriented consumption. All of these trends can be seen among consumers regardless of generation, except in a physical domain such as consumption radius.

Case Study: Keio Department Store

Keio Department Store Shinjuku opened in 1964 and is wholly owned by Keio Electric Railway Company. It is located at Shinjuku Station, which, serving ten railway and subway lines, is the busiest station in Japan. In addition, Shinjuku is the country's most competitive area for department stores in terms of number of commercial facilities, restaurants, and crowded offices. It is home to several major department stores.

At Keio Department Store, customers over 50 years of age account for about 70% of sales, and the constituent percentage of seniors is higher than at other department stores. Pioneering among department stores in Japan, Keio has its own customer membership system, giving members some privileges of discount or vouchers depending on amount of installment savings over the course of 12 months, for example. Its customers who were in their 20s or 30s when the store opened are now in their 50s or 60s. As for the number of customers (member's cardholders), according to the age groups of Keio Department Store in 2004, 55–57 is the highest 3-year bracket, and the majorities are in their 50s and 60s. Most of those who purchase are in their 50s, 60s, or 70s. The growth rate is particularly marked among people in their 40s and 50s. It is a distinction that people in their 50s and 60s purchase the most, and 73% of sales in 2004 were to those 50 or over [15].

Subdividing Senior Customers into Even Smaller Categories

When business apparel and clothing for the younger generations led women's consumption, merchandise for middle-aged or senior people was normally grouped together with full-line and full-targeted selections. However at Keio, analysis of its customer data and studies of other research results revealed clearer characteristics and trends regarding its senior female customers and subdivided them into even smaller groups: aged over 65, 55–64, and 40–54 for senior people and another category for people under 40, to correspond to the diverse values and characteristics of its senior customers.

Keio views the first group (aged over 65), the prewar generation, as having a tendency for sound consumption and a mindset for saving. They do buy new things and enjoy casual opportunities for postwar values but still need a reason for consumption each time. Keio appeals to their style with an intellectual, innovative image.

The second senior group (aged between 55 and 64), the first baby-boomer generation, shares values with the younger generation. They have information from overseas and an interest in traveling and leisure. They are authenticity-oriented but still conservative. People of this generation pay more attention to their private lives than the older generation and are not like eager beavers devoting their lives to work. This group still values individuality and word-of-mouth information from family and friends. This leads to a great deal of consumption power. Their interest in anti- and healthy-aging products is also very high. Keio Department Store feels that good-quality material that leads to good appearance is important to this generation. It also appeals to the younger generation's consciousness in an international sense.

The third senior group (aged between 40 and 54), the post-baby-boomers, are a strategically targeted generation. They have no hesitation in buying expensive, brand-name items with an international and youthful style. Actually, individual consumption unit price is higher than paid by customers in their 60s, according to Keio's data.

Then there are the junior baby-boomers, who are below age 40 and go for young career fashion. Thus, Keio has developed a clear concept of generational characteristics. However, this subdivision of seniors is a subgroup within a classification and characteristics of these divisions overlap and remain invisible.

Keio's incremental renovation in fall 2006 concentrated on the second, third, and fourth floors as a part of a 5-year renovation project (2003–2007). The following shows the arrangement of Keio's customer categories and relevant selections on each floor during the renovation.

Subdivision of Customer Category

- Category A: Prewar generation
- Category B: Baby-boomer generation (the most important target)
- Category C: Post-baby-boomer generation (a strategic target)
- Category D: Junior baby-boomer generation

Targeted Categories and Lady's Apparel Floor Layout:
The Second, Third, and Fourth Floors

- Fourth floor: Most targeted category is A (plus categories B, C, and D as A's daughters)
- Third floor: Most targeted categories are B and C (plus categories A and D)
- Second floor: Most targeted category is D (plus categories B, C, and A as D's mothers)

On the ladies' floors (from the second to the fourth floor), the department store rearranged the fourth floor in 1995, making it easier for customers in their 50s and 60s to navigate. Based on Keio's customer survey data analysis, travel was the highest-ranking purchase motive, for example. It has taken its customers' consumption habits and tastes into account and applied them to a substantiality of selection, price range, and, above all, quality customer service. As a result, sales on the fourth floor increased by 7.8% from 1995 to 2005.

The renovation on the fourth floor was aimed at improving satisfaction among existing customers. To avoid alienating existing customers with a new and unfamiliar layout but while intensifying its youthful image, the floor layout was kept intact. The image has been changed most daringly on the renovated third floor, which Keio consider important as it is supported by wide range of generations. The purpose of that renovation was to expand the brands supported by the strategic target (the post baby-boomers) and to boost sales and increase migration by the most important target, the baby-boomer generation (Category B). As a result, sales on the third floor increased by 20%, and sales on the fourth floor achieved 10% growth, according to data from 20 days after the renovation in September ([18], pp. 74–77).

Selections

Consistent with its diverse values, Keio has some items designed just for seniors (e.g., women's clothes, with subdivisions in terms of sizes, colors, and designs). Keio has also developed its own original brand for seniors. Its sweaters, for example, have the top sales in Japan. In 2007, its sales from April to September increased by 7% from 2001. Bathing-suit sales increased by 15% in the 3 years after it shifted the selection from seasonal to sport swimsuits for year-round purchases in 2002 ([17], p. 14).

After the women's hat corner was revised in 1998, it also became a big profit maker, with 300 million yen annual turnover, the top sales in Japan. Keio enlarged the selection by marketing hats as a method of sun protection and for covering hair in a fashionable way. In 1995, Keio established the walking shoes corner, which was the first of its kind among department stores in Japan. For a customer who has foot trouble, Keio is easy to access from the station. Keio's selections also correspond to different types of feet. All of these selections are based on the top-ranked values among its customers (e.g., leisure, health, relaxation, safety). For sports shoes, counter sales in 2006 increased by 80% from 2001, and sales during April to September 2007 increased by 85% over 2001 levels. Also, in 2006 sales at the town walking-shoes corner from April to September increased by 40% from the first half of 2001 and 47% in 2007 from 2001. These are also the country's top sales in this kind of section [15]. Figure 15.2 shows sales in the store and on the fourth floor at Keio Department Store Shinjuku.

After the collapse of the bubble economy, private consumption gradually recovered after the fall of 1993 and then moved up from late 1996 to early 1997, accompanied by front-loading expansion of spending prior to the consumption-tax hike from 3 to 5% in April 1997 [2]. Accordingly, Keio sees the decline of 1997 as the aftermath of the expansion of consumption in the previous year. The decline in 2004 is reaction to "the baseball team championship sale" of 2003 and full-scale remodeling construction. Typically, railway companies in Japan nowadays hold businesses in sectors such as transportation, real estate, retail, travel, and leisure. However, some railway companies used to own baseball teams in the hopes of transporting fans to and from stadiums, thus adding value to the route. Not as many railway companies in Japan today own professional baseball teams compared with the 1960s. Hanshin Electric Railway Co., owner of the Hanshin Tigers, is one of the few that still do. Keio Corporation, which is a railway company, does not own

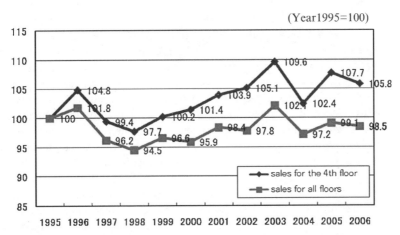

Fig. 15.2 Sales statistics of Keio department store Shinjuku (*Source*: Keio department store, Shinjuku)

a baseball team. However, because of its collaborative relationship with Hanshin Department Store, whose parent company is Hanshin Electric Railway Co., it holds a sale at the time of the championship of the Hanshin Tigers.

Sales growth for 2003 and 2005 was exceptional because of the baseball championship sales carried out in those years. Particularly, in 2003, the Hanshin Tigers won for the first time in 18 years, which created a social phenomenon involving a wide range of people cheering the team across the country. Over 120,000 people flooded into the store on the first day of the sale. The usual number is about 70,000 a day. Interestingly, the influence of these sales appeared in the middle and senior age groups that came to the fourth floor, showing a conspicuously strong reaction to the sale.

For Quality Communications

One of characteristics of Japanese consumers that Chen pointed out is that they are among the most demanding in the world regarding service and quality: complete fitness, absolute freshness of produce, swiftness of delivery, and so forth ([4], p. 234). Also, Japanese consumers have close relationships with their small neighborhood shops, and such shops offer an important opportunity for socializing. Likewise, department stores offer a similar function as centers of social life and have close relationships with customers. Therefore, Japanese shops and stores in general are highly service-oriented and place the needs of their customers as their top priority ([4], p. 228). Accordingly, word-of-mouth becomes the most reliable information for both Keio and for its customers. One research results show that seniors react less to trends and advertisements ([21], pp. 52–53). From Keio's research, it believes that the most effective way to have reliable information for senior customers is word of mouth. Therefore, quality customer service becomes especially important when its customers with diverse values rely on word of mouth. To improve customer service and communication, Keio Department Store provides full-scale training, conferring qualifications of Service Advisors on those who complete the training, and increased the number of Shopping Advisors (from 34 to 64) and of Color Advisors (from 21 to 45) in 2007. Keio plans to increase these numbers further in the coming years.

Thus, Keio Department Store strives to understand the changes in consumer values and behavior of both consumers and seniors. According to an analysis of consumers in general and of Keio's specifically, consumer values and behavior are not influenced by trends or advertisements. Consumers seek suitable merchandise for themselves. In addition, more seniors want to enjoy life, and they are shifting to a more casual, health-conscious, and beauty-conscious approach to life. One example of Keio's arrangement for these senior customers is that half of the women's clothing floor is arranged by item so that customers can choose clothes according to price, size, and color lines by themselves, not by brand. To meet with the increasing consumer values in "things for killing time," (such as trips, events, or cultural pursuit, which are increasing in popularity in department stores), what Keio focuses on are customers' stated values and purposes (e.g., merchandise to relax, or for a trip). Playground equipment and sporting goods, which were once reduced along with other merchandising systems during restructuring after the collapse of the bubble economy, have returned to Keio, creating three-generational shopping. Thus, Keio's strategy is not in creating new values or trends but in realizing its own customers' needs, anticipating what customers want and need. It repeats hypotheses and verifications from analysis based on collected information through communications with some of its 70,000 daily customers. Therefore, its renovation is carried out according to a 5- or 10-year plan.

Discussion

Department stores in Japan targeted the wealthy in their early stages and later became more popularized, turning to high-class luxury selection and multifunctionality, took on concession tenants, and installed amusement facilities. They have maintained an important position among retailers and have had an impact on the complicated distribution system since the first department store opened in Japan in 1904. However, changes in the business environment, including market change with new competitors, enactment of regulations, appearance of new retail formats, changes in consumer values and behavior, and particularly the recent long-term economic recession of the 1990s, have affected their sales.

Keio had been in great tribulation in facing severe challenges, particularly in 1996, when a new powerful competitor opened a department store in the same keenly competitive area, Shinjuku, Tokyo. Keio's challenge was to get over the sluggish business and get on the right track by employing a new, more diverse senior-targeting strategy in the face of market change due to the competitors' new business activities, demographic change toward a rapidly aging society, and consumers values and behavior.

Innovations among Keio's competitors have tended to be changes of retail formats in rapid and drastic ways. The South Building of Shinjuku Mitsukoshi was rented out to Otsuka Kagu, a furniture retailer, in 1999. The interior annex Halc of Odakyu Department Store has been tenant-occupied since 2002, by BIC camera, after poor performance of furniture sales in that space ([1] p. 29). Shinjuku Mitsukoshi reinvented itself as a miscellaneous-goods specialty shop called Shinjuku Mitsukoshi Alcott in 2005. Moreover, Mitsukoshi and Isetan merged and created, in April 2008, Japan's largest department store group by integrating their operations under a joint holding company named Mitsukoshi Isetan Holdings.

In contrast, Keio's attempts reveal the opposite innovation, focusing on internal improvement rather than external exploitation. More specifically, Keio focuses on existing customers rather than tapping new customers, recognizing and valuing its intrinsic resources and properties. Keio arranged for three-generation consumption in the 1960s rather than highlighting the newest top luxury world-brand fashion, as seen at Isetan and Shinjyuku Takashimaya, and applied a longer-term, incremental renovation project. As a result, Keio's "unchanged innovation" turned out to be a substantial distinction from other department stores.

The factors in Keio's decision on how Keio Department Store could escape from a predicament and be able to put it on track with a new senior-targeted strategy were its attempt to evolve, reviewing and making Keio's resources, including its customers, its cornerstone. The measures Keio took to cope with the changing environment and diversification of the consumer values reflected the analysis of consumption trends based on customer data from its membership and from collected information voiced daily in the store, making hypotheses and strategy, and verification to meet the customer needs.

As a result, it differentiates itself from department stores that present luxurious imported and high-priced goods in (i) a classification system according to the senior generation brackets, (ii) the serious consideration for casual and fashionable items of many kinds in small quantities that serve the purpose at reasonable prices, and (iii) making the baby-boomer generation the most important target and post-baby-boomer generation a strategically targeted bracket. Unlike younger generations, senior customers tend to stop on more floors. The approaches to shopping radius among seniors therefore would be Keio's strong point in leading to successful three-generation consumption.

Thus, the examination of Keio's measures to operate in its severe business environment demonstrates two remarkable strategies: clarification of its target customers and distinctive operation in the market. For these strategies, Keio targets senior customers, using analysis of customer data, application of supposition and inspection, and continuous information gathering to keep the consumption trends in perspective. One of these attempts is substantial theme-relevant assortments, on the hypothesis that travel, leisure, health, and safety are essential considerations. Also, the layout of each floor and allocation of the whole building are based on the hypothetical action scenario that more senior customers prefer one-stop shopping style and a wider radius inside of the building. Naturally, reliable information is supplied to both customers and Keio through reinforcement of customer services, supporting the hypothetical action scenarios at the same time. The important thing is that all innovations and efforts have to be logically integrated once a target is identified.

Keio's practice can be effective against the weakness of department stores of limited flexibility, which has surfaced since the late 1970s, particularly in the face of a changing market and consumers' changing values and behavior. It can also be effective against a lack of integrated managerial capability, which has surfaced since the early 1990s. With clear vision and targeting of customers, increased centripetal force that leads to integrated management can be expected. Also, improvement in quality service through providing a qualification system for its full-time sales staff instead of outsourcing can be expected to secure responsiveness to customers' needs and consequently to flexibility to their changing values and behavior.

An analysis of diverse consumer behavior is becoming more difficult, because it is a mixture of values reflecting life experience, aging traits, evolving traits, and individual traits. If Keio Department Store sees steady sales increases through segmentation, subgrouping of senior customers can be an effective way of corresponding to that mixture of values and can contribute to examinations of its hypothesis and verification in terms of its customers' values and behavior, as external changing business environments.

Summary and Conclusions

In this chapter, the way an organization adapts to a changing business environment was examined by exploring Keio Department Store Shinjuku as a case of a senior-focused retailer, and factors were extracted that are important in tailoring business practices to a changing business environment. To analyze a retailer's business environment, taking into account how consumer values and lifestyles and changing natural and social environments mutually influence one another is crucial, particularly when making assumptions regarding the business environment for the long term. While diversification of Japanese consumer values and behavior, reflecting the transition of the retail sector, is presented as a major factor of change in the business environment, the weaknesses of department stores in integrated management practices and innovation, which are commonly seen among Japanese department stores, limit their capability to respond to changes in the competitive environment.

For Keio, a challenge to the new powerful competitors was, at the same time, adapting to changes in the business environment. Keio took two remarkable strategies: clarification of its target customers and distinctive operation in the market. Accordingly, the key internal innovations of Keio Department Store were to improve the quality of service and communication in order to identify the values and traits of its existing customers from a long-term perspective. Some of Keio's strategies were the opposite of what competitors were doing and resulted in distinctive operation in terms of size of store, resources, speed, degree, ways of innovation, scope of target, price, and assortment; namely medium size, conventional resources, senior-targeted but considering tree generations, substantial merchandizes for reasonable price, long-term incremental change, and invisible innovation. In addition, these strategies and efforts are logically interwoven and integrated as a whole. Thus, at Keio, a clear vision of targeting customers and its logically integrated strategies increased centripetal force. This gave Keio the flexibility to adapt to the changing external competitive business environment, including consumers' diverse values and behavior.

Production technology supported Japan's industrialization and its economy. As technology developed, and products became abundant, items with intrinsic sense, value, or added value to meet personal needs started supporting the current economy. It is unknown how society and people's values change. However, for retailers like Keio, continuous efforts to gather information from customers can be helpful in satisfying customers in the even more diverse society of the future.

Appendix

Japan became an "aging society" in 1970 and an "aged society" in 1994. Now it is the most aged society in the world. However, both the public and private sectors in Japan are still underdeveloped in the area of provisions for an era of an aged society. A case study was conducted as basic research to examine the ability of organizations to cope with the changing business environment, particularly the adaptability of retailers to an aged society.

The study case was selected from among 30 retailers that had exhibited shifts toward niche business combined with quality service, based on a positioning map generated by analyses performed by a financial research institute on small- and medium-sized enterprises ([5], pp. 71–80).

With a case that met the selection criteria of an organization that (i) was already catering to seniors as its core clientele, (ii) recognizes internal and external aspects of the business environment, and (iii) has implemented innovation, this case study involved the following aspects and research methods:

- Comprehensive analysis and interpretation of changing business environments from socioeconomic and cultural perspectives, taken mainly from government statistics and interpretations, with additional research data from advertising and financial research institutes
- Exploration of conventional business practices in the retail sector, along with changes in the business environment, with research references on marketing, the retail sector, and department stores
- Examination of effectiveness and adaptability of internal functions and systems to external changes in the business environment, through a case study of one selected department store
- Face-to-face and telephone interviews and online communication with the following individuals between late October 2007 and January 2008: Sachiko Shindo, Senior Manager, Public Relations Department, Keio Department Store Co., and Yoko Yasuda, Deputy General Manager, Marketing and Sales Promotion Officer, Takashimaya Co.
- Field studies on store layout, selections, customers, services, and communication of the following department stores between August 2007 and January 2008: Isetan (Shinjuku), Keio Department Store (Shinjuku), Mitukoshi (Nihonbashi), Odakyu Department Store (Shinjyuku), Seibu Department Store (Ikebukuro), Takashimaya (Nihonbashi), Tobu Department Store (Ikebukuro)
- Data analyses provided by Keio Department Store Shinjuku

References

1. Y. Asakura, A. Ôhara, *Zenkoku hyakkaten no tempo senrhyaku* (Tokyo, Dôyu-kan 2003)
2. Bank of Japan, Monthly report of recent economic and financial developments (The Bank's View, Japan, 1998), http://www.boj.or.jp/en/type/release/teiki/gp/gp9812.htm Accessed 25 February 2008

3. Bank of Japan. *Why has Japanese private consumption remained firm?* (Research and Statistics Department, Japan, 2006)
4. M. Chen, The Japanese distribution system in transition, in *Asian management systems: Chinese, Japanese, and Korean styles of business*, 2nd edn. (International Thomson Business Press, London, 2004), chap. 19
5. Chûshô Kôko,. *Shinia shijô ni chûmokusuru chushôkigyô no Senryaku to kadai* [Strategies and challenges of small- and medium-sized enterprises in the senior market], Chûshô Kôko report no 2004–3 (Chûshôkigyô Kinyûkôko Sôgô Kenkyûsho, Tokyo, 2005)
6. Japan Student Services Organization (2005), http://www.jasso.go.jp/statistics/intl_student/data05.html#no1. Accessed 21 Jan 2007
7. M. Jinbo, Hyakkaten no Nihon-teki tenkai to mâkettyingu, in *Nihon ryûtsû sangyô-shi* (Dôbun-kan, Tokyo, 2002)
8. H. Kim, Konbiniensu-sutoa no Nihon-teki tenkai to mâkettyingu, in *Nihon ryûtsû sangyô-shi* (Dôbun-kan, Tokyo, 2002)
9. H. Meyer-Ohle, *Innovation and dynamics in Japanese retailing: from techniques to formats to systems* (Palgrave Macmillan, New York, 2003)
10. Ministry of Education, Culture, Sports, Science and Technology, Japan (2008), http://www.mext.go.jp/b_menu/soshiki2/46.htm Accessed March 17 2008 http://www.jasso.go.jp/gakusei_plan/documents/monka.pdf Accessed 17 March 2008
11. Ministry of Internal Affairs and Communications, White Paper. Information & communication statistics database, 2007
12. M. Miura, Introduction, in *Nihon ryûtsû sangyô-shi* (Dobun-kan, Tokyo, 2002)
13. K. Miyazoe (2005) *J. Market. Distribut.* Ryûtsû Kenkyû., Vol. 8, No. 1, p. 61
14. National Institute of Population and Social Security Research (2008), http://www.ipss.go.jp/syoushika/Accessed 18 Jan 2008 http://www.ipss.go.jp/syoushika/seisaku/html/a2.htm Accessed 18 Jan 2008
15. Nikkei Sangyô Shôhi Kenkyûsho, 2007-nen ritaia dankai shijô o nerae. (from Nikkei shôhi keizai seminar 29 January). *Nikkei Shôhi Mainingu*, 2006
16. Nomura Research Institute, Seikatsusha ichiman-nin ni miru nihonjin no kachikan, shôhikôdô no henka [Changes in Japanese values and consumption behaviors as seen in 10,000 questionnaires] (2004), http://www.nri.co.jp/news/2003/031215/031215.pdf. Accessed 15 Feb 2008
17. SC Japan Today, *Kenshô 2007-nen mondai. Shin-shijô to naruka dankaisedai mâketto* [Is the baby-boomer generation creating new markets?]. (Nihon Shoppingu Centâ Kyôkai, Tokyo, 2006)
18. Seni Torendo [Fabric Trend], November–December. Tôre Keiei Kenkyû-sho, 2006
19. J. Shiozaki, *Taishû-ka suru "IT shôhi." Chiteki Shisan Sôzô* (Nomura Research Institute, Tokyo, 2007)
20. J. Shiozaki, H. Nitto, N. Kawazu, *Daisan no shôhi sutairu* [The third consumption style]. (Nomura Research Institute, Tokyo, 2005)
21. M. Sugihara, Chiiki ni okeru jinkô-kôreika to kôreisha no seikatsu-ishiki: Takasaki-shi shigaichi-riyô-kôreisha ni taisuru mensetsu chôsa. Chiiki seisaku kenkyu. Takasaki Keizai Daigaku Chiiki-seisaku Gakkai. vol 6. no 4, 2004
22. H. Takei, K.-I. Kudo, T. Miyata, Y. Ito, Adaptive strategies for Japan's retail industry facing a turning point: Rebuilding corporate strength to respond to change with agility. NRI papers, no 110 (Nomura Research Institute, Tokyo, 2006)
23. K. Tateno, Sûpâ no Nihon-teki tenkai to mâketyingu, in *Nihon ryûtsû sangyô-shi* (Dôbun-kan, Tokyo 2002)

Chapter 16
Grey Power: Older Workers as Older Customers

S. Tempest, C. Barnatt, and C. Coupland

Abstract This chapter explores the increasing importance of "grey power" in the labour market and the marketplace. To fully understand grey market potential, companies need to develop an understanding of individual older customers and their broader social contexts in terms of both their varying immediate household compositions, and their intergenerational relationships. In this chapter we first challenge stereotypes and then introduce a model of older-person segmentation. The frame of analysis is then extended beyond the individual older customer in order to assess the range of "future households" in which the old will increasingly play a key role when purchasing decisions are being made. We provide a wealth/health segmentation for firms seeking to develop older customer strategies, and supplement this with a categorization of future households and the issues raised by intergenerational dynamics. This is then used to challenge false assumptions about older household compositions in the twenty-first century. In turn, this provides a segmentation of the old as workers and as customers in a variety of social contexts, which we hope offers some useful tools for companies seeking to capitalize on grey power now and into the future.

Introduction

In June 2007, YouTube asked 79-year-old web celebrity "Geriatric 1927" to provide the launch video for their UK website. A month later NASA set up a panel of retired engineers from its Lunar Module Reliability and Maintainability team to provide advice to current employees charged with returning a man to the moon by 2020. And, 2 months after that, on 23 September the US Department of Labor celebrated its fifth National Employ Older Workers Week. As demonstrated throughout this book, as population ageing continues to increase, so the "old" are increasingly being recognized as icons of consumer power, a source of key knowledge, and vital labour force participants.

This chapter explores the increasing importance of "grey power" initially in the labour market, but more significantly in the marketplace. In doing so it first challenges stereotypes and then reasserts a model of older-person segmentation of potential value to companies seeking to most successfully market their products and services. The frame of analysis is then further extended beyond the individual older customer in order to assess the range of "future households" in which the old will increasingly play a key role when purchasing decisions are being made.

Older Workers

As people live longer, rigid work retirement distinctions are becoming untenable. The Centre for Aging in London forecasts that there will be almost 700 million "elderly" people (age 65+) in the world by 2020 [12]. More people are also living to be centenarians. For example, in the USA there are 80,000 centenarians, with over 1 million forecast by 2050 [2]. Research into centenarian longevity suggests that if you have been healthy you live longer, and even amongst this very old cohort 30% have no significant deterioration in their thinking ability [2].

Widespread increases in longevity and in lifelong health necessitate a reappraisal of the work/retirement distinction and a revisiting of our stereotypes of older workers [14]. Older workers (those aged 50+) are sometimes perceived as unable to adapt to change, unable to learn new techniques and skills, and reluctant to embrace new technologies [4]. This can even become a self-fulfilling policy if older workers mentally and emotionally disengage from the workforce. Indeed, there is the danger that older people themselves internalize this socially constructed stereotyping and "discriminate against themselves" by not coming forward for training or promotion [10].

Governments are concerned about the low participation rates of older people in the workforce. This has manifested itself in concern about dependency ratios between the economically active and the economically inactive. Governments also have good reason to be concerned. Evidence suggests that many older workers are leaving the labour force on an involuntary basis. In Europe this has promoted a focus on equal opportunities and age discrimination legislation, as has been in place in the USA for many years. Companies too are becoming concerned about demographic changes, with a "war for talent" emerging as the proportion of younger people in the population in developed countries continues to fall. This has prompted debate about the optimal role and deployment of older workers. All this implies that there is a growing recognition that long-held stereotypes of older workers are unhelpful and increasingly redundant [14].

As a first step in challenging stereotypes, we would suggest a need to recognize the increasing diversity of older workers on the basis of both their wealth and their health. This concept is supported by an ongoing study by the US National Council on Aging that suggest that decisions about when to retire will in future be influenced primarily by accumulated savings and health decline [5]. Figure 16.1 illustrates our

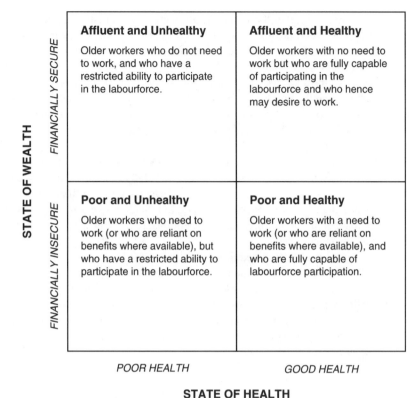

Fig. 16.1 The older worker wealth/health segmentation matrix

resultant categorization of older workers into the four quadrants of a wealth/health segmentation matrix.

In the bottom left quadrant of the wealth/health segmentation matrix we see that older people in most difficulties are those who experience poor health and who face financial insecurity. These individuals have a restricted ability to work, and are likely to be dependent on benefits where available. Research shows that workers with poor health generally retire earlier than those with good health [16]. Such individuals can find themselves in a vicious circle where health and wealth spiral downwards because affluence provides access to better housing, diet, and lifestyle which also contribute to health [5].

In the top left quadrant of the wealth/health segmentation matrix sit older people who have poor health but coupled with financial security. These individuals may not need to work, but may still have a desire to continue to do so on in order to remain socially and/or mentally active. Such workers may need technical or other support in order to remain employed. Alternatively, poor health may act as a push factor to self-employment for this older worker category [16].

In the top right quadrant of the wealth/health segmentation matrix are older people who enjoy both good health and who are financially secure. These individuals can afford to retire but may also choose to continue to work, perhaps on reduced hours and most likely on their own terms. This most fortunate group of older people is likely to have enjoyed high levels of professional success making them valuable human capital. Workers with valuable knowledge are increasingly being viewed as "customers" by employing organizations. Indeed, it has been suggested that "the most talented workers are the most sophisticated consumers, looking for the best-tailored employee deals" [8].

Finally in the lower right quadrant of the wealth/health segmentation matrix sit older people enjoying good health but who are financially insecure. These people are hence both able to work and need to do so if benefits are either unavailable or viewed as insufficient for a reasonable quality of life. Such workers are likely to be able to participate in the labour force until conventional retirement ages and possibly beyond if circumstances permit.

As our older worker wealth/health segmentation matrix helps to highlight, a diversity of health and affluence amongst older workers necessitates a move away from a single stereotype of older workers. In turn this will necessitate more customized employment practices if firms are to make the best use of their older human capital. In the UK, this is also starting to happen, with companies such as Asda, IBM, Capital One, and B&Q developing targeted retention policies and innovative retirement solutions for older workers.

Older Workers as Older Customers

An acceptance that older workers may be usefully segmented on an axis of wealth and health is no longer as radical or unusual a proposition as it was even a decade ago. It is therefore surprising that many companies seem to have forgotten that the collective word for the workers in any economy is "customers", and that any useful categorization of older workers therefore ought in parallel to drive a similar categorization of older customers.

Much of the existing marketing literature still highlights the challenge of segmenting older customers on the basis of their heterogeneity and the fact that ageing does not take away an individual's unique personality. However, whilst respecting the diversity of the individual, we would argue that it is increasingly useful to understand older people as customers by keeping in mind their parallel categorization as older workers on a wealth/health basis. We hence propose an extension of Fig. 16.1 that results in an older customer wealth/health segmentation matrix, as illustrated in Fig. 16.2.

Before considering the specific implications of the segmentation of older customers as Fig. 16.2, it is worth highlighting the importance of understanding the economic influence of the old, as well as alternative models for older customer segmentation. In the USA people aged over 50 account for nearly half of the market

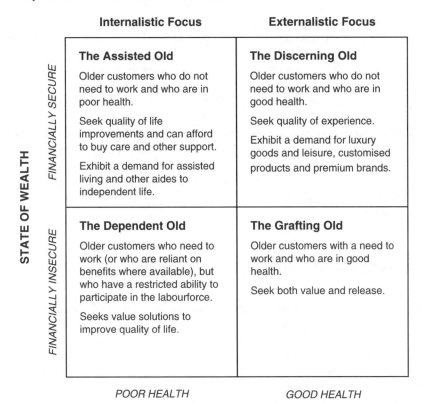

Fig. 16.2 The older customer wealth/health segmentation matrix

share for housing, food, transportation and health. The older consumer is growing in number and economic might, and yet, most firms continue to market to and design for younger people [12].

Those few and far between companies that are capitalizing on grey market opportunities are also proving highly successful. For example Saga – a UK firm specializing in leisure and services for older people – has reported a tenfold increase in the past 13 years in trekking trips booked to Nepal by older travellers (mostly aged 60–79), coupled with a surge in interest in activity holidays by mature travellers [7]. And it is not just the younger old who offer market potential. A study of centenarians in a nursing home chain found that 27% liked to watch MTV music channel, 15% played video games, and 4% knew how to use an iPod [2]. This of course all suggests that writing off the older consumer *at any age* may be a grave mistake.

Firms have been accused of ignoring older consumers for a number of reasons. One argument is that marketers are not fully aware of the potential of the grey market. However, this argument seems increasingly untenable given the growing media coverage being given to demographic ageing in the West. Alternative explanations of firms' lack of responsiveness to mature customers include older people not being categorized as a separate segment, older people being misunderstood, with misconceptions remaining about their beliefs and lifestyle [3], and older people being considered so heterogeneous that this raises challenges about how best to consider the older consumer [1].

It is known that differences of character do not change significantly with age. This means that there will be much diversity in the aging population [9], in turn making segmentation of older customers potentially challenging. Many of those seeking useful ways to categorize segments of the older population have therefore tended to subdivide the old on the simple basis of age [1]. We argue that the most useful forms of older customer segmentation need initially at least to consider the wealth and/or health factors increasingly accepted as key to the segmentation of older workers.

Internalistic vs. Externalistic Older Customers

The wealth/health segmentation matrix as presented in Fig. 16.2 subdivides older customers into four categories – the dependent old, assisted old, discerning old and grafting old – that can we believe can be effectively targeted or otherwise by specific retailers, manufacturers, and service providers. In the figure we have also chosen to highlight how those older customers in poorer health are likely to have a more internalistic focus as customers, whereas those enjoying better health are likely to be more externalistic in their market approach.

Older consumers prefer to spend on experiences rather than physical goods [11]. However, for less healthy individuals the focus becomes more internalistically focused upon living better and the maintenance of their remaining health. We of course need to be wary of portraying the older customer market too negatively as, in practice, being old does not necessarily equate with poor health. For example, in the USA only 5% of the mature market (those 55+) are in nursing homes and only 12% have a chronic illness [15]. However, changes in health such as issues of mobility, sight, or hearing can change an individual's product and service needs [12].

For companies, the customers in the top "financially secure" boxes of our grid inevitably offer the most potentially lucrative business opportunities. The *discerning old* have high customer power, being both financially secure and healthy. For this group life is for living as long as possible. They seek quality of experience and aesthetics via high quality design and brand differentiation. This externalistic focus is captured by research carried out by a specialist holiday firm Activities Abroad that revealed that older people enjoy activity holidays because they broaden their horizons, take them beyond their comfort zone, and enable the development of new social contacts [7]. In terms of aesthetics, the rise of demand for designer glasses by design leaders such as Armani and Gucci to make older people look better [6] shows design and image remain key to older people with externalistic outlooks.

The *assisted old* are financially secure but less healthy. This segment may suffer faculty decline (such as variations in sight or hearing) or chronic illnesses. This group of customers is primarily focused on quality of life improvements via products or services. They will seek quality care and technological innovations to ease the impact of their conditions and facilitate independence. They will also seek functionality rather than aesthetics and have the resources to purchase well-designed products and services. The assisted living industry (offering round the clock services from laundry services to take-out gourmet meals and doctors who make house calls) is a rapidly growing industry in the USA [6].

Within the bottom two segments of our wealth/health segmentation matrix, the less affluent old will be most concerned with value but can again be usefully separated into older customers with either an internalistic or externalistic focus based on health. Being financially insecure, the *grafting old* will not have high levels of disposable income and if they are still working may lack much spare time. However, as they are healthy they will still seek externalistic leisure opportunities that offer value for money. The Asda supermarket chain in the UK (now owned by Wal-Mart) now offers older workers, often on relatively low wages as shop assistants, "Benidorm leave" so older workers can leave the UK to spend the winter in Spain.

Finally in the bottom left quadrant of Fig. 16.2, the *dependent old* are those older customers likely to be reliant on benefits and the state due to their financial insecurity and restricted ability to work. There may be opportunities for niche providers of value products and gadgets to assist these individuals and improve their independence. However, this category of older customer is likely to be ignored by many companies due to their inability to be able to afford private care services or expensive aids. This said, opportunities will still increasingly exist to sell budget health products, as well as value products designed for ease of use by those with restricted dexterity, sight or mobility, to this large but cash-poor older customer segment.

The Older Customer Challenge

All firms need to start thinking about where their target customer groups are on the older customer wealth/segmentation matrix today, and where they will be in the relatively near future. To some extent this will be influenced by firms' actions as employers of older workers. In seeking to develop their relationships with older customers, firms need to reflect more on their diverse needs and the position of their products and services in meeting those needs.

There is also thankfully at least some evidence that a few firms are starting to think about their product and service offerings on the lines we have discussed. The Ford Motor Company, for example, has created the Third Age Suit as a product development tool. This can be worn by younger people (such as the company's engineers) to enable them to experience the mobility, strength and vision limitations of older people, and hence to help them improve care for post-50 year olds [12]. The Third Age Suit was also featured on the television program *The Gadget Show*

(2006), where it was used to demonstrate how most consumer electronics goods – and in particular mobile phones, remote controls and computers – can prove almost impossible to operate by older individuals.

One firm taking notice of the needs of older workers in the design of its offerings is Fidelity Investments. The company has been observing how older people use web sites as a key customer interface, and has sought to improve ease of navigation of its online offering for older customers as a result. Improvements have included larger text and links that are more obviously clickable [12]. Another company targeting the needs of older customers is Oxo International. This was founded to develop a line of kitchen gadget "Good Grips" in collaboration with Smart Design (a New York based industrial design firm) that would be easier to grip, twist, and squeeze but at the same time be stylish in design. The firm embraces universal design principles to produce over 350 products that appeal to a wide range of customers beyond the ageing customer [12]. Food companies and pharmaceutical firms are developing "functional foods" with medical benefits to help manage diabetes, arthritis, and heart disease.

Some technology companies are additionally starting to respond to the needs of internalistic older customers for functionality whilst also trying to meet the demands for stylish aesthetics exhibited by more externalistic older customers. For example, a lightweight hearing aid is being developed by a Danish firm that weighs less than a butterfly and fits invisibly into the ear and can be programmed to enhance the clarity of speech in noisy environments [6].

All of these developments mentioned above potentially signal what will almost certainly have to become a growing trend for a blurring of the boundaries between the healthcare sector and all other industries in product design. However, after some considerable research, what the above examples and what we could not find more obviously indicate is that more *product* development intended to assist in targeting older customers is today focused on meeting the internalistic needs of older customers with poor health. On the other side of our wealth/health segmentation matrix, service offerings, such as Saga holidays, are being developed successfully for the externalistic, healthy old. However, what is *not* happening is the development and/or redesign of products for the healthy old who nevertheless struggle to punch small buttons and read tiny text on tiny screens. The first companies in particular that mass-market phones, televisions and computers designed for older customers rather than teenagers are likely to do very well indeed!

Older Customers in Context

We would hope that our proposed wealth/health segmentation will be of value to companies trying to develop their older customer strategies. However, we would also contend that any segmentation of older customers at an individual level at best provides just a partial understanding of their market potential and position. This is because any model reliant on individual segmentation detaches its consumers from their social context.

To fully understand the grey markets of today and tomorrow, companies need to develop an understanding of the broader social contexts of older people in terms of both their varying immediate household compositions, and their intergenerational relationships. Both of these factors are largely neglected in much of the literature on ageing at present. However, only by considering the broader social context of the older customer in focus will firms be able to develop informed strategies for achieving competitive advantage in grey markets. The following section therefore provides a categorization of future households, and examines the intergenerational dynamics and challenges faced by countries with an ageing population.

The Future Household

Many products and services are purchased and used in a family context where there are competing priorities. As populations age, the nature of households is also shifting. As people live longer and the traditional nuclear family gives way to the evolving blended family, a more diverse range of households in part populated by older people emerges. More complex generational mixes within households raise issues for firms of who the product/service is designed for and with what category of customer does the spending decision reside?

We would suggest that the broad household types where older people are likely to play an influential role in purchasing decisions are as follows:

- *Pensioners with pensioners*: In such households older people reside with other older people. This is usually the family unit of the older married couple or cohabitees who are often empty nesters whose children have grown up and left home. Increasingly such household units are likely to be populated by single sex partnerships, or older friends possibly of the same sex, or older relatives living together. Much of the marketing to older people to date has tended to focus on the older married couple as the stereotypical older household where such decisions are shared if compromised. The discerning old within this household have been encouraged by leisure firms recently to "spend the kids inheritance" by enjoying their old age by prioritizing their lifestyle over those of their children.
- *Pensioners in isolation*: This is the household of the widowed, divorced, or never-married older person. Such households are characterized by older people living in isolation. Such individuals may have a wide network of friends and family, although their ability to maintain contact with them may be influenced by health and wealth considerations. Such households will be characterized by individualistic purchasing needs and decisions and segmented quite precisely by our older worker wealth/health segmentation matrix.
- *Pensioners with parents*: Older people living with very old dependent parents. As the very old increase as a proportion of the population, there is an increasing group of those aged 50+ whose parents are still alive. For the less affluent old or those who can afford domestic assistance they may wish their relatives to remain at home. But, even in the care home we may see changing household

dynamics. Indeed, Henderson [6] contends that: "It's no longer out of the question to find parents and children living together in the same nursing home." In such households the needs of the younger old and the assisted or dependent old need simultaneous consideration by firms.

• *Pensioners with teenagers*: This household type is becoming more common due to a delay in starting families, as well as blended families bringing together children from existing and previous relationships. People of traditionally pensionable age may hence increasingly find themselves living with teenagers or dependent students. This will pose some interesting questions for companies, and not least those marketing domestic products. For example, in pensioner-with-teenager households, who will the kettle and the telephone be designed for?!

As the last point above signals, as more households include older people, companies will need to increasingly think about who the products or services they are developing are actually going to be used by. Market opportunities may exist aimed at those growing numbers of families where two, three and in some cases even four generations of needs co-exist under one roof.

One approach will be to adopt a strategy of "universal design" whereby products are developed that work for people with differing physical capabilities and so benefit the population as a whole. For example, the Whirlpool Duet clothes washer and dryer is built on a pedestal that provides storage and minimizes bending when loading and emptying the machine. The enlarged door and angled basket also make use easier for all users, old and young [13].

In the workplace, as older workers become older customers, employers also need to be aware of the more diverse permutations of mature households in workplace planning. For example, research into attitudes and practices towards older workers in Scotland revealed a general attitude by employers that "as older employees were free from family commitments they could work more hours and be more flexible" [10]. Such an attitude is clearly based on a false assumption of older household compositions in the twenty-first century where older people increasingly are themselves caring for older parents and/or younger children. Left unchallenged, such false beliefs could undermine the feasibility of both a firm's HR strategy and its business models.

The Intergenerational Agenda: From Savers to Spenders to Debtors

The final thrust of the argument is that intergenerational exchanges should not be forgotten in considering grey market potential. Rather ironically, whilst many firms have been slow to see the opportunities of an ageing population, there are some signs in the media that a few organizations are beginning to pursue a heralded "gold-rush" by exploiting grey markets at the very point when the opportunities may have reached a tipping point in the West. In business and strategy timing is everything.

We know from the segmentation literature that life cohorts differ in their attitudes to consumption and saving. What has received less attention is how these differences in life cohort attitudes combine to impact upon intergenerational wealth and exchange. Intergenerational exchange is largely ignored by the current literature on grey market potential as policy-makers have focused on short-term political objectives. However, intergenerational exchange is nevertheless a vital consideration for firms developing grey business strategies if their business plans are to be realized.

For example, in the West, the generation that experienced either the depression and/or post war austerity witnessed widespread hardship first hand and remained financially cautious thereafter. This generation became *savers* who were advised "never a lender or a borrower be". This generation sought to live within their financial limits and such caution encouraged them to save to build capital for themselves and their families. For working people, many aspired to be the home owners in their families for the first time. For this generation, dying with a legacy in terms of a house or assets to pass to their children was a mark of lifetime achievement. Indeed, if we go back to 1997, 75% of mature consumers carried no debt [9]. However, in more recent years the dominance of the older savers generation is starting to give way to the *spenders*.

Baby boomers (those born between 1946 and 1964) and onwards are generally affluent because they have enjoyed a post-war boom period of relatively high employment (taking aside cyclical swings), and because many inherited or are likely to inherit from the savers. The attitude of this generation is we "have never had it so good and we are going to enjoy it." However, the high levels of conspicuous consumption by many of those currently employed, the spenders, to which much of the grey marketing is currently aimed, conceals the fact that this generation is stoking up problems for the next generation that may undermine the grey markets of the future. This generation prides itself on spending the kids' inheritance whilst benefiting from final salary pensions schemes. This generation's only legacy may be dying in debt, leaving the kids to effectively inherit the mortgage or the credit card bill.

The generations currently entering the workforce face very different prospects. In a knowledge economy, a greater proportion of this generation are remaining in higher education for longer, and starting work later, with possible stark consequences given the intergenerational legacy they will inherit. They are more likely to begin their employment with higher levels of debt and are less likely to enjoy final salary pensions. Intergenerational dynamics suggest that this generation will be less able to rely on inheritance from the spending generation. The next generation are more likely to be *debtors* as they have more debts at the start of life, are less likely to inherit or have their own equity to release as home ownership becomes harder. This will be due to house price inflation or devalued equity as baby boomers cash in their housing equity over the coming years to sustain their consumption, thereby shifting the balance of property supply and demand.

Clearly intergenerational issues are culturally relative. However, in developing strategy globally for grey markets, firms need to bear in mind the specific intergenerational dynamics at play in the countries they are targeting their products and services at if they are to fully understand future households and the forces that shape them. This requires looking at the West and monitoring the intergenerational issues in the rapidly developing economies of Asia and Latin America longer-term.

Summary and Conclusion

In this chapter, we have extended the debates about older people and business strategy in three ways. Firstly, we have provided a basis for rethinking the segmentation of older workers as older customers and for segmenting both older workers and older customers based on a wealth/health segmentation matrix. Secondly, we have extended consideration of grey market potential beyond thinking of older workers and customers in isolation by suggesting that older customers in particular need to be at least in part considered within the context of their household setting and its wider needs. Finally, we have signalled how firms need to be wary of merely jumping on the emergent "grey gold-rush" bandwagon without first taking into account intergenerational dynamics in planning their longer term silver strategies.

Whilst our research is based in Western European frame, we would argue that our wealth/health segmentation matrix and subsequent consideration of older worker/older customer profiling on a household basis, as well as intergenerational dynamics, are of direct relevance to those planning grey strategies in all countries. The household compositions in which the old reside, as well as intergenerational dynamics factors, will clearly to some extent be different and potentially unique across different nations. This will require differing approaches to grey strategy development in different countries. However, our key point of recognizing household compositions and intergenerational dynamics as key factors in grey strategy development nevertheless stands.

Older people are not all the same and will never meaningfully be able to be categorized as such. However, to conclude from this fairly obvious proposition that the old as workers, let alone as customers, cannot be usefully segmented is just plain lazy. We live in a world in which the young as a generation do not have to think because marketeers and the media do it for them. And, provided that these marketeers and the media convince the young that they are different from all other generations, the young seem fairly happy to accept this.

Unfortunately for marketeers and the media, the old are not such an easy sell. They have several things on their side, not least including experience, wisdom, and in many cases degrees of affliction in terms of health, dexterity and mobility that will lead them to base their decisions as customers on far more personal and practical considerations than the young. This said, we believe that these personal and practical considerations in large part stem from the wealth/health status of the individual, before being shaped by their domestic household context and the broader behaviour of their generational grouping. Taking these factors into account as we have herein, some sensible segmentations of the old as workers and as customers do therefore become realistic and reliable, and beyond this useful as tools for companies seeking to capitalize on grey power now and into the future.

References

1. R. Ahmad, Int. J. Mark. Res. **44**(3), 337 (2002)
2. T. Allen-Mills, Sunday Times 17 June, 20 (2007)
3. A. Alexander, IRI study shatters baby boomer shopping myths; September 11, vol. 4, p. 49 (2006). http://www.drugstorenews.com
4. W.C.K. Chiu, A.W. Chan, E. Snape, T. Redman, Hum. Relat. **54**(5), 629 (2001)
5. N. Cutler, J. Financ. Serv. Professionals **55**(2), 52 (2001)
6. C. Henderson, The Futurist Nov, 19 (1998)
7. J. Knight, The Times 15 Sept, 2 (2007)
8. M. Leibold, S. Voepel, *Managing the aging workforce: challenges and solutions* (Wiley, Germany, 2006), p. 213
9. R.C. Leventhal, J. Consum. Mark. **14**(4), 276 (1997)
10. W. Loretto, P. White, Hum. Resour. Manage. J. **16**(3), 313 (2007)
11. G. Moschis, C. Folkman Curasi, D. Bellenger, Cornell Hotel Restaur. Adm. Q. **44**(4), 51 (2003)
12. C. Pak, A. Kambil, J. Bus. Strateg. **27**(6), 18 (2006)
13. T. Purdum, The age of design: baby boomers serve as the common denominator for consumer durables manufacturers, August, 2002. http://www.industryweek.com. Accessed 11 June 2008
14. S. Tempest, C. Barnatt, C. Coupland, Long Range Plann. **35**(5), 475 (2002)
15. P. Weisz, Brandweek **37**(4), 28 (1996)
16. J.M. Zissimpoulos, L.A. Karoly, Labour Econ. **14**, 269 (2007)

Chapter 17
Older Consumers' Customer Service Preferences

S. Pettigrew

Abstract Older consumers have distinct customer service preferences that can constitute a source of competitive advantage for forward-thinking marketers who seek to attract this large and relatively affluent segment. This chapter focuses on the supermarket, financial planning, and healthcare industries to demonstrate the importance of providing personalized attention to allow for the older person's deteriorating physical and cognitive abilities and shrinking social networks. In particular, emphasis is placed on the need to allow older customers to form meaningful relationships with service staff. This strategy has implications for the recruitment, training, and retention of staff members who are able to demonstrate genuine concern for the welfare of the older consumer.

Introduction

Ageing brings with it a range of physiological changes that have implications for individuals' marketplace behaviours. Of particular interest in this chapter are the implications of these changes on older consumers' service needs. While suppliers of goods and services have typically focused on the physical adaptations of their products and premises that are required for their older customers, less attention has been given to the personal interaction elements of the exchange process. This chapter will show that older consumers can have distinct service preferences and that these have implications for suppliers wishing to differentiate themselves in the marketplace by offering superior customer service to their older clientele. Customer service is defined as those aspects of service that support the provision of the company's core products. The personal interaction that occurs in the exchange process is a primary component of customer service.

A brief account of the primary age-related physiological and social changes is provided below, followed by the findings of a large Australian study on seniors' service preferences and a discussion of the implications of these changes for marketers wishing to deliver high levels of customer service to the large and growing cohort of older consumers.

Functional Changes

Age-related physical deterioration is an inevitable aspect of the ageing process. While individuals experience this deterioration to a greater or lesser degree depending on their genetic inheritance and lifestyles, there are certain physical changes that are generally to be expected with age. For example, most people begin to notice vision impairment in their 40s and 50s. This reflects a gradual thickening and hardening of the lens and a shrinking of the pupil that in combination make it more difficult to focus the eyes [39]. Increasing hearing loss is also very common with age. Hearing impairment is of particular concern for cognitive function because it is associated with reductions in functional intelligence, especially memory [45].

Physical mobility also tends to reduce with age, largely due to decreasing muscle mass and muscular strength [8]. Reductions in mobility are particularly problematic when they result in falls as many older people suffer permanent disabilities, or even death, as a consequence of falling. Partially as a result of their smaller stature, women tend to experience greater losses of strength and mobility with age [38].

Along with these functional changes come alterations in cognitive processing. Slower processing occurs as the neural pathways to the brain deteriorate with age [45]. The outcome is that at any point in time the older person has less attentional capacity to direct at any particular stimuli and it becomes more demanding to perform the same mental tasks that used to be less challenging. As a result, new information is more difficult to assimilate, especially when it involves unfamiliar stimuli. For this reason, where new information contradicts previously learned information the older person is more likely to fail to change existing beliefs [37]. In addition, it becomes more difficult for older people to recall the source of information, which may make them more susceptible to repetitious advertising [48].

Social Changes

The physical and psychological changes discussed above have effects on individuals' social status. Deteriorating mobility, vision, and hearing shrink the older person's circle of regular contacts and make it difficult to establish new relationships. In addition, the likelihood of the death of a spouse and close friends increases with age, so older people are more likely to live alone than younger people and to have smaller social networks [6]. As a result of these factors, the incidence of loneliness increases with age. Loneliness can trigger depression in the older person, a trend that is particularly common among older women [42]. Reflecting the close relationship between mental and physical health, depression tends to be more severe amongst those experiencing lower levels of perceived physical health [2]. Depression is thus directly associated with deteriorating physical health as well as indirectly through the relationship between physical health and loneliness because failing health makes socializing more difficult. The physiological changes that occur with age can therefore impact significantly on an individual's frame of mind and his or her ability to interact effectively with others.

Understanding the Older Consumer

These functional and social aspects of ageing inevitably influence individuals' attitudes to products and their subsequent purchase decisions. The bulk of marketing research that has focused on older consumers has concentrated on their product-related attitudes and how these are manifest in purchase behaviours. Less research has been directed at analysing how these attitudes have changed over time as a result of changing physical and social characteristics. Studies are typically cross-sectional in design and as such identify variations between current cohorts but not variation within cohorts over time. The latter remains an area of untapped potential in understanding how age-related physical and social changes impact upon older consumers' preferences and choices. This will become increasingly important in the future as later cohorts of seniors can be expected to behave differently to current cohorts because of their very different life experiences [22].

Studies of older consumers' consumption behaviours have also tended to focus primarily on specific product categories, product attributes, and advertising effectiveness. For example, research has examined older consumers' attitudes to products as diverse as apparel, cars, meat products, and financial services. Packaging as a product attribute has also received attention because of the difficulties older consumers can face when coping with "senior-proof" wrapping [11].

Across most studies involving the senior segment, older consumers have been found to be similar to younger consumers in most respects. Any differences are usually in degree rather than in nature. For instance, seniors can exhibit higher levels of store loyalty [20], and tend to have somewhat smaller brand repertoires [44]. They have been found to be less price-sensitive and to have higher quality expectations [24, 43]. Older consumers are reported to be more appreciative of emotional advertisements than younger consumers, especially when the advertisements feature nostalgia appeals [14, 46].

With this emphasis on products and promotion, less empirical attention has been given to the customer service aspects of seniors' consumption experiences. While the literature on ageing consumers contains many assertions relating to customer service (e.g., the importance of recruitment and retention of older sales staff, avoiding condescension in interactions, and offering seniors' discounts carefully to prevent causing offence [11, 17, 40, 43]), these recommendations are usually unsupported with empirical data and instead reflect intuitive assessments made on the basis of the likely needs of those who experience the functional and social changes associated with the ageing process. Those studies that have explicitly addressed customer service aspects of the older consumer's shopping experience usually do so as merely one element of the consumption process and as a consequence report limited results relating specifically to customer service. One common finding among these studies is that assistance from staff is especially appreciated by older consumers [26].

Although studies of seniors' customer service preferences are largely neglected in marketing research, the health literature offers some insights on this subject as substantial work has been done on older patients' experiences when receiving medical services. In particular, the nursing literature provides numerous accounts of the physiological and social requirements of older patients and how these translate into specific needs in a service provision context [7, 19, 36]. These studies have emphasized the need to focus on older people as a specific group with specific needs, to be responsive and empathetic to older people's individual requirements, and to actively work to reduce the confusion that may occur during the various stages of the decision-making process as a result of slower cognitive processing or illness [9].

Due to the lack of empirical data relating to older consumers and their customer service preferences, most of our understanding in this area comes from studies conducted in service contexts as these exchange processes typically contain a high degree of human interaction. The health and financial services sectors tend to have been examined the most in terms of older consumers as many of their products cater specifically for this segment. There are lessons to be learned from this research, although future work that focuses on seniors' customer service expectations and preferences is needed to fill the current gap in the literature that relates to the kinds of personal interaction and other forms of customer service that are most valued and appreciated by older consumers. The section to follow outlines the results of a major Australian study into seniors' perceptions of what would constitute a "senior-friendly" business (see [35] for background details). This project identified those aspects of the service experience that were considered most important and relevant to a broad range of seniors across multiple industries.

Age-Friendly Service Providers

The Age Friendly Guidelines Project was undertaken by the Positive Ageing Foundation of Australia under the sponsorship of the then Western Australian Department for Community Development, Seniors Interests. The main objective of the project was to provide businesses with guidance on how to make their businesses more senior friendly. The research focused on Australians aged 50 years and older and involved more than 30 focus groups and two telephone surveys ($n = 1300$, $n = 505$). The first phase of the study, which comprised the bulk of the focus groups and the larger survey, identified those industries that were viewed by older consumers to be most important to their general welfare and therefore those for which it would be most beneficial to adopt age-friendly customer service strategies. These industries were found to be supermarkets, financial services, and the health sector (primarily general practitioners and hospitals). Those aspects of service delivery considered to be especially important to older customers in these industries were then explored in the remaining focus groups and the smaller of the two surveys. The results of this project offer important insights for marketers in these and other industries that target the growing senior segment. While the results are of specific relevance to Australian marketers, the tendency for most research relating to senior consumers to be conducted in the USA and the UK means that any research conducted outside these contexts has the potential to add deeper insight into the international phenomenon of ageing consumers.

Supermarkets

The need for regular restocking of provisions ensures that grocery stores are a form of retail outlet that continues to be frequently patronized by consumers in their later years. Shopping for groceries is a relatively physical pastime that requires some degree of strength and agility on the part of the shopper. For this reason, previous research has identified a range of considerations for the layout of the store and surrounding areas. For example, parking access, availability of seating, and store temperature have been noted as especially important to older shoppers [21, 23, 25]. Service considerations such as waiting times at checkouts and attitudes of service staff have also been highlighted [13, 15, 22].

The Australian research supported these priorities and highlighted the importance of customer service elements such as the demeanour and availability of service staff, assistance in locating products, and the provision of multiple delivery options to cater for different physical abilities [31, 33]. Of most importance was the ability for staff members to interact pleasantly with older customers. Almost all (99%) of older Australians surveyed noted this to be either an important or very important aspect of visiting a supermarket. Reflecting the recognized role of shopping in facilitating social interactions for isolated older people [47], focus group participants commented on their desire for "real" interactions with store employees rather than parroted, superficial greetings that they assume are the result of the training that service staff members have received. While recognizing that there is little opportunity for in-depth conversations, the participants felt that it is reasonable to expect staff to look them in the eye when greeting them and engage in friendly small talk while processing their items through the checkout.

Reflecting the physical limitations often faced by older consumers, 90% of the survey respondents felt it is important or very important for staff members to be readily available to provide assistance with product location. Some suggested that supermarkets could hire a "hospitality person" who could be given the prime role of assisting older customers. They felt that such supermarkets would be much more attractive to seniors compared to regular supermarkets that they found to be uncaring and focused on profits at the expense of customer service.

For many older people, walking around a supermarket can be physically exhaust-
ing. This discomfort is exacerbated when it is necessary to search for items that have
been moved or that are being purchased for the first time. Focus group participants
discussed the importance of efficiency, given older shoppers' physical limitations,
and therefore the need to do just one trip around the supermarket without needing to
return to previously visited aisles to search for particular items. They noted that it is
often very difficult to find staff to assist with information about the location of items
or to pass down items from high shelves. The tendency for older people to be shorter
than younger people means that they can be disadvantaged when shelves are built
to cater to average height customers. Of major concern was the danger of falling
while reaching up to high shelves. Deep freezers were also viewed as posing a significant physical challenge, with some focus group participants speaking with fear
of falling into freezers and not being able to right themselves. They were concerned
about both their physical safety and dignity in such circumstances. The provision
of additional staff dedicated to ensuring the welfare of older shoppers by assisting
with product location and product access would allow enhanced customer service
to compensate for the physical aspects of the store that can present real hardship for
the aged.

The availability of multiple delivery options was considered important or very
important by 82% of the survey respondents. These options included drive-through
and home delivery services that would reduce the need for older shoppers to manage heavy bags of groceries. While not averse to being charged for home delivery
services, those stores that provided this service on a complimentary basis were
considered to be especially senior-friendly.

Financial Planners

The financial planning sector is of increasing importance around the world due to
governments' realization that the ageing of the population is resulting in the need
for older people to become self-financing rather than reliant on the state for retirement income. In the Australian context, older consumers are particularly attractive
to financial planners as those 55 years of age and older earn around 25% of the
nation's disposable income while controlling almost 40% of the nation's wealth [1].
This combination of income and assets makes them the most financially powerful
segment in the marketplace. In addition to this segment being particularly attractive
to financial planners, the reverse is also true as older consumers are very interested
in financial services because of the need to carefully manage their income over the
remainder of their lives.

The technical nature of the information that needs to be conveyed between
financial planners and their clients can make it difficult to achieve effective communication. This means that financial planners need to possess good interpersonal skills
and to be sensitized to the perceptual abilities and limitations of their clients. In particular, the meaning of complex terminology needs to be conveyed in such a way

as to maximize comprehension. Financial planners need to be capable of assisting clients to visualize themselves in the future so they can picture themselves benefiting from the delayed gratification that is typically necessary in sound financial planning [12].

This necessary reliance on clients' cognitive skills means that financial planners should consider the effects of age-related limitations on individuals' abilities to perceive stimuli and process information. Kennet et al.'s [18] US study of financial planners and their approaches to the mature market found a strong focus among planners on the development and promotion of financial products that are useful to this segment but a general lack of appreciation of the specific service needs of older clients. Kennet et al.'s recommendations included strategies to cater for both the physical and social changes experienced by older clients. For example, they suggested using larger font sizes in documents, providing suitable access into and within the building, offering home delivery of documents, training staff to be aware and understanding of older clients' needs, and hiring older staff to liaise with older clients.

These recommendations were supported by the Australian research [28, 29], which again highlighted the customer service aspects of interactions with company personnel. Of primary importance to the respondents was the quality of the relationship formed between the client and the financial planner. Ninety-six percent of respondents rated it important or very important to develop a working relationship with their financial planner that was characterized by mutual trust and the preservation of the client's dignity. Focus group participants traded horror stories of those who had fallen victim to unethical financial planners and as a result had been financially disadvantaged. They wanted to feel confident that their financial planner had their best interests at heart as this would prevent the same happening to them.

Also of concern was financial planners' ability to determine the appropriate amount of information to deliver to clients and the manner in which it was to be conveyed. Ninety-four percent of the survey respondents rated this aspect of customer service as important or very important. Flexibility in communication style was described as an essential attribute of a financial planner because of the varying base knowledge levels and intellectual capacities of different clients. It was suggested that financial planners should be ready to provide information in both graphical and written form to allow individuals with different learning styles to have their communication needs accommodated. This flexibility should be provided in a considerate fashion as the focus group participants were adamant that older clients should not be treated with condescension simply because they lack a detailed understanding of financial planning principles.

Health Sector

The ageing of the world's population has enormous implications for the healthcare sector. As a consequence of this demographic trend and the long-standing acknowledgement of the importance of customer service in the health industry, the customer service needs of older patients have been the subject of greater attention than has been the case in other industries.

Health services are of particular importance to older people as usage of these services increases significantly with age. The Australian Bureau of Statistics estimates that per-person health expenditure is four times greater amongst those aged 65 years and older than in younger age groups [3]. The degree of dependence of older people on healthcare services is illustrated by the fact that over a 2-week period, almost 40% of Australians aged 65 and older will have visited a doctor [4].

General Practitioners

Healthcare customers of all ages are known to be particularly concerned with the quality of the personal interaction skills of their medical practitioners [7, 41]. Older patients are no exception and past research has identified the relationship between doctor and patient as one of the most important criteria used by older patients to assess their satisfaction with their doctor [21]. It appears likely that patients use their perceptions of a doctor's bedside manner as a proxy for quality of care because of their inability to assess the technical quality of the care received [5, 34]. This highlights the need for medical practitioners to ensure that they are meeting patients' relationship needs as this is likely to influence their perceptions of the quality of care and therefore their intention to comply with medication prescriptions and other behavioural recommendations [41].

The Australian research supported the emphasis in the literature on the relationship that is formed between doctor and patient [30, 32]. Ninety-seven percent of survey respondents rated a caring bedside manner and good communication skills as important or very important in their interactions with general practitioners (GPs). Many of the conditions that older patients need to discuss with their doctors can be embarrassing and difficult to articulate. A compassionate demeanour was considered essential to allow full disclosure of symptoms. One aspect of a caring bedside manner that was considered particularly critical was the time taken by doctors to genuinely listen to patients' concerns (94% agreement). The focus group participants described feeling rushed by the short appointment times typically allocated per patient. For some, this resulted in them feeling flustered and unable to focus their thoughts, which prevented them from communicating effectively with the doctor. This problem was exacerbated when patients considered their symptoms or condition to be demeaning or embarrassing.

A further aspect of customer service that was considered important by the study participants was the appropriate provision of information. Ninety-seven percent felt that doctors should make the effort to ensure that the information they provide relating to medications is readily understood by their older patients. Especially when unwell, older people can experience difficulties in assimilating and retaining information. Focus group participants noted that they preferred their doctor to write down medication instructions or details about their condition as this prevents them from getting confused or forgetting the information by the time they get home. Similarly, 90% wanted clear information concerning the costs of the services provided and any rebates that may be available to seniors. Eighty percent wanted to be given estimates of waiting times upon arrival, as even just sitting in a waiting room can be an onerous task for an older person who is feeling unwell. Knowing the length of the wait ahead of them allows older patients to mentally prepare themselves for the delay or make alternative arrangements if the wait is going to be too long for them to tolerate.

Hospitals

The findings relating to hospitals were similar to those for GPs in that trusting relationships with carers were a high priority [27]. Relationships with nurses appeared to take priority over relationships with doctors in a hospital context as patients have much greater contact with nursing staff over the duration of their hospitalization. Inpatients are in a highly dependent state and as a consequence can feel very vulnerable and desirous of empathy from those attending to their physical needs. The focus group participants expressed preference for staff members who introduce themselves, refer to the patient by name, exhibit a compassionate and friendly demeanour, and make patients feel at ease in potentially awkward or embarrassing situations. These findings mirror the outcomes of other studies of older patients' hospital experiences, where being recognized and treated with dignity were found to be primary factors influencing satisfaction [10, 16, 19].

Preference was also exhibited for staff members who take the time to get to know patients, at least a little. While acknowledging the many demands on healthworkers' time and the stresses associated with working in a hospital environment, the focus group participants expressed a desire for staff to demonstrate an unhurried demeanour and to take the time to ensure they were familiar with the older patient's condition. Seniors often take multiple medications so it is important for staff to be aware of possible negative consequences of combining different medications. This awareness only occurs when members of staff take the time to familiarize themselves with the patient's medical history.

The customer service experience in a hospital commences at admission, making this an important interaction for the older patient who is likely to be nervous and experiencing pain. It was suggested that the admissions process could be improved in many hospitals to prevent seniors from waiting for long periods. In particular, it was noted that the same information was often required at both hospital admission and ward admission, suggesting that the information collection process could be streamlined to prevent this duplication.

Implications for Service Delivery

Existing knowledge of the physical and social changes associated with ageing and the consumer studies profiled above provide insight into the customer service preferences of older consumers. These preferences can be effectively accommodated by marketers who appreciate the value of the senior segment and make it a specific focus of their attention. The aspect of customer service that appears to be most valued by older consumers is a genuine understanding of and concern for their individual needs. Older consumers appreciate those providers who take the time to get to know them as individuals and demonstrate sincere concern for their welfare. In this sense, seniors do not differ from other segments other than that the need for individual consideration is of a more profound nature, given that it partly stems from the age-related physical and social changes being experienced. Deteriorating sensory perception and cognitive processing abilities require information inputs and other forms of communication to be tailored to the specific needs of the older person. Similarly, the growing isolation that often accompanies older age can result in the need for more personalized interactions to compensate for shrinking social networks.

The provision of more tailored and personal service may appear at first glance to be a costly and resource-intensive burden on firms. However, as the large segment of baby boomers continues to enter the senior segment and experience the physical and social changes associated with the ageing process, it will increasingly be in marketers' interests to ensure their offerings are senior friendly in every way possible. In addition, achieving high levels of differentiated customer service will serve marketers well in their efforts to attract other segments that also prioritize this element of the exchange process. The relative affluence of newer cohorts of seniors will facilitate this increase in service standards by permitting higher costs to be passed on to those older consumers who are willing to pay higher prices for superior service.

The preference among seniors for service staff who exhibit sincerity and a genuine concern for their needs has implications for employee recruitment, training, and retention. Staff members will need to be selected according to their ability to demonstrate empathy with older customers. To some degree, this may require the recruitment of older workers who are capable of empathizing with the needs of seniors. Customer service training will need to cover aspects such as appropriate ways of addressing older people, appropriate physical and verbal demeanour, ways to preserve the customer's dignity, the determination of how and when to render physical assistance, and the prevention of long waiting times. In some industries it would also be beneficial to provide service staff with specific instructions about the most effective ways to convey information, such as in which circumstances information should be provided in writing and when to use pictures. Employee retention is also important as it will allow older customers to build relationships with those members of staff with whom they regularly come into contact.

Summary and Conclusion

Marketers wishing to target older consumers need to understand the strong desire among members of this segment for individualized attention. Personalized interactions are especially important to older consumers because of their deteriorating physical and cognitive abilities and their growing social isolation. Reductions in mobility, sight, and hearing leave the older person vulnerable in many consumption situations where physical adeptness is required to locate, compare, select, and carry products. Similarly, shrinking social networks can make the older person overly reliant on interactions with the providers of goods and services to obtain human contact. There is thus an opportunity for organizations to differentiate their marketplace offerings through superior customer service that recognizes and caters to older consumers' need for greater levels of physical assistance and a heightened desire to form personal relationships with those from whom they regularly purchase goods and services. Customer service targeted at the older consumer would be therefore ideally characterized by friendly but respectful interactions, the provision of physical assistance where needed, and the pacing of information to suit the customer's processing needs. Such an approach can provide a source of differentiation that is valued by older consumers and is also likely to be attractive to members of other segments that prioritize high quality service.

Given the noted similarities between the results of the Australian studies described above and those conducted in other countries and in other industries, it appears that the customer service recommendations provided here would be applicable to numerous other cultural and product contexts. The universal nature of the ageing process and the resulting implications for market-place behaviours suggest that marketers everywhere would be well served to consider how their customer service processes can be better geared to the changing physical and social needs of ageing consumers.

References

1. Access Economics, *Population Ageing and the Economy* (Commonwealth of Australia, Canberra, 2001)
2. F.M. Alpass, S. Neville, *Aging Ment. Health* **7**(3), 212 (2003)
3. Australian Bureau of Statistics, *Australian social trends 1999 – health – health status: health of older people.* (Australian Bureau of Statistics, Canberra, 2002)
4. Australian Bureau of Statistics, *The health of older people, Australia.* Australian Bureau of Australia, Canberra, 2004)
5. E. Babakus, W.G. Mangold, *Health Serv. Res.* **26**(6), 767 (1992)
6. M. Bondevik, A. Skogstad, *West. J. Nurs. Res.* **20**(3), 325 (1998)
7. M.R. Bowers, J.E. Swan, W.F. Koehler, *Health Care Manage. Rev.* **19**(4), 49 (1994)
8. M.J. Daley, W.L. Spinks, *Sports Med.* **29**(1), 1 (2000)
9. J.N. Doucette, *Nurs. Manage.* **34**(11), 26 (2003)
10. I. Ekman, B. Lindman, A. Norberg, *Heart Lung* **28**(3), 203 (1999)
11. S. Fairley, G.P. Moschis, H.M. Meyers, A. Thiesfeldt, *Brandweek* **38**(30), 24 (1997)

12. P.T. Gibbs, *Eur. J. Mark.* **32**(11/12), 993 (1998)
13. D.R. Goodwin, R.E. McElwee, *Int. Rev. Retail, Distrib. Consum. Res.* **9**(4), 403 (1999)
14. T.S. Gruca, C.D. Schewe, *Mark. Res.* **4**(3), 18 (1992)
15. C. Hare, *Int. J. Retail Distrib. Manage.* **31**(5), 244 (2003)
16. C.S. Jacelon, *Qual. Health Res.* **13**(4), 543 (2003)
17. J. Johnson-Hillery, J. Kang, W-J. Tuan, *Int. J. Retail Distrib. Manage.* **25**(4), 126 (1997)
18. P.A. Kennet, G.P. Moschis, D.N. Bellenger, *J. Serv. Mark.* **9**(2), 62 (1995)
19. T. Koch, C. Webb, A.M. Williams, *J. Clin. Nurs.* **4**(3), 185 (1995)
20. N.J. Miller, K. Soyoung, *J. Small Bus. Manage.* **37**(4), 1 (1999)
21. M. Morrison, T. Murphy, C. Nalder, *Health Mark. Q.* **20**(3), 3 (2004)
22. G.P. Moschis, *Marketing to older consumers* (Quorum Books, Westport, Connecticut, 1992)
23. G.P. Moschis, *Am. Demograph.* **18**(9), 44 (1996)
24. G.P. Moschis, A. Mathur, *Mark. Manage.* **2**(2), 40 (1993)
25. B. Oates, L. Shufeldt, B. Vaught, *J. Consum. Mark.* **13**(6), 14 (1996)
26. C. Pak, A. Kambil, *J. Bus. Strateg.* **27**(6), 18 (2006)
27. S. Pettigrew, *Aust. J. Primary Health* **12**(3), 52 (2006)
28. S. Pettigrew, K. Mizerski, R. Donovan, *J. Financ. Serv. Mark.* **7**(4), 341 (2003)
29. S. Pettigrew, K. Mizerski, R. Donovan, *Australas. J. Ageing* **23**(3), 144 (2004a)
30. S. Pettigrew, K. Mizerski, R. Donovan, *Australas. J. Ageing* **23**(3), 146 (2004b)
31. S. Pettigrew, K. Mizerski, R. Donovan, *Australas. J. Ageing* **23**(3), 142 (2004c)
32. S. Pettigrew, K. Mizerski, R. Donovan, *Aust. J. Primary Health*, **11**(3), 38 (2005a)
33. S. Pettigrew, K. Mizerski, R. Donovan, *J. Consum. Mark.* **22**(6), 306 (2005b)
34. M.Peyrot, P.D. Cooper, D. Schnapf, *J. Health Care Mark.* **13**(1), 24 (1993)
35. Positive Ageing Foundation of Australia. The age friendly guidelines project, (Positive Age- ing Foundation of Australia, Perth 2002) http://www.community.wa.gov.au/NR/rdonlyres/ 5C473211-F8E6-42FA-9C98-8492435B1351/0/DCDRPTAgefriendlyguidelines200309.pdf. Accessed 11 Jun 2008
36. M. Rantz, N.K. Davis, R.A. Tapp, *J. Nurs. Care Qual.* **9**(3), 1 (1995)
37. G.E. Rice, M.A. Okun, *J. Geronotol.* **49**(3), 119 (1994)
38. M.M. Samson, I. Meeuwsen, A. Crowe, J.Dessens, S.A. Duursma, H. Verhaar, *Age and Ageing* **29**, 235 (2000)
39. C. Stuen, E.E. Faye, *Generations* **27**(1), 8 (2003)
40. K. Tepper, *J. Consum. Res.* **20**, 503 (1994)
41. D.H. Thom, B. Campbell, *J. Fam. Pract.* **44**(2), 169 (1997)
42. P. Tiikkainen, R.L. Heikkinen, *Aging Ment. Health* **9**(6), 526 (2005)
43. H.N. Tongren, *J. Consum. Aff.* **22**(1), 136 (1988)
44. M.D. Uncles, A.S.C. Ehrenberg, *J. Advert. Res.* **30**(4), 19 (1990)
45. H. Wahl, V. Heyl, *Generations* **27**(1), 39 (2003)
46. P. Williams, A. Drolet, *J. Consum. Res.* **32**, 343 (2005)
47. L.C. Wilson, A. Alexander, M. Lumbers, *Int. J. Retail Distrib. Manage.* **32**(2), 109 (2004)
48. C. Yoon, G. Laurent, R. Gonzales, A.H. Gutchess, T. Hedden, R. Lambert-Pandraud et al. *Mark. Lett.* **16**(3/4), 429 (2005)

Chapter 18
Silver Advertising: Elderly People in Japanese TV Ads

M. Prieler

Abstract About 10% of Japanese commercials show elderly people. They advertise a relatively small range of product categories, such as pharmaceuticals/health products, financial/insurance plans, and food. Elderly people are the main target group, especially for the first two product categories, and often are the only age group that appears in the ads. In contrast, for products targeted at more age groups or for which elderly people are not the explicit targets, elderly people either do not appear at all, appear in a family setting, or in a more general way as a representative of one generation, e.g., in commercials showing that all generations use the product. This leads to the situation in which only about 20% of commercials with elderly people advertise products that are explicitly for elderly people. The representation and function of elderly people in commercials is not only connected with the age groups they are appearing with, but there also are differences within the representation of elderly people. This is especially the case of male versus female representations, in which the latter are clearly underrepresented. On the whole, most of the findings of this study confirmed previous research results from other parts of the world.

Introduction

Advertising theorists agree that if ads are to resonate with target audiences, "they need to reflect the social norms practiced in a given society" [5]. This also is certainly true in the context of elderly people. However, advertising does not just "reflect" society; it also has, together with other media, some form of influence on society. O'Barr states that "depictions of society in advertisements have their bases in the social order, and the social order is continually re-created by reference to ideals in advertisements and elsewhere about what it should be" [14]. Williamson philosophizes in a similar direction, stating that "advertisements are one of the most important cultural factors moulding and reflecting our life today" [19]. These theories naturally lead to the question of how far advertisements reflect the realities of

Japanese society; if they do not reflect society, it could be regarded as a form of distortion that might have an influence on society.

These considerations certainly are not to be underestimated by companies that think about their general image among consumers or even as a part of a Corporate Social Responsibility (CSR) strategy. The way television viewers feel portrayed by a company certainly has an influence on the overall company image. The other important question in the marketing context is how and with which models elderly people are addressed adequately in order to be reached through advertisements. Existing research findings suggest that elderly people do not necessarily want to be targeted with elderly people but with people 10 or 15 years younger than their actual age [6]; i.e., with models of their cognitive age rather than their chronological age. As a result, it can be assumed that this chapter cannot fully answer the question of what commercials target elderly people, but only the question of whether there is a connection between elderly people in and the target group of these commercials.

This chapter focuses on the use of elderly people in Japanese TV commercials, how they are represented, how far these representations reflect the realities of Japanese society, and what reasons there might be for possible differences. After showing the depiction of the elderly, as well as under what circumstances this age group is used and for what purposes, important marketing questions of this chapter include: in using elderly people in commercials, how much of this is connected with products targeted at them, and what product categories are elderly people advertising? These results will be discussed and set in a global context in order to determine if these results are special for Japan or similar in different parts of the world.

The Use of Elderly People

Although elderly people certainly are not the leading age group in Japanese commercials, a significant number of the systematically-collected television commercials (see Appendix for details) included elderly people, as can be seen in Table 18.1.

This amount, however, does not say anything about how many advertisements actually are targeted at elderly people; it only indicates how many commercials use elderly people. Within the commercials employing elderly people, the amount of commercials advertising products only for elderly people is relatively low (22.4%,

Table 18.1 Elderly people in Japanese TV ads

Type of ad	Appearance in ads (%)
All ads[a]	10.4
Ads with people[b]	13.6

[a] Number of all ads = 3352.
[b] Number of ads with people = 2557.
In summary, in 10.4% of all commercials appear elderly people. And in 13.6% of commercials featuring people are appearing elderly people. The commercials with elderly people are 348.

$n = 78$). On the other hand, various product categories are not intended solely for elderly people but can be used by them; sometimes they even are a main target group. It can also be assumed that there are various commercials not depicting elderly people that also target them as customers. This is true for a wide range of product categories that are age-neutral, such as foods, drinks, detergents, and many others.

The Representation of Elderly People

So, how are elderly people represented in Japanese television commercials? Are they shown mostly alone or together with other people and, if so, with whom and what age groups?[1] What role do they play and is there any difference in the representation of elderly people in terms of gender?

In about one-fourth of all commercials with elderly people, they appear alone without any other age group (26.1%, $n = 91$). In contrast to commercials in which other age groups also are represented, these commercials clearly are focused on advertising products that are solely for elderly people; in many cases, the merchandise is of no use to younger people. These products include pharmaceuticals and other health-related products for the elderly, such as diapers for the elderly, hearing aids, products for dentures, food supplements, and wrinkle creams. Another common product category is health insurance, which is especially created for people over 60 years. For products exclusively advertised for elderly people, the actors typically are older than 60 and mostly even older than 70. This might be an indication that the perception of age has shifted during the years and common definitions connected with retirement age have changed at a time in which elderly people live longer and are more active. In cases in which the product is not exclusively for elderly customers, elderly people still are being used for products for which they are a main target group: pharmaceuticals (including those used by younger people) and traditional Japanese food products are a few. The elderly seen in the latter case often act as an endorsement for the product and its consistent taste or quality; in other cases, they are verifying that even a cup of noodles can have the same traditional taste, convincing their critical husband of its value and encouraging him to have another cup. Naturally, there are also some elderly celebrities depicted in commercials, which appeal to a wide audience and not only to elderly people. Not surprisingly, it was observed that the use of commercials with only elderly people (in contrast to other commercials including other age groups) are connected with programs that can be regarded as clearly targeting an elderly clientele, though this question was not explicitly part of this research.

An age group with which elderly people hardly ever appear is babies (1.1%, $n = 4$; there is no commercial with *only* elderly people and a baby). Elderly people seem to be at the other end of the age spectrum and don't have much in common with babies. In contrast, elderly people appear in various cases with children (23.6%,

---

[1] Age groups in this research consist of: baby, child (age 1–17), young adult (18–29), middle age adult (30–59), old/elderly adults (60+).

$n = 82$), and at times even alone with children (2.9%, $n = 10$). In the former case, these combinations are used mostly in a general family setting, or in the latter case indicating that elderly people have to stay fit in order to play with or handle children. To do so, they need to use the advertised product, which usually is a pharmaceutical product. In one commercial, a woman is shown pushing the swing for a child but having to stop the activity because of knee pain. She can only continue after using the advertised product. In a follow-up commercial, the grandmother happily is helping the grandchild swing and is the proud consumer of the advertised product.

In cases in which elderly people are shown with young adults (31.3%, $n = 109$; with only young adults 8.0%, $n = 28$), they are shown either as members of a family or as representatives of different generations in general. In a few cases, these generations show a boss and employees. In all these representations, however, no products exclusively for elderly people are advertised.

The biggest group that appears with elderly people is middle-aged adults (62.4%, $n = 217$). Elderly people appear even relatively often alone with them (28.4%, $n = 99$). These commercials use many patterns already mentioned in other configurations. Some of them advertise products highly associated with the elderly (e.g., pharmaceuticals, hair products, insurance, wheelchairs, and hearing aids) and the appearance typically is in the form of a family group with one or two parents and an adult child. One commercial played with the assumed notion that elderly people are ignorant about recent technology. It starts out with an older mother speaking with her son on the telephone and saying that she could not connect to the Internet because it is too complicated. Then, the son appeared surprisingly some minutes later to find that the mother had not even opened the package yet, and he shows her how easy using the Internet is.

Commercials that use more than two age groups, including the elderly (34.5%, $n = 120$), mostly are in a family setting or show different generations in a general way. In one commercial, three generations of women show that they all go to the same supermarket; in another, three generations enjoy the same dish at the table, while in yet another one, all generations of a household use the same toothpaste. These commercials show clearly that the advertised product has an appeal to all generations, no matter the age. The advertised products in these commercials hardly ever target one clear age group but are accessible to all different ages. Another commercial that illustrates this point, again using the stereotype of elderly people being weak regarding technology, is for a mobile phone provider. In this commercial, grandparents called their grandchildren from a fireworks display (often taking place in the summer in Japan and connected with traditional festivals). However, they not only call but make a video call with a television mobile phone. The grandchildren are really surprised and impressed that the grandparents were able to do that, but the grandparents insist that it really is easy. This commercial indicated indirectly that the product is so easy to handle that it even can be used by the elderly; it also shows elderly people that it is a product for them to connect with the world, including calling and even seeing their grandchildren.

Looking at the representation of elderly people, there is one really significant finding besides different representations connected with different age groups – the

Table 18.2 Male versus female elderly in commercials

Sex of character in ad	Appearance in ads[a] % (number)
Male	77.3 $(n = 269)$
Female	48.3 $(n = 168)$
Only male	51.7 $(n = 180)$
Only female	22.7 $(n = 79)$

[a] Number of ads sampled = 348.

different usage of male and female characters. There is an overwhelming difference in the usage, with one-third more elderly males in commercials, as seen in Table 18.2.

Also, previous research in the Japanese context has shown that older males in adverts outnumber older females [7, 8]. It would be wrong, however, to bring this finding solely into a Japanese context, since it seems to be a global phenomenon. This was shown, for example, by Moore and Cadeau [13] in a Canadian context, by Simcock and Sudbury [17] in a British context, and in a US context by several researchers [2, 9, 16, 18]. This phenomenon is evident in society because women more than men are under pressure to remain young and beautiful and being old is often a negative trait. It must be questioned here how much such a development is based on Japanese tradition or on Western influence, but this is beyond the scope of this chapter.

What was already mentioned partly in this section should be apparent in the following in more detail, namely the different usage of elderly people in connection with different product categories.

Elderly People and Product Categories

As can be seen in Table 18.3, elderly people are used predominantly to advertise some product categories; these include pharmaceuticals, financial/insurance, and food. When thinking about the needs of elderly people, these results are not surprising. In Japanese commercials, many pharmaceutical companies target elderly people either explicitly or implicitly (i.e., they also can be used by other customers but have a strong hold for elderly people).

Financial/insurance is another category that often is targeted directly at elderly people in Japan. Although this form of advertisement is not as common in many other countries, in Japan a huge number of insurance companies especially target elderly people who want to explore new options or want to improve the conditions of their current insurance. Whereas these two product categories are usually targeted specifically at elderly people, food products are slightly different. Here, elderly people are used either as representatives of a three-generation household or as endorsers of the quality and authenticity of traditional Japanese products.

Table 18.3 Percentage of product categories in commercials with elderly people

Product category	Appearance in ads[a] % (number)
Financial/insurance	16.4 ($n = 57$)
Pharmaceuticals	14.1 ($n = 49$)
Food	11.0 ($n = 38$)

[a] Number of ads sampled = 348.

Discussion

Japanese commercials use elderly people; however, they do not reflect the actual realities of Japanese society. In Japan, 24.2% of the population is older than 59 [1], whereas in Japanese commercials the ratio is only 13.6% in commercials with people. This also is a typical phenomenon in other countries [13, 15–17]. There are several reasons for this difference. One probably is the so-called cognitive versus chronological age. It can be assumed that many elderly people in Japan feel younger than they are and therefore want to be represented by younger models. Another factor that should not be overlooked is what Greco [6] found after surveying the opinions of hundreds of advertising executives on the use of elderly people in advertising. Most of the agency executives held the same opinion, namely that advertising with elderly people works best with elderly-oriented products. This was also the case in this sample, especially in commercials using only elderly people but also partly in commercials with elderly and middle-aged people in which products that are only or mainly for elderly people are advertised. These products included pharmaceuticals and other health products, financial/insurance plans, and food. Also, the results for these product categories are rather similar to findings in other parts of the world [2, 9, 16, 17]. Most of these commercials, however, used not only the 60+ elderly, but also 70+ elderly people. This can be an indication that either the borders within society are shifting upwards, based on a longer life expectancy and a more active life, or simply that elderly people can and should be separated further into different age segments.

In this context, what Dyer [4] writes about advertisements in general should not be forgotten, namely that they "teach us ways of thinking and feeling, generally through fantasy and dreaming." Advertisements aim to show an illusion or dream, a world one can attain at least partly through consuming a product. Based on current perceptions of age in society, one of the dreams of elderly people seems to be becoming younger than they are.

So, why are elderly people not used for products not explicitly targeted at them? It is not that elderly people are not also used in other commercials; however, in such cases, elderly people either are a main target group or are shown simply as a part of a family or a more general part of a generation also enjoying and consuming the advertised product. Greco states that "the transgenerational approach incorporating persons of varying ages can be used to show the 'universal' appeal of the product" [6], and that is certainly also true in the Japanese context. Showing different age groups using the same products simply shows that they all are satisfied with the product.

One of the main reasons for seldom using elderly people is that many products are targeted at other age groups (only 22.4% of commercials with elderly people target them explicitly), and there is the risk of alienating younger customers [6]. It is assumed and partly shown in some studies [11] that younger people are not interested in products advertised by elderly people, so their use in advertisements for products for other age groups might be limited. Conversely, elderly people consider middle-aged and older models more credible than younger ones [12]. In short, advertising agencies have the difficult decision of choosing the target market they really are aiming for and have to be careful not to alienate some of their targeted groups one way or another.

Although this chapter is interested first of all in the marketing side of the representation of elderly people in Japanese commercials, one final aspect should be mentioned. As previously outlined, there is a huge gap in the representation of male and female elderly people in Japanese commercials (and also in other countries). This picture refers clearly to a general image of (elderly) women in society and especially in the media. More than men, it is women who have to look young and beautiful. Naturally, advertisements are not the creator of such images, but they also reflect social trends, and an additional medium to support and even increase such trends. Similarly, as in the cases of super-slim women in culture, media, and fashion advertisements [3], the image of elderly women is influenced partly by media and advertising. As a result, with the countertrends and discussions about the representations of slim women, there also should be more discussion about the representation of elderly women and women in general.

Summary and Conclusion

The most important findings of this research were the following. First of all, elderly people and especially elderly females are underrepresented. Elderly people are used mostly to advertise a relatively small range of product categories (financial/insurance, pharmaceuticals/health products, food) and are used in other circumstances mostly as a representative of one generation.

Just looking at these few findings, we can learn that all of them seem more or less universally applicable. This should not neglect cultural and regional specificities and certainly does not support the idea of international advertising campaigns, but these findings support the idea that maybe other findings from other studies in other countries also should be tested for their applicability in a rather different cultural and social context, such as Japan. This also is true the other way around: results from Japan, which is the most advanced country concerning demographic change, should be tested in Western environments. As could be shown at several points in this chapter, there are many similarities in how elderly people are used and targeted in Japanese commercials and in commercials in the West (especially Britain and the USA). This chapter cannot determine whether these are really based on cultural similarities or on some kind of Westernization of Japanese advertising and/or culture.

The importance of elderly people for the economy will increase during the coming years, not only in Japan, but in most industrialized countries. As a result, it must be the intention of more and more advertising researchers to deal with this topic more systematically. There have already been studies in the USA on this topic, but research is still rather scant in many countries, including Japan.

As a result, within advertising, the study of elderly people and how they want to be addressed can be one important topic for the years to come. There still is a wide field of research that can be undertaken. This study certainly can be regarded only as a first step in analyzing the usage of elderly people in Japanese TV commercials. There still are several research questions that can be addressed by follow-up research, either solely on TV commercials or on print advertising as well. One question can focus on commercials targeting the elderly, including those that do not use elderly people. Only this type of study can answer clearly the question of how many Japanese advertisements use models in the "cognitive age" of elderly people instead of their chronological age for advertising products targeted at them. A longitudinal study to see how the aging society already leads to changes in the use of elderly people in advertisements also could be useful.

It also would be interesting to learn (as was done in the USA and in Britain) what advertising executives think about the use of elderly people in advertising, what elderly Japanese think about current advertising, and what they would like to see changed. If forecasts are accurate, the market for elderly people will become more and more important during the years to come, so it is only natural for marketing researchers to put a greater emphasis on this area.

Appendix

This research is based on a total of 2 weeks recorded from four private TV stations in Sendai, Japan (each affiliated with a mother station in Tokyo). Each recording covered 20 h a day, from 6 am to 2 am, using two VCRs simultaneously. Sample 1 was recorded 23–29 August 2004; Sample 2 was recorded 4–10 April 2005. Since the overall results of the sample weeks were extremely consistent, I merged the samples here for purpose of readability. This leads to a total number of 19,805 commercials, 3352 of which were unique (2557 ads with people).

To analyze the data, content analysis using a coding sheet was used at first, since measures extend our senses, and content analysis allows a "discovery of patterns that are too subtle to be visible on casual inspection and protection against an unconscious search through the magazine for only those which confirm one's initial sense of what the photos say or do" [10]. Lutz and Collins refer here to magazines, but the same is true for any visual or sense-based text, including television commercials.

In short, an important advantage of content analysis is that it can make hidden significances visible within a huge sample; that is what I tried to do in my research. Afterward, the most significant findings of the content analysis also were analyzed qualitatively.

References

1. Asahi Shimbun, *Japan Almanac* 2003 (2003), http://adv.asahi.com/english/data/index.html. Accessed 9 Oct 2007
2. T.V. Atkins, M.C. Jenkins, M.H. Perkins, *Psychol. J. Hum. Behav.* **27**(4)/**28**(1), 30 (1990/1991)
3. S. Bordo, Identity and difference, in *Reading the slender body*, ed. by K. Woodward (Sage, Thousand Oaks, 1997), p. 167 (Reprinted from *Body/politics: women and the discourses of science*, ed. by M. Jacobus, E. Fox Keller, S. Shuttleworth (Routledge, New York, 1987))
4. G. Dyer, *Advertising as Communication* (Routledge, London, 1982)
5. K.T. Frith, B. Mueller, *Advertising and societies: global issues* (Peter Lang, New York, 2003)
6. A.J. Greco, *J. Consum. Mark.* **6**(1), 37 (1989)
7. S. Hagiwara, Nihon no terebi CM ni okeru gaikoku yōso no yakuwari [The role of foreign elements in Japanese commercials] in *Media ga tsutaeru gaikoku imēji*, ed. by K. Kawatake, A. Sugiyama (Keibunsha, Tokyo, 1996), p. 115
8. S. Hagiwara, *Media Commun.* **54**, 5 (2004) http://www.mediacom.keio.ac.jp/publication/index.html. Accessed 23 Feb 2005
9. M.M. Lee, B. Carpenter, L.S. Meyers, *J. Aging Stud.* **21**, 23 (2006)
10. C.A. Lutz, J.L. Collins, *Reading National Geographic* (University of Chicago Press, Chicago, 1993)
11. M.B. Mazis, D.J. Ringold, S.P. Elgin, D.W. Denman, *J. Mark.* **56**, 22 (1992)
12. R.E. Milliman, R.C. Erffmeyer, *J. Advert. Res.* **29**(6), 31 (1989/1990)
13. T.E. Moore, L. Cadeau, *Can. J. Behav. Sci.* **17**(3), 215 (1985)
14. W.M. O'Barr, *Culture and the ad: exploring otherness in the world of advertising* (Westview, Boulder, CO, 1994)
15. R.T. Peterson, D.T. Ross, *J. Bus. Ethics* **16**(4), 425 (1997)
16. A. Roy, J. Harwood, *J. Appl. Commun. Res.* **25**(1), 39 (1997)
17. P. Simcock, L. Sudbury, *Int. J. Advert.* **25**(1), 87 (2006)
18. M. Tupper, *The representation of elderly persons in primetime television advertising*, Master's thesis, University of South Florida, 1995, http://www.geocities.com/lightgrrrrrl/index.html. Accessed 6 Oct 2007
19. J. Williamson, *Decoding advertisements: ideology and meaning in advertising* (Marion Boyars, London, 1978)

Chapter 19
Advertising Agencies: The Most Calcified Part of the Process

C. Nyren

Abstract Today's advertising industry needs a minor revolution. Talented men and women in their 40s, 50s, and 60s must to be brought into the fold if you want to target the Silver Market. This includes copywriters, graphic artists, producers, video directors, and creative directors. If you plan on implementing a marketing strategy that includes Baby Boomers as a primary, secondary, or tertiary market, and you turn it over to only people in their 20s and 30s, you will forfeit the natural sensibilities required to generate vital campaigns.

Introduction

You can analyze marketing fodder all day and night, read countless books about marketing to Baby Boomers, attend advertising and marketing conventions around the world, and soak up everything all the experts have to say. But the bottom line is this: if the right people aren't in the right jobs, what happens is what happens in all arenas of business – failure and mediocrity.

And the reverse is true. If you had a product or service for late teens and twentysomethings, and you walked into your advertising agency and your creative team was made up of *only* people in their 50s and 60s – I would imagine that you would be very, very worried.

For over 5 years I've been writing, consulting, and speaking about advertising to Baby Boomers. Before long I realized that most follow-up questions from readers, clients, and conference attendees required answers soaked in history. Queries were usually variations of "Why do ad agencies and the media marginalize and ignore the 50+ market?" or "Why does my agency tell me that there is no need to target people over fifty? That they buy products anyway?"

The answer to all is that most agencies are not interested in nor equipped to produce vital, successful campaigns targeting this demo. Here's why:

A Very Brief History of Advertising Creatives in the United States

From the late 1800s until World War I (WWI) just about anybody could leap into advertising if they had the nerve, the verve, and a talent for persuasion. The industry was spread out geographically, culturally, ethnically. While there were advertising agencies large and small, many companies created their own ads, mostly using agencies for what is today known as media planning.

The expansion of railroads made it possible to haul consumer products and magazines/periodicals nationwide – and market nationwide. By the late 1910s advertising was becoming a very big business.

The war put a damper on this growth – but afterwards, as the USA hurriedly switched from a wartime to a consumer economy, companies garnered huge excesses of earned income. The most attractive and reasoned way to spend much of this money was on advertising [6]. Large agencies benefited because they were equipped for major campaigns.

As was the case in most businesses, the power eventually ended up in the hands of white, protestant, ivy-league educated men. Ethnic, cultural, and religious diversity was soon frowned upon. If you were Jewish, Catholic, Irish, or Italian you did your best to play it down or hide it. Women were also marginalized.

Also, to protect itself, industry headquarters settled in New York City. This was the beginning of what we refer to literally, and now metaphorically, as "Madison Avenue."

The cultural zeitgeist of the post-WWI era was "be rich," so it didn't hurt that advertising was being created by people who had a good shot at realizing this dream. It is simple common sense that the best advertising is done by people who advertise to themselves.

The 1920s was also the first time a young generation was niche-targeted. Naturally, young copywriters and art directors were assigned these accounts.

There were a few powerful, talented women. One was Helen Landsdowne, recruited by Stanley Resor, president of J. Walter Thompson's Cincinnati office. Soon, they married.

After a move to New York and a reorganization of JWT, Stanley Resor was named president, and Helen Resor quickly became one of the top copywriters in the industry. *This was a woman spearheading campaigns targeting women.* If not something new, it certainly wasn't common. Some say that Helen Resor was the primary reason JWT grew to be the largest advertising agency in the world (and it continued to be for the next 30 years).

But during her decades at JWT, Helen Landsdowne Resor was "on paper" merely the head copywriter for many major accounts, although she often presented and pitched major clients. Business propriety did not permit a woman to be an executive.

Throughout the Great Depression and WWII, the advertising zeitgeist glorified the middle class. It was bad taste to "be rich." Along with radio and a flood of inexpensive magazines, average Americans were the heroes and heroines. Smart advertising agencies added to their stables, searching and finding talented individuals with more varied, down-to-earth backgrounds.

As in the 1920s, women were still marginalized. A few couldn't be held down. A good example was Jean Wade Rindlaub of BBDO. Her campaigns for Campbell Soup and General Mills spoke directly to mothers and the middle class, and her wartime ads for Community Silver (This is for keeps) portraying wives and mothers saying goodbye to their husbands and sons were the "pin-ups" for those at home during the war. Ms. Rindlaub also created what was considered the preeminent research department in the industry, considered to be the prototype of what are now focus groups.

It wasn't until after WWII that Jean Wade Rindlaub attained V.P. status. And, it wasn't until the mid 1950s that Ms. Rindlaub was appointed to BBDO's Board of Directors, the first woman on a board of a major advertising agency.

The post-WWII era brought more changes to the advertising industry. The zeitgeist shifted from extolling middle-class values to glorifying upper-mobility, a "keep up with the Joneses" mentality.

While its roots date back to the 1920s, the 1950s also brought about a messy revolution in methodology. Hard-sell, fact-based scientific advertising collided with creative, soft-sell approaches. The best advertising was often a queasy but effective melding of the two.

Here and there, Jews, Catholics, and women began to be "officially" accepted in powerful positions. Below is a handful of the most productive and influential creatives in the early 1950s through the middle 1960s. All are on the list of the top *Advertising Age's* 100 advertising people of the twentieth Century (with their positions on the list noted):

Bill Bernbach (#1) was the first enormously successful and openly Jewish advertising creative in 30 years, spearheading campaigns for Orbach's Department Store, Volkswagen, Avis Car Rental, Life Cereal, and many others. Quotes from Bill Bernbach:

Advertising isn't a science, it's persuasion. And persuasion is an art.

Research can trap you in the past.

Logic and over-analysis can immobilize and sterilize an idea. It's like love – the more you analyze it, the faster it disappears.

Leo Burnett (#3) was a Midwesterner copywriter and creative director who only later in his career migrated to Madison Avenue. During the 1950s and 1960s he and his people created icons that are still recognized today, including The Jolly Green Giant, Tony the Tiger, The Pillsbury Doughboy, and Charlie the Tuna.

David Ogilvy (#4) is still considered by many to be the greatest copywriter of all time. During his heyday, Mr. Ogilvy boosted the branding of companies like Hathaway Shirts, Shell Oil, Sears, KLM, American Express, IBM, Schweppes tonic,

Rolls-Royce, and Pepperidge Farm. Quotes from Mr. Ogilvy:

> I notice increasing reluctance on the part of marketing executives to use judgment; they are coming to rely too much on research, and they use it as a drunkard uses a lamp post for support, rather than for illumination.
>
> Much of the messy advertising you see on television today is the product of committees. Committees can criticize advertisements, but they should never be allowed to create them.

Rosser Reeves (#5) believed in thorough research, and codified the Unique Sales Proposition (USP), a technique of focusing on the distinctive qualities of a product. His campaigns included "M&Ms melt in your mouth, not in your hand." A quote from Rosser Reeves:

> Let's say you have $1,000,000 tied up in your little company and suddenly your advertising isn't working and sales are going down. And everything depends on it. Your future depends on it, your family depends on it...Now, what do you want from me? Fine writing? Or do you want to see the goddamned sales curve stop moving down and start moving up?

Shirley Polykoff (#24) hid that she was Jewish for most of her career. As the sole woman copywriter at Foote, Cone & Belding, Ms. Polykoff was tossed the Clairol account. She came up with *"Does she... or doesn't she? Only her hairdresser knows for sure,"* and *"Is it true blondes have more fun?"* Sales of Clairol products quadrupled. Ms. Polykoff scoffed at research, and wrote from the gut.

Bernice Fitz-Gibbon (#62) was the ad manager at Macy's, Wanamakers and Gimbels. With her unique, classy copywriting and creative direction, Ms. Gitz-Gibbon was the highest-paid women in advertising in the middle 1950s.

The 1960s cultural revolution, with Baby Boomers and the youngest of the Silent Generation coming of age, had a profound effect on the industry. Doors were now open to all ethnicities, cultures, and backgrounds. Women flourished. It didn't matter who you were as long as you had the moxie, the talent. The grip that Madison Avenue had on the industry loosened. Large, medium, and small agencies were almost indistinguishable in terms of quality of output.

With the rise of multinationals during the following two decades, advertising became a truly global phenomenon. Great campaigns were now coming out of the Midwest, the West in the USA, and around the world. For the first time, a "golden age" of advertising (in the 1980s) blossomed in another country, England.

But, as with each era of advertising, there was a blind spot, a prejudice. Along with the openness of the 1960s came a new primary zeitgeist: "be young." This was fine through the 1980s. The largest market was Baby Boomers (give or take a few years), and advertising agencies were actively recruiting and handing over power and influence to creatives in their 20s. After all (if I may repeat myself for the umpteenth time), the best advertising is done by people who advertise to themselves. Why wouldn't you hire young people to create campaigns for young people? They instinctively know their market.

Ad agencies pre-1960s, while often excluding minorities and women, always had a good age mix. *This was their diversity.* While creative departments usually skewed young, they weren't made up exclusively, or even primarily, of young people.

During my presentations, the slide that always elicits gasps is the one where I slowly reveal the ages of the top creatives mentioned earlier. I say, "Many advertising historians consider the most productive phases of their careers as being between the early 1950s to the late 1960s. How old were they in the middle of their whirlwind creative periods – in 1960?"

- Bill Bernhach: 49
- David Ogilvy: 49
- Rosser Reeves: 50
- Shirley Polykoff: 52
- Bernice Fitz-Gibbon: 66
- Leo Burnett: 68

Remember: this was in the *middle* of their creative periods. Much more was to come from them. In fact, for some their most successful work was produced in the latter half of their careers. And, they surrounded themselves with people of all ages. A quote from Rosser Reeves when he was 52 years old:

> No, I don't think a 68 year-old copywriter can write with the kids. That he's as creative. That he's as fresh. But he may be a better surgeon. His ad may not be quite as fresh and glowing as the Madison Avenue fraternity would like to see it be, and yet he might write an ad that will produce five times the sales. And that's the name of the game, isn't it?

You can argue the points Mr. Reeve's puts forth. But what astounds most people about the quote is the fact that up until the 1970s there *were* 68-year-old creatives actively involved in advertising. Ask someone today about older vs. younger advertising creatives, and the quote would have to begin, "*No, I don't think a 38-year-old copywriter can write with the kids...*"

Mr. Reeves retired from the business when he was 55-years-old. It was the talk of Madison Avenue at the time. There were arguments and speculations about why he did so. Many wondered why someone would retire from advertising at such a young age.

Today, things are a bit different:

> The advertising industry is notoriously associated with young people, crazy ideas, wild parties, and general excessiveness. The average age in the industry is way below thirty... Advertising agencies are in the business of creativity. They are also in the business of managing human perceptions. It's therefore interesting that although many tactics are employed to ensure creativity, agencies have traditionally not cottoned on to the fact that a more diverse workforce, inclusive of non-discriminatory age policies, poses the potential for greater competitive advantage. (Paula Sartini) [13]

The problem is that this zeitgeist hasn't changed. It's still "be young." The advertising industry is not at all "cutting-edge," but behind the times. This is especially counterproductive now that we have complex market segmentations and new ways of reaching and targeting consumers.

From *The Business Case for Diversity* [5]:

> ... An increasing number of European companies are adopting diversity and equality strategies, not only for ethical and legal reasons but also for the business benefits they are

expected to deliver. Among the most important of these benefits are a wider pool of high quality workers, greater innovation, and enhanced marketing opportunities (The European Commission Directorate-General for Employment).

An excerpt from my book, *Advertising to Baby Boomers* [10]:

Today's advertising industry needs a minor revolution. Talented men and women in their forties and fifties must to be brought back into the fold if you want to reach Baby Boomers. This includes account executives, copywriters, graphic artists, producers, directors, creative directors. If you plan on implementing a marketing strategy that includes Baby Boomers as a primary, secondary, or tertiary market, and you turn it over to a different generation of advertising professionals, you will forfeit the natural sensibilities required to generate vital campaigns.

Truth is, you can analyze marketing fodder all day and night, read countless books about marketing to Baby Boomers, attend advertising and marketing conventions around the world, and soak up everything all the experts have to say.

But the bottom line is this: If the right people aren't in the right jobs – well, you know what happens. What happens is what happens in all arenas of business: failure and (sometimes even worse) mediocrity.

But my advertising agency says that people over fifty buy products anyway...

Sure "they" do. But do they buy *your* product instead of the competition's? Advertising agencies write off *your potential target market* because they don't know how to advertise to Baby Boomers anymore than I know how to reach a teenager or young adult who wriggles and zigzags around in his or her chair, punching, skidding, and spastically rattling something I believe is referred to as a *joystick*. (Chuck Nyren)

Not too long after the second edition paperback was released, Rance Crain, publisher of *Advertising Age*, penned some columns that mirrored much of what I had been saying for years. Two excerpts:

From *Boomer Boon* [3]:

... The ad business is woefully out of touch with baby-boomer buying power. Young ad people think older people are stuck in their ways, so it's a waste of money to try to get them to change brands...a prime-time TV show with most of its viewers in the 34-to-49 range can get 30% more per ad minute than one that caters to people 55 and older. Yet consumers age 50 and up already spend more than $1.7 trillion on goods and services a year...

Agencies like to think of themselves as the last bastion of creativity, but they're in many ways the most calcified part of the process. Enlightened clients are beginning to realize this resistance to change is holding them back; the next step is to bypass their agencies' counsel.[1] (Rance Crain)

From *You Know Who's Boss – Consumers* [4]:

... It makes all the sense in the world for ad makers (both clients and agencies) to be well-stocked with people who understand consumers, whether young people who fathom the mysteries of cyberspace, a good mixture of people who reflect the ethnic and cultural diversity of our country, and, yes, even older people who understand the vitality and buying power of the great gorge of baby boomers overtaking our land.

If the ad business is serious about regaining control of its brands, it must first understand that the "boss" is not just a 35-year-old white American. He or she is older, black, Asian or Hispanic... (Rance Crain)

---

[1] Italics are mine.

As I write this, an email pops into my inbox. It's not much different to ones I receive every week. Excerpts:

> I know you are onto something regarding the Baby Boomer business. I have enclosed a resume, and wonder if there is a way for existing ad agencies to embrace this potential, or do you see starting an ad agency devoted to baby boomers exclusively?

> I have been thinking about it, and no doubt there are a lot of other boomers who a) see age discrimination and/or b) wonder why the largest advertisers or agencies are not "getting it."

> I have submitted my resume to the top 100 ad agencies and I have received not a word. The people I know basically tell me that the agencies are looking only for young people.

This gentleman's resume (he's a graphic artist/creative director) is impressive. It includes well-known and successful national and international campaigns from 15, 20, and 30 years ago. He has the sensibility required to reach the 50+ market because he was advertising to this same market when they were in their 20s and 30s. He is one of them. He instinctively knows what their concerns are, and how to reach them now that they have matured.

But no agency wants him.

Advertising Today: Is It Only the Experienced, Older Creatives that Agencies Need to Bring into the Fold?

One other presentation slide of mine usually shocks. I talk a bit about David Ogilvy: "How old was David Ogilvy was when he wrote his first ad?" Remember, many consider him to be the greatest copywriter of all time. He is #4 on *Ad Age*'s list of the "Greatest people in advertising in the wentieth century." Many would rate him #1.

"So how old was he? Was he a child genius? Thirteen? Sixteen? Eighteen? Twenty-one?"

The answer: David Ogilvy wrote his first ad when he was *39 years old*. He spent the next 25 years actively involved in creating advertising campaigns, and another 20 involved in an executive capacity.

Here is a revolutionary thought: Agencies should also be searching for people in their 40s, 50s, and 60s who have never worked in advertising.

In the recently published book *Old Masters and Young Geniuses*, David Galenson analyzes the creative productivity of famous artists from all fields [8]:

> Experimental innovators work by trial and error, and arrive at their major contributions gradually, late in life. In contrast, conceptual innovators make sudden breakthroughs by formulating new ideas, usually at an early age. Galenson shows why such artists as Michelangelo, Rembrandt, Cézanne, Jackson Pollock, Virginia Woolf, Robert Frost, and Alfred Hitchcock were experimental old masters, and why Vermeer, van Gogh, Picasso, Herman Melville, James Joyce, Sylvia Plath, and Orson Welles were conceptual young geniuses.[2]

---

[2] http://www.davidgalenson.com/, excerpt from the publisher's book description.

Baby Boomers are finishing up the first part of their lives, and many are ready to pursue new careers. They are going back to school, learning new skills, finally following their dreams. The largest age demo for new entrepreneurs is Baby Boomers (and a bit older). They feel as if they are beginning exciting, innovative, productive lives. There are scores of books and literally hundreds of articles about "second career" Baby Boomers. I'll cite two:

From *Boomers Embark on New Midlife Careers* [9]:

According to author Marc Freedman, these (Baby Boomers) are part of a revolution that may change the nature of work and retirement in the USA – people who, instead of fading from the workforce in midlife, are embarking on second careers.Instead of the freedom from work, they are searching for the freedom to work; instead of saving for a secure retirement," they are underwriting an encore career. Freedman writes in his new book, *Encore* [7]. (Teresa Mears)

From *Baby boomers make seasoned PROs* [1]:

They were America's very first mass advertising market and a public relations officer's dream: nearly 78 million baby boomers who have come of age with radio and television. As children, they were the first consumers of breakfast cereals and baby foods. As adults, they were the biggest trendsetters in the country. But, as they started to outgrow the 18–49 year old age bracket, they are now creating a new frontier as some of the country's most established and seasoned public relations officers (PROs)... Smart PR firms are now opting to break the age-old PR model... Slick firms are now beginning to comprehend that seasoned professionals with good business backgrounds will storm the PR market. Not only do these respected practitioners treat reporters and editors with the respect that is due them, but they also have the ability to provide them with services in a fast yet professional manner.

It is this ability of the baby boomers to strategize that defines their well-advanced intellectual status, making them one of the best options in the PR industry. With their skillful ability to implement those strategies, they are known to all and sundry as the great PR practitioners. Keep in mind that executives love to have someone alongside them strategizing and managing their organizations so that they come out as winners in the marketplace. (Anna D. Banks)

But how many advertising agencies are willing to hire novices in their 40s, 50s, or 60s? You could come in with some great writing – perhaps from a different field, and/or be fresh out of "going back to college" after taking advertising courses, or be a brilliant graphic artist with a distinguished career who has never worked in advertising...

And you'll be politely shown the door.

How many Baby Boomers, ones who've always wanted to do something creative and have a secret desire to get into advertising, are opening up their own ad agencies? I doubt any would even consider it. Three decades into his career, David Ogilvy sent a memo to his staff [11]:

Will Any Agency Hire This Man?

He is 38, and unemployed. He dropped out of college. He has been a cook, a salesman, a diplomatist and a farmer. He knows nothing about marketing and has never written any copy. He professes to be interested in advertising as a career (at the age of 38!) and is ready to go to work... I doubt if any American agency will hire him.

David Ogilvy was writing about himself.

Two Successful Campaigns

Pressured by CMO's and a few forward-thinking folks in advertising agencies, things are changing. The 50+ market is now on the radar.

Unfortunately, 50+ creatives aren't. Most of the campaigns targeting Baby Boomers are clumsy and ineffective, as they take turns waving 1960s Peace Symbols while bedding moldy, psychedelic music, or portray people over 50 as smiling, vapid, mindless pod people only interested in making sure they don't have to pee while playing golf or sunning themselves at the beach, or assume that Boomers are so technologically incompetent that when confronted with a computer they press a blank piece of paper to the screen in order to "print."

However, two recent campaigns are top-notch, and take opposite approaches in reaching their target market. Both succeed. For space purposes, I will only talk about the print ads – although these coordinated campaigns use all or most media.

The Dove Pro • Age campaign has a diverse history. Hatched from the Dove Real Beauty campaign created and incubated in Europe and the USA, it consists of aesthetic, commercially viable photographs of nude women over 50. On the surface, it's pure creativity, with no facts or research.

Or so it seems.

The Crest Pro-Health toothpaste ad, at first glance, appears to be simple and dull: a picture of the product package and two columns of health and beauty benefits (but mostly health). One list refers to Crest Pro-Health, the other (with less checkmarks) to "regular toothpaste." It's pure fact-based, hard sell advertising with no creativity or emotional connection with the target market.

Or so it seems.

Why has the Dove Pro • Age campaign been so successful? Simply because of its outrageousness in daring to promote its product by using nude women over 50? It is much better than that.

Although it may appear to be purely "creative," this campaign is steeped in research. For Baby Boomer women (and a bit older), after 40 is better than before 40.

While there has always been a small percentage of women who bloomed in their later years, for Boomers it has become a generational ethos. Again, there have been major studies, scores of articles, and a handful of books on this subject. A good one is *Primetime Women: How to Win the Hearts, Minds, and Business of Boomer Big Spenders* by Marti Barletta (Kaplan Business, 2007).

Here are some excerpts from my book, *Advertising to Baby Boomers* [10]:

Contrary to popular myth, Baby Boomers do not believe that they are still teenagers or young adults...

Boomers are slyly redefining what it means to be the ages they are. Included in this new definition are some youthful attitudes, but the real change is that instead of winding down, many are winding up...

There is a big difference between thinking you are younger than you are, and not thinking that you are old. This "night and day" distinction may confuse many pundits, but it does not confuse most Boomers...

Baby Boomers do not want to be twenty again, or thirty again. They want to feel as good as they possibly can for the ages they are. They do not want to be marketed and advertised to as if they were young adults or thirty-somethings...

In fact, Baby Boom women are the real age revolutionaries. Many are feeling very empowered, very alive, and ready to take on the world. While they could do without some of the wrinkles and some of the aches, ask most women over 40 if they would like to live their 20s and 30s all over again, and they'll say, "No thanks. I'm happier and more productive now than I have ever been."...

So if an advertising agency tells you "when you target 19-to-35-year-olds, you likewise reach Baby Boomers," they are sadly out of touch with one of the largest and certainly the richest market segment today...

The second and even more important reason for this campaign's success has to do with the major two people involved in its creation and development: Shelly Lazarus (b. 1947) and Annie Leibovitz (b. 1949). Ms. Lazarus is Chief Executive for Ogilvy & Mather Worldwide (the agency that created the campaign) and has a reputation as a hands-on CEO (especially with this campaing, from what I've heard). Ms. Liebovitz has had and is having such a long and varied career that it's hard to sum it up without going on for pages. While she's much, much more, Ms. Leibovitz can certainly be described as the quintessential Baby Boomer creative.

Let's talk reality: You many not be able to find a comparable Shelly Lazarus to spearhead your campaign. You might not be able to afford Annie Liebovitz as your artistic director. But, if you are targeting women over 50, don't you think it might be a bright idea to find and hire people with similar business and creative sensibilities as Ms. Lazarus and Ms. Liebovitz?

During my presentations, I toss up a slide with some quotes and pictures from an article in *Advertising Age* – and up a hypothetical situation, playing it out as only a middle-aged wannabe ham actor can. With my tongue in my cheek towards the end, I say:

Here's a speech I liked hearing about, reported in *Advertising Age* by Lisa Sanders, from the mouth of Euro RSCG Worldwide's David Jones (age 38):

From *Ignore the Research and Trust Your Gut* [12]:

Taking a "swipe at the research and pre-testing industry," Mr. Jones next exhorted listeners to stop asking permission. Drawing on a 'truth" from British comedian Vic Reeves that "96.2% of all statistics are made up," Mr. Jones, also a Brit, argued that some of the most well-liked ads aren't based on research or focus-group results. Instead they rely on a creative director's gut instinct of what consumers will like. He cited Procter and Gamble's effort for Charmin toilet tissue created by Euro rival Publicis Worldwide that riffs off of the many euphemisms for elimination. "Publicis took a risk, and did it without a bit of research," he said.

And, by way of reinforcing the previous point, his last bit of advice was for creatives to "trust your gut." Advertising is changing fast, and to not take a risk is risky, even though it's scary to take a risk. (Lisa Sanders)

No argument from me. I love it.

But there is one big problem. When targeting Baby Boomers you have to have the right guts around to trust. That'd be 50+ creative guts.

It wouldn't be too bright to trust my gut to come up with a campaign for a product aimed at twentysomethings. My gut would tell me, "...Ummm...ummm... Wait! I got it! I got it! We get some twentysomething guy or gal or both an' spike their hair an' give'em tattoos and put rings in their noses an' iPods on their heads an' bed some hip-hop music an' have'em hold up the product! Yeah! They'll buy it! They'll buy it!"

It's fine to champion creatives and their guts and call this a "risk" – but are agencies prepared to take the common sense "risk" of hiring creatives with the best guts to trust when targeting specific demographics?

Saatchi & Saatchi, an agency famous for attempting to create "love" for their clients' products, went against their own grain with Crest Pro-Health toothpaste. On the surface it's hackneyed USP (unique sales proposition) – factual and direct, with no emotional connection. You might likewise think that such a non-evasive, non-creative campaign wouldn't have much impact anymore, but:

> Three months after its debut, Crest Pro-Health could be the most successful US toothpaste launch in the last decade... The study found two-thirds of Pro-Health buyers normally use other non-Crest brands of toothpaste, including nearly 25% who said they used Colgate Total, Crest's main rival... Pro-Health's secret? Targeting the needs of consumers who put a premium on the healthcare aspects of their toothpaste... Those who had seen Pro-Health ads were 40–50% more likely to buy it. (C. von Hoffman) [14]

No big surprise to me. About 6 months before the campaign was launched, I read about Crest coming out with a toothpaste – and targeting Baby Boomers. While they won't admit that they are (who wants to target old people?), this is it. And 2 years before that, I wrote this in the 2005 edition of my book [10]:

> Here's an example of the way Madison Avenue wants you to think: For years, pre-teens and young teenagers never paid any attention to toothpaste ads. But for the last decade or so, toothpaste has been developed, manufactured, and marketed to kids and teenagers. Forty-odd years ago toothpaste was marketed to adults only. Crest began targeting parents, claiming fewer cavities for kids with Crest, implying smaller dentist bills.
>
> Did we, as children, care? Not really.
>
> However, if you watch toothpaste ads today, you would think that people brush their teeth up until their early thirties and then all of sudden they magically turn seventy and buy only denture cream. (I guess in Madison Avenue's alternative universe, this is why all senior citizens lose their teeth. They haven't brushed in forty years.)...
>
> So what toothpaste should I buy? Anybody have any ideas? I have a trillion dollars in the bank, and 300 billion to spend as I please.And I'm sauntering around the dental care aisle, hands in my pockets, jingling a few million in loose change, looking up and down, side to side, and I'm not sure *what* I'm going to buy.
>
> As advertising agencies have told you, I'm going to *buy something*. I guess it doesn't matter to you whether I buy *your* product or not, because I'll buy something...
>
> Here's an alternative universe you might consider. And it wouldn't be such a bad one for me, either:
>
> Hmmm. What's *this* toothpaste? I think I've heard about it. Saw a commercial, read an ad about it. The person in the ad was around my age. She talked a bit about dental care, a bit about gums, about teeth, how to keep them healthy and strong. She had a nice smile, but not one that blinded me, sending me stumbling, feeling my way to the bathroom for the Visine.

> And the box doesn't look like it's an ornament for a science fiction Christmas tree. Maybe I'll buy it. (Chuck Nyren)

There is more: While it might not seem to be a visceral campaign, it resonates with Baby Boomers because these are the types of ads we saw as children. However, *it's not a retro campaign*. Saatchi & Saatchi did not try to turn it into something old, with 1950s fonts and layout. The background is metallic blue, the design fresh and modern. It's simple, factual, contemporary. It tells us what we want to know.

These two campaigns are successful because both use creativity and research. It's simply their styles and approaches have a different mix. How about a Dove Pro·Age ad with a picture of their product and a list of ingredients and benefits? Or, for Crest Pro-Health – naked Baby Boomers brushing their teeth?

I think not. Good jobs by both agencies.

With all the high-tech advances over the last 10 years comes new ways to measure how the brain works. *The Scientific News* talks about studies of older and younger and older brains.

> From *Aging Brain Shifts Gears to Emotional Advantage* [2]:
>
> Advancing age heralds a growth in emotional stability accompanied by a neural transition to increased control over negative emotions and greater accessibility of positive emotions ... A brain area needed for conscious thought, the medial prefrontal cortex, primarily influences these emotional reactions in older adults... In contrast, people under age 50 experience negative emotions more easily than they do positive ones. These younger adults' emotion-related activity centers on the amygdala, a brain structure previously implicated in automatic fear responses... This gradual reorganization of the brain's emotion system may result from older folk responding to accumulating personal experiences by increasingly looking for meaning in life. (Bruce Bower)

Summary and Conclusion

The way a product or service is perceived by a creative, and then presented to potential consumers, is the essence of successful advertising. *A diversity of creatives – and creative diversity. That's how to reach the 50+ market.*

In countries and markets where the population is homogeneous, age diversity is an even more important ingredient.

References

1. A.D. Banks, Baby boomers make seasoned PROs. *American Chronicle*, 29 July 2007
2. B. Bower, Older but mellower: aging brain shifts gears to emotional advantage. *The Scientific News*, **169**(25), 24 June 2006
3. R. Crain, Boomer boon, *Advertising Age*, 2 Apr 2007
4. R. Crain, You know who's boss – consumers. *Advertising Age*, 30 Apr 2007

5. Directorate-General for Employment, Social Affairs and Equal Opportunities, *The business case for diversity: good practices in the workplace* (European Commission, Luxembourg, 2005)
6. S. Fox, *The mirror makers: a history of American advertising and its creators* (University of Illinois Press, Chicago, 2007)
7. M. Freedman, *Encore, finding work that matters in the second half of life* (PublicAffairs, NY, 2007)
8. D. Galenson, *Old masters and young geniuses* (Princeton Univeristy Press, 2005)
9. T. Mears, Boomers embark on new midlife careers. *Miami Herald*, 11 Aug 2007
10. C. Nyren, *Advertising to baby boomers*, (Paramount Market Books, Ithaca, NY, 2005)
11. Ogilvy & Mather Agency, *David Ogilvy – biography*, http://www.ogilvy.com/history/media/biography.pdf, (Ogilvy & Mather, 2000) Accessed 13 June 2008
12. L. Sanders, Ignore the research and trust your gut, *Advertising Age*, 2 Nov 2006
13. P. Sartini, *Managing age diversity in the advertising industry*. MarketingWeb.com, 4 Sep 2006
14. C. von Hoffman, Crest Pro-Health toothpaste launch has P&G smiling. *Brandweek*, 23 Oct 2006

Chapter 20
The Importance of Web 2.0 to the 50-Plus

D. Stroud

Abstract What is the importance of Web 2.0 for older people? This paper answers this question and provides suggestions for how organizations can use Web 2.0 to improve their online interactions with the older market. The chapter analyses the differences between the historical way that Web sites have been created and used and the opportunities and dangers of using Web 2.0 technologies. Social networking and Web video are the two best known applications of Web 2.0 and are discussed in detail. The author shows that whilst both these applications are associated with young people they are intrinsically "age-neutral" and are equally appropriate to older Web users. The chapter describes how social networking and Web video are likely to develop and the resulting implications upon the channel strategy of organizations targeting the older Web user.

Introduction

There can be little doubt that Web 2.0 has been the "hot" Web topic of 2007, something it might repeat in 2008. Strangely, for something that has attracted so much attention, it remains an ethereal and ill-defined subject. For many organizations the subtleties of Web 1.0 provide enough of a challenge without grappling with the complexity of the next phase of evolution.

When all of the jargon and hype is stripped away from Web 2.0 we find a combination of exciting new ways for organizations to do the thing that should be central to their Web strategy – understanding and communicating with their users.

A question that is rarely asked and almost never answered is: "What is the importance of Web 2.0 for older people"? This paper redresses this absence of discussion and provides practical suggestions for how organizations can use Web 2.0 to improve their online interactions with the older market.

What is Web 2.0?

Most people agree that the term Web 2.0 entered the public domain following the first O'Reilly Media Web 2.0 conference in 2004. This is the only fact concerning Web 2.0 that is agreed upon. Since 2004 there have been numerous definitions and propositions about its role and importance.

In an attempt to add clarity to the debate, Tim O'Reilly produced the following definition [8]: "Web 2.0 is the business revolution in the computer industry caused by the move to the internet as platform, and an attempt to understand the rules for success on that new platform."

Whilst this definition is eloquent and brief, it lacks the specifics required for organizations to understand and apply Web 2.0 within their own, online environment.

The easiest way of understanding Web 2.0 is by contrasting it Web 1.0, its predecessor. Much of the work involved in creating this definition has been done by Fidelity Finance [2]. To understand the difference between the two generation of Web sites it is helpful to separate the Web into two components.

The first component is the Web site's *architecture*. These are the tools and techniques used to create the site. Secondly, there is the *application* of the site (i.e. the value it adds to the individual and/or organization). It is particularly important to separate Web sites into these two components when analysing how they are used by older people.

The Differences between Web 1.0 and Web 2.0

Summaries of the features involved in the architecture and applications of the two generations of Web sites are shown in Tables 20.1 and 20.2. This analysis illustrates the features that differentiate Web 2.0 from older sites. The following section considers the age-neutrality aspects of this new generation of Web sites.

Is Web 2.0 Age-Neutral?

The use of the term "age-neutral", in the context of marketing, was first used by the author Stroud [11] when describing marketing campaigns targeting consumers with a wide spectrum of ages.

When evaluating marketing creative channels and enabling technologies (like the Web) it is vital to understand if they have the power to engage both young and old alike or are limited to a narrow age group.

The Web usability Guru, Jakob Nielsen has firm views about the usability issues involved with Web 2.0 sites. His views are particularly important because a Web site's usability is particularly important to its effectiveness with older people. The

Table 20.1 Web site architecture that typifies the two generations

Architecture feature	Implication
Web 1.0	
Predominately HTML code	The formatting language of the Web site is old and was created for non-commercial applications
Hard coded static links	The linkage between regions of the Web site is "hard-wired" when the site is created
Single path through the content	The design of the site limits the user to a predetermined number of navigation routes
Limited customization	Most sites are unable to react to the user's specific requirements
Multimedia is an "add-on"	Functionality enabling users to experience audio and video content are an adjunct, not an integral part of the Web site
Web 2.0	
Inherently multimedia	Video and audio are incorporated into the fabric of the Web site
Interface adapts to the user	The interface reacts to the different behaviour of individual users
Fewer links, more actionable elements (i.e. sliders, tabs, menus and widgets)	There are multiple design techniques to enable site navigation
Created using multiple technologies (AJAX, Flex, Flash)	Web sites are constructed using an array of technologies. (i.e. AJAX enables designers to update parts of a page without the whole page reloading)

Table 20.2 Web site applications that typifies the two generations

Application feature	Implication
Web 1.0	
The Web site user passively consumes content	Users have little opportunity to respond and add value to the information provided by the Web site
Single communications channel between the user and the Web site	The application's value is limited by the information provided by the Web site owner
Web 2.0	
Users create, refine and share content	The Web site "user" can contribute information, thereby increasing the value of the site's content
A community rather than solitary experience	Applications are not limited to the interaction between the site and a single user
The scope of the application is extended by integrating data from multiple sources. This is known often called a "mashup"	The functionality of the application is not limited to the resources of the site owner

following are three of his major concerns about Web 2.0 [7]:

- *Complex interfaces can confuse the user.* This conclusion is best illustrated by the way that AJAX, one of new Web 2.0 development tools, enables part of Web a page to be updated rather loading an entirely new page. Whilst this means the transaction is faster it risks confusing users who may be puzzled or unaware of what is happening. Nielsen tested 100 AJAX-created e-commerce sites and found that shoppers often didn't notice when their shopping carts were updated. This is not an intrinsic fault of the technology but a result of the way it is being implemented.
- *Few people contribute content.* The most famous example of user-contributed content is Amazon's book reviews, launched at the beginning of the Web era (1996). Web 2.0 has resulted in making it much easier and less costly for Web sites to incorporate content sharing features. Just because sites have this facility doesn't mean it will used. This has resulted in many Web sites with sparsely populated user content areas that have limited value. What should be a user benefit can result in confusion.
- *Brand confusion caused by mashups.* Web sites containing multiple sources of information (e.g. Google maps and BBC news) can result in the site's brand identity becoming diluted. More importantly, the aggregation of multiple services can degrade the quality of the site's usability because "mashed" services are unlikely to have the same quality of usability as the host site.

Many of Nielsen's concerns are about the poor and indiscriminate use of Web 2.0 features. Anything that degrades the usability of Web sites and makes them more complicated to use will cause older people problems.

Both Nielsen [6] and Fidelity [12] have researched the effect of ageing on the speed and error rate when older people use Web sites. A summation of their conclusions is illustrated in Fig. 20.1. This shows that a 65-year-old is likely to take 60% longer and make 50% more errors than a younger person of equivalent Internet experience.

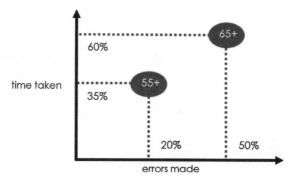

Fig. 20.1 The relationship between the time taken to use a Web site and the number of errors made and the age of the user

Because of the small sample sizes and the difficulty in comparing individuals of equivalent Internet experience, this linear relationship should be taken as a guide rather than an absolute rule. There is no doubt that age-related cognitive decline results in older people, even those with extensive Web experience, making more errors and taking longer to navigate sites.

So what is the answer to the question: "Is Web 2.0 age-neutral"?

The Web *applications* that people use are determined by their lifestyle and background, not their age (i.e. they are age-neutral). This is further discussed in Sects. 4 and 5.

The way designers are currently using the new generation of Web 2.0 tools is having a negative impact on the usability of Web sites, which has a disproportionate impact on older people. This means that the *architecture* of Web 2.0 is not age-neutral. There are no intrinsic reasons why this should be the case. It results from a lack of knowledge and concern that Web designers have for the results of physiological ageing on Web site usability.

The following two sections of this paper consider the two most important and highest profile applications that Web 2.0 has enabled and how they relate to older people.

Social Networking

Whenever the term Web 2.0 is mentioned you can be certain that the phrase "social networking" will not be far behind.

Social networking had many of similarities to the early days of texting (SMS), when adults were amazed as to why young people spent so much of their time keying messages into their mobile phones. The same bemusement exists about the ability of MySpace, Facebook and Bebo to attract vast numbers of visitors. These sites had 184 million unique visitors (worldwide) in June 2007 [3]. Table 20.4 contains the URLs and a brief description of all of the Web sites mentioned in this section.

The ability of social networking sites to generate these huge volumes of Web traffic is proof of their popularity. But, there is a hard business rationale to these sites. Rupert Murdoch, somebody who avoided investing in Web companies during the dot.com era, was so convinced of their importance that he purchased MySpace. This company entered the Japanese market in November 2007. Microsoft is also convinced of social networking's business potential as demonstrated by its purchase of a stake in Facebook.

Like all things related to Web 2.0, social networking has numerous definitions. The most useful way of explaining what it is and what it does, is by detailing its components of functionality. This is done in Table 20.3, using a set of definitions originally proposed by Danah Boyd [1].

The overarching thing about social networks is that their success is dependent on the willingness of their members to contribute and communicate. The Web site owner establishes the style of the network, provides the functionality, originates the

Table 20.3 The main components of a social networking Web site

Social networking component	Purpose
Profiles	Profiles are pages that enable individuals to describe themselves in terms of their age, sex, location, interests and a host of other variables. The profile might also contain rich content such as photographs, sound and video
Network of contacts	After joining a social network site users can identify and contact other members This might involve assigning contacts "privileges" for the types of content they can exchange
Messaging	Most social network sites also have a mechanism for users to send messages and append content to their friends' profiles. For registered members of the network this can become a replacement for e-mail
Content Sharing	This might be as simple as exchanging messages and textual content. More likely it also involves the ability to add to the site photos and videos. Increasingly it also includes the facilities for network users to construct their own blogs and wikis
Add-value content	Increasingly social networking sites are partnering with providers of content and widgets (modules of computer code) to enrich users profiles

Table 20.4 Descriptions and URLs of the Web sites discussed in this section

Web site description	Web site URL
A major social networking site that was created for students in US universities and is now available to all users in multiple geographies	www.facebook.com
A major social networking site that was acquired by Rupert Murdoch's News Corporation and is available to all users in multiple geographies	www.myspace.com
A social networking site founded in the USA and now available in multiple geographies. The site is targeted at teenagers and young adults	www.bebo.com
The largest global online employment Web site	www.monster.com
Venture funded US social networking site targeted at Baby Boomers	www.eons.com
Social networking site and portal for US grandparents	www.grandparents.com
US Web site, with imbedded social networking functionality, which is used for locating individuals providing in-home care and support services	www.care.com
A UK portal site targeted at the 50-plus	www.funkyfogey.com
A UK site providing a free service allowing people to create and maintain a memorial website for deceased family and friends	www.gonetoosoon.co.uk
A UK portal web site providing services and products for the over 50s	www.laterlife.com
Part of the John Lewis group. The first UK supermarket web site that uses elements of social networking functionality	www.waitrose.com
The largest Japanese social networking site	www.mixi.jp
Mobage-town is a mobile phone portal providing games, avatars and social networking aimed at young Japanese people	www.mbga.jp

content and sets the rules. But, it is the members' continuing levels of activity that determines the network's continuing success.

"Fogeys Flock to Facebook" was the title of an article in the August edition of Business Week [9]. This is an amusing way of describing the evolution of social networking Web sites to become age-neutral. The media portrays Facebook and MySpace as the playground of teenagers and young adults. Contrary to this popular belief, the largest age group for both sites is 35–54 year olds. The number of Facebook users age 55+ is the same as those aged 12–17 year old.

Only those who believe the 50-plus to be a homogeneous and technophobic group would be surprised by these numbers. The relationship between a person's age and their use of the Internet is complicated. For instance, as a group the 50-plus has the lowest level of Internet use. This is true in Europe, Japan and the USA.

But, if Internet uptake is analysed by socio-economic class, a more complicated and less age-related picture emerges [13]. In the UK, the average 55–64 year old, in the AB class group, uses the Internet more than all ages in groups C2DE. There are only a few percentage points different between all ages of C1s and the older group. Only 16% of the over-65 year olds are connected to the Internet, but those who are spend more time online than any other age group.

Entrepreneurs in the USA have realized the business potential of social networking sites aimed at an older market. Jeff Taylor, the founder of Monster.com, has launched eons.com, a Facebook equivalent for the 50-plus. This site has stimulated a torrent of new Baby Boomer social networking sites, all trying to capture the spending power of the 76 million Boomers in the USA. In the last year, over 20 new Boomer sites have been launched.

The limitation of these "generic" sites is that the user's age is the only thing that connects them to the other members. A more interesting and sustainable business model is where social networking is used as an enabler, not as the site's primary purpose. Grandparents.com is an example of this new breed of site that contains social networking functionality that makes life easier for the grandparent. Another example is Care.com that uses social networking to improve the process of locating care support resources.

The UK has a few examples of sites using forums and networking designed for the 50-plus market. Saga and 50connect.com have the highest number of visitors, followed by a raft of much smaller companies like Funkeyfogey, Gonetoosoon and Laterlife. More interesting than these age-specific sites is the way that major online brands, with significant numbers of older customers, are starting to use networking functionality. Waitrose, one of the UK's largest supermarkets, recently re-launched its Web site containing forums, scrapbooks and profiles, all the functionality found on a social networking Web site.

In Japan, Mixi is the leading personal portal and social-networking destination. The company was started in 1999 as an employment job site targeted at the young. In 2006 the company was floated and in July 2007 was valued at $2 billion. In the last fiscal year the company had revenues of $46 million and a profit of $10 million. Mixi's 12 million subscribers generate 15% of Japan's ad impressions, second only to Yahoo! (NetRatings).

The company's other revenue streams include job listings, with over 200,000 registered jobseekers and the premium membership services with features like additional photo storage, blog-design tools and permanent message archiving.

According to an interview between Mixi's founder and president, Kenji Kasahara, and the Financial Times [5] his social networking site is preparing for a surge in older users as the Japan's baby boomers move from work into retirement. Mixi's membership policy of "invitation only" is believed to make it particularly attractive to the older generation. The site's array of social networking functionality includes personal profiles, media sharing, blogging and online communities. This last application is expected to be popular with retirees who are expected to network with former classmates and company colleagues.

There are two opposing pressures that will change the age profile of Mixi's user base. Currently, almost 80% of users are aged between 20 and 34. The effect of more Baby Boomers members will be to increase the average age, but this will be countered by swelling numbers of mobile users, who are predominantly young. Over 58% of Mixi's mobile users are under 25, compared with 43% of PC users.

"If you want to engage with young people in Japan, you've got to have a mobile presence", says Forrester Research senior analyst Jonathan Browne [13]. For this reason, the new social networking competitors entering the Japanese market are mobile rather than PC-centric. Web sites like "Mobage-town" (mobile gaming town) rely totally on mobile access.

This doesn't mean that older people will only use PCs to access the site. The use of mobiles by older people is very high and will be further stimulated by the launch of new phone handsets, designed for older people (i.e. NTT DoCoMo new handset with a large, high-definition screen and large buttons).

How is Social Networking Likely to Develop?

The following are some of the other ways that social networking is likely to develop in Japan and other countries:

- *It will become a commodity application.* The great majority of the 50-plus will use social networking functionality and be oblivious to the fact. Unlike the current crop of age-centric sites, the real volume adoption will result from the network being part of an interest/industry/company/activity Web site. It is likely that most large, Web literate companies in retail, travel, healthcare, and consumer electronics are already considering how to use social networking to increase eye-fall and the networking effect of their Web presence.
- *There will be pressure to make the networks "open".* Facebook, MySpace and Mixi are "walled gardens". This means that communications between users and access to information is restricted to members. This is very different to the "open" nature of e-mail and the Web. Companies are starting to create more open and accessible platforms, allowing personal data to be shared with other networks and making it easier to interface with other Web service providers. For example,

Facebook is making its member profiles available to search engines so that non-members can find out who has a profile on the site.

- *It will be easier and cheaper to acquire social networking functionality.* The first generation of social networking sites were bespoke and expensive to create. This is changing. New generations of Web software companies are providing inexpensive tools that enable new sites to be created and companies to embed social networking into their existing Web platforms. The main companies providing these tools are Affinity Circles, Social Platform, Joomla and Ning.
- *Social networking is limited by the finite time users can "socialize.* It is a statement of the obvious, but there is a limit to the number of social networks a person, of any age, can join and the time they can spend online. There has undoubtedly been a "fashion" element to explain the success of MySpace, Facebook and Mixi. The demand created by the trendiness of online socializing is transient and will transfer to the next "cool" technology innovation.

Whatever way that social networking develops, its lasting success depends on delivering real benefits to customers, irrespective of their age.

Web Video

The head of creative at Avenue A | Razorfish, the largest interactive agency in the USA, believes Web video is the most exciting of the new digital technologies. Why is this?

In the same way that GIF and JPG images added richness to plain text, so video provides a new dimension to the Web's ability to communicate and entertain. Even though we have just begun the Web video revolution, the magnitude of its impact on the Internet is already staggering. Approximately half of all Internet traffic currently consists of TV shows, YouTube clips and Web animations. Within the next 24 months, video could account for 90% of all Internet traffic.

Why the Rules of Web Video Have Changed

A combination of technology developments have made the creation and viewing of Web video a mass market experience.

Firstly, the costs of video cameras and software to create and edit video have plummeted. Al Gore's Oscar winning global warming crisis documentary, *An Inconvenient Truth*, was created using standard Apple Keynote and editing software and with a video camera costing less than $4000. The production team needed to produce most Web videos has shrunk to just two people – one person to act as the journalist/interviewer and the other as the cameraman/editor.

The second development is the widespread availability of broadband. There is now a worldwide audience of 300 million subscribers who can access the Internet at broadband speeds. This number is expected to double by 2011.

According to the OECD [4], Japan has the second highest number of broadband subscribers (27 million) behind the USA. The demand for Web video and broadband access are now in a virtuous circle whereby broadband take-up is driven by the desire to view video, which in turns increases the audiences and supply of video material.

Finally, the costs and simplicity of the key determinants of Web video's success have radically improved:

- *Hosting*. There are over a 100 Web sites providing free video hosting services, double the number at the beginning of 2007. YouTube, by far the largest, contains over 60 million video clips. Aside from the USA, Japan represents YouTube's largest user base. During 2007 Sony launched a video sharing service in Japan called eyeVio, enabling users to upload and distribute their own videos. Although Sony is considering launching eyeVio outside Japan, for now it is focusing on the Japanese market. Whilst YouTube has the worldwide coverage, the Sony service has some unique features. The most important is the high quality of the video that is "near DVD quality" and far superior to that of YouTube.
- *Searching*. Google is evolving its video search capability with the development of "universal search". This will process all content; including video, images, news, and websites and then present a single, integrated set of search results.
- *Viewing*. Adobe's Flash player has become the default software used by the main Web hosting companies, including YouTube and MySpace. Adobe estimate that 99% of world's developed markets can view Flash Player content. This means that the vast majority of PCs are have the software to play video.

Web Video is Age-Neutral

Organizations must avoid pigeon-holing Web video as being a niche activity that is only used by the young and is nothing to do with older people. The fact that the average YouTube user in the USA is not a teenager but a 39 year old proves this point.

Table 20.5 shows the US breakdown of Web video users by age. The largest group of users of online video is 18–24 year olds (75%). In the oldest age group (55+) 44% of people streamed video. If the over-65s were removed from this sample it is likely that the usage level, between the ages 12 and 65, would vary by less than 20%. There will be country differences in this age profile but there are no reasons why Web video consumption will not become age-neutral in all geographies.

Table 20.5 Demographic profile of US Internet users who used Web video

Age range	Percentage of age group who have streamed video
12–17	73
18–24	75
25–34	61
35–54	56
55+	44

Source: Ipsos Insight research, December 2006

The Challenges of Web Video for Organizations

Arguably, Web video is causing the most significant changes to the way Web sites are designed and used than any other development since the Web's creation. The following guidelines are intended to assist organizations adapt to this revolution:

- Web video is a reality, it is not going away! Organizations need to plan for its use in to ensure consumers' time is spent watching video associated with their brands and marketing campaigns – not those of their competitors.
- Web video should only be used for applications where it adds significant value compared with other communications media. The temptation of treating video as "eye candy" and indiscriminately sprinkling it around the Web site must be resisted.
- The same quality standards must be applied to Web video as to any other communications technique. The novelty value of Web video will only last a short time and may already have passed. Poor quality video will then be ignored or will annoy Web users.
- Web video requires script-writing not copy-writing skills. In any 2-h feature film script there are normally only about 8000 words of dialogue. That means that in a 2 min video you would have less than 150 spoken words.
- Judging the effectiveness of Web video requires more than simple Web site analytics because the video will be viewed from multiple sources, other than the Web site. The video can be distributed as part of an e-mail campaign, pushed through RSS feeds and viewed via YouTube and Sony's eyeVio.
- The ownership of the Web video's intellectual property must be understood. As YouTube is discovering, it is very difficult to stop people loading and displaying video material they do not own. If a company's Web video uses music and actors then there might, almost certainly will, be copyright implications. The same applies if the video is sourced from a marketplace site like Mochila and Brightcove. Web video adds an extra burden on organizations to ensure their content is legal.

How is Web Video Likely to Develop?

Web video is undergoing a phase of rapid evolution that is creating new and exciting opportunities. Unfortunately, most organizations are finding it difficult to respond to these new possibilities. The following are the developments that can be expected during the coming year:

- Web video will become High Definition (HD) video. Adobe's latest version of Flash Player and Intel new chips are both optimized for HD viewing. Japanese users of Eyevio can already see the potential of high grade video.
- A new generation of Web sites are emerging that are primarily video-based, with text as a supporting medium. The limitation of only using video within the "video box" will disappear as it evolves to become the core of the Web site.
- The mobile will be equally, if not more important, as the device through which people consume video.
- 2008 could be the year when Web video reaches the tipping point and becomes a Web site necessity and not just an optional extra.

Summary and Conclusions

These conclusions are not specific to any country or region. The market leaders in social networking, Facebook and MySpace, both originated in the USA but have evolved to become global businesses with operations in Europe, Australasia and Japan.

Social networking sites, dedicated to the 50-plus, first started in the USA but all major countries now have their indigenous versions. Web video has followed the same evolution path with the US-originated YouTube remaining the largest company but with look-alikes across the globe.

The power of Web 2.0 to expand the range of applications and functionality of Web sites is as important to older audiences as any other age group. Web 2.0 enables users to experience a richness of the content and sophistication of Web applications far beyond the scope of those delivered by Web 1.0 technologies. Unfortunately, there is a negative side that we are only just beginning to understand. The same tools that enable these new applications can also create Web sites that are harder and more complicated for older people to use.

Web video and social networking are currently perceived as separate applications but will evolve to become an integral part of the fabric of Web sites. Both applications are intrinsically age-neutral. Web video will have the greatest impact on the way Web sites are designed, because of its power to explain complex, visual and emotive issues. The balance of content that is displayed in video format, compared to text and imagery, will continually increase.

The people responsible for the construction and operations of these new Web 2.0 sites, in particular Web designers, need to understand the way that physiological ageing changes the way older people interact with these applications. Unless this occurs, the ability of Web 2.0 to enrich and simplify the older person's Web experience will have the opposite outcome.

References

1. D. Boyd, N. Ellison, *J Comp-Mediated Commun* **13**(1), 11 (2007), http://jcmc.indiana.edu/vol13/issue1/boyd.ellison.html. Accessed 10 Jan 2008
2. A. Chadwick-Dias, M. Bergel, T. Tullis, Senior surfers 2.0: a re-examination of the older web user and the dynamic web, in *Universal access in human computer interaction. Coping with diversity* (Springer, Berlin, 2007), p. 868, doi 10.1007/978-3-540-73279-2_97
3. Comscore, *Social networking goes global* (Comscore, 2007), http://www.comscore.com/press/release.asp?press=1555. Accessed 2 Jan 2008
4. Directorate for Science, Technology and Industry, *OECD broadband statistics: total broadband subscribers by country* (Organisation for Economic Co-operation and Development, Paris, 2007) http://www.oecd.org/sti/ict/broadband. Accessed 2 Jan 2008
5. L. Lewis, *Financial Times*, 6 Dec 2006
6. J. Nielsen, *Web usability for senior citizens* (Nielsen Norman Group, Fremont, 2002) http://www.nngroup.com/reports/seniors/ Accessed 13 Jun 2008
7. J. Nielsen, *Web 2.0 can be dangerous...* (2007), http://www.useit.com/alertbox/web-2.html. Accessed 2 Jan 2008
8. T. O'Reilly, *Web 2.0 compact definition: trying again* (2006), http://radar.oreilly.com/archives/2000/12/web_20_compact.html. Accessed 2 Jan 2008
9. A. Ricadela, *BusinessWeek*, 6 Aug 2007, http://www.businessweek.com/technology/content/aug2007/tc2007085_051788.htm. Accessed 2 Jan 2008
10. C. Schoenberger, *How to make friends, Japanese-style* (Forbes.com, 2007), http://www.forbes.com/technology/2007/12/18/mixi-japan-mobile-tech-cz_cs_1218mixi.html. Accessed 2 Jan 2008
11. D. Stroud, *The 50-plus market: why the future is age-neutral when it comes to marketing and branding strategies* (Kogan Page, London, 2006), ISBN-10: 074944939X
12. T. Tullis, Older adults and the web: lessons learned from eye-tracking, in *Universal access in human computer interaction. Coping with diversity* (Springer, Berlin, 2007), p. 1030, doi 10.1007/978-3-540-73279-2_115 (2007)
13. R. Worcester, *Just who does the internet reach?* (Ipsos, London, 2007), http://www.ipsos-mori.com/content/just-who-does-the-internet-reach.ashx. Accessed 13 Jun 2008

Part IV
Industry Challenges and Solutions

Chapter 21
The Business of Aging: Ten Successful Strategies for a Diverse Market

H. Murata

Abstract In Japan, in the last few years, an increasing number of enterprises have been focusing on developing new products and services for older adults or for the Baby Boomer generation. In most cases, these efforts failed. One of the reasons for this is that their visions are too narrow. Many enterprises consider the older adult market or the Boomer market as a single homogeneous iceberg. However, in a modern economy, it is not sufficient to say that the Boomers represent a large part of the market just by sheer numbers. The reason is that the nature of today's market is different from that of the past. This chapter gives readers the essence to correctly view the Baby Boomer market or Senior Market and insights to success in serving such markets in other countries.

Introduction: There is No Single Baby Boomer Market or Senior Market

In Japan, in the last few years, an increasing number of enterprises have been focusing on developing new products and services for older adults or for the Baby Boomer generation. In most cases, these efforts failed. The reason why that is their visions are too narrow [2]. Many enterprises consider the older adult market or the Boomer generation as a single homogeneous iceberg. However, in a modern economy, it is not enough to say that the Boomers represent a large part of the market just by sheer numbers. The reason is that the nature of today's market is different from that of the past.

What are the key elements that affect the Boomers buying decisions today? The answer will be different for each Boomer, but the following five types of changes are the main influences on their decision making (Fig. 21.1):

1. Physical changes due to aging
2. Changes in each individual's life stage

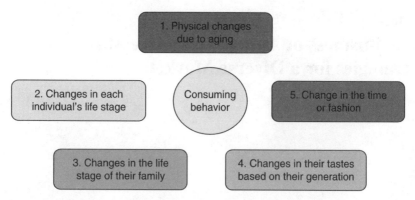

Fig. 21.1 Five key factors that influence the consuming behavior of the 50+

3. Changes in the life stage of their family
4. Changes in their tastes based on their generation
5. Changes in the time or fashion

There are, of course, other influential elements. Even so, it is easy to see how diversified the Boomers' decision making processes are just by focusing on these five elements. Their actions as consumers will be as diverse as their decision making processes. This is because those who are in their late 50s – the so-called "leading edge Boomers" – are more likely to be facing the five changes mentioned above than any other age group.

The impact of each influence is not the same for everyone. The importance of each factor will be different for each different product, service, or individual. The Boomers are so diversified as consumers that you can call the Boomers' market "an aggregate of diverse micromarkets." This is the most significant change in the nature of the Japanese Boomer's market since the time of high economic growth after WWII.

The behaviors of the Boomers as consumers are even more diverse in the modern day due to two additional factors (Fig. 21.2). The first factor is the maturity of the economy. As our standard of living increases, goods or products become superabundant. This superabundance gives us more choices and increases our expectations and demands. Then, product providers try to provide customers with more products and increase our expectations even more. This interactive relation makes consumer behavior more diversified.

The other factor that has changed the nature of the market today is the emergence of the "information society." In Japan, as of 2002, the broadband Internet costs just 18 cents per 100 Kbps, which is the least expensive in the world, while the USA with a cost of $2.86 per 100 Kbps is the most expensive among the developed countries (Fig. 21.3).

Due to this low cost, more than 50% of the people in their 50s in Japan today are users of the Internet. Also, more than 40% of the people in Japan in their 60s own a

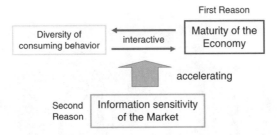

Fig. 21.2 Two reasons why the consuming behavior of the 50+ will be diverse in the modern age

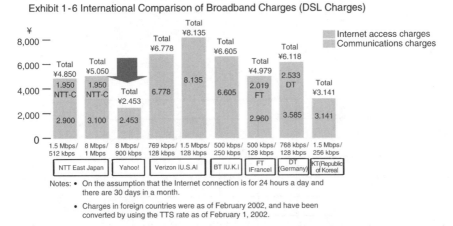

Fig. 21.3 Japan is the cheapest country in the world for Broadband access

cell phone (Fig. 21.4). As access to information increases, so does consumer choice and consumer expectations. Thus, we are living in a time of economic maturity and of the information age market. These two phenomena are still progressing and will continue to diversify the Boomers market even more.

Now what do you do to respond to these challenges? You need to widen your vision towards the world of your target customers. You must have enough adaptability for a diverse market. These are the keys to success.

To understand adaptability for a diverse market, it is useful for Japanese to look at what's going on in the US market. This is because the USA is more diverse country than Japan and is expected to have more adaptability to the diversity. Some advanced business examples in the USA may give us insights as well as inspiration since their market condition is very similar to ours. Although there are many differences between the two countries, we can see the following common characteristics in the modern economies of developed countries like the USA and Japan:

1. Demographic change due to aging of the population (Fig. 21.5)
2. Superabundance of goods
3. Shift from manufacturing industry to service industry

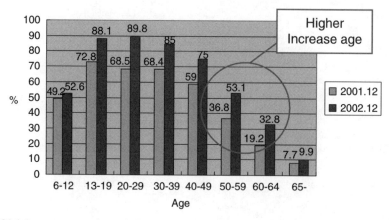

Fig. 21.4 Internet penetration ratio by age

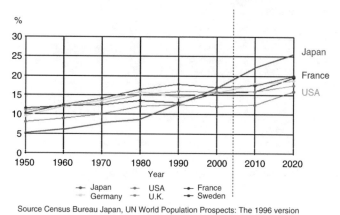

Source Census Bureau Japan, UN World Population Prospects: The 1996 version

Fig. 21.5 Aging ratio (people 65+ to total population)

4. Increase of lifestyle-related diseases such as diabetes and obesity
5. Information technology becoming an everyday affair
6. Increase in free agents and changes in working style

Based on the above, we can see many similarities between the two countries. On the other hand, there are many differences, of course. Although there are some differences, both countries are becoming similar in terms of socio-economic development. Therefore, if we have a wider vision and an open mind to other countries, we can learn mutually and inspire creative strategies for the future.

The purpose of this chapter is to give readers the essence of how to perceive the Baby Boomer market or Senior Market and insights into success in serving such markets in your country. This chapter will show you the following ten strategies [1]:

- *Strategy 1*: Become a "Finder of FUDI." New FUDI (feelings of uneasiness, dissatisfaction, inconvenience) can be found with saturated markets.

- *Strategy 2*: Become a "Need-Focused Merchandiser." The ways of service will shift from selling products to solving problems.
- *Strategy 3*: Become a "Aging-Friendly Stylist." The priority of the product will shift from function-oriented to style-oriented.
- *Strategy 4*: Become a "Refuge Temple" at the customer's home. The place for providing services will shift from the shop to the customers' home.
- *Strategy 5*: Become a "Private Concierge." Use high-tech to enable mass customization and maintain high quality.
- *Strategy 6*: Create a "Third Place" for retirees, a replacement for the workplace. The number of retirees who have no places to go everyday will increase.
- *Strategy 7*: Arrange "Intellectual Camp Experiences" in your services. Experience-learning will be more appealing for lifelong learning.
- *Strategy 8*: Become a "Knowledge Net Worker." "Nanocorps," own-sized mini-companies will increase and need sales support.
- *Strategy 9*: Use "Intellectual Tie" as the appeal of the service. Intellectual stimulation creates the chemical reaction and the attractiveness of a residential community.
- *Strategy 10*: Focus on "Loose-Tie-Big-Family." The border between individuals and groups will become blurred.

The goal of this chapter is to provide information on how to start a new business or improve existing business models. This chapter contains summaries of the ten strategies for success in serving older adults in a diverse market.

The primary focus of this chapter is the Japanese market. However, I believe it is useful for all readers in developed countries even though it includes examples of companies only in the USA and Japan. This is because those have achieved success by implementing these strategies and can be transformed among the developed countries.

Strategy 1: Become a "Finder of FUDI" (Feelings of Uneasiness, Dissatisfaction, Inconvenience): New FUDI can be Found With Saturated Markets

You may think that most markets today are saturated. Are you sure that it is true? It is not, as a matter of fact. The fitness club market is a good example. In the 1990s, the growth of fitness clubs in the USA and Japan reached a plateau. Particularly in Japan, the aging of the population and the decline in the birthrate made it necessary for the fitness club industry to find a new market among older adults and/or the Boomer generation. This effort brought a certain amount of success, but the overall growth of new members seems to have reached a peak. Still, many traditional fitness clubs missed out on countless potential customers among these target generations.

The women-only fitness company called "Curves" proved this fact. Since its founding in Waco, Texas, in 1992, Curves has spread its franchises dramatically.

Curves now have more than 10,000 franchises all over the world and represents nearly one-third of all fitness clubs. The average age of their members is 50, and most of them had never joined a fitness club before. Not surprisingly, there were millions of American women, particularly middle age or older women, who were not at all attracted to the conventional fitness clubs. They did not want to be exposed to men when they were exercising to lose weight. They also did not like the impersonal atmosphere of traditional fitness clubs that were filled with machines. And they did not want to spend long periods of time "working out."

Curves has been successful because they resolved all these concerns by offering a new service that is totally different from the conventional fitness clubs. At Curves, women do not have to worry about men. The clubs are only for women. Curves developed their original training machines, which are easy to use for older women. And, they offer an exercise program that requires no more than 30 min to complete.

One other innovation introduced by Curves is to allow its customers to workout in a small group instead of exercising by themselves. Instead of having the exercise machines facing the wall, as in a traditional fitness club, the machines at Curves are arranged in a circle facing inwards, so the customers can see and interact with each other as they workout. These innovative ideas have made Curves enormously popular among women of many different ages.

This example shows that within any apparently saturated market, you can always find countless customers who are dissatisfied with existing goods and services. To identify their negative reactions (feelings of uneasiness, dissatisfaction, or inconvenience) is the first step. If you have ideas about how to satisfy these feelings, those ideas might turn into a new successful business.

If you examine the products and services that have sold well to the older adult market, you will find that many of them offer relief from some negative element in the existing market. In Japan, a medical insurance product called "Hairemasu (You Can Apply)" by Alico has been a big hit because it was the first life insurance that anyone who is 50 or older can buy. It gives older adults relief from their feelings of uneasiness about their financial security in the future when they get sick. Kao's cooking oil, "Kenko (Healthy) Econa," is said to be good for your health because the fat will not be stored in your body as much as with other oils. This product became a big hit among those who feel uneasy about their health, especially those who are worried about diabetes or hypertension.

"Raku-Raku (easy-easy) Phone" by NTT DoCoMo, the biggest cell phone carrier in Japan, is a hidden best-selling products for older adults who did not like to use cell phones due to their small buttons and narrow displays. Raku-Raku Phone solved the inconvenience of cell phones for the older generation by redesigning their phones to be "aging-friendly."

In addition, Curves Japan was established in 2005 due to advocacy by the author. Curves Japan has opened over 640 stores nationwide in Japan during only the past two and half years. This means unbelievable success and is clear evidence that my strategy is proven.

Strategy 2: Become a "Need-Focused Merchandiser": The Ways of Service will Shift from Selling Products to Solving Problems

Consumers today have too many choices. Many older adults don't know how to make the best choices when they want to resolve their dissatisfaction. For example, where do you go when you have back pain problems?

"Relax the Back" is a US specialty store that is a one-stop solution for such people. Here is their core concept: provide customers with the means to avoid back and neck pain. If you walk into one of their stores, you will find beds, pillows, office chairs, and other products that are all designed to support or comfort your back. Their selection of products is based on the customers' needs and not on conventional product lines. This is the most remarkable characteristic of this store. You can call it a "theme store" designed for people with back problems. A back pain counselor is always available for consultation in their stores. You can also try their chairs or beds to see how they feel.

The stores are not trying to sell products. They are selling "the real experience of back pain relief" through using their products. And yet, they offer even more. They give out information on clinics or massage therapists with good reputations. If necessary, they will even give you information on products that they are not selling in their store. With their knowledge and advice, they have established their position as the back pain experts for their customers.

In Japan, The Hankyu Department Store in Umeda, Osaka opened a new relaxation and beauty zone for women called "Refre-Pit Ainee" in July, 2002. This is an area where you can find five different beauty treatments (massage, foot care etc), beauty salons, a make-up studio, a café, etc., which are all the name brands in each field. This place is extremely popular with women as a "one-stop-shop" for those who want to be pretty. All of the shops here provide services, not products.

One more characteristic is that their services are not selected by the "product-focus" (like women's clothing or men's clothing), but by the customer's "need-focus" (like wanting to be pretty or ecology-conscious) These examples show the increasing value of providing services based on the customers' needs around a single theme. The customers' needs are the basic focus, not the products.

Strategy 3: Become a "Aging-Friendly Stylist": The Priority of the Product will Shift from Function-Oriented to Style-Oriented

As we get older, we may gradually lose our physical abilities, but we never lose our fashion sense. However, most clothing and other products designed for older adults is usually unfashionable and offers only a narrow selection. From now on, products for older consumers must have an elegant style to compensate for the inconvenience that is caused by the decline of physical abilities due to age. Products must evolve from the function-oriented to the style-oriented. However, when we talk about "a real style," we are not just talking about the superficial style such as the quality of materials or design. A product with a real style must have taken the users, older adults in this case, into consideration.

A good example of this strategy is an online store called "Gold Violin." Their walking stick does not look like something that people with a walking problem hold on to. It is designed as if it were a part of a woman's fashionable accessories, just like her shoes or her handbag. Another example of a product with a strong positive appeal is "Elderhostel," which provides learning adventures for people who are 55 and over. This age limit is not discrimination. It is a positive message that older people still have lots to learn through traveling filled with outdoor adventures.

In Japan, Wacoal, a women's underwear manufacturer, created two new brands, "La Vie Aisee" for women in their 40s or older and "Gra-P" for women in their 60s or older. "La Vie Aisee," is a line of fashionable underwear that is intended to be comfortable for women whose skin gets sensitive because of menopause. "Gra-P" offers a line of nicely designed underwear, with beautiful lace and other trimmings, where the material is carefully chosen so that it is elastic and comfortable for older women's shoulders and other parts of their bodies.

The product/service provider for older generations should be a smart "aging stylist" who can provide an elegant way to overcome the inconveniences of aging. Professional skill in merchandising is required so that older adults can feel respect and consideration for their needs. If you study the products and services for older adults that have been successful in responding to their physical or psychological needs, you will feel the affection that merchandising people have for older adults. In other words, those who just try to sell products to older adults without feeling affection for them will not be successful. Never treat older people merely as consumers with lots of time and money and ignore their particular needs and interests.

The real wisdom of selling to older adults comes from having feelings of true affection, respect, and gratitude toward them. You'd better not try to tamper or use a trick. You just have to select what's best for your own parents or grandparents. The key is to make them happy.

Strategy 4: Become a "Refuge Temple" at the Customer's Home: The Place for Providing Services will Shift from the Shop to the Customers' Home

"Husband for rent" is a new business that is popular in Moscow now. In a city with a high divorce rate, many women are living by themselves. The rented husbands do all kinds of manual labor such as furniture repair and so on for these single women.

In the USA, a similar service is offered by "Mr. Handyman." They do all kinds of odd jobs, mostly for older adults who are living by themselves. Their services include anything from carpentry to the cleaning of gutters. Other enterprises offered similar services before Mr. Handyman. But, most of them were small and fragmented businesses, and the quality of their services was often unreliable.

Mr. Handyman attempts to provide reliable, high quality services as professionals. Specifically, they standardized their service menu, defining the content and the quality of each type of job with a clear price. They also equip their vans with the necessary tools and materials. Their staff visits their customers one by one, gaining their customers' trust through communication. With these efforts, they transformed this highly fragmented labor-intensive business into a new systematic service product that offers specific professional skills.

Although "Do It Yourself" is rooted in the American culture, many people give up such work as they get older. What they need then is not the "DIY shop" but the "DIY procurator service." In Japan, a new personal computer trouble-shooting service (Yokogawa Q&A) is becoming popular among older adults.

Now that broadband Internet service is available at low cost, an increasing number of older adults are using computers. However, they are not well-trained and have little understanding of the technologies, while new computer viruses and other problems keep appearing. As a result, the demand for the face-to-face computer support service is increasing.

Once you have gained the trust of your customers in this kind of business, you can get the advantage of calling on them frequently. It would be ideal to establish a stable relationship with the customers. Whenever they have a problem, you should be the "first person" that they wish to consult. In Japan, we call the function of this first person "Refuge Temple." The original meaning of the word is that the temple was the place that accepted refugees in olden days.

You should be the first "Refuge Temple" to be at their service. Since the older adults with physical declines tend to stay at home, "Refuge Temple" must visit a customer's home. It is a good sign when the customers start to tell you about other problems, including problems that are not directly related to your business. This can increase your business opportunity.

Strategy 5: Become a "Private Concierge": Use High-Tech to Enable "Mass Customization" and Maintain High Quality

Many older adults wish to live independently in their own homes as long as possible. Even so, they often feel uneasy in their everyday life. Beacon Hill Village is a membership organization that offers essential services for older people living in this historic area of Boston, Massachusetts. They have been successful in understanding and meeting their customers' needs.

Beacon Hill is an eighteenth century upscale residential neighborhood near downtown Boston. About 14% of the area's 9000 residents are 60 years old or older. Most of them do not wish to move out of this area even when they get quite old. "Village Concierge" is a popular service provided by Beacon Hill Village. A member can just call in and request services such as grocery shopping, transportation, cleaning, and other daily in-home services.

As the society is aging, the demand for concierge services will increase. Many older adults need services exclusively for them. However, it generally costs a lot to provide such time- and labor-intensive services. "Les Concierges" is a good example of how a business solves this cost problem. This San Francisco-based company provides individuals with the same kind of "concierge services" that high-class hotels offer their guests, such as access to hard-to-get tickets, restaurant reservations, etc. Their customers were initially limited to wealthy people since the membership fee for these services cost a minimum of $3540. In 1990, Les Concierges introduced a new business model. The company contracts with an employer and serves as a "private concierge" for its employees. The employer pays for the services that their employees receive. The services they provide vary from supporting an employee when a parent gets sick suddenly to arranging a family trip.

The structure of this business is similar to what we have in Japan, where an agent arranges reservations and other things for a company's employees to use the facilities and services that their company offers. The biggest difference, however, is that the "private concierge" offers truly customized services for each employee.

How can they do this? The combination of their highly trained professional staff and their own IT system makes it possible. They have built an IT system that can identify the possible needs of each customer based on all of their past service records. Thanks to this database of personal information, the staff of Les Concierges can communicate efficiently with each of the 5 million customers registered with them today.

In Japan, Suruga Bank claimed to be a "concierge bank," meaning that they will be the concierge for their customers by providing all kinds of financial services as well as support for their customers' everyday life. Specifically, they provide a service called "web concierge." Customers who have an account with them can see their account balance, the sum of their credit card payments, the balance of their loan, the sum of direct debits—all in one screen. And, you can make an inquiry by e-mail if necessary. While services such as this do offer convince to the bank's customers, the bank will have to do more if it is to fully deliver its promise to provide true concierge-type services.

The combination of quality staff and the IT system made it possible for service providers to turn a small-scale human-oriented "private concierge" business into a large-scale highly profitable high tech business. They also succeeded in enlarging their market by popularizing the services that used to be limited to wealthy people.

Strategy 6: Create a "Third Place" for Retirees, a Replacement for the Workplace: The Number of Retirees Who Have No Places to Go Everyday will Increase

Many older adults today do not consider themselves as "elderly people." As a result there are fewer people going to the so-called "elderly clubs" or "senior centers" both in Japan and the USA. Older adults do not like the elderly image of these places. On the other hand, many older adults who are retired do want to remain connected to society and are looking for a replacement for their workplace.

"Starbucks Coffee" became a big success with concept of a "third place," which means neither home (the first place) nor workplace (the second place). "Mather Café Plus" in Chicago is a new type of café that is popular among this new type of older adults. "Mather Café Plus" is called the Starbucks for seniors.

What are the reasons for their success? They don't give you the impression that it is a place for "elderly people." At the same time, they offer many different programs and ideas to respond to the varied needs of older adults.

If you go in to a Mather Café Plus, you will find that they serve good quality drinks/foods at such reasonable prices that you can drop by regularly. The atmosphere of the café is rather stylish, not like a tacky elderly club at all. In a room next to the restaurant, they offer more than 40 different programs such as computer lessons and exercise classes where you can make new friends. Their staff looks after you with great hospitality, too. Even if you go there by yourself, they will talk with you or introduce you to other guests.

The remarkable point here is that they are not making money merely as a café for older adults. Their success comes from the structure that they have built. They offer a place for older adults to get together and meet other people. And then, their customers use many of the different activities that the cafe offers. Mather Café Plus offers other services as well. For example, they take suggestions from their guests for their menu. They also offer a free telephone counseling service that provides information of all sorts; they can recommend a handyman service or provide information about the cost of an in-house caregiver. This telephone service plays an important role in their business because the information from their customers helps them to understand the potential needs of older adults. And, this helps them improve the quality of their services for their customers.

In Japan, a Japanese-style public spa called "Super Sento (public bath)" is now a popular leisure spot in many cities in Japan. It is especially popular among older adults. For a fee of around 600 yen (US$5.75), you can enjoy about ten different types of baths (jet bath, herb bath, hot spring, outdoor stone bath, sauna, etc.). Outside the baths, there are other spaces such as a restaurant, a massage center, a barbershop, a Korean body scrubbing place etc. Super Sento has established a good business model of making profits from services other than the baths. Many older adults spend their time during the weekdays in this kind of spa, helping to increase the utilization rate of these places.

Strategy 7: Arrange "Intellectual Camp Experiences" in Your Services: "Experience-Learning" will be More Appealing for Lifelong Learning

Many older adults today are looking for an opportunity to enjoy learning something. Simple recreation is not enough. In today's service industry society, people seem to have more desk work than ever before. We have fewer and fewer opportunities to learn something interactively or experientially. As a result, education today is largely passive and learning tends to be a one-way process. If you can combine intellectual experiences with leisure services like traveling, you can offer exciting learning experiences that are differentiated from the usual leisure service providers.

For example, "Elderhostel" provides learning adventures to older Americans. Their program consists of not only the lectures in the classrooms, but also real experiences outside. Their programs are based on themes that stimulate the intellectual interests of older adults. For each group, Elderhostel provides a leader who will contribute in creating a friendly atmosphere, along with an opportunity to meet with people of similar interests. This is how they maintain the high rate of repeaters.

Another good example is "Senior Summer School." Those who would like to experience today's campus life can stay on a college or university campus for a couple of weeks. They can enjoy not only attending lectures but also exploring the area and making friends with other participants with similar interests. This program attracts many older adults who are tired of the typical sightseeing tours.

In Japan, there are now travel services like "Club Tourism" by Club Tourism Company or "Otona-no-Kyujitsu (Holidays for Adults)" by East Japan Railway Company that include opportunities for the participants to learn something through real outdoor experiences during their trips.

The participants are usually involved with the planning of the trip. The travel agency arranges their plan and sells the trips. The customers can experience what they wanted. This system works well for both parties. Any type of "intellectual camp experience" for older adults must have the following elements:

1. An opportunity to meet other people with similar interests
2. An opportunity to learn through real experiences along with lectures
3. A specialized topic with professional or academic content
4. A leader who is an expert on the topic and who will create a friendly atmosphere
5. A system that allows customers to plan their own programs
6. Activities that are not a physical burden for older adults
7. A reasonable price so that older adults can participate repeatedly

Another key to the success of this kind of program is that all the participants have similar levels of interests in the topic. It is important to give detailed information beforehand and explain about the program as much as possible to enable the participants to choose the right program for themselves.

Strategy 8: Become a "Knowledge Net Worker": "Nanocorps," Own-Sized Mini-Companies will Increase and Need Sales Support

"Happy Retirement" used to be an ideal course of life, living the last stage of your life enjoying leisure on your savings. But times have changed. There are more people who wish to work even after their retirement [3]. In reality, it is often hard for a retired person to find a job. Instead, an increasing number of older adults/the Boomer generation are starting a "nanocorp" to earn an income by doing what they really want to do. A nanocorp is a small corporation usually with only one or two persons who are owners. In most cases they don't have sales people like more traditional corporations. So a new type of service has emerged to support the sales activities of nanocorps.

"Le Tip" is a membership business club where the members act as sales persons for one another. Almost all of the members are either individual "free agents" or owners of small businesses. In a weekly meeting, the members report their recent news, ask questions, exchange information, and make commitments to provide other members with access to clients. The club has strict rules to ensure that their activities are working effectively for their members' businesses. A strong spirit of mutual aid is consistently cultivated among the members.

Another outstanding example of a valuable support service for nanocorps is "High Tech Connect," a human resource agent that provides businesses that need outside help with access to a network of more than 1500 independent consultants or nanocorps to meet their specific needs.

The trend of utilizing the manpower of the retired is getting bigger in Japan. There must be many people in Japan who wish to start a nanocorp. But, they are usually lack the ability to sell their services and need help to do this. The key to successfully supporting their sales activities is to have extensive knowledge about the background of the nanocorp owners so that agents can connect the people who need sales support with the people who look for solutions. I call this new type of function "Knowledge Net Worker." A Knowledge Net Worker must have the following conditions:

1. Deep background knowledge about the "people" who use the services
2. Extensive ability to identify qualities, trust, and coordination
3. Well-structured operation rules and clear benefits to users
4. A system in which each user can use each sales network mutually

One possible source for Knowledge Net Workers will be retired business executives. In Japan, a Japanese company called "Direct Force" helps nanocorps as an agent. Direct Force consists of retired executives from large corporations. Members of Direct Force work as consultants for a small business or as instructors at a university, etc. These retired people do not have to work to make a living, but they enjoy working in society, utilizing their ability and experiences.

Strategy 9: Use "Intellectual Tie" as the Appeal of the Service: Intellectual Stimulation Creates the Chemical Reaction and the Attractiveness of a Residential Community

Life expectancy is getting longer and our standard of living is getting higher. There are also much older adults than before who want to have intellectual stimulation after retirement. On the other hand, competition is getting more intense these days both in the senior housing market and in colleges/universities. If a college/university and a residential community for older adults can cooperate, they could provide a new type of experience that will appeal to older adults. We can expect to see an increase in intellectually connected retirement communities in the near future. Intellectual ties will play a more important role than family, geographical, or career connections.

Lasell Village is a college-linked residential community for older adults in Newton, Massachusetts. The Village, which is located on the campus of Lasell College, has a built-in educational component. Cooperation between the college and the community make it possible for the residents to study at the college. The older residents are allowed to use all the facilities of the college like the regular students and the faculty. The community also offers many chances for the older adults to study with young students of the college.

Learning is the best intellectual recreation. If you place it in the center of your living environment, you will have a number of advantages. As soon as Lasell Village opened, all 210 rooms were filled, with more than 110 people on the waiting list. The residents of Lasell Village are 83 years old on average. Very few of them are bedridden. Everyone is enjoying the life there, while the young students of the college appreciate having access to their advice and experience. There are still more people who would like to live in the village based on its reputation.

In Japan, the first implementation of the college-linked community will be conducted in July, 2008 by author's initiative. "Club Encourage Mikage," located in Mikage, an upscale residential area in Kobe, will be operated through the partnership with Kansai University, one of the major private universities in Japan. It is 30 min away from the university campus. The facility provides 218 independent living units as well as 60 nursing care rooms. Every day the independent seniors will be ferried by shuttle bus to school where they will attend lessons on history, philosophy, and music alongside younger university students. By interacting with the students,the elderly are exposed to stimuli that will keep their minds active. I believe this project is one of the many creative solutions being designed in Japan to cope with its rapidly graying population.

As Confucius said, to learn and to practice is a joy of life. Using an intellectual tie is a key to differentiate a residential community for older adults. The following are the vital factors for this kind of housing product:

1. Allow residents to attend classes in cooperation with a college
2. Give residents the same access to college facilities as the students or the faculty
3. Offer as many opportunities as possible for the residents to meet with young students

Strategy 10: Focus on "Loose-Tie-Big-Family": The Border Between Individuals and Groups will Become Blurred

As you get older, your biggest worry is often the safety of living independently by yourself. Many of those without children choose to live in a full-service Continuing Care Retirement Community (CCRC). But, many of those who have children choose to move near to them. In large cities, these days we see more and more examples of a new model of "loose-tie-big-family," Older parents and their children's families live separately but in the same neighborhood. They get together often and go out as a big family of three generations.

Another type of "big family" is emerging as the population ages. In retirement communities, many older adults who are in similar situations live together, supporting each other like a loosely connected big family. For example, in a CCRC in New Hampshire called "Kendal at Hanover," the residents have set up a non-profit organization to participate in the planning and operation of the CCRC. They shape the structure of the community and the social, cultural, and intellectual life there. They determine all the management rules, how the residents get involved, how to cooperate with the local town, and all the other policies of management that are written down in a document.

One of the Japanese examples of a "loose-tie-big-family" is "Life House Tomodachi-Mura (Life House Friends Village)" in Nakaizu-cho, Shizuoka prefecture. Almost all the residents there are women who had been living by themselves. Most of them are in their 60s, all capable of living independently. The difference between this house and the usual apartment is that there are many spaces and facilities for common use. Here, you can live independently, respecting one another's privacy, while also enjoying other people's company through different activities. You will not feel the solitude or uneasiness of living by yourself, even when you get really old.

A similar example can be found in several other cities, such as "Denen Seikatsu-kan (Country Life Residence)" in Katsuura-cho, Chiba prefecture, "Co-operative House Shalom Tsukimino" in Yamato city, Kanagawa prefecture and a collective house for multi-generations called "Ashiya 17°C" in Ashiya city, Hyogo prefecture.

How can we maintain stable and friendly relationships in this new type of loose-tie big family? The key factor is whether the management can mix the individuals smoothly in a group. The management needs to do the following:

1. Establish rules to support a loosely connected big family
2. Build a system that enables each member to be involved in a loosely connected big family but also to have their privacy preserved
3. Coordinate the relationship between the local town and the loosely connected big family

Many people choose to live in a group to avoid the solitude of living by themselves. However, living with other people will bring its own problems and annoyances that you don't have when living by yourself. The ideal is to live with other people, respecting one another, being independent as an individual, and supporting one another whenever it's necessary. The mixing function of the individuals in a group will make it possible. In a loosely connected big family, each member will have an opportunity to learn from one another.

Summary and Conclusion

Many enterprises tend to look the older adult market or the Boomer market as a single homogeneous iceberg due to the large numbers of population compared to other generations. In contrast, this chapter indicates that the nature of the Boomer or seniors market is "an aggregate of diverse micromarkets," which is different from those of the past. This chapter also describes what will form each diverse micro-market and what is necessary to adapt such diverse micromarkets by referencing advanced business examples in the USA and Japan.

Strategies 1–5 give you thoughts on adapting to the diverse consumer behaviors. Strategies 6–8 give you thoughts on adapting to the diverse ways of consuming time. Strategies 9 and 10 give you thoughts on adapting to the diverse ways of living.

Some readers may ask the following question: the ten strategies you offer are very interesting; however, sometimes we ask ourselves why should these be only specific to the elderly market? Wouldn't they work well with other age groups, too? Would it be possible to say that age-neutral or transgenerational approaches are best?

My answer to the question is "partly yes, partly no." If you say "age-neutral" or "ageless" market, it is too simplified. As I explained in the Introduction, our consuming behavior is very complicated. Age is one of the most important factors to consider; however, age does not always give us the whole information.

For example, in case of customers who joined Curves, the average age is around 50. But this does not mean women automatically come to Curves at age 50. Those who come to Curves are women who don't like traditional fitness clubs but want to reduce their weight, without men and saving time. What forms each diverse micro-market is "value," not age.

References

1. H. Murata, *The business of aging: ten successful strategies for a diverse market* (in Japanese) (Diamond Corporation, Tokyo, 2004)
2. H. Murata, *Seven paradigm shifts in thinking about the business of aging: breaking the barriers in a diverse market* (in Japanese) (Diamond Corporation, Tokyo, 2006)
3. H. Murata, *Retirement moratorium: what will the not-retired boomers change?* (in Japanese) (Nikkei, Tokyo, 2007)

Chapter 22
The Discovery and Development of the Silver Market in Germany

P. Enste, G. Naegele, and V. Leve

Abstract In Germany, a paradigm shift is emerging regarding the *silver economy* and is resulting in an increasing focus on the economic potential and the economic power of the elderly. Given the much increased buying power of the elderly, the increased heterogeneity of consumption wishes and needs corresponding to the differentiation of old age, as well as the empirical evidence for an age-specific change in consumption requirements, it stands to reason to look for inherent impulses for economic growth and employment by dint of new "age-sensitive" product ranges and services and to promote their development and expansion. Today, in fact, the silver economy comprises products and services in very diverse and by no means only "social" market segments. In addition to the health economy, the silver economy affects such diverse sectors as mobility and IT. The following contribution provides an insight into the development of the silver economy in Germany and its future prospects.

Introduction

The challenges to society that accompany the demographic transition are currently being actively discussed in Germany. In the course of the debate, a paradigm shift is emerging regarding the *silver economy* and, in particular, the development of products and services for ageing and old people, resulting in an increasing focus on the economic potential and the economic power of the elderly. While in the past, older people in the role of consumers were not regarded as a financially strong and free-spending target group by German providers of products and services, this perception has changed in the meantime. The days are long gone when the concept silver market was seen to pertain only to typical *seniors' products* or *seniors' services* such as geriatric agents, elderly care products or special recreational and touristic offers (for the elderly), which for the most part form part of the classic social services of public and independent non-profit organisations (i.e. especially of the local municipalities and of the charities). Today, in fact, the silver economy comprises products and services in very diverse and by no means only "social" market segments and, in addition to the health economy, affects such diverse sectors as mobility and IT.

This "new view" of older consumers is, in particular, related to manifold, empirically observable cohort effects or (behavioural) level increases, which can be perceived especially in the fields of income, educational background, vocational qualifications and social integration [16]. They simultaneously provide important links for the implementation of the likewise new ageing concept of *active ageing* [25], which is at present also experiencing a boom in Germany. The seniors of today have many potentials and resources, which could be utilised to greater social and personal advantage than to date, e.g. in the labour market, in education, in volunteer service, in social and political participation and precisely also in and by the economy. This is also one of the core messages of the "Fifth Report on the Elderly" by the German federal government [2].

This contribution provides an insight into the development of the silver economy in Germany, while taking into account the effects of the demographic ageing of the population. To this end, the income situation of seniors as well as their consumer needs and their consumer behaviour are discussed in addition to the expected population development. By means of selected market segments, we will then outline how the development of the silver economy in Germany has already contributed and can continue to contribute to the enhancement of the quality of life and to the stronger integration of older people into society. Finally, we will point out further necessary developments in research and in practice regarding the silver economy in Germany.

Demographic Change

The constant increase in the so-called further life expectancy, in conjunction with the simultaneous constantly low birth rate (i.e. about two-thirds below the rate needed for the natural reproduction of the native population) plays a fundamental role in the demographic ageing of the population. Consequently, the number of older people is growing while the number of children is diminishing. In 1871, for example, the life expectancy of a newborn was below 40 years, this figure has continually risen in the course of the years to its present level of 80 years for a newborn boy and 84.1 years for a newborn girl. According to the available population projections, the life expectancy will continue to rise and will reach 85 years for boys and almost 90 years for girls in 2050 [22].

In contrast, the birth rate is permanently low and will continue to be so. Thus, the number of births will decrease from its present level of approximately 685,000 to around 500,000 in the year 2050. This effect is merely slightly softened by migration effects. After 2010, however, a rapid decrease in the total population is expected [20]. At present, Germany has around 82 million inhabitants, this figure will in all likelihood drop to approximately 70 million in 2050 [22].

These developments lead to profound changes in the population structure. In this connection, the so-called *triple ageing* plays a fundamental role: (i) increase in the share of the elderly in the total population, (ii) increase in the absolute number of older people and (iii) increase in the share and number of very old people (80+) [1, 7]. While approximately every fifth inhabitant of Germany was older than 65 in 2005, it is expected that by 2050 this will apply to every third inhabitant. At the same time, following the projections, the share of younger inhabitants below the age of 20 will fall from 20% (2005) to 15% in 2050. According to the data, the number of seniors (65 years and older) will increase from around 16 million at present to approximately 23 million in 2050 [22].

In the economic debate in particular, this demographic ageing of the population has been (and is in part even today) portrayed as a horror scenario (a threat to society). Besides negative implications for the social security systems and for the labour market [1], negative effects have been and are being conjured up, especially for the private demand for consumer goods and thus for growth and employment, most notably due to the declining number of consumers of private goods and services. The implied directness of the relation – fewer consumers, less consumption, declining employment and sagging growth – must, however, be rejected insofar as the private demand for consumer goods is strongly affected by the number of households and by the household structure. In this connection, one has to point to the fact that the number of one-person households has been growing for a long time. Moreover, one has to bear in mind that a restructuring or even expansion of the respective quantity and quality effects can also arise from changes in the consumer needs of the elderly reflected in the level and structure of their consumer goods demand [5, 8].

Income and Consumption of Older People in Germany

Until well in the 1980s, older people were regarded as a relatively low-income consumer group, whose consumer habits were therefore not studied in detail. This perception has changed significantly in the meantime. Numerous current studies confirm the trend that the income situation of older people in Germany as a whole has considerably improved in the past few years [1, 2]. However, the group of older people is quite heterogeneous in this respect: Some seniors can still be economically active, while others have already retired. While the majority of the 50-to-59-year-olds probably still lives in family households, or at least still has children to tend to, with increasing age most older people live in two-person or single-person households [8]. On the one hand there are many long-term unemployed seniors with only small pension rights, while on the other hand there is growing wealth, up to affluence, in old age [1]. Nonetheless it holds true that the seniors of today are on average considerably better off than earlier cohorts [2].

Income Situation of Older People

The household income of older people in West Germany has risen markedly in the period between 1993 and 2003. If one compares the income situation of the 65+ age group with that of the under 50-year-olds, further trends become apparent. While the income of the elderly rose between 1993 and 2003, the younger generation had to suffer losses of income. All in all, one can even detect a concentration of incomes in the middle and higher age groups [6]. The group of very old persons, which was in the past affected above average by old age poverty, also experienced noticeable income increases. In East Germany, the percentage increase in old age incomes in the same period was even greater due to the comparatively high wage rises and pension adjustments. Nonetheless there is still a considerable gap between the available incomes in West and East Germany [6].

Consumer and Savings Behaviour of Older People

The expenditure on private consumption in Germany amounted to around €996 billion in 2003. Compared to the expenditure in 1993 (€876 billion) an increase of 14% can be ascertained for these 10 years. In the same period, the expenditure on private consumption in households with older people (from 65 onwards) rose far above average: from €167 billion (1993) to €228 billion (2003), i.e. by approximately 37%. In 2003, the 60–65 age group showed slightly above average on consumption with €2320 per month (compared to the national average of €2180 per month). At the same time, this rise in consumption is markedly higher than the rise in income. In other words: the growth in consumption is effected at the expense of saving [6].

On the basis of the findings of the sample survey on income and expenditure, it can be demonstrated that the spending for rent and energy increases with advancing age. While only 32% of the average household's expenditure is allotted to this factor, it accounts for 35% of the spending of the 70-to-80-year-olds and for almost 40% of that of the over-80-year-olds. In comparison to younger age groups, the expenditure on health and body care as well as on recreation, entertainment and culture also continues to be above average. Of these cost factors, the recreational and cultural services as well as package tours can be regarded as the most cost-intensive [22].

The Silver Economy in Germany

Why is the Silver Economy Important as a New Socio-economic and Politico-economic Field of Activity?

The field of activity of the silver market in particular constitutes the starting-point for the economic aspirations and expectations connected with the demographic age-ing of the population. These expectations, as it were, act as a "counterbalance" to the already-mentioned horror scenarios. Given the much increased buying power of the elderly, the increased heterogeneity of consumption wishes and needs corresponding to the differentiation of old age, as well as the empirical evidence for an age-specific change in consumption requirements, it stands to reason to look for inherent impulses for economic growth and employment by dint of new "age-sensitive" prod-uct ranges and services and to promote their development and expansion. Experts regard the silver economy as an important constructive "countermessage" to the macroeconomic horror scenarios. Today it is (as if it were evidence-based) assumed in Germany that the silver economy is a sector of the future that is worth discovering and developing in the mutual interest of both the elderly and the different economic actors. There are expected to be win-win effects on both sides: an enhancement of the quality of life on the one hand and the mobilisation of growth and the creation of new jobs on the other hand. The following reasons, amongst others, support this assumption [2, 8, 10, 14]:

- For a long time, the providers in the consumer goods and services markets paid little attention to older people as consumers; this was, inter alia, due to the largely negative connotations of the term "old age" as well as to the prevalent negative stereotypes on old age. However, the elderly are increasingly beginning to object to this.
- The present cohorts of older people are increasingly interested in private con-sumption and for this purpose have a reserve at their disposal that is becoming scarcer and scarcer for other age groups, namely *time*.
- The elderly are an increasingly heterogeneous population group (differentiation of old age) and consequently also have correspondingly differentiated consump-tion wishes and needs, which can be met by a correspondingly differentiated range of products and services.
- The succeeding cohorts of older people have become both more demanding and more critical regarding their quality notions and participation possibilities as customers.
- Besides the wish for a good state of health and social integration, the desire for an enhancement of the quality of life, the maintenance of independence and the promotion of individual safety range on the top of the individual preference scale of older people. The silver market concept offers good starting-points for all these fields.
- From an economic point of view, it is moreover significant that the number of old-age households is on the rise. For it must still be borne in mind that the

private demand for consumer goods and services is not primarily guided by the number of persons but by the number of households. In other words, the demographically induced decreases in private demand due to the decline in population can be more than compensated by a likewise demographically, but also socio-structurally induced, increase in small and especially one-person households (singularisation of old age).

- Although some economic sectors, which we will examine more closely later, have in the meantime developed good products and services that meet the special needs of the elderly (e.g. regarding comfort, quality and manageability) it nevertheless holds true that most German enterprises have not yet actively discovered the silver economy as a strategic field of activity.

Political initiatives for the promotion of the silver economy, which were moreover coordinated in a cross-departmental fashion, are rather rare exceptions. In this respect we have to point to the exemplary role of North Rhine-Westphalia: In 1999, North Rhine-Westphalia was the first federal state to launch the federal initiative *Silver Economy* with the objective of spurring on the development of seniors-oriented services and products. The aim was to improve the quality of life of the elderly and, in conjunction with this goal, to promote employment opportunities [18]. Meanwhile, other federal states, regions and municipalities have followed this example, even though the setting of priorities regarding content and the degree of the cross-actor co-operation vary strongly. Schleswig-Holstein, Mecklenburg Western-Pomerania, Rhineland-Palatinate, Bremen and Bavaria have to be mentioned here. On the regional and the municipal levels, there are several initiatives on the silver economy within the scope of the local business development that are worth mentioning, e.g. in the cities of Herten, Krefeld, Dortmund (all in North Rhine-Westphalia), Kiel, Eckernförde, Rendsburg and Neumünster (all in Schleswig-Holstein) [2].

The federal level was late to react. Here one has to point to the "Fifth Report on the Situation of the Elderly" by the federal government, which focuses on the (economic) "potentials of old age for the economy and for society" and dedicates a chapter to the silver economy [2]. The federal ministry responsible for seniors policy has only recently (autumn 2007) initiated a programme "Economic Factor Old Age – Winning Enterprises Over", which set itself the target of propagating the concept of and improving the chances of success of the silver economy in Germany [3]. An important goal of the programme is to enhance the different actors' readiness to take part via "good practice" examples. Revealingly, however, this is not a programme of the Federal Ministry of Economics but of the Federal Ministry for Families, Senior Citizens, Women and Youth.

Which Areas Comprise the Silver Economy?

All in all, the silver economy should not be regarded as an own economic sector but rather as a cross-section market, in which numerous industrial sectors are involved. The following economic segments can be attributed to it [2, 10, 14]:

- IT applications in inpatient and outpatient care
- Smart living, housing adaptations and supported living services, increasingly on an IT-basis
- Promotion of independent living, likewise increasingly on an IT-basis
- Gerontologically relevant areas of the health economy, including medical technology and e-health, hearing and seeing aids technology, dental prosthetics and orthopaedics
- Education and culture (as it were in "response" to higher levels of education and more spare time)
- IT and media, in particular in conjunction with other market segments such as health, the promotion of independence and security
- Service robotics, especially in combination with the promotion of independent living in the case of older people with severe health constraints
- Mobility and the promotion of mobility, e.g. car traffic safety
- Recreation, travel, culture, communication and entertainment
- Fitness and wellness (in response to the higher health awareness particularly of the "younger old")
- Clothing and fashion (among other things, to document social integration)
- Services facilitating everyday life and other home services
- Insurance coverage, especially with regard to age-specific "risks"
- Financial services "sensitive to demography", especially in the area of capital protection, wealth maintenance and dissaving counselling

Only selected fields of activity of the silver economy will be examined in more detail.

Activity Field: Tourism

The conditions for the tourism sector to win new customers among the target group of the elderly are exceptionally good: After their withdrawal from the working force, older people in Germany have much spare time and in most cases they also have the financial means to make the most of this time. The consumer behaviour of the elderly moreover shows that older people spend a large share of their income on travelling [9].

If one looks at the travel intensity, i.e. the share of people within a population group that undertakes at least one journey of at least 5 days duration within a year, the percentage was slightly lower for older people (70%) in Germany than for the total population (74.4%) in 2004. However, if one compares the development of the travel intensity over the course of the past 10 years, it becomes clear that it increased by 5% in the age group 60-plus in the period 1994–2004, whereas the travel intensity declined slightly in the total population. The share of the 60-plus among the holiday makers has also markedly risen in comparison to the other age groups. While only every fifth traveller was aged 60 years and older in 1994, this age group accounted for 30% of all travellers in 2004 [21].

However, in the travel market too it is necessary to take into account the heterogeneity of the target group. The travel wishes of the elderly vary strongly and depend on the lifestyle, the age or the degree of mobility etc. Nonetheless they have some characteristics in common that distinguish them from the travel preferences of younger people: good accessibility, a healthy climate and tranquillity at their holiday destinations are important basic conditions that older people set great store by when planning their holidays. On the whole, one can discern a trend to upmarket accommodation, coach tours and to inland trips. Thus, for older people, Germany is an above-average popular travel destination: In 2004, 38% of the journeys of senior couples were domestic, in the case of single seniors this figure even amounted to 44%. If older German people travel abroad, they prefer journeys to adjacent foreign countries or to southern European areas. Non-European goals only have a market share of 10% among the elderly, as compared to 15% in the total population [9].

A special trend that is becoming apparent in the field of tourism for the elderly is the combination of tourism and health promotion. This encompasses all offers that fall within the scope of preventive, health-promoting, wellness-oriented, rehabilitating or curative tours, which are meeting with an increasingly great response from the elderly [9]. In order to be able to provide adequate offers for mobility-impaired persons and thus to cater for a further important target group, it is necessary to plan barrier-free, or low barrier facilities.

Experience shows that both free-market and charity organisations persist in this market segment. Mixed organisational forms arising from the co-operation of welfare organisations and commercial tour operators have proved to be especially advantageous for the development and implementation of offers such as assisted holidays [15]. Thus, like in many areas of the silver economy, the joint and cooperative action of the involved regional and supraregional actors can be regarded as a success factor.

Activity Field: Living

Living independently at home for as long as possible, even in the case of considerable physical and health impairments, or of seriously restricted mobility, is considered the top guiding maxim of old age policies and of care for the elderly in Germany. Barely 4% of the over-65-year-olds live in residential homes and the like. According to empirical findings they only do so if they (no longer) have the possibility of living independently [1]. Even in the case of need for nursing care, most (approximately 70%) of the persons concerned stay in their own homes and are cared for there [23]. With its benefits catalogue, even the German statutory long-term care insurance is basically geared to the promotion and maintenance of independent living. According to experience, however, the realisation of this goal becomes difficult if the concerned persons are very old and/or live on their own. In Germany, the so-called "singularisation of old age" is typical for around 40% of all the over-65-year-olds, of which 85% in turn are women [1].

According to representative population surveys, more than 80% of seniors indicate that they prefer to live in a normal flat. About 65% of the elderly are even prepared to put up with a move, even at advanced age, if the old flat no longer meets their wishes and requirements and if a suitable alternative (apart from residential homes) presents itself [11]. The great importance of independent living in old age also becomes evident from the fact that German seniors spend a large part (40%) of their income on housing. Furthermore, the share of the expenditure on housing has increased in the course of time.

On the whole, the housing conditions of seniors have markedly improved in Germany. Today the living space per person amounts to $54.1\,\text{m}^2$ ($40\,\text{m}^2$ in 1994). Nowadays, standard equipment includes bathrooms with showers as well as central heating. In 2004, 74% of the flats of older people had a balcony or a patio (64.4% in 1994). There has likewise been a marked rise in the ownership structures: In 2003, more than half of the elderly were flat or house owners (37.8% in 1994) [6]. Due to the effects of demographic ageing and changing family structures, it is to be expected that the number of private seniors' households will continue to increase in future, this in particular holds good for single- and two-person households.

These trends pose new challenges, particularly for the building trade and the large housing industry companies. Much of the housing on offer is not senior-friendly and to complicate matters further, a good deal of the housing supply in the conurbations from the 1950s and 1960s can only be converted into senior-friendly living space with many restrictions [26]. Moreover, it has transpired that the creation of suitable living space for the elderly cannot only be limited to housing adaptations. Instead, the whole residential environment has to be incorporated into the planning concept: This includes, amongst others, the neighbourhood infrastructure, the connection to public transport and the provision of shopping facilities and other service offers.

This activity field holds much potential for the silver economy. Thus, for instance, the conversion of flats into senior-friendly living spaces opens up new fields of activity for crafts businesses. This economic sector already covers a broad spectrum of everyday products and services and thus substantially contributes to an enhancement of the quality of life for all. Furthermore, the more than 800,000 craft businesses with almost 5 million employees and a turnover of approximately €450 billion (2005 figures) already fulfil important politico-economic and job creating functions, which could still be enhanced by additional offers of silver economy products and services.

In order to attract the target group of older people, it is also necessary to expand service and advisory service offers around the sales of the products and services. This does not necessitate an overall realignment of the business strategy but, at the most, an adjustment in various subdivisions. Generally speaking, one can distinguish three focal points:

- Qualification of the employees, particularly in the production and in the company
- Networking and co-operation with possible partners (e.g. property developers and house building companies with housekeeping and nursing service providers)
- Marketing, especially also with respect to possible forms of financing

The following activity fields represent important starting points, especially for crafts businesses wishing to gear themselves to the seniors market:

- Housing adaptation: In addition to barrier-free adaptations, this also concerns the deployment of new, partly computer-assisted technologies, such as those used in the field of assisted living [26].
- Combination of adaptation measures with supplementary services: e.g. concerning the renovation or refurbishment of living space. Here too the cross-sector networking of the individual service providers will be of vital importance in the future [4]. Networking not only enables the service providers to improve the quality of their service by bundling several skills, but also allows them to reduce their organisational and planning costs and thus to improve their profitability [19]. In addition, it also facilitates a better acceptance among older customers by offering one-stop services.

The activity field living opens up new fields of opportunity in the personal services sector too, in particular as regards household-related services. Delivery services, maintenance services and the expansion of housekeeping services can be mentioned as examples of this. In this connection, meaningful co-operation with housing associations is also conceivable. The activity field affords interesting starting points for the retail trade too (advisory and delivery services, a better access to a range of healthy food products) [4].

Despite the above-mentioned positive experiences, by far not all relevant trades are sufficiently sensitised to this issue, especially for the activity field living. This is especially true for the field of information and entertainment technology. Thus the fastest growing group of internet users in Germany are older people. Numerous new chances and challenges arise from this development, not only for the electronic industry but for other providers too. Information platforms, internet trade or travel portals, for instance, are a few examples. The entertainment electronics industry can also profit from this new target group, as is shown by the high acceptance of brain-training software for games consoles in Germany.

Excursus: Computer-Aided Independent Living as a Central Future Field of the Silver Economy in Germany

Due to the demography-related strong growth in the number of very old people in need of help, experts see great development potentials particularly in IT-aided assisted living. The Enquete Commission on Care of the federal state of North Rhine-Westphalia distinguishes between six central areas of application [13]:

- General technology for the promotion of independent living in old age (such as rotatable hospital beds, easily manageable mobile phones etc.).
- Mechanical household and mobility aids: This in particular concerns the equipment of the private households of older people with user-friendly domestic appliances as well as special technology, with which specific impairments can

be compensated, e.g. wheeled walkers or wheelchairs. In recent years, so-called service robots, such as the voice-controlled "Care-O-Bot" system, have attracted great attention.

- The utilisation of technology in connection with (age-adapted) housing adaptation: Amongst other things, this comprises measures of home automation that facilitate household management, e.g. self-adjusting blinds and blackout installations and electrical equipment that automatically switches off in the case of malfunction. Modern computer technology even allows for "intelligent" housing (*smart homes* or *digital homes* and *accompanied living*). So far, the following technical application fields are discernible: safety, simplification of everyday life, home appliances, energy management, health promotion and communication [26].
- Technology-assisted health promotion and health control: These forms of help (also referred to as e-health or health-monitoring) are still to a large extent in trial phase. They,for example, monitor the vital signs of typical high risk patients with the possibility of signalling the information to pertinent monitoring stations, or they monitor health-relevant behaviour patterns by, for instance, checking the intake of tablets and the sleeping habits. Furthermore, systems for the localisation of older patients suffering from dementia are in use.
- Technology-assisted communication: This technology is deployed in the stage shortly prior to the need for care. On the basis of home emergency call systems, the extended home emergency call system also offers additional help in the case of unexpected nursing problems as well as everyday practical support and services. Latterly, it also includes communication offers. These extended home emergency call systems can thus, all in all, be regarded as offers of activation and communication too.
- Tele-care: This term describes new forms of telematics-based care possibilities in the case of long illness and the need for care. They are mostly contemplated in connexion with other forms of intelligent household technologies and aids. Tele-care comprises the telecommunications-based long distance support or care of patients or of persons in need of care in their private homes. The idea behind this is the "virtual" old age and nursing home that assures the quality of the home care by means of a support infrastructure, which can be operated both by mobile as well as by home telecommunications.

Of essential importance for the success of IT products in the field of assisted living and home care is quite probably the question of whether the German nursing care and health funds offer advantageous refunding possibilities (which is not the case so far). Many large housing societies, which are in charge of almost half of the private housing supply for older people, have, however, recognised the potential that an IT-equipment of the flats of seniors holds for a longer independent life (and thus for longer-running lease contracts) and are currently already giving attention to the question of how to pass on possible additional costs via the lease prices.

Activity Field: Financial Services

The relationship between the group of older people and finance management is in many ways ambivalent. On the one hand, the elderly are a, comparatively speaking, high-income and wealthy group: seniors today own about 53% of the total assets. It is prognosticated that this figure will rise to two-thirds within a few years. On the other hand, it is unfortunately still common practice in the finance world to discriminate against older people or to put them at a disadvantage, e.g. within the scope of age limits for the granting of private loans. In order to make the most of the economic power of seniors, banks and insurances must therefore adapt themselves to the target group of the future in due time. Although a survey has revealed that the banks are aware of this trend, paradoxically only few of them offer age-based products [24].

Generally, financial services serve to make the income or assets available for expenditures and to transfer them to where they are needed. They therefore play an important role in each stage of life and greatly contribute to the enhancement of the quality of life of people. In principle, the financial services perform the same function for the elderly as for all other age groups. But, as the financial services change their structures and their effects in the different phases of life, there are some age-related characteristics. The demand for credit is highest in the age bracket 25–35, while the highest savings rate can be observed in the age group above 35. This differentiation also holds good for the insurance industry. Depending on the age group, there are different risks that have to be covered by an insurance policy: accidents, unemployment, death or the need of care to name but a few.

The established criteria used for the evaluation of financial services also apply for the older customers of the banking and insurance industry. For one thing, the investment must be worthwhile, i.e. the interest rate has to be lucrative. Furthermore, the investment forms should be relatively safe and it must be possible to exchange one product for another in a quick and simple procedure. The SALIS concept developed by the Institute for Financial Services (iff) complements the financial services' classic triangle of influences (which takes into account the importance of yield, liquidity and safety as assessment criteria of policyholders) by two further criteria for the analysis of financial offers, namely by *sustainabilitiy* or *social responsibility* and the *access* to financial services [17].

These criteria also coincide with the wishes and needs of older people regarding financial services. The factor *safety* plays a key role for older people: A survey of the German National Association of Senior Citizens' Organisations (BAGSO) shows, for example, that older people have a high degree of trust in their banks. This factor can, however, still be markedly improved by expanding the service and advisory functions. Moreover, older people prefer familiar and trustworthy staff members who can give them competent advice on their business matters. They are still sceptical towards online-banking. Only 16% do their banking business via the internet [12].

The factor *rate of return* plays a minor role for most senior citizens, this is also reflected in their investment behaviour. Most older people would rather put money into a safe but little profitable savings account, than choose a high-risk but potentially more profitable investment form (e.g. shares, property funds). Of much greater importance seems to be the criterion of short-term availability: Products with a long maturity or long commitment periods tend to be rejected by the elderly. In the case of senior citizens, the criterion of accessibility must be explored from different angles. For one thing, their mobility is often restricted due to age-related physical impairments. This aspect plays an increasing role, especially in rural areas as many small bank branches there are closing. In this connexion, one has to consider other offers that continue to facilitate the access to finance (mobile branches, house calls etc.). Another aspect that falls within the scope of the subject *access* is age discrimination. While it is true that 95% of the older people polled in the above-mentioned BAGSO survey indicate that they have never been refused financial services on grounds of age, it is in fact often a different story when it comes to obtaining a loan. If older people are granted a loan, the terms and conditions of the loan are often much more unfavourable than those for younger people with a comparable asset situation [12].

If one has a closer look at the wishes and needs of older people, one realises that the basic needs of older people regarding the classic financial services sector can often be met with the already existing products. Instead, it is all about optimising the already offered products and services for the silver market. In the silver economy (as well as elsewhere) it has proven to be of value to count on one-stop services, i.e. on services that bundle formerly single or partial services to a complete service package that can thus be tailored to the wishes and needs of the individual client.

Summary and Conclusion

This overview of the subject area "the economic power of older people" has shown that there is also great potential in sectors other than the classic health market for products and services that are sensitive to demographic change. There are already some sensible offers and approaches that have to be expanded, refined and, if need be, redeveloped in future. A critical synopsis of the experiences gained so far in the field of the silver economy leads to the following recommendations for a socio-politically sensible, and at the same time economically positive, further development of the silver market:

- Customer-oriented enhancement of the range of products as well as of services, and a differentiated market development
- Sensitisation and co-ordination of the actors
- Further development and increased deployment of senior marketing
- Provision for the consumer needs of poor older people
- Empowerment and a better representation of the interests of older consumers
- Dialogical product and services development
- Enhancement and expansion of the existing products and services
- Further development of user-friendly and seniors-oriented design

- Promotion of a consumer protection for older people

As the experience in Germany has shown, the increasingly heterogeneous consumer group of the elderly shows an increasing interest in private consumption as well as differentiated consumption wishes and needs, which can be met by a correspondingly differentiated range of products and services. The silver market needs to be regarded as a strategic field of activity for social integration, the maintenance of independence and the promotion of individual safety, and therefore for the enhancement of the quality of life of older people.

References

1. G. Bäcker, G. Naegele, K. Hofemann, R. Bispinck, *Sozialpolitik und soziale Lage in Deutschland, 4th edn., vol. 2* (VS, Wiesbaden, 2008)
2. Bundesministerium für Familie, Senioren, Frauen und Jugend, *Fünfter Bericht zur Lage der älteren Generation in der Bundesrepublik Deutschland* (BMFSFJ, Berlin, 2006)
3. Bundesministerium für Familie, Senioren, Frauen und Jugend, *Neues Unternehmensprogramm Wirtschaftsfaktor Alter – Unternehmen gewinnen* (BMFSFJ, Berlin, 2007), http://www.bmfsfj.de/bmfsfj/generator/Kategorien/aktuelles,did=99658.html. Accessed 06 Nov. 2007
4. M. Cirkel, P. Enste, *Handwerk für Ältere Menschen* (FFG-Bericht, Dortmund, 2006)
5. Deutscher Bundestag, *Abschlussbericht der Bundestags-Enquete-Kommission "Demographischer Wandel"* (Zur Sache, Bonn, 2002)
6. Deutsches Institut für Wirtschaftsforschung,, *Auswirkungen des demographischen Wandels auf die private Nachfrage nach Gütern und Dienstleistungen in Deutschland bis 2050* (DIW, Berlin, 2007)
7. P. Enste, R.G. Heinze, V. Leve, *Finanzdienstleistungen und Seniorenwirtschaft* (FFG-Veröffentlichung, Dortmund, 2006)
8. V. Gerling, G. Naegele, K. Scharfenorth, Der private Konsum älterer Menschen. *Sozialer Fortschritt* **11**, 292–300 (2004)
9. Gesellschaft für Konsumforschung, *50plus* (GfK, Nürnberg 2002) 11. R. Heinze, Der Demographische Wandel als Wirtschaftsmotor, in *Alter hat Zukunft* ed. by F. Schönberg, G. Naegele (LIT, Münster, 2005), pp. 341–358
10. R. Heinze, Der Demographische Wandel als Wirtschaftsmotor, in *Alter hat Zukunft* ed. by F. Schönberg, G. Naegele (LIT, Münster, 2005), pp. 341–358
11. R. Heinze, V. Eichener, G. Naegele, M. Bucksteeg, M. Schauerte, *Neue Wohnung auch im Alter: Folgerungen aus dem demographischen Wandel für Wohnungspolitik und Wohnungswirtschaft* (Schader-Stiftung, Darmstadt, 1997)
12. B. Keck, *Die BAGSO Umfrage: "Ältere als Bankkunden"* (The elderly as bank customers) (German National Association of Senior Citizens' Organisations, BAGSO, Bonn, 2005) http://www.bagso.de/startaktuell+M534e265543e.html. Accessed 13 Jun 2008
13. Landtag Nordrhein-Westfalen (eds), *Situation und Zukunft der Pflege in NRW. Bericht der Enquete Kommission des Landtages Nordrhein-Westfalen* (Eigenverlag, Düsseldorf, 2005)
14. G. Naegele, J. Hilbert, Perspektiven der "Seniorenwirtschaft" – Anmerkungen zur Nutzung der "Wirtschaftskraft Alter". *Theorie und Praxis der Sozialen Arbeit* **3**, 12–18 (2003)
15. G. Naegele, R. Heinze, J. Hilbert, A. Helmer-Denzel, *Seniorenwirtschaft in Deutschland – Tourismus und Wellness im Alter* (FFG-Veröffentlichung, Dortmund, 2006)
16. G. Naegele, J. Mitarbeit von Hilbert, V. Gerling, M. Weidekamp-Maicher, *Perspektiven einer produktiven Nutzung der "weichen" Folgen des Demographischen Wandels im Rahmen der Nationalen Nachhaltigkeitsstrategie. Expertise, erstellt für das Bundeskanzleramt* (FFG-Vervielfältigung, Dortmund, 2003)

17. U. Reifner, Alter und Finanzdienstleistungen, in *Produkte, Dienstleistungen und Verbraucherschutz für ältere Menschen* ed. by Deutsches Zentrum für Altersfragen (LIT, Berlin, 2006), pp. 283–348
18. A. Roes, Die Landesinitiative Seniorenwirtschaft NRW, in *Alter hat Zukunft* ed. by F. Schönberg, G. Naegele (LIT, Münster, 2005), pp. 359–374
19. A. Schilde, D. Salzig, C. Liedtke, *Unternehmenskooperation– was ist dran am neuen Zauberwort* (Institut für Klima, Umwelt, Energie, Wuppertal, 2002) http://www.wupperinst.org/uploads/tx_wibeitrag/ws26.pdf. Accessed 13 Jun 2008
20. B. Sommer, Bevölkerungsentwicklung in den Bundesländern bis 2050. *Wirtschaft und Statistik* **8**, 834–844 (2004)
21. U. Sonntag, A. Sierck, *Urlaubsreisen der Senioren*. (Forschungsgemeinschaft Urlaub und Reisen, Kiel, 2005)
22. Statistisches Bundesamt, *Bevölkerung Deutschlands bis 2050 – 11. koordinierte Bevölkerungsvorausberechnung* (Statistisches Bundesamt, Wiesbaden, 2006a)
23. Statistisches Bundesamt, *Pflegestatistik 2005 Deutschlandergebnisse* (Statistisches Bundesamt, Wiesbaden, 2007)
24. R. Syre, Finanzindustrie – Weckruf "55 Plus". *Manager Magazin* 31.05.2006 (2006)
25. A. Walker, The principles and potential of active ageing, in *Facing an ageing world – recommendations and perspectives* ed. by S. Pohlmann (Transfer, Regensburg, 2002), pp. 113–118
26. D. Wilde, A. Franke, *Die "silberne" Zukunft gestalten. Handlungsoptionen im demographischen Wandel am Beispiel innovativer Wohnformen für ältere Menschen* (Driesen, Berlin, 2006)

Chapter 23
India: Emerging Opportunities in a Market in Transition

S.P. Antony, P.C. Purwar, N. Kinra, and J. Moorthy

Abstract India is in the middle of its demographic transition. The 60+ age group is projected to treble by 2050 while the 0–14 group remains stagnant. India's population structure and distribution would then closely resemble that of nations like Russia and the UK, as seen now. Their high aging index indicates that the 60+ age group is larger than the 0–14 group. Such changes in the size, structure, and distribution of the population will have implications for public policy as well as business. The Government has launched a slew of initiatives to meet this challenge. On the business front, many products and services have been launched that specifically target the elderly. However, there are many other products and services used by all age groups. These may have to be repositioned if the motivations of the different age groups are not similar. Both from the angle of public policy and business, decision makers in India should closely examine the experience of nations with a high aging index and respond to the challenges of demographic transition.

In the developed countries, the dominant factor in the next society will be something to which most people are only just beginning to pay attention: the rapid growth in the older population and the rapid shrinking of the younger generation [10].

Introduction

The world is aging rapidly. The population median age has increased from 24 in 1950 to 28 in 2005, and is projected to increase to about 38, by the year 2050. The elderly[1] is the largest growing segment, growing five times faster than the total population. The elderly by 2050 will constitute 22% of the population from under 10% in 2005, and 8% in 1950 (see Table 23.1).

---

[1] We use the term "elderly" to refer to those aged 60+.

Table 23.1 Population aging by regions 1950–2050 [36]

Region	Year	Age group (%)			Median age	Aging
		0–14	15–59	60+	(years)	index
World	1950	34	58	8	24	24
	2005	28	61	10	28	36
	2050	20	58	22	38	110
More developed regions	1950	27	61	12	29	43
	2005	17	63	20	39	118
	2050	15	52	33	46	213
Less developed regions[a]	1950	37	56	6	22	17
	2005	31	61	8	26	26
	2050	21	59	20	37	98
Least developed regions	1950	42	54	5	20	12
	2005	41	53	5	19	13
	2050	28	61	10	28	37

[a] India's population parameters fall within those of the less developed regions.

Population aging[2] worldwide will operate at varying levels of intensity, and in different time frames (see Table 23.1). In the more developed regions, the aging index will double to 213 in 2050. In the less least developed regions (like India) and in the least developed regions it will quadruple to 98 and 37 respectively. The median age during the same period, will rise from 39 to 46 in the more developed regions, from 26 to 37 in the less developed regions, and from 19 to 28 in the least developed regions. The aging index[3] worldwide has increased from 24 in 1950 to 36 in 2005 and is expected to increase to 110 in 2050. This indicates that the younger population is shrinking. This also indicates that the population in the more developed regions has aged earlier, but the process has been accelerated in other regions of the world.

We examine in this chapter the facets of demographic change in India. We also discuss the strategic role of demographic analysis in market planning. Demographic change has two important implications for marketing – development of new products and services, and repositioning of existing products and services. Here we highlight some of the responses of marketers in India. Finally, we draw some lessons for countries in the early stages of demographic change.

---

[2] Population aging is the process by which older individuals become a proportionally larger share of the total population. At the root of population aging is demographic transition, the process by which mortality rates decline, followed by fertility declines [35].

[3] Aging index is the proportion of 60+ to the 0–14 age group. An index of 100 would imply that the 60+ population equals the 0–14 population. An index higher than 100 would indicate that the 60+ is larger than the 0–14 population [35].

The Indian Context

India has traditionally been a low growth economy. However, it has shown signs of vibrancy over the last few years and has been able to sustain high growth. Disparities in income levels that do exist vary across states, and urban and rural markets. Over a third of all consumer expenditure is by about 100 million people, the top 10% of the population. They could be classified as big-ticket buyers and may be fuelling the growth in the economy. India has the world's largest middle class of 200 million, the top 20%, which may also have high consumption levels. The penetration of "utility" goods is much higher than luxuries, comfort, and high lifestyle commodities [16].

India, with the world's second largest elderly population next only to China, is in the middle of its demographic transition [26] (also refer to Table 23.2). Its population parameters fall within those of the Less Developed Nations of the world (Table 23.1). The aging index is expected to rise to about 111 in 2050, from 15 in 1950 and 22 in 2005. The median age of 39 in 2050, is higher than the averages for the world and the less developed regions.

Since the beginning of the twenty-first century, the 60+ age group in India has grown faster than the total population. This growth rate is expected to be sustained until 2050, for which projections are available. Despite this high growth rate, the population numbered just about 20 million in 1950. However, by 2005, while the total population doubled to over 1 billion, the 60+ trebled to 84 million. The 15–59 age group, the working population, has grown as much as the total population, while the 0–14 group has grown at a much lesser pace (Table 23.2).

In the next 50 years, while the total population and also the working population will increase by half, and the 0–14 group will not grow, the 60+ will again treble. The population of elderly at about 335 million would be larger than the 0–14 population at 302 million. The elderly would become the second largest group after the working population (Table 23.2). This indicates that the younger population in India too is shrinking.

Table 23.2 India's aging population 1950–2050 [36]

Year	Age group[a]			Total	Median age	Aging
	0–14	15–59	60+		(years)	index
1950	139	212	21	372	21	15
	(37)	(57)	(6)			
2005	374	676	84	1134	24	22
	(33)	(60)	(7)			
2050	302	1021	335	1658	39	111
	(18)	(62)	(20)			
Growth (1911–1950)	–	–	9	120		
	–	–	(74)	(48)		
Growth (1950–2005)	235	464	63	762		
	(169)	(219)	(300)	(205)		
Growth (2005–2050)	−72	345	251	524		
	(−19)	(51)	(299)	(46)		

[a] Figures in millions and percentage in parentheses.

344   S.P. Antony et al.

Within the country, however, there are variations. The proportion of elderly to the total population in rural areas is higher than that in urban areas. Kerala state in South India has the highest proportion of elderly to total population. The proportion of the elderly to the population is higher in the southern states and relatively lower in the eastern and north-eastern region. It is also higher in Punjab, Haryana and Himachal Pradesh, which are economically better-off states, relatively. These states and also the southern states have done well on a number of socio-economic indicators and have also been successful in bringing down their population growth rates. Among the poorest states, Orissa has a high proportion of elderly to total population. The regional pattern is more or less similar for both rural and urban areas.

Moreover, there is a significant change of socio-economic circumstances for the elderly with the breakdown of the traditional joint and extended family system [26]. The joint family as a traditional social unit took care of the elderly, sick, widows and orphans. The old age dependency ratio has seen a marginal increase between 1981 and 1991. Here again, there are variations. The dependency ratio[4] is somewhat higher for females than for the males and much higher in the rural areas than in the urban areas. The higher ratio for rural areas may be explained by the migration of individuals in the working age population to urban areas.

India's population age distribution in 2005 closely resembles the distribution available in the less developed regions of the world. India's population by 2050, however, will more resemble the distribution as seen in the more developed regions today (see Tables 23.1 and 23.2). This also indicates that the age structure of the population is changing.

This larger problem of aging has two critical concerns. Galbraith states: "The first is how the individual should respond to the mature years. The second is how the larger community, including the government, should respond to the needs of the old" [13]. Drucker [9] has noted that such demographic transition and changes in the population age distribution have far-reaching implications for retirement and pensions, housing, public policy, health care, labor markets, business, and marketing, among others. The fiscal gaps that are widening for instance in the USA, Europe, and Japan could become worse as the baby boomers[5] retire [11]. One illustration of the impact of population aging is the case of Kerala in India, where the pension bill grew more than the salary bill, and is causing nightmares [38].

At the public policy level, India has responded to the population aging at least in recent times. Formulation of the National Policy on Older Persons [23] is a case in point. The Government of India also proposes to launch the National Programme for the Elderly [9] with a planned outlay of Rs. 4 billion[6] (US$100 million).

---

[4] The ratio is expressed as the number of persons in the age group 60+, per 100 persons in the working population (age group 15–59 years).

[5] Baby boomers are those born post-war between 1946 and 1964 [25]; this definition is applicable for those born in the USA.

[6] US$1 is worth about Rs. 40.

The Government launched the Senior Citizens Savings Scheme in 2004. The scheme offers higher differential rates of interest and garnered over Rs. 80 billion (US$2 billion) in less than a year [28]. In the latest budget [7] the Government proposes to extend income tax concessions for investments made under this scheme. The objective is to offer safety and reasonable returns to this vulnerable group, which saw erosion in real incomes due to falling interest rates.

This has become critical to the welfare of the elderly as many of them, more so in the unorganized sectors of employment, do not enjoy pension benefits and depend on interest income derived from investment of retirement benefits. Moreover, social security measures in India are in a nascent stage.

The National Old Age Pension Scheme was introduced by the government in 1995 to address the issue of social security for the destitute. The rechristened Indira Gandhi National Old Age Pension Scheme enlarged its scope in 2007 to cover all aged 65+ below the poverty line. Some 16 million aged persons, about 20% of India's elderly, will benefit [29]. In the union budget, the government has proposed an allocation of Rs. 34 billion (US$861 million) for this scheme [7].

Another related issue has been the lack of liquidity for the elderly. To own a home is a fundamental aspiration for the great majority of the Indian populace. And, many manage to acquire one while in employment. Much of these acquisitions are funded by housing loans that are freely available. Late in the family life cycle, many families spend large sums on the education and marriage of children. Finally, after retirement, many are left with few options that give a steady stream of cash inflow. The Government of India has recently launched the Reverse Mortgage Scheme to provide financial income for the elderly who own homes, but who do not have sufficient income [1]. The government has further proposed that revenue streams received by senior citizens would not be treated as income for tax purposes [7]. This would make the scheme much more attractive.

The government plans to allocate Rs. 7 billion (US$175 million) for public health to focus, among others, on the national program for care of elderly and their rehabilitation [6]. During the eleventh plan period 2007–2012, the government proposes to set up two National Institutes of Ageing with eight regional centers, in addition to a department of geriatric medicine with one center each in every state. Some private hospitals have already added geriatrics wings [22].

The impact of demographic transition on the structure and age distribution of our population will also impact consumer markets. We discuss this impact in the following section.

Demographic Analysis

Demographics explain 2/3rds of everything. They help predict which products will be in demand... (David K. Foot, Canadian demographer cited in [3], p. 188)

Demographics, the most important variable, describe and provide statistics that study population in terms of size,[7] structure and distribution.

Market Planning

Demographic analysis is the first step in market planning. Demographic trends are more reliable than other variables in the study of consumer behavior [3]. Demographic profiles are relatively straightforward, and a great deal of information is available on the various characteristics of various segments, for instance, the size and economic power of teenagers. Consumers buy products like many others of the same age group or life stage. They have many commonalities like shared values and cultural experiences [30]. But, responses to offers within age groups may differ [24, 25, 31]. While within-age-group differences may be large, between-age-group differences may equally be large and significant.

Demographic profiles are useful when we do not have enough knowledge about a market or when a market is evolving [3]. It lends itself relatively efficiently to media targeting, since data is available on the demographic characteristics of most media audiences [27].

When marketers need more insights than can be obtained from demographics, psychographics and personality variables help to identify, and define a segment. Demographic profiles are combined with other profiles like psychographics to form market segment descriptors. In such a sense, age is used as a proxy for other fundamental differences in consumer behavior [3, 4].

Demographic analysis also raises questions about macro-marketing, marketing from the society's point of view. Issues like consumer vulnerability and other consequences of marketing action become critical here. While the study of consumer behavior is focused mostly on micro issues, its roots are in macro-marketing [3].

As the population ages, demand for healthcare, nursing, retirement homes and such products and services targeted specifically at the elderly is bound to increase. While the share of the younger (0–14 aged) population in the total population is shrinking, its importance may not decline. With small families becoming the norm, parents may be more able to spend on high-quality products and services.

The elderly or "young-again" market is a rapid growth segment worldwide (see Tables 23.1 and 23.2). Empty nests, more disposable income but less opportunities to spend, the luxury of time, and accumulated chronological age and experience characterize this segment [3]. On the flip side, rising inflation could cause a drop in real incomes.

---

[7] Size is determined by fertility and birth rates, life expectancy and death rates, and migration, and refers to the number of individuals in our population. Structure describes the population in terms of variables like age and gender. Distribution refers to the geographic location of individuals in the population [18].

It is clear that this demographic transition opens up opportunities as some age groups increase in size and economic power, and threatens as others decline at least in size. We discuss the implications of this transition in the following section.

Marketing Implications of Demographic Change

Two important dimensions of the marketing implications are discussed here – new product and service development, and repositioning and branding strategies.

New Product and Service Development

If the needs of the elderly are not met in full, or only partially, and if the segment is substantial and profitable, marketers may choose to offer new products and services targeted specifically at the elderly. Offerings for instance could be refurbished and elderly-friendly bathrooms, special tour packages, cosmetics, healthcare, retirement homes, and pension funds. Marketers it would appear have responded well to this dimension.

A scientist at the Bangalore-based National Institute of Mental Health and Neuro Sciences (NIMHANS), for instance has reportedly developed an herbal drug to arrest cognitive decline in the elderly [15]. A magazine for the elderly, *Harmony*, has been launched by Tina Ambani with India Today [14]. Four-seater electric cars called buggies and low-floor buses that make it easier for the elderly are some of the launches [2, 5]. Housing is another area that has seen a slew of initiatives. A variety of projects catering to different economic levels have been launched across the country [8, 19, 20].

Many tour and hotel packages specifically targeted at the elderly have been launched [32, 33]. Leading tour operator Cox & Kings reports a rise in the number of foreign tour package bookings by the elderly [34]. Informal discussions with financial services industry professionals indicate that the elderly form a growing and influential client base for such services as online share trading and mutual funds.

In-depth interviews with leading retailers of consumer durables in Lucknow[8] revealed that retailers were familiar with the demographic group of the elderly consumer. This had two nuances. Firstly, that the elderly were identified as a distinct segment, with differing motivations. Secondly, that the elderly were being seen visiting showrooms in sizeable numbers, and making purchase decisions jointly.

The question "What do senior citizens buy from your store?" elicited spontaneous responses: "Oh they buy almost everything that younger persons buy." The

---

[8] Lucknow is the capital city of Uttar Pradesh state in North India.

assortment was as varied as refrigerators, air conditioners, microwave ovens, house-hold furniture (including computer tables), relaxation products, toasters, and audio and video products. In addition to watches, jewelry, garments, sweetmeats and gifts.

We were then interested to know whether younger consumers bought the same type of products. This question also drew insightful responses. For instance, in the Godrej store: "the elderly prefer the Storwel brand of almirahs,[9] and the younger the Slimline brand." Slimline is sleeker and sports a modern, sophisticated look. We could surmise that the elderly prefer Storwel, it being a retro and well-established brand. It is plausible that Slimline has chosen not to target the elderly. We do not know whether this is a well-deliberated dual brand strategy by Godrej to distance the two brands in an apparently age-neutral[10] product category.

Other product categories with similar age differences are dining tables and sofa sets. While the younger prefer tables with glass tops, the elderly prefer wooden tops. In sofa sets, the younger preference was for plushier, luxurious sets. We could gather that similar differences in preferences exist in the Titan range of watches. The Regalia and Royalle brands of watches, in the price range of Rs. 2000 (US$50) to Rs. 5000 (US$125), were preferred by both the younger and the elderly. However, there appears to be a distinct preference by the elderly for the Nebula brand. The prices range from Rs. 21,000 to Rs. 80,000 (US$525–2000). We do not know if they are being bought to be given away as gifts, as in the case of sweetmeats. Blackwell et al. [3] also notes that the elderly make excellent prospects for luxury goods, travel-related products and services, and financial services.

There are also other product categories that are relatively new, like cell (mobile) telephones and digital cameras, and probably with a high degree of technology where surrogate decision-making is indicated. Many of these products are popular with the elderly. However, for instance to store phone numbers or to make deci-sions like renewals of service, purchase of instruments, the elderly rely on younger members of the family.

These insights are anecdotal and need to be validated with rigorous research. It is significant to note that at least the retailers are aware of age-related differences in product preferences. However, a holistic and concerted strategy designed by the manufacturer is not evident as yet. For instance, we have not observed any special sale for the elderly or signage that better accommodates the needs of the elderly.

Economic Times notes that the elderly are being targeted by marketers but that understanding the requirements of the elderly is difficult [37]. This could imply that marketers are comfortable marketing products and services specifically used by the elderly like old-age homes. They, however, might not have paid attention to under-stand their differing motivations, and so have not come to terms with marketing

---

[9] Almirahs or cabinets may be made of wood or metal. The Godrej range is made of metal. Almirahs are a must-have in every Indian home. They are used to store precious jewelry and garments.

[10] Product categories that are commonly used by all age groups are said to be age-neutral, like the common variants of toothpaste, or almirahs. In contrast, other product categories like adult diapers are age-specific.

products and services in age-neutral categories. We discuss in the following section the need for repositioning in such categories.

Repositioning and Branding Strategies

The shrinking of the younger population "will change markets in fundamental ways. Growth in family formation has been the driving force of all domestic markets in the developed world" [10]. Marketers would then have to make significant reorientations. Loudon and Bitta [21] recount the case histories of companies like Walt Disney, Gerber, and Coco-Cola, which shifted focus from younger age groups to an older customer franchise. Such drastic reorientations were necessitated by the reality of a shrinking young population.

In India, Cadbury Dairy Milk as a brand has extended its customer franchise, from the traditional children segment to include youth. In a telephone interview, the company spokesperson suggested that Cadbury Dairy Milk was at present targeting the youth franchise. Its advertisements in recent times feature, as the brand spokesperson the film star, Amitabh Bachchan, considered a youth icon in India. It is remarkable that he is seen with graying hair and beard. An analysis of the advertisements for Cadbury Dairy Milk over the last few decades clearly indicates the transition that the brand has made from a child to an adult customer franchise. Many other advertisements also carry Amitabh Bachchan as the brand spokesperson. This also has to be viewed in the context of old-age stereotypes in society.

Household consumer expenditures will change significantly due to the varied product assortments demanded by different age groups. For instance, the elderly may spend more on over-the counter drugs and personal care products [21]. It is important to note that while the two age groups may share many assortments, its size may vary.

Products typically targeted at the younger consumer like chocolates could be repositioned as an elderly consumer offering. The offering may thereafter become unattractive to the current younger customer franchise if the elderly consumer were also to be targeted. This is a critical issue that cannot be glossed over, since for many marketers the younger customer franchise is the predominant segment being served currently.

Summary and Conclusion

Not many marketers are sure of the strategies to be employed [25]. Kennett [17] observes that compared to other industries, the financial services industry is slow in implementing strategies targeted at the elderly. The highly regulated nature of most services, like telecommunications, land and mobile telephony, and financial products may make it inherently difficult to vary services. However, this observation may be true of other industries as well.

The younger age group presently accounts for a large share of consumer expenditure and also receives a large share of marketing attention. With many product assortments shared by different age groups, marketers would have to examine whether products need to be repositioned for the elderly consumer. It then becomes critical to understand the motivations of elderly consumers. Given this demographic and marketing context, can the existing knowledge on behavioral responses be extended to elderly consumers? It is plausible that marketers lack knowledge and experience to develop a marketing strategy targeted at the elderly, more so for product and service assortments shared across different age groups.

It is plausible that many marketers, at least in India, are yet to come to terms with an aging population, it being a recent phenomenon. This age group has not been large enough to merit attention earlier – 21 million in 1950, 85 million in 2005, and 335 million in 2050. The proportion is steadily increasing and is estimated to reach 20% in 2050, larger than the 0–14 age group (see Table 23.2). Their numbers have trebled in the last 50 years and are expected to treble again in the next 50. The total population though would increase only by half. Even worldwide, their numbers and proportions have not been large until now, more so in comparison with the younger age groups.

"Older" Indians may yet account for a quake in life-cycle spending patterns. Their spending is expected to rise faster than in any other age group, fuelled by a more educated and affluent generation entering senior citizen status [12]. However, it is to be recognized that not all older Indians may account for the quake.

Financial insecurity in old age is an area of concern that has been articulated in detail in the National Policy on Older Persons [23] and that also has implications for marketing. The situation has been exacerbated by a number of reasons: the growth of small and nuclear families, migration to urban areas, and the changing role of women in the workplace, among others. One-third of the population is below the poverty line, which is the bare minimum for subsistence. Another one-third is above it but still belong to the lower income group. That leaves the middle class and upper income groups.

The National Policy on Older Persons [23] recognizes the fact that a large proportion of the 60+ would be:

> ...middle and upper income groups, be economically better off, with some degree of financial security, have higher professional and educational qualifications, lead an active life in their 60s, and even first half of the 70s, and have a positive frame of mind looking for opportunities for a more active, creative and satisfying life.

It is comforting that the Government of India has affirmed to develop policy instruments for the elderly disadvantaged. As noted earlier, in the last several years several initiatives have been taken. A large beginning has been made in the latest Union [7]. Cumulatively, these could possibly have a cascading effect on consumer spending and open up hitherto unexplored markets – provide staples at affordable prices. The numbers at the bottom of the pyramid are huge, over 100 million by 2050. It is an opportunity and challenge that marketers in India cannot afford to miss.

Anticipating such trends is not enough. It is to be seen how society at large and marketers in particular will respond to the demographic transition. While some initiatives on the public policy front are clearly visible, concerted efforts are still needed to address the issue of aging in India, more so given the large inequalities in income levels, dependency ratios, and aging index, across regions and gender in particular. It will be instructive to share the experiences with other nations in the less and least developed regions in particular.

More importantly, the aging index in India by 2050 is expected to exceed 100 and the structure and distribution of her population would resemble nations like Russia, the UK and Ireland, and Sweden as seen today; these nations presently have an aging index higher than 100. It can be safely surmised that India is about 50 years behind such nations in demographic transition.

Therefore, both from the perspective of public policy and business, it would be expedient for countries in the early stages of demographic transition (like India) to closely look at the situation and experience of these nations. Secondly, measures should be put in place to meet the consequences of population aging.

References

1. Aged can earn from property. *Business Standard*, 01 Mar 2007, p. 3
2. BEST plans to buy 30 low-floor buses *Auto Monitor*,15 Nov 2004, p. 28
3. R.D. Blackwell, P.W. Miniard, J.E. Engel *Consumer behavior*, 9th edn. (Thomson Asia, Singapore, 2002)
4. P.F. Bone Identifying mature segments. *J. Consum. Market.* **8**(4), 19–32 (1991)
5. Buggy comes to aid of elderly, disabled, *Times of India*, 29 Apr 2007, p. 4
6. Centre allocates over Rs. 700 crore for public health, *Chronicle Pharmabiz* 29 Mar 2007, p. 32
7. P Chidambaram, *Budget 2008–2009: Finance Minister, P Chidambaram's speech before the Parliament* (Ministry of Finance, Government of India, New Delhi, 2008) 1. P.F. Drucker, *The daily drucker: 366 days of insight and motivation for getting the right things done.* (HarperCollins, New York, 2004)
8. Corsendonk hospitality arm extends to elderly in India, *Economic Times*, 25 May 2005, p. 8
9. P.F. Drucker, Population trends and management policy. *Harvard Bus. Rev.* **29**(5), 73–78 (1951)
10. P.F. Drucker, *The daily drucker: 366 days of insight and motivation for getting the right things done.* (HarperCollins, New York, 2004)
11. P. Engardio, C. Matlack, Global aging, *BusinessWeek Online* 31 Jan 2005
12. Euromonitor, *Consumer lifestyles in India*, (Global Market Information Database) (Euromonitor, Singapore, 2004)
13. J.K. Galbraith, John Kenneth Galbraith's notes on aging. *Encyclopædia Britannica Online* (1999) http://search.eb.com/eb/article?tocId=9344838. Accessed 2 July 2005
14. Harmony – a magazine for senior citizens launched by Tina Ambani, India Today group to distribute, *Insight Media* (2004, Jun 14)
15. Herbal drug to arrest cognitive decline, *Express Pharma Pulse* 8 Oct 1998, p. 11
16. Indicus Analytics, *The size of the Indian market: 2000 and beyond – Final report for Reebok India Limited* (Indicus Analytics, New Delhi, 2000). http://www.indicus.net/Home.aspx?id = Studies& submid = Consumer%20Economics%20%26%20Market& sr_no=10005. Accessed 10 Aug 2007
17. P.A. Kennett Marketing financial services to mature consumers. *J. Ser. Market.* **9**(2), 62–72 (1995)
18. B.R. Lewis Demographics, in *The Blackwell Encyclopedia of Management* ed. by C.L. Cooper (Blackwell, Oxford, 2007)

19. LIC subsidiary plans to set up communes for senior citizens, *Times of India*, 5 Jul 2002, p. 13
20. LICHFL launches retirement village, *Realty Plus*, 30 Apr 2006, p. 14
21. D. Loudon, A.J. Della Bitta *Consumer behavior: concepts and applications*, 3rd edn. (McGraw-Hill, New York, 1988)
22. Manipal hospital adds geriatrics department, *Business Standard* 26 Feb 2007, p. 5
23. Ministry of Social Justice and Empowerment, *National policy on older persons* (Government of India, New Delhi, 1999) http://socialjustice.nic.in/social/sdcop/npop.pdf. Accessed 10 July 2007 http://www.moneycontrol.com/mccode/news/article/news_article.php?autono=328612. Accessed February 29, 2008
24. G.P. Moschis Marketing to older adults: an overview and assessment of present knowledge and practice. *J. Consum. Market.* **8**(4), 33–41 (1991)
25. G.P. Moschis, E. Lee, A. Mathur Targeting the mature market: opportunities and challenges. *J. Consum. Market.* **14**(4), 282–293 (1997)
26. Planning Commission, *National human development report 2001*. (Government of India, New Delhi, 2002)
27. C.D. Schewe Marketing to our aging population: Responding to physiological changes. *J. Consum. Market.* **5**(3), 61–73 (1988)
28. Senior citizens' saving scheme proves a hit. *Economic Times*, 8 Apr 2005, p. 3
29. M. Singh, PM launches Indira Gandhi National Old Age Pension Scheme (Prime Minister's Office, New Delhi, 2007). http://pmindia.nic.in/speech/content.asp?id=614. Accessed 19 Nov 2007
30. M.R. Solomon *Consumer behavior: buying, having, and being*, 5th edn. (Prentice-Hall of India, New Delhi, 2002)
31. P.T. Sorce, P.R. Tyler, M.L. Loomis Lifestyles of older Americans. *J. Ser. Market.* **3**(4), 37–47 (1989)
32. Taj hotels unveils new package for the elderly. *Financial Express*, 5 Aug 2003, p. 4
33. TCI launches senior citizen holidays. *Express Travel & Tourism*, 31 Aug 2004, p. 13
34. The I and me consumer. *India Today*, 12 Jul 2004, p. 20
35. United Nations, *World population prospects: the 2004 revision* (Population Division, Department of Economic and Social Affairs, United Nations, 2004). http://esa.un.org/unpp. Accessed 21 Jan 2006
36. United Nations, *World population prospects: the 2005 revision (medium variant)* (Population Division, Department of Economic and Social Affairs, United Nations, 2005). http://esa.un.org/unpp. Accessed 21 Jan 2006
37. Urban-rural split impacts senior citizens. *Economic Times*, 13 Nov 2004, p. 1
38. M.S. Varma, Pensions growth a nightmare, *Financial Express* 31 Jul 2006, p. 5

Chapter 24
Silver Markets and Business Customers: Opportunities for Industrial Markets?

P. Mertens, S. Russell, and I. Steinke

Abstract Demographic change will pose distinct challenges for companies. The ratio of people over 65 years of age will rise in all triad countries. At the same time, the number of younger people, and thus recruits in all education levels, will drastically decline in Japan and Germany. In the USA, a shortage of highly skilled and educated workers is expected. The employment rate of aged people will therefore rise. Companies can react on many different levels. On the one hand, they can make it a business opportunity by developing and selling products and services that support older people. On the other hand, companies will have to cope with fewer younger workers. We discuss several ways to do this: (i) to prevent loss of skills from retirement, (ii) to accommodate older workers, and (iii) to survive with fewer workers. These could lead to B2B products and services that can help companies to solve the issues involved. We look at these possibilities in turn and find that they each lead to ideas that have one or more of the following properties: (i) they are actually B2C products, (ii) they are management or organizational solutions or services, or (iii) their benefits are not specific to older workers but benefit all employees. Thus, we are led to the conclusion that the technical products best suited for the B2Industry silver market will not be "silver-specific" products, but products "designed for all" with an emphasis on usability and problem solving.

Introduction

Demographic statistics show that the ratio of people over 65 to those under 65 will increase by a factor of two in all triad countries (Fig. 24.1)

This effect will have a severe impact on many parts of society. There will be challenges in the financing of retirement and health care, and there will be shifts in the purchase behaviors of shifting consumer groups. In this chapter, however, we will concentrate on the impacts on companies. These impacts include a shortage of younger workers, and a shift towards a higher numbers of older workers. We will

Ratio "over 65" to "15 to 65"

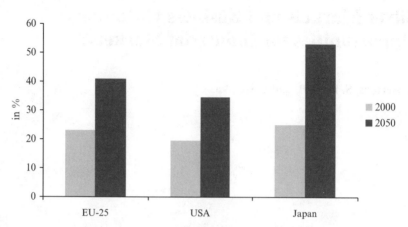

Fig. 24.1 Dependency ratio; defined as the percentage of people over 65 (retired) compared to people between 15 and 65 (working age population) [3, 20]

briefly summarize our conclusions on the consequences, and how these may lead to B2B (business-to-business) business opportunities. However, we first would like to take a more detailed look at the statistical data.

Although the forecast above requires assumptions on future birth rate statistics and migration, implications for companies with regards to their workforce are unambiguous, because the 20 year olds to be hired in 20 years have already been born. A look at the age "pyramids" of Japan, Germany, and the USA tells an undisputable story.

In Japan, a very pronounced baby boom in the years after World War II led to a maximum population increase. This group is now going into mass retirement. Accordingly, one of the major concerns about demographic change in Japan is the retention of the knowledge and skills of these retiring baby boomers (see, for example, [12]). This situation is very similar in the USA.

In Japan, an additional effect can be seen: although the baby boomers had fewer children than their parents, their sheer number produced an "echo baby boom." However, the birthrate has kept declining, leading to an extremely low birthrate for echo baby boomers. The number of newborns is still shrinking, and in 2006, Japan has seen the first year of negative population growth.

This effect is less pronounced in the USA and Germany. However, although the number of children in the USA seems to be more stable, companies there still report shortages of highly skilled and educated workers.

This can also be seen very strikingly in Japan, where we already see a decline of engineering students. From 2001 to 2006, this number declined from 463,000 to 425,000, a decline of more than 9% [9]. This is in spite of growing numbers of foreign students, especially from other Asian countries, accepted to engineering departments in Japan.

In Germany, the baby boom was later than in either Japan or the USA, so that some of the challenges treated here will become acute about 5–10 years later. However, it is forecast that when the population in Germany begins shrinking after around 2010, their labor force will shrink twice as fast [7, 8].

As a prosperous economy requires growth, this situation requires a solution. As the example of the USA shows, immigration and higher female participation in the workforce can be only partial solutions.

Therefore, in all countries mentioned, the employment rate of older workers is expected to rise. To get a feeling of the severity of the change, we offer some telling data [20, 21]:

- In the USA, more than 25% of the working-age population will reach retirement age by 2010, resulting in a potential worker shortage of nearly 10 million people.
- The number of the total US workforce aged 55 or more will increase from 21.8 million in 2003 to 31 million in 2010, a growth rate four times faster than that of the overall workforce.
- In the European Union (EU), the number of elderly people (age 60+) will increase by almost 50% between 2005 and 2050. In absolute numbers this means around 151 million in 2005, around 198 million in 2025, and around 226 million in 2050 [20].
- The EU workforce with ages from 15 to 59 will shrink from 462 million in 2005 to 405 million in 2025, and down further to only 330 million in 2050.

Figure 24.2 shows that Japan and USA already have a quite high rate of employment of older workers. However, in the EU, an increase of this rate will be needed in order tap the big potential of the additional older employees.

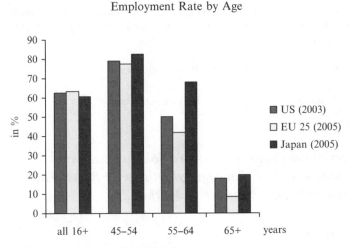

Fig. 24.2 Employment rate by age [3, 10, 20, 21]

The facts of demographic change pose both challenges and opportunities for companies. Responding to the challenges for companies is now a very active research field, and it has been treated in many publications, for example [2,5,13,14]. According to Mertens et al. [13], the challenges can be grouped in five categories:

1. Ensuring innovativeness
2. Retaining older workers and expertise
3. Accommodating older workers
4. Reducing company costs and risks
5. Other issues

The paper also contains a number of recommendations for company actions. The present paper aims at discussing business opportunities for companies arising from demographic change, but restricted to the B2B case. We see two broad categories of B2B business ideas that can be defined as:

1. Improving business success by supporting employees in older age groups.
2. Improving business success by helping companies cope with the challenges posed by demographic change.

We will address these two areas in turn.

B2B Business with Products Supporting Employees in Older Age Groups

This idea relates to products that older people use or are confronted with, or that are designed specifically with them in mind. Some of these products are not bought directly by the older persons, but instead by companies selling or catering to them. We briefly look at two big categories of this kind:

1. Components for products, where these products are ultimately bought and used by older people
2. Products for the healthcare and elderly care markets

Components for Products That are Sold to Customers – Where These Customers Use, Package, or Otherwise Resell These Products Ultimately to the Silver Market

In this first category, some examples are:

- Automotive components: As retired people become more numerous, and also much healthier than they used to be in most of the twentieth century, they will demand self-determined mobility and will use cars in much greater numbers than before. Still, on average, this customer group will have specific requirements to cope with diminishing eyesight, decreased flexibility in body movement, reduced ability to concentrate for long periods of time, etc. For this group of customers, car companies as well as automotive supplier companies are developing features and devices that make it easier and safer to use vehicles. Examples include seats and doors that make entry more comfortable, safety devices like night vision enhancements, parking aids, distance radars, and easy to see and interpret signs and instruments in the car.

These components are usually developed by a supplier OEM (original equipment manufacturer) for the car company.

- Increasingly, older people will become accustomed to the lower costs and the higher convenience achieved with digital appliances. For instance, ATMs (automatic teller machines) and other digital public-use equipment (like airline check-in machines, vending machines for tickets, and so on) have low or zero usage fees, yet they help to reduce the complexities and time burdens of banking and travel.

These consumer-support products are usually bought by businesses that are service providers. The service providers in turn often heavily influence the direction of further developments in conveniences.

So, both groups of examples have in common that, although they are B2B products, they share the following characteristics:

- They are designed with a "silver" end user in mind. As such, when looking at end user requirements, market research, market acceptance, and so on, they should instead be treated like B2C (business-to-consumer) products. This assertion is further supported by the need to extensively test these products for safety, utility, and usability with the intended customer group.
- The B2B customer has a lot of influence on the product design. In fact, this B2B firm is the customer that deals directly with the end customer.

Therefore such "OEM B2B products" cannot be viewed as a typical B2B business situation.

Another point of view would stress that many successful B2B companies, emphasize that the best way to help improve the business of the industrial customers is to obtain an in-depth understanding of the end customer's needs. This puts us back into the B2C area, which will be covered elsewhere in this book.

Products for the Health Care and Elderly Care Market

This market will be driven by the following demographic and scientific facts:

- The proportion of the world population over 65 will increase.
- The life expectancy will increase in all countries. The most dramatic increases of life expectancy, as well as number and relative proportion of older people, will happen in Asia, Africa, and South America.

- Age-related diseases like Alzheimer's, Parkinson's, diabetes, many forms of cancer, and others, will increase.
- The health care systems in most developed countries are already financially stressed.
- Most people needing special care as elderly citizens will be living in poor or emerging economies, where health and elderly care is challenging even today.
- Dramatic progress in biology and medicine, using genomics, proteomics, and other technologies will extend life and health.

Today's hope is that with current technological developments, we will develop ways to substantially improve the health and care provided to elderly persons. The focus of efforts here lies in new treatment ideas, as well as efficiency improvements such as:

Preventive medicine
- It is much better for the patient, and much more cost effective, to prevent disease than to rely on remedial medicine. Promising ideas to do this include an increase of in vitro diagnostics and telemedicine, as well as novel testing and screening methods. For example, health officials in Scotland want to help prevent blindness resulting from diabetes by conducting special tests for all diabetes patients. Authorities are using software from Siemens to call the approximately 300,000 people in Scotland at risk into screening centers, and then to analyze the test results. In the centers, a screening of the ocular fundus enables doctors to detect alterations in the blood vessels of the eye very early. Such alterations can indicate, for example, calcification of the veins, which can be related to cardiovascular disease. In the eye, the veins are very small, so that changes can be detected very early. The images are automatically analyzed with image recognition software, which identifies alterations and classifies them for the use of the doctors.
- Some examples following this approach are especially well suited for emerging economies, as portable, simplified devices for testing are being developed that take advantage of the growing ability of wireless communication in many countries. The availability of efficient, high tech but affordable diagnostics can have an enormous impact, both on developed and on emerging economies.

Personalized medicine
- Progress in medical science gives us hope that treatments based on the patient's personal genomic and proteomic makeup will allow more targeted treatments, which are more effective and also cheaper. Figure 24.3 shows an example: A combination of blood tests (in vitro diagnostics) and imaging technology (molecular imaging) enables personalized medicine. (1) A fluid analysis is performed. (2) In vitro tests indicate disease markers. (3) PET/CT scan localizes and characterizes the abnormality. (4) Data integration. Thanks to knowledge-based IT, doctors determine the ideal combination of medical treatment. (5,6) Follow-up with in vitro and in vivo tests indicating steadily diminishing concentrations of disease biomarkers and shrinking tumors. This allows personal targeting of treatment, which promises not only to be more effective, but also helps to select very

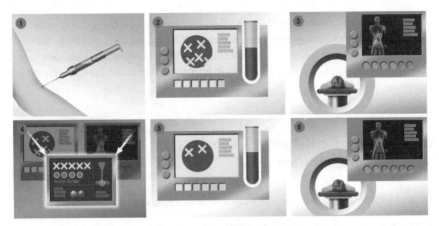

Fig. 24.3 Outline of tomorrow's molecular-based healthcare: *1* fluid analysis, *2* in vitro tests, *3* PET/CT scan, *4* data integration, *5, 6* follow-up with in vitro and in vivo tests

precisely which of the many (possibly very expensive) treatments is most promising. It therefore is both a promise of better treatment and of cost efficiency in health care.

- Healthcare IT: Today, in most hospitals, patient data are kept in many different forms and places: the manual patient file, X-ray photographs, letters and data kept in PCs, CT and NMR image files in computers, etc. The hospital personnel have to review these disparate sources and mentally combine them to form a state-of-the-art picture of the patient's situation. The combination of these disparate data sources across fields of medical specialty is supported by emerging approaches to computer-based collaboration, automatically translating field-specific terminologies, and focusing on the key issues in a particular patient's time-course of symptoms and treatments. Leveraging modern IT and communications technologies promises to dramatically improve efficiency in hospitals and health administration, in cost reductions for patient communication and monitoring, and in improving the quality of diagnosis and effectiveness of treatment. Today's healthcare IT enables the physician to pull together data from different examinations onto one PC in order to make a diagnosis. At the same time, the graphical nature of the presentation allows the physician to discuss diagnosis and treatment with the patient.

In conclusion, the health care and elderly care sectors will be strongly influenced by demographic change. We believe that companies providing solutions that aim at efficiency in healthcare will be successful providers for doctors, hospitals, health insurance agencies, and governments. Thus, the health care and elderly care markets are important opportunities for the B2B and B2G (business to government) market.

The driving characteristics of these markets will be determined by sheer numbers – demographic and financial – and scientific and technical progress mainly in biomedicine and information technology. These larger scale drivers will be far more important than any finer-grained personal characteristics of elderly consumers such as individual health history, exercise behavior, or budgeting and spending choices.

The assessment of business opportunities in these markets therefore requires a very specific approach, drawing heavily from knowledge of health care economics and biotechnology.

B2B Products for Helping Companies Cope with Demographic Change

To deal with this field, we suggest a division into three separate categories:

1. Prevention of the loss of skills from retiring workers
2. Accommodations for older workers
3. Survival strategies for business operations with fewer workers

We will analyze each of these categories in turn.

Prevention of the Loss of Skills from Retiring Workers

The area has been addressed in many publications [5, 13, 14]. The two principal action areas are:

• Delaying the time when employees retire
• Preparing for the fact that they will eventually leave

The first of these two has been addressed in detail in the publications cited above. They call foremost on companies to begin to implement a program addressing the special needs of older workers. The measures employed are typically human resources (HR) department-based management systems, incentive programs, and sustained training programs. For example, apart from the protected legal status sometimes afforded to older workers to discourage age discrimination, HR programs can reduce distracting business situations like injuries and inter-employee complaints. Also, by emphasizing the benefits and mandates for cooperativeness and respect, HR can lay the foundation for a more productive inter-generational set of contributors. Incentives for sales or production achievements can be accompanied with recognition for teambuilding and idea sharing in social networks of contributors, for instance. As training technologies evolve, novel opportunities arise for acquiring and recovering expertise – such as in virtual world simulations and game-like scenarios or role-playing rehearsals of likely business situations.

These actions do not lead directly to B2B sales opportunities, with the exception of consulting and training to help companies set up their own programs.

The latter business opportunity, preparing for experienced employees to leave, will require both management solutions (for example intergenerational teams) and technical solutions (for example knowledge management). Here, we observe that many US and European authors, like the ones cited above, stress that any solution must be embedded in the company culture, especially in its HR management processes.

For example, retaining knowledge when people leave a company can be best dealt with by transferring knowledge to younger workers. For this, it is necessary to have both a culture where sharing knowledge is encouraged, both for the experienced people to share with others, and also for the younger people to respect and appreciate receiving the information. The development of a more sharing office or manufacturing-line culture does not follow a simple prescriptive flowchart. Instead, managers have to be trained and specifically rewarded to make measurable progress in these inter-employee interactions. Instituting the programs and progress metrics calls for skills derived from operations research and the social sciences, as well as a careful study of enhanced employee motivation in successful enterprises. Applying these findings as older employees retire, the entering groups of younger workers can thereby more fluidly integrate and absorb a larger portion of the possibly lost lessons and heuristic guidelines.

Next, since companies are subject to competitive pressure, to ensure cost efficiency of the knowledge transfer, a specific process should be in place [5, 13, 19].

Finally, the knowledge transfer process can be aided by knowledge management and training software and tools. Managing knowledge takes many forms, from better training manuals and search interfaces to contextually sensitive tools for ensuring company policy compliance and the focused application of previous business lessons learned. There are some simple recent approaches that show promise – like end-user document and email tagging, mapping of common domain terminology dependencies (taxonomies and folksonomies), and visual connectivity-mapping for circles of friends and reliable information sources. It is often more important to know how to get a human-experience-contextualized answer through a small set of personal contacts than to try to look up an isolated fact in a vast words-only database. So, implementing and improving a set of know-how tools and methodologies will likely give significant competitive advantages to tomorrow's globally-contending firms.

Thus, the knowledge transfer process can be aided by knowledge management and training software and tools. This is an approach that is especially favored by Japanese companies [11]. The emphasis on knowledge transfer is currently especially high in Japan because of the severity of the baby boomer mass retirement phenomenon.

In conclusion, helping companies prevent loss of skills from retirement provides B2B business opportunities for:

- Companies offering consulting and training for people and knowledge retention programs
- Companies offering knowledge management software and consulting

Obviously, these are niche opportunities rather than being capable of driving a large company's business.

Accommodations for Older Workers

Today's older workers are healthier and more motivated to continue working than those of 20 years ago. Today's 70 year olds are in this manner more like yesterday's 60 year olds.

Since there have always been employees aged between 60 and 65, they are not a new, unknown group in the workforce. Only the ratio of older to younger workers is changing. Consequently, we do not expect completely new product requirements, but rather a shift in the relative importance of requirements.

When looking at the literature cited above, it is a very wide field that addresses this area. Issues addressed include:

- The working environment
- The social working environment (intergenerational teams, travel, etc.)
- Payment schemes, insurance, and pension
- Work schedules: part time, retirement
- Health management
- Lifelong learning and training

All but the first of these issues require solutions in management and processes, focusing on the HR system of the particular company. Again, this leads to business ideas for specialized consulting companies, but not for companies dealing in technical products.

Learning and training are key factors for assisting older workers in their productivity and self-esteem. Solutions addressing this include knowledge management systems, which have already been discussed.

Working Environment

Older employees experience deterioration of physiological capabilities and to some extent cognitive abilities. Workplace design that takes account of an aging workforce has to address the specific needs of elderly. Age-related constraints have to be compensated for in order to maintain efficiency of work and accessibility of tools. It is necessary to design a work environment that makes allowance for the wide range of capabilities of the elderly.

Accessibility – defined as a product's capacity to be used by everyone, regardless of abilities or disabilities – is important at two levels:

- Older employees need an appropriate physical working environment
- Accessibility of hardware and software at the workplace has to be assured

Physical Working Environment

The major requirements and business opportunities for the design of an appropriate physical working environment come from the specific health-related needs of older workers and from various regulatory requirements. Considerations may address:

- Diminished visual or hearing acuity
- Diminished physical strength and endurance
- Higher risk of injury from repetitive work and mobility-related accidents
- Lower tolerance for heat, humidity and noise

Many of these issues can also be addressed by appropriate staffing, and by very simple measures like:

- Good ventilation, air conditioning, and temperature control
- Increased illumination of the environment
- Availability of transport equipment (carts, shelves, cranes, etc.)
- Reduced ambient noise
- Increased levels of luminance contrast

Accessibility of Hardware and Software

The efficient use of tools for work by older employees requires appropriate human/ system interactions. Besides sensorial (visual, hearing, haptic) and fine motor skills restrictions, design for an aging workforce has to consider age-related cognitive changes. Not all facets of cognition deteriorate with age. Semantic memory, for instance, including factual knowledge, is not affected by age. Some older people actually show better performance in this respect than younger people [15]. Age-related impairments and capabilities do not apply to all elderly people to the same extent. They vary from person to person and may occur in different combinations. Examples of age-related cognitive changes are:

- Decrease in selective attention. Older people have more problems in filtering out irrelevant information [17].
- Decrease in working memory capabilities [4]. This involves short term memory for temporarily storing and simultaneously managing information. It is required to accomplish complex cognitive tasks (comprehension, learning, reasoning).
- Divided attention, which allows completion of more than one task simultaneously (e.g. operating a machine and talking on the phone), decreases with age.
- Fluid intelligence, including information processing (capabilities to differentiate, compare, classify), is reduced [1]. This is necessary for solving new problems.
- Reaction times get longer.

Creation of work environments that are accessible to an older workforce starts with the analysis of user requirements and needs. This includes consideration of specific sensorial, fine motor, and cognitive capabilities as well as an analysis of the context of use in the daily work of older employees. Analyzing the usage context of interactive products includes looking at goals, workflows, task characteristics, equipment (hardware, software, materials), and the physical and social environment. The results of this analysis, supplemented by usability and accessibility standards, provide the basis for the definition of usability (including accessibility) goals. They are crucial for the subsequent design of the user interface. In the design process, use may be made of specific interaction technologies and recommendations that turned out to be supportive for elderly workers. Some examples:

- Multimodal user interfaces allow compensation of reduced sensorial and/or fine motor abilities. For example, visual impairments can be compensated by assistive audio technology such as audio output in addition to textual output. Voice recognition as an input mode might substitute keyboard typing.
- To offset reduced working memory faculties, the interface should present a reasonably limited number of interaction options at any one time [6, 16]. Extended periods of time looking for information or possible user/system interactions should be avoided. The placement of visual cues in user interface design can reduce search time.
- Recommended means of counteracting reduced visual abilities are high-resolution computer monitors, high color contrasts, and minimal demands on peripheral vision [18].
- Cues as user interface elements can be used to facilitate detection of task-critical information (e.g. indicating potential or actual hazards). Multimodality (using e.g. acoustic or haptic vibro-tactile cues) increases the effectiveness of cues. Cues lead to a change from selective to focused attention, which is, unlike selective attention, not age-related. Incorporation of cues is also advisable because elderly people show reduced abilities regarding divided attention and fluid intelligence.
- To overcome reduced sensorial-motor skills, different input modes to control a device can be offered (e.g. keyboard, mice, trackballs, head trackers, hand trackers, voice).
- Individualization of the interface allows the interface to be adapted to the specific abilities and needs of the user. This may cover font size, selection of input and output devices, the speed and size of the pointer, the color and blink rate of the pointer, background and display colors, and the volume and speed of audio output.
- Personal preferences on one device at the workplace should be portable to other devices.
- Accessibility features should be easy to activate or deactivate.

In designing work tools suitable for older employees, consultancy by user interface experts at early stages of the planning of hardware and software is essential. This approach avoids the need for costly posterior adaptations. Existing workplaces should be evaluated. Usability tests of hardware and software in reference to requirements analyses and usability/accessibility standards are fundamental to improving workplaces for an aging workforce.

Incorporating accessibility features and measures in the working environment supports effective task performance by elderly workers. The majority of accessibility features for the elderly also benefit younger employees. Needless to say, all of these measures would benefit all employees.

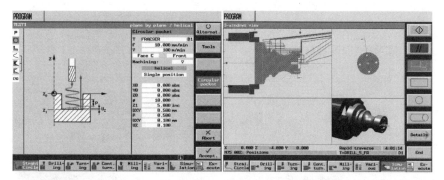

Fig. 24.4 Innovative graphical programming of machine tools, with examples from milling (*below left*) and turning (*below right*). The figure shows using these features when transferring knowledge from older to younger employees

Another group of more specific ideas for enhancing the physical working environment is based on innovative solutions from the IT and automation areas:

- Automation products that allow workers to program in terms that are natural for their workplace, namely drawings, measurements, and metal working processes. Figure 24.4 demonstrates one example: Workers do not have to program in programming languages, but can interact with the machine controls in terms of drawings, measurements, and metal working processes including simulation. This not only makes it easier to put in the desired work to be done on the workpiece, but also allows easier use of the experience older workers can bring to the workplace. In addition, the simulation allows one to check the results, again in a graphic form, leading to better quality of work results.
- Adaptive automation systems to prevent repetitive input and facilitate knowledge transfer; integrated knowledge management.
- Force-assist robots and other devices, automation equipment.
- Integrated PLM (product lifecycle management) software including engineering, design, manufacturing, and others, leading to improved working conditions in engineering and R&D (research and development).

On a closer look, all of these ideas will benefit not only the older workforce, but will improve working conditions and productivity for all employees. This echoes findings about barrier-free or universal design before: The liftMatic oven is an example of design for all (Fig. 24.5). The design of the product takes into account the needs both of the elderly and of people with disabilities. It mounts on the wall like a cabinet. At the push of a button the entire oven floor can be moved up and down. The liftMatic is very easy to operate because it is filled from below and food is always at eye level. The user can reach the cooked food from three sides and the controls are easy to reach. Illumination is optimal. The self-cleaning mechanism eliminates the need for cleaning inside the oven. The design of this product is appealing to all consumers.

Fig. 24.5 The liftMatic (Siemens) is an example of design for all

In conclusion, accommodating older workers can lead to business ideas in:

- Consulting and knowledge management
- Working environments focusing on accessibility for the aging workforce (ease of use, design for all)

Survival Strategies for Business Operations with Fewer Workers

As said in the beginning, especially for those companies in Japan and in Western Europe, there will need to be a high degree of coping with fewer workers in their home bases, even when taking immigration into account. This will increase the demand for automation equipment and robotics in manufacturing, and will also increase demand for integrated PLM software to streamline the product lifecycle from development and design through to manufacturing, including design of manufacturing equipment and automation software.

This last approach will require a suite of software tools that enable a seamless integration of all those processes (Fig. 24.6). Modern PLM software allows

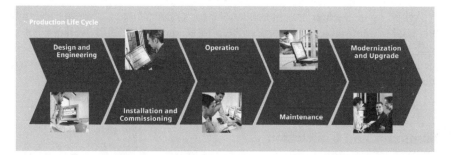

Fig. 24.6 Schematic view of the seamless integration from engineering through installation, commissioning, asset management and plant operation

Fig. 24.7 Simulation of production setup and environment

for the production of a new product simultaneously with planning its future production. In a production site it will be very important to be able to simulate not only the production itself, but also the automation (to survive with fewer workers) and the ergonomics (to accommodate a growing percentage of older workers). Figure 24.7 shows an example combining automation, ergonomics, and the human–machine interface (HMI) mentioned in Section on "Accommodations for Older Workers". The virtual production scenario can be optimized regarding automation, ergonomics, visualization, and HMI, and more. Thanks to simulation technology, the complex processes of a complete factory can be optimized and downtime can be drastically reduced.

Again, as in Section "Accommodations for Older Workers", we observe that this kind of innovative products does help to accommodate older workers, but as well benefits all employees and makes sense for the younger demographic segments. Therefore, there will be multiple incentives for industry customers to use this equipment and software, independent of the Silver Market phenomenon.

Summary and Conclusion

In this chapter, we have analyzed whether the silver market phenomenon will lead to opportunities for businesses to provide business products and services.

The statistics tell us that not only will average age rise and lead to new requirements, for example in health care and for complex industrial products such as cars and ATMs, but also that the workforce will change, leading to a shortage of young, highly skilled workers, and a higher percentage of older workers.

We have analyzed these effects in turn. Putting it all together, we find several types of product ideas that can be addressed as being related to the silver market phenomenon. These examples fall roughly into six categories:

1. Supplying OEM companies that in turn serve the B2C silver market (as in automotive equipment, ATMs, ticket machines, etc.). This category is closely associated with B2C market ideas.
2. Products for the health and elderly care market. This is a very important issue. It has to be considered within the very different context of national health management systems and progress in medicine and biology.
3. Knowledge management software and consulting. Business-critical know-how must be captured from retiring workers, and transferred efficiently to younger replacements. Also, familiarity with the aging population is needed and their ways of thinking will be valuable. This familiarity can be promoted with specific knowledge-focused tools and targeted business process consulting. The increasingly knowledge-dependent marketplace will reward the increases in awareness of aging consumer and worker demands, and businesses that offer methods for improved knowledge utilization will also be rewarded. Knowledge management advances driven by these issues will then help to promote a richer environment for corporate diversity and innovation in goods and services overall. This category is a specific answer to the silver market phenomenon, but will probably remain a niche markets for specialized (and presumably mostly small) companies.
4. Automation equipment, including new possibilities of simulating production. This category is already a well-defined and big market, independent of the silver market phenomenon. Nevertheless it is supportive for the silver market/aging workforce, and is a major contribution for companies that have to cope with a shortage of workers.
5. Workplace products with an emphasis on ease of use and accessibility (design for all). The workplace products of this category have yielded examples like user

interfaces – universal design, adaptive automation, robotics and force-assist systems, learning and training systems, and knowledge management. All of these seem to benefit from a careful analysis of silver market requirements. However, this will not lead to completely new requirements, only to a higher emphasis on the usability issues. Thus, we expect that all users will benefit.

Category 5 comes closest to constitute a kind of B2B silver market. Thus, our summarizing conclusion is that the products best suited for the B2Industry silver market will not be silver-specific products, but well designed products with an emphasis on usability and problem solving, benefiting all sectors of the employee demographic.

References

1. P.B. Baltes, U. Lindenberger, U.M. Staudinger, Die zwei Gesichter der Intelligenz im Alter. *Spektrum der Wissenschaft* **10**, 52–61 (1995)
2. P.T. Beatty, M. Visser (eds.), *Thriving on an aging workforce: strategies for organizational and systemic change* (Krieger, Melbourne, FL, 2005)
3. Commission of the European Communities, *Confronting demographic change: a new solidarity between the generations*, Green Paper COM(2005) 94 (CEC, Brussels, 2005) http://ec. europa.eu/employment_social/news/2005/mar/comm2005–94_en.pdf. Accessed 16 Jun 2008
4. F.I.M. Craik, Age-related changes in human memory, in *Cognitive aging: a primer* ed. by D. Park, N. Schwarz, (Hove Psychology, Hove, 2000), pp. 75–92
5. D.W. DeLong, *Lost knowledge: confronting the threat of an aging workforce* (Oxford University Press, Oxford 2004)
6. A. Dickinson, R. Eisma, P. Gregor, Challenging interfaces/redesigning users, in *Proceedings of the 2003 conference on universal usability,* Vancouver, 10–11 Nov 2003 (ACM, New York, 2003), pp. 61–68
7. Federal Statistical Office, *Germany's population by 2050.* Results of the 11th coordinated population projection (Statistisches Bundesamt, Weisbaden, 2006) http://www.destatis.de/jetspeed/portal/cms/Sites/destatis/Internet/EN/Content/Publikationen/SpecializedPublications/Population/GermanyPopulation2050. Accessed 16 Jun 2008
8. J. Fuchs, D. Söhnlein, *Vorausschätzung der Erwerbsbevölkerung bis 2050*, IAB project no. 16/2005, (Institut für Arbeitsmarkt- und Berufsforschung, Nürnberg, 2005) http://doku.iab.de/forschungsbericht/2005/fb1605.pdf. Accessed 16 Jun 2008
9. Japanese Ministry of Education, *Basic school survey* (MEXT, Tokyo, 2007) http://www.mext. go.jp/b_menu/toukei/001/003/csv/tk1102.csv. Accessed 16 Jun 2008
10. Japanese Statistics Bureau, *Annual report on the labour force survey* (Ministry of Internal affairs and Communications, Tokyo, 2005)
11. JARA (Japan Robot Association), 2007 Mass-retirement (I) and (II), *ROBOT* **2007/03** p. 1 ff, **2007/05** p. 1 ff
12. F. Kohlbacher, *Knowledge retention and HRM: insights from the "year 2007 problem" in Japan*, Paper presented at the Association of Japanese Business Studies (AJBS) conference, Indianapolis, June 2007
13. A. Kuebler, P. Mertens, S. Russell, R. Tevis, Enterprises face the aging demographic – some options to overcome demographic challenges in a multinational company, *Int. J. Hum. Resour. Man. Dev.* (2008) (in press)
14. M. Leibold, S.C. Voelpel, *Managing the aging workforce: challenges and solutions* (Wiley, New York, 2007)
15. M. Martin, M. Kliegel, *Psychologische Grundlagen der Gerontologie* (Kohlhammer, Stuttgart, 2005)

16. C. Reynolds, S.J. Czaja, J. Sharit, Age and perceptions of usability on telephone menu systems, in *Proceedings of the of the Human Factors and Ergonomics Society 46th annual meeting*, Baltimore, 30 Sept–4 Oct 2002 (HFES, Santa Monica, 2002) pp. 175–179
17. W.A. Rogers, Attention and aging, in *Cognitive aging: a primer* ed. by D.C. Park, N. Schwarz, (Hove Psychology, Hove, 2000), pp. 57–73
18. F. Schieber, Human factors and aging: identifying and compensating for age-related deficits in sensory and cognitive function, in *Impact of technology on successful aging* ed. by K.W. Schaie, N. Charness (Springer, New York, 2003), pp. 5–99
19. Tenessee Valley Authority, *Knowledge retention: preventing knowledge from walking out the door* (TVA, Knoxville, 2006) http://www.tva.gov/knowledgeretention/pdf/overview.pdf. Accessed 16 Jun 2008
20. United Nations Population Division, Department of Economic and Social Affairs, Expert Group meeting on social and economic implications of changing population age structure, Mexico City, 31 Aug–2 Sept 2005, (UN Population Division, New York, 2005) http://www.un.org/esa/population/meetings/EGMPopAge/EGMPopAge.htm. Accessed 16 Jun 2008
21. H. Wan, M. Sengupta, V.A. Velkoff, K.A. DeBarros,, US Census Bureau Current Population Report, P23–209: *65+ in the United States: 2005* (US Government Printing Office, Washington, 2006) http://www.census.gov/prod/2006pubs/p23–209.pdf. Accessed 16 Jun 2008

Chapter 25
Business Chances in Personal Transportation: Traffic Safety for Older Adults

K. Mitobe

Abstract Japanese society has many problems regarding the aging population. This paper discusses safety changes in personal transportation for older adults. According to the statistics, the risk of traffic accidents among older adults is extremely high. In order to achieve traffic safety, it is important to address declining sensory and cognitive functions. We discuss three business chances aimed at reducing traffic accidents among elderly pedestrians: inspection technology, training technology, and assistive devices that compensate for cognitive functions. From the human factor study using virtual reality technology, the detailed situations of pedestrian traffic accidents become clear. Effective assistive technology can be developed based on risk factors for traffic accidents.

Introduction

The Akita prefecture is rapidly becoming an aging society in Japan. Medical care expenditures for the elderly, a shrinking number of working people, and increasing traffic accidents have emerged as social issues. Akita University has been studying the human factor in order to prevent traffic accidents. In this article, we discuss engineering techniques to enhance safe transportation for the elderly. Additionally, we describe business changes designed to address problems of personal transportation for older adults.

Automobiles are a popular means of personal transportation, but many older adults must stop driving due to declining cognitive functions to avoid the risk of traffic accidents. In general, the elderly are more aware of safety concerns than the younger generation. In 2004, traffic accidents caused over 55 billion dollars of social loss in Japan [3].

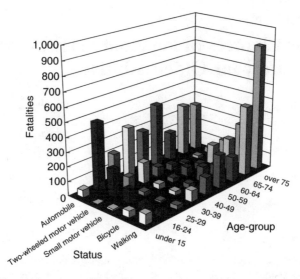

Fig. 25.1 Relationship between traffic fatalities, age group, and transportation devices

In 2005, there were 78.8 million people with driver's licenses in Japan [13]. Adults over 65 accounted for 12.4%. Statistical predictions indicate that the number of older adults will approach 34 million in 2020 [2]. This creates a huge market for assistive technology. Currently, there is no assistive safety device that can compensate for the declining cognitive abilities of older drivers. Therefore, most older drivers must give up their licenses in favor of walking, which increases the risk of falling. Figure 25.1 shows the relationship between traffic fatalities, age group, and transportation devices [13]. Statistical data shows that older pedestrians account for the majority of fatalities. To reduce traffic accidents among the elderly, preventing pedestrian traffic is key.

In the latest study of human factors, one third of subjects displayed declining risk avoidance (capacity of balance, oversight, cognitive ability of speed, estimative ability of self speed etc.) [7–10, 15, 17]. Those declining functions might induce traffic accidents.

It is difficult to assist pedestrians using safety devices, because many people do not want to carry the devices. Currently, safety devices are mounted inside of vehicles and alert only the driver. However, devices that alert the pedestrian of traffic danger might be better able to reduce accidents.

Usually, the active safety devices on a car sound an alarm only to a driver. However, if the active safety devices can convey the danger of an approach of a car to a pedestrian in advance, it might be able to reduce traffic accidents of pedestrian. We named this concept to Car-to-Pedestrian Friendly Interaction System.

Transportation System for Older Adults

To reduce traffic fatalities among older adults, we propose a three-step strategy involving active safety technology, public transportation, and risk avoidance. The invention of active safety and assistive technology is key to boosting vehicle sales among the aging population.

Assistive Technology for Drivers

Active safety technology in Japan is not only useful for elderly drivers but also for other age groups. Table 25.1 presents active safety devices that are currently on the market. Assistive technology is divided into two types: stand-alone and cooperative. Standalone systems are self-contained devices, while cooperative systems can communicate with other vehicles and can be embedded in roads. Unfortunately, there are no available active safety devices that can assist with declining cognitive functions.

Electric Wheelchairs

Electric wheelchairs (maximum velocity 6 km/h) do not require a driver's license under Japanese law and thus provide a useful form of transportation for older adults [12]. However, traffic accidents involving electric wheelchairs are increasing. In 2006, all fatalities and 60% of injuries resulting from electric wheelchairs involved older adults [21]. This shows that older adults are at risk of traffic accidents even at low speeds such as for wheelchairs. Future electric wheelchairs should have sensors that can detect pedestrians and vehicles. Furthermore, wheelchairs should have an automatic warning system in order to establish a friendly interaction with automobiles and pedestrians.

Public Transportation

Community buses that are subsidized by the local government enhance convenience for older adults and handicapped persons. If more older adults use community buses,

Table 25.1 Active safety devices that are currently available

Intelligence	Technology
Stand alone system	Lane-keeping system [17]
	Active headlights [6]
	Honda Night Vision [1, 19]
Cooperative system	Intelligent transportation system [20]
	Advanced cruise-assist highway systems [4, 5]

then the possibility of traffic accidents will decline. This administrative service functions effectively in downtown residential areas [16]. However, operation is difficult in local communities with dwindling populations.

Consideration of Transportation Systems for Older Adults

Providing a safe transportation system for older adults is important for preserving their quality of life. Public transportation is a good solution for older adults, but it is inconvenient in local communities with dwindling populations. Many types of assistive technology for drivers have been developed, but it is generally difficult for older adults to deal with multiple information sources. The human interface that sends information to older adults is an important consideration. Technologies that can compensate for the decline of cognitive functions must be developed, but we must first determine which functions to compensate for.

Pedestrian Safety

Older adults without driver's licenses often choose walking as a method of personal transportation, which increases their risk of falling. Unlike drivers inside their vehicles, there are no steel shields to protect them from the physical impact of an accident. Older adults, who constitute 25% of the population, are a vital part of the local economy. Social participation by older adults is very important for revitalizing the economy. Therefore, ensuring the safety of older pedestrians is an important issue.

Assistive Technology for Older Pedestrians

Traffic safety depends on capturing the attention of both drivers and pedestrians (Table 25.2). Typical policies by the National Police Agency in Japan instruct older pedestrians to wear bright clothing or reflective stickers. A warning device to alert the pedestrian using a cellular phone, and vehicle navigation systems have been developed but are not yet in practical use [14]. Full-time lighting devices have also been used to improve pedestrian visibility. Auditory cues, such as the sound of a car engine, can be helpful. Overall, however, there are few effective approaches to pedestrian safety in Japan. Thus, we propose the use of an active safety device, called the Car-to-Pedestrian Friendly Interaction System (CPFIS), to alert pedestrians to danger. Using a pedestrian simulator, we examine human factors in order to find the best method for CPFIS.

Table 25.2 Approach from a driver's side and a pedestrian's side for traffic accident prevention

Strategy	Measures
Alert for driver	Bright clothing for pedestrian
	Reflective sticker for pedestrian
	ITS with pedestrian's cellular phone [14]
Alert for pedestrian	Full-time lighting devices on a car
	Auditory cue of car's existence
	Car-to-Pedestrian Friendly Interaction System

Table 25.3 Applications of VR techniques for the traffic safety

Application	Social meaning
Practice	Traffic safety education
Screening	Checkup of physical fitness and recognition test
Rehabilitation	Training for the declining function
Human factor study	Analysis of traffic accident's factors
	Design of a safety car for pedestrians

Training System Using a Virtual Reality

Virtual reality (VR) is a useful method for evaluating the cognitive abilities of older adults as well as the risk factors that induce pedestrian traffic accidents. The results can help us to develop a method that draws a pedestrian's attention to a vehicle.

Advantages of Using a VR Technology

Table 25.3 summarizes the advantages of applying VR technology to prevent traffic accidents [11]. In cyberspace, it is possible to fully control time-varying environmental conditions such as visibility conditions, traffic environment, and the velocity of automobiles. VR techniques can reproduce traffic situations that are more likely to lead to accidents involving pedestrians based on records of past accidents. This leads to a priori training by experience, enabling pedestrians to avoid accidents by their own efforts.

While it may seem to be a simple matter, sophisticated perception, recognition, and decision abilities are required in order to avoid accidents while crossing streets. One must notice approaching cars, estimate their speed, and act on the basis of an accurate understanding of one's own position relative to each car. This depends on one's own walking speed, under all weather conditions and times of day. If the motion of a subject can be measured during practice, it can be used as an indicator of various abilities needed to avoid accidents. There is a possibility of identifying recognition and physical functions that have been degraded due to aging without being noticed (screening). If a degraded ability is identified, then a cyberspace environment is used as a training device to complement the lowered ability (rehabilitation). Data on the relation between accidents and human motion that are accumulated in the above processes will help to analyze factors leading to traffic accidents that cannot be obtained directly from on-the-spot investigations.

Designing cars that operate in cyberspace will help to enhance pedestrian safety (human factor). In cyberspace, the visual and audio information presented to the subjects can be reproduced, and the recognition, decision, and action of the subject can be investigated. Furthermore, cyberspace can connect via a fiber-optic channel, allowing extension to a client-server remote inspection system with existing technology. Figure 25.2 shows the block diagram of an inspection system constructed with the pedestrian simulator system. The inspection system is composed of a video presentation unit displaying the virtual traffic environment and measuring the motion

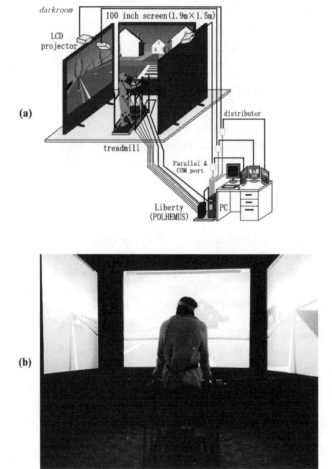

Fig. 25.2 Pedestrian simulator system: (**a**) block diagram of inspection system, (**b**) experiment scene

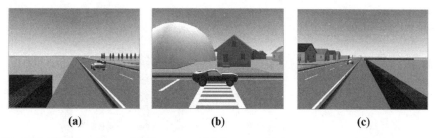

Fig. 25.3 Virtual road scene in cyberspace: (**a**) left screen, (**b**) front screen, (**c**) right screen

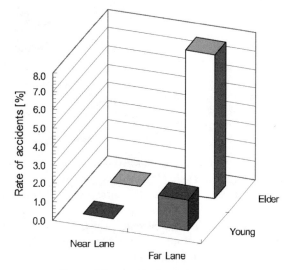

Fig. 25.4 Rate of accidents in each lane

Place of the accident

of the subject and a control computer [11]. Figure 25.3 shows the virtual traffic environment used in this system.

Human Factor of Older Pedestrians

Experiments were carried out with 15 subjects (nine younger subjects, six elderly subjects) in a total of 282 trials (excluding dropouts in the course of measurements and cases of violation of instructions) with the pedestrian simulator. There were 11 accidents, eight of which involved elderly subjects. A dangerous crossing was defined as a case in which a car passed within 1 m to the front or rear of the subject. Under the conditions of this experiment, most traffic accidents occurred in the daytime. There was only one accident at night.

Figure 25.4 shows the rate of traffic accident occurrence in each lane. The rate of accidents was five times higher for the elderly (1.7% for the younger subjects and

Fig. 25.5 Rate of accidents
and car velocity for each
group

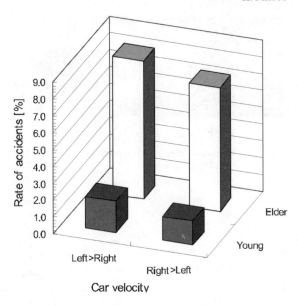

7.8% for the older subjects). All of the traffic accidents were due to a car approaching from the left side of the subject; accidents occurred in the far lane. Figure 25.5 shows the rates of accident occurrence for the elderly and young subjects as functions of the speed of cars approaching from the left (far) side and right (near) side. The rate of accident occurrence was higher when the speed of the car approaching from the left was higher that of the car approaching from the right. That is, traffic accidents were 1.3 times more likely to occur for the younger subjects under this condition and 1.1 times more likely for the elderly subjects.

Consideration of Strategy of Pedestrian Safety

Many of the traffic accidents reported for pedestrians occurred near their homes. From the human factor study using VR technology, the detailed situations of pedestrian traffic accidents become clear. Based on the risk factor of traffic accidents, we can develop effective assistive technology.

Business Chances in the Future Technology

There are three business chances in the process of reducing the traffic accidents of pedestrians in an aged society. The first business chance is the establishment of inspection technology. Health checkup technology using VR technique will be able to find the older adults who have risk factors of traffic accidents based on human factor study. This technique is not only useful for the prevention of traffic accidents but is also effective as a checkup technology for cognitive function. The second business chance is the establishment of training technology. Based on the results of tests, a proper training or rehabilitation program can be proposed in order to recover the declined ability of older adults. Recuperation of the cognitive function prevents older pedestrians from dangerous situations of traffic accidents. The third business chance is the establishment of the market of assistive devices that can compensate for older adult's sense and cognitive functions. The bottom line is that the assistive devices should be developed based on each older adult's declining function. In the case where it is impossible to recover the ability, we will be able to develop assistive devices in order to compensate for the declined function. The important point is that the assistive technology has to be developed based on each declined function, and it doesn't have to be based on latest technology.

Summary and Conclusion

Japanese society faces a lot of problems with the aging of the population. The percentage of elder people in traffic fatalities might be increased in all aged societies. However, we have been continuing the challenge in order to make an aging society affluent and vibrant. In this chapter, business chances in personal transportation for older adults has been discussed.

According to the statistics, the risk of traffic accidents involving older adults was extremely high during walking. In order to achieve traffic safety for older pedestrians, it is important to support the declining sense and cognitive functions. Unfortunately, there are no active safety technologies that can compensate for declining sense and cognitive functions of older pedestrian. One of the strategies for the prevention of pedestrian traffic accident is an enhancement of sensibility (visibility and audibility) of older adults to harmful cars. For example, a lot of business automobiles in Japan have mounted additional LED devices on the front grille in order to increase their visibility for older adults. However, it is not enough for prevention of all pedestrian traffic accidents. I believe that we can develop more intelligent "Car-to-Pedestrian Friendly Interaction Systems" based on the human factors of older pedestrians.

Three business chances existing in the process of reducing pedestrian traffic accidents have been discussed. The first business chance is the establishment of inspection technology. The second business chance is the establishment of training technology. The third business chance is the establishment of the market of assistive devices that can compensate for older adult's sense and cognitive functions. From the human factor study using VR technology, the detailed situations of pedestrian traffic accidents became clear. Effective assistive technology might be developed based on the risk factors of traffic accidents [18].

References

1. T. Aoki, H. Kitamura, K. Miyagawa, M. Kaneda, *Development of active headlight system*, SAE paper 970650, 1141 (1997)
2. Cabinet Office, *Annual report on the aging society 2006* (Government of Japan, Tokyo, 2006), http://www8.cao.go.jp/kourei/english/annualreport/2006/06wp-e.html. Accessed 13 Jun 2008
3. Cabinet Office, *Surveillance study on economic loss by traffic accident* (Government of Japan, Tokyo, 2007), http://www8.cao.go.jp/koutu/chou-ken/h19/houkoku.pdf
4. H. Hatakenaka, T. Hirasawa, K. Yamada, *JSAE Trans.* **38**(3–07), 15 (2007)
5. S. Hirai, H. Hatakenaka, I. Yamazaki, *JSAE Trans.* **38**, 6 (2007)
6. S. Ishida et al., in *Proceedings of 10th ITS World Congress*, Madrid, 16–20 Nov 2003 (IBEC, Birmingham, 2003)
7. K. Mitobe, T. Akiyama, N. Yoshimura, M. Takahashi, T. Ifukube, *J. ITE* **51**(6), 850 (1997)
8. K. Mitobe, T. Akiyama, N. Yoshimura, M. Takahashi, *T. IEE Jpn.* **118-A**(3), 245 (1998)
9. K. Mitobe, M. Kojima, Y. Terata, M. Takahashi, N. Yoshimura, *Soc. Mater. Eng. Resour. Jpn.* **12**(1), 16 (2004)
10. K. Mitobe, N. Yoshimura, B. Reimer, J.F. Coughlin, *J. Jpn. Council Traffic Sci.* **5**(1), 23 (2005)
11. K. Mitobe, J.F. Coughlin, N. Yoshimura, *IEICE* **J89-D**(10), 2174 (2006)
12. M. Mizohata, H. Kitagawa, *Papers City Planning* **38**, 41 (2003)
13. National Police Agency Japan, *Police white paper*(2006), http://www.npa.go.jp/hakusyo/h18/honbun/hakusho/h18/pdfindex.html
14. Nissan, *Nissan to test intelligent transport system using cell phones*, Nissan press release 17 Apr 2007, http://www.nissan-global.com/EN/NEWS/2007/_STORY/070417-01-e.html. Accessed 13 Jun 2008
15. N. Ooarata, K. Mitobe, N. Yoshimura, *J. Jpn. Council Traffic Sci.* **5**(1), 16 (2005)
16. A. Taniguchi, S. Fujii, *J. Jpn. Soc. Civil Eng. D* **62**(1), 87 (2006)
17. Y. Terata, K. Mitobe, N. Yoshimura, *IEICE* **J87-A**(2), 296 (2004)
18. Y. Terata, K. Mitobe, N. Yoshimura, *TVRSJ* **10**(1), 111, (2005)
19. T. Tsuji, *IEICE*, **89**(3), 272 (2006)
20. T. Tsuji, H. Hattori, M. Watanabe, N. Nagaoka, *IEEE Trans. ITS* **8**(3), 203 (2002)
21. K. Yonemitsu, S. Tsunenari, *J. Jpn. Council Traffic Sci.* **4**(2), 21 (2004)

Chapter 26
In-Vehicle Telematic Systems and the Older Driver

J. Meyer

Abstract The car is rapidly changing. In addition to its traditional driving-related functions it is becoming a platform for various services and devices. Some of these are involved in the driving task and can improve its ease, comfort, and safety. Others are unrelated to driving and allow the driver to engage in various activities while driving. The aging of the driving population and the tendency of older people in many parts of the world to continue driving for as long as possible pose major challenges regarding the design of such devices and their deployment in cars. Some advantages, as well as some limitations these devices may have for older drivers are pointed out. Design of future in-vehicle telematic systems will have to consider these issues in order to provide maximum benefits for the older driver.

Introduction

The Aging Driver Population

One of the major topics that will concern older people in the foreseeable future is transportation. It determines mobility and the ability to maintain adequate personal relations, to obtain services, and to engage in various activities outside the home. This issue becomes particularly important, considering the suburbanization of many countries. Fewer people tend to live in high-density housing environments that can easily be serviced by public transportation. When living outside these areas, transportation becomes almost exclusively a matter of using one's privately driven car. The consequence is that older people increasingly tend to continue driving for as long as possible.

The USA, as one of the countries with the highest use of personal vehicles for transportation, indicates some of the trends. A recent analysis of data from the National Household Travel Survey showed that 89% of older Americans (age 65+)

conduct their travel in personal vehicles. Older adults take fewer trips, travel shorter distances, and have shorter travel times than younger adults. However, the individually driven car remains the main means of transportation. Only 2% of travel is done by means of transportation other than using a privately owned car and walking [2].

The trend to continue driving for as long as possible is reinforced by a number of factors. Today's older generation is the first generation that grew up with almost universal driver's licenses and private cars. Also, there is a tendency towards active aging, which is supported by a steady decrease in disability with age. Even though more people may be diagnosed as suffering from diseases, such as hypertension or diabetes, the adequate management of these diseases allows them to function appropriately and without real disabilities [10]. In addition, today's older people are better educated than previous generations, which makes it likely for them to strive for continuing independence and mobility.

These trends pose significant challenges to the automobile industry as well as to society, which both need to decide how to cope with the changing characteristics of the driving population. It may have implications on transportation planning, the design of urban areas, the licensing and monitoring of drivers, and many other aspects.

The Changing Car

Not only is the driver population changing, but the car is also undergoing major changes. In fact, driving a car today differs for the first time greatly from driving early mass-produced cars. In the past, the driver obtained all information necessary for driving by looking through the windshield or the windows. There was little in the car a driver needed to direct attention to, except perhaps passengers. Today, drivers obtain more and more information for driving through alerting systems. Also, judging from trends in research, future cars will have enhanced and augmented vision systems that will support drivers when visibility is impaired and will enhance the likelihood the driver will see obstacles or other relevant information. The driving task itself is becoming automated to some extent, with features such as cruise control (which maintains constant speed) and intelligent cruise control (which also maintains constant headway from preceding cars). In addition, the car becomes a platform for various devices that combine computation and communication. These devices are often referred to as telematic systems.

The novel devices introduced into cars belong to three categories according to their relevance for the driving task:

1. *Vehicle control devices* are devices that are immediately involved in driving. They may provide information through enhanced vision systems, backward or blind spot cameras, or they may alert the driver about potential dangers through various types of warnings. Other systems are involved in the control of the vehicle. These include adaptive cruise control systems or intelligent braking systems.

2. *Driving assistance devices* provide information that is relevant for driving, but does not immediately affect vehicle control. Examples are navigation and traffic advisory systems that provide information on congestion or accidents on the route.
3. *Driver infotainment devices* allow the driver or passengers to receive entertainment, allow communication, or support driver comfort. These devices are unrelated to the driving task itself. Examples for these systems are car entertainment systems, cellular phones, email and web access from the car.

The three types of devices are not independent, and are, in fact, often implemented in the same system, using the same displays and controls. These devices can potentially interfere with safe driving, but they may also support driving safety in that they allow the driver to obtain information in ways that are optimally designed for the driving environment.

The changes in driving and the introduction of telematic systems in cars are likely to pose major challenges for older drivers. They will have to adapt to these new technologies. This may be particularly problematic for older drivers, whose main advantage may be their long experience with driving, which makes them, overall, very safe drivers. New devices may require the learning of new skills and may make previous experience obsolete. Also, these devices are often initially introduced into high-end cars, which are usually bought by more affluent (and usually older) costumers. Thus the older driving population (50+) will be the first to gain experience with these systems and will have to deal with technologies that are still not mature.

The automotive industry and system designers will have to face these challenges when designing in-vehicle devices, as well as the services that will be provided through them. In order to make them appeal to costumers, they must be of value for the older drivers. But, perhaps, the characteristics of the older driver may make the use of these devices particularly dangerous. This is a major dilemma with which manufacturers and societies have to cope. Below are some of the issues relevant for this dilemma and pointers to possible solutions.

Why Are Older Drivers Special?

Older people may differ from younger ones in numerous aspects (see [12], for an analysis of aging and driving). They belong to a different generation, which grew up with a different education system, different cultural values, and different technologies. This effect is often referred to as the cohort effect. Other differences may be related to the higher frequency of diseases and the consequent use of medication among older people. Some diseases and medication, such as medicine against hypertension or psychopharmacological drugs can negatively affect driving. A third, and probably the most important, reason for age-related differences are changes in sensory and cognitive functioning.

Particularly prominent are changes in vision. The decrease of visual abilities begins after the age of 20 and continues throughout a person's life. Shinar and

Schieber [16] already stated that all visual functions deteriorate with age, the amount, rate, and onset of deterioration varying widely between individuals and functions. While static acuity begins to deteriorate in the 60s, other visual abilities deteriorate earlier and performance differences between individuals increase with age (see [12] for a more detailed description of age-related changes in vision). Major visual abilities that decline with age include visual acuity (i.e., the ability to resolve small details when viewed from a distance), dynamic visual acuity (i.e., the ability to observe the direction and speed of a moving object), and the ability to focus on near objects. Particularly severe are age-related changes in night vision, contrast sensitivity, and recovery from glare. Night vision, for instance, starts to decline when a person is in his or her 20s, and continues to decline at an increasing pace throughout a person's life. Another visual property that is relevant for driving and decreases with age is the useful field of view (UFOV), i.e., the width of the visual field over which information can be acquired in a quick glance.

Other age-related changes that may affect driving and the use of in-vehicle devices include progressive decrease in hearing, which may start as early as 40. There are also complex effects of aging on attention. There is evidence that older adults have greater difficulty in dividing attention effectively, compared to middle aged and younger adults [1]. This is particularly relevant for in-vehicle devices, which almost necessarily require the driver to divide attention between driving and using the device. Some evidence for these difficulties was expressed in a UK survey of older drivers [7], many of whom indicated having problems with their car radio, while others stated that they don't have a problem with their radio, because they simply never used it when driving. Older drivers will be more strongly affected by the use of in-vehicle devices. Their driving is likely to be somewhat impaired by these systems, and they may compensate for this by driving slower and with longer headway [11].

The existence of age-related changes in memory is well established [8]. The memory difficulties may affect the use of new in-vehicle technologies, for instance by making it more difficult to remember procedures for using the system or by interfering with the recall of names and codes that are used in speech-activated systems. Another domain where age-related changes may impact performance is skill acquisition [3]. Generally, skill acquisition becomes slower with age, and a person will find it difficult to alter familiar ways of performing certain tasks. On the other hand, the procedural memory for familiar tasks and skills may remain intact up to a very advanced age. Thus a person is likely to be able to perform complex sets of actions, such as playing a musical instrument or driving a car. However, he or she may find it difficult to acquire some new skills that require changes in well-established routines.

Aging is also accompanied by a general slowing in processing speed. This causes a lengthening of response times and slower actions and in particular slower responses to unexpected events [4]. However, with respect to driving, studies on braking responses actually showed that response time was unaffected by driver age, as long as drivers expected the event to occur. Responses took longer and response time increased with age when events were unexpected [13].

A major problem for many older people is lowered flexibility. A recent extensive postal survey in the UK with more than 1000 respondents identified as major problems that cause difficulties for older drivers issues such as turning the head and looking out of the rear windows (56.1% of drivers reported this as a problem), as well as vehicle ingress and egress [7]. The lowered motility of the neck and head is a likely cause for accidents in which an older driver either collides with an object that is behind the car when backing up or fails, when changing lanes, to see a vehicle that comes up from behind in a parallel lane. This, in particular, is an issue for which adequately designed in-vehicle devices, such as alerts and visual aids, can provide clear benefits for the older driver.

It is important to develop a sound understanding of the causes for differences between age groups, because the different causes will make it more or less likely that certain differences will continue to exist in the future. If an age-related difference is caused by a physiological process, it will probably remain an issue that will require consideration in the future. If, however, a difference is due to cohort effects, the difference will exist only for a limited period of time, and it will eventually disappear. One possible example may be the use of computerized devices. Today's older population is often reluctant to use these devices, but this may not be the result of an age effect. The widespread use of computerized devices began in the 1980s, which may have been relatively late in the careers of current older people. Hence these people did not acquire the skills necessary to use these devices as part of their education or work. People who now approach the age of retirement are much more likely to have experience with computers and may eventually find computer-based devices in the car and in other domains very useful.

Designing Telematics for Older Drivers

A number of points need to be considered when designing and evaluating telematic systems and other in-vehicle devices for older drivers.

The Importance of Long-Term Evaluation

A major challenge for designers and manufacturers of new in-vehicle devices is the need to predict how these systems will affect driving (and in particular safety) and driver satisfaction. This prediction is particularly difficult because the effects of new technologies may change dramatically over time and may differ from the predictions derived from preliminary testing. Some technologies (such as the ABS system) had initial negative impact on safety and some time had to pass before people learned to use the new technology correctly. During this learning period, drivers may misuse the new technology, which may cause it to constitute a safety hazard in the short run. Thus technologies need to be evaluated in the long run. Even then, a device that was shown to be potentially useful may not improve safety and perhaps even lower it. This may be due in part to changes in the way people use the technology after the device is introduced. It is therefore crucial to evaluate the costs and benefits of technologies in the long run and assess what intervention or policy change is most likely to generate the desired positive effects.

User-Centered Design

The introduction of new technologies for older drivers should be based on the notion of "user-centered design" [14]. It requires the entire design process to be driven by the attempt to address the needs of the user and to adapt the product to the user characteristics. Usability considerations are of major importance for consumer acceptance and satisfaction in the design of almost all consumer products. However, in the context of in-vehicle technologies they are particularly important because of the inherent safety issues related to these devices [5].

The design of novel in-vehicle devices requires the application of knowledge and insights from a number of disciplines. These devices are by and large computerized, and theories, research, and recommendations from the field of human-computer interaction (HCI or CHI), cognitive engineering, ergonomics, and human factors engineering should be considered (for sources, see, for example, [6, 17, 18]). The different areas of research overlap, but the approaches and theoretical systems that were developed in each of them are sufficiently distinct to warrant a closer look at all bodies of literature. Even though there is extensive research in each of these fields, there are still large gaps in our knowledge on how to design in-vehicle devices, especially if these devices are to be used by older drivers.

Considering Older Drivers' Sensory Capabilities

As mentioned above, older drivers are likely to have diminished sensory capabilities, compared to younger people. Design for older users should therefore strive to maximize contrast and illumination. Also, most older people have presbyopia and require the use of corrective lenses to view close objects. Hence in-vehicle displays and devices that require vision of small details may be problematic. Drivers will not put on reading glasses to use a system and may find driving with bi- or multifocal glasses unpleasant.

One possible way to avoid the problems that arise with visual information displays for older drivers may be to choose auditory displays instead. However, hearing difficulties are fairly common among older adults, and they need to be considered when auditory displays are designed. Overall there is some evidence that older drivers may particularly benefit from multi-modality displays that combine visual and auditory information [9].

The Promise of Telematics for Older Drivers

The question of how to provide older drivers with an opportunity to drive for as long as possible, while minimizing the risks due to incapacitated and unsafe drivers, is a crucial topic that will require increasing attention in the future. One possible way to deal with this problem is through appropriately designed technologies. As Pauzie [15] pointed out:

1. Reducing the complexity of the driving task reduces the performance differential between young people and the elderly
2. Optimizing in-vehicle systems (improving the legibility and intelligibility of information, simplifying dialogue) with regard to the functional capacities of older drivers generally also benefits the rest of the user population

There is ample evidence that older people will not automatically reject new technology that provides information and assistance, in particular if interaction with the system is intuitive. This acceptance extends even to technologically highly complex systems, if these are easy to use.

It will be necessary to develop cars and technologies that can help older drivers deal with some of the changes that occur with age. Such systems, if designed and introduced properly, may allow an older driver to maintain her or his mobility for a longer time, improving their quality of life. These considerations are also crucial for the automobile industry, which needs to consider the characteristics of the changing driver population. Manufacturers who will adapt their cars to the needs of this population are likely to have a foothold in a growing and affluent market.

Clearly the issues will not be simply the development of new technological solutions. Rather, the successful implementation of these technologies will require the collaborative effort of specialists from a variety of disciplines. It will be necessary to implement the idea of user-centered design into the design process of these devices, considering the user from the very beginning. This will require the close involvement of specialists in the research of life styles, demographics, and consumer behavior who need to pay special attention to older consumers.

The new technologies will also require entirely new ways of thinking about methods for testing these devices. It is by no means assured that a technologically sound device that provides some benefits for the user will eventually be adopted. It is necessary to develop new models and methodologies to predict users' complex reactions to a new technological system and to adapt the system accordingly. One can, for instance, not simply assume that a system analysis that applies for the current usage patterns of a device will also apply when the device is altered. The benefits that are to be expected from a new technology have to be considered very carefully. A lane change warning system can serve as an example. It alerts the driver when she or he intends to move into a lane in which there is another car. Such a system provides great benefits for older drivers who often find it difficult to turn their head. The installation of such a system should help drivers avoid collisions and should make driving safer. However, drivers can potentially develop strong reliance on such systems. In extreme cases drivers may initiate a lane-change maneuver without bothering to look, waiting for the warning system to cue her or him if the lane is occupied. Given that the warning system will not be perfect (no system ever is), collisions are still likely to occur, and in these cases manufacturers may be held liable. Thus the introduction of such systems requires a careful analysis of all aspects of the use of such a system, a task that requires the development of adequate predictive tools.

The same applies to the design of telematic systems. Here, too, we are facing many unknowns regarding the effects of these technologies on drivers in various situations. The design of the device, the allocation of functions to it, and the design of the interface all require a thorough understanding of the interaction between users and technologies. This goes clearly beyond our current knowledge in this field. We need to expand the empirical basis for our work by collecting both field and laboratory data. In addition, we need to develop appropriate design methodologies that take into account the unique characteristics of the driving situations and the needs and properties of the driver. This will be particularly important for older drivers, who may have less ability to adapt to non-optimal design of the system. Finally, we need models of the use of the automation and devices for predicting how users will respond to a certain system design. Such models will allow us to move from the unsystematic engineering of human-vehicle systems that is practiced today to a more systematic and model-driven technique that approaches the methods used in other fields of engineering.

But, not only the design process needs to be reconsidered. The introduction of the new technologies into cars for older drivers also makes it necessary for car manufacturers to reconsider their roles. More attention will have to be paid to the familiarization of the new driver with the technologies in the car. The best ways to do this are still fairly unclear. Possibly car sales will have to include the use of a simulator or test track to teach the driver how to respond to different events with the complex technologies. In addition, older drivers in particular will need to have the technologies customized to their particular needs. This can be done by the driver, but with all likelihood optimal customization should be based on the objective evaluation of a specialist. This will require the development and validation of tools to determine the optimal configuration for a driver. Also, specialists for customizing cars to the needs of individual customers may have to be trained. It is unlikely that current sales personnel can be expected to do this job appropriately, unless they receive the tools and knowledge for this additional service.

Summary and Conclusions

This paper discusses some of the major issues that are relevant for the design of in-vehicle telematic systems for older drivers. The appropriate design of telematic systems for older drivers is a delicate balancing act. It needs to consider the requirements of older drivers and their characteristics, but it may also involve changing

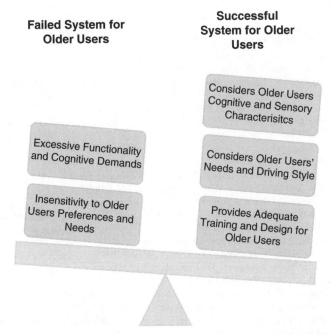

Failed System for Older Users

Excessive Functionality and Cognitive Demands

Insensitivity to Older Users Preferences and Needs

Successful System for Older Users

Considers Older Users Cognitive and Sensory Characterisitcs

Considers Older Users' Needs and Driving Style

Provides Adequate Training and Design for Older Users

Fig. 26.1 Factors affecting the successful or failed introduction of an in-vehicle telematic system for older users

usage patterns and needs through appropriate training and support. A schematic depiction of some of the relevant points is shown in Fig. 26.1.

The introduction of new in-vehicle technologies for older drivers requires us to expand the boundaries of our knowledge and our understanding in a wide variety of fields. It is likely that the insights gained here will be important in various domains, beyond the design of vehicles. Thus this may be an opportunity to develop some of the major technologies for the twenty-first century.

The new in-vehicle technologies, when designed for older users, are also likely to be one of the major business opportunities in the twenty-first century. Developing in-vehicle systems that are designed with the older user in mind and that are responsive to older drivers' needs can provide an important service for the older drivers and society, by increasing mobility and driving safety. They may also give manufacturers a major advantage over competitive brands that are less attuned to this rapidly growing market.

References

1. W. Brouwer, J.G. Ickenroth, R.W.H.M. Ponds, P.C. van Wolfelaar, Divided attention in old age, in *European perspectives in psychology, vol 2*, ed. by P. Drenth, J. Sergeant, R. Takens. (Wiley, New York, 1990), p. 335
2. D.V. Collia, J. Sharp, L. Giesbrecht, *J. Safety Res.* **34**, 461 (2003)

3. F.I.M. Craik, L.L. Jacoby, Aging and memory: implications for skilled performance, in *Aging and skilled performance: advances in theory and applications*, ed. by W.A. Rogers, A.D. Fisk, N. Walker (Erlbaum, Mahwah, NJ, 1996), p. 113

4. L.L. Falduto, A. Baron, *J. Gerontol.* **41**, 659 (1986)

5. M. Flyte, *Int. J. Vehicle Des.* **16**, 158 (1995)

6. M.G. Helander, T.K. Landauer, P.V. Prabhu, *Handbook of human–computer interaction*, 2nd edn. (North Holland, Amsterdam, 1997)

7. P. Herriotts, *Appl. Ergon.* **36**, 255 (2005)

8. L.L. Jacoby, J.F. Hay, Age-related deficits in memory: theory and application, in *Theories of memory, vol 2*, ed. by M.A. Conway, S.E. Gathercole, C. Cornoldi (Hove Psychology, East Sussex, 1998) p. 111

9. Y. Liu, *Displays* **21**, 161 (2000)

10. K.G. Manton, E. Stallard, L. Corder, *J. Gerontol. A Biol. Sci.* **53**, B59 (1998)

11. N. Merat, V. Anttila, J. Luoma, *Transport. Res. F* **8**, 147 (2005)

12. J. Meyer, Personal vehicle transportation, in *Technology for adaptive aging*, ed. by R. Pew, S. Van Hemel, National Research Council, Board on Behavioral, Cognitive and Sensory Sciences and Education (The National Academies, Washington, 2004), p. 253

13. P.L. Olson, M. Sivak, *Hum. Factors* **28**, 91 (1986)

14. A. Owens, G. Helmers, M. Sivak, *Ergonomics* **36**, 363 (1993)

15. A. Pauzie, *Recherche Transports Sécurité*, **81**, 203 (2003)

16. D. Shinar, F. Schieber, *Hum. Factors* **33**, 507 (1991)

17. B. Shneiderman, C. Plaisant, *Designing the user interface: strategies for effective human–computer interaction*. 4th edn. (Addison Wesley, Reading, MA, 2004)

18. C.D. Wickens, J.G. Hollands, *Engineering psychology and human performance*, 3rd edn. (Prentice-Hall, New Jersey, 1999)

Chapter 27
Taking Advantage of Adversarial Demographic Changes to Innovate Your Own Business

E. Osono

Abstract Any company faces the challenge of adapting to demographic change. In this chapter, we focus on adversarial change. What if a new customer segment emerges but has a very different set of needs? What if the growing customer segment brings subtle shortcomings in your offerings to the surface? Such is often the case with the silver market segment. These changes bring with them great opportunities for the company to innovate itself. The question is how? The distance of the organizational units and the leaders who are in charge of both the new and old businesses is critical. Also, when a company starts a new business, it has to carefully manage these three processes, namely: borrowing, forgetting, and learning. Focusing on organizational distance and the three processes, we have conducted comparative case studies of Toyota's adaptation to demographic changes in the USA, which has led to an insight about how organizational distance has contributed to innovation.

Introduction: Challenges of Demographic Changes as Opportunities for Innovation

The growing importance of the silver market in the aging society presents new business opportunities to many companies. However, when approaching a new customer segment, a company should consider what new processes and values it should *learn* for the new business [2], what it would like to *borrow* from the existing business if it would like to enjoy a competitive advantage over green field competitors [8], and at the same time, it should *forget* about the business processes and value of the existing system [2].

Silver customers will have unique needs, about which the company should learn. It is said that when baby boomers get old, their needs will be very different from the current elderly customers. However, approaching the silver market would be especially beneficial to a company's overall performance if the silver segment constitutes the leading customers in that other market segment, and this would enable the company to share the learning. The silver market for automobile companies is such a case. The physical limitations of older customers, which include weaker muscles, stiffer joints, diminished hearing and eyesight, and slower reaction times, require more user-friendly interior and exterior designs. These include knobs, switches and door handles that are easier to manipulate, wider door openings, higher seats and bigger, more visible numbers and letters on gauges and radio interfaces, as well as more intelligent support for their driving in the form of a semi-automatic parking system to help drivers parallel park and a monitoring system that attracts drivers' attention when it detects that their attention is not on the road. All these arefeatures thatwould be helpful for all drivers. It is reported that Ford helps young engineers to experience the physical limitations of elderly people by having them wear a special suit, goggles, and gloves that make movement more difficult, impedes their sense of touch when pressing buttons and turning knobs, and diminishes their vision [1]. As a result, now the door handles of most Ford cars and trucks can be gripped with a full palm-grasp [3]. Toyota asked the US design firm IDEO to study cars for elderly people. Also, it conducts research with professor Ryuta Kawashima, at the Institute of Development, Aging, and Cancer affiliated with Tohoku University, Japan, to develop a car that can keep elderly drivers alert to prevent accidents. Kawashima is the neuroscientist who designed Nintendo's megahit "brain-training" game.

These features are not overly emphasized because elderly customers do not want to be treated as elderly. However, by precisely meeting their needs, the company sheds light on the degree to which conventional products and services fail to even consider the needs of this target audience.

When the silver market segment grows large enough, overall business processes – not only product features but also sales and maintenance processes – will be geared towards them. Thus, the question is how to develop a new business that targets the silver market. Tushman and O'Reilly [11] noted that the distance of the organizational units and the leaders who are in charge of both the new and old businesses, in their words, "ambidextrous organizations and ambidextrous leaders," is critical.

Since no car company has developed an entire business geared toward the silver market, I would like to introduce comparative case studies of Toyota's adaptation to the US demographic changes, focusing on organizational distance and the three processes. Both cases can be said to have been successful, yet Toyota adapted different approaches in terms of organizational distance, which resulted in different challenges. The first case is Toyota's proactive courtship of Generation Y as automobile customers who apparently disliked the company's reliable but dull product image and the industry's unfriendly sales process [6]. Toyota launched a new product line, the Scion, which targets young customers, with a new marque, a new product development process, a new marketing approach, a new sales process, and a new business model. The second case is the Lexus, Toyota's way of accomodating baby boomers as they mature and expand into the US luxury segment [5]. For reasons of space, we will not discuss the Lexus case in as much detail as the Scion case, however, a comparison will be made to draw implications.

Scion, a New Business to Change the Old

Toyota grew up with the baby boomers in the USA. In the 1960s, baby boomers who had just come of age found Toyota's lineup of small cars with low prices and a low number of defects very attractive. In the 1970s, when the world experienced two oil shocks, Toyota as well as other Japanese automobile manufacturers established their position in the US market with fuel efficiency.

As the baby boomers aged, Toyota added bigger cars, such as the Camry, to its product lineup. As a result, Toyota's sales composition in the USA changed. Small cars and sports cars, which had occupied 74% of sales in the 1980s, decreased to 22% in 2000. Small pickup trucks halved from 18 to 9% during the same period, and medium and large cars increased from 7 to 32%.

In 2000, Toyota was no longer a popular brand for the younger generation. Young people thought of Toyota as an "old people's" car. The average age of Toyota's customers was 48 and getting older as the baby boomers aged (see Fig. 27.1 for Toyota's customer profile in the USA).

On the other hand, the youth market was expected to grow because a growing number of children of baby boomers, known as Generation Y (born between 1980 and 1994), were becoming old enough to buy cars. Generation Y comprises 63 million people, and is comparable to the 75 million baby boomers (the largest single group of US consumers until now) and is three times the size of Generation X (born between 1965 and 1979). In 2010, the youngest Generation Yers (those who were born in 1994), will reach 16, becoming old enough to drive. Each year until 2010, 4 million people will become 16 years old, and become potential new customers.

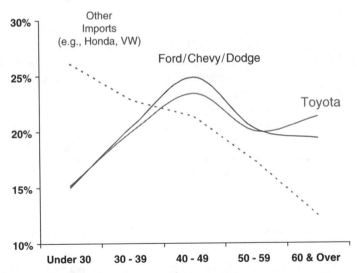

Fig. 27.1 Toyota's customer profile in the USA (Source: Toyota Motor Corporation)

Generation Yers will purchase 25% of the US small car market in 2010, and 40% of the US new car market (accounting for 6.5 million new cars out of a total 16 million in the new car market) in 2020.

Generation Y

Numerous studies have found Generation Y to be very different from Generation X. On the whole, they have more advanced educational backgrounds than any previous generations, especially among the women. Ethnically, they are more diverse, with over one-third being non-white. They have an optimistic outlook of their future income, and can expect, to some extent, economic support from their parents. As consumers, they are difficult. Widely exposed to various marketing techniques from childhood, they are more skeptical than other generations about the messages coming from TV commercials and magazine advertising. A new marketing approach would be required. Furthermore, they have high expectations for their cars, with design, quality, safety, and advanced technology all being taken for granted. They tend to consider cars as a means of self-expression much more than other generations do (refer to Fig. 27.2 for the characteristics of Generation Y.).

It was bad news for Toyota, whose cars were well liked for their reliability, fuel efficiency, and value for the money, but which were often said to lack of personality. To make matters worse, younger customers under age 35 were more dissatisfied with the automobile purchasing process, and Generation Y would surely be much less tolerant (refer to Fig. 27.3 for young customers' attitudes toward the car purchasing experience). Toyota's customer satisfaction index for the purchasing process repeatedly fell below the industry average.

No car company had ever developed a business geared specifically to Generation Y. Generally, companies such as the Big Three and Toyota, which sold to the mass market, were not popular among young people, who did not want to drive the same cars as their parents. Car companies tended to take a similar approach in their development of cars for young customers, merely offering an edgy exterior design at an affordable price, and providing favorable financing and insurance packages. In the case of Toyota, in Germany, the Yaris was positioned to win over a new type of customer – the young, educated, and financially well-off consumer. University students were offered new financing schemes with lower down payment requirements, longer loan periods, and discounted insurance policies that included free repairs.

Genesis: Experimentation of a New Marketing Approach

There was a predecessor to the Scion. In 1998, Yoshio Ishizaka, President of Toyota Motor Sales, USA. (hereafter TMS), Toyota's national sales and marketing company, suggested that a project team be organized to figure out a new marketing

	Generation Y	Generation X
Birth date	1980–1994.	1965–1979.
Age in 2004	9–23 years old.	24–38 years old.
Lifestyle	Busy and hectic, oriented to being constantly busy.	Busy but not as involved in continuous activities as Generation Y.
Activities	Music, sports, recreation, entertainment, relaxing, hanging out with friends.	Embrace daily routines with less enthusiasm than Y does—more free time.
Careers	Confident, risk-taking, entrepreneurial	Less focused on career than Y, more conservative
Social/Lifestyle goals	Good life is balanced life. It is possible by smart planning and flexibility.	Balance is critical for an overall good lifestyle.
Buyer behavior	Very image conscious, also very financially practical, high wealth expectation will reinforce spending habits.	Relatively more pragmatic and value conscious.
Diversity	Open and accepting of different ethnicities and lifestyles.	More deliberate about accepting diversity; not as comfortable overall.
Family	High regard for family.	Skeptical about the concept of family as a result of high divorce rate.
Self-reliant	Take responsibility for own activities, solve problems (group or individual basis).	Desire for self-reliance, but primarily on an individual basis, not group.
Optimism	Ever optimistic, as a result of early accomplishments while growing up.	Reasonably optimistic, less confident of ability to solve issues beyond themselves.
Community	Strong sense of community, desire to solve social issues as a group.	Less involved, more focused on resolving personal and career issues.
Rewards and success	Success is living happy and balanced life. Money is expected.	Similar to Y yet, yet with greater focus overall on financial rewards.
Role played by cars	Freedom, means of transportation, viewed as image statement, like part of their wardrobe.	Though this attitude was present in X, it is much more pronounced in Y.
Image of cars	Image is even more important to Y than it was to their Boomer parents, importance will grow.	X was also somewhat image driven in their decision-making.
Purchase process of cars	Rely on parents for assistance with decision making, but in the future will add a substantial amount of information gathering, especially online and via word-of-mouth	X slightly more accepting of traditional purchase process, though appeal of negotiation/significant time spent declines with buyer age.

Source: Nextfriend Report 1999 in Youth Market Overview, pp. 1–2.

Fig. 27.2 Characteristics of Generation Y [4]

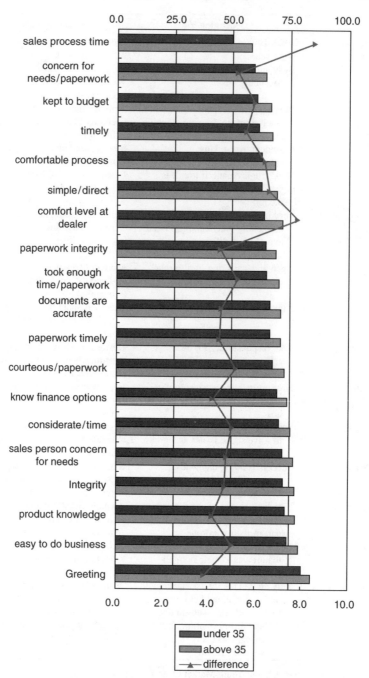

Fig. 27.3 Young customers dislike the car purchase experience. The bar graph (*upper scale*) shows the satisfaction rate. The lower the number, the less satisfied customers are. The line graph (*lower scale*) shows the difference in satisfaction rate between under-35s and over-35s. Larger difference indicates that it is a unique dissatisfaction factor for under-35s are especially dissatisfied. (Source: Toyota Motor Corporation)

approach for the youth market. TMS created the "Genesis" team within Toyota's Marketing Division. Its mission was to develop marketing strategies to convince the youth market to purchase the three cars that they had already decided to introduce to the US market: the Echo, a sub-compact car, (sold in Japan under the name Platz); the Celica, a two-door sports coupe; and the MR Spider, a convertible sports coupe.

The Genesis team developed some unprecedented marketing techniques. They put unique displays on the dealers' sales floors, and most of the TV commercials were not on the major television channels, but instead appeared on MTV, VH1, Comedy Central, and other cable television programs popular among the target youth market. They emphasized the Internet and made music and 360-degree videos freely available. They also sponsored concerts, extreme sports, and other events. By the end of November 1999, 2 months after the Genesis initiatives, the average age of the customers of the newly launched Celica and Echo was lower than that of their previous models, (33, compared with 42 for the Celica, and 38, as opposed to 43 for the Echo).

The three cars that the Genesis team had launched sold 100,000 units in total, but marketing alone could not continue to attract the youth market. The sales volume of the Celica halved after 2 years, and the Echo decreased to one-third. The average age of the Celica and Echo customers in 2003 rose to 37 and 45, respectively.

Genesis, however, enabled TMS to conduct an intensive study of the youth market, understand it thoroughly, and experience success with viral marketing, which was new to them. At the same time, TMS learned that to succeed in the youth market, a new marketing approach alone was not enough, and the choice of cars, product concept, and business model all had to be tailored to meet the needs of the targeted customer segment.

Toyota applied the learning from Genesis to the marketing of its Matrix, a car that targets main-stream young customers with a Toyota marque. In July 2002, TMS added an interactive game called "Road Rush" to its website directed at individuals between the ages of 15 and 24. The viewer chooses a Toyota vehicle (Matrix, Corolla, Celica, or Tacoma), the music, and a driver to speed through short animated videos set in New York, London, and Los Angeles. Toyota vehicles and the brand symbol appear in dynamic and unexpected ways. After visiting the site, the adjectives visitors used changed from "dependable" to "youthful" and "fun-to-drive" [10].

Birth of Scion: A New Business Model

In July 1999, when Yoshimi Inaba took office as the TMS President, approaching the youth market was one of the four challenges of his tenure, which was expected to be 3–4 years. Inaba explained his thinking behind the challenges:

> I kept watching the situation for a while, considering what initiatives were necessary for TMS. The No.1 enemy of TMS was its own success. It had a long history, and some of the top managers had thirty-year careers at TMS. It was even more Toyota-like than Toyota in

Japan. Its sales system was based on good relationships with the dealers, and was sales-volume driven. I called it a "conventional model at its prime." TMS was one of the best results of the traditional Toyota Model. It was easy for us to try to avoid anything that might disturb TMS, including its dealer relationship, since TMS was doing so well and contributing a significant amount of profit to Toyota.

In February 2000, the Scion team was established in the Corporate Planning Department with six TMS associates, each in their 30s or 40s. A few members from the Genesis project joined the Scion team as experts in the youth market and Internet marketing. Jim Lentz was appointed as the Scion team leader.

In January 2001, Scion organized the Dealer Advisory Board, which consisted of eight dealer representatives. At the beginning, the board was split, with some members for the initiative and others against it. The Scion team convened board meetings every 4 or 5 months, and consulted with the board on all major issues.

After a year, they set the goals of this initiative, which were to: (i) attract young customers, which Toyota had not been able to do thus far; (ii) transform the sales process so that TMS could offer to young customers the new type of purchase experience they wanted; and (iii) transform the sales process of the entire Toyota organization. The new sales process they proposed included the discontinuation of price negotiations and extensive use of the Internet.

They decided to start this initiative with two models, and chose them from existing cars to lighten the financial burden. This, however, was done only on the condition that they would develop a new model specifically for this initiative within a few years. They engaged in lengthy discussions to decide how independent from Toyota this operation should be, if a new brand name other than Toyota was necessary, and other issues.

As basic objectives and approaches to Scion were confirmed and Scion moved closer to operational status it became part of the Toyota Marketing Department in the TMS Toyota Division, which had 250 employees. Although the Scion team had its own budget and moved out of the main building where the Marketing Group was located, it was required to obtain the approval of Toyota's Marketing Group, and Lentz continued to report to both the Toyota Division's Marketing Manager and the Toyota Division Head.

In June 2002, Lenz was promoted to Marketing Manager of the Toyota Division, and Jim Farley was chosen to be his successor and Scion team leader. Farley felt that it was very important for the Scion team that Lentz had a great deal of knowledge about Scion and that he was in charge of both Toyota and Scion marketing.

Scion Cars: The Birth of xA and xB

The Scion team visited Japan and examined every model. They were looking for cars that only young people would want, at less than US$18,000, with style, versatility, and an element of surprise. As soon as the team saw "bB," which had just been introduced in Japan, a small boxy wagon that looked like "an ambulance from World

War I" or a car that appears in Japanese *manga* or animation, they believed that American young people would love it immediately, even though there was nothing like it in the USA. They also decided to include a small hatchback, "ist," which was under development and had yet to be introduced to the Japanese market.

Both bB and ist needed some modifications to cope with the US emissions regulations, safety regulations, etc. Tetsuya Tada, who was the assistant to the chief engineer of bB, was assigned as chief engineer of the two cars. The development process he employed was very different from others. Usually, the Engineering Department would develop a car aimed at certain target customers. Then, the sales organization, after taking a look at the car, would start thinking about how to sell it and, finally, the Accessories Development Division would develop accessories for it. However, in this project, the chief engineer, collaborating with the TMS Scion team, started the process by thinking about the marketing approach and sales process first, and then letting the sales process guide development.

The bB was very unique because it clearly targeted the hip-hop culture within the Japanese youth market. It offered more options in terms of accessories, which made customization by each customer possible. The Scion team decided to adopt this idea for Scion although in the USA, tuning had been limited to a small number of avid fans. They felt that there would be a large enough number of young people who would want to customize their cars, because they were exposed to Japanese tuning culture and this matched Generation Y's tendency to use one's car a means of self-expression.

In order to avoid having to develop new parts for Scion, they selected, from the materials used for all Toyota and Lexus seats and dashboards, materials that had a luxurious and high-tech image. Fortunately, bB and ist were based on the same platform that was being used for many other small-sized models, of which about 1 million cars were produced per year.

It was the sound system to which Tada paid most attention, because field research in the USA revealed that Generation Y could not live without music. Tada ignored common sense arguments about how much could be distributed to the sound system for cars in Scion's price range. Advanced model speakers and noise absorption materials were adopted from the Lexus, which were provided as standard equipment, and a sub-woofer was offered as an option. With all these changes, bB and ist became Scion xB and xA (refer to Fig. 27.4 for photographs of xA and xB).

The xA and xB offered as many as 40 accessories as options, which were common to the two cars. A choice of red or blue floor lights, and shift lever knobs that were made of chrome were just a few of the available options. For the first time in its history, the TMC Engineering Department shared drawings with the Specialty Equipment Marketing Association (SEMA) before their launch to encourage the independent accessory manufacturers and tuners to develop accessories for Scion.

Fig. 27.4 Scion xA (*left*), xB (*right*), and tC (*center*) (Source: Toyota Motor Corporation)

New Sales Process

The target customers of Scion were the trendsetters of Generation Y, who were estimated to be about 15% of Generation Yers, while Toyota approached the mainstream
members of Generation Y.

Young customers showed extreme dissatisfaction with the car purchasing experience. They felt that it took too much time, and that price negotiations were unfair
(refer to Fig. 27.3). Therefore, the Scion team considered it critical to introduce a
new sales process, so as to create a more pleasant purchase experience.

The first thing they tried to do was eliminate the price negotiation process. Therefore, the Scion business model asked dealers to adopt "pure pricing." Under this
model, dealers publish prices on the Internet or in their store fronts, and stick to
those prices to allow customers to know them in advance and make the sales process transparent, thereby eliminating in-store negotiations and reducing customers'
anxiety.

However, pure pricing as a concept was new to the automobile industry, and to
its customers. Therefore, the Scion team realized that communicating the concept
of pure pricing to customers and having them expect it was critical. Also, the price
structure of the products and services had to be simplified. Scion cars came with
fewer options, specifically model type (xA or xB), transmission (automatic or manual), and body colors. TMS developed simple but satisfactory insurance and loan
products for Scion.

Next, the Scion team requested dealers to assign one sales consultant to handle
the entire sales process, which previously had been divided among receptionists,
sales associates, sales managers, and finance associates. Under the old process, customers often had to repeat the same story or start new negotiations every time a
different person took over. It took 4 h under the old process, and the Scion team was
aiming to reduce this to 2 h.

Since Generation Y wanted more information from the carmakers, Scion created an official Scion site and provided detailed information about the cars. Dealer sales representatives were trained with CD-ROMs, and educational programs were offered at TMS so that they could have a thorough knowledge of the products.

Finally, the Scion team introduced new logistics based on the demand-pull system, which involved fewer inventories at dealerships but larger inventories at TMS. This was the opposite to the conventional system, in which dealers kept larger inventories so as not to miss a sales opportunity. However, by keeping dealer inventory low, Scion discouraged discounts and push sales, which sometimes ignored customers' preferences. To provide customers with the pleasure of customizing their own cars, dealers were requested to put accessories on the cars only after the customers chose the desired options and accessories. Then, customers would be required to wait several days to obtain the products. Scion developed an information system that allowed dealers to track the port inventory and notify the customers of when they could deliver the cars.

Choice of Sales Channel

It would have been much easier to implement Scion's new sales process if Scion had operated a direct sales channel. However, it did not open direct retail stores. It was Toyota's long-standing policy not to operate dealerships but to let local entrepreneurs demonstrate their initiative.

Given that independent dealers were the primary sales channel, there were still some approaches that were possible, and this was the issue that required the longest debates. First, Scion could be sold by dedicated sales representatives in separate buildings. All Lexus stores had separate buildings from Toyota's and the same exterior and interior designs. Second, Scion could be sold in a dedicated corner within the Toyota stores, which was called shop-in-shop. In the end, Scion and TMS decided to go with the second option: the shop-in-shop approach (refer to Fig. 27.5 for the Scion corner). They also decided they would not offer Scion business to all the existing Toyota dealers, but only those who volunteered.

The Scion operation shared with Toyota such activities as order processing from the dealers, logistics management, and regional office operations. This approach made the Scion group lean, and it was able to start out with only ten members. At the regional offices, the same associates were responsible both for Scions and Toyotas. Lentz explained the logic as follows:

> For us, Scion is a portal strategy, which leads new customers to Toyota. If this isn't made, Toyota must shrink in the long run. Generation Y consists of only 5% of the car market now, but will be 40% in 2020. Toyota must turn them into its customers in any case. We can set up experiments by starting Scion as a shop-in-shop operation within Toyota dealerships. Through this experiment, Toyota dealers can learn how to deal with these new customers. The more Toyota dealers participate in Scion, the more desirable it is for Toyota in the long run.

Fig. 27.5 The Scion Corner (Source: Toyota Motor Corporation)

TMS Scion was able to get a sense of whether the Scion Covenant was being observed through various means, including daily communication between the twelve regional offices and dealers, mystery shopping conducted by marketing research firms, customer surveys on the Internet, e-mails sent to the Scion official site, and conversations about Scion on the Internet in official and unofficial Scion sites. The regional office evaluated the observance of the Scion Covenant every 4 months, and rewarded those dealers who did exceptionally well by allocating more cars than originally planned. Dealers who repeatedly violated the Covenant would feel the results directly in decreased allocations.

Viral Marketing

One year before the Scion launch in California, the team displayed posters with such slogans as "No Clone Zone" and "Ban Normality" without mentioning the Scion name. The same slogans were projected on buildings at night. The Scion team held test-drive events by setting up a tent and banners near the entrance of the expressway, and arranged venues at things like hip-hop events. Scion's pamphlets were distributed with alternative culture magazines such as Urb, Asian Culture, and Tokion. Music CDs, gift certificates for hip-hop apparel brands were given to those customers who demonstrated a strong interest in Scion.

After the launch, Scion's viral marketing tried to provide topics that would attract word of mouth. First, Scion tried to fuse their cars with music, art, and fashion so that posters, events, test-drive events, and magazines were designed with that in mind. Events were held at nightclubs, break dance tournaments, and exhibitions of graffiti art. Advertisement through the mass media was focused on midnight music programs on cable TV, as had been done with the Genesis initiative before. Second, Scion's viral marketing approached the tuning culture, sponsoring 17 tuning events in 2003 in cooperation with tuners and accessory makers. Third, it was done through grass-roots efforts. During the weekends, eight Scions, four xAs, and four xBs car-avanned the streets where young people hung out, with Scion associates driving the cars. All these initiatives worked in conjunction with the official Scion site on the Internet.

Scion encouraged people to create Scion communities by starting the official site and aggressively providing detailed information. At the official site, the associates at the Scion Customer Experience, a call center for Scion, chatted with the customers so that inquiries and discussions were handled in a lively and speedy manner. More than 300,000 people visited the official site each month, of which more than 70% were under the age of 35 (refer to Fig. 27.6 and Fig. 27.7 for the viral marketing of Scion).

Scion chose new partners to develop and implement these new marketing techniques. They did not choose the established advertising agent with whom TMS had been working for years, but rather contracted with small advertising agents, one for each marketing channel (the Internet, magazines, and events).

New Business Model

The MSRP for xA was US $12,480, and xB, was US $13,680. These were in the same price range as the Korean automakers, and lower than any other Japanese automakers. Scion even came out with full options as part of the standard offering so that the MSRP was very reasonable.

The dealer margin for Scion cars was set at 6%, about half that of the usual Toyota car, yet almost the same as the actual dealer margin after the price discount. Moreover, Scion customers were expected to spend much more on accessories than Toyota customers, who spent only US $300 on average. Dealers could enjoy a fat margin on accessories rather than on new car sales. In addition, dealers could reduce inventory costs, advertising expenses, and sales promotion expenses. As a result, dealers enjoyed one of the highest profits per car with Scion among all the Toyota cars. The TMS Scion team expected that dealers would recover their initial investments and become profitable after 3 years.

New Wine in Old Bottles

About 10% of the dealers were very positive about the Scion from the beginning. For those dealers who had stores in the areas where young people hung out, such as Santa Monica, or those who wanted their children to take over the dealership, Scion seemed likely to provide great opportunities. Many dealers were skeptical, though. Was it possible to implement new concepts such as pure pricing and 15-day inventories? Would the xB sell? Would Toyota start to decrease dealer margins on Toyota-branded cars once Scion was accepted? Toyota had been very successful so far. Why should the dealers change anything? Some of the dealers were put off by the fact that TMS specified the details of the sales process. The retail business was

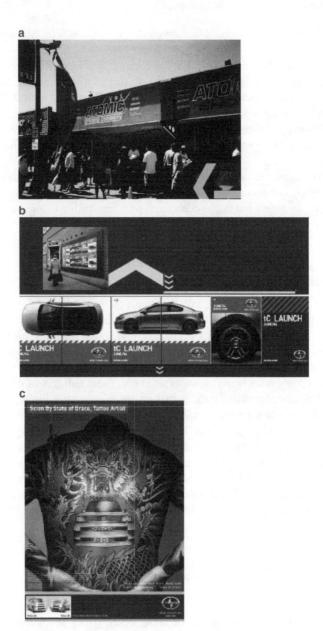

Fig. 27.6 Viral marketing of Scion: (**a**) street rally, (**b**, **c**) posters (Source: Toyota Motor Corporation)

not TMS' business; why would the dealers have to follow TMS' instructions in the retail world?

To obtain their cooperation, TMS Scion explained repeatedly to the dealers that the new customers would be very different from the traditional customers, and that

a

b

Fig. 27.7 (**a**) Scion magazine, (**b**) paint event (Source: Toyota Motor Corporation)

they were dissatisfied with the sales process. Consequently, this posed a great opportunity for Scion to differentiate itself from its competitors through the introduction of an entirely new sales process.

Cascade Launch and Initial Uphill Struggle

In order to master the entire process, dealer representatives were required to attend a 1-week educational program in addition to the regular 2-day sessions on product features. To make the process work, Scion was gradually introduced to different geographic areas of the USA during the first year, while the Scion team closely watched to see if the new process worked and made any necessary changes. Scion was first introduced in California in June 2003, then in the South and on the East Coast in February 2004, and finally in the central states in June 2004.

In the first 3 months, from June 2003 to August 2003, Scion sold more than expected (sales of 4770 units against a forecast of 4600 units). Scion expected that sales ratio of xA to xB would be six to four, yet it turned out to be three to seven. Most of the xB customers made up their minds to buy the xB before visiting the dealership. In contrast, the xA did not show such strong appeal. The pre-launch focus interviews showed that the xB had polarized appeal. Scion had projected more sales with the xA because it was more affordable and less radical in design.

At the beginning of July, Scion asked the Takaoka Plant in Japan to cease production of the xA. Also, it increased inventory at the port so that dealer inventory did not pile up further. For Toyota, who kept production levels stable for enhanced quality and lower manufacturing costs, halting production was the rarest of exceptions. Scion increased its advertising activities to raise the recognition of the xA. For example, it put up 80 billboards featuring the xA in metropolitan areas, with the xA surrounded by numerous accessories and dubbed "Scion by LJ, Tuner" (LJ Garch is a famous professional tuner).

Dealers could not get enough xBs and carried too much xA inventory. Still, the pure price policy successfully took root at the dealers. At the very beginning, customers called or visited several dealers, and checked to see if they could get a discount. Most of them found that they could not, and after these stories were shared among the customers, this kind of shopping around decreased significantly within 2 months of the launch. As expected, customers' expectations about pure pricing restrained dealers from violation. Some dealers suggested a price discount to customers, and those customers complained about it on the Internet.

The biggest challenge in the new sales process was in finance and insurance (F&I). At most dealerships, F&I was conducted by a specialist rather than a Scion case manager. The person in charge of F&I had to understand the regulations and prevent any mistakes in documentation, otherwise dealers and customers were potentially at risk, both legally and financially. F&I managers usually handled about 100 contracts a month, and Scion sales were not large enough to assign a separate F&I manager. Another possible reason could be the organizational and political problems that dealers might face when resulting F&I profits moved from the F&I department to the new car sales department. F&I was a significant source of income for dealers. On a busy weekend, Scion customers sometimes had to wait as long as a few hours when being handed over to the F&I manager. Some F&I managers, not knowing about Scion's inclusive, simple guarantee package, tried to sell extended warranties, and others just ignored it.

Having designated sales representatives for Scion had mixed results. Some dealers assigned three designated Scion sales representatives, yet at most dealerships, the same sales representative sold both Scions and Toyotas. Some dealers requested its sales representatives to sell both Scions and Toyotas after realizing that sales representatives made much less money if they sold only Scion cars.

Attracting Young Customers

About 74% of the Scion customers were new to Toyota. The average age of the Scion customer was 36, while the average Toyota customer was 48. The average age of customers of Scion's third model, the tC, at the end of September 2004 was 24, which was much lower than that of Nissan Sentra or Honda Civic Coupe customers. The Scion attracted a more diverse ethnic group – only 57% of Scion customers were white, as opposed to 81% of Toyota's customers. Scion had successfully opened a door to the New World.

Despite the problems mentioned in the section above, most of the customers were satisfied with their purchase experience at the dealerships, and almost 93% expressed a willingness to recommend the dealership to others, compared with only 88% of Toyota customers. Some of those customers satisfied with their Scion purchase experience told others, "I never had such an enjoyable experience buying a car."

Communications among Scion owners on the Internet sometimes resulted in owners clubs, with some active owners clubs meeting more than once a month to exchange information or ideas about tuning. Scion not only talked with some of the owners directly, but also listened carefully to what they had to say about Scion at the owners club site, and quickly adopted any good suggestions. The owners liked this very much, and felt like they were a part of Scion.

Further Improvement

The managers of Scion felt that it was critical to keep moving ahead in order to keep attracting the trendsetters of Generation Y. Product cycles would have to be shortened to keep them fresh and eliminate price discounts. For example, the xB went through a minor change in March 2004, 9 months after its introduction. Limited production versions of each model would be created often.

The tC was introduced in June 2004, a year after the Scion launch. The tC was a sports coupe that was lower and wider in posture than other small-sized coupes, equipped with a large, panorama moon roof united with the ceiling. It had a large engine and offered firm handling, like a German sports coupe, to emphasize power and the joy of driving (refer to Fig. 27.4 for photographs of the tC). The development approach to tC was similar to that of xA and xB: a common platform that was used broadly within the company, and parts that were already being used in other models. The MSRP (manufacturers' recommended selling price) of the tC was extremely low for its contents. This was also true of the xA and the xB. The US $15,950 MSRP (with manual transmission) was US $5000 to US $10,000 lower than its equivalent rival, and the tC attracted many more orders than expected, forcing customers to wait several months to receive delivery of their cars.

Sixteen months after the launch, when the author revisited the Scion headquarters, TMS had made several adjustments, including the addition of dealer training programs and an improvement in its retail sales forecasts. However, most significant was the separation of the field activities from Toyota. The Scion team assigned two or three Scion field managers to its Regional Offices. Successful Scion dealers understood, from the top management to the frontline associates, why they had started their Scion business and in what ways Scions differed from Toyotas. To impress upon dealers the difference between Scions and Toyotas, the field managers from the regional offices handing Scions were required to be different from those managers handling Toyotas, and they had to be thinking about Scion 24 h a day.

Scion and Toyota

Lentz, Marketing Manager of the Toyota Division, talked about learning from the Scion:

> Scion will change the new product development process at Toyota as well as the sales process. The tC's development lead-time is already drastically shorter than before. Shorter development lead-time is necessary for the shorter product life cycle of Scion. In addition, we might be able to develop new product development processes for radical products.

In the sales and marketing areas, Toyota Division and the dealers adopted the new approaches developed by Scion, such as selecting music and magazines, setting an overall tone, and building associations. Don Esmond, Executive Vice President in charge of the Toyota Division, commented:

> The sales process of Toyota will change. For example, some dealers already started to let one sales consultant handle all the sales processes, and they were wondering why they did not do this much earlier. It is indispensable for the long-term success of Toyota to change Toyota's operation by doing good things for Scion. Camry should change so that Generation Y likes it when they get older.

Yuki Funo, who succeeded Inaba as the president of TMS, talked about the Scion's strategic meaning to Toyota:

> The retail process of the automobile has a problem of not appealing to young people, to which Toyota is not an exception. However, it is very difficult to transform Toyota. So, we created an experiment with the sub-brand Scion to attract young customers with the hope that when they graduate from Scion, they might move to Toyota. Dealers would not follow the automakers' instructions to transform the sales process unless it made business sense. The Toyota dealer franchise should be able to attract Generation Yers when they get older and make up the biggest market segment several decades from now. Changing Toyota is not the goal. Not to be left behind the customers' changes is.

Finally, Jim Farley, Vice President in charge of the Scion team, expressed his thoughts on Scion as of October 2004:

> Before starting Scion, I personally thought an independent franchise from Toyota was an ideal strategy for Scion, but I changed my opinion 180 degrees. In order not only to change Toyota, but also to keep Scion different from Toyota and as a niche brand, it had to be shop-in-shop. By being part of Toyota, we don't have to worry about dealers' sales growth and

can avoid expanding the product line to the mainstream market, while being part of Toyota makes it more difficult to conduct operations in the Scion way. We had to fight against people at the Toyota Division and dealerships, and made many people uncomfortable. We also made mistakes in how to implement the Scion model in almost all the operational areas, which made a long list, and we are going to correct them in the coming 12 months. This is the very reason why I believe only Toyota can do Scion successfully, no other car companies. It requires good dealer management, logistics management, manufacturing, and product development.

We need good people in our team to make Scion successful. By making work at Scion team rewarding, I'm trying to keep attracting capable associates. One approach is to send them out to Toyota operations with a promotion quickly after they achieve something on the Scion team so that we can reward them while at the same time share our learning with the Toyota Division. By moving people between Scion and Toyota, we could have both independence and interdependence, which are necessary for innovative projects within a large organization.

Learning from Scion, the effectiveness of which was proven in the USA, was transferred to Toyota in other countries. Toyota Canada used a Matrix website to build a relationship with the youth market by getting young people actively involved, by giving them the "Graffiti your Matrix" tool. Visitors made Matrix look like either an angel or a devil, with jaws or with a Superman's cape (see p. 15 in [10]). Toyota del Peru provided new accessories with the Yaris to let young customers personalize their cars (see p. 16 in [10]). However, Toyota did not introduce the Scion marque to other countries, including Japan, despite it being the bB's mother country, in order to avoid diluting the marketing budget by adding another brand worldwide.

Scion Case Revisited

As described above, Scion was a new innovation for Toyota, intended as a means for approaching Generation Y, with its very different needs. Scion *borrowed* from Toyota by sharing processes in product design, product development, procurement, manufacturing, across-the-ocean shipping, and field people, as well as after-sales service and supportive functions at dealers. Also, Scion *borrowed* from Toyota by transferring know-how in dealer management, logistics management, and the viral marketing of the Genesis project. On the other hand, Scion had to *forget* Toyota's policy of not offering factory accessories, logistics and an evaluation system that encourages sales volume, and its dealers' sales process. Finally, Scion *learned* new practices for its sales process at dealerships, such as pure pricing, a pull not push sales style, and the need to communicate directly and frequently with customers via Internet. Toyota's *learning* from Scion happened in two routes. The first route was by sharing activities with Scion, and the results included the designing of products that appealed to the opinion leaders, developing closer relationships with third parties to provide more accessories to customers, and developing products in a shorter lead-time. The second route was by transferring know-how, such as viral marketing and case manager sales systems, to name a few.

Among the various new practices of Scion, the most challenging to learn was the new sales process because it was totally different from the old one. It tried to impart new values and practices in the shop-in-shop environment, which made learning harder because it was more difficult to forget those of the Toyota operations. On the other hand, the shop-in-shop approach made it easier for Toyota to learn from Scion and change itself through the transferring of know-how. Why is it easier to learn when organizational distance is closer? If Scion operations were conducted in a separate shop, people at Toyota shop would see Scion operations as being something totally different from their business and emphasize differences and trade-offs [9] rather than considering what could be learned from Scion.

Lexus: A New Business to Learn New Skills and Improve the Old

Another attempt by Toyota to adapt to demographic change was the Lexus, which was launched in October 1989 in the USA as its second brand to approach the luxury segment. It won the number one market share in 2000, and has stayed at the top (at least until this case study was written).

When it was launched, two American brands stood out – Lincoln with a market share of 24%, and Cadillac with 18%. Import brands followed (Mercedes Benz with 6.8%, and BMW with 5.8%). American cars were popular for their brand heritage and extensive network of dealer outlets, (1648 and 1605 respectively for Lincoln and Cadillac, against Mercedes' 422 and BMW's 413), but people were concerned about their dependability and durability. European cars, appealing to customers with their performance, offering high top speed and firm handling, were very expensive due to the currency exchange rate and gas guzzler tax for low fuel efficiency.

Lexus entered the market with clear differentiation from the incumbents. The LS400 was extremely smooth and silent, with a top speed comparable to German cars but with a reasonable price tag and fuel efficiency. Also, customers could expect to have an excellent experience in every one of the Lexus dealerships. Dealers kept a record on each car sale and after-sales service, and developed strong relationships with customers. As Lexus expanded its product line, some customers had a second and third Lexus in their garage.

Lexus shared with Toyota product design, product development, procurement, manufacturing, and across-the-ocean shipping. However, TMS created a Lexus division as a new business unit, established designated field offices and a dealer franchise, and developed educational programs for TMS associates and Lexus dealers. Having a separate division, field activities and a dealer franchise contributed to the excellent service at dealerships, which made many people Lexus' loyal customers.

Sharing activities allowed Lexus to adopt a reasonable price tag, which appealed to those who could tell the difference between cheap and valuable. However, it also caused confusion. Lexus models were manufactured in the same production line with Toyota models. When Lexus introduced the RX300 in 1998, its quality rating for new cars was significantly damaged. The factory that manufactured the RX300 had never manufactured any Lexus vehicles before, and the workers did not thoroughly understand the expectations regarding Lexus quality. It was not enough to distribute teaching manuals and increase inspection points. The factory began inviting the employees from Lexus dealerships to come in and speak to factory workers about the customers' expectations. It also posted pictures and messages from Lexus customers on the factory floor. This event demonstrates how difficult it is to manage two different businesses in the same process.

Toyota also faced physical challenges by having Lexus and Toyota models in the same production line. The production manager at the Tahara plant told the author that the best assembly processes for Lexus and Toyota were quite different. The former emphasized avoiding scratches, while the latter put the priority on manufacturing efficiency. In the end, priority was given to the best process for the Lexus models, which logically resulted in improved over-all quality for Lexus cars and higher manufacturing costs for Toyota cars. With continuous improvement, they will gradually be able to lower the manufacturing costs and produce Lexus cars without scratches at a lower cost, and Toyota cars at the Toyota cost without scratches. Thanks to Toyota's well-trained capability for continuous improvement, mixing different businesses contributed to both businesses in this case.[1]

Summary and Conclusion

We have considered how a company can take advantage of demographic change to improve itself. The cases of Scion and Lexus have brought us some insights, which can be applied to companies planning to approach the growing silver market in other industries:

- Approaching the silver market is especially beneficial if the new customers are more demanding than the current target customers, and if their dissatisfaction raises an alarm. By meeting elderly customers' needs, you can better satisfy your target customers' needs.
- Leaders should encourage people to ring the bell to overcome cognitive inertia. People tend to believe that the past continues into the future, and because of the tendency to focus on evidence that supports your hypothesis and ignore any evidence that does not (the so-called "confirmation bias"), it is difficult to realize that the future may be different. Toyota was keenly aware of its weakness in the youth segment, and took action ahead of its competitors. In Scion's case, leaders played a significant role. Ishizaka started the Genesis project and Inaba launched Scion. In Toyota, leaders are expected to propose difficult challenges that require a leap [7].

---

[1] When Toyota introduced Lexus models in Japan in 2005, it provided separate production lines for Toyota and Lexus vehicles. Other activities once shared, such as product design and product development, were also separated to emphasize specialization and differentiation between the two.

- To learn new practices, experiment. Genesis, which used ordinary Toyota cars, was an experiment in the efficiency of viral marketing. It was a partial solution to a bigger problem, but it was not a failure. Toyota has a culture that appreciates experimentation, and encourages learning from it [7]. We see the same attitude in Scion's cascade launch.
- To learn new practices, be open. Scion learned from new advertising agencies, Lexus leaned from dealers who had been selling other luxury brands and enhanced Lexus' uniqueness.
- Clarify the strategic purpose of the new business and choose the right organizational distance. This point is elaborated below.

Management thinking has been advising companies to separate organizations when different businesses have different strategies, because the most suitable processes, evaluation systems, and values are different. Nobody argues against the claim that Wal-Mart needs a very different organization from Nordstrom's. However, who would recommend Nordstrom to operate Wal-Mart? These two are too different. Being able to leverage your unique capabilities in the old business is the source of competitive advantage against others in the new business. Nordstrom may not have anything valuable for significantly enhancing Wal-Mart operations. Hence, if a company has a good corporate strategy, it must consider the processes of "borrow, forget, and learn." Please note that the "make them separate" argument emphasizes forgetting and learning, but not borrowing.

Some companies might take this a step further. A comparative case study of Toyota's Lexus and Scion presents two new patterns:

1. Companies may aim to change their old business based on the experience of the new businesses. To achieve this goal, organizational distance should be closer, as we have seen in the case of Scion's shop-in-shop operations, although it makes forgetting more difficult for the new business.
2. Companies aim to upgrade each business by sharing new capabilities among different businesses, as Toyota did with the mixed product line of Lexus and Toyota. In this case, even the confusion that arises due to the mixing of different values and practices may be necessary. This is another type of learning, mutual learning, and is beyond borrowing because both businesses benefit.

How can a company take advantage of demographic change that seems adversarial? In a sense, your weakness looks weaker because the new market segment emerges as a result of demographic change, yet responding to this change should take precedence over concerns about your weakness. The company might need to put up with confusion, but by carefully managing organizational distance and the four processes of borrowing, forgetting, learning, and mutual learning, it may be able to re-innovate itself.

Finally, an implication to those who are in other countries. In Scion's case, the USA was the leading market for Generation Y, where music and extreme sports trends were created, and needless to say, these young people owned more cars. Toyota, a Japanese car company that makes careful listening a priority, won the trust of

Generation Y in the USA, but not in Japan. If you want to approach the silver market, you should go to Japan and other leading markets, listen carefully and conduct experiments, and then apply that learning in other countries.

References

1. Ford Motor Company, *"Third-age suit" helps Ford to understand mature drivers*, (Ford, Brentwood, 1999) http://media.ford.com/newsroom/release_display.cfm?release=624. Accessed 16 Jun 2008
2. V. Govindarajan, C. Trimble, *Ten rules for strategic innovators: from idea to execution* (Harvard Business School, Boston, 2005)
3. T. Incantalupo, Automakers say aging consumers' tastes vary widely, *Knight Ridder Tribune Business News*, 15 Nov 2003, p. 1
4. Nextfriend, Report 1999, in *Youth Market Overview* (1999), p. 1
5. E. Osono, Lexus: The challenge of the U.S. luxury car market. *ICS case studies* (Graduate School of International Corporate Strategy, Hitotsubashi, 2002)
6. E. Osono, Can Toyota attract young customers? *ICS case studies* (Graduate School of International Corporate Strategy, Hitotsubashi, 2004)
7. E. Osono, N. Shimizu, H. Takeuchi, *Extreme Toyota: radical contradictions that drive success at the world's best manufacturer* (Wiley, New York, 2008)
8. M.E. Porter, *Harv. Bus. Rev.* **65**(3), 43–59 (1987)
9. M.E. Porter, *Harv. Bus. Rev.* **74**:61–78 (1996)
10. Toyota Motor Corporation, Promoting the Toyota way in sales and marketing, *Team Toyota*, **5**, Mar/Apr 2003
11. M.L. Tushman, C.A. O'Reilly III, *Winning through innovation: a practical guide to leading organizational change and renewal* (Harvard Business School, Boston, 2002)

Chapter 28
The Golden Opportunity of Silver Marketing: The Case of Housing and Financial Services

K.A. Grossberg

Abstract The unprecedented aging of Japan's population presents costs and opportunities for its future as a society and as a major economic power. Japan's seniors already control the largest portion of the nation's wealth,[1] but in the very near future they will also consume the lion's share of the social expense for care and living as they age and their proportion in the total population increases. In this chapter we examine two areas which promise major commercial opportunities because of such a vast socio-demographic change linked to a huge pool of liquid assets.[2] Those areas are, firstly, catering to the financial needs of the country's senior citizens and, secondly, responding to their particular preferences and requirements for housing. In Japan's generally sluggish market for housing and financial services, the "silver market" provides one of the richest segments available, but successfully offering such services to this population requires skill, sensitivity and an understanding of the evolving consumer mindset in Japan.

Introduction

Japan is not unique among post-industrial societies in having an aging society, but it is surely *primus inter pares* in the extent to which the country's demographic bulge has shifted from youth to old age. As of 2005, the percentage of Japan's population at age 65 or older (20.1%) was higher than such "old" European nations

---

[1] Dai-ichi Life Research Institute estimates that assets of Japanese baby boomers total ¥130 trillion, which is equivalent to 10% of all personal financial holdings in Japan. In addition to the amount of assets that they hold, between now and 2009, companies will also be paying out about ¥50 trillion in retirement severance as workers reach age 60. According to a Dentsu survey, baby boomers are expected to spend about ¥11 trillion on travel after retirement, of which 90% would be for travel outside of Japan [12].

[2] Financial assets held by Japanese households rose to a record high of ¥1.56 quadrillion as of 30 June, 2007, with cash and deposits constituting 50% of that amount, a considerably higher percentage than in other advanced economies [4].

as Italy (19.7%) and Germany (18.8%) and far higher than the relatively "young" USA (12.3%) [5]. By September 2007, the 65 and older population had grown to 21.5% of the population, with the number of Japanese of at least 80 years old topping 7 million for the first time, 5.6% of all Japanese [10]. And, as time passes, Japan's character as the world's most geriatric society will likely become even more pronounced. From a public policy perspective, there are big problems ahead for Japan as the global community's eldest nation, but from a business and marketing point of view, such lemons can be the stuff of lemonade for the right industries. This research will examine two sectors that are related to each other – financial services and housing – which are already counting on the silver market to earn them substantial profits. "Housing" in this chapter refers to real estate offerings specially designed with the priorities of older Japanese in mind.

That the baby boomers are a veritable "pig in a python" demographically speaking is not news, and the looming opportunities presented because of their retirement from full-time employment and progressive aging have not eluded the attention of Japanese businesses. But, seeing opportunities and developing appropriate strategies to exploit those opportunities are not the same thing, and not every attempt to grow rich from the assumed needs or projected demand of Japanese baby boomers will succeed. Still, many enterprises are intent on turning that "silver" into gold. The banks, a major actor in this market, are trying to capture as much of the boomers' retirement pensions and savings as they can, and the residential housing developers have used a number of strategies to entice these older citizens to buy housing designed with them in mind (both in Japan and abroad) or to renovate (reform) their existing dwellings to make them more user-friendly for elderly residents.

The fortunes of many companies are riding on the extent to which their assumptions about senior citizens' consumption behavior turns out to be correct. Some firms have miscalculated as to the potential popularity of their innovations, and end up paying the price for not satisfying their targeted customers. One example of such a strategic error is the multi-generation house (*nisetai jutaku*) in its original incarnation, described later in this chapter. It was assumed by real estate developers that an appeal to the Japanese idea of togetherness – of having grandparents, children, and grandchildren all occupying the same house – would have great resonance with the Japanese. But, what they did not count on was the fact that the elder residents, whose financial contribution (of both land and down payment) was what usually made such expensive houses possible in the first place, would feel cheated and neglected after the three generations were actually living together in such housing for some length of time.

One example of the profits anticipated from the silver market can be seen in the financial arena. Companies have created financial instruments that cater to this market or, in the case of Goldman Sachs' Baby Boomer Basket E-Warrant, hope to profit in other ways from its growth. The ultimate success of some of these new products or services remains unclear. Goldman Sachs Japan designed the Baby Boomer Basket E-Warrant product to capitalize on the anticipated boom expected to result from the changing consumption preferences and needs of the elderly. Performance of the Baby Boomer Basket E-Warrant is linked to the share price of a basket of eleven companies that are predicted to gain disproportionately from the boomers' new lifestyle. Some of the 11 companies included are East Japan Railway (leisure travel), Konami (fitness clubs), Mitsbishi UFJ and Mizuho banks (financial management of boomers' pension and retirement nest eggs), and Toto (toilets and bathrooms) [15].

While the areas represented by these and other companies stand to gain from elder-spending during the next decade, it is still not clear how much this thrifty but status-conscious Japanese generation will actually spend, or where they will finally decide to put their hard-earned savings. The banks and brokerages assume that they will have to put the money somewhere, and are intent on getting the lion's share of those funds. Likewise, the real estate companies are certain that the silver market is ready to take the plunge to buy or renovate property that more fully satisfies their desires for comfort, privacy, and a richer life experience as they grow older.

Financial Services in Japan: Rethinking Customer Needs

It is almost a cliché to say that Japanese financial service firms (including banks, brokerages, and insurance companies) are behind the curve when it comes to offering state-of-the-industry, efficient service to their clients. Although the lost decade that followed the bursting of the economic bubble in 1990 led to some soul-searching on the part of the large institutions as well as ambivalent efforts to renovate their antiquated systems and priorities, culturally determined attitudes still prevent the rapid introduction of many internationally accepted practices. For example, banks still rely on the traditional seal (*inkan*) rather than customer signatures for official documents and have done little to transition to paperless systems. It must be acknowledged, however, that elder Japanese grew up with this archaic system based on the use of *inkan* seals instead of signatures, and with passbook-based bank accounts with paper documentation used for every small transaction, so they are not necessarily seeking the same type of internet-based, automated service that has become popular with their younger compatriots. But, these seniors can recognize good service when it is offered to them, and the financial institutions are learning that to provide that service they must be more flexible than is their habit.

Change does not come quickly. After all, it took the better part of a decade before the excessively low interest rate returns on bank and pension accounts finally pushed Japanese seniors to explore new and riskier investments that offered the possibility of higher returns. There are 8.4 million Japanese baby boomers slated to retire starting in 2007, which has spurred the banks to expand their sales efforts into territory that is traditionally the province of stockbrokers. The domestic banks will not be alone. Foreign institutions also intend to compete for the Japanese boomers' yen. Prominently, Citigroup acquired Nikko Cordial's brokerage business and, with its 108 branches throughout Japan, could become a formidable rival [8].

Another longtime player in the Japanese market, HSBC, plans to open branches in Tokyo, Osaka, and other large cities to grab a greater share of private assets [18].

Subject to Japanese government approval, the bank wants to offer wealth management services starting in January 2008 throughout its network. It began offering private banking in Japan in 1996, catering to individuals with financial assets of more than ¥300 million, but the new service will target the 6.3 million people in Japan that the bank estimates have liquid financial assets of at least ¥10 million. This will bring it squarely into the middle-class boomer segment in direct competition with Japanese banks. Meanwhile UBS, the world's biggest money manager, opened its third branch in Japan in July 2007 and said it would target the ¥300 trillion in assets held by half a million Japanese households with assets of ¥200 million or more. According to the Bank of Japan, Japanese households still have 50% of their assets in cash or deposits, compared to 13% in the USA, so there is substantial room for growth in this business. Still, the BOJ admits that individuals are shifting their assets from deposits to higher-risk, higher-return government bonds and investment trusts. In 2007 investment trusts captured a record high of 5% of the total under management, expanding from 3.7% the year before [4].

Not only are the foreigners getting into the act, but the restructuring of Japan's financial services industry will bring complete deregulation of insurance product sales by the end of 2007. That means that the banks can offer one-stop shopping to customers interested in mutual funds, Japanese government bonds, and insurance policies, as well as the traditional bank products – loans and deposits. This will include a broadened mandate for the type of insurance products banks will be permitted to sell, beyond just the savings-type insurance that they traditionally have handled, and will include policies that offer payouts for illness or death. Bank of Tokyo-Mitsubishi UFJ, which owns the largest branch network in Japan (660 branches), is preparing to offer nearly every type of insurance to its customers. Mizuho Bank will sell medical insurance policies, but all the banks know that they must recruit experts from insurance companies who are knowledgeable about these products in order to ensure the success of this initiative [1].

The Japanese providers of financial services are aware that this silver market has unique needs and wants and they are experimenting with different ways to attract senior citizens to their different company banners. In this, they are trying to leverage the boom in services, which now accounts for some 30% of Japan's GDP and almost 60% of total consumption spending. Health-related services, such as fitness, golf, and various self-indulgent therapies and treatments are of course very popular, but entertainment and lifestyle-related recreation is also in heavy demand [3]. That being the case, some of the marketing attempts used by the banks still seem to be counter-intuitive, but that is what makes the Japanese market so fascinating and difficult in general. For example, banks have created affiliation groups for different types of diversions that enable the clients to share experiences with others who are retired or semi-retired, or empty nest couples with reduced obligations to their children and workplace. Sumitomo Mitsui Banking Corporation set up an organization called "Next Club 50s" to appeal to this particular segment. To join the club, a bank customer must have more than ¥5 million yen on deposit and be at least 54 years old. On the pretext of having a wine-tasting or learning how to make sushi, these customers are introduced by SMBC to the company's investment trusts. These are products that the bank is using to get this age and income cohort accustomed to putting at least some of their savings into instruments riskier (but potentially more rewarding) than time deposits. With some 8.4 million Japanese baby boomers expected to retire soon, banks like SMBC want to be able to retain as much of their retirement pensions in-house as possible [9]. Since the newly retired share many generational experiences, it makes sense to consider their needs as forming a cohesive core, and since they have more leisure time than any previous Japanese generation, they can be appealed to by combining financial concerns with recreational activities. In addition, as the least individuated of Japan's current generations, they are considerably less resistant to being treated as a group. It might even reduce apprehension to accepting the investment trust because others of their generation are also being solicited at the same time and during the same recreational activity.

The past decade has seen many of Japan's leading banks and insurance companies merge into ever larger entities to protect themselves from the financial ruin that threatened when the financial bubble burst in the 1990s. As a consequence, the number of institutional choices available to Japanese seniors continues to narrow, and is considerably more limited than the options available to their American or European counterparts. Since those institutions traditionally moved "in convoy" it was hard for those consumers to find any point of differentiation in the products on offer. In addition, the fact that the return on savings during the past decade has been infinitesimal compared to what it will take for the increasingly long-lived baby boomers to be self-supporting means that a note of desperation has crept into Japanese seniors' search for a way to fund their retirement needs, which also encourages the financial institutions to create new products for them.

Even the conservative Japan Post, the world's biggest financial institution with €1164 billion (¥187,000 billion) of customer monies has launched a suite of investment trusts from a variety of domestic and foreign asset managers (including Nomura, Daiwa, Goldman Sachs, Nikko, DIAM, Sumishin, and Fidelity). After struggling internally with such a major shift in strategy, it then took Japan Post a lot of time and effort to try to persuade its traditionally risk-averse customer base to buy the new products. The fact that a real market for them now exists, however, is seen in the results: Japan Post actually exceeded its annual sales target for 2006–2007 a month ahead of schedule, and will double that target for 2008 to ¥1100 billion. What is perhaps most important is that Japan Post has proved something no one would have believed possible only a few short years ago: that Japanese are willing to buy riskier investments than just savings accounts at their local neighborhood post office [16].

One reason why the financial service firms have been at all successful in selling the new investment trusts is because the long upward trend of global equity and property prices has calmed investor fears. A rising tide raises all ships. But, their success to date is also attributable to the fact that the banks and Japan Post have committed a lot of resources to the task. The insistent drumbeat of their sales pitch that Japan's retirees must begin to invest and not just save has begun to move older Japanese to reallocate their asset portfolios towards a higher risk/reward profile.

Because interest rates in Japan have remained at historic lows for the past decade it has been relatively easy to persuade older depositors to take advantage of the more attractive returns currently available from even the most conservatively managed investment trusts.

There is a double-edged sword inherent in marketing these riskier products, and the danger signs are already evident. As of 2007, 25% of Japanese customers who purchased investment trusts from major banks or brokerages were not satisfied with the service rendered because of sales fees that are too high or a dearth of post-purchase information and insufficient explanation of the risks associated with the products. Significantly, the level of customer satisfaction was much higher when investment trusts were bought from online brokerages or directly from the mutual fund company [7]. So, the giants of Japan's financial community must not underestimate this target market as they did for so many decades when a highly regulated system gave them the advantages of an oligopoly without the possibility of credible foreign competition. The world is changing, and the silver market is a cohort that will vote with its assets and take its wealth elsewhere if not treated properly.

The banks have had extra motivation since October 2007 to improve their service because a new law was passed whose intent is to protect elderly customers from sharp practices when buying investment trusts and other risk products. Now, selling risk instruments to seniors without first confirming that they understand how the products work could subject the seller to government penalties, so banks are working to ensure compliance. Sumitomo Mitsui Banking Corp. requires that customers aged 70 or older be accompanied by a family member when purchasing a variable annuity. Bank of Tokyo-Mitsubishi UFJ explains the risks involved at least twice to customers over 70 when selling investment trusts and variable annuities. Some banks are also strengthening their after-sales service, such as Mizuho Bank, which is starting to increase the frequency of visits to customers over 70 to explain the investment performance of their holdings to less than 6 months between calls [6].

The sub-prime mortgage bubble, which burst in late 2007 and continues to work its way through the international financial system, affecting Japan as well as the USA and other advanced economies, only serves to strengthen the call for caution and attention to legal and ethical constraints on financial product marketing to elder citizens on limited or fixed incomes. There are no doubt older Americans in danger of losing the roof over their heads in the fallout from the sub-prime mortgage implosion, and this issue must also be taken into consideration when marketing housing to retirees in Japan.

Marketing Real Estate to Older Consumers

One's house is truly one's castle, and this becomes even more so as we age and our mobility declines. Sometimes, when children grow and leave the family home, it becomes obvious that we might be happier, more comfortable, or better served by a different type of housing. This sentiment became the stimulus for a mass movement in the USA over the past quarter century, with a major shift of retirees to properties that had been developed with them in mind, in Sun Belt states like Florida, Texas, and California where they were offered adults-only communities that promised them a carefree lifestyle. Japan has not been immune to the impact of this cultural shift, but the importance placed on family members as caregivers of their own elderly at first created a somewhat different twist on the concept of senior housing.

The high cost of living in Japan proper has also created an opportunity for marketing housing solutions outside of Japan to Japanese baby boomers. This movement occurred in the UK on a large scale, where thousands of retired British subjects became permanent expatriates in Spain and Italy. Also, in the USA increasing numbers of American retirees on fixed incomes have been buying condominiums in Panama and Costa Rica because they provide cheaper alternatives for growing old comfortably than are currently available in the USA proper.

However, housing alternatives for the silver market must take into account both the economic and the social aspects of their lives. For most Japanese boomers, their peak earning years are over and, depending on their financial situation, they will either have to live on a limited fixed income or be able to call on rather substantial liquid assets for their retirement lifestyle. In either case, the issue of appropriate housing requires a consideration of the fact that the strength of the Japanese family unit is in fact weakening, though perhaps not to the degree that can be seen in the USA. Hard evidence about how much more these baby boomers want to distance themselves from their children's lives, and vice versa, than was thought possible only a few years ago can be found in the data on the decline of co-residential living arrangements among contemporary Japanese families.

Between 1975 and 1995 the proportion of Japan's over-65 population living together with their children fell from 72 to 49% and there was a corresponding increase in the percentage of older Japanese living alone (from 7 to 12%) and in couple-only households (almost doubling, from 15 to 28%) [11]. These trends have continued and, if anything, may have even accelerated. Developers and marketers of residential properties saw an opportunity to sell a type of housing to these older Japanese that fused the ideal of keeping the entire family under one roof with the reality that parents and married children are frequently less willing to compromise their privacy than in previous generations. The existence of such contradictory emotions led to the creation of the multi-generation house.

The "two-generation house" (*nisetai jutaku*) was a concept that was supposed to provide parent and child with separate housing units under the same roof, and the Japanese government added its seal of approval for this model by legally stipulating that the two families in the dwelling had to be related to each other. Of the ten major housing companies, the three largest in 1994 (Sekisui House, Misawa Home, and Daiwa House) reported that approximately one third of their orders were for *nisetai jutaku* (see pages 60–61 in [2]). Similar to the pace and direction of deregulation in financial services, with housing policy as well, the not-so-subtle influence of the Japanese government is apparent in the way the industry is allowed to develop and the specific products it offers to fulfill the anticipated needs and desires of the baby boom generation. A not irrelevant issue encouraging the proliferation of *nisetai jutaku* housing was the fact that the housing company would be able to secure an advantageous "two-generation loan" to finance the construction of this type of residence (see p. 62 in [2]).

But, there was trouble in paradise that within a decade led to questioning the very rationale for the two-generation home. The parents felt cheated, because their assets had been a major reason why such housing could be created, but they perceived little benefit from the close proximity with the family of their offspring. The marketing of this housing involved promoting an unrealistically harmonious view of three generations living together in an almost idyllic environment. The reality was that "the anticipation of the elderly couple in the sharing of their grandchildren was not matched by the reality of being left alone with them" as perpetually available babysitters (see p. 64 in [2]).The adult children gained more from this arrangement than did their elderly parents, who felt their freedom of movement was constrained by the expectation that they would always be willing to take care of their grandchildren, even as their own grown-up children paid them little attention except when they were needed.

In a reaction to the negative feedback from the multi-generational home, the real estate industry began to realize that a change in marketing strategy was needed. Out of this necessity was born the promotion of technologically advanced and user-friendly housing for the elderly. Behind such an initiative lay the recognition that elderly parents had been the financial senior partner in the joint household situation from the start, often because they owned the very land upon which the house was built (see p. 65 in [2]). So, in the mid-1990s homes with safer, more convenient features for elder residents began to appear in Japan. Some of these amenities included wider corridors (to accommodate wheelchairs), the elimination of thresholds and steps within the house between rooms, installation of railings in bathrooms and along walls, and the use of extra large and easy-to-read switches for lights and fixtures (see p. 66 in [2]).

The development companies learned that the ideological emphasis on a multi-generational family living together as in the past is not the great selling point they had assumed it would be. Japanese seniors are waking up to the altered emotional landscape of the family in the twenty-first century and are more interested in finding a housing solution that suits their own needs, rather than one which keeps the family "together" under terms unfavorable to their autonomy and freedom. This altered emphasis matches the government's recognition that families can no longer be shamed into taking care of their elder members, a technique for social control that had been used successfully countless times in Japan's recent past. Public agencies or private services increasingly will have to pick up the slack as fewer young Japanese are willing or able to make the sacrifices required to take care of their aging parents.

A third type of solution for the housing needs of the baby boomer generation – besides the multi-generation home or the "reformed" dwelling – lies not within Japan itself but beyond its borders. Although Japan has the world's oldest population, it is not the pioneer in this activity. The British have long been relocating outside of the British Isles to the warmer climes and cheaper living available on the coasts of Spain and in Italy, as well as other Mediterranean locations. The USA has the advantage of being a large, continental country with its own Sun Belt perfectly suited for the golf courses, hot tubs, outdoor pools, tennis and shuffleboard courts, and the easy living touted by retirement communities consisting of homes and condominiums built specifically for the older buyer. Language and culture, of course, are not a problem for Americans and Canadian "snowbirds" who simply migrate south or west. Nevertheless, the high cost of living in the USA has encouraged Americans to look abroad too, mainly south of the border in Central America and the Caribbean, for environments boasting both a warm climate and a low cost of living. Panama, in particular, has become extremely popular as a long-stay destination for such retirees.[3]

For the Japanese who choose to move abroad to find pleasant and affordable surroundings, the different languages, cultures, and level of health and other services available are important considerations and constitute substantial obstacles to the marketing of this real estate option. To date, not many older Japanese have actually migrated to the Philippines, Malaysia, Thailand or other countries that have tried to attract them in order to bring their foreign exchange into the various domestic economies. Nevertheless, the idea keeps growing, and these three Southeast Asian countries in particular seem to think that attracting the Japanese baby boomer expatriate is a viable marketing proposition. Each has devised a different program with varying financial and visa requirements (see Table 28.1 below).

The concept of overseas migration for the retired was introduced to the Japanese population in 1986, when the Japanese government proposed a project called "Silver Colonies" to build towns and villages for Japanese pensioners in Australia. That project never materialized because of Australian opposition. In 1992 the Japanese

---

[3] Sinpatanasakul [13] describes in detail why Panama is the number one destination for Americans seeking a low cost of living country to retire. The visa program offered by Panama, known as the "pensionado" program, provides retirees with discounts that have no serious competition anywhere else. As long as retirees are able to document a minimum monthly pension of US$500 (in addition to US$100 for each dependent), they are eligible for the pensionado visa offering the following benefits:

Import duty exemption for household goods
Tax exemption to import a new car every 2 years
50% off entertainment anywhere in the country (movies, theaters, concerts, sporting events)
30% off in-country bus, boat, and train fares
25% off in-country airline tickets
50% off hotel stays Monday through Thursday
30% off hotels stays Friday through Sunday
25% off restaurant bills
15% off at fast-food restaurants
15% off hospital bills (if no insurance applies)
10% off prescription medicines
20% off medical consultations
15% off dental and eye exams
20% off professional and technical services
50% reduction in closing costs for home loans
25% discounts on utility bills
15% off loans made in your name
1% less on home mortgages for homes used for personal residence
20-year property tax exemptions on all newly constructed homes

Table 28.1 Long-term Japanese expatriate resident requirements and conditions in three Southeast Asian countries [13]

	Thailand	Malaysia	Philippines
Visa name	Thai second home	Malaysia my second home	Special resident retiree's visa
Visa duration	Permanent	10 years	Permanent
Financial requirements	Monthly income of US$1650 or deposit of US$25,000	Local deposit of US$87,000 (under 50); US$43,000 (over 50)	Monthly pension of US$800+local deposit US$10,000 (over 50)
Property ownership	60/40 Thai/foreigner	Yes	60/40 Filipino/foreigner
Tax policy	Offshore income is tax-free	Offshore income is tax-free	Offshore income is tax-free
Cost of living	Rank 127th	Rank 114th	Rank 141st
Health care	Outstanding	Advanced	Advanced
Politics and crime:			
Political stability	0.55	0.51	−0.49
Terrorism index	1	1	4
Crime index	Ranked 14th	Ranked 34th	N/A
Language	Thai	English, Malay	English, Filipino

Long-Stay Foundation was established to facilitate long-stay tourism abroad. Southeast Asian countries began to see the economic virtue of this idea after the slump caused by the economic crisis of 1996. The crisis proved a stimulus for Malaysia, Thailand, and the Philippines to launch individual programs that created special visa categories for retirees. But, purchase behavior and incentives vary with different income groups. Japanese with higher incomes prefer to travel to various countries for a "look-see" before they decide on where to eventually settle, while less affluent retirees tend to move directly to a country because of the lower cost of living there ([14] as cited in [13]).

For these various initiatives to succeed, a health and welfare infrastructure that is Japanese-friendly must be erected. Having healthcare facilities staffed with Japanese speakers is one way Thailand has tried to make itself more attractive to the potential Japanese long-stay prospect. The relative lack of security in some of these countries when compared to Japan is another issue that must be tackled to set the risk-averse Japanese baby boomers' minds at ease. So, this is still a work in progress, but if economic conditions continue to favor an overseas cost-of-living, it is one option that Japan's silver citizens may well begin to take more seriously.

Summary and Conclusion

Enabling Japan's aging population to (i) sustain and support itself from its accumulated savings and (ii) enhance its quality of life are two goals that can best be served by innovative product development on the part of the financial services and real estate industries. Key points that have been discussed in this chapter include the following:

- The rapidity with which Japan is becoming a geriatric nation means that it must be a pioneer in creating solutions for enabling its elderly to grow old in physical comfort and financial security, or suffer the consequences of failing to do so. In this chapter we have examined some of the initiatives that promise to reward the creative marketer, while simultaneously fulfilling this promise of a better life for the country's seniors.

- One area of these innovations is designing financial instruments that answer the need for higher returns without unduly increasing the older investor's risk. This issue has taken on new urgency with the global sub-prime mortgage crisis currently rippling through the developed world's banking and securities industries and jeopardizing not only the retirement nest-egg of millions of senior citizens in the USA, Japan, and the European Union, but the very financial structures of those countries as well. The new cautious environment means that marketing financial services to the elderly will increasingly emphasize legal and ethical constraints on risk exposure. This will be in addition to the current Japanese focus on designing products that offer an attractive return and on providing ancillary services that attract seniors to particular banks or financial institutions in order to capture a larger share of their investment business.

- Another initiative involves creating new and renovated housing options that are elder-friendly, including the packaging of practical offerings that would make it possible for seniors to move abroad in order to enjoy an affordable retirement lifestyle not possible on a fixed income in Japan proper. Quality of life issues relevant to older Japanese will receive increasing attention from Japanese firms that develop real estate and renovate (reform) older properties. This trend may also influence the way the residential real estate industry evolves elsewhere in the world, such as in the USA and Europe, where the population is aging more slowly but will have similar needs in the not-too-distant future as they bulk larger in those countries' total populations, and where inexpensive overseas housing alternatives might become more mainstream choices.

Time will tell which of the many options will capture the imagination – and the pocketbooks – of Japan's aging boomers. But, they are so important to the Japanese economy that their needs cannot be denied. The more attentive and creative marketers will win the competition for their patronage, as the financial services and residential real estate industries continue to transform themselves to accommodate this major consumer market.

References

1. Banks gear up for insurance deregulation, *The Nikkei Weekly* (September 3, 2007)
2. N. Brown, Under one roof: the evolving story of three generation housing in Japan, in *Demographic change and the family in Japan's aging society* ed. by J.W. Traphagan, J. Knight, (SUNY, New York, 2003), pp. 53–71

3. Consumers splurging on services, *The Nikkei Weekly* (19 Feb, 2007)
4. Household assets hit record ¥1.56 quadrillion in June, *The Japan Times* (19 Sept, 2007)
5. Japan has highest ratio of elderly, government, *International Herald Tribune* (11 July, 2007)
6. Law prompts banks to heighten protection for elderly customers, *The Nikkei Weekly* (1 October, 2007)
7. Mutual fund buyers express discontent with banks, brokerages, *The Nikkei Weekly* (27 August, 2007)
8. M. Nakamoto, Bid reflects a shifting climate, *Financial Times* (7 March, 2007)
9. M. Nakamoto, Pension attention: why the investment pots await Japan's big savings switch, *Financial Times* (12 January, 2007)
10. People age 80 and over top 7 million, *The Japan Times* (17 September, 2007)
11. J.M. Raymo, T. Kaneda, Changes in the living arrangements of Japanese elderly: the role of demographic factors, in *Demographic change and the family in Japan's aging society* ed. by J.W. Traphagan. J. Knight, (SUNY, New York, 2003), pp. 27–52
12. P. Rial, Around the markets: leisure companies may benefit as Japanese baby boomers retire, *International Herald Tribune* (23 February, 2007)
13. A. Sinpatanasakul, *Senior expatriate tide: marketing overseas housing to the retired,* MBA thesis, Waseda University, (2007)
14. M. Toyota, A. Bocker, E. Guild, Pensioners on the move: social security and trans-border retirement migration in Asia and Europe, ASEF-Alliance Workshop, spring 2006, *IIAS Newsletter* no. 40 (2006)
15. D. Turner, Money follows Japan's baby boomers, *Financial Times* (31 January, 2007)
16. D. Turner, Japanese experiment lures the risk-averse, *Financial Times* (23 April, 2007)
17. S.K. Vogel, *Japan remodeled: how government and industry are reforming Japanese capitalism* (Cornell University, Ithaca, 2006)
18. M. Yasu, F. Flynn, HSBC to expand in Japan, *International Herald Tribune* (6 September, 2007)

Chapter 29
Medical System Reforms and Medical Information Systems in Japan

N. Kishida

Abstract Japan is undertaking medical system reforms in order to suppress the ballooning national medical expenses of the aging society. Medical computerization is one of the focal issues for this. The government has stated a plan to mandate the online billing of medical service fees for all medical institutions. The prevalence of electronic medical records (EMR), which has been delayed due to unsophisticated information technology (IT) and the limited IT literacy of elderly medical staff in general, should be promoted. Without the prevalence of EMR, several social innovations, the regional coordinated medical service, and the future National Health Record service etc., will not become reality. The author advocates inducing newcomers to innovate business models by means of deregulations, so as to promote more investment in the medical information market from the business sector, and to accelerate the build-up of regional medical information networks based on networked EMR systems.

Introduction

The most popular Japanese word for the electronic medical record (EMR) is *Denshi karute*. *Denshi* means electronic in Japanese, while *karute* has its origin in the German *karte,* which means a card. Japan had learned so much from German medicine since the nineteenth century that Japanese medical personnel still use some jargon of German origin. Besides *karute* for medical records, there are *kuranke* (kranke) for a patient and *ento* (entlassen) for the discharging from a hospital, for example [6].

Nowadays, Japanese medicine is under a strong influence from US medicine, which leads the medical science of the world, and English is used frequently among Japanese medical experts. Nevertheless, jargon of German origins still survives in practical medical institutions, which have long been sustained by the personnel who learned a lot from German medicine.

In this chapter, the development and the implementation of medical information systems in Japan, especially EMR for clinics, is discussed from a view point of possible business opportunities and required innovations, which have appeared in dealing with the national healthcare issues of the coming aging society.

Japanese attempts to develop EMR started in the 1980s. These were local attempts by limited university hospitals or voluntary practitioners. In those days, EMR was generally regarded as a tool to decrease paperwork and for the filing of stocks of films in medical institutions. With the remarkable progress in IT, deepened discussions on medical information systems by the various experts concerned were made during the 1990s. Medical computerization was gradually accepted as one of the important means for the institutional reform of the public healthcare system to cope with the aging society. Now, the penetration of EMR is considered as a relevant indicator of the computerization of medical institutions.

In order to arrange conditions for introducing EMR to medical institutions, the government made a notification in April 1999 and allowed the keeping of medical records. These were mandated by medicinal law and dentistry law, in electronic media, provided each medical agency was responsible for certain requirements. Then, in December 2001, the IT Strategy Headquarters of the Cabinet Office released "The ground design for computerizations in the healthcare sector" as a part of "e-Japan Priority Policy Program." It set as policy objective that the EMR system penetration would be 60% of all hospitals with 400 beds or more and 60% of all clinics by the end of 2006. However, a recent survey suggested that 30% of hospitals with 400 beds or more (6% of all hospitals) and merely 7% of clinics would have introduced EMR systems by that date [9].

The Ministry of Health, Labor, and Welfare (MHLW) renewed the ground design for medical computerizations in March 2007. New ground design basically inherited the outline and the achievements of the old one, and stressed the importance of the integration and the optimization of medical computerization for the whole society. But, it was devoid of numeric targets, and made no mention of financial resources. The computerization of Japanese medical institutions is still underway.

Public Healthcare System Reforms for the Aging Society

The Japanese public healthcare system reforms to handle ballooning medical expenses are found against the background of these medical computerization issues.

In Japan, an universal care policy was established in 1961 and various public healthcare insurers have been sustaining this policy. Under this policy, every Japanese is insured by one of the public insurers, and may equally enjoy the benefit of high quality medical services in any region of Japan, of those expenses mostly covered by one's healthcare insurance. Medical institutions care for patients first, then bill the insurers. The government sets the prices of medical service fees in every other year, while insurance rates differ among insurers depending upon their financial conditions. As the baby boomers have begun to retire, the burdens of the government-managed Employee's Health Insurance and the municipalities-managed National Health Insurances are getting heavier. Because of this, the new health insurers for the "late-stage elderly people" (those who are 75 years old or more) are going to be established, one for each prefecture by all municipalities in 2008. In the new system, medical expenses are paid 10% by the insured, about 40% by local governments and the treasury payment, and about 50% by other insurers (e.g., corporate health insurance societies). Also, new price tables for the new insurers will be optimized for geriatric care.

The 2007 financial year (FY2007) state budget of Japan was JPY 83 trillion (US$720 billion, when US$1 = JPY 115). About 25% of this, JPY 21 trillion, was spent on the redemption and interest payments of government bonds, which would amount to JPY 547 trillion by the end of March 2008. Another JPY 15 trillion was distributed among local governments. The general policy spending was limited to JPY 47 trillion, and the social welfare spending, which included the public medical spending, shared 43.4% of it, a total of JPY 20.4 trillion [14]. The ratio of national medical expenses to GDP was 8%, which ranked Japan in the 18th place among the OECD countries in 2003 [24]. Although this figure does not seem so extreme, it is expected to get worse in the future without adequate countermeasures. The Japanese government had discounted 3.16% of the medical service fee since April 2006, the largest price cut ever made, only to find a slightly (0.1%) increased estimated national medical expenses of JPY 32.4 trillion in FY2006 [20]. This shows the difficulties in decreasing the national medical expenses of an aging advanced country, because novel expensive advanced therapies are often accepted.

The government is setting forward a medical expense moderation total plan based on the Medical System Reform Act of June 2006. To prepare this act, MHLW made a long-term forecast for the public medical spending in October 2005. This forecast predicted that JPY 28.3 trillion of the public medical spending in FY2006 would be JPY 56 trillion in FY2025 without the reform, while it could be moderated to JPY 42 trillion with the reform [16]. The computerization of healthcare, such as EMR, is considered to leverage the plan in enabling a higher transparency of medical treatments, as well as a higher operational efficiency.

The reform also aims to decrease prolonged hospitalizations of elderly people. Instead, bedfast old persons will be cared for jointly by three actors. Acute hospitalizations will be covered by health insurances, and the home care of the convalescence or the terminal stage will be supplemented by household efforts and the long-term care insurances managed by municipalities. Because multiple medical and nursing teams will take care of the same patient in such a system, the prevalence and the sharing of EMR are desired for the regional healthcare partnership.

Moreover, the computerization of medical institutions is relevant to human resource purposes. It is said that there are enough medical doctors in Japan, although some problems, such as the shortage of medical practitioners in underpopulated areas, unevenly located specific departments like gynecology or pediatrics, and the overworking of hospital doctors are observed [17]. The medical computerization is not a silver bullet, but is expected to relieve these symptoms by the telemedicine technology and ameliorations in operational efficiency.

The shortage of nursing staff is also serious. The Japanese Nursing Association reported that roughly 38,000 fresh nursing personnel started working in hospitals in April 2006 while about 10,000 nursing students had failed or given up being nursing staff. About 100,000 nurses out of 810,000 in all Japanese hospitals leave their jobs every year, because of both retirements and career changes. It is estimated that latent nurses, those who have nursing licenses but have not been working as nursing staff since leaving hospital jobs, amount to about 550,000. The causes of this situation are described as health or family problems due to hard work, fears of medical accident risks, and misgivings about one's own vocational capability [7]. Medical computerization will contribute not only to suppress nurses from early retirements, but also to revitalize latent nurses by ameliorating the operational efficiency, sharing the best nursing practices, and clarifying responsibility in case of medical accidents.

Online Billing and the National Health Record Data Base

The bill statement for medical service fee, which is called the "receipt" generally in Japan, is another principal output of medical computerization. A medical accounting system in the Hospital Information System (HIS) usually handles receipts in hospitals. A HIS consists of several sub-systems, such as the clinical assay, the prescription, the reservation, and the ordering. The ordering system is considered the basic HIS function, while EMR is an important option. Regardless of EMR functions, the penetration of HIS was 22% in October 2005, and 73% for hospitals with 400 beds or more, inclusive. The larger the hospitals were, the more of them had developed HIS [15]. The top EMR vendor for HIS was Fujitsu that shared 32% in April 2007, followed by NEC, CSI, and Software Service. Those four vendors shared over 70% of all HIS with ordering systems in operation [23].

The so-called *resekon*, the receipt computer, is used in 66% of clinics and 97% of hospitals [3,13]. While a resekon is an integrated medical accounting sub-system in many HIS, the resekon for a clinic is basically a PC workstation in which medical accounting software is installed. The software is a strong entry barrier, because not only medical service fee calculations require special knowledge and know-how about complicated logics and minute exceptions, but the fee table is revised biyearly and version update services are necessary.

The typical minimum resekon system for a clinic, which consists of a server, a client, and a printer, costs roughly JPY 1 million for the hardware and JPY 3 million for the software. It is a prominent investment for a startup medical practitioner, who often leases it for 3–5 years. These expensive resekons had outputted only paper-printed receipts before. MHLW approved digitized receipts in December 2001, but only in FD or MO forms. MHLW argued that this elementary computerization, however, had halved the overtime work of medical accounting clerks, saved JPY 480,000 per month, and decreased clerical mistakes in receipts by 40% in a hospital with 250 beds [21]. It shows how evidently the medical computerization contributes to ameliorations in operational efficiency, though only 38.6% of receipts were digitized by the end of 2006 [19].

Hospitals and clinics render receipts to the check and payment organizations (CPO) monthly. CPOs make formality checks on all receipts they received, then sort and forward them to the various insurers concerned. Each insurer inspects receipts forwarded from CPOs and sends back suspicious ones to CPOs for reviews. Insurers pay determined amounts insured to CPOs and each CPO distributes it to corresponding hospitals or clinics. CPO business is a semi-oligopoly market, which is almost shared by 47 National Health Insurance Organizations (one for each prefecture) and the Social Insurance Medical Fee Payment Fund (SIMF). In FY2006, SIMF dealt 846,640,000 receipts, of which the determined amount insured was JPY 10,226.8 billion. All the digitized receipts were printed out on paper so as to suit traditional clerical works in CPOs. SIMF spent JPY 65 billion annually to sustain these works by 5000 clerks and 4500 doctors [4].

SIMF charges a fee of JPY 110 per receipt to cover those costs, but some medical institutions are unhappy about paying for these old-fashioned labor-intensive methods and some insurers sometimes blame the SIMF for the quality of its services.

Reflecting on those longstanding complaints, MHLW allowed the CPOs to make their receipt checking and payment works online in 2006. Now, some of large hospitals have started to render their receipts online to CPOs and formality checks are done partly by software. So far, because some CPOs accept receipts online while other CPOs do not, medical institutions are forced and annoyed to prepare various kinds of receipt, such as on paper, in FD/MOs, and via online networks. In April 2006, the government showed a timetable and stated that receipt submission online would at last be mandatory step-by-step for all medical institutions by 2011.

It is ideal to substitute the whole current labor-intensive receipt checking work by doctors and experts to the AI expert system that may judge fraud billings or unnecessary tests and medications. However, development of the "electronic point table" for the online calculation of the medical service fee had just started in 2007. Works to simplify the huge current medical service fee point tables, as well as arguments to clarify the complicated calculation logics so as to suit requirements of the future online AI expert systems, are undertaken in MHLW. The first electronic point table is to be released by the spring of 2008.

Also, to build up medical databases by gathering information from online receipts is very promising as a source of epidemical studies and policies. Since April 2007, MHLW had already started a challenge to shorten the average length of a hospital stay, of which the goal was set based on the data achieved from analysis of paper/MO receipts. When the real-time online receipt database enables quick and total surveys in the future, effective health and epidemic prevention systems based on detailed geographical and/or demographical analysis will be possible.

Prevention of diseases will also cut the medical expenses. The concept of the NHR is under discussion in Japan. NHR is a personalized total health database managed at the national level. Under the NHR system, each person uses a single NHR account throughout their life, while the authorities may consult and analyze health information of the nation as a whole. Some kinds of NHR are being developed in

Canada, UK, USA, and the Nordic countries, but Japan has been reluctant because of issues concerning personal information and the development costs. A recent scenario for NHR in Japan [27] regards the development of regional EMR networks as a step of the NHR implementation process.

Before the NHR concept arose, several attempts of the regional medical information network for coordinated healthcare had been made. There are publicly funded projects on issues like cerebral strokes [28] or obstetrics [13]. These have been put into trials on some regional EMR networks, and owe a lot for their developments to the strong private initiatives of certain doctors or local governments. On the base of the precedent regional EMR networks, the coordinated medical care services may show a sizable progress.

Troubles On-Site: Calling for Innovations

Unless EMR is prevalent in clinics, effective coordinated care services in regions will be spoiled. Effects on smoother care-team management are often pointed as a merit of EMR, as well as fewer mis-prescriptions, the easier search for specific records, and cost-cutting in archives or clerks.

A survey [22] showed that the top-share EMR vendor for clinics was BML at 23%, the second was Hitachi Softech at 22%, followed by Sanyo at 21%, and Labotech at 11%. Despite of the imperfectness of these figures because major HIS EMR vendors, like Fujitsu etc., did not disclose their sales performance in the clinic market, the top four ranking above is believed to be accurate. But, the penetration of EMR in clinics was only estimated to be 7% by 2006.

A survey [25] described the reasons why "e-Japan Priority Policy Program" failed to fulfill its target in the EMR penetration, especially in the clinic segment. More than 40% of the EMR-negative doctors and dentists agreed with three reasons: (i) the low operability (49%), (ii) the high introduction cost (48%), and (iii) the uncertain merits of adoption (45%). Because the EMR penetration in clinics (7%) did not reach the "average minus 1σ" line of the normal probability distribution, it is estimated that not all opinion leaders or early adopters had accepted EMR yet, according to the Rogers curve theory [26]. It means that the majority of Japanese medical practitioners valued EMR as not being value for money. EMR systems require more innovations.

Standardizations are inevitable because medical computerization is an application of the advanced network information technology. Many of the trailblazing HIS and EMR were developed for closed systems, and were incapable of connecting networks due to their unique medical codes, lack of communication protocols, and differences in system architectures. Early challenges of the standardization of the EMR networking appeared during 1990s. MHLW and the Medical Information System Development Center (MEDIS-DC), supervised by the Ministry of Economy, Trade, and Industry (METI), played major roles in the standardizations of terminology and the coding. Some made attempts to establish Japanese standards such as the

MML (a Japan-made EMR language) at first, but in the end, international standards were gradually accepted for the sake of the versatile connectivity. Although a set of standards for EMR have almost gained a consensus now, the launch of standard EMR systems and the replacement of old ones are still going on.

The Japanese Medical Association (JMA), the largest physician's organization in Japan, developed a standard online resekon system for clinics so as to establish an on-site standard platform of medical computerizations, according to "The JMA Declaration of Medical Computerization" in 2001. In this project, which is called ORCA (Online Receipt Computer Advantage), JMA proffers a free standardized network resekon (the JMA standard receipt software) and materials for standardized EMR developments as an open source stock footage. Also, JMA trains and organizes volunteer software houses and value-added resellers all over Japan as JMA-certified IT support shops, striving after the diffusion of the standardized online resekon with EMR (which operates on a Linux PC workstation of the multi-vendor delivery platforms). There were 135 JMA-certified IT support shops in September 2007 [10]. A total of 5139 medical institutions had introduced the JMA standard receipt software in January 2008 [11]. This is only about 4.7% of 107,790, the total of Japanese medical institutions in February 2007 [18]. The ORCA project is considered a successful attempt because almost all the vendors of resekon and EMR have adopted the ORCA standard now.

BML, the numberone EMR vendor for clinics, is the second largest clinical laboratory firm in Japan. BML has featured the smooth integration of its laboratory test services and its EMR products, and occupies the current market leading position. The number two EMR vendor Hitachi adopted a practitioner-designed software (by MD Masahiko Yoshihara) as the prototype of its EMR product for clinics. Surpassing some major medical equipment makers like Toshiba or Shimadzu, a home electronic appliance company, Sanyo, is the number three EMR vendor for clinics, due to its tactful product designs and services. Some EMR-specialized emerging companies (EMR VB) fare better in this market, like the number four EMR vendor, Labotech.

The low operability, which is the worst obstacle to EMR prevalence, is of a combined etiology. While there had been actually many EMR software systems with terrible user operability before, the computer literacy of the medical professionals was also highly individual. Computer illiterate doctors had a voice in those days, partly because early EMRs that originated as early as the 1980s were said to be created mostly through the initiatives of some enthusiastic doctors, those who we would now call nerds. Almost all early products were designed to operate on classic Japanese PC architectures, like the PC98, have faded out, but a few early EMR VB have managed to survive in niches like Apple Doctor and Yui Consulting. The early trailblazing PC-based EMRs for clinics left sour reputations in general. On the other hand, a user-friendly EMR for HIS was rarely developed because trouble shooting of the ordering system, which was often developed by system engineers unfamiliar to hospital works, were the primal mission of the computing staff on early HISs in large hospitals [1].

Whether it is due to individual capabilities or poor system designs, if an EMR system with low operability were actually introduced to a doctor's office on-site, the doctor's workloads and the consultation time per patient would be increased, and it would end in lower medical service and poorer business conditions for the medical institution. This is why the number one reason for denying the adoption of EMR was the low operability.

Various Innovations and Business Chances

So far, conventional new EMR product developments have been incremental product innovations, focused on ameliorating the operability in order to sophisticate new products to suit the practical on-site purposes. Some EMR VB's products featuring a superior operability share around 2% of the clinical market [22]. Three ways for differentiation are observed: (i) smooth linkage with other medical devices (Agape), (ii) integrated resekon and ordering functions as if it were a mini-HIS (Sanei Medisys, Medical Information), and (iii) unique data entry technologies (Labotech, Yuyama).

Expecting the future NHR network, EMR systems for clinics will soon compete at the higher level, the regional medical information network level. In a METI and MEDIS-DC joint program "The regional medical information network system standardization and demonstration project," a perinatal EMR network system, which is based on a Kagawa prefecture-developed prototype, was put into trials in 2006 for 3 years in four areas (Tokyo, Chiba, Iwate, and Kagawa). Systems developed thorough such programs will become the Japanese standard.

Because the physician in charge and the patient are to legally share one's personal EMR in Japan, each clinic is expected to operate its EMR server. Those clinical EMR servers connect by wide area network (WAN) or the web-based virtual private network (VPN) to the regional medical information network servers that are operated in the regional core hospitals, and constitute a regional network system. The Kagawa perinatal EMR network provides a standardized EMR application by the web, although the networked clinics may use their own EMR systems as long as they are standardized products. For this network system, Shikoku Electric Power group serves for the server management, while Fujitsu integrates the core EMR network server. Because Fujitsu has gotten a late start in the clinical EMR race, it plans to turn the game around at once in this opportunity of the coming regional medical information network build-up phase.

Kameda Medical Center, which hosts the perinatal EMR network trial in Chiba, is known for its trailblazing efforts to organize a private regional medical information network in its home town, Kamogawa city. More than 150 licenses for Kameda's network-capable HISs and EMRs have been distributed by IBM Japan or Apius, an EMR VB established by the Kameda and Sumitomo Corporation [2]. A successful trial in Chiba will guarantee the success of the network systems, in several regions, of those core hospitals that have already adopted Kameda's HIS.

Some small software houses have found their place in niche, user interface-related segments of the networked EMR system market when they worked with large HIS integrators as partners. For example, Mitla developed the web-based EMR system for the Kagawa perinatal EMR network with the NTT docomo group. Interface Technology developed a mobile EMR client system for Ehime University Hospital with Hitachi and Casio.

Apart from these server-centralized approaches for the regional medical information networking, there is another approach which will preliminarily distribute standardized medical information applications to hospitals and clinics widely in the region, while waiting for the maturity of the platform technology and infrastructures. The Shizuoka prefectural EMR was developed by SBS Information Systems and four other IT firms for Shizuoka prefecture. It is a referral editor module attachable to HISs of major vendors. It reads out and backups EMR data from the attached HIS periodically and prepares the issue of digitized referral forms in CD-ROMs on demand. Referrals may be read in an ordinary PC because the viewer is bundled into the CD-ROM. This is an attempt to accelerate the standardization of EMR in clinics by supplying a practical standardized application that is useful even in an environment with inadequate network infrastructure. It also makes sense when the network has broken down, in case of a large earthquake for example. MHLW adopted this Shizuoka EMR in 2006 as the prototype of the new standard EMR software SS-MIX, and is planning to distribute it nationwide.

Theoretical Aspects of the Innovations

In some prominent innovation theories, the relationship between a novel technology and an existing one is understood dynamically by utilizing a sort of learning curve [5, 12]. A general principal is shown in Fig. 29.1. The performance of an

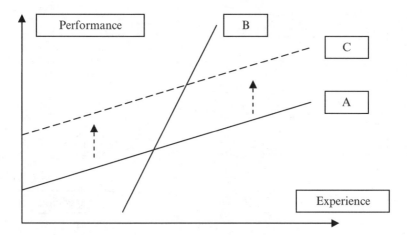

Fig. 29.1 Relative performance change between old and new technologies in general

existing technology A will move up along the curve A as operational experiences are accumulated. Moreover, *Kaizen*, the Japanese favorite incremental innovations will shift the curve A gradually upward, in this figure, to the curve C. On the other hand, the curve B, which represents the performance of a novel technology B has a steeper rising slope than A's. The performance of B is smaller than that of A initially, but the more B's experiences are accumulated, the greater B's performance will be, and the technology A will finally be replaced with the technology B.

The existing Japanese healthcare is sustained by highly labor-intensive efforts of medical staff. This system is so matured that its learning curve is expected to be marginally ameliorated from now on. The cause of the delay in the medical computerization is assumed to be that the curve B of the novel IT-supported healthcare is supposed to take on an irregular stepwise pattern because of its complexity. The new technology is, in fact, a set of services by various actors coordinated by networked EMR. If it is ideally optimized, its learning curve would have a constant steep rising slope like the curve B in Fig. 29.1. But, if a constraint appears somewhere in the complicated operations, the growth of the performance will be deterred. The stair-like flat part of curve B in Fig. 29.2. represents this.

Because healthcare is a public service equally guaranteed to every Japanese in any region of Japan, any computerized healthcare in which performance is not up to the existing level of care will not be adopted at all. Under such circumstance, neither learning curve effects nor incremental innovations are possible. The very beauties of the current Japanese healthcare system, such as sophisticated care levels by existing integrated medical systems and the universal care policy, seem to hinderrapid medical computerization. In other words, the core issue is that of reforming the healthcare system of Japan to an IT-supported one that is suitable for an aging society, while minimizing the tradeoff on burdens and service qualities.

So far, current trials have focused on urgent diseases like brain stroke or on maternity care, whose service levels have been of concern recently due to human resource

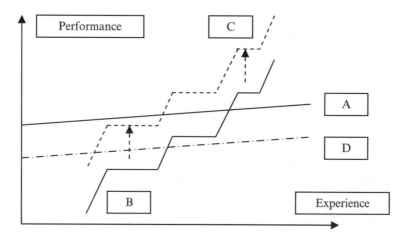

Fig. 29.2 Strategy to implement a new technology with a stair-like learning curve

problems. The trials can be interpreted as the development of incremental innovations for the new IT-coordinated regional healthcare by well- trained IT personnel in regions with highly network-capable environments. This means applying new technology to the sectors whose existing learning curves are D, then shifting up the new technology's curve B to the level of the curve C by means of incremental innovations. When applying the new technology, which is ameliorated to the curve C, to the general medical sectors whose existing curves are A, it is obvious that the timing in technological replacement will come one stair earlier.

An Innovation Paradox: Retrenchment Requires Investments

The mandatory online billing by 2011 is a strong driving force for medical computerization in Japan. The next issue is that how and to what extent promotes the medical computerization in exploiting this opportunity. At first, investments to buildup the regional EMR networks will be required. Retrenchment requires investment. According to economics, a nation's economy consists of three sectors, the domestic accounts, the public finance, and the business.

Scenario 1: Investment from the Domestic Account

This scenario is to pass the medical computerization cost to the medical service fee paid ultimately from the domestic accounts. An additional JPY 30 has been paid for the first consulting in properly computerized medical institutions since 2006, but it is too little to be an effective incentive for medical institutions [25]. Escalating this approach and paying ample bonus to well-computerized facilities is an idea, but the rise of the insurance premium is not welcomed. Hence, the current situation, the gradual diffusion of network-capable EMR systems, which is sponsored by the medical institution's own retained earnings, will not change drastically. Obsolete stand-alone resekons will be replaced to new network resekons within 3–5 years when their lease periods have ended. Only the total online receipt submission will be completed by 2011.

Scenario 2: Investment from Public Finance

Both the Japanese central and local governments have made a good deal of long-standing investments in promoting medical computerization. Many were invested in the research and development projects for the standardizations, though ample subsidized charges have been paid for HISs of several large hospitals since 2001. The outcomes of this policy were unsatisfactory, as mentioned before.

In this scenario, the public finance will aggressively make further investment in the standardized medical information networking projects, anticipating the future NHR service. Because those projects will offer the MEDIS projects developed network systems, they will provide standardized EMR applications via networks. As a result of this scenario, the EMR penetration in clinics will increase drastically, regardless of the operability of their EMR.

Scenario 3: Investment from the Business Sector

Mobilizing business firms of wisdom in order to break out of such a stalemate is the third scenario. The main arena will be the network platform on which regional medical information networks are operated. To invite corporate investments in this business, as well as to strike a good balance between the building of high quality social infrastructures and the healthy market mechanism, it is necessary to maintain a solicitous administration that cares especially about trade-offs between standardizations and liberalizations, or deregulations and enhancing supervisions.

There are two possible measures to vitalize this market. The synchronizations of the regional medical information network developments with the coming competition among new network technologies is one, and the deregulations that will enable various creative new business models is the other.

The existing regional medical information networks are operated on expensive leased circuits or the internet-based VPN, which has insufficient capability for its future purpose. The NTT group has announced the launch of a strategic new service, New Generation Network (NGN), in early 2008. NGN has a network system architecture that guarantees every transmission through it the security of VPN level and enough throughput to transmit high-resolution digital medical images. NGN is expected to be suitable for the regional medical information network platform. Also, KDDI is preparing its own NGN service, and VPN technology on the internet is making progress. The competition for the regional medical information networks will be among various network technologies.

The standards and the requirements for the networked EMR VPN-ISP (Internet Service Providers) or the EMR server hosting centers will make the corporate investment easier. In 2005, 12 prominent HIS vendors organized HEASNET (the Healthcare Information Secure Network Consortium). It has issued guidelines for the security management of medical information systems, and is undertaking the development and the popularization of an on-demand VPN technology, which enables secure medical information networks on the internet [8].

Furthermore, some deregulations will make various new business models possible. Just for an example, online advertising on the network-based EMR browsers will be attractive for healthcare-related industries. In this case, firms without network technology may sponsor regional medical information network providers.

The Choice: Creative Initiatives Promote Social Innovations

Among the three scenarios above, the first scenario is the most likely one, but this is a passive choice for overall medical computerization in Japan. The regional medical information networks will not be completed for years. The sufficient prevalence of EMR in clinics will not be attained until the time when the Japanese medical jargon *karute* has become obsolete, i.e., when the generations of physicians that learned mainly German medicine have aged and retired from medical institutions and the average IT literacy of care staff is improved, though it will not be long before this occurs.

The second scenario would be ideal, but MHLW must deal with several issues for the coming aging society, such as pensions, the falling birth rate, and women's labor. Therefore, a renewed privilege costing for medical computerization will be difficult.

Some would avoid the third scenario, because it is reminiscent of the overheated cellular phone or ADSL selling in the past IT bubble era. However, the medical information market is no bubbly consumer market. Experts offer specialized systems and services to professionals there. Trusting in the selective functions of the professional market, as well as the long-matured concept models and technical standards, Japan ought to have leveraged the corporate creative initiatives in the medical computerization business by means of deregulations. Remember, the EMR developments have been promoted by several innovations created by initiatives of various actors, such as EMR nerds, voluntary hospitals, and some local governments.

Summary and Conclusion

Medical computerization is a key leverage to suppress the national medical expense of the aging society in Japan. But, the existing labor-intensive integrated healthcare system is so sophisticated that it has hindered the prevalence of the emerging IT-supported healthcare. Hoping to prove their benefits, some service/disease-specific networked EMR-supported care systems are under public field trials, which will make the systems practically operational. For the quicker build-up of regional networked EMR infrastructures, deregulations and pro-competitive policies are desirable to induce more business investment in these markets.

Some Japanese firms are exploiting the global scope to innovate their products. Fujitsu is participating in one of the British NHR projects. Panasonic and Sharp initiated Continua Health Alliance, an NPO for the global standardization of wireless networked care devices, with Intel, Phillips etc. An EMR VB, "Order-Made Souyaku," introduced a Swedish technology for its new EMR in 2006.

Japan will invest in effective foreign medical IT or experiences abroad not only for business or international corporations, but to improve her own. Even a developing country may be an adequate incubator for the emerging telemedicine. In any case, a creative initiative is the requisite condition, and the sufficient conditions are the amelioration and the implementation.

References

1. N. Akiyama, *The practical "theory of EMR"* (in Japanese), (Shizuoka Shimbunsha, Shizuoka, 2006)
2. Apius, *About us* (in Japanese), (Apius, 2007). http://www.apius.com/aboutus.htm. Accessed 26 Sept 2007
3. M. Asonuma, The mandatory online billing system of the medical service fee (in Japanese), in *White Paper on healthcare*, ed. by Health Policy Institute, Japan (Japan Medical Planning, Tokyo, 2007), pp. 117–123
4. Cabinet office, *Materials for the medical sector: open discussion of Promotion Committee for Focal Issues, Council for Regulatory Reform (17 May 2007)* (in Japanese), (Cabinet office, Tokyo, 2007)
5. C.M. Christensen, *The innovator's dilemma,* (Harvard Business School Press, Boston, 1997)
6. H. Etoh, R. Kishi, et al., *Bull. Nagano Coll. Nurs.* **4**, 31 (2002)
7. M. Furuhashi, K. Saito, The "7 to 1" nursing staff allocation and the shortage of nurses (in Japanese), in *White paper on healthcare*, ed. by Health Policy Institute, Japan, (Japan Medical Planning, Tokyo, 2007)
8. Healthcare Information Secure Network Consortium, *Activities* (in Japanese), (HEASNET, Tokyo, 2007). http://www.heasnet.jp/index_J.htm. Accessed 24 Sept 2007
9. Japanese Association for Healthcare Information Systems Industry, *Mon. New Med.* **33**(7), 166; **33**(8), 180; **33**(9), 180; **33**(10), 136; **33**(11), 122 (2006)
10. Japan Medical Association, *The list of JMA certified IT support shops* (in Japanese), (JMA, Tokyo, 2007), http://www.orca.med.or.jp/orca/nintei/_reference/pdf/nintei-list-2007-04-09.pdf. Accessed 13 Jun 2008
11. Japan Medical Association, *JMA standard receipt software deployments on 15 January 2008* (in Japanese), (JMA, Tokyo, 2008). http://www.orca.med.or.jp/orca/nintei/nintei_png/2008-01-15-deployment.png. Accessed 20 Jan 2008
12. R. Landau, N. Rosenberg, Innovation in the chemical processing industries, in *Exploring the black box*, ed. by N. Rosenberg (Cambridge University Press, New York, 1994), pp. 190–202
13. I.Mihara, *Studies on the review of the problems in promoting the application of EMR to the healthcare coordination* (in Japanese), (MHLW, Tokyo, 2004)
14. Ministry of Finance, *Financial data reference* (in Japanese), (MOF, Tokyo, 2007) http://www.mof.go.jp/zaisei/con_07.html. Accessed 23 Aug 2007
15. Ministry of Health, Labour, and Welfare, *Summary of the survey and the report (static and dynamic) on medical facilities and hospitals (2005)* (in Japanese), (MHLW, Tokyo, 2005). http://www.mhlw.go.jp/toukei/saikin/hw/iryosd/05/kekkal-3.html. Accessed 4 Sept 2007
16. Ministry of Health, Labour, and Welfare, *Tentative proposal for the institutional reforms of healthcare (October 2005)* (in Japanese), (MHLW, Tokyo, 2005)
17. Ministry of Health, Labour, and Welfare, *White paper on health, labour, and welfare* (in Japanese), (MHLW, Tokyo, 2006)
18. Ministry of Health, Labour, and Welfare, *Medical Facility census (February 2007 est.)* (in Japanese), (MHLW, Tokyo, 2007). http://www.mhlw.go.jp/toukei/saikin/hw/iryosd/m06/xls/is0614.xls. Accessed 27 Sept 2007
19. Ministry of Health, Labour, and Welfare, *performance review form I-11–1 (August 2007)* (in Japanese), (MHLW, Tokyo, 2007). http://www.mhlw.go.jp/wp/seisaku/hyouka/dl/i-11-b.pdf. Accessed 14 Jan 2008.
20. Ministry of Health, Labour, and Welfare, *Report for the central social insurance council (8 August 2007)* (in Japanese), (MHLW, Tokyo, 2007)

21. Ministry of Health, Labour, and Welfare, Social Insurance Medical Fee Payment Fund, All-Japan Foundation of National Health Insurance Organizations, *Billing by digitized receipts: the digitized receipt processing system for clinics* (in Japanese), (MHLW, Tokyo, 2005)
22. Monthly New Medicine of Japan, *Month. New Med.* **34**(9), 134; **34**(10), 165; **34**(11), **170** (2007)
23. Monthly New Medicine of Japan, The hospital information systems (HIS) in operation (in Japanese), in *White paper on electronic health record & picture archiving and communication systems 2007–2008*, ed. by Monthly New Medicine of Japan (The ME Association, Tokyo, 2007), p. 120
24. OECD, *Health data 2006* (OECD, Paris, 2006)
25. Plamed, Japan Business Management, *Survey on the introduction of EMR* (in Japanese), (Plamed, Japan, 2006), http://www.plamed.co.jp/activity/research/r060006/. Accessed 6 Sept 2007
26. E.M. Rogers, *Diffusion of innovations,* (The Free Press, New York, 1995)
27. H. Tanaka, *The electronic health record and the computerized healthcare* (in Japanese), (The ME Association, Tokyo, 2007)
28. J. Yoshida, *The Regional Medical Coordination Network in Nagoya area: lecture material* (in Japanese), (Japan Healthcare IT Initiative, 2007), http://www.jahis.jp/it-board/H19sympo_pre/07-1yoshida.pdf Accessed 27 Sept 2007

Chapter 30
The End of Mass Media: Aging and the US Newspaper Industry

M. Miller

Abstract The Baby Boom generation – the largest in US history – grew up with mass media and is by far the largest constituency for newspapers, television, and magazines. But, as audiences age and fragment, the economic foundation of these traditional media are challenged. The pain is especially sharp in the newspaper industry, giving rise to worries about the future of American journalism.

Introduction

The Baby Boom generation represents the last gasp for mass media in the USA. Boomers – the largest generation in American history – grew up with television, newspapers, and magazines, and they are the largest constituency of traditional media. But, the generations following Boomers are far less loyal, spreading their time across a wide array of new digital information choices. The pain of audience erosion has been felt most sharply in the newspaper industry, which has had the greatest difficulty attracting younger readers. Surprisingly, even older audiences (Boomers and seniors) have begun to shift their attention away from printed newspapers towards new media choices. That erosion, along with advertiser perception that older consumers are less desirable marketing targets, has rocked the economic foundation of the US newspaper publishing industry. Revenues from advertising and circulation are falling at an accelerating rate. Investors have fled newspaper stocks, leading to a wave of industry consolidation via mergers and acquisitions.

It's ironic that the newspaper industry finds itself being punished for its audience, since Boomers are by far the most affluent American demographic segment. But, quality of audience hasn't helped newspapers convince youth-obsessed advertisers to stay on board. And investors worry – correctly – that newspapers simply won't be able to replace Boomer readers as they age and die. Indeed, a good deal of evidence points to continued fragmentation of audiences for news, entertainment, and other content as Boomers age out of the market in the coming decades. Large, mass audiences will be harder to find for all traditional media companies. Instead, media companies will find themselves responding to customer demands for customized access, and serving niche markets. The newspaper subscriber gives way to Internet users who access a story or two on a website via news integrators like Google News. Television viewers who once sat down for 2–3 h of programs at a time now download just one show they want from the Internet. Music lovers don't buy the full CD of their favorite artists, just the individual songs they want.

Fragmentation poses a threat to all traditional media, but the threat to newspapers is especially alarming. The large editorial budgets and staffs of newspapers historically have been the most important source of unbiased fact gathering that is the foundation of news information flow in the US. As newspapers fall victim to fragmentation and ebbing revenue streams, it's not yet clear what new form of robust newsgathering organizations will take their place.

Newspapers face a long, difficult transition from print to success in digital media. In order to survive that transition, they will need to find a way to retain their core, older print audience as long as possible – and to convince advertisers of their value.

The US Boomer Market

Baby Boomers have dominated and shaped America's economic, political and social scenes, partly due to their sheer numbers. Born in the post-war years 1946 to 1964, Boomers account for 78 million adults, the largest generation in US history. But, the impact of Boomers also stems from a unique perspective shaped, in particular, by the coming-of-age experience of older Boomers. As young adults in the 1960s and 1970s, Boomers led the charge in massive social and political upheaval that included the civil rights and anti-war movements, feminism and women's rights, sexual freedom, drugs, and rock music. As they have moved through different stages of life, they've continued to remake their social environment. From an economic perspective, Boomers have driven sales of various industries: baby food in the 1950s and 1960s; blue jeans, fast food and rock music in the 1970s and 1980s; mutual fund companies and retirement funds in the 1990s.

In the same sense, the Boomer generation identity is linked with the explosion and dominance of mass media in the second half of the twentieth century, particularly television:

> Television separated the Boomers from every previous generation. Mass production and technological advances in the 1950s allowed most American families to own a set...in 1948 there were fewer than 400,000 TV sets in the country. Four years later there were nearly 19 million. By 1960 nine out of every ten American homes had a TV, and the average set was turned on for at least six hours every day...according to the political scientist Paul Light, the average Baby Boomer had viewed between 12,000 and 15,000 hours of television by age 16. [4].

Now, media companies face the stark reality that their most loyal audience is aging, and that the US population profile is turning more gray. The oldest Boomers turned

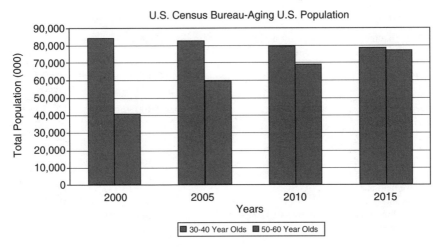

Fig. 30.1 US census bureau – aging US population

60 in 2006; by 2011, the number of the country's adults age 50–69 will be roughly equal to the number of adults age 30–49, according to the US Census Bureau (Fig. 30.1)

An aging customer base generally is a worry for any business, and mass media is no different. The industry relies on revenue from advertisers who, in turn, typically are hunting for young customers. The idea is to capture "customers for life" when they are in their prime as consumers. Marketers tend to see older consumers as set in their brand preferences, winding down their activities and pursuits – and not really buying much of anything [10].

The Boomer generation puts such traditional marketing thinking to the test. Just as they have put their unique stamp on every other phase of life, Boomers show signs of remaking life beyond 50. Most tell researchers and journalists that they envision an active and engaged post-50 lifestyle. Most Boomers tell pollsters they intend to continue working in "retirement," while pursuing new passions such as travel, learning, and volunteer activities [5]. Boomers are the most affluent US demographic segment; they account for 36% of the adult population, but account for a disproportionate share of wealth and consumer spending in a wide array of categories, ranging from vacation home purchases to luxury cars and gourmet food. From a financial services industry perspective, they are more active investors and borrowers than younger segments of the population (Table 30.1)

Newspapers have an especially commanding share of these readers, who should be a premium marketing target for advertisers. Among adults age 50–59 years of age, 52% read a newspaper daily, and 60% are regular Sunday readers [8].

Still, newspapers have had trouble selling what should be a premium-marketing target to advertisers. Just the opposite, in fact media buyers extract discounts from publishers due to the aging of their audiences [10].

Table 30.1 Baby boomer investments

Baby boomers index above adults in general with diverse investments and expenditures. Hence, they are more likely to:

Investments	Adults in general index	Baby boomers 40–59 index
Have home-improvement loan	100	132
Have home-equity loan	100	131
Have home mortgage	100	125
Used discount stockbroker past 12 months	100	122
Plan to buy second vacation home next 12 months	100	119
Plan to pay $35,000+ for a used vehicle next 12 months	100	119
Have mutual funds	100	119
Have 401-K plan	100	118
Stayed in upscale hotel/motel past 12 months	100	117
Have money market funds	100	117
Shopped at any gourmet food store past 12 months	100	115
Plan to pay $35,000+ for a new vehicle next 12 months	100	114
Plan to buy a major appliance next 12 months	100	114

Source: Scarborough Research, 2005 Release 2 (Top 50 Market Report) Prepared by NAA Business Analysis and Research Department [8]

The Fragmenting Media Audience

At the heart of the newspaper industry's dilemma is the explosive growth in the number of consumer information options. The Internet, PDAs and MP3 players, video games, and social media websites all compete for the time and attention of consumers. And, they take time away from traditional media. Consider the following trends [9]:

- Prime-time network television declined 30% in the 10-year period ending in 2005, and the number of hours watching broadcast television overall dropped 15%
- Total magazine circulation has been sliding since 2000

Meanwhile, overall US Internet penetration is now at 60%. Some 45% of Americans now spend 4 h per day or more online *outside of their working hours,* a figure that rivals television usage: 65% of Americans watch 4 h or more of television per day (Fig. 30.2) [6].

Social media and websites where users create their own content also are seeing soaring use that steals time from traditional media. About 45% of Americans now use sites such as MySpace and Facebook.[1]

Although younger Americans are leading the charge in adopting new media, Boomers are definitely along for the ride. And why not? Boomers have embraced – and invented – all sorts of new technology and information platforms in their

---

[1] IBM Corp.

Nearly 45% of users spend over 4 hours/day online for personal
use; TV rivaled in attention, though 65% still watch over 4 hours/day

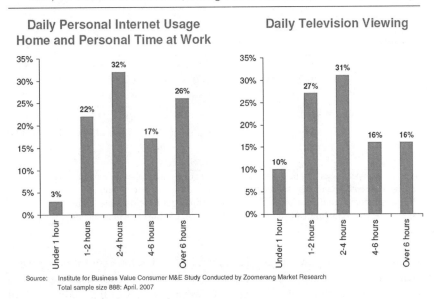

Daily Personal Internet Usage Home and Personal Time at Work

Daily Television Viewing

Source: Institute for Business Value Consumer M&E Study Conducted by Zoomerang Market Research
               Total sample size 888: April. 2007

Fig. 30.2 Nearly 45% of users spend over $4h$ day^{-1} online for personal use; TV rivaled in attention, though 65% still watch over $4h$ day^{-1}

lifetimes: the personal computer, e-mail, cell phones, video cameras, MP3 players and DVDs, just to name a few examples. Why would a generation so comfortable with new technology turn away from it just because they've started turning 50 or 60?

So, it should come as no surprise that 65% of Americans age 50–64 are online [12], or that time online is pulling them away from print media. As recently as 1999, 72% of US adults aged 55 and older read a daily newspaper; by 2006, that figure had slipped to 67% [14].

It's not just new media that are fueling that decline. There's striking evidence that older consumers are simply losing interest in following news. As Table 30.2 shows, the number of older Americans who feel the need to "get the news every day" fell sharply over the period 1995 to 2005. Although the reasons for this decline aren't entirely clear, some analysts point to a general societal turnoff to political and media institutions:

> Over the last 17 years, consumers of news and information have come to perceive the media as biased, inaccurate, and un-professional. While at least one-half of all adult Americans in 2004 tended to believe their daily newspaper, believableity ratings have been falling over the last several years and lag behind network television. According to the Pew Center for People and the Press, 'the public's evaluations of media credibility also are more divided along ideological and partisan lines. Republicans have become more distrustful of virtually all major media outlets over the past four years, while Democratic evaluations of the news media have been mostly unchanged.' [9]

Table 30.2 "I need to get the news every day": change in percentage from 1995 to 2005 by income group

"I need to get the news every day"	Total	Young[a]			Family[b]			Mature[c]		
	(%)	UY	MY	LY	UF	MF	LF	UM	MM	LM
1995	50	52	39	39	50	44	37	66	61	59
		(100)	(76)	(76)	(97)	(85)	(73)	(127)	(117)	(115)
2000	44	33	36	34	44	35	31	56	55	56
		(100)	(107)	(101)	(131)	(109)	(94)	(167)	(165)	(167)
2005	42	38	32	32	45	35	32	59	48	47
		(100)	(83)	(85)	(118)	(93)	(83)	(154)	(127)	(123)
Point change, 2005–1995	−8	−14	−8	−7	−5	−8	−6	−7	−12	−12

Source: Newspaper Association of America, Synovate Consumer Opinion Panel.
[a] *UY* Upper-income young, *MY* middle-income young, *LY* lower income young.
[b] *UF* Upper-income families, *MF* middle-income families, *LF* lower-income families.
[c] *UM* Upper-income mature, *MM* middle-income mature, *LM* lower-income mature.

The shift away from news is an especially negative development for newspapers, which have counted older Americans as their stronghold audience. The picture doesn't get any brighter when one projects forward to look at the media habits of younger age cohorts.

People form their news and information habits at a fairly young age, and those habits tend to stick as they age. Since 1972, the National Opinion Research Center at the University of Chicago has been asking Americans whether they read a newspaper daily as part of its well-regarded general social survey (GSS). The data reflect falling readership levels across age groups. The number of Americans age 20–29 who say they read a newspaper every day has fallen from 46% in 1972 to 21% in 2002. Clark Martire and Bartolomeo, an industry research firm that has analyzed the GSS data, predicts that 9% or fewer of 20–29 year olds will be daily newspaper readers by the year 2010 [1]. The age groups maintain a fairly consistent newspaper-reading habit as they age, but no age groups showed sizeable gains in readership as they grew older. In essence, newspapers are failing to replace readers as they age and die.

Impact on the Industry

The impact of falling readership has been unmistakable, using any number of yardsticks:

- *The number of newspapers*: There were 1457 daily newspapers in the US in 2004, compared with 1763 in 1960 [7].
- *Circulation*: Total morning and evening daily circulation stood at 52.3 million in 2006, down from 58.8 million in 1960.

- *Market penetration*: In 1950, 123% of US households bought a newspaper daily [13]. That's not a typographical error; rather, 1.23 newspapers were bought per household. By 1990, penetration had plunged to 67%, and in 2000 it was just 53%.
- *Advertising*: Total print newspaper advertising revenue stood at $47.4 billion in 2005. But, spending is declining as much as 3% annually, depending on the category of spending measured (national, local, or classified). At the same time, overall US advertising expenditures are rising about 3% annually [2].
- *Market valuation*: Investors have fled newspaper stocks in recent years. For example, the average monthly adjusted price of shares in New York Times Co., fell 29% from September 2005 to September 2007, to $19.80 per share. Over the same period, shares of Tribune Co. were down 16%. Over the same period, the S&P 500 index rose 21%.[2]

Newspapers have tried to get into the act online, but with mixed results. Major global news brands such as the New York Times have built substantial online audiences, but traffic for most mid-sized and smaller newspapers has been flat since 2005 [11], a period when overall web traffic grew substantially. One reason for the unimpressive audience growth at newspaper sites is their mediocre web site design and content. In fairness, newspaper websites operate in a vastly different competitive environment than their print counterparts. Most American cities today have just one major newspaper; a handful still have two or three local print competitors. On the Internet, newspapers find themselves competing with a vast array of news providers in a truly global market. Some of the most successful are aggregators and search engines such as Google News and Yahoo!, which flourish by leveraging content the newspapers themselves create. Yahoo!, for example, has the largest audience for news online, with 25 million unique visitors monthly in November 2005, compared with 5.1 million for the New York Times website [9]. And, while there's a proliferation of sources, a great deal of traffic is aggregating around a few large, global online brand names, such as CNN and the New York Times [11].

Even when newspapers do win the battle for online eyeballs, the revenue generated is far less than in print. Newspapers need two to three dozen web users to replace the revenue generated by a single print reader [11]. That reflects not only the loss of newspaper print circulation revenue, but online ad rates that are far lower than in print.

Future of Print Journalism

The threat to newspapers raises serious concerns about the future of serious, research-based journalism in the USA. Although magazines and some television news organizations remain committed to maintaining substantial reporting and research staffs, large editorial budgets at newspapers historically have provided

---

[2] Finance. yahoo.com

the information underpinning most independent journalism in the USA. Overall newsroom employment is already slipping [13] and battles between editors and corporate management have occurred repeatedly in recent years at major newspapers such as the Los Angeles Times as economic pressure grows. New York Times Co., which is well-known in the industry for lavish editorial budgets and high quality journalism, has faced increasing pressure from investors seeking improved financial results [3]. Many industry observers believe the pressure will accelerate as the industry's economic underpinnings continue to weaken in the years ahead – and that news-gathering will suffer.

"The core issue is, who will pay for the reporting that is the fundamental basis for public discourse?" says Ken Doctor, president of media consultancy Content Bridges, a prominent blogger on newspaper industry trends (http://www.contentbridges.com), and a former top editor and executive with newspaper publisher Knight Ridder:

> There is a fundamental difference between reporting and commentary. The emergence of blogging has made it possible for people outside newsrooms with real knowledge to comment and analyze, and get their thoughts to audiences. The problem is the original source reporting. What do people opine about? The news. The best reporting on that news feeds the commentary. Newspaper journalists have a different legacy than other journalists. They come to work every day to find out what is happening, and they don't tilt their reporting to suit advertisers, politicians or business executives. Their value system is one of no fear or favor, and that's what is threatened here.[3]

Summary and Conclusion

Newspapers may be able to survive in a highly-competitive digital environment, but the transition to success will be painful and long. While fighting that battle, newspapers would do well to re-focus on their core audience of Boomers, the last loyal mass audience and one with demographic characteristics advertisers *should* love. For a start, newspaper publishers need to find ways to halt the erosion of that older print audience. Then, they should lead a media industry charge to convince advertisers that Boomers have the money, want to spend it – and that newspapers are the place to reach them.

References

1. J. Bartolomeo, *Time bomb: the challenge of the next generation* (INMA, Dallas, 2002), http://www.inma.org/members/ppt/bartolomeo.ppt. Accessed 18 Jun 2008
2. R. Coen, *Insider's report: Robert Coen presentation on advertising expenditures* (Universal McCann, New York, 2007), http://www.mccann.com/news/pdfs/Insiders6_07.pdf. Accessed 18 Jun 2008

---

[3] Author's personal communication with Ken Doctor on 26 September, 2007.

3. S. Ellison, How a money manager battled New York Times, *The Wall Street Journal* (21 Mar, 2007), http://online.wsj.com/public/article/SB117441975619343135-n166azU72Y6Gkd Tvlv4nWSeWWWo_20080319.html. Accessed 18 Jun 2008

4. S. Gillon, *Boomer nation: the largest and richest generation ever, and how it changed America* (Free Press, New York, 2004)

5. Harris Interactive, Merrill Lynch, Age Wave, *The New Retirement Survey* (Merrill Lynch, New York, 2005), http://www.ml.com/?id=7695_7696_8149_46028_46503_46635. Accessed 18 Jun 2008

6. IBM, US Consumer Research Digital Entertainment and Media (IBM Institute for Business Value, April 2007), http://www.ibm.com/iibv

7. Media Management Center, Northwestern University, http://www.mediamanagementcenter. org/

8. Newspaper Association of America: *The source: newspapers by the numbers* (NAA, Vienna, VA, 2006) http://www.scribd.com/doc/2293801/Newspapers-by-the-numbers-2006. Accessed 18 Jun 2008

9. Newspaper Association of America. *Growing audience: understanding the media landscape* (NAA, Vienna, VA, 2006) http://growingaudience.com/downloads/GALandscapeExec Summary.pdf. Accessed 18 Jun 2008

10. P.L. Norton, The Last Laugh, *Barron's*, 26 Feb 2007

11. E.T. Patterson, *Creative destruction: an exploratory look at news on the internet* (Joan Shorenstein Center on the Press, Politics and Public Policy, Harvard University, 2007), http://www.ksg.harvard.edu/presspol/carnegie_knight/creative_destruction_web.pdf. Accessed 18 Jun 2008

12. Pew Internet and American Life Project, *Older Americans and the internet* (Pew, Washington, 2004), http://www.pewinternet.org/report_display.asp?r=117. Accessed 18 Jun 2008

13. The Project for Excellence in Journalism. *The state of the news media 2004: an annual report on American journalism* (PEJ, Washington, 2004). http://www.journalism.org. Accessed 18 Jun 2008

14. The Project for Excellence in Journalism. *The state of the news media 2007: an annual report on American journalism* (PEJ, Washington, 2004) http://www.journalism.org. Accessed 18 Jun 2008

Chapter 31
Material Innovation in the Japanese Silver Market

J. Tomita

Abstract By means of a case study, this chapter argues what the material innovation process in the Japanese silver market should be like. Material suppliers are continuously attempting to contribute to an aging society through material innovation. Although they are not always successful in their intentions to meet the needs of users, they at times discover the actual needs of the users, which are slightly different from the perceived needs.Subsequently, these suppliers work on improving the new materials so as to meet the actual needs of users by developing a close contact with them. The case of superabsorbent polymer (SAP), studied in this chapter, is a typical example of this. We term this material innovation process an emergent process. The SAP "AQUALIC CA" launched on the market by Nippon Shokubai Co., Ltd., in 1983 is a raw material that facilitated the popularity of disposable diapers in the Japanese market. It also currently holds a large share in the American and European markets. However, it was not originally designed for use in disposable diapers, and the process it underwent from development to marketing was not linear. This case study describes how after failure in its technological development and supply agreements, success was finally achieved. Further, it indicates the effectiveness of developing evaluation technologies in the process through an end-user oriented approach. As a result, this study should prove to be a valuable aid in helping material suppliers in understanding effective innovation management.

Introduction

What should the material innovation process be like? What is effective innovation management for material suppliers? In recent times, the silver market is growing in Japan, and material suppliers are required to contribute to an aging society through material innovation. For example, nursing care goods such as furniture, food, and sanitary products are composed of several materials. Material suppliers often attempt to develop new materials. Although they are not always successful in their intentions to meet the needs of users, they at times discover the actual needs of the users, which are slightly different from the perceived needs. Subsequently, these suppliers work on improving the new materials so as to meet the actual needs of the users by developing a close contact with them. The case of superabsorbent polymer (SAP) studied in this chapter, is a typical example of this. We term this material innovation process as an emergent process.

Disposable diapers first appeared in Sweden during World War II as an alternative to cloth diapers. After the war, panty-type disposable diapers were sold in the USA and became highly popular. In the USA and Europe, with the abundant availability of wood as a resource, flocculent pulp was used as an absorbent material in these diapers. As many women had already advanced into playing active roles in society, the use of disposable diapers instead of those made of cloth allowed such workingwomen to save time. Consequently, disposable diapers became highly popular in the USA and Europe before they attained similar popularity in the rest of the world. In Japan, however, the widespread use of disposable diapers came about much later, and until around 1980, most diapers were made of cloth.

Under such circumstances, the SAP "AQUALIC CA," launched on the market in 1983 by Nippon Shokubai Co., Ltd. (hereinafter Nippon Shokubai), began to be used as a diaper material due to its low cost and excellent absorption characteristics. As a result of the adoption of this material, disposable diapers have become highly popular in Japan, and, at the same time, the use of SAP has increased in the American and European markets.

Moreover, at present, the demand for adult disposable diapers is growing in order to support the independence of elderly people, improve the comfort level of incontinent patients, and minimize the workload on nursing care.

Currently, more than 1 million tons of SAP products, including AQUALIC CA, are consumed worldwide. Based on the estimation 10 g SAP/diaper, 1 million tons of SAP can amount to 100 billion disposable diapers. Assuming that each child uses an average of four diapers per day, or an average of 1500 diapers per year, these 100 billion diapers cater to the needs of as many as 65 million children.

Thus, SAP has now become the primary raw material used in disposable diapers. However, AQUALIC CA by Nippon Shokubai, one of the major SAP products, was not originally developed for use in disposable diapers. The process it underwent from development to marketing was not linear. Nippon Shokubai experienced many failures during technological development and subsequent supply agreements before finally meeting success.

Here, we examine the factors underlying the successful development of this product as well as the process it underwent that led to its success. Further, this study indicates the effectiveness of the accumulated evaluation technologies in the process by an end-user oriented approach.Consequently, it is supposed that this study will be a valuable aid to material suppliers in understanding effective innovation management.

Market and Product

Market

Figure 31.1 shows the production volume of disposable diapers in Japan during the past 10 years. In comparison with the production volume for adults, the production volume for children is much larger. However, the former has been increasing rapidly over the past 5 years. Moreover, the population structure in Japan has currently witnessed drastic changes in that the number of births has declined; but the number of elderly people over the age of 65 has increased. According to a report of the Ministry of Internal Affairs and Communications in Japan, by 2030, there will be 35 million elderly people, comprising 30% of the entire population of Japan. Further, the number of elderly nuclear families has also increased. Under these conditions, disposable diapers for adults will be more important in supporting the independence of elderly people, improving the comfort level of incontinent patients, and reducing the workload on nursing care.

Currently, approximately 10 g of SAP is used to produce one diaper. Therefore, 20 billion disposable diapers for children can be manufactured with 200,000 tons of AQUALIC CA. A child uses an average of four diapers per day or an average of 1500 diapers per year. Hence, these 20 billion diapers can fulfill the needs of as many as 13 million children.

In 1983, Nippon Shokubai launched AQUALIC CA on the market as a SAP product. It is a type of powdered polymer that is a lightly cross-linked acrylic acid polymer; moreover, for the first time in the world, it is being manufactured by employing the bulk aqueous solution polymerization method. Ninety percent of the AQUALIC CA manufactured is currently used in the production of disposable

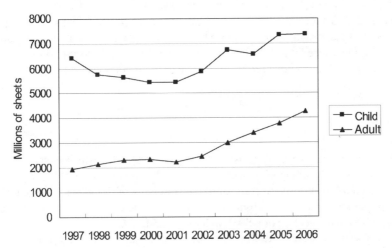

Fig. 31.1 Production volume of disposable diapers in Japan. Source: Japan Hygiene Products Industry Association

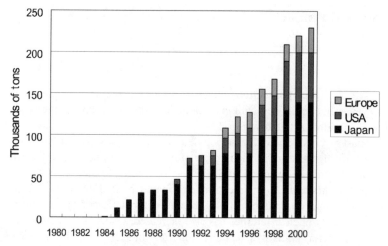

Fig. 31.2 SAP production capacity of Nippon Shokubai (volume in tons) [8]

diapers. In terms of the production volume of disposable diapers, 79% of the total manufactured quantity is used for children's diapers, 11% for adult diapers, and 1% for sanitary napkins. Other uses include pet products (as an alternative to sand for cats, pet sheets, etc.), food-related products (drip-absorbent sheets), household products (disposable portable body warmers), cables (waterproof tapes for optical cables), water-retention materials for soil management, etc.

Due to its unique characteristics, described in a later section, the market share of AQUALIC CA was about 25% of the global SAP market as of 2004; it was competing with BASF of Germany for the leading position in the market. The size of the global market has reportedly reached around 1 million tons, or approximately 150 billion yen in value based on a rate of 150 yen kg^{-1}.

Over the past decade, the global demand for SAP has been growing at a pace exceeding 10% annually, and Nippon Shokubai has increased its production capacity accordingly (see Fig. 31.2). In 2005, the company planned to start production at a new plant in China with a production capacity of 30,000 tons $year^{-1}$.

Product

Disposable diapers basically consist of a top sheet through which water can pass freely, a water-absorbing core, and a back panel that is impermeable. AQUALIC CA is used in the absorption core. Until the beginning of the 1980s, approximately 70 g of pulp was used in the absorption core. Later, the core weight was reduced to 40 g with the introduction of a SAP such as AQUALIC CA.

The use of AQUALIC CA provides advantages such as free absorbency, high maintenance capacity, high complementarities, and low cost.

First, it can swell considerably in volume by absorbing water (strong absorbency), and yet, it does not leak the absorbed water even under constant pressure. For this reason, when used in diapers it not only prevents the leakage of urine but also prevents the buttocks of children from becoming soiled.

Second, its capacity to disperse liquid is excellent. To increase liquid dispersion, the absorption concentration of the polymer should not be too high and the absorption speed should not be too fast. If the absorption concentration is further increased, the efficiency of the diaper decreases due to gel blocking. If the absorption speed is too fast, absorption occurs only at that portion of the diaper that has come into direct contact with urine and thus decreases the sustainability of the diaper. AQUALIC CA serves as a balance between such factors.

Third, it complements the urine absorbency of pulp. SAP can further absorb the urine after it has been absorbed by the pulp, thereby drying up the pulp and enabling its reuse.

Fourth, its cost of production is low because it can be easily mass-produced. The conventional manufacturing method (i.e., the reverse phase suspension polymerization method) was inferior in terms of its process ability after polymerization, drying ability, and mass production. The novel polymerization system and manufacturing method developed by Nippon Shokubai have greatly improved productivity.

AQUALIC CA is now widely used in the manufacture of adult disposable diapers. According to Kajiwara and Osada [4], these diapers can be divided into four types: panty-type, flat-type, supplementary pad-type, and pad-type. The panty-type diaper is an adult diaper that is most widely used. The adult panty-type diaper is similar in structure to the disposable diaper manufactured for children. The flat-type is used along with a diaper cover or a net panty. The supplementary pad-type is placed onto a diaper in order to improve the absorption capability of the diaper. These three types exhibit strong absorption and are thus used for those who require considerable protection. In contrast, the pad-type diaper has weak absorption capacity and is used by those who do not face a serious problem. The production volume of pad-type diapers has tripled over the last decade because of its high usability and low cost.

History of SAP and the Development of Disposable Diapers

SAP has evolved alongside the development of disposable diapers for children. Disposable diapers first appeared in Sweden during World War II as an alternative to cloth diapers. As in those days cloth and detergents were scarce in Sweden, the feasibility of using the country's abundant wood resources for diapers was studied. Disposable diapers are said to have originated from tissue disposable diapers.

After the war, panty-type disposable diapers were sold in the USA and became highly popular. In the USA and Europe, where there existed abundant wood resources, flocculent pulp was used as an absorbent material in diapers. As many women had already advanced into playing active roles in society, the use of disposable diapers enabled such working women to save the time that would have otherwise been spent washing cloth diapers. Consequently, disposable diapers became highly popular in the USA and Europe before they attained similar popularity in the rest of the world. In Japan, however, the widespread use of disposable diapers came about much later, and until around 1980, most diapers were made of cloth.

The development of SAP itself dates back to the 1960s in the USA. In those days, research on SAP in the USAfocused on the water-retention materials used in soil management. The first patent for the use of SAP in disposable diapers was filed in the USA in 1972. Subsequently, in 1974, a research laboratory affiliated with the S Department of Agriculture published a report stating that starch-acrylonitrile graft polymer, which used starch, was useful as a SAP.

Based on this report, Sanyo Chemical Industries, Ltd., began research on SAP. In 1978, it commercialized a SAP, and Daiichi Eizai Co., Ltd., began using this material for sanitary napkins. At around the same time, Procter & Gamble (P&G) entered into the Japanese market and began selling its disposable diapers named "Pampers." In those days, SAP had not yet been used in disposable diapers; applied research on SAP was also underway in Japan.

In such an environment, Unicharm Corp. began selling disposable diapers using SAP in 1981. Although, the product contained only a small amount of SAP, it stimulated the disposable diapers market in Japan. In 1983, Nippon Shokubai commenced the commercialization of its SAP product and in 1984, successfully launched a production plant with a capacity of 10,000 tons/year, a considerably large mass-production plant. Sanyo Chemical Industries, Ltd., the largest SAP supplier in Japan at the time, had a plant with an annual SAP production capacity of only several hundred tons.

In 1985, following the example of Kao Corp, P&G began selling disposable diapers using a large amount of SAP. As mass production commenced, the price of SAP began to decline, and the volume of SAP usage increased. Since then, the popularity of disposable diapers has sharply risen in Japan and, at the same time, the use of disposable diapers with SAP has also increased in the USA and Europe (see Fig. 31.2).

More than 90% of SAP is currently used for sanitary materials such as disposable diapers; moreover, most of this SAP is composed of lightly cross-linked acrylic acid polymers. Since this material has characteristics suited to disposable diapers and is low in cost, it has become the mainstream material used in the production of SAP. Other types of SAP have limited usage in industrial applications.

Background of the Development of AQUALIC CA

Development of Sodium Polyacrylate

As its name suggests, Nippon Shokubai (literally, "Japan Catalyst") is a company that specializes in catalyst-related technology. Since its inception, it has manufactured phthalic anhydride from naphthalene (1941), maleic anhydride from benzene

(1952), and ethylene oxide from ethylene (1959), using catalyst-based vapor-phase oxidation technology in each case.

In 1970, for the first time ever, the company succeeded in the development of acrylic acid from propylene. The research began with the aim of developing propylene acid, but failed. Instead, it developed acrylic acid. Tsubakimoto and Shimomura, both polymer (high-molecule) researchers, repeatedly developed and modified prototypes based on such accidental findings, finally succeeding in developing sodium polyacrylate (also known as polysodium acrylate or PSA).

Today, acrylic acid is an accessible material. However, until Nippon Shokubai developed a new manufacturing process, it used to be expensive because of the considerably complex methods used in its production. Specifically, acrylic ester was formerly compounded using acetylene and alcohol (in a process known as the improved Reppe method). The compound was then hydrolyzed to extract acrylic acid. This method was used by Rohm and Haas Company, Toagosei Co., Ltd., and other suppliers.

On the other hand, the manufacturing method developed by Nippon Shokubai extracts acrylic acid directly through vapor-phase oxidation of propylene and is suited to mass production, enabling the manufacturing of acrylic acid at a low cost. Interest in polymer-based materials as alternatives to water-soluble phosphoric acid-based compounds increased due to a movement in Japan that was aimed at reducing the use of phosphorous, for example, the amount of phosphoric acid contained in detergents. Under these circumstances, Nippon Shokubai succeeded in developing a low-molecule weight PSA (a product named AQUALIC L) in 1972, and sold it as a detergent builder or colorant dispersant.

In 1973, the company succeeded in developing a high-molecule weight PSA (HPSA), and marketed it for use as a flocculation and viscosity enhancer as well as a food additive. The technological experience gained in developing HPSA led to the subsequent development of a SAP. HPSA was initially difficult to mass produce. However, as mentioned later, the manufacturing method of HPSA was similar to that of SAP. Nippon Shokubai developed a super-low molecular weight PSA in 1976 and a medium-molecule PSA in 1982, increasing the sales of the AQUALIC family of products.

Development of Polymer for Sanitary Napkins

After the commercialization of HPSA, Yoshida, who was in charge of development, supplied samples to help identify new applications other than those mentioned above. Subsequently, he received the following request from a sanitary product manufacturer: We want sanitary napkins (leakproof sheets) that can be flushed away with water, and would like to try HPSA as its leakproof sheet. Sanitary napkins were made with plastic film in those days, and this made it impossible for users to dispose of them by flushing them down the toilet.

Three researchers including Shimomura commenced work on the development of a prototype using a compound of HPSA and the cross-linked acrylic acid polymers. As the alkalinity of HPSA was too strong, the product was bad for skin; therefore, researchers mixed the cross-linked polyacrylic acid with HPSA in an attempt to neutralize it. After a leakproof test was performed by Shimomura – his wife consented to be a test sample – a prototype sheet satisfying the target specifications was developed. However, some problems were encountered in the method used to manufacture the sheet for use in sanitary napkins, ending in its commercial failure.

Although the prototype could not be commercialized it was named AQUALIC CA, with the second element of the name being derived from an abbreviation of "catamenial absorbent." The research on SAPs continued; this was because it coincided with the research policy (domain) of Nippon Shokubai: "Efficient use of our own raw material (acrylic acid) and our own technology (HPSA)."

The researchers' focus on absorbency was based on the fact that the development of HPSA had repeatedly failed due to swelling, as it was not water-soluble. Shimomura believed that this characteristic could be exploited by using it as an absorbent and a leakproof material. This is a typical example of an accidental byproduct being created while developing a possible new application, just as in the development of the "Post-it."

Later, Shimomura discussed with Yoshida the possibility of using it as an absorbent; Yoshida suggested that it may be able to replace the flocculent pulp used in disposable diapers. Thus, the development of AQUALIC CA for disposable diapers began.

At the time, approximately ten suppliers in Japan were planning to launch SAP businesses using their own raw materials and their own manufacturing methods. Nippon Shokubai had already begun selling acrylic acid to customers, and some of these customers were developing SAPs. Some people within Nippon Shokubai voiced their opposition to the launching of its SAP business, arguing, "We will have to compete with our customers." For these reasons, the researchers decided to look for new customers who had no conflicting interest or to sell AQUALIC CA to customers by stressing the advantages it offered over rival products.

Development Process of AQUALIC CA

Invention of a New Manufacturing Method

The development of AQUALIC CA for use in disposable diapers began in 1978 and involved three researchers including Shimomura. These three researchers had developed cross-linked acrylic acid polymers in the previous year. At the time, they belonged to the No. 3 Laboratory of the Central Laboratory, which consisted of approximately 30 researchers. All of the researchers had a bachelor's or master's degree in chemistry. As the mainstream research themes at the laboratory were focused on the study of other high-polymers, SAP research was considered relatively offbeat and was not recognized as an official research theme. However, since Shimomura could boast of having commercialized two research outcomes by 1973, the three researchers were able to work on SAP research without facing major constraints.

During the initial stage of development, SAP was also used in a method in which it was mixed with flocculent pulp in the manufacture of disposable diapers. First, Tsubakimoto, the manager of the No. 3 Laboratory, proposed a method that involved immersing an acrylic acid monomer into flocculent pulp by employing a special mixer. However, due to certain problems with the process, the method was not successful. Subsequently, Shimomura polymerized a monomer–water solution alone, employing a special mixer designed for different purposes. The process was successful and, it resulted in creating a polymer that had a texture similar to that of cooked rice. This was in 1980. A bench-scale plant was established in that year and the number of research members was increased to four.

This aqueous solution polymerization method was an epoch-making manufacturing method that greatly improved the productivity of SAP. Under the conventional method, referred to as stationary gel polymerization, drying the polymerized gel was to some extent difficult and the gel had to be cut into small pieces. Further, the gel had to be polymerized slowly and sliced thinly in order to dissipate heat, which would otherwise result in the degradation of the performance of the gel; the heat that was released during the process of polymerization increased the temperature and significantly lowered productivity.

The manufacturing method developed by Shimomura, on the other hand, could create a polymer that was of the size of a grain of rice during the initial process itself, eliminating the necessity to cut the gel into smaller pieces. Moreover, heat was readily dissipated, as the size of the particles was small. For these reasons, Shimomura's method was suited to mass production. This manufacturing method resolved most of the problems faced in the conventional manufacturing method. However, a problem was discovered in the absorption mechanism. Specifically, the diaper became wet and sticky at points subjected to the weight of the child after it had absorbed urine, making proper absorption impossible. To ensure that urine was absorbed properly, it was found necessary to disperse the urine evenly throughout the diaper.

Shimomura suggested making the surface of the gel particles "as hard as an eggshell." Moreover, he proposed a method of cross-linking the gel by adding a food additive to the polymerized particles. If the surface of the gel when swollen with water is solid, gaps are readily created, making uniform dispersion easier. His idea of adding a food additive was derived from his past experience in the development of SAP for sanitary napkins. In the development of the napkins, he compounded HPSA that was used as a food additive, successfully polymerizing and cross-linking HPSA in the presence of other food additives.

Since sanitary napkins are classified as quasi-drugs, approval from the then Ministry of Health and Welfare (now the Ministry of Health, Labour and Welfare) was necessary before they could be marketed. Shimomura believed that the use of food additives would make it easier to obtain government approval and instructed his subordinate researchers, including Irie, to try this surface cross-linking method. As a result, the surface was successfully cross-linked using this method, considerably increasing its absorption capacity. In subsequent research involving a different theme, Irie and Masuda succeeded in achieving granulation using only water, improving the appearance of its surface.

Thus, the competitiveness of the SAP product was enhanced by improving its productivity through the new aqueous solution polymerization method and by improving its properties through the surface processing method. These inventions were eventually extremely beneficial to the future of the SAP industry. However, as mentioned earlier, government approval for quasi-drugs was necessary in order to market SAP for use in sanitary napkins. The researchers visited universities and hospitals to collect data on safety, stability, analysis methods, etc. and repeatedly visited the ministry for negotiations. They finally received approval in 1983.

Development Cancellation Crisis and an Opportunity for a Large Contract

Subsequently, Nippon Shokubai received an inquiry concerning AQUALIC CA from a major sanitary product manufacturer. The researchers including Shimomura continued their development work; they were all highly motivated. Approximately 6 months later, however, the manufacturer in question announced that it would produce SAP on its own. Following this announcement, the response of the top management was to discontinue the development of SAP. Nevertheless, the researchers including Shimomura opposed this idea and persuaded their manager to not discontinue the development. As a result, a decision was made to continue with the research, but only with a few research members.

Subsequently, Nippon Shokubai received an inquiry from a major Japanese cosmetics company regarding the use of AQUALIC CA in sanitary napkins. This prompted a decision by the top management of Nippon Shokubai to commercialize AQUALIC CA by aggressively creating sample products; moreover, a pilot plant with a production capacity of 1000 tons was constructed in 1983. However, the company initially received very few inquiries and the operating ratio of the plant was at a very low level.

In late 1983, an inquiry was received from another major global sanitary product manufacturer, "P," for 10,000 tons of SAP. The production of 10,000 tons of SAP was considered to be a massive operation in the functional polymers industry where an annual production of 1000 tons was considered large.

Shimomura and the other researchers looked for a new manufacturing method to further improve productivity. During this process, his manager Tsubakimoto suggested continuously polymerizing the material instead of using the conventional batch method. Shimomura began developing a continuous polymerization method using various approaches, including modifying machines and visiting food industry exhibitions, food processing plants, etc. Subsequently, he suggested applying automatic sushi-making robot technology and developed a prototype polymerization system. The prototype system turned out to be highly practical, and the number of researchers working on the continuous polymerization method was then increased to six – three researchers each on the day and night shifts – in order to develop the production system. Finally, the continuous polymerization system was completed.

Although they were all researchers, these six people worked on the entire process from finding new applications to approaching the users. Undoubtedly, it is the workers who are on the site who actually manufacture the product; however, it is the researchers who determine the facility conditions and product quality. Researchers with such experience have reportedly been able to develop a broad range of expertise in areas such as surveys, users, manufacturing methods, and patents in addition to expertise in their own special fields. Such a development method can be very effective with regard to functional chemical products, which require close contact with users.

Risks Involved in the Massive Supply Agreement

In February 1984, Nippon Shokubai shipped samples to company P for evaluation of the performance of AQUALIC CA produced by the continuous polymerization method and received approval with regard to the specifications from P. In March, Nippon Shokubai signed an agreement to deliver 10,000 tons of the product and began construction of a new production facility at the Himeji Plant. The researchers including Shimomura received an internal company award for their achievements.

In June of that year, however, P requested Nippon Shokubai to increase the order by an additional 10,000 tons to a total of 20,000 tons. A majority of the Nippon Shokubai directors opposed the request, saying that the risks were too high. Shimizu, the then director of the laboratory, and Shimomura were asked to attend the board meeting and were requested by President Ishikawa to offer their opinions. Shimomura emphatically replied, "No problem. We should do it." President Ishikawa received the acquiescence of the board and signed the agreement for an additional 10,000 tons in September.

By October, the new facility at the Himeji Plant, which had a production capacity of 10,000 tons, had almost been completed. Subsequently, on 31 October, while attending the regular end-of-month technical meeting, Tsubakimoto and Shimomura were suddenly called in by their superior and informed that a telex had been received from P reporting that a serious problem had been discovered. The message stated that the performance of Nippon Shokubai's SAP was inferior to that of rival products.

The researchers – Tsubakimoto, Shimomura, and Irie – immediately flew to the USA. Andy Scott, the contact person for P, informed them that although the required specifications were met, the performance of the product when used in diapers was poor. What they had meant by "specifications" referred to the properties of SAP and not the performance of the diapers; moreover, P was unaware of the actual performance of the diapers until the SAP was actually applied to the diapers that it had produced.

For Nippon Shokubai, this raised the risk of losing the investment in the new 10,000-ton facility and putting the entire company in a difficult situation. The researchers' manager instructed them to improve the continuous polymerization method without making any changes to the production facility. However, the researchers including Shimomura felt that the texture of the gel created by the continuous polymerization method differed from that created by the batch method. They therefore decided to work on improving productivity by using the batch method in parallel with the continuous polymerization method. Further, they decided to keep this a secret from their manager. The researchers frequently traveled back and forth between the laboratory in Suita and the plant in Himeji, maintaining close correspondence with the manufacturing group. During the months of November and December, they carried out improvement work on weekends as well, as if each week consisted of "two Mondays, Tuesday, Wednesday, Thursday, and two Fridays."

As a result, they discovered that the productivity could be improved by using the conventional batch polymerization method. This result was reported at the end of the year to Vice President Nakajima, the head of the project. The researchers again flew to the USA with the new samples on 8 January. P reportedly performed a sample test using babies as test subjects. Test users had not meant "lead users," but common end-users. The test sample of babies couldn't suggest an idea of new diapers. The test proved that AQUALIC CA was overwhelmingly superior in performance to the rival products, and the researchers including Shimomura were finally successful.

Nippon Shokubai commenced the delivery of SAP to P in mid-1985, approximately 6 months after the agreed date. The agreement had stipulated that failure to deliver or purchase SAP by a predefined date would involve the payment of a penalty as large amounts of capital investment had been made by both parties. However, as both parties had encountered problems of their own such as quality and defects in production lines in the initial stages, Nippon Shokubai was fortunate to be spared the burden of paying a huge penalty. From around August onwards, the company began to produce and deliver SAP smoothly.

First-Mover Advantage by Developing Evaluation Technologies

As mentioned later, the production of AQUALIC CA increased alongside the growth in demand. One of the reasons for the increase in production was the evaluation technology that the company had developed ahead of its competitors. The simplest evaluation method used for testing disposable diapers is the teabag method. In this method, a teabag is first emptied; subsequently, it is filled with the prototype polymer and immersed in water. Following this its weight is measured to determine its absorption strength. This measuring method was first developed by Nippon Shokubai and is now used throughout the world.

The "test of absorption strength under constant pressure" is said to be considerably more important for diapers. A diaper is subjected to pressure when used by a child who is lying down; therefore, it should be able to properly absorb urine under such pressure. Moreover, the absorbed liquid has to be uniformly dispersed throughout the diaper. Nippon Shokubai focused on such functions in the initial stages of development itself and developed the surface cross-linking technology well before users (diaper manufacturers) requested such specifications.

Using this pressure test, the analyses by Nippon Shokubai proved that the request by diaper manufacturers for a fast absorption speed was, in fact, erroneous. The absorption speed was generally considered as "the faster the better." However, a polymer that hardens within a short period, if used in a diaper, will intensively absorb urine only where the diaper has actually come into contact with the urine. This makes the life span of the diaper shorter, even though the absorption speed will be faster. Nippon Shokubai learned through its tests that the polymer used in a diaper should gradually absorb and disperse the liquid throughout the diaper and dry the absorbed liquid.

The company later clarified another misunderstanding concerning absorption capacity – represented by claims such as "absorbs 1000 times its volume." A polymer is generally conceived to be better if a larger amount of liquid can be absorbed by a smaller quantity of polymer. However, after absorbing the liquid, a polymer with high absorption capacity will swell and transform into a gel-like object that is as soft as tofu. This gel block prevents further liquid from being absorbed into the diaper. For this reason, Nippon Shokubai reduced the absorption capacity to only 300–400 times its volume.

Even if the specifications provided for the polymer are met, it does not necessarily guarantee that the performance of the diapers will be satisfactory. Since diapers are used over extended periods, they have to absorb urine repeatedly instead of only once. Specifications generally define values that apply to momentary use; however, it is also necessary to collect evaluation data pertaining to long-term use.

As mentioned above, premises that were initially considered to apply to the disposable diaper industry successively turned out to be inaccurate. As illustrated by the example of company P, diaper manufacturers also did not have a sufficient understanding of the functions that were actually required of diapers nor the technology to effectively use polymers. Shimomura stated: "That is why Nippon Shokubai's new ideas and technologies were accepted by customers."

Subsequently, Nippon Shokubai developed and improved its SAP by understanding the potential needs of children with respect to disposable diapers; moreover, it offered these new features and improvements to disposable diaper manufacturers while developing evaluation technologies by collecting feedback data. This suggests the importance of such perspectives as an end-user oriented approach, which takes into consideration the hierarchical nature of customer relationships. Specifically, in developing its products, Nippon Shokubai, a SAP supplier, not only had to listen to the requests from diaper manufacturers, its immediate customers, but also had to consider the performance of the diapers that were actually used by children, the end-users of the diapers.

Becoming the De Facto Standard

Since P, the world's largest sanitary product manufacturer, had decided to use Nippon Shokubai's SAP, major chemical suppliers throughout the world followed Nippon Shokubai's methods such as the use of acrylic acid as a raw material and the adoption of the aqueous solution polymerization method, and the surface cross-linking method. Thus, AQUALIC CA became the de facto standard in terms of both product and manufacturing method.

On reminiscing, Shimomura stated the following:

> Company P purchased AQUALIC CA for 10 years without any complaints. During that period, P did not mention anything about the product's performance – good or bad. They simply said that it was about the same as any new rival product. However, as the rival products did not utilize the surface cross-linking method, the researchers at Nippon Shokubai were confident that such rival products were inferior to AQUALIC CA in performance. But, as other companies started to catch up with AQUALIC CA after about 10 years, P, for the first time, started to request SAP suppliers to change their SAP specifications by incorporating the advantages of AQUALIC CA. In retrospect, it is apparent that AQUALIC CA boasted the highest performance among all SAP products at that time.

The production of AQUALIC CA has steadily increased in Japan since 1985. Production capacity grew at a rate of 10,000 tons annually until 1988 (see Fig. 31.2). Subsequently, in 1990, Nippon Shokubai began production abroad. In 1990, it established a joint venture (NAII) with Alco of the USA and constructed a plant in Tennessee. In 1993, it established a joint venture with BASF of Germany and began SAP production there. Subsequently, in 2000, it constructed its own SAP plant and began production in Belgium. During these years, the global demand for SAP increased at an annual rate of more than 10%; Nippon Shokubai expanded its production capacity to meet this rising demand. At present, the company boasts the world's largest production capacity, amounting to 320,000 tons annually, from facilities that include a plant under construction in China and other plants in Japan, Europe, and the USA that are currently being expanded.

Moreover, currently, the demand for adult disposable diapers is growing in order to support the independence of elderly people, improve the comfort level of incontinent patients, and reduce the workload on nursing care. The adult panty-type diaper is similar in structure to the disposable diaper meant for children. The amount of SAP used is in the range of 13–20 g and that of pulp is in the range of 50–70 g. The concentration of SAP used in adult diapers is lower than that used in the ultrathin disposable diapers meant for children [4].

Many diaper manufactures are presently developing adult disposable diapers that have better leakage prevention and reduced thickness, through the improvement of the absorption core. Moreover, improvements in product design to make the use of diapers more comfortable are also being carried out by using test sample of adults. A high gel strength and fast absorption speed are two indispensable properties of SAP when developing high-performance cores meant for adult diapers. Moreover, many SAP suppliers including Nippon Shokubai are developing such polymer gels.

Improvement in the comfort level reduces the amount of workload on care providers and further protects the privacy of the individual.

Summary and Conclusion

This case study demonstrated the innovation process of the SAP AQUALIC CA developed by Nippon Shokubai. AQUALIC CA is a raw material that has helped to increase the popularity of disposable diapers in Japan and currently holds a share of about 25% of the global market; thus, making it one of the most internationally competitive functional chemical products in recent years (see [2,5] for the definition of functional chemical products).

Recent research on product development has demonstrated that "team 'kimeko-makai' management (detailed management)" [7], "'customer of customers' strategy" [6], "management of customer system" [11], and "assessment capability" [10] are potentially effective with regard to functional chemical products.

This case study describes the innovation process that led Nippon Shokubai from repeated failures in the technological development and supply agreements of PSA, HPSA, etc. to eventual success. It was not a linear process, but an emergent one. Further, it suggests the gaining of a first-mover advantage by developing evaluation technologies through the end-user oriented approach. Moreover, since users do not have sufficient technological capabilities to appropriately evaluate and use raw materials embodying a novel technology such as AQUALIC CA, raw material suppliers have to develop evaluation technologies by maintaining close correspondence with users right from the early stages of development in order to gain a competitive advantage. This study should prove to be a valuable aid in helping material suppliers understand effective innovation management. In other words, they need knowledge and know-how beyond their product coverage [1].

It could be also applied to other industrial goods such as components or equipments. Innovation for new final products or new system products needs both component knowledge and architectural knowledge that integrates multi-components or equipments [3]. Generally, component suppliers have the former, system manufacturers have the latter. However, the innovative technology needed for system product innovation, like in the auto industry, is not the same as the broader and deeper knowledge needed for components innovation [9]. So, component suppliers also have to accumulate evaluation technologies by close contact with users from the early stages of development. It should be a valuable aid for various industrial goods suppliers to understand effective innovation management.

It could be also important for system manufacturers to try to differentiate their new products from the early stages of development by close contact with suppliers having high evaluation technologies.

References

1. S. Brusoni, A. Prencipe, *J. Manage. Studies*, **38**(7), 1019 (2001)
2. K. Fujimoto, K. Kuwashima, in *Kinousei kagaku* (Functional chemicals), ed. by Kinousei kagaku sangyou kenkyuukai (Kagaku kougyo nippou, 2002), pp. 87–143 (in Japanese)
3. R.M. Henderson, K.B. Clark, Admin. Sci.Q. **35**(1), 9 (1990)
4. K. Kajiwara, Y. Osada (eds), *Gels Handbook* (Academic, New York, 2000)
5. Kinousei kagaku sangyou kenkyuukai (Functional chemical industry research group) (eds.) *Kinousei kagaku* (Functional chemicals), (Kagaku kougyo nippou, 2000) (in Japanese)
6. K. Kuwashima, Kenkyuu gijutsu keikaku (*J. Sci. Policy Res. Manage.*), **18**(3/4), 165 (2003) (in Japanese)
7. K. Kuwashima, *Akamon Manage. Rev.* **4**(9), 459 (2005) (in Japanese)
8. T. Shimomura, in *Koukyuusuisei polymer no gijutsu to kaihatsu monogatari*. (Technology and development story of superabsorbent polymer.) Catalyst symposium of The Japan Petroleum Institute, 3 March, 2004 (in Japanese)
9. A. Takeishi, *Bungyo to kyoso*. (Division of labor and competition) (Yuhikaku, Tokyo, 2003) (in Japanese)
10. J. Tomita, Keieiryoku sousei kenkyuu. (*J. Creat. Manage.*) 15 (2007) (in Japanese)
11. J. Tomita, T. Fujimoto, The customer system and new product development in *Management of technology and innovation in Japan*, ed. by C. Herstatt, C. Stockstrom, H. Tschirky, A. Nagahira (Springer, Berlin, 2005), pp. 73–84

Chapter 32
Potholes in the Road to Efficient Gerontechnology Use in Elderly Care Work

H. Melkas

Abstract The use of information and communication technologies (ICT) including safety alarm technologies is increasing. Its influence on service personnel in elderly care has implications on the possibilities of rooting technological innovations into care work. Human impact assessment methodologies have been employed to assess competence related to technology use, needs for orientation into technology use, and well-being of care personnel. Safety alarms are considered useful both for actual care work and for the administrative part of the care organization. Care personnel appeared not to be fully informed as to technical characteristics and the resulting organizational changes. At individual and work community levels regular human impact assessment of new technologies may stimulate their adoption by the professional carers. This chapter is based on empirical research in a large research and development project in Finland. The research focused on safety telephones and high-tech well-being wristbands.

Introduction

Implementing information technology requires changes in work practices and in collaboration among organizations, as well as in knowledge and skill levels of personnel [3, 5, 8, 15, 17, 18]. Since technology and care service are commonly not felt as being connected [1], the introduction of such technologies leads to fatigue, loss of work motivation, additional costs, unwillingness to use the technology, and a decrease of well-being at work [4,8,12,16], resulting in premature loss of experience and professional skills of elderly workers in the workforce [6, 21].

This chapter includes results of empirical research on the impact on workers and workplaces within elderly care in Finland of safety telephones and a high-tech well-being wristband that monitors vital signs, in order to find factors to speed up adoption of technological innovations in care organizations.

The Finnish population is aging rapidly. According to population forecasts, one out of four Finns will be aged over 65 in the year 2030. High pressure is placed on services for the elderly. Safety telephones and wristbands that enable a call for help by pushing just one button increase the possibilities for an aging person to continue to live in her or his own home, even when there is a need for assistance. Aging people usually wish to live at home as long as possible, and safety alarm systems are part of today's structure of elderly care in Finland. Feelings of insecurity and fear are among the most common reasons for moving into a block of service flats or an old-age home. Safety alarm systems increase the user's feeling of safety and security, and their use has increased in private homes. They are also utilized in institutional settings to facilitate the work of care personnel, who can provide help more quickly in cases of need, such as when an aging person has fallen on the floor and is unable to get up without assistance [12].

Of the some 70,000 safety alarm systems in use in Finland today, more than half have been acquired by private citizens at their own expense. The rest are owned or maintained by municipalities as part of the public service provision. Safety alarm services are offered by private companies (in specific geographical areas or nationally), municipalities, foundations, non-governmental organizations and co-operatives [12].

The system of safety alarm services includes a call center that receives alarm calls and gives guidance to customers or, if necessary, calls out a service provider who goes to the aging person's home to provide help. The call center also receives notifications concerning technical faults or service needs related to alarm appliances. Call centers may be tiny internal units in old-age homes or blocks of service flats that serve only the residents, large centers that serve thousands of customers from all over the country, or something between, such as municipal centers [12]. The services focused on in this chapter are provided within blocks of service flats or in home care.

A safety alarm customer may call for help by pushing the button on her/his wristband or pendant. The customer is then connected to the call center and may communicate by speech with the person in charge at the center. The service provider must arrange a quick and effective response to an alarm signal at all times. The type of response depends on the type of reason for alarm call. Typical responses are verbal advice, visit by a safety helper, or calling out emergency services (such as ambulance) [12].

Safety alarm systems are concrete examples of gerontechnology. Gerontechnology means research, development, and implementation of specific technologies (devices or environments) for the benefit of the whole aging population or its parts [2, 7]. Gerontechnology has five roles in supporting aging people [9]:

• Preventive: gerontechnology solutions aim at preventing weakening of health
• Supports strengths: gerontechnology develops methods and devices that help in reaching a wider benefit from aging people's strengths at work, in leisure time, in learning and social interaction

- Compensates for weakening abilities: gerontechnology produces methods, devices and products that compensate for weakening senses or ability to move
- Supports care work: gerontechnology provides technology for care workers to support their work
- Furthers research: gerontechnology helps aging people indirectly by supporting scientific and clinical research

This chapter focuses on the fourth role – the role that supports care work. The research methodology is described in the Appendix. Altogether 78 workers were targeted in their relation to current and future use of safety alarms. Their customers were using a traditional safety telephone or a high-tech well-being wristband that automatically monitors 24 h a day the user's activity level by measuring micro- and macro-movement, skin temperature, and skin conductivity. It contains a manual alarm button, but will also trigger an alarm if and when the user is unable to do so. If desired, the system also provides an automatic notification when the wrist unit is removed or reattached (Fig. 32.1). The wrist unit continuously monitors its own performance, automatically transmitting alarms of any connection problems.

Effects of safety alarm use were investigated with the help of human impact assessment methodologies [10, 11]. Questions asked related to, for instance, linkage of technology to health (including perceived health) and to social effects such as trust and commitment, time use, information flows and network collaboration [12, 13], feelings of participation, as well as economic situation at the workplace. Results are presented qualitatively.

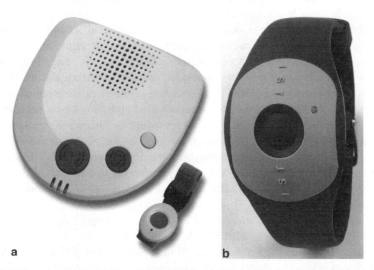

Fig. 32.1 The safety telephone (**a**) and the well-being wristband "Vivago WristCare" (**b**) that were tested (photographs by IST Oy and Miratel Oy)

Results of Empirical Research on the Use of Safety Alarms

Organizational Issues

In certain blocks of service flats, the safety technology is felt to be useful and vital for work, whereas in some others, it is felt to cause harm and a notable amount of extra work – instead of help. Extra work is caused by so-called needless alarms made by customers, and false alarms made by accident or due to technical failures, such as false routing of alarm calls due to the structure of the building (walls, etc.). The caregiver also has to prepare a written statement on received alarms on a personal computer.

In addition to general organizational issues, substitutes and managers were specifically addressed. Lack of abilities among substitutes influences time use, as the permanent staff has to spend time on guiding them and supervising their work. Disagreements in the work community may be caused by a situation where some of the personnel are more committed to use of an appliance or a system and know it better.

Some typical positive answers concluded that unnecessary visits to customers have ended; work motivation has increased; tasks and time use at work can be planned better if the system is well learnt; welcome changes are brought to work; and customers feel that they are heard and get help. The work of the care worker on the night shift is felt to become easier if she/he can deal with the matter on the phone with the customer. Customers have the possibility to live a peaceful life of their own and receive services only when they wish.

The safety technology provides increased tools for managers. They can monitor the needs for help of customers and the reactions of care workers, and assess whether these meet. They can also monitor overall workload better. It is motivating for both care workers and managers that when a care worker writes an alarm record, including the work done to respond to it, it makes her/his work visible in a new way.

Some typical negative answers concluded that due to safety alarms, the work schedule and thoughts get mixed up. Recording of alarm calls causes extra work. All personnel at the workplace are not committed and do not bear responsibility for this matter. Substitutes usually do not know the customers, so there are easily misunderstandings, and the information received on the phone cannot always be trusted. Substitutes in very short employment relationships have difficulties in being able to participate in the system and utilize it properly due to lack of time to get acquainted with it. Those among the personnel who have good knowledge must be ready to answer the questions of substitutes.

Negative answers also revealed that customers are visited at 2 h intervals (in blocks of service flats), but still they call; the meaning of the wristband is forgotten or misunderstood. The financial cost of the system in comparison with the real benefit was felt to be in contradiction, and this could cause pressure in managers' expectations concerning employees and their work.

Ethics of technology were also addressed. Customers may feel lonely when there is only the safety phone and no-one comes to visit them. The care worker cannot always come right away to help the customer, and some customers may not call even if they have a real need for help.

Trust, Skills and Motivation

There may be problems in answering an alarm call made by a customer. Transferring calls for help from one caregiver to another through the phone that first receives them has been problematic. This transfer requires pushing a series of numbers in a situation where the caregiver may just be helping another customer.

False guidance from producers of alarm systems, concerning waterproofness and the use during washing, bathing and a sauna visit, threatened secure functioning. Care workers do not have accurate and sufficient knowledge of these technical characteristics that have a significant impact on secure functioning. They may give the elderly user guidance such as that using the alarm device is all right in all circumstances. Care workers feel that it is a great benefit that the device can be carried at all times; when they trust that the customer can get help anywhere, they are slightly less concerned about the customer's well-being. This is, however, based on inaccurate information. Such matters highlight the importance of continuous orientation and training of personnel as well as responsibility from the producers of appliances.

Still, the impact of introduction of new technology on professional self-esteem is considerable. Lack of adequate skill and knowledge levels leads to feelings of insufficient capabilities. This, in turn, leads to decreased motivation, fear, and distress.

Some typical answers concerning trust, skills, and motivation included decreased work motivation, because you cannot trust the system completely. Senior personnel felt more uncertain in using technological aids and even have fears. Senior personnel may feel that new things are "useless" and difficult to learn. Technology causes a feeling of ignorance and "insignificance." Constantly keeping up with development of technology is difficult to bear, also for managers. Senior personnel may hand these tasks over to younger and more capable workers. Managers are concerned with how care workers cope at work.

Workers thus ask for more or better training. Different professional groups' needs must be mapped to find out who really benefits from training. It is important to try to organize different study plans for people with different backgrounds and abilities. There must be cooperation in learning: the young learn from the older, and the older learn from the younger. Everyone at the workplace should be able to take part in training, as safety alarm systems have an impact on different professional groups. The system is burdensome if orientation into use is not given, to substitutes, for instance.

Inability to analyze different kinds of sleep diagrams of the well-being wristband exists quite often. An experienced nurse may be able to analyze a customer's health condition on the basis of the curves and assess the impact of medication, but this is not self-evident. The curves are felt to be partly easy but partly difficult to understand and making use of them efficiently requires training.

Services Rendered

Additional effects of safety telephones and well-being wristbands are, inter alias, effects on feeling of health, atmosphere at the workplace, time use, attitudes, as well as effects on opportunities to participate in, contribute to and influence the work community. A well-being wristband may be seen as a uniting factor in the work community – "our thing" that influences the atmosphere in the workplace positively.

Some typical answers were those highlighting everyone's commitment to respond to alarm calls. Safety alarm systems enhance coping at work, and in line with training, they function as a creator of community feeling at work. Systems keep the brain vigorous and give an opportunity to develop one's competence. On the other hand, junior personnel felt that "one can feel to be 'above others' when this area at work is well learnt."

However, the service system outside the workplace should also be taken into account. Its practical significance depends on the type of the safety telephone system – whether it is an internal system in one municipality or based on services purchased by a municipality from a commercial company [12]. Also, caring family members and relatives are addressed. Some typical answers concluded that near relatives are satisfied because they know that safety is secured. Some relatives suppose that the "machines" play a bigger role in monitoring of customers' health condition than they actually do.

Discussion: How to Avoid Potholes?

New Individual Competence Requirements

In spite of problems and drawbacks, the employees focused on often feel that receiving and recording safety alarm calls is easier than normal use of computers. This may be due to regarding safety systems as a help and a tool for elderly care and seeing the ability to utilize them more as a professional skill than the use of computers as such. Safety alarms are assistive devices in daily use, accepted as part of work. They are felt to save time and financial resources; bring smoothness to planning of work; and maintain customers' independence and self-management. Experiences of using safety alarm systems may, however, be quite different depending on the individual employee. Some feel that a certain procedure such as recording an alarm call is cumbersome, while others do not think so.

Fears and doubts of personnel are mainly related to situations where the safety technology does not function, or customers are unable to use it with personnel on duty far away. In many workplaces, a safety telephone is "the caregiver" of an elderly person at night, their only link to the surrounding world. Some employees feel distressed because of this situation, as they suspect that all elderly people cannot manage with a mere safety telephone, but need another human being to be close by. In short, the technology is not fully trusted.

Still, the ability to use safety alarm technologies has become a central competence area. It has been found in earlier research that conditions are present to involve home nurses more explicitly in the introduction of assistive devices to their patients [20]. This finding is supported by our results. It is not only a question of care in this competence area, but also of the ability to guide customers in their technology use. Professional carers such as nurses are indeed important contributors to the use and integration of technological innovations in social and health care [22].

Strength of Orientation

Most of the negative effects of safety alarm technology use could have been eliminated or relieved by means of good orientation, based on foresight information and assessment, as reported earlier [14, 16]. Introduction of technology into the workplace may have a significant impact on professional self-esteem. Without an appropriate level of skills and knowledge, feelings of insufficiency and incapability arise, leading to lowered motivation, fear, and distress. Poor abilities and possibilities to use technology have caused severe conflicts in some workplaces. The conflicts may, on the surface, seem to be due to something other than technology use, so solving them may be very difficult and depart from false assumptions.

The most significant factor related to introduction of technology that motivates an individual employee is the benefit that she/he gets from using it. Different types of impact of technology use are often indirect and difficult to identify. The skill level of each employee is different, and employees have different attitudes towards changes at work. Introduction of technological innovations to the workplace is development work in the same way as creating a quality management system or introducing team work. Technology does not function in a vacuum, so also typical problems related to project work and development efforts should be taken into account [19]. It is especially important when orientation is taken care of by an outside consultant or trainer. Producers of appliances and systems often organize initial training, but that kind of training rarely takes into consideration the specific needs of an individual workplace. It is even more problematic to find a common language and a suitable starting level for a trainer who does not work in the care sector.

Orientation into technology use is one central area in introduction of technological innovations into work. Orientation should depart from individual employees' needs and cover all the aspects of assessment of work processes, technical orientation, and security issues, as well as support after the introduction of a device or a system. Continuous orientation is especially important for those in temporary employment relationships.

Orientation should not stop where technology has been brought to use and the necessary skills have been learnt. A well-managed orientation system includes assessment and updating of skills, when systems or devices are updated and renewed. The different stages of the continuous orientation process need to have a clear beginning and end but, as a process, it should go on in the workplace in one way or another all the time [16].

When considering the necessary skills, relevant questions are views of the role and usefulness of technology in the workplace. A foresight assessment should also cover the necessary level of competence of individual employees. Is it sufficient if basic skills are learnt or should every employee also be able to take care of more demanding tasks, such as taking out various types of reports from the system of well-being wristbands?

Importance of Impact Assessment

Areas that are directly or indirectly related to technology use may be well identified with the help of human impact assessment methodologies. If a decision is made to introduce well-being wristbands, including their accessories, in a block of service flats, this implies changes in work processes. Impact assessment produces information to support decision-making and development. In the case of technology use, an assessment to be made before its introduction is the most beneficial. A central principle in impact assessment is collaboration; it gives personnel an opportunity for participation and dialogue. Impact assessment takes into consideration views of different groups of workers and of individual workers.

According to experiences from empirical research, results of impact assessments make attitudes, expectations, fears, and values visible – ready to be discussed and targeted in development efforts [11, 14]. In the use of technological innovations, experiences and views are highly varied. Impact assessment processes also give a lot of information for the benefit of planning orientation and training that were found to be essential. The social and health care sector is hierarchical, and a positive assessment culture has hardly been developed for individual workplaces of this sector in Finland.

The impact of technology use on care workers may be dependent on the ways in which customers use technology. Safety alarms are a typical example. If a customer uses the safety alarm too often or too seldom, it has an impact on the care worker. If the customer forgets to use the alarm altogether, perhaps due to beginning dementia, it has an impact on the care worker. According to the empirical research results – rather than drawing conclusions on impacts of technology use at a general level – it is essential to pay detailed attention to impacts on care workers at an individual workplace and thereafter to weakening of negative impacts and strengthening of positive impacts.

In introduction and impact assessment related to technology, managers have a central role in many ways. They must be able to assess and supply useful technologies at a suitable pace of introduction into the work processes of each individual employee. This would be a big step on the road to effective adoption of new, innovative technologies. In addition, regular human impact assessments of technology are expected to lead to savings in acquisition, training, orientation, and other costs; however, they are still commonly seen as an unnecessary extra cost. There is still a lot to be done to further sober application of technological innovations, including a holistic view of their suitability for customers and employees alike.

Other Factors

In order to avoid potholes in efficient use of technological innovations, ethical questions and acceptability of technology use in care work should be targeted in discussions at workplaces. Care workers have many questions and concerns related to these themes, and they need attention in joint discussions between and among workers and managers. This was found to enhance sober and efficient application of technology as well as well-being at work.

Awareness among municipal authorities of preconditions of technology use in elderly care is one further factor to be developed if potholes are to be avoided. In Finland, municipal decision-makers draft strategies for elderly care, but managers at workplaces may have difficulties in implementing them. Care workers usually have no knowledge of the strategies, although they should provide the guidelines for practical work. Issues related to use of technology in elderly care are described at a superficial level, if at all. Impacts of technology use are not taken into account. There are most often formulations that technology use will be increased, but considerations of what this means in practice in the daily lives of care workers and customers are missing.

Increased use of technological innovations in elderly care requires comprehensive and coherent transmitting of actual attitudes and practices from decision-makers and managers to care workers. Wrong or inappropriate decisions lead to expensive solutions that may even weaken the quality of the service experienced by customers and lead to burn-out among care workers, as their work processes change.

Summary and Conclusion

Healthcare and social care form a large, societally highly important sector. It is especially large in Northern European countries in comparison with others but, anywhere in the world, questions concerning social and healthcare interest both scientists and the general public. The sector is also an important employer, whether organizations represent the public, private, or the third sector. In many countries, this sector is undergoing major changes and suffers from lack of financial resources as well as of personnel. Many other types of changes take place in individual organizations of the sector: technological innovations are introduced in an increasing amount to cope with the workload, collaboration between the three sectors is increasing, and the existing personnel often face problems in coping at work.

This chapter has focused on issues that typically cause potholes in the introduction and use of technology. In care work, abilities related to technology use have not yet become a central competence area at work, but the most important abilities are knowledge and skills related to care work itself and to illnesses. The view of competence in technology use as part of care work should, however, be widened. On the basis of results of empirical research conducted in Finland on safety telephones and high-tech well-being wristbands, this chapter illustrates the multi-faceted influence of technology use on service personnel in elderly care. This influence has implications on the possibility of rooting technological innovations into care work.

Regular human impact assessment of new technologies may stimulate their adoption by professional carers. Most of the negative effects of safety alarm technology use could be eliminated or relieved by means of good orientation based on foresight information and assessment. The effectiveness and economic significance of technology use consist of the impact of well-being at work, on productivity, and of sober utilization of technology in work processes. Detailed attention has to be paid to impacts on individual care workers and thereafter to weakening of negative impacts and strengthening of positive impacts.

This chapter shows what technology use may mean in practice in the daily lives of care workers and their customers. When employees become familiar with technological innovations by having enough time and space to learn, they can also adjust technology to their own needs. Impact assessments and related needs for orientation are not as such tied to any particular sector, workplace, profession, or theme or change being assessed, so their potential usability and applicability in developing and investigating services and work communities are much larger than can be described in this chapter. It is a question of rooting a general positive assessment culture into services, workplaces, and the development of one's own work.

Acknowledgments This research was financially supported by the National Workplace Development Programme Tykes of the Finnish Ministry of Labour.

Appendix: Methodology

The research focused on eight workplaces of care personnel, of which seven are blocks of service flats (sheltered accommodation) and one is a unit providing home care. Financing was public (four cases) or other (four cases: foundations and nongovernmental organizations). Some of the organizations included are eager to try out new technologies, others are not for or are against, while some resist new technology use or have very little experience so far. The workplaces are located in different parts of Finland and employ 7–60 persons from different professional groups (mainly assistant nurses and nurses). The care workers focused on have both permanent and temporary employment relationships. Altogether, 78 workers are targeted in their relation to current and future use of safety alarms. The customers were given a traditional safety telephone or a high-tech well-being wristband (Vivago WristCare) that automatically monitors 24 h a day the user's activity level by measuring micro- and macro-movement, skin temperature, and skin conductivity. It contains a manual alarm button, but will also trigger an alarm if and when the user is unable to do so. If desired, the system also provides an automatic notification when the wrist unit is removed or reattached (Fig. 32.1). The wrist unit continuously monitors its own performance, automatically transmitting alarms of any connection problems.

Effects of use of safety alarms have been investigated with the help of human impact assessment methodologies that were originally developed for the planning of physical environments. They consist typically of four phases: (i) identification of different types of impact by filling in forms, discussing, and/or interviewing, (ii) assessment of significance of the different types of impact, (iii) planning concerning weakening or strengthening the different types of impact, and (iv) drafting action plans [10, 11, 14]. From May 2005 to September 2006, eight impact assessment processes were undertaken in the care organizations by three researchers. A typical assessment process lasted for approximately half a year with several assessment events.

There was only one man among the professional carers involved, as the work-places were female-dominated. The share of aging employees over 45 years of age was fairly large. The employees participated in the assessment processes by filling in pre-prepared forms in groups of 2–3 employees, or individually in certain cases. They also participated in subsequent discussions on the results of the assessment. Questions asked related to the linkage (impact) of technology to health (includ-ing perceived health) and to social effects, such as trust and commitment, time use, information flows and network collaboration [12], attitudes and disagreements, feeling of participation, meaningfulness of work, need for training, services, eco-nomic situation at the workplace, and otherpossible types of impact (image of the workplace, and private live of the professional). Results were analyzed qualitatively.

References

1. A. Barnard, *Nurs. Philos.* **3**(1), 15 (2002)
2. H. Bouma, Gerontechnology: emerging technologies and their impact on aging in society, in *Gerontechnology: a sustainable investment in the future*, ed. by J. Graafmans, V. Taipale, N. Charness, (IOS, Amsterdam, 1998), pp. 93–104
3. R.B. Cooper, R.W. Zmud, *Manage. Sci.* **36**, 123 (1990)
4. T. Cox, A. Griffiths, S. Cox, *Work-related stress in nursing: controlling the risk to health.* Working paper CONDI/T/WP.4/1996. (International Labour Office, Geneva, 1996)
5. F.D. Davis, R.P. Bagozzi, P.R. Warshaw, *Manage. Sci.* **35**, 982 (1989)

6. N.S. Ghosheh Jr., S. Lee, D. McCann, Conditions of work and employment for older workers in industrialized countries: understanding the issues. *Conditions of work and employment series* no. 15. (International Labour Office, Geneva, 2006)
7. T. Harrington, M. Harrington, *Gerontechnology: why and how* (Shaker, Maastricht, 2000)
8. H. Jurvansuu, J. Stenvall, A. Syväjärvi, *Information technology and workplace practices in health care: An assessment of TEL LAPPI project* (in Finnish). (Ministry of Labour, Helsinki, 2004)
9. J. Kaakinen, S. Törmä, *A pilot study on gerontechnology: The ageing population and opportunities related to technology* (in Finnish). (Office of the Parliament, Helsinki, 1999)
10. T. Kauppinen, K. Nelimarkka, *J. Environ. Assess. Policy Manage.* **6**(1), 1 (2004)
11. T. Kauppinen, K. Nelimarkka, *Human impact assessment (HuIA) as a tool of welfare management* (National Research and Development Centre for Welfare and Health, Helsinki, 2004) http://info.stakes.fi/NR/rdonlyres/8028AF2D-4E9D-4965-B9B9-E3E2FF6626DB/0/huiatrainingmaterial.pdf. Accessed 20 January 2008
12. H. Melkas, *Towards holistic management of information within service networks: Safety telephone services for ageing people.* Doctoral dissertation (Helsinki University of Technology, 2004). http://lib.tkk.fi/Diss/2004/isbn9512268868/. Accessed 6 January 2007
13. H. Melkas, Analyzing information quality in virtual networks of the services sector with qualitative interview data, in *Challenges of managing information quality in service organizations*, ed. by L. Al-Hakim (Idea Group, Hershey, 2007), pp. 187–212
14. H. Melkas, A. Raappana, M. Rauma, T. Toikkanen, *Human impact assessment of technology use in workplaces of elderly care services* (in Finnish), (National Workplace Development Programme Tykes, Helsinki, 2007)
15. R. Miettinen, S. Hyysalo, J. Lehenkari, M. Hasu, *From product into tool at work? New technologies in health care*, (in Finnish), (Stakes, Helsinki, 2003)
16. A. Raappana, M. Rauma, H. Melkas, *Gerontechnology* **6**(2), 112 (2007)
17. G.L. Rafnsdottir, M.L. Gudmundsdottir, *Work* **22**, 31 (2004)
18. G.L. Rafnsdóttir, L.R. Sigurvinsdóttir, in *Cyberfeminism in the Nordic lights: digital media and gender in a Nordic context*, ed. by J. Sundén, M. Sveningsson, (Cambridge Scholars, Newcastle, 2007), pp. 223–242
19. M. Rauma, A. Raappana, H. Melkas, T. Toikkanen, *Työpoliittinen aikakauskirja* **50**(1), 66 (2007)
20. M. Roelands, P. Van Oost, A.M. Depoorter, A. Buysse, V. Stevens, *J. Adv. Nurs.* **54**(2), 180 (2006)
21. J. Siltala, The short history of worsening work life (in Finnish) (Kustannusyhtiö Otava, Helsinki, 2004)
22. J.Webster, J. Davis, V. Holt, G. Stallan, K. New, T. Yegdich, *J. Adv. Nurs.* **41**(2), 140 (2003)

Chapter 33
Senior Educational Programs for Compensating Future Student Decline in German Universities

D. Schwarz, J. Lentzy, and C. Hipp

Abstract Most industrialized countries are currently facing a shrinking and aging of the population. Germany's population is expected to fall from about 82.4 million people to between 69 and 74 million people in 2050. Simultaneously, the average age of the population is increasing. In particular, the coming years in Eastern Germany will be characterized by a strong decline in the number of young people and a significant increase in the number of elderly. However, demographic change does not automatically imply negative consequences but also creates room for opportunities. In this chapter, we explore opportunities to enlarge the purpose of the educational silver market by an economic component due to two developments: (i) current and upcoming generations of seniors increasingly spend their spare time studying intellectual and cultural subjects, and (ii) traditional universities suffer from a low number of students. We make considerations regarding incentives to include more people aged 65 and over in educational issues, and thus to create a win–win situation for third agers and institutions of higher education.

Introduction

Europe has just entered a critical phase in its demographic evolution, and each additional decade that fertility remains at its present low level will imply a further decline in the European Union of 25–40 million people, in the absence of offsetting effects from immigration or rising life expectancy [25].

As the German Federal Statistical Office for the German case reported, the share of people aged 19 years or less will fall from nearly 20% in 2001 to about 15% in 2050, while the share of people aged 20–64 years will fall from 61 to about 52%, and the share of people aged 65 and older will rise from 19 to 33% (see p. 5 in [12]). The results are based on the assumptions of the "middle variant" of the population projection, i.e., a constant birth rate of 1.4 children per woman on average, increased life expectancy of an infant male to 83.5 years and of an infant female to

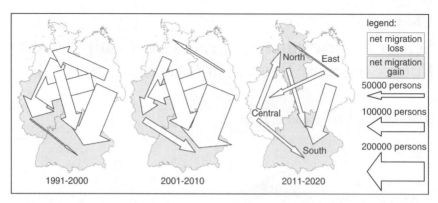

Fig. 33.1 Germany's internal net migration from 1991 to 2020. Source: Federal Office for Building and Regional Planning [4]

88.0 years by 2050, and annual net migration of a minimum of 100,000 and maximum of 200,000 people (see pp. 6–7 in [12]). This indicates that the average age of the population will rise from 42 years in 2005 to about 50 years in 2050, and that the population will fall from about 82.4 million in 2005 to between 69 and 74 million in 2050 (see p. 5, 17 in [12]). The situation in Eastern Germany seems to be even more dramatic. While the shrinking of the population in Western and Southern Germany is more moderate, the shrinking of the East German population is so great primarily due to internal labor migration and secondly due to the collapse of the birth rate after 1990. As Fig. 33.1 shows, migration from Eastern Germany to the old Federal States (North, Central and South of Germany) is not forecasted to stop during the next few decades.

People aged between 18 and 30 years seem to be the most mobile; in contrast, people aged 50 years and over show the least mobility. Therefore, the East German population will first shrink, caused by the missing potential parents and thus a new generation of children, and second by age. The share of people aged 65–74 living in the new Federal States will increase by 8% from 2002 to 2020, while the share of people aged 65 and over will increase by 31.3%. Simultaneously, the East German population will shrink by almost 8%, which means a loss of slightly more than 1.3 million people between 2002 and 2020 [4]. In contrast, the share of people aged 65 and over living in the old Federal State will increase proportionally by only 22.6% from 2002 to 2020 while the total number of people will rise from 65.5 to 66.4 million people in the same period [4].

"The triumph of public health, medical advancements, and economic development over diseases and injuries that had limited human life expectance for millennia" has brought many challenges regarding aging societies (see p. 5 in [21]). This development means thinking about the inclusion of older people at all levels of society, as well as economic issues. Thus, the authors of this chapter look at the educational market for retired people and the benefits for institutions of higher education in East Germany, which suffer from a low number of young students.

The Third Age

In the literature, there are many categorizations of "age" and the decades of life. Regarding elderly adults, the terms "young-old" and "oldest-old," or "third age" and "fourth age," have become popular [8,23,33,34,36]. It is also a fact that there is no agreement about the lower and higher age limits of the respective classifications. Figure 33.2 gives an overview of a few existing definitions (Fig. 33.2)

While statisticians hardly criticize these categories, gerontologists have argued about this subject for several years. Apart from research problems in defining groups of interviewees, they fear that the extreme category is associated with negative stereotypes and the period of final dependence, decrepitude, and death (see pp. 369–370 in [8], p. 6 in [21]).

Regarding the topic of this chapter, we prefer to apply a more open definition of age. Following the arguments from Swindell, third agers "are no longer tied to the responsibilities of regular employment and/ or raising a family" (see p. 419 in [36]), as they are in relatively good health, retired, socially and politically engaged (see p. 217 in [13], p. 409 in [27], p. 192 in [28], p. 643 in [39]), and aspire to achieve personal self-fulfillment (see p. 28 in [43]). They enjoy a more vigorous life than previous generations (see p. 409 in [27]) and are willing to engage in honorary work and to spend time in consumptive activities like education. A survey initiated by the Federal Statistical Office of Germany listed the daily activities of people aged 60–69. Besides time spent on physical recreation and sleep, older people mainly spend their time in voluntary work and personal hobbies. About 31% of senior citizens aged 60–69 are experienced in performing or currently perform voluntary services, which indicates that elderly people are willing to participate in educational courses in preparation for these services (see p. 13 in [5]) (Fig. 33.3).

Even if some researchers ascribe the mentioned characteristics to the term "third age" (e.g., [34,36]) and others to the term "young-old" (e.g., [28]), the age of retirement seems to be the lower limit of both terms. While eligibility for social security benefits in Germany has dropped to between 58.5 and 60 years (see p. 177 in [7], p. 9 in [16]), the collapse of the German social security system leads to a successive

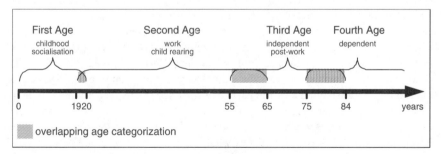

Fig. 33.2 Visualization of age categorizations. Author's illustration according to the definitions from [8,34,39]

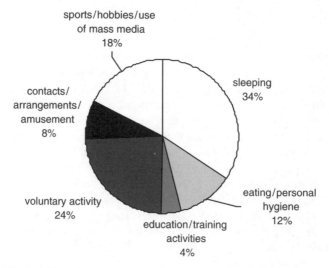

Fig. 33.3 Daily activities of senior citizens aged 60–69. Author's illustration according to data from [14]

rise in the regular retirement age to 67 years from 2012 on. Thus, the lower limit of the third age category will shift naturally.

As we have already pointed out, the number of people aged 60 and over will increase in the future. The relevance of the "silver market" is rising and results, among others, in the University of the Third Age (UTA) movement (see p. 409 in [27]).

Universities of the Third Age

Historical Survey

Models of learning for elderly people have a history of at least 40 years. The first generation of senior educational services came up in 1960 to serve as a cultural leisure activity in order to occupy seniors and promote their social interaction (see p. 338 in [24]). The Institutes for Learning in Retirement (ILR) seem to have resulted from this generation, established in 1962 in New York City (see p. 54 in [17]). The second generation of senior educational services originated in the 1970s and focused on the development of life experiences of seniors to prepare them to intervene in social issues (see p. 338 in [17]). The activities of the University of Toulouse probably belong to this generation, as the term "University of the Third Age" was proposed first in 1973 by Pierre Vellas when the University offered low-cost summer programs for retired persons (see p. 57 in [17], p. 410 in [27], p. 178 in [44]). This French model of UTA was characterized by engaging retired adults in forms of self-programmed learning, organized and presented by university staff and funded by the government (see p. 178 in [44], p. 57 in [17]). This first UTA had four major objectives [41]:

1. To contribute to raise the level of physical, mental, and social health and the quality of life of older people
2. To provide a permanent educational program for older people in close relation with the other age groups
3. To initiate research into age issues
4. To set up education programs in gerontology for present and future decision-makers, including Community Information Programs to promote the awareness of age issues in each person in our society

Lemieux identified a third generation of senior educational services, or better, a next generation of UTAs, which emerged in the 1980s (see p. 338 in [24]). The aim was to develop a curriculum for seniors who are retiring earlier and earlier, are better educated, and are demanding credited university courses for their tuition.

The UTA models spread rapidly around the world, including Australia, New Zealand, Canada, USA, Argentina, Germany, Czech Republic, Poland, UK, Scandinavia, China, and Japan (see p. 57 in [17], [37]). However, they are different in regard to the organization objectives, form of organization, approach of learning, field of study, admission requirements, and offers of certificates like a baccalaureate or diploma (see p. 411 in [27], pp. 5–8 in [13]).

Case Box 1

One example for the different UTA concepts is the "University of the Third Age Online" (U3A Online). The idea to use the internet to deliver UTA services was born in 1997 by a group of UTA leaders from Australia, New Zealand, and the UK (see p. 418 in [36]). It was originally funded by the Australian Government in 1999 and has continued to receive funding from the Australian Government and considerable help from other supporters to provide educational services for older people anywhere in the world who are isolated either geographically, or through physical or social circumstances [40]. The courses are generally organized as follows: they require no previous knowledge of the subject areas, there are no exams and no degrees are awarded, they have been developed by knowledgeable volunteers, they require Internet access and basic computing skills [40]. The original concept of the virtual UTA has been reinforced by co-operative activities with UTA colleagues in other parts of the world who run their courses online with participants, e.g., from UK, Australia, New Zealand, the USA and Germany (see p. 427 in [36]).

The UTAs in China are another example. "Since the end of the Cultural Revolution, Chinese governments have regarded education as important for helping the more than 100 million older Chinese to adapt to social change" (see p. 434 in [37]). China was supposed to be the country that has the largest number of UTAs, namely 19,300 UTAs and 1.81 million members by the end of 2002 [38]. A wide variety of UTAs have been set up since the 1980s, supported by government help with funding, premises, and guidelines for the management of UTAs [38]. The first UTA was established in Shangdong Province in 1983 [19]. Swindell and Thompson figured out that there are both very prestigious and more traditional universities, and the majority of China's UTAs are associated with recreational centers (see p. 434 in [37]).

To promote the development of UTAs in China, the China Association of Universities for the Aged (CAUA) was established in 1988, now has 207 member UTAs, publishes a magazine on lifelong learning, and has set up a research group on the development of textbooks for UTAs [19].

The demographics of an aging society and the increasing demand for social activities have posed new educational challenges (see p. 173 in [44]). There is great potential, first, because of the baby boomer generation that is already retired or will retire in the next few years. Second, there are many interested learners resulting from increased longevity (see p. 537 in [22]). Moreover, there are positive psychological and medical findings related to education in later life phases regarding the maintenance of well-being and productivity [10, 37], enhancements of coping strategies, and prevention of unnecessary decline (see p. 448 in [9], p. 403 in [27]). According to UNESCO, which has initiated the concept of lifelong education, it is assumed that "learning is something that all people do and want to do for reasons which are intrinsically valuable to their human existence and quality of life" (see p. 174 in [44]). Additionally, elderly people have a need for appropriate services and material goods, and education is itself one of those services (see p. 313 in [31]) or, in a new term, one of those "silver market" services. All of these facts could be a sign of a fourth generation of educational services – a generation that focuses on the following aspects:

- From a social perspective to ensure the quality of life of older people, to meet their potential of interests and their demand for participation in social life through learning and honorary teaching [41].
- From an economic perspective to support public institutions of higher education that suffer from a low number of young students caused by demographic effects through study fees and allocation of governmental funds.
- From a socio-political perspective (see p. 78 in [43]) to gain a future-oriented voting public (see Chap. IV, p. 2 in [26]), and to improve the level of physical, mental, and social health to reduce costs of the health care system.

Senior Educational Services in Germany

The supply of education for retired adults in Germany is manifold and somewhat confusing (see p. 153 in [43], p. 23 in [35]). Wenzke listed the big five providers of educational services in Germany (see p. 158 in [43]):

- Institutions for senior citizens, like day-care centers, senior clubs, and service centers (20%)
- Admitted senior groups (13%)

- Educational institutions, e.g., senior universities (13%)
- Adult education centers (12%)
- Cultural and municipal institutions (9%)

While the number of providers, and thus the complexity of offers, has increased during the past few years, the participation of third agers and obviously their learning motivation are still relatively low (see p. 24 in [35]). This raises the question of whether the low participation is caused by the inactivity of elderly people and/or caused by unavailable or unattractive offers [35].

Focusing on UTAs, Saup [32] provided an overview of study offers for seniors at German institutions of higher education. A few universities in the former Federal Republic of Germany (e.g., Dortmund, Oldenburg, Mannheim, Frankfurt, Bielefeld, Münster, and Marburg) started in the 1980s with educational services for third agers. The number steadily increased from 35 universities in 1994 to 42 in 1997 and 50 in 2001 (see p. 13 in [32]). Meanwhile, this number of senior universities has increased further.

Considering the past years, younger third agers are increasingly interested in educational programs (see p. 15 in [32]). The average age of seniors participating in the offered programs in 2001 dropped to 63 years, possibly due to the lower age of retirement in the past (Fig. 33.4)

Older adults have three possibilities to study at UTAs (see p. 18 in [32]). Firstly, interested persons can register as *ordinary* students, presupposing the university entrance diploma, participating in required courses, and taking examinations. Saup estimated that 3500–6000 senior citizens (age not specified) were registered in 2001. Secondly, third agers can participate in education as *regular* guest auditors. Normally, no entrance certificate is required and the training finishes without

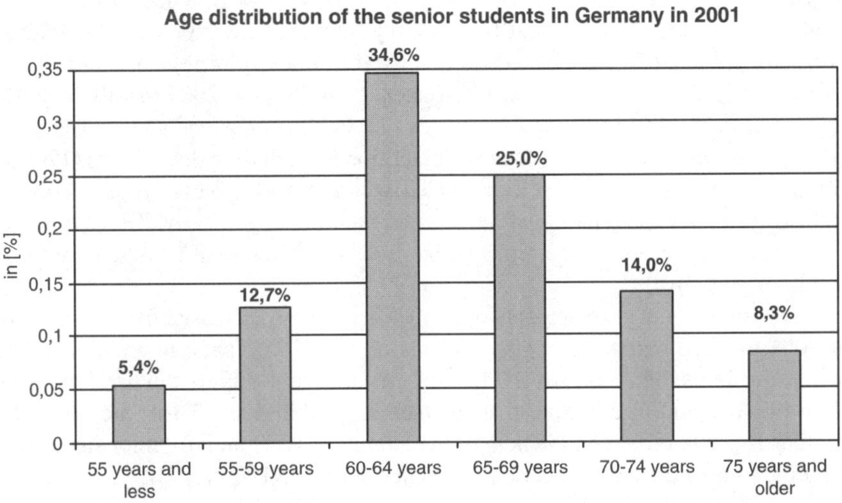

Age distribution of the senior students in Germany in 2001

Fig. 33.4 Age distribution of senior students in Germany in 2001 [32]

any examinations or educational achievements. The participants are free to choose generally offered fields of science without entrance limitations. Thirdly, UTA candidates can register as *specific* guest auditors. This program provides special advisory courses, regular courses, post-professional training, and lecture series. The content and duration of study is not determined. These and other factors regarding this kind of senior study differ from university to university. Being a specific guest auditor seems to be the most attractive program, since about 25,000 students were registered in that group in 2001.

The current generation of third agers has an agenda for studying. They, for example, intend to study to compensate for the gap in previous education, to renew study abilities, to qualify for honorary work or even to extend employability, to satisfy the need for participating in a desired study, to improve image, to keep able to communicate with younger generations or their grandchildren, to discuss philosophical questions, to keep physical and mental mobility, and simply to avoid loneliness (see p. 59 in [18], p. 15 in [32], Chap. IV, p. 4 in [26]).

Teaching these competencies (regarding competence profiles in senior education see [20]), German UTAs are primarily university-linked and quite academic in nature, because often university professors conduct these programs [37]. They finance their senior programs from their own resources as well as participation fees (see p. 186 in [42]), because they get no financial support from the government (see p. 12 in [11]).

Case Box 2: UTA at the University in Cottbus

The UTA at the Brandenburg Technical University in Cottbus, located in the south east part of the Federal State Brandenburg, was founded in 2001 to establish a place for education, meeting, and activity (see p. A11 in [43], [46]). Since 2001, the program includes arrangements that focus on the building of competencies helpful in everyday life and of competencies to qualify for honorary or regular employment (see p. 117 in [43]). The offer for third agers from 2002 to 2005 mainly included (see p. A179 in [43], [46]): sports courses (23.8%), lectures and series of lectures (19.3%), lectures held by professors or practitioners including discussions (17.3%), computer courses (15.7%), self-organized working and project groups (10.5%), sightseeing (8.1%), and participation as guest auditors in generally offered lectures. There are no admission requirements, but a semester fee of €30 is required (see p. 339 in [43], [46]).

In recent years, the participants of this UTA program increased from 87 persons in 2001 to 1186 registered senior students in 2006 [45]. This, in addition to the increasing demand for courses and lectures, means that lecturers can hardly accomplish this demand in addition to their main responsibilities. Therefore, the UTA Cottbus is partly reliant on the help of the alumni of BTU and of senior students to refer their knowledge and experience to others (see p. A190 in [43]).

According to the assumed fourth generation of UTAs, there are two main aims: firstly from a social point of view, to meet the demand for senior education caused by the increasing potential (e.g., see p. 9 in [30], p. 24 in [5]) of third agers in the next 5–15 years. Since German UTAs are mainly university linked (see p. 436 in [37]), the second aim is to help universities that suffer from a low number of students. This means compensating for the decreasing number of young students and, thus, the decreasing funds of the federal government through senior students' tuition charges and other currently undefined funds. In short, there is a need to create a win–win-situation.

Strategies to Enlarge the Benefit for German Universities

As mentioned in the "Introduction," both the number of third agers and probably the number of senior students – ceteris paribus a constant share – in East Germany will increase. Simultaneously, the net income will decrease, caused by the demographically required reforms in the German social pension program (see p. 197 in [6]). Thus, expensive educational offers will probably not be affordable for the majority of UTA clientele. This dilemma leads to the consideration of strategies to finance this social responsibility of educating and developing retired persons through attractive leisure activities, and thus to recruit senior students and raise the total number of students at universities.

Application for governmental support. Education must be seen as a form of social policy (see p. 410 in [27]) and should, at least partly, be financed by the government. It is a social responsibility to care for elderly people and to protect them as long as possible from age-related impairment. That, in turn, could positively affect the social security system through reduced health care costs, and should be a main incentive for the government to bankroll.

Realization of a unique program. The UTA needs to have a competitive advantage compared to other providers of senior educational services. A competitive advantage is manageable if many competitors have the respective resources (see p. 155 in [1], p. 6 in [3]). As Barney defined: "Even if a resource is valuable, rare, and costly to imitate, if it has strategically equivalent substitutes that are themselves not rare or not costly to imitate, then it cannot be a source of sustained competitive advantage" (see p. 47 in [2]). This unique selling proposition (USP) campaign (for example by establishing a unique and attractive program) comes along with an adequate price policy. When the university succeeds in creating a competitive advantage, it improves its reputation. Thus, sponsors will potentially support this concept. For example, learning activities for seniors at Canadian UTAs are sponsored by federal initiatives, provincial initiatives, or community-based programs (see p. 454 in [9]).

Analysis of demand. UTA clientele should be interviewed to find out their intention and learning preferences regarding content (see Chap. II in [26]), time (see p. 409 in [27], [29]) and so on. For example, it does not seem conducive to run adult education programs in the evening, when some older people may be reluctant to leave home. Senior students have an "autonomous educational will" (see Chap. IV, p. 2 in [26]) that could be realized in the above mentioned unique program.

Enlargement of the offer. In addition to the regular program, a virtual UTA that provides intellectually challenging courses for isolated or handicapped older people as well as for conventional UTA members could be interesting (see p. 414 in [36]). In Australia, the first "UTA online" started in 1999 and by the end of the first year, nearly 300 members belonged to that organization [36]. Regarding the limited mobility and the circuitousness of the trading area, this enlarges the target group as well as the inclusion of unemployed and interested people. They should have the possibility to participate in educational courses in order to use the whole capacity of the UTAs. UTAs in France have done this already (see p. 5 in [37]).

Establishment of an incentive policy. Elderly people aspire toward self-fulfillment, individualism, immediacy, and community (see p. 177 in [44]). Some adults have not had the chance to study or to study a desired scientific field. As Picton (see p. 409 in [27], [29]) identified, many retired persons left school at a very early age, perhaps due to socioeconomic imperatives or lack of opportunity to pursue education beyond the basic level. Thus, it is relevant to develop a specific curriculum for senior students like a "bachelor of arts" (see pp. 339–341 in [24]) or a Ph.D. program. These educational achievements allow senior students to teach, such as in adult education centers, or even to work as senior consultants. Maybe there is a demand for more than low-cost learning opportunities. Additionally, this prompts universities to think about different tuition fee strategies.

Establishment of network. Cooperating with municipal senior institutions could reduce costs through the use of synergies or declining administrative tasks. Besides the divided effort in organizing programs and marketing campaigns, a clear and convincing concept of senior educational services would result (see p. 117 in [43]).

Improvement of information. While conducting research for this article, it was difficult to get up-to-date information about the respective UTA programs, or even to find the respective UTA websites. The fact that today's third agers are mostly unpracticed in working with computers, and that these sites are not very user-friendly or self-explanatory is problematic. Improving the availability of information could be an important step toward improve the image of UTAs.

Boost of honorary work. Last, but not least, voluntary work should be mentioned. Specific offers could be operated by experienced senior students themselves (see p. 414 in [36], p. 644 in [39], p. 454 in [9]). Often they are motivated to transmit their life experiences (see p. 182 in [44]) and feel self-fulfillment (see p. 357 in [15]). It is necessary to boost honorary work (see p. 19 in [5]) to enlarge the variety of educational courses and simultaneously reduce costs.

Summary and Conclusion

This chapter began by discussing the demographic change regarding a shrinking of the population, particularly in Germany and East Germany. The projections of statistical offices have shown that the number of people living in Germany is expected to shrink. Simultaneously, the average age will increase in East Germany, caused by the migration of young people, and thus of potential parents, to other parts of

Germany. Therefore, there seems to be a high potential for educational offers for older people. In the second section, we focused on the definition and classification of the term "third age." Many statisticians and gerontologists deal with that topic, but there is no agreement about the limits of each age category. Therefore, we defined retired people who are interested in intellectual free time activities and social engagement as third agers. These individuals are interested in gaining new competencies, in particular in the field of social science, and in exchanging life experiences. For these people, UTA were established. In the section "Universities of the Third Age," we briefly outlined the history of these UTAs and hypothetically enlarged Lemieux' three-generation concept of UTAs by a fourth generation. We argued that there could be at least the following main aims of today's UTA, particularly in East Germany: Firstly, to ensure the opportunity for older people to continue to live in dignity, to ensure conditions and contexts that are at least equal to those available for younger age groups (see p. 461 in [34]), and to meet their potential of interests and their demand for participation in social life through learning and honorary teaching. A second aim is to support public institutions of higher education that suffer from a low number of young students, through senior students, the study fees of UTA clientele, and the additional allocation of governmental funds. This compensation seems to be possible since German UTAs are often university linked.

Next, we described the German system of educational services for senior citizens. As a short case and example, we mentioned the UTA at the Brandenburg Technical University Cottbus.

In "Strategies to Enlarge the Benefit for German Universities," we focused on the creation of a win–win situation for third agers, who may choose attractive educational services from a wide palette, as well as for universities that get steady low funds for registered students from the federal government. Therefore, we proposed some strategies to enlarge the benefit for universities and thus to be able to ensure and steadily improve the UTA program. As Swindell reasoned, keeping the brain active in later life may lead to measurable improvements in health and well-being (see p. 427 in [36]). Elderly people have a need for appropriate services like education (see p. 313 in [31]) and, therefore, education must be seen as a form of social policy and social responsibility that is at least partly financed by the government.

What we learned from this chapter about UTAs and in particular the East German difficulties to recruit students, or rather UTA clientele, is not easily transferable to other countries. That is because the UTAs all over the world differ in their organization objectives, form of organization, approach of learning, field of study, admission requirements, offers of certificates (see p. 414 in [27], pp. 5–8 in [13]), and support of the government. But, we pointed out that the motivational factors play a key role in raising the number of senior students. Our remarks regarding the analysis of demand, virtualization of educational courses, and improvement of the availability of information about the UTA could also be valuable impulses for other countries, on the one hand to satisfy senior students' needs and, on the other hand, to use institutions of higher education to their full capacity.

References

1. L. Argote, P. Ingram, *Organ. Behav. Hum. Decis. Process.* **82**(1), 150 (2000)
2. J.B. Barney, *Acad. Manage. Rev.* **26**(1), 41 (2001)
3. J.B. Barney, E.J. Zajac, *Strateg. Manage. J.* **15**(special issue), 5 (1994)
4. BBR, Federal Office for Building and Regional Planning.*Raumordnungsprognose 2020/2050: Ausgabe 2006*. (BBR, Bonn, 2006)
5. BMFSFJ, German Federal Ministry of Family, Seniors, Women and Youth (eds.), *Bildung im Alter: Ergebnisse des Forschungsprojektes.* (BMFSFJ, Berlin, 2004
6. BMFSFJ, German Federal Ministry of Family, Seniors, Women and Youth (eds.), *Fünfter Bericht zur Lage der älteren Generation in der Bundesrepublik Deutschland: Potenziale des Alters in Wirtschaft und Gesellschaft: Der Beitrag älterer Menschen zum Zusammenhalt der Generationen.* (BMFSFJ , Berlin, 2005)
7. A. Börsch-Supan, R. Schnabel, *Am. Econ. Rev.* **88**(2), 173 (1998)
8. B. Bytheway, *J. Soc. Issues*, **61**(2), 361 (2005)
9. B.S. Clough, *Educ. Gerontol.* **18**(5), 447 (1992)
10. M.W. Drotter, *Educ. Gerontol. Int. Q.* **7**(2), 105 (1981)
11. I. Dummer, *EFOS News* **1**, 12 (2004)
12. Federal Statistical Office Germany (ed.), *Bevölkerung Deutschlands bis 2050: 11. koordinierte Bevölkerungsvorausberechnung* (FSO, Wiesbaden, 2006)
13. European Federation of Older Students at the Universities (eds.), *EFOS News*, **1**, 5 (2007)
14. H. Engstler et al., in *Alltag in Deutschland: Analysen zur Zeitverwendung: Conference Proceeding Zeitbudgeterhebung 2001/02, 16–17 Feb 2001*, ed. by Federal Statistical Office Germany (FSO, Wiesbaden, 2004), pp. 216–246
15. M.J. Graney, W.C. Hays, *Educ. Gerontol. Int. Q.* **1**(4), 343 (1976)
16. J. Gruber, D. Wise, Social security programs and retirement around the world, in *NBER Working Paper Series*, Working Paper 6134 (National Bureau of Economic Research, Cambrigde, MA, 1997)
17. L.K. Hebestreit, *An evaluation of the role of the University of the Third Age in the provision of lifelong learning.* Dissertation, University of South Africa (2006), http://etd.unisa.ac.za/ETD-db/theses/available/etd-06042007-115106/unrestricted/thesis.pdf. Accessed 18 Jun 2008
18. H. Hirsch, *Altern. Higher Educ.* **5**(1), 57 (1980)
19. ICT, *ICT-in-Education Toolkit, sustaining lifelong learning, 2007.* http://www.ictinedtoolkit.org/usere/p_page.php?section_id=175#footnote47. Accessed 18 Jun 2008
20. S. Kade, Altersbildung und Kompetenz, in *Altersbildung an der Schwelle des neuen Jahrhunderts*, ed. by R. Berghold, D. Knopf, A. Mörchen (Echter, Würzburg, 1999), pp. 129–135
21. K. Kinsella, D.R. Phillips, *Popul. Bull.* **60**, 1 (2005), www.prb.org
22. F. Kolland, *Educ. Gerontol.* **19**(6), 535 (1993)
23. P. Laslett, *A fresh map of life: the emergence of the third age* (Harvard University Press, Cambridge, MA, 1991)
24. A. Lemieux, *Educ. Gerontol.* **21**(4), 337 (1995)
25. W. Lutz, B.C. O'Neill, S. Scherbov, *Science* **299**, 1991 (2003)
26. D. Meynen *Lässt sich das Seniorenstudium modularisieren? Ansätze zu einer wissenschaftsdidaktischen Theorie des Studiums im Alter* (Learning in Later Life, 2003) http://www.uni-ulm.de/LiLL/5.0/aufsaetze/daniel_meynen/seniorenstudium_modul.htm. Accessed 19 Jun 2008
27. V. Minichiello, *Int. Rev. Educ.* **38**(4), 403 (1992)
28. B.L. Neugarten, *Ann. Am. Acad. Political Soc. Sci.* **415**, 187–198 (1974)
29. C.J. Picton, *Trans. Menzies Found.* **8**, 113–118 (1985)
30. J.U. Prager, A. Schleiter, *Älter werden – aktiv bleiben: Ergebnisse einer repräsentativen Umfrage unter Erwerbstätigen in Deutschland*, (Bertelsmann, Gütersloh, 2006). http://www.bertelsmann-stiftung.de/bst/de/media/CBP_Umfrage_03.pdf. Accessed 18 Jun 2008
31. D. Radcliffe, *Educ. Gerontol.* **8**(4), 311 (1982)
32. W. Saup, *Studienführer für Senioren*, ed by Bundesministerium für Bildung und Forschung, (BMBF, Bonn, 2001) http://www.bmbf.de/pub/studienfuehrer_fuer_senioren.pdf. Accessed 18 Jun 2008

33. R.A. Settersten, K.U. Mayer, *Ann. Rev. Sociol.* **23**, 233 (1997)
34. J. Smith, *Eur. Rev.* **9**(4), 461 (2001)
35. C. Sommer, H. Künemund, *Bildung im Alter: Eine Literaturanalyse*. Forschungsbericht 66 der Forschungsgruppe Altern und Lebenslauf (FALL). (Freie Universität Berlin, 1999) http://www.fall-berlin.de/index.html?/fdl3.htm. Accessed 18 Jun 2008
36. R. Swindell, *Int. J. Lifelong Educ.* **21**(5), 414–429 (2002)
37. R. Swindell, J. Thompson, *Educ. Gerontol.* **21**(5), 429 (1995)
38. J. Thompson, *The amazing university of the third age in China today*, (U3A, UK, 2002). http://worldu3a.org/worldpapers/u3a-china.htm. Accessed 18 Jun 2008
39. E. Timmer, M. Aartsen, *Soc. Behav. Pers.* **31**(7), 643 (2003)
40. U3A Online, *A virtual university of the third age*. (Griffith University, Queensland, 2008) http://www3.griffith.edu.au/03/u3a/. Accessed 18 Jun 2008
41. P. Vellas, *The first university of the third age*, http://worldU3A.org/aiuta/vellas-uk.htm, 2007-10-31
42. K.P. Wallraven, in *Handbuch Altenbildung: Theorien und Konzepte für Gegenwart und Zukunft*, ed. by S. Becker, L. Veelken, K.P. Wallraven (Leske + Budrich, Opladen, 2000), pp. 186–188
43. B. Wenzke, *Produktivität im Alter: Bildung zwischen Institution und Selbstorganisation*, Ph.D. thesis, (Brandenburg Technical University Cottbus, 2007)
44. A. Williamson, *Int. J. Lifelong Educ.* **16**(3), 173 (1997)
45. ZfW (ed.), *Vortrag zum 5jährigen Bestehen der Seniorenuniversität* (BTU, Cottbus, 2006)
46. ZfW (ed.), *Seniorenuniversität*, (BTU, Cottbus, 2008) http://www.tu-cottbus.de/btu/de/weiterbildung/kindersenioren/seniorenuniversitaet/. Accessed 18 Jun 2008

Lessons Learned and the Challenges and Opportunities Ahead

C. Herstatt and F. Kohlbacher

> Concerning ageing, we are talking too much about technology and not about innovation. But what counts is not what is technically possible. What counts is what people want.
>
> Professor Joseph F. Coughlin, Director, AgeLab, MIT

After two prefaces, one introduction, 33 full chapters and one afterword to come after this concluding chapter, we would like to keep this chapter short and concise. Nevertheless, we don't want to fail to mention that, despite this vast amount of valuable information, insights and analyses, there still remain many questions unanswered and a great deal of work to be done. But, as we explained in the Introduction, we did not – and could not – aim for completeness but rather for variety and to highlight the differences between distinct industries and countries. Thus, we could only present a first fraction of the global silver market phenomena and some of the industries working on ways of catering for the needs of elderly people. The need for further research, as well as practice, is obvious.

Lessons Learned

The lessons learned are of course legion. We won't repeat all the lessons learned from each individual chapter here and it would be somewhat unfair to stress only the lessons learned from some chapters. But one of the most crucial insights is without doubt the fact that the silver market is by no means a homogenous market segment in that the so-called 50-plus market covers a wide range of different customers and consumers with an equally wide range of values, attitudes, needs and wants. Thus, the silver market actually consists of various different silver markets. In a similar vein, we should not forget that marketing has, for a long time, already gone beyond the simplistic segmentation by age and that, despite the tremendous business potential of the 50-plus, we should resist the temptation of merely looking at a person's age.

The second crucial insight is that the silver market is not necessarily restricted to the silver generation only. Or, put differently, who is silver is not determined by age (alone) and that younger consumers can also have silver hair, so to speak. This of course refers to the powerful concepts of universal and transgenerational design. Managers and scholars alike should bear in mind that the best products, services and solutions are often those that can be attractive to a variety of customers regardless of their age and that they can also be used or consumed regardless of age and physical or mental condition. Beware of ageism, think transgenerationally!

Challenges Ahead

Of course, the challenges ahead are numerous. Ever more countries are affected by demographic change. Think about China, for example. The population structure continuously shifts from young to old due to the effects of the one-child policy for example. Even currently very young countries such as Vietnam and Thailand are also aging, even though the population is not going to shrink over the next decades. However, despite the importance and the vast implications of population aging and shrinking in many nations, we should not forget that population growth still remains a major challenge in many developing countries. Lord Adair Turner of Ecchinswell, Former Chairman of the UK Pensions Commission, for example argues that:

> . . . .across the world the biggest demographic challenge is rapid population growth in parts of the developing world, not the manageable problems of aging in rich developed countries. [3]

Even though this issue goes beyond the scope of this book, this fact should not be forgotten when discussing demographic change.

Another crucial challenge derives from a combination of the financial situation and the health condition of senior people. Especially with the, mostly affluent, baby boomer generation that is approaching age 60 and beyond in many countries, the focus of most silver market strategies are the "rich and young-at-heart" elderly, while the "poor and weak-of-limb" elderly are often neglected. True, there are ever-more helpful gerontechnologies and assistive and supportive devices etc. available, but these are often costly. What happens to those who cannot afford to pay by themselves and are at the same time not sufficiently covered by social and welfare systems? We believe that there might be a new silver market phenomenon on the horizon, which will even be more challenging to governments, policy makers and corporations. The number of those elderly people whose financial and health situation is not favourable might strongly increase over the next decades. Prahalad [2] has written a book "The Fortune at the Bottom of the Pyramid", where he refers to those consumers at the bottom of the income and wealth pyramid, especially those in developing countries. Kohlbacher and Hang [1] were the first to apply this idea to the silver market, where those in need will be those at the top of the population pyramid (while being at the bottom of the income and wealth pyramid). They warn:

Firms should be careful not to exclude those customers at the bottom of the innovation pyramid, not only because – as is the case with many baby boomers – the fortune at the bottom of this pyramid is enormous, but also because of corporate social responsibility, as they can benefit both individuals and societies with "gerontechnologies" and related products and services. [1]

Bringing the issue of (corporate) social responsibility and social innovation to the discussion of the silver market, or bringing the silver market phenomenon onto the agenda of the CSR and social business debate, will be an important development for both areas.

Opportunities Ahead

Finally, the opportunities ahead will not be less than the challenges. The baby boomers will continue to age and retire and so will their children in the future. The silver market phenomenon will not only be an opportunity for business but also an opportunity for innovation and invention, creativity, learning, and social response and responsibility. The lead market Japan could certainly serve as an interesting role model, as can other countries such as the USA, Germany and the Scandinavian nations, but also India and China.

We strongly hope that this book has contributed to this opportunity for business, innovation and invention, creativity, learning, and social response and responsibility. We also hope that it will be a helpful tool in making sense of the silver market phenomenon and that it will encourage an active and creative debate as well as real action in tackling the challenges and opportunities of demographic change.

References

1. F. Kohlbacher, C.C. Hang, in *Proceedings of the 2007 IEEE International Conference on Industrial Engineering and Engineering Management (IEEM)* (2007), p. 1915–1919
2. C.K. Prahalad, *The Fortune at the Bottom of the Pyramid: Eradicating Poverty Through Profits* (Wharton School Publishing, Upper Saddle River, 2006)
3. L.A. Turner, Population ageing or population growth: what should we worry about? The WDA–HSG Discussion Paper Series on Demographic Issues, St. Gallen, No. 2007/5, 2007

Afterword

H. Tschirky

In the January 2008 issue editorial of *Ageing & Society*, one of the top-ranking journals in social gerontology, the editor in chief proudly puts the rapid expansion of his journal in parallel to the distinct "... transformation of interest in applied gerontology from a rare academic enthusiasm to an active pursuit of policy makers and several professions in ever more countries" [9]. This statement reflects on one side the rapidly burgeoning significance of the aging phenomenon in society. On the other side it illustrates the imperative need to tackle the theme from a highly interdisciplinary perspective.

This dual emphasis accurately characterizes the content of the book publication at hand. While focusing on market aspects, it corresponds to the vivid awareness in recent years of the facts and consequences of demographic change and at the same time captures this theme with a highly refreshing plurality of dimensions. These range from political aspects, social implications, innovation trends and require-ments, and changing consumer behavior to the so-far underestimated potentials of services and service innovations, and industrial challenges and solutions. Moreover, the authors cover the view from the major global economies, yet put the accent on Japan.

This accent indeed illustrates, as in numerous other aspects, the quite particular situation of the second largest economy. Demographic change in fact has a pri-mordial significance in Japanese society. A discussion on age-related phenomena is not missing in any qualified publication on Japan's socio-cultural background. On one side, societal characteristics are highlighted, which manifest the deeply rooted respect for age. Early references are typically made to Confucianism, which is assumed to have gained ground in Japan in the later part of the third century. This moral system is attributed to the Chinese philosopher Confucius, who lived from 551 BCE to 479 BCE. Aiming at social harmony, Confucianism teaches the "vertical society," representing a social structure that is characterized by respect for the elderly and company seniors and, vice versa, by benevolence and care toward younger family members and the company employees. The social and political order at its core identifies five major relationships of responsibilities and duties:

sovereign–subject, parent–child, husband–wife, elder sibling–younger sibling, and friend–friend.

Particular expressions of Confucianism-based age–status relationships are *senpai–kohai* relations. *Senpai* (先輩) consists of the two Chinese characters (or so-called kanjis) *sen* (先, meaning earlier) and *pai* (輩, meaning colleague) and can be translated as "senior" or "mentor." *Kohai* (後) contains *ko* (後, meaning after, later) and again *hai* (or *pai*, 輩) and means "junior, undergraduate." In companies or sports clubs, *senpai–kohai* relations refer to related members with different time-related affiliations to the organization, where the *senpai* has a mentor function and the *kohai* performs, naturally, serving functions for his *senpai*. Quite often this is a lifelong relationship outlasting the original company affiliation.

A similar reflexion lies in the word *sensei* (先生), which is used in a honorific way to refer to a person with educational competencies. It consists again of *sen* (先) and *sei* (生, meaning life) and therefore allows the interpretation that someone is qualified with a distinguished level of knowledge based on their longer life experience.

The veneration of ancestors is a manifestation of age-respecting relationships as well. This consists of commemorative rites in homes or temples, which are based on the belief that the ancestors do return at selected times of the year and are listening to specific concerns, requests, and wishes of the still-living family members. For example, *O-bon* (お盆[1]) is such a traditional celebration, held in July or August, depending on the geographic area.

Finally, since recently, the third Monday of September, the *Keiro no Hi* (敬老の日) or "Respect for the Aged Day" is a national holiday in Japan. It celebrates the value of respect for elderly people, which is expressed by the kanjis *kei* (敬, meaning respect) and *ro* (老, meaning become old).

On the other side, this book brings up themes that illustrate the age-related demographic changes. According to recent studies reported by Kohlbacher [7], the median age of the Japanese population will sharply increase from 41 years in 2000 to 54 years in 2050. At the same time, the total population will shrink from 126.7 million to 93.7 million. This also means, for example, that by 2015 roughly 25% of the population will be 65 and older. At the same time, Japan enjoys the worldwide highest life expectancy at over 81 years of age.

In parallel, the various purchasing power segments are undergoing major shifts. From studies of the Fuji Research Institute it can be concluded that consumption by the elderly will grow to ¥72 trillion in 2010. This figure corresponds to 34% of the nation's total consumption or, in monetary value, more than double within 10 years. Also, it is expected that the number of elderly needing nursing care will amount to 4 million, representing a nursing-care market of roughly ¥6.9 trillion.

After all, this simultaneous "shrinking *and* aging" phenomenon, combined with the purchasing power shift, is the reason for the specific focus of this publication.

An additional focus deserves to be emphasized: Among the numerous solutions aimed at coping with the demographic change in Japan, the options of rendering

---

[1] *o* (お) is a honorific term expressing respect and *bon* (盆) has the meaning of "tablet" and may refer to offering tablets used in Buddhist funeral ceremonies.

existing services to the rapidly emerging Silver Market and the creation of new services for this market are in the fore. In fact, the theme "services" is clearly experiencing increased attention in applied academic research, and "service innovations" have been particularly chosen as a focus of intensified research. According to Chesbrough [1], who coined the term "open innovation," services in 2003 represented 80% of the gross domestic product of the USA. According to the OECD, they account for a similar percentage of economic activity across all advanced industrial economies. Despite this, most analyses of innovation tend to focus on products, not services. He highlights: *"It is now time to update our curriculum for teaching and researching innovation to address the dominant sector of economic activity"* [1].

Facing this major challenge for academia as well as entrepreneurial practice, it is not surprising that Japan is among the main movers. On one side, however, the service culture in Japan already has a level of competence that may hardly be topped by any other economy. Everyday service experiences in Japanese department stores speak for themselves.

On the other side, it is also not surprising that a former chairman and president of Canon has successfully been teaching and practicing his conviction: "the biggest room on earth is the room for improvement!" – a statement that is representative for the entrepreneurial spirit of numerous Japanese leaders.

In this spirit of *kaizen* (commonly translated as "continuous improvement"), some reflections may be appropriate on the future potential of further developing and innovating services in Japan:

Services, in comparison to material products, are different in many essential respects. Overall, the main distinctions are given by the facts that services are immaterial and that they are produced and consumed simultaneously. Typical examples are nursing-care services. The immaterial nature makes it quite difficult to precisely quantify the quality of services in such a way that they fully fulfill the customer's expectations. In other words, specifying service quality is challenged to quantify not merely *explicit knowledge* but in addition and to a large extent *implicit or tacit knowledge*. In rendering nursing-care services, the amount of services, their nature, and the equipment to be used allow them to be specified explicitly. However, the mindful way of handling patients and the regardful modality and content of required communication are primarily of implicit nature.

As a consequence, the final service quality depends to a large extent on the specific behavior of the person rendering the service. Behavior can be considered to represent a visible expression of invisible values. Therefore, the intention to provide a high quality service has to focus, in the first place, on best-suited personal and organizational values, which ought to determine the behavior of the service-rendering people. In other words, since in an organization shared values represent the company culture, its appropriate value constitution, compatible with a chosen business strategy, comes to the fore.

According to Schein [8], the company culture represents a "unique pattern of shared basic assumptions." Such basic assumptions or values are, for example, an assumption concerning the organization–environment relationship about whether it is environment-dominant, organization-dominant, or symbiotic. Another assumption concerns task orientation: whether it is primarily task-oriented, primarily relationship-oriented, or task *and* relationship oriented [8].

Among the numerous managerial functions and responsibilities, influencing the company culture is no doubt among the most fundamental. However, in entrepreneurial reality this priority is rarely a striking characteristic of management practice. One reason may be that, for example, working out a business plan is primarily a challenge for management techniques, whereas influencing the company culture requires competencies well "beyond" mastering such techniques and are rather centered around personality strength and leadership qualities.

In other words, the common saying: "today's companies seem to be over-managed and under-led" refers to an apparent leadership gap in practice. Assuming that leadership can be considered synonymous to "cultural management," this gap refers to a clearly underestimated significance of the company culture and its behavior-determining values.

In this light of leadership and cultural management, the future potential of further developing and innovating services in Japan shall now be dealt with. The anticipated conclusions are as follows: Given the current quality level of rendered services and taking into account Japan's traditional cultural values, the future competitive opportunities for Japanese organizations to excel in providing services are clearly ahead of organizations from any other industrialized economy.

Main reasons for this positive outlook are given by the fact that Japanese employees enter an organization a priori with a personal value system, which is to a large extent coined by a service and innovation mind that is an inherent constituent of Japanese tradition, culture, and society. These are typical examples:

1. In Japanese, "work" is often translated as *shigoto* (仕事). The first kanji (*shi*, 仕[2]) has the meaning "serve," whereas *goto* (事) can be translated as "matter, something." In other words, a working attitude is intrinsically related to a serving attitude.

2. The above mentioned *kaizen* (改善) refers to a concept of continuously improving given structures and processes. Basically it attempts to eliminate any kind of waste, in the broadest sense. Three kinds of waste are distinguished: *muda* (無駄,unproductiveness), *muri* (無理, unreasonableness), and *mura* (斑, unevenness). *Kaizen* is the core concept of the most successful Toyota Production System and consists, literally translated, of the two terms *kai* (改, reform) and *zen* (善, good). In the context of cultural values, *kai* reveals an interesting fact: the first part of the kanji, 改(*kai*), is also an independent kanji, 己(*ko*), and has the meaning "self." The second part is a so-called radical and can, according to De Roo [2], be interpreted as "action." In other words, "reform" consists primarily of an action on the human "self." This is a perception that is in contrast to the situation in Western cultures, where reform is usually considered to be an affair outside one's own self.

3. The deeply rooted tradition and practice of the tea ceremony (*cha-do*, 茶道) is a formidable expression of Japanese service culture. It represents a highly sophis-

---

[2] Translations according to Hadamitzky [4].

ticated and intimate ritual of preparing and serving tea for guests. The historical roots of cultivating and drinking tea in Japan are traced back to the ninth century, when a Buddhist monk, Eichu, returned from China. Today's high degree of perfection of the art of tea ceremony is related to Sen no Rikyu, who lived from 1522 to 1591. The principles underlying this art are harmony (*wa*, 和), respect (*kei*, 敬), purity (*sei*, 清), and tranquility (*jaku*, 寂). They dominate the entire event from the esthetical architectural design of the tea room, the tasteful wall decorations, the selection of the tea ceremony equipment, the disciplined preparation of tea, and the soundless movements of the host and his helpers until the culminating act of handing the tea cups over to the guest of honor and the other guests. In other words, being the guest of honor at a tea ceremony represents the ultimate experience of receiving a service in a way that is expressing highest respect and reverence. Therefore the metaphor "tea ceremony," being enshrined in the Japanese way of life for centuries, can serve as a directing "polar star" for further perfecting services of any kind according to a leadership vision such as: "let's make our customer feel like the guest of honor at a tea ceremony when receiving current and new services from our company!"

4. *Ichi-go-ichi-e* (一期一会) is a widely known cultural concept closely related to the tea ceremony. It consists of the four kanjis *ichi* (一, one), *go* (期, time), *ichi* (一, one), and *e* (会, encounter). The meaning of this saying emphasizes the uniqueness of any get-together between people representing a "once in a lifetime chance." The situational parallel to rendering services is quite obvious: As mentioned above, producing and consuming services are simultaneous sequences and factually represent the setting of *ichi-go-ichi-e* situations. Therefore, using this metaphor in order to emphasize the challenge to make rendering and receiving services a "once in a lifetime event" for customers, can represent a further stringent leadership vision. It expresses symbolic management, which is understood by Japanese, and only by Japanese, quite well.

5. As a final example, a social concept will be presented that had been developed by Hamaguchi [4, 5] in order to explain the peculiarity of the Japanese social structure in contrast to Western societies. Whereas Western societies have their basis in individuals representing separate subjectivities, the situation in Japan is fundamentally different. In fact, the Japanese system cannot be interpreted in terms of the "individuum," but rather in terms of the "relatum" [4]. This means that the Japanese society is not merely a sum of loosely related individuals but rather a closely related network of subjects. Therefore, the opposite of individualism can be described as relationism Accordingly the nature of human interactions is necessarily different (Fig. 1).

In Hamaguchi's concept, two human models are distinguished, the *individual* and the *contextual*. It is assumed that people like A and B act from within their life-space, defined as the personal horizon of awareness within which decisions are taken and activities are initiated. In the case of individuals, the life-space closely encompasses the person. Interactions take place outside this life-space and have their origin primarily from a solipsismic view. In the case of interacting contextuals, the situation is categorically different since their life-spaces include the interpersonal

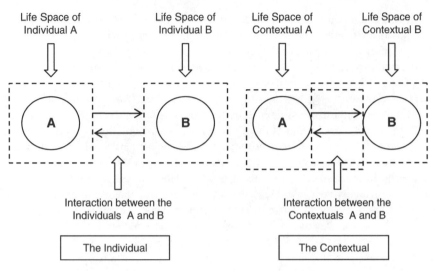

Fig. 1 Interactions of individuals and contextuals [4]

context. Therefore "... *The contextual find the basis of its own existence not within itself but in the relations between ego and others. It is what may be called a social molecule, and interactions between ego and others are developed within the life space to which they both belong*" [4].

In the case of rendering and at the same time receiving services, this mutually focused perception on others has far-reaching consequences. On one side it guarantees (on line and real time) practicing a true "customer orientation" while services are provided and simultaneously consumed. Such a customer view is certainly more authentic than the one that is included while developing new products and services in the laboratory. Also, it allows a situational and behavioral flexibility when rendering services to other people. On the other side it includes the empathic way of receiving services, representing the other essential part of service culture.

What do these five examples tell us? As mentioned above, developing a business strategy has to be accompanied by an evaluation of the company culture and in particular of its "cultural fit" with the aimed at strategy. For example, the Global CEO Study [6] conducted by IBM revealed the fact that 80% of the interviewed CEOs acknowledged the necessity to change their business strategy from mainly cost-cutting to revenue growth. And, 60% of them expect growth coming from new products and services. At the same time, 90% of the CEOs anticipated the urgency to transform their enterprises to become more responsive in order to implement the planned new growth strategies.

This is obviously a situation that requires leadership to bring about the required new cultural fit. Even though this is a highly challenging task, it is not an unsolvable one. However, the task is facilitated if the value system of the employee joining an organization exhibits an affinity with the cultural values required for a new strategy. This is certainly a fortiori the case if the new strategy has a primary focus on services and service innovations. Due to the higher quota of tacit knowledge and corresponding behavioral qualities needed, bringing about the required cultural fit is certainly less difficult than focusing on products and product innovations. For these reasons, the opportunities for Japan to excel in the emerging field of service innovations are most promising.

To sum up: coping with the demographic change is certainly a fundamental societal challenge requiring pervasive solutions from government, academia, and the economy. However, confidence is justified that Japan will develop appropriate solutions in time and thus confirm the true nature of Japan's vitality. Japan's strength, as commonly emphasized, may well be based on characteristics like lifelong employment, long working hours, and discipline. In a long-term view, however, it appears that it is primarily the meta-competence to successfully solve existential problems that accounts for Japan's impressive longevity and survival capability. Typical examples are the rapid industrialization and rebuilding of the economy after World War II, overcoming the bubble economy hype, and, in a prospective view, coping with the demographic change.

With a multifaceted perspective, this book is pioneering a promising attempt in this direction. In addition, emphasizing the service side of potential solutions upgrades its significance well beyond the original focus on the silver market.

References

1. H. Chesbrough, A failing grade for the innovation academy. Financial Times, 27 Sept 2004
2. J.R. De Roo, *2001 Kanji*, 2nd edn. (Bonjinsha Distribution Center, Tokyo, 1982)
3. W. Hadamitzky, *Kanji und Kana 1 Handbuch*, 5th edn. (Langenscheidt, Berlin, 1999)
4. E. Hamaguchi, in *Masuda Foundation, Japanese Systems – An Alternative Civilization?* (SECOTAC LTD, Yokohama, 1992)
5. E. Hamaguchi, S. Kumon, R.C. Mildred, J. Jpn. Stud. **11**(2) 289 (1985)
6. IBM, *Global CEO Study 2004* (IBM Almaden Research Center, Almaden, 2004)
7. F. Kohlbacher, *How Companies Deal with Demographic Change – Systematic Overview and Examples* (Lecture at Tsukuba University, 18 Feb 2008)
8. E.H. Schein, *Organizational Leadership and Culture* (Jossey-Bass Inc., San Francisco, 1992)
9. T. Warnes, Ageing Soc. **28**, 3–4 (2008)

Printing: Krips bv, Meppel, The Netherlands
Binding: Stürtz, Würzburg, Germany